✳ RITUAL KINSHIP ✳

✳ RITUAL KINSHIP ✳

Ideological and Structural Integration of the Compadrazgo System in Rural Tlaxcala

✳ VOLUME II ✳

HUGO G. NUTINI

PRINCETON UNIVERSITY PRESS
PRINCETON, NEW JERSEY

Contents

List of Figures

List of Tables

Abbreviations

ANDC   *Acostada del Niño Dios en casa* (bedding of the child Jesus at home)

ANDI   *Acostada del Niño Dios en la iglesia* (bedding of the child Jesus in church)

AOI   *Apadrinación de ornamentos de iglesia* (sponsorship of church paraphernalia)

BCC   *Bendición de coche o camión* (blessing of a new car or truck)

BM   *Bendición de los Misterios* (blessing of the Holy Manger)

BOI   *Compadrazgo por bendición de obras de la iglesia* (compadrazgo relationship contracted by the blessing of church repairs or improvements)

BSI   *Bendición de santo o imagen* (blessing of a saint or image)

CABP   *Compadrazgo por apadrinación en bodas de plata* (compadrazgo relationship contracted on the occasion of a silver wedding anniversary)

CCCA   *Compadrazgo contraido por el casamiento de los ahijados* (compadrazgo relationship contracted by the marriage of one's godchildren)

CCCH   *Compadrazgo contraido por el casamiento de los hijos* (compadrazgo relationship contracted by the marriage of one's children)

CEON   *Compadrazgo por el estreno de objetos nuevos* (compadrazgo relationship contracted by the handsel of new utensils)

CSV   *Coronación de la Santísima Virgen* (coronation of the Holy Virgin)

FC   *Compadrazgo de fruta cuata* (compadrazgo relationship contracted when a person finds a twin fruit or vegetable)

JJ   *Compadrazgo de jícara o jarrito* (compadrazgo relationship contracted by drinking partners)

PCA   *Parada de cruz de Actiopan* (erection of the cross at Actiopan)

PCE   *Parada de cruz de entierro* (erection of a burial cross)

Preface

In the preface to the first volume of *Ritual Kinship* I expressed my gratitude to the many individuals and institutions who helped make that work possible. That gratitude remains as warm today. For the generous financial support that enabled me to gather the ethnographical and ethnohistorical research on which this work is based I would like to thank the National Science Foundation (GA-32451-1-2-3), the Wenner-Gren Foundation for Anthropological Research, the American Philosophical Society, the Pittsburgh Foundation, the University of Pittsburgh Center for International Studies, and the University of Pittsburgh Humanities Research Fund. Without their assistance I could have completed neither the specific studies on Belén nor the more general comparative work on Tlaxcala. (As in *Ritual Kinship* I, 1970 will be regarded as the ethnographic present throughout this monograph.)

What also remains true today is that there is no way to single out every individual or institution to whom I am indebted, but once again I would like to thank some of those to whom my debt is greatest: the Instituto Nacional de Antropología e Historia in general, and its former directors, the late Dr. Eusebio Dávalos Hurtado, Dr. Ignacio Bernal y García Pimentel, and Dr. Guillermo Bonfil Battala in particular; the authorities of the state of Tlaxcala during the years 1966-1976, particularly former governors Licenciado Don Anselmo Cervantes H., the late General Don Antonio Bonilla Vásquez, Dr. Don Luciano Huerta Sánchez, and Don Emilio Sánchez Piedras; the bishop of the diocese of Tlaxcala Dr. Don Luis Munive y Escobar; and the municipal authorities of the Tlaxcalan communities in which I have worked for twenty years.

I would like to thank again for their intellectual and professional support the following people: Rolando Alum, Lilyan Brudner-White, Fred Eggan, Barry L. Isaac, Timothy D. Murphy, Triloki Nath Pandey, John M. Roberts, Thomas S. Schorr, Henry A. Selby, Doren L. Slade, Alexander Spoehr, James W. Taggart, and Douglas R. White. They contributed richly to the development and the expression of the ideas contained in this book. To my friend and colleague the late Angel Palerm I owe particular gratitude for his insightful ideas on ritual kinship, particularly as they related to its magico-symbolic functions and the elements of risk that permeate the system.

Over the years the informants in the more than thirty Tlaxcalan communities in which I have worked have always been generous and friendly. To the people in the towns where most of the comparative information in this study was collected—Santa María Belén, San Bernardino Contla,

Santa María Atlihuetzian, Santa Cruz Tlaxcala, San Juan Totolac, San Rafael Tepatlachco, San Pablo del Monte, and San Esteban Tizatlán—a special expression of thanks is due. My wife and I have contracted over 120 ritual kinsmen (*compadres, comadres, ahijados,* and *ahijadas*) in our twenty years of fieldwork, and the deep bonds we have formed have been an inspiration to this work.

Again, let me make special mention of my compadre Desiderio H. Xochitiotzin and of the members of the Reyes family, who since 1968 have made my family part of theirs.

To Betty Bell, coauthor of Volume One, I am indebted for the map, the diagram, and the glossary. She also edited the original manuscript and was a fruitful source of ideas and insights related to the analytical framework. Finally, I would like to thank Barbara Westergaard, the editor of the manuscript for the Princeton University Press. Her creative work has enabled me to present a better book.

h.g.n.

✳ RITUAL KINSHIP ✳

Introduction

Ritual Kinship II in Perspective

This book is the continuation of Volume One of *Ritual Kinship* (Nutini and Bell 1980) which is concerned with *compadrazgo* (ritual kinship), one of the most widespread institutions in Latin America. Together the two volumes constitute a comprehensive treatment of compadrazgo. Although each is essentially a self-contained monograph, a certain amount of background information will help the reader. Therefore, in this introduction I summarize the most salient points and the general themes discussed in *Ritual Kinship* I. I should emphasize that this volume contains enough ethnographic detail to make the analysis of compadrazgo intrinsically meaningful; the reader who wishes to pursue a particular ethnographic or historical point in depth should, however, consult *Ritual Kinship* I.

In the Introduction of that volume I present the comparative, regional, and historical foundations of the compadrazgo study. I pay particular attention to the ethnographic and ethnologic setting of structural studies, emphasizing the nature of compadrazgo from the standpoint of short-range and long-range historical perspectives. I delimit and analyze the role of compadrazgo, the central institution in the conceptualization of transitional peasant communities, as the functional equivalent of kinship. I discuss the ontological and epistemological bases of the study's theoretical and methodological framework. I address myself especially to the diachronic-synchronic continuum, the ideological-structural dichotomy, and the internal and external perspectives of structural studies. Finally, I present an integrated analytical framework centered on the institution of compadrazgo as a comparative concept.

Part One of the first volume constitutes the ethnographic description of compadrazgo in Santa María Belén and rural Tlaxcala. Specifically, I present the following information about the compadrazgo system as a whole and about particular compadrazgo types: a detailed description of the social, religious, and symbolic rites, ceremonies, and celebrations and the economic dimensions associated with each type; the chain of events for each type from its inception until the rite or ceremony that terminates its formal dimensions; the manner in which the social, religious, and economic domains impinge on the discharge of the rights and obligations in the compadrazgo system, as exemplified by each type; the primary and secondary meaning of each type for Belén society and the operational constraints in the discharge of specific attributes caused by these meanings; some general information pertaining to the compadrazgo system as a whole, such as the relative ranking of types, summary descriptions of principles of operation, and the like; an explicit and detailed description of the permanent bonds and obligations obtaining in some of the most important compadrazgo types (especially baptism and marriage), and by reference to these types, the nature of the permanent bonds and obligations obtaining in the lesser types; the symbolic, social, or religious nature of the mediating entity, and the resulting implications for the structuring of relations and the general functioning of compadrazgo types; the structure of action and behavior patterns of all primary actors (in dyadic form) involved in each type, and their religious, social, and symbolic participation in every rite, ceremony, and celebration of the compadrazgo cycle; the less detailed, general description of the social, religious, and economic participation of secondary actors and related personnel such as kinsmen, other ritual kinsmen, neighbors, and friends; a general account of some of the mechanisms for recruiting primary and secondary actors and the constraints of participation governing related personnel; finally, some of the general attributes of the extension of ritual kinship ties and behavior.

In Part Two of *Ritual Kinship* I, I analyze the structure of compadrazgo choice and the system's regional components. The main topics discussed are: the preliminary steps leading to the establishment of the different compadrazgo types; the personal and societal characteristics associated with the recruitment of ritual kinsmen and with ritual behavior patterns; the web of obligations at the operational and functional levels, and the ways in which they are modified by specific structural constraints; the socioeconomic and religious positions of the personnel involved in the various types of compadrazgo and how these affect the functioning of the system; the spatial, territorial, and regional aspects of compadrazgo and their influence on the functioning of the system itself; and the extracommunal dimensions of compadrazgo as an expression of the differential acculturation of rural Tlaxcala during the past century. The compadrazgo system of Belén is analyzed within the context of the region and viewed within what I have called the short-range historical perspective.

Part Three is concerned with the comparative, ideological, and long-range implications of compadrazgo in rural Tlaxcala and, by extension, in Mesoamerica and many regions of Latin America. In this endeavor I analyze the theory and process of syncretism and acculturation as they have affected rural Tlaxcala from the Spanish Conquest to the present. At the same time, I analyze the compadrazgo system within the wider socioreligious order and general ideology of which it is an inextricable part, namely, the *ayuntamiento religioso* (local religious government) and the cult of the saints. I demonstrate the growth of the compadrazgo system and its functional adaptation to community and region during the past 450 years. As a result of the analysis, I sketch a limited-range theory of rapid sociocultural change centered on the concepts of modernization and secularization.

Finally, in the Conclusions I address myself to several topics having to do with the compadrazgo system of Belén in particular and rural Tlaxcala in general, which have significant implications for the conduct of similar studies in Latin America: the way in which the compadrazgo system of Belén is embedded at the communal and regional levels, and its conceptual role for ethnographic and general studies elsewhere; the nature of Belén's compadrazgo in transition, and the mechanisms of secularization and modernization that are affecting the process; in passing, I generalize to analogous situations at the communal and regional levels which are undergoing similar accelerated processes of change; a synoptic comparison of compadrazgo in Latin America. In the appendix I examine a representative sample of the ethnographic literature to determine what has been done and what needs to be done.

In the balance of these introductory remarks, I present the conscious paradigm that the average well informed adult in Belén has about the institution of compadrazgo, and the developmental account of compadrazgo types from inception to formal resolution. (This material appeared in slightly different form in *Ritual Kinship* I. The reader is referred to pages 53-62 and 198-201 of that volume.) These constructs should facilitate the reading of this book and make the ensuing arguments and analyses wholly intelligible.

The Beleños' Conscious Paradigm of Compadrazgo

There are thirty-one occasions in the life, ceremonial, and socioeconomic cycles of the people of Belén when a man, a woman, and even in some cases a child, can enter into a compadrazgo relationship, either as an individual or as a member of a group. Each of these occasions results in a specific compadrazgo type with specific social, economic, religious, and ceremonial aspects. The types vary in their intrinsic and symbolic importance and in the degree to which their concomitant events and activities are institutionalized.

A compadrazgo relationship is established between two individuals, couples, or a fixed number of related people (kinsmen and nonkinsmen) through the link of a person, image, object, or occasion (the mediating entity). The mediating entity is central to the system from the structural viewpoint, for no compadrazgo relationship can be established without it, yet it is not itself of primary functional importance. As the Beleños themselves point out, this is true even when a person serves as a mediating entity. Once the initiation ceremonies are over, the godchild becomes a passive figure in the ensuing social and economic network, which is dominated entirely by parents, godparents, and their extensions. This is more obvious, of course, in types with a religious image or a material or symbolic object or occasion as the mediating entity, for in these types the mediating entity serves only as a means for establishing the relationship. Formally speaking, then, the subject-object link of compadrazgo is structurally passive, whereas in the ensuing web of compadrazgo behavior, the subject-subject link is dominant. Beleños recognize this explicitly, and what is uppermost in their minds in any compadrazgo relationship is the extension of certain social, religious, and economic patterns of behavior, which have relatively little to do with the reasons for establishing the original relationship. If the initial social and religious requirements—the need to find, say, godparents for a child's baptism or a sponsor for an important social occasion—were to disappear suddenly from Belén society, the system would remain basically the same, for the people would seek out in other realms of social behavior requirements that would enable them to maintain the basic function of the compadrazgo relationship. In other words, the structural function of compadrazgo is not the same thing as its structural form.

The basic compadrazgo terminology is standard throughout Tlaxcala. Sponsors are universally addressed and referred to as *padrino* (godfather) and *madrina* (godmother) of the mediating entity, who (or which) is designated by the term *ahijado* (godson) or *ahijada* (goddaughter). Even if the mediating entity is an image or object, it is referred to as the ahijado, and the compadres are referred to as the padrinos of the object. The godparents and the parents, kinsmen, or owners of the mediating entity refer to and address each other as compadre ("cofather") and *comadre* ("comother"). (Unless otherwise indicated, I use the plural term *compadres* to refer to both compadre and comadre. This is not only standard Spanish usage, but appropriate to the fact that most of the economic, religious, and social dealings are conducted by the compadre-comadre dyad. I also use *ahijados* to refer to both ahijado and ahijada.)

This terminological triad obtains for all compadrazgo types, although some significant terms of address and reference vary with the type, as does the extension of the ritual kinship terminology. But the human, religious, and material composition of the triad does not, structurally speaking, alter its symbolic and functional content.

Beleños classify the various compadrazgo types along several dimensions, distinguishing, for example, between those that involve a sacrament and those that do not. The latter they further subdivide into primary and secondary, though perhaps not quite as categorically as the following typology would suggest: *compadrazgo sacramental* (sacramental compadrazgo); *compadrazgo no-sacramental primario* (primary nonsacramental compadrazgo); and *compadrazgo no-sacramental secundario* (secondary nonsacramental compadrazgo). In chart 1 Belén's thirty-one types are listed according to this classification scheme. (A few of the interchangeable types could be subsumed under one another, but they are listed separately because the option of choosing one or the other is available.)

CHART 1
Compadrazgo Types and Their Variants

Compadrazgo sacramental
1. Bautizo (baptism)
2. *Casamiento* (marriage, including ten subsidiary compadrazgo relationships, brought about by the following objects or events: three *padrinos* [godfathers] and *madrinas* [godmotherrs] of *velación* [nuptial benedictions], *arras* [earnest money], and *anillos* [wedding rings]; and seven madrinas [only] of *lazo* [ornamental tie], *ramo* [bouquet], *libro* [prayer book], *rosario* [rosary], *pañuelo* [scarf], *pastel* [wedding cake], and *cola* [train for wedding dress])
3. *Confirmación* (confirmation)
4. *Parada de cruz de entierro* (erection of a burial cross, PCE)
5. *Primera comunión* (first communion)
6. *Compadrazgo contraido por el casamiento de los hijos* (compadrazgo relationship contracted by the marriage of one's children, CCCH)
7. *Compadrazgo contraido por el casamiento de los ahijados* (compadrazgo relationship contracted by the marriage of one's godchildren, CCCA)

Compadrazgo no-sacramental primario
8. *Acostada del Niño Dios en casa* (bedding of the child Jesus at home, ANDC)
9. *Acostada del Niño Dios en la iglesia* (bedding of the child Jesus in church, ANDI)
10. *Apadrinación de ornamentos de iglesia* (sponsorship of church paraphernalia, including *palio* [pallium], *imágenes* [images], *sagrario* [ciborium], *estandartes* [banners], *altares* [altars], *lienzo de Cristo* [Christ's tunic], *cáliz* [chalice], *ornamentos sacerdotales* [priestly ornaments], *reclinatorio* [pew], etc., AOI)
11. *Bendición de santo o imagen* (blessing of a saint or image, BSI)

12. *Coronación de la Santísima Virgen* (coronation of the Holy Virgin, CSV)
13. *Escapulario* (scapular)
14. *Graduación* (graduation, including graduation from *kinder* [nursery school], *primaria* [grade school], *secundaria* [junior high school], *preparatoria* [high school], *enfermería* [practical-nursing school], and *comercio* [business school])
15. *Parada de cruz de Actiopan* (erection of the cross at Actiopan; this takes place at the community spring, on the patron saint's day, PCA)
16. *Quince años* (celebration of a girl's fifteenth birthday)
17. *Sacada a misa* (taking a mother to hear mass on the fortieth day after she has given birth)
18. *Compadrazgo de evangelios* (presenting a child in church at the age of three)
19. *Compadrazgo de limpia* (compadrazgo relationship contracted by the ceremonial cleansing of a sick person)
20. *Compadrazgo por bendición de obras de la iglesia* (compadrazgo relationship contracted by the blessing of church repairs or improvements, including *pisos nuevos* [new floors], *ventanales* [windows], *atrio* [atrium], altares, *bautisterio* [baptistry], *banquetas* [benches], etc., BOI)

Compadrazgo no-sacramental secundario
21. *Bendición de casa* (blessing of a new house, including also the blessing of a new *sitio* [house site], *tienda* [store], *baños* [baths], *panadería* [bakery], *taller de costura* [sewing shop], and *peluquería* [barbershop])
22. *Bendición de coche o camión* (blessing of a new car or truck, BCC)
23. *Bendición de los Misterios* (blessing of the Holy Manger, BM)
24. *Parada de cruz* (erection of a cross for a variety of occasions including the inauguration of an item of property or ceremonial object, and a thanksgiving or intensification rite for such as: *horno* [oven], *molino de nixtamal* [ground-corn mill], tienda, *pozo* [well], *lavadero* [washing place], *campo* [cultivated field], *campanario* [belfry], *sementera* [first seeds], *almiar* [first haystack], *primeras crías* [first litters], *huerta* [orchard], etc.)
25. *Primera piedra* (setting the foundations of a house)
26. *Compadrazgo de amistad* (compadrazgo relationship contracted for reasons of close friendship)
27. *Compadrazgo por apadrinación en bodas de plata* (compadrazgo relationship contracted on the occasion of a silver wedding anniversary, CABP)

28. *Compadrazgo de aretes* (compadrazgo relationship contracted when a baby girl is given her first pair of earrings)
29. *Compadrazgo por el estreno de objetos nuevos* (compadrazgo relationship contracted by the handsel of new utensils, including primarily coche, camión, *muebles* [furniture], *televisión* [television], *estufa* [stove], *instrumentos musicales* [musical instruments], *arado* [plow], *pala* [shovel], etc., CEON)
30. *Compadrazgo de fruta cuata* (compadrazgo relationship contracted when a person finds a twin fruit or vegetable, FC)
31. *Compadrazgo de jícara o jarrito* (compadrazgo relationship contracted by drinking partners, JJ)

Another distinction made by the people of Belén is that between prescriptive and preferential compadrazgo types. Beleños feel they must comply with the requirements of the prescriptive types, and an individual who fails to do so faces religious, social, and sometimes economic sanctions. Failure to comply with a preferential type, on the other hand, does not result in social or economic sanctions. This does not mean that all preferential types are judged equally important, and an individual's evaluation of the importance of a preferential type is in fact the primary factor determining whether or not he will establish the relationship. Indeed, two or three of the preferential types are considered so important that definite pressures are placed on those who fail to establish these compadrazgo relationships.

Certain of the thirty-one types stand out because they are considered of unusual importance in terms of intrinsic religious and social attributes related to the ceremonial and life cycles or because they epitomize traditional practice and are particularly appropriate for the establishment of satisfactory and durable compadrazgo ties. There are eleven such types: baptism, marriage, confirmation, first communion, primera piedra or bendición de casa (these two are interchangeable and are here counted as one), BSI, PCE, parada de cruz, ANDC, ANDI, and PCA. Of these, baptism, marriage, confirmation, first communion, BSI, ANDI, PCE, and PCA are prescriptive; and parada de cruz and ANDC are preferential. Although the remaining types can be thought of as secondary from the social and religious viewpoints, in perhaps half of them pressure is brought to bear on someone who does not comply. This means that the average Beleño contracts something over two-thirds (ca. twenty-two) of all the compadrazgo types and that only about one-third are truly optional.

The people also divide compadrazgo types into religious and social. Of the eleven important types just cited, all but marraige, PCE, and parada de cruz are classified as religious. This does not mean, however, that the religious types are intrinsically more important, either analytically or behaviorally. Nor does it mean that the quality or intensity of behavior associated with the religious types is necessarily more important structurally than that associated with the social types. In fact, it is not entirely clear why the people classify as social rather than religious such apparently religious types as casamiento and PCE.

A distinction between public and private compadrazgo types is also made by the people of Belén. In private compadrazgo types, the relationships between two individuals or sets of individuals (mediated by the ostensible object of the relationship) do not involve social or religious implications beyond their spheres of action. Public compadrazgo types, on the other hand, involve not just individuals or sets of individuals, but either the community as a whole or religiously or socially significant numbers of individuals who participate, at least temporarily, in the events and activities of the primary actors (the compadres). In public types the compadrazgo relationships are permanent only for the primary actors; for the rest the associated obligations and patterns of behavior are discontinued once the occasion for which the relationship was established is over.

Much about the structure of compadrazgo is mechanical: in each type the component parts are well integrated, thoroughly known by the people, and highly institutionalized. In addition, for the prescriptive and highly preferential types, the actors' behavior is highly uniform, and people over a certain age know exactly what is expected of them at each stage. In other words, the norms and ideals that regulate the selection of godparents, the appropriate time and occasion to establish a compadrazgo relationship, the duties and obligations involved in the relationship, the extension of patterns of behavior, the alternative options for discharging rituals, and in general all the structural aspects of compadrazgo are well known. When deviations from the norms occur, they are governed by the desire of the primary actors to maximize other goals. In terms of function the people make a rather sharp distinction between primary actors (those immediately involved in the relationship) and secondary actors (those who by extension are affected by the relationship).

The duties, obligations, behavior patterns, and associated ceremonial and social events are specific to each compadrazgo type. The behavior patterns associated with each type can vary in quality and intensity, depending both on the importance of the type in the Beleños' conscious hierarchy of types and on the aims of the individual who established the relationship. Thus each compadrazgo type has some intrinsic and extrinsic attributes, independent of the cause for establishing the relationship, that must be considered in deciding with whom to establish the relationship. When an individual enters a compadrazgo relationship, he makes a firm commitment to comply with the constraints the relationship imposes upon him. And, in fact, when people are unable, individually or collectively, to discharge properly the contractual obligations involved in compadrazgo relationships, a serious potential for discord exists.

Yet another distinction the Beleños make regarding compadrazgo relationships is that between the person asking someone to enter a relationship and the person being asked. In the first place, the structural position of the person asking someone to become his ritual kinsman is quite different from the position of the person being asked. (This applies by extension to all related personnel associated with the main actors.) When A asks B to enter a compadrazgo relationship, A is asking B to incur certain economic, social, and religious obligations. Though A will later reciprocate, the initial obligations are often higher for B than for A, and this inequality has a bearing on the future of the relationship. In the second place, the person requesting the relationship by definition places himself in the debt of the person being asked, and this too influences the relationship. This imbalance, of course, more or less evens itself out in any individual's total web of compadrazgo, for over his lifetime compadrazgo career, the average Beleño is asked to become a compadre approximately as many times as he asks others.

Two interrelated principles regulate the system: no one should refuse to enter into a compadrazgo relationship of any type, and one must always know in advance that those one is asking will accept. This is not simply an idealized conception, and it is considered extremely bad manners to violate these principles. Compadrazgo relationships are seen as sacred, not just in a religious sense, but (no doubt more importantly) in a social sense as well. The institution serves as one of Belén's most important mechanisms for social control, and people are careful to conform to its mechanical structural form.

The Beleños' clarity about the system's form does not extend to their understanding of its function. Beleños are perfectly aware that compadrazgo relationships (and the system in general) serve a variety of functions, yet when asked to explain the system's place in the social structure of the community, or the value of some particular type, they tended to answer uncertainly and evasively. They were happy to describe the specific activities or behavior patterns associated with particular types, but they did not volunteer information about the function of the system. That the people were unaware (unconscious) of the significance of the form and the structured behavior patterns they were able to describe so well should come as no surprise; anthropologists engaged in this kind of work have found this the rule rather than the exception.

To understand how Belén's compadrazgo structure works, one must first establish how the system regulates the various men, women, and children who participate in compadrazgo relationships. When and how do they participate as primary or secondary actors, as those who initiate or those who accept a relationship, or as mediating entities? The different types can be characterized in terms of the structural positions and roles of the people involved. (Children, as I have mentioned, are not just mediating entities, but can engage as primary actors in several types; the analysis of these instances can help clarify the symbolic and material functions of compadrazgo; see Forbes Tanner 1971.)

I have described, in somewhat simplified form and using slightly more abstract terms, the conscious paradigm of compadrazgo held by the people of Belén. It is a faithful picture of the ethnographic reality insofar as the formal structure and the behavior patterns associated with the institution go. In terms of the system's functions within the community's general social structure, however, it is not a faithful portrait, and these functions must be inferred from the analysis of the structure.

Clearly, the conscious and unconscious paradigms in Belén differ substantially, and one aim of the analysis is to determine why. Generally, the more mechanical a system or subsystem, the smaller the discrepancy between the people's conscious paradigm and the anthropologist's structural or functional analysis. Conversely, the more statistical (stochastic) the system, the greater the discrepancy. Furthermore, since function is inferred from structure, at least at the analytical level, discrepancies between conscious and unconscious paradigms are more apt to show up in discussions of function. (What I am saying applies not just to Belén, but to all of rural Tlaxcala as well.)

Developmental Summary of Compadrazgo

The ethnographic information presented in *Ritual Kinship* I, as well as some of the general principles of the system sketched there (pages 62-194), are graphically summarized in diagram 1. What remains to be done in the structural domain before I can make a functional interpretation of the compadrazgo system is also apparent in the diagram.

The diagram makes it possible to trace the events connected with the formal aspects of compadrazgo types in Belén and rural Tlaxcala from their inception to their formal resolution. The event and relationship nodes show all the important occasions with social, religious, or symbolic meaning in the formal compadrazgo cycle. The personnel interaction nodes show the people associated with each occasion and the direction of their obligations.

The preliminary steps or previous compadrazgo ties, and sometimes both, determine the selection of padrinos and the constraints affecting

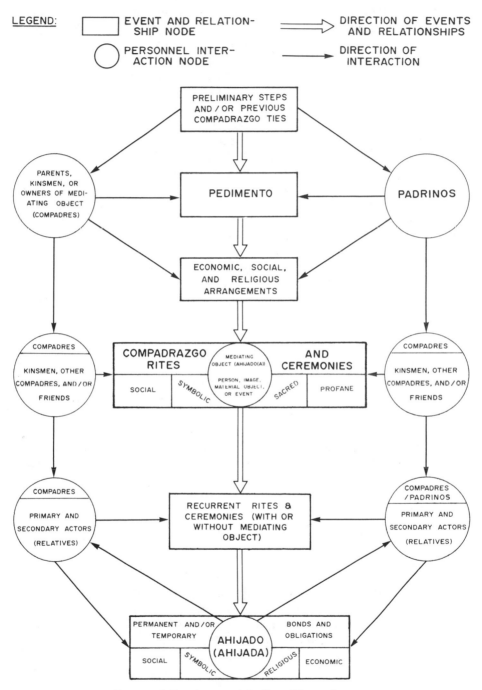

DIAGRAM 1. Developmental Outline of Compadrazgo

both those who do the asking and those who are being asked to enter into a relationship. This node leads directly to the *pedimento* (formal request of sponsorship). This essentially symbolic and social node is not necessarily important in itself, but because it is a microcosm of the future compadrazgo relationship it acquires structural importance. The next node is primarily economic in that the arrangements and preparation involve immediate economic obligations that both compadres and padrinos must fulfill according to the terms agreed on in the pedimento. (The arrangements node also has religious and social aspects, but these are usually less important than the economic ones.) Since the economic obligations of the arrangements node define and underlie many of the ensuing ceremonies, and play a role in shaping any future permanent bonds as well, it is in many ways the most important one in the cycle. In social, religious, and ceremonial terms, however, the compadrazgo rites and ceremonies node is the most important one. During these activities the primary actors are linked by the mediating entity and the future character of the relationship is established. Analytically, this node can be thought of as the axis of the relationships, which defines the structural and functional development of the participating personnel.

The recurrent rites and ceremonies node involves the reinforcement and intensification of the relationship and is generally associated with the types having a primarily symbolic meaning. Recurrent rites and ceremonies can take place with or without the intervention of the mediating entity. They can take place from a week to a year or more after the principal rites and ceremonies. Although recurrent rites and ceremonies are part of less than 30 percent of the compadrazgo types in rural Tlaxcala, all types have some sort of reinforcing and intensification mechanisms. The final node appears on the diagram to accommodate the personnel interaction associated with the nodal chain.

In the top personnel interaction node, most of the people involved are primary actors—on the one hand the parents, kinsmen, or owners of the mediating entity, and on the other the padrinos or sponsors (called padrinos throughout for simplicity's sake). Although a few kinsmen or other compadres and friends on both sides may participate in the activities connected with this node, they are not included in the diagram because their roles at this stage are subsidiary. Those associated with this node are involved in the first three nodes of social, religious, and economic obligations leading to the main part of the cycle.

At the second node are all those involved in the main compadrazgo rites and ceremonies (that is, the fourth node of the event chain): the padrinos, compadres, their respective kinsmen, other compadres, friends, and neighbors. At this node can be found the largest number of primary and secondary actors and related personnel whose participation in the compadrazgo cycle is structurally binding.

The bottom node involves mainly the primary and secondary actors whose chief function is to discharge the recurrent rites and ceremonies (the fifth node of the event chain). Like the first personnel node, this node can include related personnel whose obligations are not binding, for only the primary and secondary actors of the last personnel node are subject to the binding obligations of the last node of the event chain. This is the residue of the compadrazgo cycle; in the future either the relationship becomes an enduring one, or, if the obligations are temporary, it is almost invariably transformed into another, usually more important, relationship.

In Volume One the emphasis was on the detailed description of compadrazgo types and their internal organization in terms of rites, ceremonies, duties, obligations, constraints, and general events. In other words, Chapters One to Eight of *Ritual Kinship* I were concerned with what I have called the four central nodes of the developmental chain of events of the compadrazgo cycle. This volume is concerned primarily with the compadrazgo system as a whole and the permanent dimensions of compadrazgo after the central rites and ceremonies have been discharged. Part One contains the structural analysis of compadrazgo and its multidimensional levels of meaning. I discuss compadrazgo as a system and how it impinges on or is related to other systems of community culture and society. Part Two constitutes the functional analysis of the institution at the different levels of local and regional integration. The appendix presents the theoretical foundation of the entire study, centering on the epistemological and ontological requirements of the analytical framework; in passing I discuss there the ideology of anthropological investigation.

A word to the reader about repetitions, length of exposition, and the primary aim of this monograph. I wish I could have written this study more elegantly and concisely. This, unfortunately, has not been possible, for which I have the following reasons. First, there is no model for what I have attempted to do with the institution of compadrazgo. I borrowed, of course, many modes of analysis from kinship studies, but just as many I had to develop as I proceeded with the discussion. Second, the compadrazgo system of Belén and rural Tlaxcala, at least as I have analytically and methodologically defined it, is extremely complex and encompasses practically every domain of local culture and society. Thus, the problems of description and analysis in *Ritual Kinship* I have been compounded several times in dealing with the ramifications of thirty-one compadrazgo types. Third, in this study I look at the compadrazgo system from several perspectives and levels of analysis, and this *modus operandi* required the frequent change of frame of reference in order to position compadrazgo in its proper substantive domain. In summary, the conceptual task that I have undertaken in this study does not lend itself well to elegance and conciseness, and I have sacrificed the pursuit of these worthy aims for clarity and completeness of exposition. The repetitions that the reader will encounter are not there for emphasis, but rather to facilitate the reader's task of understanding the nature of each compadrazgo type and properly embedding the compadrazgo system in local culture and society. Finally, whatever the merits and contributions of this monograph, it is my earnest hope that the reader will regard it as an exercise in how and under what conditions the compadrazgo system, rather than kinship, can be regarded as the central institution in the analysis of many transitional folk communities throughout most culture areas in Latin America.

∗ PART I ∗

The Structural Analysis of the Compadrazgo System

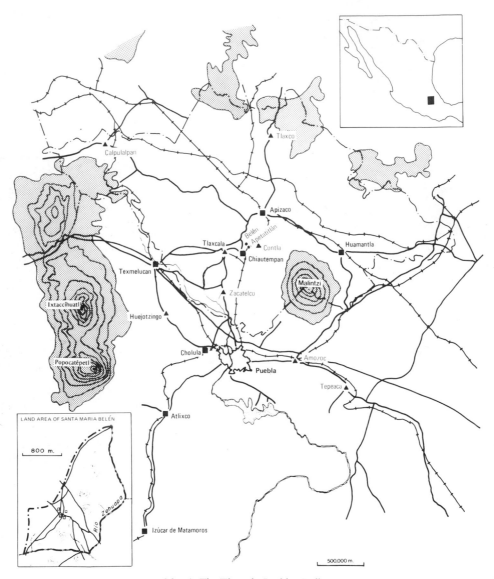

Map 1. The Tlaxcala–Pueblan Valley

The Sacred Nature of Compadrazgo in Belén and the Characteristics of the Mediating Entity

Ritual Kinship I described and analyzed the compadrazgo system of Santa María Belén and rural Tlaxcala (see map 1) in its regional (Part Two) and historical (Part Three) contexts, and it dealt structurally with the mechanisms of recruitment, selection, and initially associated constraints (Chapters Seven and Eight). It is now time to analyze the main attributes and domains that structure this subsystem within the context of Belén culture and society. The first such complex that comes to mind is the nature of the compadrazgo system, and what this means structurally and operationally. (Once again I must remind the reader that, although the analysis is centered on Belén, it applies equally to most of rural Tlaxcala, that is, to all traditional and transitional communities which constitute more than 70 percent of the total population of the state.)

The Social Meaning of Sacredness

Beleños regard both the institution of compadrazgo and the obligation to discharge its various types as sacred to themselves and to the community as a whole. The key term here is "sacred." The concept of sacredness does not have primarily a religious meaning; just as important is its social meaning, for it acquires specific significance within the sociomoral context of individuals in action. To say that compadrazgo is a sacred institution means largely that, because it acts as an imperative to social action, Beleños must comply with its constraints and directives in order not to break the continuity of the sociomoral order and bring down upon themselves natural and supernatural sanctions. The concept of sacredness is closely tied to religion insofar as compadrazgo is an institution with a large religious component, but the institution per se also partakes in considerable measure of the supernatural aspects of religion and rests upon the same ideological foundation. Hence Beleños are structurally compelled to enter the compadrazgo system either as active initiators or passive actors in a complex network of socioreligious events in the community's life and ceremonial cycle.

The sacred ideology of the compadrazgo system is well attested to by a sizable complex of legends and quasi-myths in which the central theme deals with the consequences of failing to comply with the requirements of the compadrazgo system. It is not surprising, then, that Beleños seldom refuse to enter into a compadrazgo relationship when they are asked to (the only notable exception being marriage compadrazgo because of the *años noviciados* or dangerous years; see *Ritual Kinship* I, pages 75–77), even for the types that, within the system itself, are not necessarily prescriptive. However, the sacredness of the compadrazgo system, which I have construed as an institution belonging to the moral-supernatural order with certain sanctions and rewards, refers to the system as an abstract and general entity and not to specific types or instances of it. The sacred nature of compadrazgo—the activation of the social or supernatural order as an object of reward and punishment—comes into play when an individual or group of individuals is drawn into a compadrazgo network by being asked to enter into a compadrazgo relationship. Once the main ritual and ceremonial events have been properly conducted, we can say that the specific actors have complied with the sacred prescription of the compadrazgo system. What happens afterward may or may not fall within the sacred nature of the system, depending mainly on the prescriptive or preferential nature of the compadrazgo type, as can be seen in the description of the various postritual behavior patterns associated with the thirty-one types in Belén. The sacred nature of compadrazgo in Belén was most clearly expressed by one of my informants when he said that "above and beyond personal feelings and sentiments there exists the permanent and unchanging bond of being compadres, and the physical and moral obligation to respect that bond. It is because of this sacred relationship that compadres must trust [*tenerse confianza*] and respect [*respetarse*] each other, and treat each other ceremoniously and without using the familiar *tu* [*tutearse*]." This attitude is shared by most Beleños, and this is one of the main reasons that the compadrazgo system has continued to function more or less traditionally despite ever-increasing contact with the outside world and strong social and economic pressures against it.

The sacred nature of compadrazgo may best be characterized as the ideology that shapes the structural matrix of the institution, as well as actual statistical discharge. Two things must be mentioned in this connection. First, the ideology of compadrazgo has an important diachronic component (see Part Three of *Ritual Kinship* I). It is evident that the manner and circumstances in which the compadrazgo system (basically of European origin) was internalized by the Indian population of Tlaxcala, and the resultant syncretic institution, have much to do with its ideology, which developed as a process of action and reaction vis-à-vis other social and religious elements of Indian culture and within the changing social structure of Indian communities for more than 300 years. A second synchronic point, perhaps more relevant, is that the ideology of the compadrazgo system extends beyond its sacred character and is related to the concepts of *confianza* (trust), *respeto* (respect), and reliability. These, however, are primarily expressed in a structural form, and are dealt with separately.

Choice, Acceptance, and Compadrazgo Sacredness

The compadrazgo system is regulated by two interrelated principles, namely, that one should not refuse to enter into a compadrazgo relationship of any kind, and that one always asks people who one knows in advance will accept. The first is made operationally meaningful by the sacred nature of compadrazgo per se. The second, however, can be made operational as a structural principle only by determining how it is discharged: we must determine how people know what is proper and socially adequate in entering into a compadrazgo relationship. In its broader aspects this question has been answered in Chapters Seven and Eight of *Ritual Kinship* I, which deal with the structure of compadrazgo choice and the social, religious, and economic statuses of primary actors, by describing the range of choices available to the individual. But it remains to ascertain the social mechanisms and immediate actions employed by individuals or groups in actualizing a given choice and ensuring that it has social and religious acceptability.

The structure of compadrazgo choice presents Beleños with a series of alternatives. This context we must regard as the most primitive substratum determining how, with whom, and under what circumstance individuals will enter the system. At a more immediate level we have a second set of constraints which determine whom one can ask to enter into a compadrazgo relationship, and under what circumstances. These are related primarily to the general social and religious positions and characteristics of prospective candidates. Thus, beyond the most primitive substratum, the average Beleño is presented with at least one, and most often several, individuals who may comply with the cultural and ideological requirements for an adequate compadre, but the final decision is governed by the more immediate set of constraints. It must be noted, however, that considerations that are inherently part of the structure of the compadrazgo system (e.g., the age of compadres, the specific qualifications for each compadrazgo type, the specific positions of prospective compadres in the life cycle) have been held constant here. In a sense, these would constitute a third—and the most superficial—set of structural constraints in the operation of the system. (I have discussed this point in the description of each compadrazgo type, and the information is synthesized in the chapters on the developmental cycle of the compadrazgo system; see Part One of *Ritual Kinship* I.)

To qualify for entering into a compadrazgo relationship, a Beleño must be in good social and religious standing in the community, in the sense of complying with the culturally determined norms that regulate its social and religious structure. Prospective compadres must possess certain important social and religious attributes if a successful compadrazgo relationship is to be established (see Chapter Seven of *Ritual Kinship* I). To a large extent this is an idealization, for it is never entirely possible to have all the attributes, so two qualifications must be specified. First, these requirements are less likely to apply to compadres chosen from outside the community, and the Beleños themselves tend to be much more lax about looking for desirable attributes. Second, even in the case of endogamous choice, few if any prospective compadres have all the desirable attributes, and Beleños have a definite set of priorities: social considerations always come before religious ones; it is always more important, say, to be properly married or to be a good family man than to be pious or to be a man who properly fulfills his communal religious obligations. In any event, all these constraints play a definite and important role in the structure of compadrazgo choice at this second level, and the people of Belén carefully weigh and consider all the possibilities and alternatives whenever they engage in a compadrazgo relationship. From this viewpoint, and given definite ends in view, the compadrazgo system in Belén is definitely rational.[1]

It remains to determine how people decide, in the face of a series of alternatives, whether a given individual will willingly agree to become a compadre. The average Beleño knows that even if he asks a person with whom he is not on particularly good social terms to enter into a compadrazgo relationship, that person must accept the invitation or risk the social disapproval and perhaps outright antagonism of the community. Even today, when the compadrazgo system is beginning to depart from its traditional ideological matrix, very few people would dare contravene this social imperative. The matter, then, is largely a question of etiquette: whom does one ask to enter into a compadrazgo relationship so that a minimum of immediate negative feelings are incurred. Even people well disposed toward contracting a compadrazgo relationship may find it temporarily impossible for social or economic reasons, so the Beleño needs to know in advance whether a prospective compadre can agree to enter into the relationship without undue social or economic hardship. He must therefore obtain the following information: is his prospective compadre in reasonable economic shape for the forthcoming compadrazgo activities; does he have other economic *compromisos* (obligations) that will interfere with his compadrazgo obligations; is he in good standing with his immediate and extended family so that they will not object to his accepting the compadrazgo; are there any social reasons such as mourning, a death in the family, illness, or other impending social compromisos that could seriously interfere with the proper conduct of the compadrazgo relationship; and so on?

It is on the basis of this information that Beleños finally decide whom they should ask to enter into a compadrazgo relationship. Such information is not difficult to gather in such a small community, for most of the social and economic affairs of the average famiy are well known to the people at large. When in doubt as to this information, or about any deep-seated, negative feelings that friends or neighbors may have, Beleños try to assess the situation by using friends and relatives as intermediaries to sound out the prospective compadres. This method never fails, and the etiquette of this aspect of the compadrazgo system is complied with scrupulously, thereby averting many unpleasant situations. This aspect of the system applies perhaps exclusively to endogamous compadrazgo, for in cases of exogamous compadrazgo, informants unanimously agreed, Beleños do not hesitate to risk a refusal, thereby recognizing that people from outside the community (especially those in urban areas) are probably not bound by an ideology that does not permit refusal. With respect to endogamous compadrazgo, we must point out that the *modus operandi* described here does not apply in the same fashion to all compadrazgo types, and that there is a definite gradation of compliance with its requirements. The more important the compadrazgo relationship, both structurally and ideologically, the more carefully will people comply with the requisites. For example, in the case of important types like baptism, marriage, or PCE, those who select the compadres take great pains to determine their adequacy and their ability to accept; the selection is much less rigorous in less important types such as graduation, FC, or aretes; and preliminary investigation is nonexistent in such a minor type as compadrazgo de amistad. Furthermore, it is important to note that considerations of adequacy and ability to accept are perhaps even more important in public-communal compadrazgo types, inasmuch as the entire community, at least theoretically, has a voice in the selection of compadres for these types. In summary, one of the main reasons selection functions smoothly in the compadrazgo system in Belén is that the people are willing to comply with the etiquette that prospective compadres must only be asked under optimum circumstances.

The Mediating Entity: Necessary and Sufficient Conditions

Compadrazgo relationships come into being through the link of a mediating entity, be it a person, an image, an object, or an occasion, and while this link is necessary to the structure of compadrazgo, it is not of primary importance to its functioning. Many ethnographic studies have overemphasized the importance of the mediating link to the detriment of the broader structural extensions of the compadrazgo system. Historically, it is true that the compadrazgo system was based on the parent-godson-godparent triad, but synchronically it represents a much broader structural context (see Part Three of *Ritual Kinship* I). The primary function of the mediating link is to serve as the immediate, ostensible motive for establishing a compadrazgo relationship, but it sinks into comparative or total unimportance after the central ritual and ceremonial complex has been completed.

One reason for the overemphasis on the mediating entity has been confusion between the necessary and sufficient conditions that shape a social unit or institution. The historical antecedents of the compadrazgo system have led many anthropologists to confuse the necessary and sufficient conditions of the synchronic situation.[2] When the compadrazgo system was introduced to the New World in the first half of the sixteenth century only persons were mediating entities, and at that time the mediating entity was not only the system's central, primary element, but its necessary and sufficient condition as well. This is no longer true today. Ahijados may still be a necessary condition for the compadrazgo system, but they are not a sufficient condition, for the system now includes such a variety of mediating entities that the concept of ahijados no longer suffices by itself. There are as many compadrazgo types today as there are occasions in the life and ceremonial cycles that people wish to make important by contracting ritual kinship ties.

Nevertheless, most anthropologists working in Latin America assign the same function and structure to all mediating entities, be they persons, religious images, or utilitarian objects. They assume implicitly that the nature of the mediating entity makes little difference to the structure of specific compadrazgo types, and compound the conceptual misunderstanding of compadrazgo by maintaining that in the synchronic situation the mediating entity is the central part of the system, as it was at the start of the system and for at least 150 years thereafter (see the appendix of *Ritual Kinship* I).

As we approach the contemporary situation, however, the original function of the compadrazgo system—the ritual and ceremonial help (sponsorship, intercession) afforded to the ahijados by the padrinos on the difficult and essentially dangerous occasions of the social and religious cycle—begins to recede rapidly as the primary, central part of the system. The primarily social aspects embodied in the compadre-compadre dyad begin to acquire major importance, and this is expressed to a large extent by the emphasis on fulfilling the duties and obligations that persist after the central ritual and ceremonial complex has been discharged. Furthermore, as we move from the inception of the compadrazgo system in most parts of the New World to the contemporary situation, there is a marked change in the character of the mediating entity. Instead of persons who were generally connected with the important occasions of baptism, marriage, and the orthodox religious cycle and folk life cycle, saints and images were institutionalized as mediating entities, and finally within the past 200 years, so were objects (see Part Three of *Ritual Kinship* I). (Here I also include occasions of danger or importance in everyday life, leading to such compadrazgo types as primera piedra, parada de cruz, or graduación.) The process is still going on, for if we are to judge by the history of Belén since the 1940s the number of compadrazgo types with an object (or occasion) as a mediating entity is still growing. The strongest evidence for the shift in importance from the padrino-ahijado dyad to the compadre-compadre dyad is the expansion of mediating entities from persons to images and objects. This seems clearly to be a manifestation of new motives and reasons for the expression of structural features that continue to have a great effect on the total societal framework, and that are in the long run expressed most strongly in the post-ritual and ceremonial duties and obligations of a social and economic nature.

The Ideological and Structural Components of the Mediating Entity

The ideological changes that the mediating entity has undergone during the development of the compadrazgo system over the past 450 years are set forth in detail in Part Three of *Ritual Kinship* I. From a strictly synchronic viewpoint, however, the mediating entity has several important aspects that must be explored in order to understand parts of the compadrazgo system such as private and public compadrazgo relationships, individual and communal relationships, primary and secondary compadrazgo types, primarily symbolic and primarily socioreligious types, and so on. First of all, it should be evident that in terms of both form and content, each compadrazgo type depends on the nature of the mediating entity, and the types in the system have therefore been classified according to whether they involve a person, a saint or image, or an event or physical object. The mediating entity—the ostensible reason for establishing a compadrazgo relationship—has primarily two structural aspects. On the one hand, it defines the nature of the ensuing relationship with respect to whether or not it will have a social padrinos-ahijados dyad which may be functionally discharged in a certain way. Thus, one could speak in terms of *compadrinazgo* (Ravicz 1967) only in cases in which the mediating entity is a living person. On the other hand, the nature and quality of the mediating entity to a large extent determine the total arrangement of ensuing functional relationships. In other words, the quality of being a person, image, or object; the social, economic, or religious characteristics of the mediating entity; and the conditions under which it has become the ostensible reason for establishing a compadrazgo type, are the attributes that define the global structural form and functional discharge of that type. The obvious flexibility of the compadrazgo system, which has often been pointed out by anthropologists who have dealt with the concept diachronically, comes precisely from constant change and from the increasing adoption of new mediating entities in order to adapt, sanction, or accommodate social, religious, economic, or symbolic behavior to changing conditions. In any event, the structural importance of the mediating entity must be kept separate from the functional interpretation of the assessment of the compadrazgo system as a global institution. This confusion between the structural and functional dimensions of the compadrazgo system has at times contributed to the mistaken idea that the central functional aspect of the institution is the padrinos-ahijados dyad, not—as I maintain—the compadres-compadres dyad. In terms of structure, the padrinos-ahijados dyad—or perhaps more accurately, the sponsor-sponsored entity—defines the compadrazgo type, but functionally this is not the case. It is quite evident that in nearly half the types (all those in which the mediating entity is an image or object) there is no ensuing, living padrinos-ahijados relationship, and in the other half the padrinos-ahijados relationship grows cold after varying periods of time.

The argument can be summarized by scaling the natural properties of the three basic types of mediating entities present in the compadrazgo system of Belén, which, it might be added, are the same in all compadrazgo systems found in the ethnographic literature. This will give a clearer conception of the natural constraints of all types of mediating entities, and of the subsequent modifications that give rise to the various categories of compadrazgo types. The most basic intrinsic properties of mediating entities are given by the position they occupy in the ideological order of the compadrazgo system, and a scaling of mediating entities is coterminous with the Beleños' conscious ideological scaling of compadrazgo types. In this context, the importance of a type is predicated on the ideological value of its corresponding mediating entity, and the distinction that the people of Belén make between sacramental and nonsacramental compadrazgo (which I have further subdivided into primary and secondary for heuristic purposes, a subdivision that is to some extent recognized by the people) indicates the ideological value they place upon the various compadrazgo types (see Part One of *Ritual Kinship* I). It is evident that this tentative threefold classification of all compadrazgo types in Belén, and the fact that the people attach significance to it, reflect the natural scaling of mediating entities: from persons, to saints and images, to objects and events. In descending importance, mediating entities (and their corresponding compadrazgo types) are primarily social, primarily religious, and primarily economic.

Analysis of the range of compadrazgo types in Belén shows that all of the types classified as sacramental compadrazgo have persons as mediating entities and have primarily a socioreligious matrix. Only five out of thirteen primary nonsacramental compadrazgo types have a person as a mediating entity; the other eight have a saint or an image, or religious event, and the matrix of this category too is primarily religious. Four out of eleven secondary nonsacramental compadrazgo types have persons as mediating entities. Two have a religious object or event, and five have physical objects; the matrix of this last category is primarily economic. In summary, the ideological ordering or scaling importance of mediating entities and corresponding compadrazgo types in Belén is arranged along two axes: the person-image or saint-object or event continuum; and the socioreligious-religious-economic matrix of structural-functional discharge. The high correlation between the two in the form and content of the compadrazgo system of Belén makes it appear that the ideological and the structural-functional orders are much the same, but this is not the case. Anything more than a superficial analysis reveals a new series of dimensions which show their divergence, and this is manifested in the discrepancy between the threefold classification discussed above (which is mainly an ideological classification) and the classification of those eleven compadrazgo types (1-5, 8, 9, 11, 15, 24, 25; see chart 1) that the people of Belén explicitly consider most important (which is mainly a structural-functional classification; see Chapter Two of *Ritual Kinship* I). (When I refer to the ideological foundation of the structural-functional system as primarily diachronic, I mean that it has resulted from the long process of action and reaction through which a social institution acquires its form as an expression of changing social, economic, religious, and political conditions, and, more important, that it cannot be properly conceptualized within a strictly synchronic matrix. Part Three of *Ritual Kinship* I makes it clear that the ideological order underlying the structural-functional discharge of the compadrazgo system today cannot be properly understood and conceptualized without reference to 450 years of Tlaxcalan acculturation.)

I maintain that the ideological order must be separated from the structural-functional order in analyzing a social institution, for otherwise it is difficult to formulate adequate explanations. The intrinsic assessment of compadrazgo types, and the total assessment of the system, are predicated on interinfluence between the ideological and the structural-functional orders. Thus, there is a certain ideological matrix that orders mediating entities and their corresponding compadrazgo types along a continuum of degrees of importance, but this continuum is modified by exogenous considerations that result primarily from the articulation between the structural-functional order of the compadrazgo system and the global framework of Belén culture and society. Neither the ideological classification embodied substantially in the threefold classification, nor the structural-functional classification embodied in the eleven most important types explicitly acknowledged by the people is adequate alone for assessing the absolute or relative importance of compadrazgo types in Belén. Furthermore, since we know both the ideological classification of the people and the overt structural ranking it is important to ascertain the considerations (exogenous to the compadrazgo system itself) that constitute the sufficient causes for the working and discharge of the system. These exogenous considerations are social, religious, economic, and symbolic, and they represent not only the ostensible functions in which the structure is exemplified, but also the conditions for expanding the system and articulating it with the total framework of Belén culture and society.

The Synchronic and Diachronic Dimensions of the Mediating Entity as an Index of Change

The mediating entity has been discussed extensively because it represents a microcosm of the compadrazgo system in form and content, and is thus analytically profitable to investigate; that is, the properties of the system and the conditions underlying its functional discharge emanate from this core. Paradoxically, the mediating entity is not intrinsically important or interesting either as a structural entity or in its functional implications, but it embodies a series of synchronic and diachronic dimensions that the investigator is well advised to analyze before he begins to expand his structural analysis. Diachronically, the mediating entity is the best indicator of the acculturative development of the compadrazgo system, for it not only shows the growth of the system by the addition of new persons, images, or objects as ostensible reasons for establishing new compadrazgo relationships, but perhaps more important, it indicates the extent to which the compadrazgo system is responding to the general process of change being experienced by the total sociocultural system. Thus, the diachronic analysis of mediating entities sketches a picture of the structural development of the compadrazgo system as well as the emergence of the ideological order underlying that development. No other structural aspect of the compadrazgo system occupies such a central or analytically significant position.[3] From the synchronic viewpoint, on the other hand, the mediating entity is an adequate concept around which to organize the structural and functional analysis, for it involves many focal aspects of the compadrazgo system as a global entity. Finally, the value of the mediating entity as an analytical threshold can also be extended to the articulation of the compadrazgo system and the general framework of community culture and society, for the flexibility and adaptability of the system should be taken as indicators of the degree to which it is an expression of the changing and acculturative conditions at any given point. Thus, every appearance of a new compadrazgo type is an indication of socioeconomic change and of the response of traditional mechanisms to pressures and influences from the outside world, and this in turn marks the position that the compadrazgo system has in the overall sociocultural system.

In the case of Belén in particular, and Tlaxcala in general, and by extension many areas of Mesoamerica, the synchronic and diachronic dimensions of the mediating entity constitute a significant measure of change and acculturation. This is not surprising, given the universality of compadrazgo and its pervasiveness within the sociocultural system of which it is a part, but this very universality and pervasiveness make it either a rather vague institution to use as a conceptualizing entity or a kind of unconscious clearinghouse (from the standpoint of the investigator) for analyzing a series of behavior patterns pertaining primarily to the social and religious domains. Conceptually, then, the compadrazgo system may be regarded either as a field of social and religious action which is so vast as perhaps to be worthless to the investigator, or as a very narrow field usually confined to what I have called ritual kinship sponsorship. Anthropologists who have given accounts of specific compadrazgo systems, as well as those who have addressed themselves to the institution as an ethnological, comparative institution, have tended toward one or the other extreme (see the appendix of *Ritual Kinship* I). My position is that neither of these stands is tenable; the former leads to valueless generalizations while the latter unnecessarily restricts the compadrazgo system by emphasizing the mediating entity as a structural-functional entity per se.[4]

One very important aspect I have not touched on so far, which is closely connected with this analysis, concerns the necessary variables and sufficient causes that operate in the introduction and adoption of new mediating entities resulting in new compadrazgo types. What dynamic principles govern the adaptability and the expansion potential of the compadrazgo system? The answers lie outside the compadrazgo system itself and are related primarily to its functional dimensions, and they depend on how the system itself is articulated in the general framework of Belén society. A large part of the functional analysis of the compadrazgo system is concerned with elucidating the operative principles underlying it, and only in this context can we answer these questions.

Compadrazgo and Compadrinazgo

A few words might be said about the heuristic and methodological implications of the mediating entity, especially the misplaced emphasis on it as the all-important element of the compadrazgo system. This way of looking at the compadrazgo system has become increasingly popular in recent anthropological literature, and the view can best be exemplified by the concept of compadrinazgo (Ravicz 1967). Compadrinazgo holds that the most important relationship that structures and shapes any compadrazgo type is that obtaining in the padrinos-ahijados dyad. Those who look at the compadrazgo system from this viewpoint do make the distinction between "*compadrinazgo*" (a barbarous corruption of Spanish) and "*compadrazgo*," but they confuse the centrality of the mediating entity with its structural and functional importance in the total system. This confusion of the structural and functional roles of the mediating entity is compounded diachronically in the sense that those who think that the compadrazgo system may best be conceptualized in terms of compadrinazgo mistake the genesis of the institution with its synchronic expression at a given point in time. The development from compadrinazgo (which can be defined essentially as the functional and direct expression of ritual kinship sponsorship as applied exclusively to individuals) to compadrazgo (which can be defined as the overall application or extension of ritual kinship sponsorship to persons, images, objects, or any important social, religious, or even economic occasion or event) is primarily determined by the addition of increasingly diversified nonindividual and ramified mediating entities. It may be unrealistic to employ the concept of compadrazgo to cover this broad range of socioreligious phenomena, and used properly the concept of compadrinazgo can no doubt be employed to refer to a part of the compadrazgo system. There are, however, some heuristic and practical disadvantages to using the term compadrinazgo for the vast range of phenomena described in Part One of *Ritual Kinship* I as the various types of compadrazgo.

First, anthropologists have not been all that interested in the institution of compadrazgo, even though they recognize its universality in Indian, peasant, and even urban Latin American societies.[5] In fairness I should point out that anthropologists who have used the concept of compadrinazgo as standing for compadrazgo (Ravicz 1967:238–242) have gone on to describe the extra–padrinos-ahijados dimensions of the institution; none of them really maintains that the padrinos-ahijados dyad exhausts the web of duties, rights, and obligations; they argue, rather, that everything is structured and functionally discharged on the basis of that dyad. In a sense, then, I have used the term compadrinazgo explicitly to denote the inadequacies that inevitably derive from undue emphasis on the padrinos-ahijados dyad as the primary aspect of the compadrazgo system, an overemphasis that has some important methodological implications:

1. It leads us to regard compadrazgo not as a system but rather as a series of dyadic relationships with specific functions and activities. There is nothing wrong with conducting a social analysis on the basis of dyadic relationships, but when such relationships are taken as conceptual ends in themselves (see Foster 1961) and are not articulated with other dyadic relationships or with other subsystems, then this seems to me a rather empty analytical procedure which can lead only to monistic, disjointed descriptions and explanations. The advantage of regarding compadrazgo as a system is primarily that it helps us to articulate this block of socioreligious behavior and associated activities with other systems in the total framework of Belén society, and of countless other communities like it.

2. It assumes a priori that the initial occasions of ritual kinship sponsorship, and especially baptism (the original ritual kinship sponsorship model), are the intrinsically most important compadrazgo types in the system (whereas in Belén, and Tlaxcala in general, several other types are equally important) and that other types with nonhuman mediating entities are naturally of secondary importance and often insignificant. While this a priori scaling of the institution may not be harmful if we regard compadrazgo as a series of unrelated types, it is unacceptable if we view compadrazgo as a system with its own operational principles. Furthermore, this assumption makes the mistake of confusing the ideological and structural-functional orders—that is, confusing what people should do with what they actually do (Nutini 1965b:718).

3. Finally, perhaps the most serious shortcoming of looking at the institution in terms of compadrinazgo is the implicit notion that social units and institutions can be studied in isolation so long as we establish their form and content and the immediate web of bonds and obligations that link their personnel. This *modus operandi* (which pervades not only studies of compadrazgo but most studies of kinship and socioreligious institutions in Mesoamerica) can lead only to an atomistic account of social structure and process.[6]

CHAPTER 2

The Personnel of the Compadrazgo System

I have already described the networks of personnel that participate in specific compadrazgo types (see Chapters Three through Five of *Ritual Kinship* I), and here I would like to put the structure of personnel in perspective vis-à-vis the total compadrazgo system. In this chapter I also analyze those anomalous situations that involve the addition or deletion of personnel, plus a few anomalies in the organization of personnel that are significant in the general structure of the system. Thus, these topics are analyzed: (1) the organization of personnel in terms of primary, secondary, and tertiary actors or ritual kinsmen; (2) personnel and their extensions in compadrazgo types that require only one sponsor (padrino or madrina), and the relative positions of these types; (3) the web of ritual kinship in compadrazgo types that include personnel who function at the same time as ahijados and compadres, and the structural implications of such situations; (4) the implications and extensions of personnel in compadrazgo relationships in which the padrino and madrina are not husband and wife; (5) the role and nature of children as primary actors in the compadrazgo system, as both subjects and objects, and the permanence of the relationship established; (6) the personnel of compadrazgo types in which multiple dyads obtain between the padrinos and ahijados and among compadres, and the structural implications of this situation; (7) the endogamous and exogamous (with respect to the community) dimensions of the personnel of the compadrazgo system, and their implications for the acceptable discharge of given compadrazgo types.

Primary, Secondary, and Tertiary Actors

The primary actors of any given compadrazgo type are all those persons who participate directly or are immediately involved in any of the three basic dyads, namely, padrinos-ahijados, compadres (padrinos)-compadres (kinsmen or owners of mediating entity), and ahijados (mediating entity)-parents (kinsmen, owners). Thus, the following combinations of primary actors are possible: (1) Under normal circumstances, the primary actors of a compadrazgo type involve two padrinos (male and female), one ahijado or ahijada, and two parents (male and female) or kinsmen, for a total of five persons. (2) When the mediating entity is a deceased person, an image or saint, or an object or event, there are only two fundamental dyads and four primary actors, that is, the two padrinos and the two parents (or kinsmen) or owners of the mediating entity. (In Belén, at least, all of the nonindividual mediating entities require two padrinos, one male and one female, as well as two owners, usually husband and wife.) (3) When the mediating entity is an individual but the compadrazgo requires only one padrino-madrina, all three fundamental dyads exist but with only four primary actors. (4) A final combination can be added in the form of multiple-dyad compadrazgo types—for example, marriage and ANDI compadrazgo—in which there are multiple dyads between padrinos-ahijados and compadres-compadres. This combination of primary actors can include ten or more compadres-compadres or padrinos-ahijados dyads, and the total number of primary actors involved in these cases depends on the total number of multiple dyads. The dyadic relationships in multiple-dyad types are structurally individual and ego centered, and by themselves do not constitute a subsystem. For example, in marriage compadrazgo there are ten possible subdyadic relationships, because the couple can have ten subsidiary padrinos (see Chapter Three of *Ritual Kinship* I). In this case, the ahijados (that is, the married couple) are dyadically related to as many padrinos as sanctioned by the marriage with subsidiary ritual events, and the parents of the married couple also stand in a dyadic relationship to all of them. But all the various marriage padrinos (couples) are not necessarily unrelated to each other, except under certain circumstances. The same situation obtains in ANDI compadrazgo, in which the padrinos de acostada become compadres of all the sponsors of this activity of the religious ayuntamiento (*mayordomos* and *fiscales*, the principal officials), but the mayordomos and fiscales do not necessarily become compadres to one another. It should be noted, furthermore, that this public-communal compadrazgo type offers as many possible dyadic relationships as there are inhabitants in Belén, with the padrinos playing the central role, but this is primarily symbolic and is not activated socially or economically in any important way (see Chapter Four of *Ritual Kinship* I).

There are twelve compadrazgo types in Belén that involve multiple dyads (see table 1). The most elaborate are the two mentioned above, but in general all compadrazgo types involving primarily religious sponsorship and of a public-communal nature are potentially as elaborate as the marriage and ANDI compadrazgo types. Moreover, some multiple dyads—for example, marriage compadrazgo—may be said to involve as many different compadrazgo types as there are sponsoring events or things associated with the marriage ceremonies (that is, arras, anillos, lazo, and so on). I have chosen to regard marriage compadrazgo

TABLE 1. Compadrazgo Types with Single or Multiple Relationships

Type	Single Dyads	Multiple Dyads[1]
Bautizo	x	
Casamiento		x
Confirmación	x	
PCE		x
Primera comunión	x	
CCCH		x
CCCA		x
ANDC	x	
ANDI		x
AOI		x
BSI	x	
CSV		x
Escapulario	x	
Graduación	x	
PCA		x
Quince años	x	
Sacada a misa	x	
Compadrazgo de evangelios	x	
Compadrazgo de limpia		x
BOI		x
Bendición de casa	x	
BCC	x	
BM		x
Parada de cruz		x
Primera piedra	x	
Compadrazgo de amistad	x	
CABP	x	
Compadrazgo de aretes	x	
CEON	x	
FC	x	
JJ	x	

[1] These are collective relationships with more than one compadres-compadres or padrinos-ahijados dyad.

as a single type, with as many as ten possible subtypes, because the Beleños themselves view it as a unit, and also because there is considerable leeway regarding the establishment of the subsidiary sponsorships (see *Ritual Kinship* I, pages 74-87). With respect to the number and organization of personnel, then, the first three combinations present no problems and require no further clarification. The fourth combination, on the other hand, needs considerable elucidation, for multiple-dyad compadrazgo types are perhaps the best examples of how the compadrazgo system can at times approximate the structure of a true kinship system.

Secondary actors are defined as all those individuals who are primary relatives (real kinsmen) of primary actors, namely, siblings, parents, children, and spouses. All these categories of kin stand in well-defined relationships to primary compadrazgo actors, and of course the range of application of well-defined behavior patterns, rights, and obligations varies among the compadrazgo types.

The rubric of tertiary actors covers a rather broad category of individuals who may or may not be related through kinship to primary or secondary actors, but who do play a certain, albeit minimal, role and engage in fairly well defined behavior patterns in a few of the most important compadrazgo types. The web of ritual kinship behavior and the extension of rights, obligations, and behavior patterns that characterize these types are dealt with separately, for at the moment I want only to delineate the categories of ritual kinsmen as they enter into the general organization of compadrazgo types. Further, the category of tertiary compadrazgo actors is most significantly embodied in the incest prohibitions associated with each type of the compadrazgo system. In this light, tables 2 and 3 are quite significant. Table 2 shows that well-defined behavior patterns as well as ritual kinship terminology are extended to tertiary actors in five compadrazgo types; in sixteen types they are extended to secondary actors only; and in ten types they are extended to primary actors only. Table 3 indicates that the incest taboo of compadrazgo (that is, marriage prohibitions) extends to tertiary actors in two compadrazgo types, to secondary actors in four types, and to primary actors in eleven types; fourteen compadrazgo types carry no marriage prohibitions, except among padrinos and ahijados.[1]

At this point it is important to draw attention to those junctures at which compadrazgo, as a system of ritual kinship, most closely resembles the true kinship system in structure of personnel and general organization. In a kinship system there are basically two types of relationships: those among individuals in a dyadic pattern; and those among all individuals who are exocentrically united by the web of kinship. A kinship system thus involves ego-centered as well as global-exocentric re-

TABLE 2. Extension of Ritual Kinship Terminology and Behavior
by Compadrazgo Type

Type	Primary	Secondary	Tertiary
Bautizo			x
Casamiento			x
Confirmación		x	
PCE			x
Primera comunión		x	
CCCH		x	
CCCA		x	
ANDC		x	
ANDI		x	
AOI	x		
BSI		x	
CSV		x	
Escapulario		x	
Graduación	x		
PCA		x	
Quince años	x		
Sacada a misa		x	
Compadrazgo de evangelios		x	
Compadrazgo de limpia		x	
BOI	x		
Bendición de casa			x
BCC	x		
BM		x	
Parada de cruz			x
Primera Piedra		x	
Compadrazgo de amistad	x		
CABP		x	
Compadrazgo de aretes	x		
CEON	x		
FC	x		
JJ	x		

lationships (that is, relationships binding upon the members of the total aggregate). The general organization of a kinship system depends on the interplay of these two types of relationships, which together define the structural parameters of the system. From this formal standpoint, the compadrazgo system is not unlike a real kinship system, for although the former involves primarily ego-centered relationships, within

TABLE 3. Extension of Incest Prohibition to
Compadrazgo Actors by Type

Type	None	Primary	Secondary	Tertiary
Bautizo				x
Casamiento			x	
Confirmación			x	
PCE				x
Primera comunión			x	
CCCH		x		
CCCA		x		
ANDC		x		
ANDI		x		
AOI	x			
BSI		x		
CSV	x			
Escapulario	x			
Graduación	x			
PCA		x		
Quince años	x			
Sacada a misa		x		
Compadrazgo de evangelios		x		
Compadrazgo de limpia		x		
BOI	x			
Bendición de casa		x		
BCC	x			
BM	x			
Parada de cruz			x	
Primera piedra		x		
Compadrazgo de amistad	x			
CABP	x			
Compadrazgo de aretes	x			
CEON	x			
FC	x			
JJ	x			

certain contexts there arise global-exocentric relationships binding upon the system as a whole. It is incorrect to say simply that compadrazgo is composed entirely of a series of ego-centered relationships in a dyadic pattern, for there are instances when we can speak of specific networks of compadrazgo as defined in terms of global-exocentric relationships. This is especially the case in such compadrazgo types as marriage, ANDI, and PCA, and probably in all public-communal types. While dyadic relationships among compadres predominate in them, there is a certain dimension in which the compadres-compadres dyad is transcended, and functionally—though perhaps not permanently—the sum total of such dyads must to some extent be regarded as a corporate whole, with the dyads standing in a global-exocentric relationship. In essence, then, the structural and functional differences between the compadrazgo system and a real kinship system are not categorical, but rather a matter of degree; ego-centered relationships predominate in the former, global-exocentric relationships in the latter. Further, we are speaking at the moment about the compadrazgo system with reference to individual compadrazgo types; that is, the system here is defined by the total number of relationships, both ego-centered and global-exocentric, among all primary actors and their extensions. Under these conditions the ego-centered dimensions of compadrazgo loom the largest, and this is probably what has made anthropologists view the institution as little more than a series of isolated dyadic relationships.

When, however, we move on to the two more important structural aspects of compadrazgo, more global-exocentric dimensions become apparent. The first of these aspects appears when we consider the total number of compadres (from all the different compadrazgo types he has contracted) a given individual has; with all their extensions, they may number hundreds of individuals and involve a very complicated web of rights, duties, and obligations. In this case, ego-centered relationships may still predominate, but at the same time there is a significant increment of global-exocentric relationships that make the compadrazgo system function not unlike a true kinship system on a variety of occasions. I have in mind here the continuing rights and obligations entailed by certain types of compadrazgo, which make the global system function as a corporation (see Chapters Three and Four of *Ritual Kinship* I)—the web of relationships resulting from compadres who double or triple in a series of compadrazgo types that are structurally complementary or functionally involve communal obligations. The second structural aspect of compadrazgo emerges when we regard it as an important aspect of community life, and as organizing, or helping to give form to, a rather vast portion of social, religious, and even economic behavior. From this standpoint, the compadrazgo system most resembles the real kinship system, and in several aspects the former may be regarded as an extension or complement of the latter. Finally, while it is heuristically adequate to keep in mind the predominance of ego-centered relationships in the compadrazgo system as distinct from the predominantly global-exocentric nature of the real kinship system, the former must necessarily be regarded as a system functionally organized in a similar fashion to the latter.

The major criticism, therefore, of most of the literature on compadrazgo is that the institution has never been analyzed as a system. Most anthropologists have regarded compadrazgo as an important aspect of community life, but they have failed to assess its conceptual importance (see the appendix of *Ritual Kinship* I). This standpoint, of course, is much the same as that exhibited in most community studies in Mesoamerica (and perhaps the whole of peasant Latin America), which implicitly assume that kinship is not very important in the organization of primarily peasant communities. From a conceptual viewpoint, a social institution or social unit is as important as the investigator wishes to make it, if—and only if—he takes the trouble to redefine it and place it in the wider societal framework, so that its analysis becomes a core around which he can assemble a wide range of social, economic, religious, and even political behavior in order to explain that behavior more adequately. It is in this light that this study of the compadrazgo system must be assessed. I am not so much interested here in the compadrazgo system per se as in how it can be used for getting at other more fundamental aspects and processes of Belén culture and society (and, by extension, Tlaxcalan society)—for example, the nature of the ideology underlying the structural order, and the interactions between the two; the nature of change and acculturation in Belén and Tlaxcala in general; the interconnection of the social, religious, and economic spheres; the role of economics in situations of rapid secularization, and so on. I am trying to look at the sociocultural system of Belén from the vantage point of the compadrazgo system as an all-pervading aspect of community life, much as the British social anthropologists made use of kinship systems in their studies of the social life of African tribes. The only significant difference here is that this study involves important diachronic dimensions, and I have tried to analyze the global situation in terms of the intimate relationship between the synchronic and diachronic variables.

Compadrazgo Types Requiring Only One Sponsor

Several compadrazgo types in Belén require only one sponsor, a padrino or a madrina depending on the sex of the mediating entity, for only compadrazgo types with persons as mediating entities can exhibit this anomaly. Table 4 shows that there are nine such types: confirmación, primera comunión, escapulario, graduación, sacada a misa, compadrazgo de evangelios, compadrazgo de limpia, compadrazgo de aretes, and FC. In addition, six of the subtypes of marriage compadrazgo re-

TABLE 4. Compadrazgo Types Sponsored by a Couple or an Individual

Type	Couple	Individual
Bautizo	x	
Casamiento		Madrina (six of the subtypes)
Confirmación		Madrina or padrino (sex of child)
PCE	x	
Primera comunión		Madrina or padrino (sex of child)
CCCH	x	
CCCA	x	
ANDC	x	
ANDI	x	
AOI	x	
BSI	x	
CSV	x	
Escapulario		Madrina or padrino (sex of person)
Graduación		Madrina or padrino (sex of graduate)
PCA	x	
Quince años	x	
Sacada a misa		Madrina
Compadrazgo de evangelios		Madrina or padrino (sex of child)
Compadrazgo de limpia		Madrina or padrino (sex of person)
BOI	x	
Bendición de casa	x	
BCC	x	
BM	x	
Parada de cruz	x	
Primera piedra	x	
Compadrazgo de amistad	x	
CABP	x	
Compadrazgo de aretes		Madrina
CEON	x	
FC		Madrina or padrino (sex of finder)
JJ	x	

quire only one sponsor. In seven of the nine cases the sex of the ahijados determines the sex of the sponsor: in compadrazgo de aretes, of course, the sponsor is always a madrina, and in sacada a misa compadrazgo the sponsor is also always a madrina, whether the infant is a boy or a girl. The other exception is that the sponsor in all six subsidiary compadrazgo types of marriage is always a madrina (lazo, ramo, libro, rosario, pañuelo, and pastel).

What does it mean substantively to have only one padrino or madrina in any given compadrazgo type, and what does it involve structurally? First, the central activities of the compadrazgo type, from pedimento to recurrent rites and ceremonies (see diagram 1), do not require the presence of the sponsor's spouse; there are no structural injunctions about his or her direct participation in any event or activity of the type. In practice, however, spouses do participate in subsidiary roles, primarily giving social and ritual support to the padrino or madrina. After the main rites and ceremonies are over, there is virtually no difference between this group of compadrazgo types and the other compadrazgo types in Belén. For example, in confirmación, unless there are serious impediments, the padrino or madrina is accompanied by his or her spouse throughout the religious ceremonies and subsequent events, and this can be said of virtually all the other types noted above. The only exception is sacada a misa compadrazgo, in which only the madrina accompanies the mother and infant to church. Structurally speaking, these compadrazgo types are fundamentally the same as those that require both padrino and madrina, and there are no significant differences beyond that of personnel. All other things being equal, compadrazgo types with only one sponsor always involve less personnel than do normal types with two sponsors, and thus are worth noting specifically. The people themselves make no distinctions, however, and behave toward one-sponsor compadrazgo types as if they were normal types. Under these circumstances, there are no structural or functional reasons for isolating a category of compadrazgo types with a single sponsor, for no meaningful correlations obtain with respect to the extension of ritual kinship behavior, ritual kinship terminology, the extension of incest prohibitions, or any of the significant structural characteristics.

It must be realized, however, that seven of the nine types concern religious events in the life cycle, while the other two involve secular aspects of the life cycle, and that the ahijados, with two possible exceptions, are children. These are perhaps the only significant correlations associated with this group of compadrazgo types that I am not able to explain adequately ideologically or structurally. It is important to explain this anomaly and its associated aspect, namely, that there are no compadrazgo types in Belén with only one sponsor when the mediating entity is an image or object. This is a typical case in which the synchronic matrix fails to yield a meaningful explanation and in which the answer may emerge from analysis of the diachronic matrix. Although it is possible that with new ethnographic data, the synchronic matrix could reveal a solution, the assumption that the diachronic and synchronic matrices are never sharply separated is far more likely to lead to results. The ethnographic and ethnologic literature shows many instances of manufactured structural or functional explanations (strictly synchronic by the standard definition of these concepts) for cases such as the one under consideration, in which a solution is forced because of lack of a diachronic dimension, whereas either a combination of synchronic and diachronic elements or a sequence of strictly diachronic elements would be the only possible means of eliciting an explanation.

A good reason, however, for regarding the nine compadrazgo types with only one sponsor as analytically significant is that they afford an example of the sometimes serious discrepancies between the ideological and structural-functional orders. The people are fully aware that the ideology of the compadrazgo system prescribes that only one sponsor, male or female, is necessary in these nine types. They also know (and this is verbalized by most Beleños) that there need not be any direct compadrazgo relationships with the sponsor's spouse. In practice, however, the sponsor's spouse and extensions are accorded the same structural position and functional discharge as in any normal compadrazgo type. Thus, Beleños are aware that they should do such and such, but they *actually* do thus and so. Let us say here that Beleños are aware of both the ideology—what they should do—and the structure (in a Pickwickian sense) of the system—that is, what they actually do. This should be qualified, however: what Beleños actually do must in turn be looked at from the viewpoint of what they ultimately do (that is, as the outcome of a series of considerations), and of how their structural behavior is modified by a series of constraints that are not necessarily part of the phenomenon at hand. But what Beleños are not aware of is the discrepancy between the ideological order itself and the structural order and its two domains (the structural order per se and the structural order in action as modified by exogenous constraints), and this is the key to and the interesting aspect of the discrepancy. Most anthropologists are well aware of the two parameters—ideal and actual behavior—that govern sociocultural systems, and they know that to understand how a system or institution works, we must analyze both the imperative to action and the action itself. It is not enough to say simply that the people know that ideologically only one sponsor is needed in these nine compadrazgo types, or that these types are structurally and functionally undistinguishable from normal compadrazgo types. The crux of the matter is to explain and understand, first, how the ideological order is articulated with both aspects of the structural order; and second, why the people are unaware of the discrepancy that is so obvious to an observer outside the system, and to determine what constraints are operative at this juncture. I have not solved the problems envisaged here, but in the appendix I have sketched a tentative, limited-range theory regarding the articulation of these orders which may help us to understand them.

Compadrazgo Types Including Personnel Who Function as Ahijados and Compadres at the Same Time

Several compadrazgo types in Belén require that certain primary actors function at the same time as padrinos, ahijados, and compadres, or that any of these three categories of primary actors be transformed into another category in the development of the compadrazgo relationship— most commonly, ahijados to compadres. There are eleven compadrazgo types in this category (see table 5): six subtypes of marriage compadrazgo, plus CCCH, CCCA, ANDC, ANDI, CSV, escapulario, sacada a misa, compadrazgo de limpia, CABP, and FC. In marriage compadrazgo, the six subsidiary madrinas (lazo, ramo, libro, rosario, pañuelo, and pastel) are usually of the same age group as the bride and groom, and are generally chosen by the bride. Immediately after the wedding ceremonies, these madrinas often become the comadres of the bride with all the appropriate extensions; that is, they become ritually related to the bride and groom in a manner equivalent to that of the compadres-compadres dyad. Both CCCH and CCCA compadrazgo include several padrinos-ahijados dyads that may be transformed into compadres-compadres dyads, which operate along generational and economic lines. In ANDI, ANDC, and CSV compadrazgo, the young madrinas important to these three types are always of a different generation from that of the adult participants, and after the ceremonies are over, they are individually or communally transformed into ahijadas. The padrino or madrina in escapulario compadrazgo becomes compadre or comadre of the ahijado or ahijada after the ceremonies are over if the latter are adults; but if they are children, the padrinos continue permanently in that status. The madrina for sacada a misa compadrazgo automatically becomes the comadre of the woman who has been presented in church as the final rite in the purification cycle, with the corresponding extensions of ritual kinship behavior. In CABP, the padrinos become compadres of the ahijados after the ceremonies are over. If the ahijado or ahijada in compadrazgo de limpia is an adult, he or she automatically becomes the compadre or comadre of the padrino or madrina, with the corresponding extensions; an ahijado(a) who is a child retains the status permanently.

TABLE 5. Transformation of Primary Actors' Roles
by Compadrazgo Type

Type	Fixed Role	Transformed Role[1]
Bautizo	x	
Casamiento		Six of the subsidiary madrinas become comadres of the bride
Confirmación	x	
PCE	x	
Primera comunión	x	
CCCH		Several padrino(a)–ahijado(a) dyads are transformed into compadres-compadres dyads
CCCA		Several padrino(a)–ahijado(a) dyads are transformed into compadres-compadres dyads
ANDC		Young madrina becomes ahijada
ANDI		Young madrina becomes ahijada
AOI	x	
BSI	x	
CSV		Young madrina becomes ahijada
Escapulario		Adult ahijado(a) becomes compadre or comadre
Graduación	x	
PCA	x	
Quince años	x	
Sacada a misa		Ahijada becomes comadre
Compadrazgo de evangelios	x	
Compadrazgo de limpia		Adult ahijado(a) becomes compadre or comadre
BOI	x	
Bendición de casa	x	
BCC	x	
BM	x	
Parada de cruz	x	
Primera piedra	x	
Compadrazgo de amistad	x	
CABP		Ahijados become compadres
Compadrazgo de aretes	x	
CEON	x	

TABLE 5 (cont.)

Type	Fixed Role	Transformed Role[1]
FC		Adult ahijado(a) becomes compadre or comadre
JJ	x	

[1] All mediating entities function as ahijados throughout the central rites and ceremonies. The transformation of roles takes place immediately or shortly after this event.

The same is true of FC: an adult who finds a twin fruit becomes compadre or comadre to the padrino or madrina; a child permanently retains the status of ahijado or ahijada.

On the whole, the most important principle underlying the structure of ritual kinship behavior and personnel in these anomalous compadrazgo types is generational; that is, no cross-generational relationships, with corresponding behavior patterns, endure beyond the ritual, ceremonial, and social and economic activities associated with the core of the compadrazgo type. After the central complex of the compadrazgo relationship is over, the padrinos-ahijados and the compadres-compadres dyads must be transformed if they include primary actors of a different generation; padrinos are transformed into ahijados, or ahijados are transformed into compadres. The fact that the three main categories of primary compadrazgo actors must function for a short time in cross-generational roles is simply an operational constraint that specific mediating entities impose upon the compadrazgo type, given the nature of the ritual occasion.

The economic implications of this anomalous situation are also of some importance, in that whatever permanent bonds and obligations are involved in the compadres-compadres dyad, children (who are involved in the majority of these types) cannot very well fulfill them. Furthermore, since these compadrazgo types, with the exception of ANDI and ANDC, are not among the most significant in Belén, the strength and longevity of the padrinos-ahijados dyad are not great, and the compadres-compadres dyad is bound to become the core of the compadrazgo type, on the basis of which it acquires a relative status within the total compadrazgo system of Belén. We should also note that in the general organization of these types there is sometimes a significant transposition or inversion of roles for the central ceremonies, which differentiates them from normal compadrazgo types. For example, young children play the role of ritual sponsors in the truly ritual and ceremonial sense (in ANDI and ANDC); adults make the pedimento in the role of compadres for themselves as sponsored mediating entities (in CABP and escapulario compadrazgo), and so on. With the exception of the six subsidiary compadrazgo types (or madrinazgos) of marriage, the most significant of these types within the total compadrazgo system are preeminently of a ritual and ceremonial nature (ANDI, ANDC, and CSV), in which the ostensible mediating entity is an image occupying a central place in the religious-ceremonial organization of the community, which requires the sponsorship of children as associated with purity and the nature of the occasion. The primarily ritual-ceremonial meaning of these compadrazgo types makes them somewhat different from the other eight types of this category. Compadrazgo types such as CABP, compadrazgo de limpia, escapulario, or sacada a misa are simply the result of certain recognized events in the life and religious cycles which do not make the mediating entity an intrinsically significant sponsored object, and the fact that they entail either adults or children is taken by the people as a natural constraint.

These eleven anomalous compadrazgo types have in common a clearly dualistic element in which there is a transposition of roles and a crossing of generations during the principal rites but an almost automatic reversal of roles once these are over: child padrinos become ahijados, and adult ahijados become compadres. In at least three of these compadrazgo types the change to natural generational roles is fairly well institutionalized, as in CABP, when the padrinos give the ahijados (those who are celebrating their twenty-fifth wedding anniversary) the prescribed present. During this formal, final ritual occasion the padrinos and ahijados exchange speeches and thanks, and it is verbally established that thenceforth they will be compadres in accordance with Belén custom. In general, this set of compadrazgo types is significant not so much because its form and content differ substantially from normal compadrazgo types in Belén, as because it shows the principle of not crossing generations in operation, as well as some of the functions of children in the compadrazgo system of Belén.

Compadrazgo Relationships in Which the Padrino and Madrina Are Not Husband and Wife

In some compadrazgo relationships in Belén the padrino and madrina are not married. The ideology of the system holds that it is best for sponsors to be married couples, but there is a gradation of permissible departures from this rule. Approximately 90 percent of all compadrazgo relationships in Belén involve sponsors who are husband and wife, and the remaining 10 percent covers virtually the whole spectrum of the compadrazgo system. It is important to determine how departures from the ideological rule are related to compadrazgo types, the reasons and conditions under which the unmarried sponsors are selected, and the implications for the extensions of ritual kinship terminology and behavior.

Although the injunction is clear, structurally speaking—and given certain exogenous considerations—any compadrazgo type in Belén can involve sponsors who are not married. This has occurred at least once in each compadrazgo career in the sample. The ideological rule is binding in varying degrees, however, with the result that certain compadrazgo types predominate in this anomalous structure. Obviously, the nine types that require only one sponsor (padrino or madrina) are most often found in this category of relationships, since it does not matter whether the sponsors are married or not. In fact, these nine types could also be categorized under the present heading of nonmarried sponsors. Next in the gradation come the nonsacramental compadrazgo types that have an object or event as mediating entity, such as AOI, BOI, BCC, CEON, and so on; the exceptions here are the compadrazgos of bendición de casa, primera piedra, and parada de cruz. All these types fairly often involve sponsors who are not married to each other. Next come various nonsacramental compadrazgo types that involve primarily images or persons, but also objects, which have a primarily symbolic or religious meaning (see table 6); among these are included such types as BSI, compadrazgo de evangelios, bendición de casa, BM, parada de cruz, and primera piedra. There are few nonmarried sponsors in these compadrazgo types, and Beleños believe that it is best to avoid such relationships if possible. Finally, the people are very reluctant to establish compadrazgo relationships with nonmarried couples in all cases of sacramental compadrazgo (with the exception of primera comunión, which belongs to the previous category) and in the two most important public-communal compadrazgo types, ANDI and PCA. In these cases they are effectively constrained ideologically, and only under extreme or very special circumstances will they engage in an anomalous relationship. This gradation of breaking the ideological rule is clearly verbalized; the preceding categorization of compadrazgo types is an expression of what the people actually say, and analytically I could not improve upon this explicit scale. What is interesting here is the question of why the people are sometimes so conscious of the subtle interplay of the ideological and structural orders, while in other instances they are unaware of discrepancies that are immediately obvious to the anthropological observer.

A variety of reasons can be adduced for the anomalous practice of contracting compadrazgo relationships involving nonmarried couples;

TABLE 6. Primary Meaning of Compadrazgo Types

Type	Primary Meaning
Bautizo	Religious-social
Casamiento	Social-religious
Confirmación	Religious
PCE	Symbolic-religious
Primera comunión	Religious
CCCH	Social
CCCA	Social
ANDC	Social-symbolic
ANDI	Symbolic
AOI	Symbolic-religious
BSI	Religious-social
CSV	Symbolic-religious
Escapulario	Symbolic-religious
Graduación	Social
PCA	Symbolic
Quince años	Social
Sacada a misa	Religious-social
Compadrazgo de evangelios	Symbolic-religious
Compadrazgo de limpia	Symbolic-social
BOI	Symbolic-religious
Bendición de casa	Symbolic-social
BCC	Symbolic-social
BM	Symbolic
Parada de cruz	Symbolic
Primera piedra	Symbolic
Compadrazgo de amistad	Social
CABP	Social
Compadrazgo de aretes	Symbolic-social
CEON	Symbolic-social
FC	Symbolic-social
JJ	Social

at the same time, these reasons are shaped by a series of social and economic conditions. It is, then, the conjunction of these reasons and conditions that determines the selection of a nonmarried couple as sponsors of a given compadrazgo type. The reasons for this anomalous practice can be characterized as primarily functional, that is, designed to produce certain results, the most important of which are: the desire, and sometimes the need, on the part of those asking for the compadrazgo relationship (these may include personnel beyond the primary actors, or compadres, making the pedimento) to reconcile factions in a neighborhood or among kinsmen; the personal desire of a couple to bring certain friends within its orbit of compadrazgo; the inability of the parents of a person or the owners of an image or object, and their kinsmen, to secure a married couple as the sponsors of a given compadrazgo type; and the communal need to generate rapport among various factions or groups within the community (for example, among the members of the ayuntamiento religioso, or between the halves into which the community is territorially divided) and with nearby communities. The conditions under which these reasons are activated are primarily social and economic, as their subject matter clearly indicates. They are social in the sense that the matrix in which the reasons become operative is determined by considerations of social action and the conflict of personal or communal interests. They are in lesser but still significant degree economic, in that the reasons involve an economic goal, on the one hand, or the absence of an economic base, on the other. Some examples may help to explain this conjunction, and the way in which the mechanisms of compadrazgo choice operate in these anomalous relationships.

A married couple is about to enter into one of the normal compadrazgo types. They live in a *paraje* (territorial unit) that is factionally divided, in which serious conflict may sometimes take place. The couple belongs to one of the factions of neighbors or kinsmen, but hoping to bring about rapport between the antagonistic groups, decides to establish the compadrazgo relationship by choosing the padrino from one faction and the madrina from the other. This act, with its symbolic quality, may automatically be regarded by the other faction as an overture from their antagonists to bring hostilities to an end. It should be added, however, that the faction to which the couple belongs usually suggests—and sometimes presses for—this move, which is almost invariably an effective way to end dispute in Belén. This example, which involves neighbors who may or may not be related by kinship ties, shows one of the several social-symbolic functions of the compadrazgo system, the implications of which are analyzed in Part Two.

The second example is basically the same in content, but involves only primary actors rather than groups of individuals. Here the function of establishing the compadrazgo relationship with two unmarried sponsors is to bring about rapport between two sets of independent couples and their normal extensions; it does not necessarily involve factionalism or conflict, but rather the desire to have closer social, economic, and even religious relationships. Statistically speaking, this is unquestionably the most significant reason for establishing this anomalous type of relationship, and the resulting compadrazgo network is one of those

instances in which the typical dyadic pattern of interaction is transcended, for the three interacting sets of primary actors (compadres)
form a kind of corporate group in the functional sense of the term.

The third example is that of the parents of a child or the owners of
an image or object that needs to be sponsored who cannot secure the
sponsorship of a married couple because of their disadvantageous social
and economic position; that is, they belong to the lowest socioeconomic
stratum in Belén. These families are among the poorest in the community and their members rarely participate in its religious life. Such
couples usually select a madrina from among families on their own socioeconomic level, and a padrino from among the most affluent people
in Belén; he is bound by tradition to accept, and he also gains social
status by acquiring compadres whom he can regard in a sense as clients.
Thus, the asking couple combines in this selection a person of its choice,
the madrina, with a padrino dictated by its social and economic position, for the padrino will not only pay his own part of the expenses but
will also help his poor compadres with their part. This reason for establishing the anomalous relationship is the second most common in Belén,
but it is decreasing as the overall economic well-being of the community improves, and the members of its lowest economic levels are finding new opportunities open to them.

The last example pertains in part to the exogamous aspects of the
compadrazgo system in Belén, but it is really a variation of the first two
reasons and conditions; in fact, the only difference is that the last reason
leads to the establishment of public-communal compadrazgo relationships in which the good will generated pertains to the entire community
or a large part of it. With regard to the exogamous compadrazgo relationships in this category, I have in mind primarily the longstanding
ties between the people of Belén and those of a few neighboring communities, especially section 1 of the neighboring municipio of San Bernardino Contla (see Nutini and White 1977:376). I know of two well
documented cases of compadrazgo relationships established with section
1 of San Bernardino Contla in which the sponsors were nonmarried
couples, and these were for ANDI and PCA compadrazgo—that is, for
the two most important public-communal types. Beleños have always
maintained friendly relationships with neighboring communities through
the establishment of compadrazgo relationships, and in the two cases
under consideration asking nonmarried couples to be sponsors was purposely designed to increase the number of actors from section 1. The
most important consideration in this primarily symbolic compadrazgo
relationship is community participation, and asking a padrino and a madrina from two different families achieved this more effectively than
asking a married couple. Both cases occurred at times when the inter-

action between Belén and section 1 appeared to have deteriorated, and the Beleños consciously sought the most effective means the compadrazgo system offered them for restoring it. In cases such as these, which aim to improve community relationships, only public-communal compadrazgo types such as ANDI or PCA are used.

Some generalizations are in order regarding the reasons and conditions connected with the establishment of anomalous compadrazgo relationships involving nonmarried couples. First, two main themes dominate the structure and functioning of these relationships, namely, the generation of rapport and the lessening of conflict, and the desire or need to produce a certain economic result, although other subsidiary themes may be adduced. At the same time, and except for those who cannot easily establish a normal compadrazgo relationship for reasons of low economic and social status, the majority of these anomalous relationships have a communal dimension, which can encompass a small group of neighbors or kin or the community as a whole. As a corollary, the communal interest in establishing the anomalous compadrazgo relationship always involves the participation of personnel other than the primary actors who do the asking, and the participation increases in direct proportion to the communal dimension. In cases of small groups of kinsmen or neighbors, the couple that either volunteers or is selected to engage in the anomalous relationship consults with the prominent members of the group to arrive at a consensus regarding the persons in the opposite group whom they will select as compadre and comadre, but this is usually done rather informally. But when the establishment of the compadrazgo relationship is of considerable or total communal interest (the members of the large neighborhoods in dispute, the two halves of Belén, or the community as a whole), then selection of the padrino and madrina is discussed formally and in detail by an assembly of those concerned. In one specific instance of selecting the sponsors for ANDI compadrazgo in 1946, when land disputes had brought relations between Belén and section 1 of San Bernardino Contla to the breaking point, the Beleños gave wider than usual expression to this anomalous manner of establishing a compadrazgo relationship. They selected a padrino and a madrina from different families of section 1, and the young madrina from a third family (when nonmarried couples are sponsors in compadrazgo types that require a young madrina, she is usually the daughter of the padrino), thereby affecting a maximum representation of personnel from section 1 as primary actors. These proceedings were discussed very thoroughly by the people of Belén at a general meeting called by the fiscales and the entire ayuntamiento religioso.

It should be emphasized that while it is theoretically possible for any compadrazgo type to be used to create rapport and lessen tension, in practice only public-communal types are used for occasions involving either the community as a whole or major segments of it; at the individual and neighborhood levels, private-individual compadrazgo types can achieve the same result. People belonging to the lowest economic and social strata of Belén, of course, may choose nonmarried couples for any type of compadrazgo. Second, the compadrazgo types chosen to create rapport or diminish tension through the selection of nonmarried couples as sponsors are commensurate with the gravity of the situation the relationship is supposed to alleviate. Third, the general structure and activities of anomalous relationships obviously differ from normal compadrazgo relationships, primarily in the greater elaboration and repetition of rites and activities; two separate pedimentos must be made, and the peripheral rites and activities must be duplicated. These quantitative differences do not result in qualitative difference, however, and on the whole these anomalous relationships are simply more elaborate and complicated because they can include more than twice the usual number of primary actors and subsidiary personnel.

One final point concerning these anomalous compadrazgo relationships concerns the extension of ritual kinship behavior patterns and ritual kinship terminology. Here a distinction must be made between anomalous relationships involving only individuals and their immediate extensions, and groups of individuals at different levels of communal integration. In the former case, compadrazgo rights and obligations, as well as ritual kinship terminology, are ideologically extended, or may be extended, to all the primary and secondary relatives of the nonmarried padrino and madrina—that is, to their spouses and secondary actors—and the total web of compadrazgo bonds is considerably augmented. In practice, however, the situation is asymmetrical with regard to the padrino—that is the affluent man, who is supposed to make the relationship economically feasible—at least for the duration of the central complex of rites and ceremonies. The padrino is seldom willing to extend ritual kinship terms to compadrazgo actors beyond the primary actors, and in this way the total compadrazgo relationship is somewhat balanced with respect to the number of participants when compared with the normal compadrazgo relationship. The bonds and obligations between the asking couple and the madrina and her husband and extensions are the most effective and lasting aspect of the anomalous compadrazgo relationship; in time they are transformed into a normal relationship, especially if one or both sides of it improves its economic or social position in the community, while the relationship and the bonds between the asking couple and the padrino grow progressively colder. In an anomalous relationship involving groups of individuals at the various levels of communal integration, there is usually duplication of the primary actors—those who make the pedimento and are parents, owners, or symbolic custodians of the mediating entity (individual couples, mayordomos, fiscales, etc.), the padrino and his wife and primary relatives, and the madrina and her husband and primary relatives. All of them behave very much as in a normal relationship involved in any public-communal type, and the ensuing duties and obligations are also of the same strength and intensity, for they must be maintained if long-lasting rapport between antagonistic groups is to be achieved. The primarily symbolic bonds established between the two groups are much like those in the normal public-communal compadrazgo types, or perhaps even more intense.

The Role of Children as Primary Actors

The role of children as mediating entities has been outlined in the preceding description. Children, however, also play a significant role as subjects in the compadrazgo system of Belén and rural Tlaxcala. As can be seen in table 7, they participate as primary actors in sixteen compadrazgo types, and in twelve of these they are mediating entities or objects. These types are related to a series of occasions in the ritual and life cycles, and to three other occasions that Beleños have seen fit to ritualize (graduación, compadrazgo de aretes, and FC). As the ostensible reason for establishing a compadrazgo relationship, children are no different structurally from adults or from any other kind of mediating entity, and normal bonds and obligations shape the relationship. (Children are defined here as those below marriageable age: up to eighteen for girls, and about twenty-two for boys. Structurally, we can define as children those individuals who cannot initiate a compadrazgo relationship by themselves, that is, those who are not married, but there are a few exceptions.) As mediating entities, children are governed primarily by the generational principle, which permits only superordinate cross-generational behavior patterns and prohibits the use of cross-generational ritual kinship terminology. Thus, in any compadrazgo relationship established among the three primary dyads of the system, children have a fixed and permanent position as ahijados. The dividing line is marriage. Being a mediating entity in any compadrazgo relationship up to and including marriage compadrazgo carried a fixed status as ahijados vis-à-vis the other primary actors and their extensions. Conversely, participation as a mediating entity after marriage does not carry a fixed status, for it changes to that of compadre or comadre after the principial ceremonies are over.

Three points must be noted and qualified here. First, there are exceptions to the first injunction; bachelors and spinsters can become com-

TABLE 7. Categories of Primary Actors by Compadrazgo Type

Type	Category
Bautizo	Adults as compadres, children as ahijados
Casamiento	Adults as compadres and ahijados (transitional)
Confirmación	Adults as compadres, children as ahijados
PCE	Adults as compadres, adults and children as ahijados
Primera comunión	Adults as compadres, children as ahijados
CCCH	Adults as compadres and ahijados
CCCA	Adults as compadres and ahijados
ANDC	Adults and children as compadres, young madrina
ANDI	Adults and children as compadres, young madrina
AOI	Adults as compadres
BSI	Adults and children as compadres, often with a young padrino or madrina
CSV	Adults and children as compadres, young madrina
Escapulario	Adults as compadres, children as ahijados
Graduación	Adults as compadres, children as ahijados
PCA	Adults as compadres
Quince años	Adults as compadres, children as ahijados
Sacada a misa	Adults as compadres and ahijados, children as ahijados
Compadrazgo de evangelios	Adults as compadres, children as ahijados
Compadrazgo de limpia	Adults as compadres, adults and children as ahijados
BOI	Adults as compadres
Bendición de casa	Adults as compadres
BCC	Adults as compadres
BM	Adults as compadres
Parada de cruz	Adults as compadres
Primera piedra	Adults as compadres
Compadrazgo de amistad	Adults as compadres
CABP	Adults as compadres and ahijados
Compadrazgo de aretes	Adults as compadres, children as ahijados
CEON	Adults as compadres
FC	Adults as compadres and ahijados, children as ahijados
JJ	Adults as compadres

padres or comadres in a variety of compadrazgo types; this can be construed as another reason or condition under which compadrazgo relationships are contracted with nonmarried couples. This is not a serious contravention of the injunction, however, for few people in Belén remain unmarried past the age of twenty-five, the age initiating their active compadrazgo careers. Second, the generational principle becomes inoperative after a person marries. As I have discussed in detail, any individual or couple who becomes a mediating entity after marriage (for example, in sacada a misa, CABP, or FC compadrazgo) is transformed from ahijado(a) to compadre or comadre after the main ceremonies are over, even if the padrinos for the occasion are one or even two generations older. The strict application of this injunction is even more obvious when we realize that immediately after marriage a couple can theoretically engage in any compadrazgo type as the asking couple, and may seek padrinos who are considerably older. Third, the change of roles from ahijados to compadres, or vice versa, is not determined so much by generational affiliation as by the passage from single to married status. But since for the average person in Belén this passage more or less coincides with the merging of the second and third generational categories (that is, the categories of young adults and mature adults), I have chosen, mostly for purposes of exposition, to describe the situation in terms of nongenerational crossings.

What I have said so far also applies, of course, to the role and function of children as subjects or sponsors, the details of which have already been discussed. What I want to discuss now is the role of children as embodying symbolic value and as social models of the general structure of the compadrazgo system. In five of the sixteen types involving children as primary actors, they participate as ritual sponsors; the six madrinazgos of marriage compadrazgo, and ANDC, ANDI, BSI, and CSV. There are two important points here. First, four of these five types require the sponsorship of young madrinas only, that is, girls between the ages of twelve and eighteen; and only one, BSI, may involve young padrinos as well. In the BSI compadrazgo type, the owners of a saint or image often insist upon adding to the adult sponsorship that of a young padrino or madrina, depending on the sex of the image or saint; this will always be the son or daughter of the adult sponsoring couple, or if they are not a married couple, of the padrino. Although the incidence of BSI compadrazgo relationships that include a young padrino or madrina is fairly high, it is still negligible compared to that of the other four types requiring children as ritual sponsors, and we can disregard it and concentrate on the role and function of young madrinas. Second, the six madrinazgos of marriage compadrazgo also constitute a special situation in that these madrinas do not necessarily have to be children—that is, single—for often the bride chooses a recently married friend. There is nothing significant to note in the latter case. In the former, the madrinas fall into the structural category of children, but after the marriage ceremonies they do not revert to the role and function of ahijadas, inasmuch as they are the sponsors of a couple in the same age group.

Strictly speaking, in only three compadrazgo types (ANDC, ANDI, and CSV) do children exhibit what might be termed the highest or purest expression of symbolic ritual sponsorship in Belén. In this context they stand as a model for what Beleños regard as the most efficacious form of ritual sponsorship in the religious domain, and also as a social model for future sponsorship. ANDI and CSV compadrazgo are certainly the most important public-communal compadrazgo types in the category of religious sponsorship, and ANDC compadrazgo is equally important among the religious private-individual types. There are other primarily symbolic-religious compadrazgo types, both private-individual and public-communal (for example, escapulario and PCA), that could involve children as sponsors, and I do not know why Beleños confine the sponsorship of children to just three types.[2] It is interesting and significant that, beyond the obvious meaning of children as unspoiled and symbolically pure subjects, there is a more important dimension in regarding them as conducive to producing the best results in any symbolic or ritual act in which they are involved as sponsors. Beleños believe that children are the favorites of the saints and all the supernaturals in the Catholic pantheon; this view is not peculiar to Belén but is part of the general folk Catholic ideology of Mesoamerica, and to some extent it is shared in urban areas. Children are also thought to be the favorites of non-Catholic, pagan supernaturals as well. The people believe, for example, that the agency of children, in combination with specific ritual or ceremonial acts, is necessary to counteract evil influences in a variety of contexts involving witchcraft and sorcery; or that *tetlalchihuics* (sorcerers) and *tlahuelpuchis* (witches) must be especially careful not to antagonize children once they begin to talk, or, as the people put it, "cuando les llega la razón" (when they become endowed with reason).[3] This intrinsic symbolic efficacy of children is not something they are aware of, but rather something immanent in them, and the people feel that they are justified in using it. Thus, children acquire this symbolic and ritual property as soon as they begin to talk, and it remains with them until approximately the age of courtship. It appears, however, that they are at their most efficacious between the ages of twelve and fifteen, and this is borne out by the fact that virtually all madrinas for ANDC, ANDI, and CSV compadrazgo are in this age group.

Beleños are quite explicit about this symbolic and ritual property of children, but they are not at all explicit as to why they have confined its use to these three primarily ritual-religious compadrazgo types. It appears, however, that the use of children for preeminently religious-ritual types represents only their formal use in the compadrazgo system. Children are informally used on many other occasions that are ritually and symbolically sanctioned by the establishment of a compadrazgo relationship, but either their use falls outside the compadrazgo system per se, or they take more peripheral roles in it. For example, children play a role in the ceremonies of several compadrazgo types such as baptism, marriage, parada de cruz, primera piedra, and most public-communal types. They offer flowers and the chiquihuites of pedimento, help to decorate altars and other ceremonial objects, carry flowers and incense in processions, and are physically present in specific rites and ceremonies, thus reflecting their immanent symbolic and ritual importance in generating the appropriate conditions for the success of the ceremonies. This aspect of the role and function of children in the compadrazgo system is not formally incorporated into the web of permanent bonds and obligations and repetitive patterns of behavior that bind together primary, secondary, and even tertiary actors, but it is nevertheless an important part of the ritual and ceremonial activities that surround many compadrazgo types in Belén.

From the structural viewpoint, the role of children in the compadrazgo system of Belén involves a dimension that is perhaps more important than their symbolic and ritual efficacy: they serve as role models. Beleños feel that from an early age, children must learn certain things about compadrazgo behavior. Even today, when certain aspects of the compadrazgo system are changing, and when the general atmosphere surrounding compadrazgo is no longer as constrictive as in traditional times, the people still consider it important to teach children how to behave in future compadrazgo relationships. Whenever a child becomes a padrino or madrina, parents are quick to point out to their own children that they themselves may become young padrinos or madrinas, but above all parents use such opportunities to teach their children what it means to engage in a compadrazgo relationship as adults. Parents not only tell children about their future roles as ahijados, and reinforce the roles of ahijados that they are already playing (baptism, confirmation, and so on), but more important, they teach their children (in part by encouraging them to participate as spectators and in minor roles) the meaning of respeto, confianza, and reliability, and emphasize the roles they will later play as compadres. This attitude, by the way, is an overt ideological manifestation of the primacy of the compadres-compadres dyad over the ahijados-ahijados dyad in the compadrazgo system of Belén.

Parents also encourage their children to establish mock compadrazgo relationships among themselves, and a rather complex pattern of play develops among children revolving about the compadrazgo system. Parents often use the terms of endearment *compadrito* (little copadre) and *comadrita* (little comadre) to refer to their children in a variety of contexts, but always with the idea of underlining a certain relationship or bond pertaining to the compadrazgo system. Under these circumstances, most children grow up fully cognizant of what is involved in a proper compadrazgo relationship, and by the age of about eighteen they have usually participated directly or indirectly in several compadrazgo types. Thus, it is evident that the participation of children as ritual sponsors serves as a social role model for their future compadrazgo careers, and as a means of early indoctrination into the compadrazgo system. In terms of age, children in Belén are most interested in participating in compadrazgo relationships, mock as well as real, between the ages of nine and fifteen. After the age of fifteen, especially in the case of girls, they begin to think seriously about the time when they will become real sponsors in their own right, which may come soon after the madrinazgos of marriage. In summary, then, although the formal role of children as ritual sponsors is confined to only five compadrazgo types, the symbolic, ritual, and social importance of children in the compadrazgo system is far wider than this, and in terms of participation in the system, there is no sharp break between childhood and adulthood.

The Web of Ritual Kinship in Multiple-Dyad Compadrazgo Types

One particularly important aspect of the anomalous structure of personnel has significant implications for the conceptualization of compadrazgo beyond its mere analysis in terms of patterns of dyadic relationships. This is the group of compadrazgo types that have multiple dyads, that is, more than one padrinos-ahijados or compadres-compadres dyad. I have already stated the basic aspects of this structural situation at the beginning of this chapter, and here I make a few preliminary generalizations; the topic can only be analyzed in connection with the articulation between compadrazgo and real kinship, and the way in which the former operates as a system and functions beyond the mere efficacy of a pattern of dyadic relationships. There are twelve compadrazgo types in Belén (see table 1) with multiple dyads, sometimes as many as ten for a single type. While there is no doubt that dyadic relationship patterns predominate in the structure of compadrazgo in Belén and rural Tlaxcala, or in any other instance of compadrazgo, description in terms of them must be considered a first level of analysis; dyadic relationships

per se, as the manipulable blocks of behavior for the analysis of compadrazgo as a system, represent in turn a second level of analysis.

It is easy to visualize and delineate the compadrazgo system of Belén
by looking at its two extremes. At one extreme, at the level of individual, normal compadrazgo types, are those instances that involve the
three basic dyads and a total personnel of five primary actors (i.e., the
first combination; see "Primary, Secondary, and Tertiary Actors," this
chapter). These cases represent a microsystem; there are no ego-centered
relationships, as the three basic dyads are related directly to one another,
and we have therefore a minimal system—a structural situation in which
there are more than two one-to-one relationships. In practice, furthermore, every individual instance of any compadrazgo type in Belén does
indeed function as a microsystem. (This also obtains for the third combination but not for the second, which has only two basic dyads, that
is, the compadres-compadres dyad.) At the opposite extreme, at the
level of the global compadrazgo system vis-à-vis the total structure of
Belén, there is no question that compadrazgo must be regarded and
conceptualized as a system, inasmuch as it involves multiple relationships that directly or indirectly impinge upon each other, and articulate
a large block of social behavior in the communal life of Belén. This is
what I have called the broader, articulating dimensions of compadrazgo,
which so far have not been discussed or conceptualized, either in specific
compadrazgo studies or within the context of broad village studies in
Mesoamerica.

Between these extremes are two junctures in the compadrazgo system
that must be clarified to determine how they themselves form a system,
at a lower level but beyond the simple collection of dyadic relationships:
the sum total of compadrazgo relationships that a given couple has asked
or been asked to enter into at any given point in time; and compadrazgo
types that involve multiple dyadic relationships (that is, the fourth combination). With respect to the former, I have already granted that dyadic
relationships are primarily ego-centered, but that these cannot be taken
to constitute the whole dimension of analysis; on the next level of analysis, they cease to be conceptual units in themselves and become appropriate blocks of behavior organized in some form of a system. Furthermore, the system is best seen in operation on specific occasions in the
life cycle of individuals and the ceremonial cycle of the community,
where groups of compadres, regardless of their egocenteredness, do in
fact behave as a corporate group, hence as a system. The compadrazgo
career of the average married couple approaching old age may include
as many as 60 or more sets of compadres (roughly 100 asking plus 99
being-asked relationships, with slightly more than one-third being repeated sets of compadres). Individually, there is no question that these

120 relationships are dyadic and ego-centered. But when one starts to look beneath the surface for the combinations, alliances, and specific bonds that develop among these dyadic relationships with reference to a certain couple—that is, ego-centered, but also from two, three, or many other ego-centered loci—then a new dimension begins to emerge. This can be embodied in well-delineated networks of bonds and obligations and general behavior patterns that transcend the dyadic relationship pattern, and the total situation must be regarded as an operational system. The analysis of this networklike, systematic aspect of compadrazgo has not been undertaken for the ethnographically reported instances of compadrazgo anywhere in Latin America (see the appendix of *Ritual Kinship* I); instead, anthropologists have confined themselves to describing compadrazgo entirely in terms of dyadic, ego-centered relationships.

Compadrazgo types with multiple dyads probably provide the best examples of how compadrazgo in Belén functions as a system with corporate dimensions. In "Primary, Secondary, and Tertiary Actors," when I talked about the fourth combination, I purposely emphasized that the ego-centered dyadic relationships in multiple-dyad compadrazgo types do not by themselves form a system since structurally speaking they have an ego-centered locus. But it is misleading to say simply this and end the analysis. There are occasions and specific events in which all the personnel tied by these dyadic relationships cease to be tied solely to the ego-centered locus, and the operation becomes a multilocus one in which all or most of the dyads impinge upon each other. On these occasions in the life cycle and ceremonial cycle of individuals and the community, the multiple compadres-compadres dyads of such compadrazgo types have very specific corporate functions. They involve reciprocity and some form of exchange of goods and services, and the appropriate ritual kinship terminology is applied to primary actors and their extensions. It is probably this aspect of compadrazgo in Belén and rural Tlaxcala, together with certain sequences of compadrazgo types (that is, types that lead progressively into other types), that are most amenable to conceptualization in systematic terms—as a network of well-defined mechanisms of reciprocity, exchange, and bonds and obligations among groups of ritual kinsmen as corporate or semi-corporate groups (even though they are not constantly maintained as such), in which dyadic relationships emanate from many ego-centered loci. These systematic aspects of compadrazgo in Belén are not always permanent, however, but are activated whenever the occasion requires them, and this is perhaps the most important difference between the compadrazgo system and the real kinship system. Any instance of the compadrazgo system can be conceptualized correctly only in terms of the appropriate combination of dyadic and systematic dimensions, emphasizing one or the other as we move from one level of analysis to another. (The elaboration of these and the final analysis are presented in Chapters Eleven through Fourteen.)[4]

The Endogamous and Exogamous Dimensions of the Compadrazgo System

The final point of discussion in the anomalous structure of the compadrazgo system concerns primarily the exogamous aspects of the institution, and the effects that the personnel of such aspects have on the proper structural and functional discharge of specific compadrazgo types, and on the articulation of the system as a whole within the global framework of Belén culture and society. The exogenous structure and implications of the compadrazgo system were analyzed in Chapter Nine of *Ritual Kinship* I in the context of the pan-Tlaxcalan incidence of the institution. There we addressed ourselves to the exogamous and exogenous considerations that enter into the extracommunal dimensions of the compadrazgo system, but primarily from the standpoint of its place in the wider framework of Belén culture and society in particular, and rural Tlaxcala in general. I now want to narrow the analysis to the immediate implications of the exogamous dimensions of the compadrazgo system, and the resulting constraints that are apt to lead to significant changes in its structure and functions. While there have always been many exogamous compadrazgo relationships in Belén, this aspect of the compadrazgo system can be regarded as anomalous—at least from the viewpoint of the local ideology. Given the fact, then, that for a long time a balance between the exogamous and endogamous aspects of the compadrazgo system has been maintained, I want to determine what will happen if this balance is upset, and in what ways this change will in turn affect the total structure of the compadrazgo system.[5]

Participating in exogamous compadrazgo relationships has for at least two centuries been part of community life in Belén, and although local ideology dictates that endogamous compadrazgo relationships are most appropriate and efficacious, at a higher level the practice is sanctioned by the general ideology of the compadrazgo system in Tlaxcala—the product of more than 400 years of acculturation, which includes several sociocultural communal aspects (of which the compadrazgo system is one of the most important) with a pan-Tlaxcalan incidence. For the approximately 100 years for which we have reliable data on the quantitative aspects of the compadrazgo system the number of exogamous compadrazgo relationships in Belén has remained fairly constant at about 40 percent. Despite this ideological discrepancy (at the local and the regional levels), from a formal viewpoint exogamous compadrazgo relationships in Belén work out rather well, and in this sense the degree of anomaly is rather small. Exogamous compadrazgo relationships do not differ significantly from endogamous relationships in Belén for two reasons: the entire rural Tlaxcalan area has a high common cultural denominator, and the compadrazgo system is remarkably uniform among the *municipios* and communities with which Beleños have traditionally exchanged compadres. For example, the ideological rule that dictates in Belén that normal compadrazgo relationships are contracted endogamously also operates in the majority of other Tlaxcalan communities.[6] Thus, the basic operating principles of the compadrazgo system, together with such important attributes as the method of recruitment, the roster of types, the functions and activities of each type, the rites and ceremonies, and so on, are shared to a high degree by most of the municipios and communities that exchange compadres with Belén. Nevertheless, participation in exogamous compadrazgo relationships in Belén does involve a certain amount of social and psychological anxiety for primary actors; hence we must regard such relationships as anomalous. Under these circumstances, structural and functional differences are bound to appear, and in the final analysis, the ideological and structural similarities—but especially the latter—underlying the global compadrazgo system in Belén and rural Tlaxcala indicate that it is best conceptualized and heuristically balanced in terms of the *normal* and *anomalous* classification of endogamous and exogamous compadrazgo relationships respectively.

What I have said here pertains primarily to the place of structure in the wider societal framework, and to the differences that are likely to occur, given certain well delineated exogenous considerations. We must also look at the exogamous dimensions of the compadrazgo system insofar as they affect the participating personnel, and, concomitantly, the changes that may result from changes in the articulation of the ideological and structural orders. The latter point involves primarily a shift of analysis from structure to ideology, so I deal first with the former. The primary actors involved in exogamous compadrazgo types are the same as in types contracted endogamously. This is true both ideally and actually, at least for the principal ceremonies. It is not the case, however, for secondary actors, and much less so for tertiary actors. Seldom if ever do tertiary actors play any significant role in the major events, in the ensuing activities, or in the general shaping of the compadrazgo relationship. A possible exception is the compadrazgo relationships that the people of Belén contract with very close neighbors such as those from section 1 of San Bernardino Contla or the barrio of Tlatempa (also within the municipio of Apetatitlán); in these, Beleños make every effort to carry out all functions and activities and to encourage all personnel to participate in the fullest and most traditional way. But in any case only five compadrazgo types in Belén extend behavior patterns and ritual kinship terminology to tertiary actors (which doubly constrains an exogamous compadrazgo type; see table 2).

For secondary actors there is, however, a gradation of participation in the principal ceremonial events and activities and in the shaping of the ensuing bonds and obligations, regulated largely by two variables: distance from Belén, and the compadrazgo type under consideration. Secondary actors participate to a considerable degree in sacramental compadrazgo types, especially marriage, and in public-communal types, especially ANDI and PCA. Many secondary actors are intimately involved in the rites and ceremonies of these types, and are later drawn into the web of bonds and obligations as extensions of primary actors. This differs little from the normal, endogamous situation for similar types. The people of Belén, as well as those from the communities with which they exchange compadres, make an effort to attend each other's activities and celebrations after the main ceremonies are over, and try to comply scrupulously with ensuing bonds and obligations, much as if they were engaged in an endogamous relationship. Such cases may involve some economic and social hardship because of the travel involved, and the fact that compliance may involve much time and effort; however, the people of Belén, and rural Tlaxcalans in general, like to travel and ordinarily do a good deal of intercommunity visiting. In any event, this positive feeling about the exogamous aspects of the compadrazgo system seems to indicate that it is still strong and a viable mechanism for social integration and to some extent for economic contact on a pan-Tlaxcalan level, despite elements working against it—for example, secularization and increasing permanent contact with the outside, urban world. This "normal" situation with regard to exogamous compadrazgo affects approximately seven or eight compadrazgo types, but it does not obtain in those compadrazgo types ranked by the people as secondary, (see table 8). In these there is a noticeable decrease in the active participation of secondary actors, and in the strength of and compliance with the bonds and obligations tying the personnel of these types. Beleños feel that the active participation of primary actors is sufficient, and that secondary actors should be left to participate according to their will. This situation, then, departs noticeably from normal, endogamous compadrazgo relationships. With regard to the types ranked by the people as tertiary (see table 8), only the primary actors are effectively drawn into the compadrazgo relationship in every aspect and activity, and both ideally and in practice, exogamous compadrazgo relationships in this category are confined to them. This is the case with such minor compadrazgo types as quince años, BCC, CABP, FC, and so on. Beleños

TABLE 8. Beleños' Unconscious Classification of Compadrazgo Types

Type	Primary	Secondary	Tertiary
Bautizo	x		
Casamiento	x		
Confirmación		x	
PCE	x		
Primera comunión		x	
CCCH		x	
CCCA		x	
ANDC		x[1]	
ANDI	x		
AOI			x
BSI		x	
CSV		x	
Escapulario		x	
Graduación			x[2]
PCA	x		
Quince años			x
Sacada a misa		x	
Compadrazgo de evangelios		x	
Compadrazgo de limpia		x	
BOI		x	
Bendición de casa	x		
BCC			x
BM		x	
Parada de cruz	x		
Primera piedra		x	
Compadrazgo de amistad			x
CABP			x
Compadrazgo de aretes			x
CEON		x	
FC			x
JJ			x

[1] Doubtful: sometimes secondary and sometimes primary.
[2] Doubtful: sometimes tertiary and sometimes secondary.

seldom contract these compadrazgo relationships exogamously, however, so this possibility is not often realized.

Finally, distance plays a constraining role in the effective participation of secondary actors across the spectrum of all compadrazgo types. Distance itself is not an independent variable, but is affected by several factors. The most important is labor mitigation, which leads to the establishment of friendships that finally result in compadrazgo relationships; less important factors are historical considerations and the traditional social and sometimes economic bonds between Belén and several other Tlaxcalan communities. In general, success in fulfilling the duties and obligations of exogamous compadrazgo relationships is always directly proportional to the distance from Belén of the community in which the compadres live. Beleños prefer to engage in compadrazgo relationships with people who live no more than a half-hour's walk or bus ride from Belén, and this is the case for more than two-thirds of the communities with which the people of Belén have traditionally exchanged compadres.

This picture has been changed by the greater participation of rural Tlaxcalans in labor migration and other economic ventures outside their communities since the 1930s and 1940s, which has brought about more extracommunal contacts at places of work and in other extracommunal environments, and in turn has led to the establishment of compadrazgo relationships independent of distance or the ranking of the compadrazgo type. This new element has significant consequences for the compadrazgo system in Belén, and those involved in such exogamous compadrazgo relationships will have an impact on the future articulation between the ideological and structural aspects of the system. Traditionally the personnel of exogamous compadrazgo relationships have been governed, in functions and activities and in duties and obligations, by the importance of the compadrazgo type and the distance to Belén. This is now disrupted by a new variable that cuts across the traditional variables and throws the structure of exogamous compadrazgo in Belén rather out of balance; in time it will probably throw the entire system out of balance and hence into a new structural-ideological matrix.

The preceding paragraphs constitute a brief look at the exogamous dimension of the compadrazgo system in Belén with respect to the personnel involved, as a complement to the view (the general articulation of extracommunal compadrazgo and the fabric of Belén culture and society) presented in Chapter Nine of *Ritual Kinship* I. I have determined how, and the extent to which, the personnel of exogamous relationships depart from those of endogamous relationships with respect to two main variables, departures that did not affect the traditional balance between the exogamous and endogamous dimensions until the appearance of a third variable—the labor migration or secularizing variable. The traditional balance is still to a considerable extent in effect, but the global compadrazgo system of Belén is beginning to show strain. Discussing this aspect of the system in terms of its personnel is the most appropriate way in which to approach the major point involved here:

that is, what changes in the compadrazgo system will ultimately result from the upset of the traditional exogamous-endogamous balance—first, in the articulation between its ideological and structural orders, and ultimately, in the rise and consolidation of a new compadrazgo ideology? This task is undertaken in terms of personnel and not in terms of social, religious, or economic attributes per se, because the participation of personnel in a dynamic context is always more visible than such attributes in process, and changes in personnel and their behavior seem to be a more direct way to get at the basic operational principles of change. (Part Three of *Ritual Kinship* I illustrates how this approach is implemented in connection with the acculturative development of the ayuntamiento religioso from the time of the Conquest to the middle of the seventeenth century, and the development of the compadrazgo system from the Conquest to the present.) Thus, from this particular viewpoint, all *anomalous* structural and functional contexts involving personnel—all those contexts that depart from an operationally (but never absolutely) defined or postulated state of equilibrium (as with the anomalies and extensions discussed in this chapter)—are promising means of ascertaining the dynamic principles that govern sociocultural systems.[7]

Anomaly and Operationally Defined Normality

Throughout this chapter, my aim has been to present all those situations in which the personnel of the compadrazgo system function anomalously, in a manner different from what I have operationally defined as normal—situations in which there is a significant discrepancy between what, structurally speaking, people should do and what they actually do, which leads to differences in functional discharge. The addition or omission of personnel from the three basic dyads and extensions, the transformation of roles, or the enlargement of roles and functions, constitute what I have termed the anomalies or departures from the normal, traditional structure and function of the compadrazgo system in Belén. They affect the structure and functions of given compadrazgo types, but may or may not significantly affect the system as a whole or its interconnection with Belén culture and society. There are two reasons for the rather extended analysis presented in this chapter. First, discrepancies between what people should do (structural rules) and what they actually do (statistical norms) are always important in understanding the whole of a system or subsystem in operation, and an adequate conceptualization must include both. For this reason, departure from structural normality must always be included in the description and analysis of any system or subsystem, and this is best done in terms of departures from an operationally defined situation in which personnel are directly involved. This makes it easier, among other things, to visualize and assess the system in action, and in turn helps us to more clearly perceive and understand what has operationally been defined as normal. Second, and more important, the analysis of anomalous departures from operationally defined normality is one of the best means for reaching a proper understanding of a second and more fundamental distinction, namely, that between the ideological and structural orders. It is therefore important to describe and briefly analyze all the significantly anomalous aspects of the compadrazgo system's personnel before proceeding with the structural analysis, as most of these anomalies are used to illustrate specific structural and functional aspects of the system in the remainder of this study. This chapter, however, also helps us understand the statistical variations and structural alternatives with which the people of Belén are presented. This is a significant point, and it is important to keep in mind in sociocultural systems—like Belén's—that are undergoing rapid change, for it is one of the implicit assumptions of this study that although the compadrazgo system has so far resisted the onslaught of secularization, Belén is now at an economic threshold that will undoubtedly disrupt the accommodations and adjustments that the compadrazgo system has hitherto been able to achieve. Thus, the practical methodological value of this chapter is greatest with regard to predicting the direction that socioeconomic change in Belén is likely to take within the next generation.

The Structural Implications of Asking and Being Asked to Enter into a Compadrazgo Relationship

Another major task in the structural analysis of the compadrazgo system is to clarify the implications and ramifications of the two basic ways in which relationships are contracted and come into being, namely, asking and being asked to become a compadre. The structural implications of asking or of being asked to enter into compadrazgo relationships represent a fundamental distinction which has repercussions throughout the whole system, and which makes itself felt in the functional attribution of every type. In the following pages I address myself to the areas in which this distinction plays its most significant role. First, however, I give a general account of the distinction with respect to both its structural and ideological components.

Subordination and Superordination of Compadrazgo Actors

Beleños are aware that asking or being asked to enter into a compadrazgo relationship involves different attributes with regard to discharge, intrinsic social and economic positions, intensity of contracting bonds, subordinate-superordinate positioning, and expectations. This general complex applies to all compadrazgo types, but varies according to the socioeconomic, religious, and symbolic importance that the people attach to each type. However, the overall orientation and generalized practices associated with this distinction always operate when a compadrazgo relationship is established, and the distinction can be analyzed operationally for the system as a whole.

The basic attribute of the asking–being asked distinction is that, ideologically, the petitioner is automatically placed in a position of subordination, and different expectations are involved in each case. Translated into structural terms, this assertion means that while the person being asked is constrained to accept because of the sacred ideological nature of compadrazgo in Belén, it is felt that the individual who asked is placed in his debt. Thus, the burden of making the relationship a successful one falls on the person who requests it. Both the person asking and the person being asked have precise duties and obligations, of course, and are bound by certain canons of behavior which they must obey to comply with the minimum requirements of any of the compadrazgo types in Belén. We are not talking about these first-order structural requirements, but rather about the intangibles that are not spelled out by the structural-ideal framework of compadrazgo. Thus, the individual who is asking will be expected to take the initiative (especially with regard to whatever permanent bonds and obligations are established after the core of rites and ceremonies comes to an end) in every activity that requires the social, religious, and economic interaction of the compadres and their extensions. At the same time, he is required to place himself in a position of subordination to the compadre whom he asked, and to show him publicly the respect that their differential positions entail. The same applies to primary actors and their extensions, and the whole spectrum of behavior associated with the asking–being asked distinction applies also to the web of ritual kinship established by the compadres-compadres relationship. This structural attribute of the distinction is naturally modified by considerations extrinsic to the situation itself, such as the relative age of the compadres, their relative social position, their wealth, their religious standing within the community, and so on. For example, in the case of a rich, fairly old individual who asks a rather poor, religiously undistinguished individual (that is, one who does not have an outstanding record of religious sponsorship in the community) to become his compadre, the former will not necessarily be placed in a position of overt behavioral subordination to the latter, as demanded by the ideology of the asking–being asked distinction. In this case, extrinsic considerations have obviously superseded the proper discharge of the requirements of the asking–being asked distinction. In any compadrazgo situation, of course, the intrinsic ideological requirements of the asking–being asked distinction are or can be modified by the extrinsic structual requirements mentioned above. Assessment of the discharge of the distinction must always involve this interplay between the ideological and structural orders—in the present context, interplay between the intrinsic subordination of the person asking and the extrinsic attributes of contracting compadres. It goes without saying that this applies to every similar juncture in the compadrazgo system of Belén.

Adopting a unidimensional approach in the present example would not lead to determining what structural elements produce a situation in which an individual who is higher in socioeconomic, or even religious position, would ask an individual in a subordinate position to be his compadre, thereby superseding or counterbalancing the inherent superordination of the person being asked. Only when all differential variables are analyzed, can problems of choice and decision making in systems such as compadrazgo be solved. We can sum up the differential attribute of the asking–being asked distinction by saying that it colors the most significant aspects of the compadrazgo system, and the best way to see it in operation is to outline the most important aspects and occasions of its developmental cycle.

The Dynamic and Temporal Implications of the Asking–Being Asked Distinction

The various compadrazgo types in Belén have specific developmental cycles, and the system as a whole also has a definite developmental cycle with respect to primary actors and their extensions. For the moment let us take for granted that such cycles involve specific situations and occasions that may not only change the intrinsic discharge of compadrazgo types (that is, the roles and expectations of primary actors and their extensions) but at the same time develop into other compadrazgo relationships (that is, be transformed into other compadrazgo types). In this general context the asking–being asked distinction has signficant implications. Furthermore, under the rubric of the developmental cycle of compadrazgo we must also include individual compadrazgo careers, and the asking–being asked distinction unquestionably has its most significant effect in the shaping of these careers. Since these matters are dealt with extensively in Chapters Thirteen and Fourteen, this analysis can serve as an introduction.

First of all, the asking–being asked distinction shapes the developmental cycle of an individual or a couple's compadrazgo career to the extent that an individual or couple always starts by asking other individuals or couples to enter into compadrazgo relationships.[1] The distinction then shapes, or is a structural indicator of, the individual's compadrazgo career with reference both to particular compadrazgo types and to compadrazgo as a system. I can plot this development in a fairly even inverted elliptical curve in the following manner. An individual starts his compadrazgo career by exclusively asking to enter into compadrazgo relationships. This usually happens soon after marriage, when a couple begins to have children who must be baptized and perhaps ritually cleansed. As the individual enters into other aspects of the life and ceremonial cycle, as well as other requirements of community living, he engages in an increasing number of compadrazgo relationships, and by then not only asks but also is asked. The operating principle here is that as the person grows older and, in the eyes of the people, becomes more responsible and reliable, he will be asked more and more often to enter into compadrazgo relationships. Somewhere slightly past middle age the apex of the curve is reached, and at this point the average individual reaches approximately an even frequency of asking and being asked. As the individual approaches old age, the curve begins to descend, since the number of requests made of him rapidly and steadily outnumbers his requests to enter into compadrazgo relationships. By the end of his compadrazgo career (usually between ages seventy and seventy-five) he is still being asked but no longer make requests of his own. Obviously there are fewer and fewer occasions for the average individual to ask to enter into compadrazgo relationships, while his desirability as a compadre is on the rise because of many factors connected with age, religious prestige, and the like. This curve is a statistical notion, of course, but it does convey the structural-actual discharge of the developmental career cycle of the average person in Belén. Here again, what makes this curve a statistical representation of the social reality of compadrazgo are variables extrinsic to the system itself.

The second area in which the asking–being asked distinction has significant repercussions is in the central complex of rites and ceremonies associated with each particular compadrazgo type, and in the preliminaries leading to it. First, the parents, kinsmen, and owners of the mediating person, image, or object are the prime movers in these two all-important aspects of the compadrazgo relationship, and its permanence depends significantly on their success in discharging the social, economic, and religious activities and the rites and ceremonies involved. To a large extent, and especially from a functional standpoint, interaction between the individuals asking and those being asked (between parents, kinsmen, or owners and the padrinos, during the preliminaries and the core of the ceremonies) marks the total scope of the relationship throughout. Thus, the asking–being asked differential character of any compadrazgo type will determine the course of the relationship in its permanent, semipermanent, and recurrent rites and ceremonies, based essentially on the way in which the preliminaries and the core of the ceremonies are carried out, that is, on the degree to which primary actors adhere to the ideological constraints of the distinction. If the affect is positive, then the compadrazgo relationship will probably develop into a close, successful, and long-lasting association; conversely, if the affect is negative, this kind of association will not result. Repeatedly, Belén informants reiterated that it is the compadres' behavior during the preliminaries and the core of the ceremonies that determines the quality of the more lasting aspects of the compadrazgo relationship, and that when relationships come to an end shortly after the ceremonies, it is because the constraints of the asking–being asked distinction were not complied with. All other things being equal, then, it is obvious that the more closely people adhere to the ideological order underlying the distinction, the more successful will the compadrazgo relationship be.

Given the fact that the ideological component of the asking–being asked distinction means primarily that responsibility falls upon the person asking, and that he is at least slightly subordinate to the person being asked, what structural attributes must be complied with during the preliminaries and the core of ceremonies to ensure a successful and lasting compadrazgo relationship? These attributes fall primarily into social and economic categories. First, the individual in search of padrinos must make sure that he finds the right person or couple for the compadrazgo relationship, and that the chosen padrinos will not be embarrassed when the pedimento takes place. The prospective padrinos must be informed so that they can ready themselves for the occasion, or else, in the customary roundabout fashion, let the petitioners know that the compadrazgo cannot be accepted—thus making it against the rules to ask. Second, throughout the pedimento and the core of ceremonies, it is imperative that the padrinos always be treated with the consideration due their inherent position of superordination, and this type of behavior must also be extended to secondary and even tertiary relatives. In practice, such behavior is manifested primarily by extending participation in the ceremonies to the largest possible number of secondary and tertiary relatives of the padrinos, as dictated by the structure of the specific compadrazgo type, and by always giving the places of honor to the padrinos and their entourage. The padrinos, of course, will automatically be addressed in terms indicative of behavioral superordination. This superordination slowly disappears as the relationship progresses to its semipermanent or permanent stages, however, and in time the compadres-compadres dyad is marked by overt positional equality. Indeed, this situation is an indication that all constraints have been complied with, and that the relationship is successful. Third, at this stage the economic realm is perhaps most important to the future success and durability of a compadrazgo relationship. In most compadrazgo types, the expenses of the persons asking are higher than those of the padrinos, but the difference may not be substantial. Moreover, the padrinos are performing a religious, social, and/or symbolic service which is sanctioned only by the sacred nature of compadrazgo and does not confer any other reward, so it is structurally proper that they be helped to discharge their economic obligations if need be. In other words, the differential distinction of subordination dictates that individuals asking to enter into a compadrazgo relationship extend economic courtesies. In perhaps the majority of cases this economic differential remains latent, of course, for padrinos are able to discharge their economic obligations without any help (most people seek padrinos who are able to bear the economic responsibilities without difficulty), but they must know that they can count upon help if they need it.

An example will show how this is manifested. Not infrequently, when an individual is asked to enter into a compadrazgo relationship he may at the moment lack the cash or other economic resources needed for the preliminaries and the ceremonial core of the compadrazgo type. Wanting to accept, he lets the petitioner know of the situation in the usual roundabout fashion. The petitioner can either proceed with the pedimento, implicitly assuming responsibility for the padrino's economic deficiencies, or he can seek another compadre. In the former case, assumption of the economic obligation means that all expenditures in cash and kind will be reimbursed in specified ways which may include payment in cash, goods, or services. In such cases, the rapport thereby generated between the compadres tends to lessen their differential status, and to bring about a greater closeness in the relationship. Implicit in this analysis is the deep-seated ideological belief that the success of any kind of social relationship is predicated upon its having as egalitarian a basis as possible. In this example, economic assistance to the prospective padrino serves to counterbalance the inherently subordinate position of the petitioner, thereby structuring a more egalitarian situation. When the padrinos do not need economic assistance from the person seeking the relationship, other intangible economic requirements within the prevalent ideology of the asking–being asked distinction must still be complied with. Examples of such intangibles are generosity in the various expenditures, the quality of the food, clothing, and other items associated with the core of ceremonies, extension of participant invitations, and so on. In many ways, the discharge of economic obligations, predominantly on the part of the person seeking the relationship, is little more than the generation of confianza and reliability, as we shall see in the next chapter. In one way or another, however, the asking–being asked distinction colors, and in some instances clearly structures, the future development of compadrazgo relationships after the ceremonial core comes to an end.

The Permanent Implications of the Asking–Being Asked Distinction

The third domain of the Belén compadrazgo system in which the asking–being asked distinction has significant consequences consists of the network of bonds and obligations that survives the ritual core. The way in which these bonds, duties, and obligations are discharged obviously depends upon how the relationship was initially structured, as described above. Of greater importance to the overall structural analysis is the determination of how the asking–being asked distinction goes beyond the functional discharge of the system and permeates the various aspects both of compadrazgo per se and of its relationship to other systems

within Belén culture and society. The distinction has structural consequences for several domains that come into being after the ceremonies
have ended: ritual kinship behavior, and the extension of bonds and
obligations beyond primary actors; the structure and function of recurrent rites and ceremonies; the recruiting mechanisms of compadrazgo,
in which certain compadrazgo types lead to other types; the duration,
intensification, and sometimes termination of compadrazgo relationships; and so on. All these subdomains of compadrazgo in Belén are
deeply embedded in larger, more encompassing domains such as the
developmental cycle of compadrazgo as a whole and individual transformations, the functional system in operation in terms of private-individual or public-ceremonial complexes, and so on. It is therefore more
appropriate to discuss the fundamental asking–being asked distinction
within the context of these larger segments, not only to help eliminate
repetition but also to give a more integrated picture of the components
of compadrazgo as a system.

I have emphasized the obvious, namely, that the asking–being asked
distinction corresponds to the different structural positions of the personnel of the compadres-compadres dyad (or, if you wish, the com-
padres-padrinos dyad), because it has received little or no attention in
the literature on compadrazgo. Few accounts of compadrazgo, not even
our best reports, (see, e.g., Foster 1953; Gillin 1945; Mintz and Wolf
1950; Paul 1942), have concerned themselves with the structural positions of the contracting parties in compadrazgo relationships, or with
the implications for the system in operation. Almost invariably, compadres and padrinos have been regarded as occupying equal reciprocal
positions within the network of compadrazgo—in basically egalitarian
situations, that is—and I think this has been one of the main reasons the
functional aspects of the institution remain basically unintelligible. To a
considerable extent this results from conceptualizing compadrazgo as a
basically dyadic structure, and neglecting the institution's systematic aspects.

Chapter 4

Confianza, Respeto, and Reliance

The Conceptual Configuration of Dynamic, Activating Principles

So far I have discussed what may be regarded as essentially the static attributes and mechanisms of the compadrazgo system. To proceed to the analysis of some of the most important structural attributes of compadrazgo, I must discuss what I regard as the dynamic, activating principles of the system in operation. Substantively, the dynamic, activating principles are no different from any other component of a system under investigation; that is, their content is on the same empirical level as the more visible elements that we become acquainted with at the data-gathering stage. Such dynamic, activating principles do, however, become substantively more signficant once we pass to the analytical stage. Thus, what I have called the activating principles of confianza, respeto, and reliance were no different from many other social, religious, economic, and symbolic components of the compadrazgo system in Belén and rural Tlaxcala at the moment the data were being collected. But when preliminary analysis of the raw data was undertaken, the substantive content that fell under the rubric of what the Beleños themselves call confianza, respeto, and reliance began to emerge as something special within the general substantive context, and this necessitated a different conceptual handling. Thus, in the preliminary stages of analysis different conceptual dimensions may begin to take shape, and at this point we may need to think in terms of different anayltical tools. The concepts of confianza, respeto, and reliance clearly began to take form when I realized that conceptually they had to be treated differently from several other attributes and general properties of the compadrazgo system that at the data-gathering stage looked homologous.

From the strictly conceptual viewpoint, on the other hand, dynamic, activating principles should not be regarded as in any sense apart from the social structure. The term "principle" suggests that such entities may fall outside the formal content of a system, and that this ontological status gives them whatever explanatory dimensions one associates with the term. On the contrary, dynamic, activating principles are an integral part of any sociocultural system under consideration, although they constitute a very special part of its conceptual mechanisms. From a strictly descriptive standpoint there is no reason to assign a special status to dynamic, activating principles such as confianza, respeto, and reliance. It is only at the analytical level, where explanation begins to emerge, that we should be concerned with the search for, and elucidation of, those substantive junctures that can be construed into activating, dynamic principles. Every sociocultural system that can be studied will have potential dynamic, activating principles that we may be able to discover and conceptualize. I can say little about the methodology for discovering such junctures, except that even at the strictly substantive level, certain empirical elements will always stand out as having greater potential significance for the formulation of dynamic, activating principles. Such is the way in which I regard confianza, respeto, and reliance. The literature on compadrazgo bears me out, to the extent that confianza and respeto are among the most frequently mentioned attributes of compadrazgo. The trouble is that these two concepts have not been given the status of principles, yet clearly they have a much more signficant dimension than their common-sense meaning within the strictly ethnographic context.

A dynamic, activating principle, then, is a conceptual entity that can be successfully operationalized (to some extent even in the formal or mathematical meaning of operationalization), and that will serve to establish the form that causal entailment can have within the system under consideration. In a broader, less formal sense, dynamic activating principles are those junctures or variables or complexes of variables that denote a high common substantive denominator; that is, that they can be construed as embodying a high degree of semantic homogeneity applying to a large body of sociocultural phenomena. Thus, there are two principal reasons for seeking to discover dynamic, activating principles: they can help us to formulate causal relationships, hence taking us beyond purely functional relationships; and they serve as covering terms for large bodies of substantive sociocultural phenomena whose parts can be seen as forming a more structured whole. As explanatory mechanisms, dynamic, activating principles are most useful in structuring specific (or even general) contexts in terms of interaction between the ideological and structural orders—namely, in terms of how the former may be efficacious over the latter. In part, these mechanisms are referred to as dynamic, activating principles to differentiate them from other structural components of a system by endowing them with an extra substantive dimension. More important, however, they embody explanatory dimensions we can construe into a causal relationship—that is, into the microcosm that shows us how to measure the degree of influence that a certain ideological order has over its corresponding structural order. In brief, then, and with specific reference to the present context, confianza, respeto, and reliance as dynamic, activating entities are operating principles that enable us to explain in terms of causal relationship.[1]

The Covering Nature of Confianza, Respeto, and Reliance

Before examining and discussing in detail what confianza, respeto, and reliance imply for the discharge of the compadrazgo system of Belén and rural Tlaxcala, let us analyze what they mean qua principles with respect to their theoretical and methodological components. I begin with the latter. The concepts of confianza, respeto, and reliance are universal aspects of the compadrazgo system in the more than 200 communities that comprise the rural sector of the Tlaxcalan part of the Tlaxcala-Pueblan valley. In every community with which I am well acquainted (approximately 35), these concepts are very much in the minds of the people, and are readily verbalized as a significant component of the structure of compadrazgo in a large variety of contexts and situations. Even at the lowest, data-gathering level, the concepts of confianza, respeto and reliance have a certain substantive-empirical component that makes the ethnographer take note of their special status vis-à-vis other homologously and analogously collected materials. Thus, even before preliminary analysis the ethnographer in rural Tlaxcala is directly impressed with the significance of confianza, respeto, and reliance as potential organizing principles. How do the people themselves verbalize these potential principles, or rather the substantive content that the terms denote structurally? To begin with, the three terms, and especially confianza and respeto, are almost invariably covering terms for a wide variety of behavior extending across the entire structure of the compadrazgo system. When the people of Belén and rural Tlaxcala in general tell the ethnographer, say, that compadrazgo relationships are marked by varying degrees of respeto, they are expressing a series of ideological imperatives or constraints that may entail social, economic, religious, or symbolic components characterizing specific ways of behaving on specific occasions. The same holds true for confianza and reliance, but the semantic component of these terms is mainly structural; that is, they are not exacting imperatives or constraints to action, but rather refer to the actual discharge of a compadrazgo relationship, which may be extended to the system as a whole. It is therefore difficult to get at the semantic meaning or interpretation of what is denoted by the terms confianza, respeto, and reliance when they are uttered by the people, and this may well be the reason these terms have retained their common-sense meaning as well as their almost universal incidence in the ethnographic literature on compadrazgo. Analysis of material on compadrazgo behavior soon begins to show the covering nature of confianza, respeto, and reliance, when one realizes that each term stands in the consciousness of informants for a wide variety of attributes, patterns, and components that for one reason or another the people are not usually able to verbalize.[2] Here, then, lies the extrasubstantive dimension of confianza, respeto, and reliance that I want to construe as bundles of special structural attributes.

At this point, two generalizations are in order. First, the semantic nature of those terms that involve extrasubstantive dimensions—covering terms—is most often of an unconscious kind and hence more difficult to discover. And second, since there are always unconscious phenomena that our subjects denote under the rubric of specific terms, it is always possible, at least theoretically, to construct what I have called activating, dynamic principles. Not all dynamic, activating principles have an unconscious base, and it is quite possible to construe them on the basis of conscious phenomena. What I am maintaining is that the most effective dynamic activating principles are those construed on an unconscious substantive-empirical base; at the same time, these have the widest possible covering dimensions, since it is their unconscious character that gives them this property. In summary, then, the substantive composition of dynamic, activating principles has inherent properties that make them specially suited for getting at those thresholds that are amenable to two or more levels of analysis.

In the specific case of confianza, respeto, and reliance, two alternatives are possible from the substantive viewpoint. On the one hand, we can regard the substantive composition of the terms as a unidimensional empirical whole which does not involve any unconscious, covering properties. This has been the common-sense conceptualization of the terms in the traditional ethnographic literature of compadrazgo, in which confianza and respeto are not accorded any special status either ontologically or epistemologically. On the other hand, we can, as I have already suggested, operationalize the substantive components of confianza, respeto, and reliance. I have already discussed what this means theoretically in a general context, and I confine myself here to filling in various procedural and formative details. Once it has been decided that a certain substantive-empirical corpus of behavior or specifically delineated attributes within a well-structured system can be construed into a dynamic, activating principle or principles, the main concern is with systematically delineating the extent of the covering properties, and the extent to which the principle or principles can be operationalized in at least my informal meaning of the concept. The covering dimensions are given at the substantive level, and what must be done at the analytical level is to ascertain how various attributes and behavior patterns that are unconsciously subsumed under the principle can be made into a homogeneous whole. With respect to operationalization, the main concern is with causal relationships, that is, with ascertaining how the ideological order is efficacious over its corresponding structural order, and with measuring the relationship to some degree. Let us leave this point for the moment and concentrate on the first point and related matters.

Taken by themselves, the attributes and behavior patterns covered by the principle are conceptual categories that are too low to be operationalized by themselves, and must therefore remain strictly substantive-empirical components with a primarily descriptive value. It would be a waste of time, for example, to try to construct a covering term for a concept such as friendship or locality, as I discussed these terms in connection with the structure of choice. From this viewpoint, then, the essential basis of the concept of operationalization is the ability to pinpoint those covering terms that stand for a much broader substantive basis and that can be analyzed at a higher level, thereby structuring the situation in a position of causal superordination. In terms of covering properties, the principles of confianza, respeto, and reliance have enough theoretical weight to enable us to establish a hierarchy of behavior patterns among the covering elements subsumed under them. The construct denoted by the principles of confianza, respeto, and reliance is not composed of fixed entities or specific attributes, but rather of relational properties holding among structural attributes. Only under these conditions can we call these concepts principles, for otherwise the construct denoted by any of them is little more than a refinement of the functional system. Here, then, I have ostensibly defined a dynamic, activating principle. More formally, a dynamic, activating principle is a conceptual device by means of which we try to transcend functional causality by placing the principle at a higher conceptual level. Thus, a dynamic, activating principle, by virtue of its substantive-empirical homogeneity, is a model for a specific system or domain. It plays the conceptual role of *explanandum* to the extent that, given specific behavioral attributes, we are able to explain why and how it will affect other parts of the construct—the body of sociocultural phenomena denoted by the covering term. Perhaps an example will help to clarify this.

Let us take the principle of confianza. I have established that when Beleños use the term, the conscious payload denoted by confianza includes also a much wider unconscious range of behavior. (I discuss this behavior in detail in Chapter Twelve.) Let us say that the principle of confianza—or rather at this level, the covering concept of confianza—stands for behaviorial patterns and structural attributes V, W, X, Y, and Z.[3] When these behavioral patterns and structural attributes have been empirically determined by a variety of techniques which may include indirect elicitation, indirect observation, and inferences from previous analysis, it is not enough to say that the covering term is explicit (conscious) and what it denotes is implicit (unconscious). We must go on to establish how V, W, X, Y, and Z are arranged in a certain specific order with respect to the priorities that confianza entails vis-à-vis other principles in the discharge of compadrazgo relationships, and with respect to the degree of intensity that the principle displays in each compadrazgo type. In other words, once we determine what the behavioral and structural components of V, W, X, Y, and Z are, we must then measure their degree of inclusiveness and the ways in which they may influence one another. If we do not do this, then we might as well analyze V, W, X, Y, and Z individually, and not as parts of a higher integrative, analytical device. In the former case, we are giving equal weight to V, W, X, Y, and Z, and the analysis is functional and unidimensional. It is, however, the actual measuring, scaling, ranking—whatever one wishes to call the process of establishing the interaction of behavior patterns and structural attributes V, W, X, Y, and Z—that constitutes the significance of confianza as a dynamic, activating principle.

At the outset, let me say that while I have isolated the behavioral and structural components of confianza, I have not been able to measure or scale their interlocking efficacious dimensions. Nor do I think this study is the place for it, for here it is only possible to operationalize in the informal sense. But the job of fully operationalizing in the formal mathematical sense is half-completed, and any mathematical anthropologist can apply formal techniques to the quantitative material presented here (and much material that I have not been able to present, such as thousands of compadrazgo relationships extending over fifty years, the compadrazgo careers of several dozen individuals, and the like) and be on firm ground in the sense of operating within an already structured situation—for I do not think that behavior by itself can serve as the raw material for the application of deductive techniques that will yield generalizations. (The mathematical, formal treatment of confianza and many other attributes of compadrazgo are the main subject of a forthcoming monograph by White and Nutini n.d.) Unless one knows the parameters that govern the ideological-structural interplay, one cannot formulate the correlations or relations of invariance that are the essence of generalization, and which are more than simple enumeration at the level of specific ideological-structural systems.[4] What I am seeking is causal relationships, and these can primarily be found in terms of ideological-structural interaction. The behavior patterns and structural attributes denoted by V, W, X, Y, and Z must be handled with this end in view, for otherwise one is simply quibbling about whether certain kinds of data have a more fundamental semantic content.

Before leaving this subject, I would like to point out why the components of an activating principle need not be differentiated with respect to their behavioral and structural dimensions. In my conceptual view of sociocultural phenomena, the behavioral level always represents what is immediately observed, that is, what people actually do, while the structural level is not directly observed and represents rather the immediate expression of imperatives and commands that govern what people actually do. My conception of the organization of human behavior and action involves the interaction of three levels or domains of analysis that I call the structural-actual order, or what people actually do (sociocultural perception); the structural-ideal order, or what people consciously think they should do (sociocultural perception once removed); and the ideological order, or what people unconsciously believe they should do (sociocultural perception twice removed). Furthermore, my analytical approach seeks explanation in the causal links that unite these three levels of analysis (this is discussed in the appendix).

For purposes of simplification the last two orders can be combined into one, which I call the structural level of analysis. Thus we have observable behavior conditioned by structural imperatives, rules, or commands, which—translated into behavioral action—means that what people actually do cannot be meaningfully separated from what they should do, since our concern is to find out how one conditions or determines the other. In other words, while the ontological composition of behavior and structure is quite different, the epistemological properties that unite them into an efficacious whole compel us to treat them as an undifferentiated analytical complex. Thus, the covering properties of any of the principles under discussion here include behavior and imperatives (structural rules) that are inextricably related. Specific structural components correspond to specific bundles of behavior, but it is often very difficult to place such components in a relationship of cause and effect, or to gauge their causal relationship. My theory, of course, assumes that structural rules and imperatives "cause" actual behavior, at least to the extent that the former are imperatives to action that in one form or another are expressed in actual behavior. To explain, then, means in my view mainly to measure the degree to which actual behavior deviates from what the structural rules and commands specify, in addition, of course, to establishing extrasystemic reasons (causes) for the deviations. But since we cannot always determine which is the cause and which the effect, and yet we can clearly determine the expression of behavior and action, it stands to reason that we cannot conceptually separate the oscillation of our two orders unless new evidence is brought to bear upon the situation at hand. On the other hand, the problem is not always as difficult as it appears, for while the situation may be unclear at one level of analysis, at another level the structural-behavioral distinction may appear quite clearly. I do not mean "level of analysis" to refer to the ideal-actual distinction, but to different configurations of data which involve different standpoints and must be analyzed at different levels of complexity.

The Behavioral-Structural Scaling of Confianza, Respeto, and Reliance

Next I want to scale the principles of respeto, confianza, and reliance with respect to their behavioral-structural payload, and determine what these entities as covering terms embody in the way of ontological and epistemological properties. Respeto is mostly an ideological entity, confianza a combination of ideological and structural attributes, and reliance mostly a behavioral or structural-actual entity. By scaling these activating principles, I can first ascertain their degree of inclusiveness within the total compadrazgo system, and at the same time determine the direction of the causal relationship. Scaling them also enables me to determine the role they play in structuring specific compadrazgo types, and the degree of constraint or imperativeness they are able to effect. Let us take each principle in turn.

When I say that respeto is primarily an ideological entity, I want to denote that its V, W, X, Y, Z . . . , N components are all or nearly all configurated in terms of imperatives to action in the highest sense of the term; that is, they represent the most basic value components that a sociocultural system is able to express in action. When we analyze the principle of respeto and isolate V, W, X, Y, Z . . . , N, we discover that they are seldom if ever expressions of behavior or actions, but rather directives that specify the way people should behave in a complex set of situations. One cannot observe respeto directly. It must be inferred from behavior that is the direct expression of highly diverse complexes, such as the pedimento ceremonies, in several specific situations of the life cycle of any compadrazgo type. But what is most signficant here is that the structural-ideal nature of V, W, X, Y, Z . . . , N is in many ways the most clearly verbalized by the people when they specify, either under questioning or spontaneously, the forms that these attributes take in the discharge of certain compadrazgo types. This is indeed an odd situation, for I have established that the ideological aspects of any situation involving human interaction are always the most unconscious phenomena that we have to deal with. How is it possible, then, that respeto is well verbalized by Beleños and rural Tlaxcalans (see Chapter Ten)? The difficulty can be solved only by distinguishing between social and individual consciousness, for what may be socially unconscious at one level may be expressed quite consciously by individual members of the group at another level. In the case of respeto, the principle itself is unconscious; the people as a group are not aware either of its covering nature or that it represents a complex of imperatives and commands to action, but they are quire aware of, and can readily specify, the individual imperatives and commands and how they are discharged in practice. Two things are clear: the people recognize respeto as an all-important ingredient of the compadrazgo system of Belén in action, but they are not aware of the fact that it stands for all the specific attributes that they can name in detail. From this viewpoint, the principle of respeto is the most inclusive in the compadrazgo system of Belén, for it not only shapes behavior and action, but also affects the discharge of confianza and reliance.

The principle of confianza is a combination of ideological and structural attributes, involving both imperatives and commands to action and the organized behavior that results from them. Confianza, like respeto, does not denote observable behavior. Here again, people talk about confianza and it can be elicited indirectly in a variety of contexts, but one cannot say that it can be identified by recording what people do in specific contexts. The main difference between respeto and confianza is that the people know what confianza means specifically with respect to component attributes. Thus, they are quite aware of the degree of confianza involved in most compadrazgo types in Belén, whereas they are not aware of the degree of respeto attaching to the same types. In other words, the covering nature of a principle, from more to less inclusive, is always gauged by people's awareness of its component attributes. I must add, however, that the implementation of my analytical framework is most difficult here, for how can we detect and measure degrees of awareness? At the moment I can only assume that it can be done accurately, and that to some extent I have done so here.

Finally, the principle of reliance is essentially a behavioral or structural-actual entity, and here we are dealing primarily with observable behavior. The only significant difference is that, unlike undifferentiated behavior (that is, observable behavior that does not fall under the rubric of a covering term), it is interconnected, for its various components have a core of meaning that ties them together. Thus, the people are not only fully conscious of what the principle of reliance stands for, they can also specify the actual operation and contexts of most of its components. Even the principle of reliance, however, must have a modicum of ideological or structural elements; that is, it must involve imperatives and commands, for otherwise the interconnection of its behavioral attributes would not obtain. The proportion of these structural elements is never large, and they are elicited indirectly, as in the case of confianza. The principle of reliance is the easiest to pinpoint, and such concepts should be constructed first in a structural analysis, but this should not keep us from searching for the more abstract, unconscious principles denoted by confianza and respeto. Were we to operate simply on the basis of essentially behavioral principles, we could never demonstrate causal relationship, and the analysis would remain unidimensional.

It should be clear by now that a structural analysis that aims to show causal relationship must necessarily take cognizance of all three domains denoted by respeto, confianza, and reliance. Explanation, or even mere description, cannot be achieved on the basis of any one or two of the three fundamental ontological-epistemological domains into which I have separated sociocultural phenomena. Two are well recognized by most anthropologists today, namely, actual and ideal behavior—what people actually do, and the rules that "cause" or condition their actions. The third domain comes into being by taking cognizance of the conscious or unconscious character of ideal behavior, thereby creating what I have called the ideological domain (mostly unconscious) and the structural-ideal domain (mostly conscious). Traditional anthropologists believed that we could understand human behavior only, or primarily, in terms of conceptualizing the rules that conditioned or caused it. At the opposite extreme, traditionalists have also maintained that the rules, imperatives, and commands of a sociocultural system are not significant, and that explanation can be achieved by the manipulation of behavioral data alone. In more recent times, many anthropologists have come around to the view that description and explanation are impossible without taking into consideration both what people should do and what they actually do, and explanation will consist in determining why and to what extent people's behavior deviates from or adheres to the ideal rules. The next step, then, after having scaled the ontological-epistemological nature of the principles of respeto, confianza, and reliance, is to determine how they are interrelated so as to provide a basis for explanation, both with respect to individual compadrazgo types and as general principles operating at the level of the compadrazgo system as a whole.

The principle of respeto in Belén plays the overriding role of giving the compadrazgo system a certain unitary meaning (but at the strict ideological level), and it is largely this function of respeto that enables us to isolate compadrazgo as a fairly well delineated system, distinct from several associated or related systems such as the kinship system and the ayuntamiento religioso—an open-ended but effective system which embodies a homogeneous substantive base. The internal consistency of the compadrazgo system derives from the fact that the actors involved in any compadrazgo relationship are bound by the imperatives and commands subsumed under the covering nature of respeto. But the principle of respeto in operation, through its covering attributes, does not specify the intensity, degree of deviation, adherence, or associated constraints obtaining between the imperatives and commands to action and actual behavior at the individual compadrazgo level. This is what I mean by saying that respeto is the most inclusive of the three principles. Every individual in Belén who enters into a compadrazgo relationship, regardless of the type, knows that respeto is forthcoming, but what he does not know is that this universal constraint will be modified at the individual compadrazgo level by other less ideological and more structural principles. Under these conditions, respeto stands as a principle that is able to generate causal relationships only at the systemic level; that is, it specifies (or may specify) the boundaries of action for all compadrazgo types taken together. Thus, eliciting and manipulating the covering attributes of respeto give us the range of structural and behavioral interaction required to talk about compadrazgo as a system. Although at the substantive level this is the last domain to be delineated, given the fact that its composition is indirectly and inferentially established, at the analytical level it is the first step that must be taken to delineate the system.

Confianza, on the other hand, is probably the key operational principle with which I have to contend in the bulk of the analysis. It operates most effectively at the individual compadrazgo level, for, unlike respeto, the principle of confianza definitely specifies the degrees of confianza associated with individual compadrazgo types. It represents the pivotal kind of principle that a truly sophisticated analysis requires. By itself, however, confianza is not an effective medium for generating efficacy; rather, it must be regarded as a bridge between the rules and imperatives embodied in essentially ideological principles such as respeto, and the essentially behavioral principles such as reliance. The principle of confianza constitutes a body of rules and imperatives that specify the degree of efficacy involved in every compadrazgo type; at the same time, it conditions the behavior associated with every compadrazgo relationship, thereby affecting the operation of behavioral principles such as reliance. When Beleños enter into compadrazgo relationships, they know how the covering attributes of confianza will be discharged and the prescribed degree of intensity. Thus, a couple entering into a PCE compadrazgo relationship knows that the relationship includes certain prescriptions that are quite different from those for first communion, BCC, or BSI compadrazgo relationships. I am not referring to general prescriptions, of course, but to those falling within the covering nature of confianza. It goes without saying that at any given level of analysis more than one (usually several) covering principles exist. I have isolated only confianza, but perhaps a more exacting analysis could isolate other principles. Moreover, what I am doing in this chapter is exploratory. My aim is primarily to show how a more sophisticated structural analysis in terms of covering attributes embodied in activating principles, and in terms of three distinct but interconnected levels of analysis, will not only be more economical but will eventually be more amenable to formal operationalization.

Finally, reliance is not so much a principle as strictly a covering term that distinguishes a corpus of behavioral data from other behavioral data that do not fall into a systematic pattern. It is the most specific of the principles under consideration; hence it must be regarded as a means of measuring the efficacy of the other two domains as expressed by respeto and confianza, rather than as having efficacy in itself. From a different standpoint, reliance must be considered as an effect of the efficacy of respeto acting at the level of the global compadrazgo system, and confianza acting at the level of individual compadrazgo types, for when we interdigitate the covering attributes of respeto and confianza we get specific behavior denoted by reliance. As the most empirical of the three covering principles, reliance is of course the easiest to formulate, but at the same time it is least useful from the theoretical viewpoint. (I am speaking about reliance as an analytical tool and not, of course, about its purely substantive composition.) The substantive composition of reliance is indeed the observable behavior that we want to explain in terms of the efficacy of the two other levels of analysis, but as an analytical tool it does not offer significant possibilities. In other words, we must not confuse the ontological and the epistemological properties of any level of analysis or the analytical constructs that we can build at such levels. In any event, at this stage of methodological sophistication reliance can be an adequate tool for analysis, and for practical purposes I have placed it on essentially the same level of abstraction and theoretical adequacy as respeto and confianza.

Multidimensional Analysis, Causal Relationship, and Measurement

The foregoing discussion indicates the nature and composition of the principles of respeto, confianza, and reliance, as exemplifying my three analytical levels, and how they are interconnected in the process of generating efficacy or causal relationship. Three signficant points are involved: first, the basic aim of structural analysis is to discover and formulate a hierarchy of behavior patterns and relations of invariance (structual variables) in the form of covering terms. This can best be achieved through a multidimensional approach that specifies a series of interconnected levels of analysis, which are inked in a way that permits us to determine the direction of cause and effect. The function of this multiplicity of analytical levels is solely to subsume empirical data (observable behavior) under the rubric of increasingly more abstract principles, which I have denominated covering terms. The determinant characteristic of covering terms is that the more abstract they are, the less behavioral they become; as we ascend the hierarchy of levels, the covering terms become more ideological and therefore potentially more amenable to demonstrating causal relationships. The trick in this approach is *measurement*, that is, our ability to give quantitative value to a causal relationship in terms of adherence to or deviation from the rules, imperatives, and commands that each successive level of analysis has with respect to its counterpart on the next lower level. The whole approach rests on two fundamental assumptions: first, sociocultural behavior alone cannot constitute the primary, most primitive data for our conceptualizations; indeed, raw behavior does not exist in the sociocultural universe, and only psychology can observe it (see Nutini 1971b). Second, all sociocultural systems make fundamental assumptions about the universe in order to ensure successful societal living, and these constitute the rules, imperatives, commands, values, or ideology (what I have called the ideological domain) that condition observable behavior; more specifically, what people actually do is intelligible only in the light of what they should do. As a corollary of the second assumption, I postulate that the rules, imperatives, or general ideological system underlying observable behavior are always discoverable, no matter how remote or hidden they may appear to be at the strictly empirical level. If these assumptions are correct, then my approach follows logically, and the only need it has at the moment is adequate quantitative implementation.

The second point is closely related to the first, and has to do with the demonstration of causal relationships, that is, with explanation. I have said that this is achieved by measuring the interconnection between any two or among all three levels of analysis. What this means primarily is that an explanation is forthcoming if we are able to determine and specify how and why a set of behavioral or structural attributes deviates from or adheres to a metalevel of analysis—that is, a higher set of covering attributes. Once we have established a level of analysis that is connected to a metalevel of analysis by a covering term, the explanation consists in determining why, under what conditions, and to what extent the rules, imperatives, and commands specified in the metalanguage are not complied with at the object-language level of analysis. This I have expressed by saying that ascending levels of analyses have efficacy in a downward direction. Thus, I have come full circle, and connected all parts of my analytical approach into a logically coherent whole. Criticisms to the effect that this approach cannot be implemented at present because we have neither the appropriate substantive-empirical base required by the multidimensional analysis, nor the required measuring techniques, are not to the point. It is true that the burden of proof is placed on me, but even if I cannot verify the analytical framework in its entirety, at least the conception of metalinguistic levels of analysis is worth testing.

The third point is essentially a practical one, having to do with the inherent advantage in approaching the conceptualization of whole systems or well-delineated bodies of behavior in terms of multidimensional levels of analysis. When we accept the conceptual possibilities of the ever more inclusive integration of behavior denoted by specific analytical levels, our task of abstraction is greatly facilitated, and in this way we can reach the level of abstraction at which theoretical terms can be formulated. In methodological terms this can be expressed by the establishment of the junctures at which we can realistically operationalize a concept of covering terms. It is in the substantive nature of any concept, no matter how small its semantic payload, that it can always be made to subsume more primitive behavior at a different level of analysis. The task of the anthropologist searching for junctures to operationalize is always conditioned both by the substantive composition of the concept he wishes to operationalize, and by his ability to subsume related behavior under the widest possible covering. This ability consists exclusively in structuring the concept being operationalized in such a way that it can be measured successfully. Thus, the practical advantage of my approach is that it guides the selection of appropriate chunks of behavior for operationalization, and conversely, that it prevents us from choosing inherently low-level concepts that are difficult or impossible to operationalize realistically.

Let us take, for example, the operationalization of compadrazgo choice in terms of friendship, locality, and a few similar concepts discussed in Chapter Seven of *Ritual Kinship* I. Such an operation would be a thankless one, and in the end impossible to accomplish, for as I hope to have demonstrated, these concepts can be accommodated under the rubrics of respeto, confianza, and reliance. Friendship, locality, generosity, cooperation, honesty, and several such terms cannot be placed at the same substantive and analytical level as our three principles, which for measuring purposes carry a much larger semantic payload. Structural-functional anaylsis, because of its unidimensionality, assigns the same semantic value to all behavioral data. Obviously, structural-functional analysis is a useful step in the scientific procedure leading to successful operationalization. My conception of one of the most important aspects of anthropology as a science consists of a series of steps in which a variety of analytical tools is applied in order to arrive at a body of

behavior sufficiently distilled (or abstracted) to permit operationalization, that is, the formulation of adequate relations of invariance. Neither
functionalism nor structuralism can by itself provide these conditions.
From observed behavior to achieved operationalization there are several
stages of analysis, but in themselves they do not produce the required
results. The object of this chapter is to indicate what we must do, and
how we can expand structural analysis, to achieve such a goal. By extension, the study as a whole advances from behavioral description, to
functional analysis, to structural analysis, and finally, I believe, the stage
is set for a truly formal operationalization. It is at this point that any
mathematical anthropologist can take over and successfully use his bag
of deductive tricks.[5]

The Covering Properties of Confianza, Respeto, and Reliance

Before leaving the analysis of the principles of respeto, confianza, and
reliance, I must analyze in some detail their actual covering properties
and the roles they play in the strictly structural and functional analysis
in progress. Respeto as a covering term is the most universal analytical
attribute of the compadrazgo system in Belén. It not only unifies compadrazgo into a well-structured system, it also delimits the boundaries
of actual behavior, within which, to be sure, there is considerable leeway. In essence, it ideally prescribes the fundamental nature of compadrazgo in Belén. When the average Beleño declares that compadres must
respect each other or that respeto is the necessary condition for a compadrazgo relationship, these utterances cover a wide range of imperatives and commands, the highest expression of which is embodied in
what I have called the sacred nature of compadrazgo. Respeto is not
only an imperative to action, but also a command that conditions a wide
variety of behavior. To this extent, at least, respeto can be said to influence and mold every successive level of integration well down into observable behavior. The multiphasic nature of respeto in Belén is shown
by the variety of ways in which Beleños and rural Tlaxcalans express
its semantic content; for example, "los compadritos deben respetarse"
(compadres must respect each other), "el respeto es esencial para mantener una relación de compadrazgo" (respeto is essential to maintain a
compadrazgo relationship), "si deja de haber respeto ya no hay compadrazgo" (if respeto comes to an end, compadrazgo ceases to exist),
"el respeto es la fuente del éxito y buen fin de un compadrazgo" (respeto is the source of the success and good ending of a compadrazgo),
"el respeto en el compadrazgo es algo muy diferente a tenerse respeto"
(respeto in compadrazgo is something very different from respecting
one another), "el respeto es sagrado y sin él no habría compadrazgo"

(respeto is sacred and without it there would not be any compadrazgo), and so on. In fact, it was this variety that led me to a more thorough investigation of respeto, with the result that it became the embodiment of most of what I can call ideological at this level of verbal expression. The semantic payload of the principle of respeto covers a wide range of rules, commands, imperatives, and constraints, which are the closest approximation to an ideological construct at the subsystem level. Respeto embodies many aspects of the ideological order of Belén culture and society as a whole, and by speaking of respeto in isolation I have assigned to its components the status of independent ideological entities, when in fact they are themselves conditioned by the highest semantic level of Belén culture and society (that is, the ideological order affecting the total entity).

In order of relative inclusiveness, respeto encompasses the following components: (1) The bonds of compadrazgo are supernaturally sanctioned, and contraventions and undue deviations from established directives may bring down the wrath of both Catholic and non-Catholic supernaturals. (Supernatural punishment can take a variety of forms, but the most common are illness, poor crops, and bad luck in business ventures. The symbolic and mythological underpinnings of the injunction are explicit in dozens of legends in which La Malintzi, the patron saint, El Cuatlapanga, and several other pagan and Catholic supernaturals play the role of cosmic mediators or upholders of the moral order.) (2) Compadrazgo relationships, and the compadrazgo system as a whole, are sacred institutions without which Beleños would be discontented and unhappy: their culture and society would become disorganized, and they would see many of their significant social and religious institutions come to an end. (3) Compadrazgo relationships of every type perform specific functions in facilitating the structural embodiment and actual discharge of the most diverse institutions, social and religious units, and associated behavior and activities in Belén culture and society. (4) The range of compadrazgo relationships is indefinitely expandable, from both the individual and the societal viewpoints, and the creation of any new compadrazgo type is a measure of the differential significance of the associated institution or formal activity in Belén. (5) The central rites and ceremonies of every compadrazgo relationship, and the subsequent economic, social, and religious rights and obligations, are equally important to successful compliance with the moral order supporting the compadrazgo system. The central rites and ceremonies impress upon compadrazgo actors the need for the relationship itself, primarily by what can be called magico-symbolic reinforcements, and the subsequent rights and obligations validate the relationship in the eyes of the society as a whole. (6) The compadrazgo system in general, as well as each of its types in particular, is above all a bridging mechanism and a social catalyst which has two main functions: it facilitates the interaction of society and the supernatural; and it helps to smooth the interaction between the ritual-ceremonial and the secular dimensions of religion and the social structure. (7) The compadrazgo system is ultimately a value in itself, because, regardless of its functions and roles within Belén culture and society, it gratifies the individual and in a variety of ways gives him a measure of security not supplied by other institutions.

These seven ideological injunctions do not in themselves take the form of rules, commands, or constraints, but they are definitely expresed as such in specific injunctions which implicitly take the form of "thou shall" or "thou shall not" imperatives. The most directly expressive of these imperatives are: (1) perform all rites and ceremonies, and discharge all social, religious, and economic rights and obligations in order to live at peace with yourself, the supernatural, and society; (2) comply with compadrazgo prescriptions, for failure to do so leads to unpleasant consequences for which only the individual is responsible; (3) contract prescriptive compadrazgo relationships even if the economic or social price is high, for in the long run they will result in your general well-being; (4) give to your compadres for you will receive in equal measure from them, and above all do not try to cut corners (the Spanish word *escatimar* clearly expresses this concept) in discharging your obligations, for you will be treated in the same way; (5) whenever an important occasion requires establishment of a compadrazgo relationship, do not hesitate, and in the process choose your compadres on a basis of equality; (6) do not engage in compadrazgo relationships for the sake of gain per se, but only with the aim of generating personal security and smoothness in your relationship with the world; (7) it is your duty, as a member of Belén society, to discharge your compadrazgo obligations properly, for this results in general well-being for all; (8) discharge your compadrazgo obligations (and your participation and general sponsorhsip within the ayuntamiento religioso as well) to the best of your abilities, for you will ultimately be judged on the basis of how well you have done this.

Lest I be misunderstood, I must reiterate that this body of "native categorical imperatives" (which are strongly conditioned by the golden rule of Christianity, and quite symmetrically implemented) is not part of the observable behavior or empirical corpus that I obtained from the people of Belén. These native categorical imperatives are in a real sense a model of the compadrazgo system in Belén, which are worked out in behavioristic terms with respect to lower levels of analysis. The seven main semantic components of the principle of respeto, expressed in the specific injunctions, can be regarded as a theory of the compadrazgo system of Belén which, by the appropriate manipulation, enables us to predict certain results of compadrazgo behavior at lower levels of analysis. From this viewpoint, the principle of respeto is in part a deductive construction; that is, it represents the articulation of certain assumptions that I make about the compadrazgo system of Belén as a meaningful unit of study, activated, of course, by the inductive configuration of compadrazgo in action. In such a situation there is no need to ask whether respeto as a principle is part of the data under observation; all one need ask is whether such a principle enables us to explain or predict something about the observable data. In other words, the principle of respeto is adequate for this construction because it embodies a significant substantive semantic payload which, although not directly traceable to the nuclear meaning of the concept, can be made into a theoretical term by a certain amount of deductive manipulation. Without this operation, all the attributes subsumed under respeto (the components and imperatives listed in the preceding paragraphs) seem to have only a tangential connection, and what is worse, they appear to operate at only one level of analysis. From this view of the compadrazgo system in operation, the principle of respeto in its behaviorally worked out injunctions (not exclusively recorded) provides the system with the necessary parameters to action—that is, moral directives, the deviation from which leads to certain consequences that can be theoretically measured, thereby producing explanations.

The principle of confianza, which embodies a different level of analysis, presents a different set of problems which at this stage of methodological development is harder to handle. First of all, confianza in Belén has a less covering nature than respeto. It operates at the level of individual compadrazgo types, where it plays a role analogous and homologous to that of respeto at the level of the total compadrazgo system. Here we can see the more restricted nature of confianza as an activating principle; but because of the state of current measuring techniques I have made it pivotal to the analysis. The principle of confianza can be adequately handled within the structural analysis, and in fact Volume One can be regarded as an implementation of similar principles involving commensurable quantities of semantic payload. One cannot forget, however, that what confianza represents as an activating principle is conditioned by respeto, so that under no circumstances can we confine ourselves exclusively to the former. Confianza, on the other hand, does have certain general attributes that pertain to the compadrazgo system as a whole. In the first place, it can be considered as a potential attribute of any compadrazgo relationship, which permits its actors to ask each other favors of an economic, social, and religious nature. This does not mean that this potential is always actualized, but rather that it can be actualized given certain specific circumstances. What is important here is to establish when such circumstances come to bear upon confianza as a principle. Confianza can also be seen as conditioning the allocation of social, economic, and religious resources so as to minimize conflict with the proper discharge of other systems within Belén culture and society. In this light, confianza is another rule or injunction which must be subsumed analytically under respeto. This is only one of two or three similar general attributes of confianza that made me regard the principle as a combination of primarily structural components with a few ideological attributes. We can therefore disregard the latter as having already been explained.

The covering nature of confianza is easier to elicit from informants, but at the same time its semantic content is much greater than that of respeto—in fact, nearly as many times greater as the number of compadrazgo types. Needless to say, I am not yet in a position to deal with this highly complex problem. To do so would require more sophisticated data-collecting techniques (which must certainly involve intensive teamwork and the use of various recording devices), and the development of computer programs to handle the analysis. But since I am more concerned here with exemplifying a certain analytical framework than with actually showing results, I need only show with one or two examples of specific compadrazgo types how the structure of confianza affects actual behavior. In the first place, the degree of confianza can be more or less specified for each compadrazgo type, and I have the data to show that this is perhaps the most significant attribute in scaling the thirty-one compadrazgo types in Belén from structurally more important to structurally less important by several classificatory devices—by, for example, the prescriptive-preferential distinction; social, economic or religious importance; the nature of the mediating object; and so on. Furthermore, the fact that confianza is what I have called a conscious, or mostly conscious, principle makes it easy to manipulate empirically. In summary, then, confianza in its ideological aspects must be manipulated in the same fashion as respeto, or rather as one of its covering attributes, whereas in its structural dimensions it assigns a specific position to every compadrazgo type, and as such each type becomes a microcosm of the compadrazgo system.

Let us take the PCE compadrazgo type as an example. I have stated that the principle of confianza in its nuclear meaning signifies the potential attribute for the allocation of economic, social, and religious resources, and that this universal dimension (that is, universal within the global compadrazgo system) fixes the scaling position of any compadrazgo type. In terms of degree of confianza in the above sense, PCE compadrazgo ranks low on any of the scales that can be constructed.

One cannot ask overt favors involving economic or social expenditures from a PCE compadre, but this is more than counterbalanced by the high symbolic content that compadres can draw upon. But in terms of the principle of confianza in its broadest covering nature, PCE compadrazgo ranks among the highest in Belén with respect to most scales that we can construct on the basis of the structural attributes specified in tables 1-11, 13-24, and 26-33. It is this aspect of confianza that I want to exemplify here.

These structural-actual aspects of confianza can be expressed in terms of the specific injunctions and imperatives covered by the principle, which are: (1) the occasion of death requires that the rites and ceremonies of the compadrazgo relationship as prescribed by tradition be scrupulously followed (there are no alternatives, and this is borne out by the fact that the highest ideal standards are adhered to and that the situation has not changed since the 1930s or so); (2) one must always have a close friend, neighbor, or previous ritual kinsmen prepared for an emergency, for death is almost always sudden in Belén; (3) the ritual sponsorship afforded by PCE compadrazgo requires that the chosen compadres generate the highest possible magico-symbolic support for the deceased; (4) special "respeto" must be shown to PCE compadres for their high symbolic value, especially in the case of baptism padrinos who must bury their dead ahijados; (5) one cannot select as PCE padrinos individuals who have a poor record in the sponsorship of mayordomias or in fulfilling positions in the ayuntamiento religioso; (6) one cannot engage in exogamous relationships in PCE compadrazgo; (7) PCE compadres will always be given preferential treatment over other compadres at any social, religious, or ceremonial occasion.

Although my data would enable me to elicit similar sets of injunctions and imperatives for another eight or nine compadrazgo types in Belén, it would be repetitious to list them all. What is of interest at the moment is that every compadrazgo type in Belén is immediately regulated and conditioned by a particular set of confianza injunctions and imperatives similar to that of PCE. All thirty-one confianza sets can be scaled by assigning numerical value to the two or three universal attributes of confianza, which together with the measurable efficacy of respeto in operation, will give us the total ordering of compadrazgo types in Belén in terms of (or in the direction of) the overall structural importance of each type and its positional properties within the compadrazgo system.

Finally, the principle of reliance, which represents the lowest level of analysis, is the easiest to envisage conceptually as well as substantively. It is only one of several principles at the third level of analysis in an essentially similar position within the compadrazgo system of Belén. Some of these principles are friendship, locality, and religious participation. These are essentially structural-actual elements, but I call them principles because just as in the case of reliance, they have a certain covering nature of their own. For purposes of simplication, I have included them under the rubric of reliance, although in a more exacting structural or formal analysis they would have to be considered separately. Moreover, reliance is unquestionably the most central of all the principles that I was able to isolate at the observational level of analysis, because it embodies the mechanism of compadrazgo selection which is at the heart of the structure of the compadrazgo system in Belén. I therefore analyze only reliance in its restricted role, with the understanding that the analysis applies to all other isolable principles at this level.

Reliance may be defined as the ability, willingness, and readiness of an individual in Belén to contract the duties and obligations of a compadrazgo relationship. The term has not only a nuclear meaning, but also a roster of behavioral attributes, expressed in structural form, to the effect that such behavior must be properly discharged in the correct order dictated by the conjoined action of respeto and confianza. This can also be expressed by saying that the discharge of reliance is the *normal* result of all that respeto and confianza (and equivalent principles) represent as efficacious mechanisms. Second, reliance is specifically determined at the level of individual compadrazgo; that is, there are different degrees of reliance associated with each of the thirty-one types in Belén. Furthermore, reliance must be measured and scaled in the same way as confianza. Third, the covering semantic content of reliance includes a long list of both individual and social characteristics which, properly interdigitated, will produce the overall efficacy of reliance in linking structural-actual behavior, and the numerical value of reliance for each compadrazgo type. The most significant covering properties are: generosity, frankness, cooperativeness, helpfulness, honesty, enthusiasm, social sponsorship, mediating ability, and communal service. All these properties or attributes take the form of specified behavior which conditions and guides individual choices and courses of action. As the last and most substantive level of analysis, they can be arranged into paradigmatic sets; that is, reliance as a whole is really a paradigm of actual behavior viewed from a more abstract position. I have demonstrated this in the analysis of compadrazgo choice and the determinants of compadrazgo structure presented in Chapters Seven and Eight of *Ritual Kinship* I.

The Exploratory Nature of Multidimensional Analysis

I have shown the substantive and analytical composition of the concepts of respeto, confianza, and reliance as embodying the three levels of my analytical approach, and have also indicated why I call them activating principles by demonstrating that they have a semantic content that can be put to good analytical use. This has not been an exhaustive study of all the principles in each of the three levels; rather, I have illustrated their extent by taking respeto, confianza, and reliance as typical at each level of analysis. This is essentially an exploratory chapter designed primarily to demonstrate how a thorough structural analysis can lay the foundations for implementing mathematical and formal methods by putting the raw data of sociocultural experience into a distilled, more simplified form before engaging in deductive manipulations. It is important to this approach that not all substantive-empirical data are assigned the same structural composition, and by this I mean that we must search for those junctures at which it is possible to subsume certain behavior and substantive components under increasingly encompassing terms. Each of the three principles represents a model of actual behavior at increasingly abstract levels of analysis, which are substantively composed of bundles of attributes that can be isolated by giving apparently flat, unidimensional phenomena a certain numerical value. It is not yet possible for me to show how scaling and measuring techniques are actually applied, but I have determined the requirements and assumptions necessary for implementing this multidimensional approach. This chapter may be regarded as a discussion of how the latent analytical properties of respeto, confianza, and reliance, as the most important representatives of similar principles on their respective levels of analysis, can be actualized in the explanation of actual behavior. The inclusion of, say, such attributes or variables as friendship, neighborhood ties, extracommunality, and so on, under the rubric of confianza will seem inappropriate to the reader only if he confines himself to thinking about them in terms of their nuclear meanings. But if we can express numerically all that these attributes or variables represent as conditioning and guiding behavior, there should be no difficulty in understanding how confianza becomes the covering term encompassing all of them. In other words, I have chosen to deal with the conditioning aspects or causal properties of friendship, neighborhood ties, extracommunality, and several other attributes and variables in terms of a reduction to confianza, that is, in terms of how this principle (in a Pickwickian sense) represents an adequate common denominator.

Before I conclude, a few remarks are in order. The reader may ask why I interrupted the normal structural analysis with this exploratory chapter. The answer is that I wanted to implement, at least in a preliminary way, some of the major aspects of the theoretical framework presented in the appendix with direct reference to a compadrazgo domain. At the same time, the interposition of this chapter partway through the structural analysis on the one hand indicates where I go after the static

TABLE 9. Strength of Respeto and Confianza

Type	Respeto	Confianza
Bautizo	Strong	Strong
Casamiento	Strong	Strong
Confirmación	Medium	Medium
PCE	Strong	Strong
Primera comunión	Medium	Medium
CCCH	Medium	Medium
CCCA	Medium	Medium
ANDC	Strong	Strong
ANDI	Strong	Medium
AOI	Weak	Weak
BSI	Medium	Medium
CSV	Medium-strong	Weak
Escapulario	Medium	Medium
Graduación	Medium	Weak
PCA	Strong	Medium
Quince años	Weak	Weak
Sacada a misa	Medium-strong	Medium
Compadrazgo de evangelios	Medium-strong	Medium
Compadrazgo de limpia	Medium	Medium
BOI	Medium	Weak
Bendición de casa	Strong	Strong
BCC	Weak	Weak
BM	Medium	Weak
Parada de cruz	Strong	Strong
Primera piedra	Strong-medium	Medium
Compadrazgo de amistad	Strong (but temporary, until another compadrazgo results)	Weak-medium
CABP	Weak (intrinsically, but strong if there are other compadrazgo ties)	Medium
Compadrazgo de aretes	Weak (intrinsically, but becomes stronger with other ties)	Weak-medium
CEON	Medium	Weak
FC	Weak (intrinsically, but becomes stronger with other ties)	Medium-weak
JJ	Medium (but temporary, until another compadrazgo results)	Weak

dimensions of the compadrazgo system have been analyzed, and, on the other, endows the remainder of the analysis with a more dynamic component. It shows the differences between a transitional structural analysis (Chapters One–Three) and a mature structural analysis (Chapters Five–Ten). With respect to the immediate analytical value of the chapter, it is obvious that the configuration of structural elements that remain to be analyzed will most certainly be affected in several ways by the threefold analytical framework. Take for example, table 9. Here I have scaled the strength of respeto and confianza with respect to all compadrazgo types in Belén, but obviously this is not a very accurate scaling. First, table 9 takes into consideration only the rough value of these two principles in terms of their overall efficacy, and not, at least in the case of confianza, in terms of their relative intensity and strength at the individual compadrazgo level. Second, the actual behavior denoted by the row itself is constituted by the nuclear meaning of respeto and confianza, and not by the conjoined efficacy of these principles in both their specific and universal constituents. And third, the value (strong, medium, weak) given to the nuclear meaning of respeto and confianza is itself approximate. In consequence, were I to scale the thirty-one compadrazgo types in Belén in terms of a meaningful composite construct of respeto and confianza, I would have to endow these concepts at the global and the individual compadrazgo levels with a much higher degree of substantive accuracy and analytical refinement.

Basically the same obtains at the level of the total compadrazgo system of Belén. The content of tables 1–11, 13–24, and 26–33 is certainly not an exhaustive description of the major structural-actual attributes of the thirty-one compadrazgo types in Belén; I could add another dozen, for which I do not have the necessary substantive base.[6] But let us suppose for the sake of argument that these thirty-one tables represent the total number of significant structural attributes of the compadrazgo system. In such a structurally bounded system, an analysis leading to measurable explanations undertaken in terms of my three activating kinds of principles is especially appropriate. Once I am able to scale each compadrazgo type in terms of individual properties of respeto, confianza, and reliance, the interdigitation of the universal properties of these three principles will transform the compadrazgo system of Belén into a domain in which explanation will be the function of the specific numerical value combinations that respeto, confianza, and reliance are able to generate. This means, of course, a gigantic task of scaling and measuring each entry in the rows and columns of all thirty-one tables (961 entries) multipled by as many combination scales (a minimum of five or six) as it is necessary to apply to the matrix. Unfortunately, the substantive data for this matrix are not under control, and to complete them would probably require a team working at least three years. Furthermore, such a volume of data can only be handled by computers, so the analytical step of the inquiry would also have to be a cooperative effort. This is at present (1974) a soluble problem, and in the future the use of computers will no doubt become part of the standard operational procedures of anthropology, but at the moment I can implement only part of this general scheme. I do control considerable data that can be used within the context of a few specific compadrazgo types, and data that are pertinent to four or five aspects of the joint efficacy of respeto, confianza, and reliance for the total compadrazgo system. I can do this schematically and without necessarily assigning specific quantification, a job that must be left to a separate study (White and Nutini n.d.). In the remaining chapters of the structural analysis, I try to exemplify some of the methods, ideas, and procedures discussed in this chapter, and at the same time illustrate with examples what I have here discussed more or less abstractly.

CHAPTER 5

The Preferential and Prescriptive Structure
of Compadrazgo

In this and the five following chapters I analyze the most important formal structural attributes of the compadrazgo system in Belén, paying special attention to their dynamic aspects in shaping the discharge of individual compadrazgo types. My aim is to show how these structural elements, individually and in combination, shape and condition compadrazgo relationships in Belén. The point of reference continues to be tables 1-11, 13-24, and 26-33, and the analysis oscillates between the global compadrazgo system and individual compadrazgo types. Through this interdigitation of the particular and the general, the actual dynamics of compadrazgo in Belén will emerge.

The Conscious and Unconscious Paradigms

In the Belēnos' conscious, explicit paradigm of the compadrazgo system, one of their principal distinctions is between prescriptive and preferential compadrazgo types; in the words of many informants, "los compadrazgos en Belén, o son obligatorios y se tienen que cumplir por ley y costumbre, o son por gusto y se cumplen más o menos a voluntad propia" (compadrazgo relationships in Belén are either obligatory and must be complied with by law and custom, or they are for pleasure [optional], and compliance is left to one's own will). The situation is much more complicated structurally, of course, and I try here to expand on this native paradigm and elucidate its substantive and analytical implications. I begin with what the people have in mind when they say that certain compadrazgo types are obligatory (which I have translated as prescriptive) and others optional (which I have temporarily translated as preferential). Essentially, Beleños clearly express the distinction between prescriptive and preferential compadrazgo types when they say that if the former are not complied with, certain religious, social, and sometimes even economic sanctions for the individuals concerned ensue. The latter do not involve such sanctions, although several types in this category do approach prescriptive status in the sense that there is strong private and public disapproval when they are not complied with. What informants do not state explicitly are several associated aspects of the distinction, the most important one being the form, nature, and effectiveness of the sanctions for noncompliance with prescriptive compadrazgo types. There is no sharp break in the people's ideological conception of the thirty-one compadrazgo types corresponding to their actual separation into prescriptive, highly preferential (those that approach prescriptive status), and preferential. All compadrazgo types are arranged on an ideological scale from 1 to 31, with a decreasing degree of religious, symbolic, and social importance. Thus, the ideology of compadrazgo in Belén dictates that all compadrazgo types must be complied with, but many extracompadrazgo variables can impede this ideal, and the scale reflects the fact that an increasing number of options exists. The people of Belén find it convenient to break the scaling continuum at certain points, to produce the three categories of compadrazgo compliance indicated above, which is a good paradigm of the structural-actual situation. But this is as far as the paradigm goes. For insight into the compadrazgo system at work we must turn to the specific religious, social, and symbolic sanctions attached to prescriptive and sometimes to highly preferential compadrazgo types, which in the last instance determine the status of specific types along the continuum.

Natural and Supernatural Sanctions for Noncompliance

The sanctions that the compadrazgo system specifies for noncompliance fall primarily into two categories: natural and supernatural. Supernatural sanctions, meted out by Catholic and non-Catholic supernaturals alike, can be expressed individually or collectively. The individual and his immediate family are deprived of the everyday protection of the supernaturals (the patron saint, the most venerated images in the community, La Malintzi, and a few other pagan entities) against envy, evildoers, and malignant spirits (which, according to the people's beliefs are always lurking—*acechando*—ready to do one harm if not properly propitiated). Overall, they are deprived of the guarantee that the supernaturals will not in any way aggravate the natural difficulty of living in peace with one's kinsmen and neighbors by withdrawing their support.[1] When this happens, there is a serious (as ideologically conceived by the people) breach of the natural order. Furthermore, if one individual (or several) fails to contract prescriptive compadrazgo sponsorships, he assumes a collective responsibility, in that the entire community may suffer from a lessening of collective rapport with the supernatural. Therefore, it is the responsibility of the group to urge individual members of the community to follow as closely as possible the ideological directives of the compadrazgo system of Belén. Supernatural sanctions can also affect a particular individual's family without extending beyond it. The most common form of individual sanctions is for particular supernaturals to refuse to grant favors to people not in good standing with them, because they have not been properly propitiated. Since Belén's particular ideological system results in people always asking favors of the supernaturals, this form of sanction is an effective coercive mechanism. In more serious breaches of compadrazgo compliance, the supernaturals may of their own volition mete out sanctions in the form of illness, bad crops, and bad luck in business ventures. It should be remembered also that the supernatural sanctions that maintain the ideologically coercive power of compadrazgo are part of a wider system, which includes the mayordomía system and the ayuntamiento religioso, and are underlain by the most fundamental ideological complex in Belén society. The manifest validation of this form of supernatural coercion underlying the ideological system is expressed clearly in the case of a man in Belén who became seriously ill for no apparent reason; at the same time, his *milpas* (cultivated plots) yielded very little, while everyone else in Belén had a bumper crop that year. It was the consensus that this had happened because he (hence his wife and daughter, also) had refused to sponsor the ANDI compadrazgo for that year, even though he was one of the richest and most prominent men in the community. In the eyes of the people, refusal to become ANDI padrinos, one of the most important communal compadrazgo types, necessitates a drastic show of coercive power, and this instance is well remembered by all adults in Belén as a paradigm of what happens to those who chance the refusal of compadrazgo or religious-ceremonial sponsorship. In addition, the latent content of many legends in Belén clearly enact the moral consequences of not following the ideological directives of socioreligious sponsorship.[2]

Natural sanctions can be social and economic, and they are meted out by individuals, groups of indivduals, and even the community as a whole. Natural sanctions are not in themselves powers or mechanisms of coercion that regulate and guide the discharge of the compadrazgo system in Belén. Rather, they are a corollary of supernatural sanctions. The people of Belén operate under the general assumption that failure to comply with specific socioreligious and symbolic sponsorships, be they of the compadrazgo type or pertaining strictly to the religious domain, involves collective responsibility. It is the business of the community as a whole to see that everyone in Belén complies with his ritual, ceremonial, and symbolic obligations. In serious breaches of ritual and ceremonial sponsorship this ideal is actualized, and the whole community may engage in coercive sanctions. Such extreme cases seldom occur, however, and therefore natural sanctions are meted out by individuals or groups of individuals—which at times may be fairly large. These individuals are usually kinsmen, neighbors, and couples directly or indirectly related to offenders by previous compadrazgo ties. Of course, the seriousness of the sanctions and the number of people applying them are directly proportional to the category of the compadrazgo type and its position on the ideological scale.

Social sanctions, which are better regarded as coercive mechanisms, take three main forms: verbal admonition and disapproval, withdrawal of social participation, and gossip. When any individual in Belén fails to undertake a compadrazgo relationship that rates as sanctionable, one of the effective ways of coercing him into compliance is verbal admonition and disapproval by close friends, kinsmen, and previous compadres. (Although I am referring to individual culprits, this status is extended to his wife and children as well; those who must suffer the direct consequences of sanctions are couples and their nuclear families—to be more exact, entire households. In the most serious breaches of compliance, sanctions can be extended to a wider range of kinsmen.) The individual is approached and told outright that he must mend his ways and undertake the ritual sponsorship, however difficult this may be. If he has failed to establish the compadrazgo relationship because of lack of means, he will probably be offered economic help in kind or cash by one or several of his critics. This is often an effective means of coercion, for there are few people in Belén who can afford to antagonize neighbors, kinsmen, and other compadres to the extent of breaking or curtailing social relations with them—the inevitable results in such cases. The critics themselves, especially if they are kinsmen, are selfishly interested in forcing compliance because it reflects badly upon them to have relatives who are not in good standing with the supernaturals and with the community as a whole. In a wider context, verbal disapproval may be expressed by a variety of people, even by children, and individual culprits may on various social occasions be harassed to an almost unbearable degree.

Withdrawal of social participation is really a consequence of verbal admonition. If an individual does not heed advice and verbal coercion, the next step is to deny him and his household participation in social, religious, and ritual occasions. This is the most extreme coercive measure that can be applied in Belén, and Beleños universally agree that no one has been able to withstand this kind of pressure without becoming totally alienated from the community or leaving it. But given the high compliance with the ideological directives of the compadrazgo system, the extreme measure of withdrawing social participation is seldom applied.

Finally, gossip—independent of the other coercive measures—is an effective means of forcing compliance. When word gets around that a certain couple failed to comply with such and such a compadrazgo type (and the people purposely intensify the ever-present undercurrent of gossip for such occasions) there is a quick reaction, and in a dozen ways—jokingly, confidentially, patronizingly, and in double-entendre—a wide variety of people let the culprit know how much they disapprove. This can be a very bothersome form of coercion and also a very effective one, for even before formal admonition is given, the offender has already reacted to the gossip aroused by his failure to comply. Since the occasions for prescriptive and highly preferential compadrazgo types are highly visible and immediately identifiable, the gossip circuit is informed almost immediately, and in a small community like Belén it is only a matter of a day or so before everyone knows. In chronological order, the average offender is subjected first to the coercion of gossip, then to verbal admonition, and last to withdrawal of social participation. Although a few cases do involve the second stage of coercion, gossip is usually sufficient, for its disagreeable consequences are enough to force the offenders and their families into the proper behavior.

Again, economic sanctions are not in themselves coercive measures but rather a corollary of social sanctions, and more specifically, of withdrawal of social participation. If the coercive process has reached the third stage, it is obvious that a man will not easily be able to borrow money, or to engage in labor exchange or in the exercise of any activity with an economic component. In fact, this economic factor is one of the most effective deterrents to letting coercion reach the last stage. Two additional factors relating to economic sanctions must be taken into account. First, supernatural sanctions have a significant economic component when they take the form of bad crops and bad luck in business ventures, which more than any other aspect of the ideological belief system of Belén deters people from deviating from prescribed rules. Second, when an individual has been coerced—sometimes with the enticement of *ayuda* (mutual help or aid)—into complying with a compadrazgo type, there is a lingering economic effect. People will often hesitate to give such individuals assistance of any kind, nor will they be willing to establish mechanisms of economic interaction or seek them as compadres in the future. Awareness of this aspect of economic sanctions is one of the single most powerful stimuli to comply with all important prescriptive and highly preferential compadrazgo types in Belén.

To a considerable extent, these remarks about the system of sanctions and the coercive process apply also to the mayordomía system and the ayuntamiento religioso, inasmuch as all three have fundamentally the same ideological component. The only noticeable difference is that now, when Belén is undergoing a significant process of secularization, the compadrazgo system seems to have remained more conservative than the mayordomía system and the ayuntamiento religioso, and this is most clearly expressed in its greater adherence to their common ideological system. While deviation from the ideological order in the mayordomía system and the ayuntamiento religioso (refusal to accept mayordomias, reluctance to assume ritual and ceremonial sponsorship, or refusal to become an officer in the ayuntamiento religioso) is becoming steadily more common, there is seldom failure to comply with prescriptive and highly preferential compadrazgo types. I do not know exactly why this is so, but it is evident that the compadrazgo system is proving more adaptable to the secularizing trends now sweeping the Tlaxcala-Pueblan valley.

Sanctions, Traditionalism, Secularization, and Change

These remarks make it clear that the complex of natural and supernatural sanctions endows the compadrazgo system in Belén with an effective compound of coercive mechanisms, which must be taken into consideration in analyzing the adaptive persistence of the system in the face of strong secularizing forces. In fact, I can demonstrate that the two principal reasons the compadrazgo system has remained one of the most constant aspects of Belén culture and society during the past thirty or so years are, first, the inherently adaptive nature of its ritual and ceremonial dimensions; and second, the effective system of sanctions and coercion that buttresses it. The latter, of course, is not in itself an efficacious mechanism, but rather the result of the compadrazgo system's position at the core of Belén's ideological order. This is also true of the religious system (including both the mayordomía system and the ayuntamiento religioso), but despite this common ideological denominator, the compadrazgo system has remained closer to the ideological order because of its better adaptive mechanisms, which are more suitable structurally to the contemporary secularization trends, the increasing contact of Belén with the outside world, and the rather drastic economic changes that the Tlaxcala-Pueblan valley has undergone during the past half-century. Thus, the compadrazgo system lends itself well to the transitional period in which eventually the traditional ideology of Belén will be transformed into what I have called a secular ideology (see Chapter Eleven of *Ritual Kinship* I). The compadrazgo system is better able to adapt because of its ability to incorporate all that is most sacred and mechanical in the traditional ideological order within a behavioral matrix that does not involve abuse of the economic domain (economic resources) for its own sake. In these circumstances, then, the ideological order of the compadrazgo system is still traditional, for, on the one hand, the people do not think it requires an excessive expenditure of economic resources that they are beginning to internalize in terms of capitalization; and, on the other, the system of sanctions and coercions is an immediate deterrent to serious deviations from its directives and injunctions. The compadrazgo system in Belén and rural Tlaxcala can even be used as an index of secularization and change. What I have in mind here is that the appropriate discharge of compadrazgo is, or can be used as, a mechanism of invariance holding between the traditional ideological system and the modern conditions of its discharge, in the face of several identifiable variables such as contact with the outside world, new economic conditions, demographic and land pressures, and so on. It is assumed that the best way to measure sociocultural change, leading to control of the variables that will enter into the formulation of an adequate theory of change, is to ascertain the efficacious relationship between the ideological order and the structural-actual order, for the key mechanisms of change operate at the ideological level.

Let me briefly illustrate this viewpoint, and at the same time give more insight into the prescriptive mechanisms of the compadrazgo system in action. It became quite apparent early in the fieldwork and analysis that the double action of natural and supernatural sanctions sometimes performed combined coercive functions in the discharge of the compadrazgo system. On the one hand, those individuals in Belén (still the majority) who believe that natural sanctions are merely the human, societal expession of supernatural sanctions, and serve to complement them, are obviously traditionalists who, for a variety of reasons, must be regarded as well within the orbit of the traditional ideological order. On the other hand, an increasing number of people in Belén, also for a variety of reasons, no longer believe in direct supernatural action over human affairs, and consequently do not believe in supernatural sanctions for failing to comply with the directives and injunctions of compadrazgo. These individuals are to a considerable extent (at least with respect to the compadrazgo system) outside the influence of the traditional ideological order; they are, so to speak, in transition toward being effectively influenced by a new ideological order that is not yet part of the community as a whole. This transitional group (at a rough estimate, about 10 to 15 percent of all couples in Belén), however, is still under the influence of the traditional ideological order to the extent that natural sanctions, and the coercive power associated with them, are still an effective mechanism of compliance. While transitional individuals overtly express some disbelief in the coercive powers of the supernatural (in particular, they ridicule the folk philosophy associated with these powers, and the morality enactment expressed in the legends), they are not outside the coercive mechanisms embodied in the various social and economic sanctions. Directly or indirectly, then, Beleños are effectively guided and constrained by traditional directives and injunctions.

Scaling such a situation would produce this gradation of ideological adherence: first come those for whom the ideological order is in full force and who see natural and supernatural sanctions as inextricably connected; for them, natural sanctions are a warning of the more serious supernatural sanctions needed to bring people into compliance. Second, are those who are still traditionalists, but who do not think in terms of the intimate interconnection of supernatural and natural sanctions; they regard compadrazgo compliance more as a social responsibility of the individual than as a means of creating rapport with the supernatural. Third come those who think that rapport with the supernatural is of strictly individual significance, and the compadrazgo compliance is again a strictly social mechanism aimed at facilitating community living. Fourth are those who do not believe in supernatural sanctions for anything at all (the 10 to 15 percent described above), and who cannot easily conceive of a connection between the supernatural and the individual and society; furthermore, they are beginning to think that the compadrazgo system is no longer a very useful institution at the community level, though they may regard it as a mechanism for extracommunal ties with a considerable economic dimension. Fifth and last, there will be those (I express this in the future tense, for there are no individuals in Belén now in this category) who will totally reject the compadrazgo system, at least in its sacred, community form, and for whom the social value of the institution will lie primarily in the way it can improve the individual's social and economic status; this in turn will destroy the horizontal egalitarianism of the compadrazgo system and transform it into an institution with a significant vertical component, expressed primarily in extracommunal form. Let me note, however, that a certain traditional ideological component will linger on, and even at this fifth stage the symbolic, ritual, and ceremonial value of the compadrazgo system will retain a certain efficacy. People will continue to practice many compadrazgo types, no longer within the traditional ideological order, but rather underlain by a new ideological order which will be determined primarily by economic variables. When the majority of Beleños reach the fifth stage, the community will have achieved a secular or urban-oriented status, for want of a better term, in which the ideological-structural articulation will have a totally different basis. If it were possible to scale the decreasing efficacy of the traditional ideological order, measure the time that each stage takes to complete, and give numerical values to individuals and their increase in secularization in each of the categories, we would have all the elements needed for a limited-range theory of change on a conceptual topic that is shared by the majority of rural communities in the Tlaxcala-Pueblan area.

Refusal to Comply with Prescriptive-Preferential Injunctions

The next problem to consider is that despite the still effective traditional ideological order, people sometimes do not comply with its directives and injunctions, and must be brought into line by the application of coercive measures. All of the forty or so informants whom I interviewed in depth stated that at least once, and sometimes two or three times, that they had tried to refuse to comply with certain prescriptive or highly preferential compadrazgo types. This cannot be interpreted as a phenomenon resulting from the secularizing trends that have affected the Tlaxcalan area for several decades. Rather, it is part of the traditional culture and society of Belén, for some of my oldest informants, several of them past the age of eighty-five, recall this happening more than sixty years ago. Why, then, do individuals in Belén refuse to comply with a given compadrazgo, in view of the strong system of sanctions and coercive mechanisms? Until about 1960 or so, no one in Belén got away with refusing to contract a compadrazgo relationship for the prescriptive and highly preferential types; only very recently have people been able to do this successfully, though they still pay a rather high price. But now as the traditional system is beginning to break down, it is especially illuminating to see how the traditional mechanisms operate in coercing people into reversing their initial refusal.

Individuals initially refuse to enter into a compadrazgo relationship for three main reasons. First, in all societies there are individuals (innovators belong to this category) who for a variety of reasons that I cannot even begin to delineate here—many of them psychological, no doubt—will drastically depart from ideological rules and directives and come into direct conflict with something that the majority of the group holds dear. Such individuals have appeared occasionally in Belén for as long as my oldest living informant (who was ninety-five) can remember. Several cases (approximately ten in this century) well remembered by the people—one of them the couple noted above, who refused to become ANDI padrinos—were related to the compadrazgo system. They involved either refusal to accept a compadrazgo, or refusal to ask for a compadrazgo relationship in the baptism, marriage, PCE, CSV, and PCA types. These people simply did not believe in the sacred nature of compadrazgo, and clearly stated that it was so much nonsense. Consequently, they faced the whole spectrum of natural and, according to the emphatic assertion of informants, supernatural sanctions and coercive mechanisms. In all cases, either the individuals concerned were driven out of the community, or their lives were made so miserable that after a prolonged period (in one case four years) they were forced to comply. Of the approximately ten cases remembered by informants, seven left the community shortly after their drastic refusal (in fact, I was able to interview one of them in Santa Ana Chiautempan where he established residence after leaving Belén), while the other three stayed in Belén.

It is not immediately apparent why such drastic sanctions and coercive measures have been successfully applied to the compadrazgo system, while neither the equally important (perhaps more important) mayordomía system or ayuntamiento religioso has ever had such effective mechanisms. This suggests, among other things, that the compadrazgo system stands at the ritual-ceremonial core of Belén culture and society—or, if you wish, at the center of what I have called the magico-symbolic domain. Noncompliance is numerically insignficant and its structural implications are not important, but it exemplifies very well the coercive power of sanctions.

The other reasons do not exactly involve refusals to comply with a given compadrazgo type, but rather consist of stratgegies that the people employ to achieve certain economic advantages or increase their economic well-being. The second occurs when a couple genuinely does not have the economic resources to contract a given compadrazgo relationship at a specified time and according to tradition. The strategy here is that the couple expects that the pressures applied by kinsmen, neighbors, close friends, and other compadres will ultimately result in economic assistance. The strategy usually succeeds, for rather than see a kinsman, neighbor, friend, or compadre decline in ritual-ceremonial status and be penalized socially, the people applying the pressure will supply what is needed to discharge the compadrazgo obligation. The refusal consists simply in not looking for a set of padrinos in the form prescribed by each prescriptive and highly preferential compadrazgo types. It goes without saying that given the rapid diffusion of information in Belén, the pressures resulting in economic help will always follow the sponsoring occasion itself. For example, if a couple baptizes a child without benefit of a compadrazgo relationship, it may be two days before the pressure makes itself felt. There may be rumors or gossip that the couple did not search for padrinos, but nothing can be done until the baptism takes place, for its is always thought that at the last moment the parents will make an effort to do things according to prescription. In this case, the coercion is in fact nominal. The parents do hold out for a while for the sake of appearance, but when the economic help becomes a reality, padrinos are selected and there are special rites of atonement, for obviously the baptism itself cannot be repeated. Each of the prescriptive and highly preferential compadrazgo types has its own specific rites of atonement. In general, they consist of a reenactment of the actual rites and ceremonies of sponsorship (if these cannot be repeated) but with a strong infusion of asking forgivenes (*pedir perdón*) on the part of the offenders. In some cases, the overall rites and ceremonies are repeated, as in the bendición de casa compadrazgo type.

The third reason for refusal is economic gain. A couple with the resources for undertaking a compadrazgo relationship without help may plead economic disability and heavy financial obligations to elicit assistance. Kinsmen, neighbors, friends, and other compadres often suspect that the couple is playing the refusal strategy for economic gain, and if they can prove it they can apply the whole range of sanctions and coercive measures. If they do not suspect or cannot prove that the couple's economic resources are adequate, then the third reason for refusal is resolved in the same way as the second. If, however, friends and kinsmen can establish their case, the pressures may be so strong that the offenders give way. A husband and wife who cannot convince their critics that they are economically unable to discharge a given compadrazgo obligation are in an uncomfortable position, for it is difficult to go back on their original stand, but finally they succumb to the mounting coercion.

While the second reason for refusal is rather common in Belén and does not involve many disadvantages, the third is a real gamble on the part of adventurous couples on the lookout for ways to save their own resources. Both strategies of refusal can, however, be regarded as somewhat irrational. The social disadvantages of refusing to contract a compadrazgo relationship outweigh the economic assistance given in either real or faked cases of economic deprivation. It is far better to exhaust all means of generating resources (borrowing money, soliciting help from kinsmen and neighbors, and so on) and comply fully with the directives and injunctions of the compadrazgo type, than to choose the refusal strategy. Once people have refused, they have a reputation for being socially irresponsible and economically unreliable, even miserly, and it may be some time before they can erase the stigma of even a single refusal. The second and third reasons for refusal are strictly temporal, however, for the system of sanctions and coercive measures will eventually make people comply.

Finally, a few remarks about which compadrazgo types are not initially complied with for the second and third reasons, a category that includes only private-individual prescriptive and highly preferential compadrazgo types, are in order. Prescriptive public-communal compadrazgo types fall entirely in the first context of refusal, and they involve the application of the strongest sanctions and coercive measures in Belén—as in the example of the ANDI padrinos' refusal. In fact,

Beleños find it almost unthinkable that couples will refuse to become sponsors of the four prescriptive and highly preferential public-communal compadrazgo types, especially since rich, prominent people are almost invariably asked. The private-individual compadrazgo types that can be initially refused are baptism, confirmation, first communion, ANDC, BSI, bendición de casa, and parada de cruz. Marriage and PCE compadrazgo are never initially refused—the former because marriage itself presupposes a large expenditure in which compadrazgo expenses can be more or less accommodated; the latter because ideologically this is probably the most sacred compadrazgo type in Belén, and sponsorship most needed on this occasion (see table 12).

Prescriptive, Preferential, and Optional Compadrazgo Types

The thirty-one compadrazgo types in Belén must now be scaled with respect to their intrinsic degree of compliance. But instead of using the threefold classification of prescriptive, highly preferential, and preferential I now refer to the last as optional, its native term, for this better denotes its status within the global classification. Highly preferential types are henceforth often referred to simply as preferential. Before these three taxonomic categories can be scaled, however, they must be defined and amplified in terms of underlying sanctions and coercive mechanisms. The ideological order of the compadrazgo system requires that all types be complied with, but structurally this is translated into a hierarchy of adherence to injunctions and directives. The compadrazgo types can be heuristically divided into three categories based on the degree of force with which sanctions and coercion are, or potentially can be, applied. The conscious paradigm of the people of Belén clearly expresses the main distinction between prescriptive and optional compadrazgo types as those in which noncompliance results in sanctions, and those in which no sanctions are forthcoming. To determine the intrinsic structure of compadrazgo compliance by itself, and in relation to other aspects of the system in action, I start with this native paradigm and expand, refine, and scale it.

First, I define prescriptive compadrazgo types as those in which refusal will call into action the entire roster of natural and supernatural sanctions, and their corresponding coercive mechanisms, thereby forcing compliance. Prescriptive types are the most mechanical in the system (indeed, this is the most mechanical aspect of the entire range of Belén culture and society), and permanent refusal to comply results in placing the offenders outside the compadrazgo system—which in turn means either total social ostracism or expulsion from the community. This situation, then, expresses the categorical imperative of the compadrazgo system in its most pristine form. As I have explained, however, at the structural-actual level, there are temporary strategies that couples employ with well-defined economic aims in mind, and within the category of prescriptive compadrazgo there are types that can and types that cannot be used in such strategies. Thus, within the prescriptive category itself there is a significant division into those compadrazgo types that can be temporarily refused for strategic reasons, and those that can never be refused. Among private-individual types, marriage and PCE compadrazgo belong in the latter division, and among public-communal types, ANDI and PCA. Prescriptive compadrazgo types are characterized by their unequivocal structural discharge in accordance with a clearly defined complex of sanctions and coercions. Beleños are very much aware of the directives and injunctions, and of what they must expect from failure to comply. The ritual-ceremonial discharge of prescriptive compadrazgo types has remained constant since the 1900s and only recently have a fair number of people begun to deviate, thereby moving Belén toward at least an incipient secular or economic ideology. But while the ideological injunctions and directives of this most pristine form of the system will go first, they will remain longer in the social consciousness of the people (and will be buttressed by natural sanctions), and it is within this context that the compadrazgo system of Belén will become adapted to a new ideology under quite different economic and social conditions.[3]

Second, preferential compadrazgo types occupy a position between prescriptive and optional types. They are defined as those in which non-compliance will bring natural sanctions and their associated coercive mechanisms into play, but not supernatural sanctions. They rank lower than prescriptive compadrazgo in the ideological scale, given the fact that no supernatural interference is necessary to force compliance, and therefore are of less total significance to the well-being of society as a whole. Despite the lack of supernatural sanctions, several types in this category must be classified as essentially prescriptive, for natural sanctions in the ideological scale are sufficient to enforce compliance. Thus, we have a dual division of preferential compadrazgo types: those in which social and economic pressures are strong enough to force compliance upon people who refuse initially; and those in which social and economic pressures are not strong enough, thereby allowing people to escape without complying. Among the former are types such as parada de cruz and ANDC, while in the latter are types such as primera comunión, escapulario, and graduación.

The difference between these two divisions is essentially a matter of the effectiveness of the social and economic sanctions and coercive measures, which depends on the position of the type in the ideological scale. Highly preferential compadrazgo types, which can ultimately enforce compliance, can be ranked as more or less equal to the second division of prescriptive compadrazgo types, but they must be placed lower on the idoelogical scale because they do not involve supernatural sanctions. The structure of natural sanctions and coercion is much like that of prescriptive compadrazgo, with perhaps the difference that the pressures are seldom as strong or applied by as many people. Beleños make every effort to comply voluntarily with the prescriptive compadrazgo types, whereas the lesser pressures associated with highly preferential compadrazgo types make it easier to employ refusal strategies. A significant number of preferential compadrazgo types, however, cannot ultimately be enforced, regardless of pressures, and here the situation is different. People who undertake to apply pressure know the relative ranking of these types in the ideological scale, and do not apply any coercive measures that could be effective; if their pressure does not produce compliance, they also know that this falls within customary behavior. In practice, a few kinsmen or friends will apply pressure as a matter of custom, for thier own personal reasons (such as maintaining an image of themselves as enforcers of the moral-sociological order or as members of groups that pride themselves on being traditionalists), but knowing that the offenders can persist in their refusal to comply. Hence, pressures and coercion are seldom applied with much heart. If a couple refuses to contract a compadrazgo relationship in the present category, pressure does not go beyond gossip and verbal admonition. Still, most preferential compadrazgo types in Belén occur frequently, and many couples dare not refuse them, for disagreeable social and economic consequences follow upon refusing too often. People in Belén are very conscious of community feeling and social pressures of any kind, and they will incur expenses that they cannot afford rather than face the consequences of initial noncompliance, even when they cannot really be forced to comply.

Third, optional compadrazgo types can be defined as those in which refusal to comply involves neither natural or supernatural sanctions of any kind—at least not directly, as in the two other categories. But the ideology of the compadrazgo system is such it makes itself felt, indirectly, thereby forcing compliance with a high number of compadrazgo types in this category. The indirectness of the pressures has already been explained, and they can be summarized as the fear that specific individuals and the community as a whole may brand one as socially uninterested, miserly, and lacking in esprit de corps. Under normal circumstances, then, couples in Belén do comply with as many optional compadrazgo types as their social and economic means permit, and often they will exhaust their resources in order to be considered traditional, upright members of the community. The overall incidence of compadrazgo types in Belén presented in table 10 supports this ideological perspective of the compadrazgo system. Of the thirty-one types, nine are classified as having universal incidence; nine as having high incidence (that is, more than 80 percent of the couples contract the compadrazgo type); eight as having medium incidence (that is, between 50 and 60 percent compliance); and only five as having low incidence (that

TABLE 10. Community Incidence of Compadrazgo Types

Type	Universal	High	Medium	Low
Bautizo	x			
Casamiento	x			
Confirmación		x		
PCE	x			
Primera comunión			x	
CCCH		x		
CCCA			x	
ANDC		x		
ANDI	x			
AOI			x	
BSI	x			
CSV	x			
Escapulario		x		
Graduación			x	
PCA	x			
Quince años				x
Sacada a misa		x		
Compadrazgo de evangelios			x	
Compadrazgo de limpia		x		
BOI				x
Bendición de casa	x			
BCC				x
BM	x			
Parada de cruz		x		
Primera piedra			x	
Compadrazgo de amistad				x
CABP			x	
Compadrazgo de aretes		x		
CEON			x	
FC		x		
JJ				x

TABLE 11. The Conscious Prescriptive-Preferential Paradigm
of Compadrazgo Types

Type	Prescriptive	Preferential	Optional
Bautizo	x		
Casamiento	x		
Confirmación	x		
PCE	x		
Primera comunión			x
CCCH			x
CCCA			x
ANDC		x	
ANDI	x		
AOI			x
BSI	x		
CSV	x		
Escapulario			x
Graduación			x
PCA	x		
Quince años			x
Sacada a misa	x		
Compadrazgo de evangelios		x	
Compadrazgo de limpia		x	
BOI			x
Bendición de casa	x[1]		
BCC			x
BM	x		
Parada de cruz		x[1]	
Primera piedra			x[1]
Compadrazgo de amistad			x
CABP			x
Compadrazgo de aretes			x
CEON			x
FC		x	
JJ			x

[1] With an alternative.

is, less than 40 percent compliance). Moreover, types with a medium
or low compliance include several selective compadrazgos—that is, by
numerical necessity or by the nature of the occasion, not everyone can
participate—so obviously the pancompadrazgo degree of compliance in
Belén is extremely high.[4]

The Structural Scaling of Compadrazgo Types

I am now in a position to scale the thirty-one compadrazgo types and to indicate their subdivisions as breaking points in the continuum. Table 11 presents the people's conscious distinction between prescriptive or obligatory types, and preferential or optional types. It shows that there are eleven prescriptive, five preferential, and fifteen optional compadrazgo types. This paradigm of the prescriptive-optional distinction is fairly accurate, but it needs to be refined on the basis of the structural analysis. By correlating the actual behavioral discharge of all compadrazgo types with their degree of adherence to or departure from the stated ideological order, and taking as a taxonomic index the complex of sanctions and coercions, I am able to scale the situation with a significant degree of accuracy. Table 12 presents the scaling in a straightforward manner, but to complete the structural analysis it is necessary to discuss the table in some detail and to furnish additional information.

In table 12 I first separated all the compadrazgo types into private-individual and public-communal, for its is obvious that both the ideological content and the structural attributes of these two categories are quite different. Second, I followed the breakdown more or less naturally suggested by the foregoing analysis, except that I referred to compadrazgo types in which sanctions and coercive mechanisms are not strong enough to enforce ultimate compliance (types 12 to 16) simply as preferential. Third, I ranked the thirty-one types, segregated into private-individual and public-communal, from 1 to 25 and 1 to 6 respectively. Thus, the arabic numeral to the left of each type in table 12 represents its ranking in the overall prescriptive-preferential-optional scale of the compadrazgo system. Fourth, in arriving at this ranking of the compadrazgo system, I employed several additional structural attributes roughly quantified in tables 1-11, 13-24, and 26-33. Since I have discussed at length the operation of the system of sanctions and coercive measures, the people's conscious paradigm, and the major breakdowns themselves, the analysis for the remainder of this section is centered on these extrastructural attributes.

To begin with, table 12, by itself, represents as exact a scaling of compadrazgo types as is now possible, given the general corpus of structural-actual attributes of the compadrazgo system in Belén summarized in tables 1-11, 13-24, and 26-33, and taking as the analytical matrix the ideal-structural articulation of the system. The numerical position represents the degree of ideological compliance with the compadrazgo system in terms of actual behavior, in that the position of all compadrazgo types in this scale is determined by the effectiveness of the complex of sanctions and coercive mechanisms in enforcing what

TABLE 12. The Prescriptive-Preferential-Optional Scaling
of Compadrazgo Types

	Private-Individual	Public-Communal
Prescriptive (can never be refused) Prescriptive (can be temporarily refused)	1. PCE 2. Casamiento 3. Bautizo 4. Bendición de casa 5. Sacada a misa 6. BSI 7. Confirmación	1. PCA 2. ANDI 3. CSV 4. BM
Highly preferential (sanctions enforce ultimate compliance)	8. Parada de cruz 9. ANDC 10. Primera piedra 11. Compadrazgo de limpia	
Preferential (sanctions are not strong enough to enforce ultimate compliance)	12. Compadrazgo de evangelios 13. Primera comunión 14. CEON 15. Escapulario 16. Graduación	5. BOI 6. AOI
Optional (refusal to comply does not entail direct pressures)	17. CCCH 18. CCCA 19. Compadrazgo de amistad 20. JJ 21. FC 22. Compadrazgo de aretes 23. BCC 24. CABP 25. Quince años	

the ideological order dictates. Table 12, then, is essentially a shorthand expression of the structural-actual discharge of compadrazgo in Belén permitted by the inherent constraints of the underlying ideological order. At the same time, and given the highly mechanical nature of this aspect of the compadrazgo system, table 12 is an accurate representation of the ideological model that underlies much of the system. The conscious paradigm of the people of Belén corresponds fairly accurately to the mechanical model exhibited in table 11, and the discrepancies between these two constructs can always be explained with reference to specific constraints or variables external to the compadrazgo system.

Here we have a case of a mechanical model (unconscious to the people) based on a conscious paradigm, which permits us to map structural-actual behavior, given certain specified conditions. This model not only predicts the degree of deviance from the jural rules of the system, but also determines the underlying but immediate considerations that enter into the actual choices and decisions that the people must make. All we need to know to activate the model is the specific constraints (sanctions and coercive mechanisms), and the position of a given compadrazgo type (in the private-individual–public-communal scale). By activating the model, I mean specifying the processes that lead to making a decision about establishing a compadrazgo relationship. This is an efficient model, for the variables are few and easy to control; at this point a mathematical anthropologist could formulate the variables of the system into a formal construct.

I can best discuss the relation of table 12 to the foregoing analysis by describing the mechanisms and steps that led to the scaling of compadrazgo types. The scaling of both private-individual and public-communal compadrazgo types was immediately given by the ideological effectiveness of the system of sanctions and associated coercive mechanisms, which is such that all compadrazgo types in Belén fall into the five categories of table 12 (prescriptive-prescriptive-highly preferential-preferential-optional). The ideological-structural articulation only indicates, however, that certain types fall into certain categories—if specified steps are not taken in the discharge of a particular compadrazgo type, certain sanctions and coercive mechanisms will come into operation and enforce compliance. How did I in that case, arrive at the scaling of the compadrazgo types within these categories? Why, for example, is baptism compadrazgo number 3 in the scale, while confirmation is number 7? Before answering, I must amplify what I have said about the content of tables 1-11, 13-24, and 26-33.

Tables 1-11, 13-24, and 26-33 are essentially a summary of the significant structual attributes of the compadrazgo system (not an exhaustive one, to be sure, but at least commensurate with our still rather crude data-gathering techniques), directly or indirectly elicited. The ideological content of each of these tables is not explicit, and can only be determined by other techniques, as I have done here by establishing the rules and directives connected with that specific aspect of the compadrazgo system. For example, table 8 shows the people of Belén's implicit classification of the overall importance of compadrazgo types in terms of a primary-secondary-tertiary scale. (The same is true for most of the structual-actual attributes mapped in tables 1-11, 13-24, and 26-33, except for those in which the classification or the payload itself is consciously known.) I call this classification unconscious because it is

TABLE 13. Independent and Dependent Compadrazgo Types

Type	Independent	Dependent
Bautizo	x (but with different types; sacada a misa)	
Casamiento		x (includes several subtypes)
Confirmación	x	
PCE	x	
Primera comunión	x	
CCCH		x (casamiento)
CCCA		x (casamiento)
ANDC	x	
ANDI	x	
AOI	x	
BSI	x	
CSV	x	
Escapulario		x (may be included in limpia)
Graduación	x	
PCA	x	
Quince años	x	
Sacada a misa		x (may be subsumed in baptism)
Compadrazgo de evangelios		x (may be subsumed in sacada a misa)
Compadrazgo de limpia		x (may be included in escapulario)
BOI	x	
Bendición de casa	x (may be part of primera piedra)	
BCC	x (may be considered red part of CEON)	
BM	x	
Parada de cruz	x (may be part of bendición de casa or primera piedra)	

TABLE 13 (*cont.*)

Type	Independent	Dependent
Primera piedra	x (may be part of bendición de casa)	
Compadrazgo de amistad		x (leading to other compadrazgo relationships)
CABP	x (but the result of other compadrazgo relationships)	
Compadrazgo de aretes		x (leading to other compadrazgo relationships)
CEON		x (but the result of other compadrazgo relationships)
FC		x (leading to other compadrazgo relationships)
JJ		x (leading to other compadrazgo relationships)

arrived at by the analysis of several complexes of compadrazgo behavior, and rarely elicited verbally from informants. It might be asked why I have chosen the structural payload of table 11 rather than that of table 8 as embodying the core of the ideal-structural articulation. Is not the prescriptive-preferential-optional classification of the people one of the several equally significant structural attributes of the compadrazgo system? The answer is yes. The structural payload of table 11 is no different from that of several other tables, but I chose the prescriptive-preferential-optional paradigm as the core of the ideal-structural articulation because it is the most mechanical, that is, the one that deviates least from the ideological order. Thus, while I could have taken as the ideological-structural referent tables 8, 9, 13, or several others, they would not have been as effective for analytical purposes as the prescriptive-

TABLE 14. Strength of Permanent Bonds and Obligations

Type	Strong	Medium	Weak
Bautizo	x		
Casamiento	x		
Confirmación		x	
PCE	x		
Primera comunión		x	
CCCH		x	
CCCA		x	
ANDC	x		
ANDI	x[1]		
AOI			x
BSI	x		
CSV		x[1]	
Escapulario		x	
Graduación			x
PCA	x[1]		
Quince años			x
Sacada a misa	x		
Compadrazgo de evangelios		x	
Compadrazgo de limpia		x	
BOI			x
Bendición de casa	x		
BCC			x
BM		x[1]	
Parada de cruz	x		
Primera piedra		x	
Compadrazgo de amistad		x	
CABP		x	
Compadrazgo de aretes		x	
CEON			x
FC		x	
JJ		x	

[1] No economic obligations.

preferential-optional paradigm. While the analysis of table 8 has direct significance for specific aspects of compadrazgo in action, I consider this of relatively less importance. I could not have scaled the compadrazgo system adequately on the basis of any other structural attribute shown in tables 1-11, 13-24, and 26-33, for their mechanical component is either not high enough, or not demonstrable to me. Fundamentally, what I

TABLE 15. Initial Economic Obligation by Compadrazgo Type

Type	Very High	High	Medium	Low
Bautizo			x	
Casamiento	x			
Confirmación				x
PCE			x	
Primera comunión			x	
CCCH				x
CCCA				x
ANDC			x	
ANDI	x			
AOI				x
BSI			x	
CSV			x	
Escapulario				x
Graduación			x	
PCA		x		
Quince años			x	
Sacada a misa				x
Compadrazgo de evangelios				x
Compadrazgo de limpia			x	
BOI		x		
Bendición de casa			x	
BCC				x
BM		x		
Parada de cruz			x	
Primera piedra				x
Compadrazgo de amistad				x
CABP		x		
Compadrazgo de aretes				x
CEON				x
FC				x
JJ				x

am saying is that not all structural or behavioral attributes of a system or institution are at the same level, and that some have a greater potential analytical yield. In any event, while the structural content in tables 1-11, 13-24, and 26-33 is in each case relative and analytically important to specific aspects of the compadrazgo system, the rough scaling involved in several tables is important to the definitive ranking of com-

TABLE 16. Strength and Permanence of Padrinos-Ahijados Dyad by Compadrazgo Type

Type	Relationship
Bautizo	Strong–medium
Casamiento	Medium
Confirmación	Medium
PCE	None
Primera comunión	Medium–weak
CCCH	Weak
CCCA	Weak
ANDC	None after the third year
ANDI	None after the third year
AOI	None
BSI	None
CSV	None
Escapulario	Weak structurally, strong to medium personally
Graduación	Weak
PCA	Strong for eight years
Quince años	Weak or none
Sacada a misa	Medium structurally, strong personally
Compadrazgo de evangelios	Medium
Compadrazgo de limpia	Weak structurally, strong personally
BOI	None
Bendición de casa	None
BCC	None
BM	None
Parada de cruz	None after the third year
Primera piedra	None
Compadrazgo de amistad	None
CABP	Strong but short-lived
Compadrazgo de aretes	Strong
CEON	None
FC	None
JJ	None

padrazgo types in table 12. The compadrazgo types of at least six tables (8, 9, 14–16, and 32) are ranked on a scale showing relative importance. This represents an incipient, natural scaling on which to build a more sophisticated paradigm or model in roughly the same fashion as I have done for table 11 and the model thereof. Ideally, then, the global operationalization of the compadrazgo system requires interdigitation of the scaled content of tables 1-11, 13-24, and 26-33. I cannot do this at present, for I do not command the substantive data to undertake for all these tables the operation illustrated in table 12.

The operational model of table 11 presented in table 12 was possible because I command the necessary data (gathered after I realized that the rough prescriptive-preferential-optional paradigm of the people constituted one of those thresholds yielding to analysis centered on the ideological-structural articulation). For my purposes here, however, operationalization of the prescriptive-preferential-optional paradigm is enough; there is no point in multiplying examples with asymptotic results. It should be realized, of course, that the primary function of structural analysis is only to lay bare the arrangement of elements and variables that will enter into the formal operationalization of a construct. (At least in the present context, this is what I mean by structural analysis, although it may have other equally significant meanings with the broad, almost ideological domain of anthropological practice). The structural analysis itself does not yield any quantitative results. In the model of the prescriptive-preferential-optional paradigm I have only stipulated the general arrangements of the construct, and on this basis certain operations can be performed, such as predicting compardrazgo compliance within the range of my five major categories; but actual compadrazgo choices cannot be predicted, nor can the mechanisms of decision making that underlie such choices be controlled. This can only be done (once the variables and elements of the construct are controlled) in terms of relations of invariance, and their positional and relational properties. This task cannot be undertaken without the help of mathematics. Any nonmathematical operationalization of constructs such as my model of the prescriptive-preferential-optional paradigm will yield only minimal results.

I can now complete the structural analysis by describing how the scaling within the five groups of compadrazgo types in table 12 was arrived at. Once I accurately placed all thirty-one types into the five categories (see table 12: 1, 2, 1, 2; 3-7, 3, 4; 8-11; 12-16, 5, 6; 17-25), the position of each type within its category was determined by the interdigitation of the structural content of tables 2, 3, 8-10, and 14. (As explained, the principal reason for choosing these tables was that they were already incipiently scaled.) The higher the overall threefold interdigitation of the tables per each type in the category, the higher the rank of the type in the total scale. Let us take, for example, the private-individual prescriptive compadrazgo types that can be temporarily refused: baptism, bendición de casa, sacada a misa, BSI, and confirmation. For each of these five types, a numerical value was assigned to the structural contents of tables 2, 3, 8-10, and 14. Furthermore, the six tables themselves were scaled as follows: 8, 9, 10, 14, 2, 3; that is, the primary-secondary-tertiary classification of overall importance was intrinsically higher than the strength and intensity of respeto and confianza, which in turn, was intrinsically higher than overall incidence of compadrazgo types, and so on. If we take the primary-secondary-tertiary classification (table 8) we see that baptism and bendición de casa are primary types, while sacada a misa, BSI, and confirmation are secondary types. This immediately divides the group into two subcategories. In turn, the interdigitation of the other five structural contents (tables 9, 10, 14, 2, and 3) gives us the final position of the five types within the prescriptive (can be temporarily refused) category. The same procedure was applied to the five categories covering both private-individual and public-communal compadrazgo types in Belén. In this fashion, the ideal-structural articulation, as shown by the complex of sanctions and coercive mechanisms in action, was complemented with the interdigitation of selected structural-actual attributes of the compardrazgo system, thus enabling me to construct a fairly accurate model by establishing a precise scaling of compadrazgo compliance. The difficulties of interdigitating the simple scaling of just six structural attributes can give us an idea of how much more complicated it will be to interdigitate thirty structural-actual attributes, if and when I possess the necessary data. For the moment, however, I feel certain that a well-defined segment of the compadrazgo system in Belén has been adequately analyzed and is ready to be formally operationalized. At least, I have outlined in some detail a practical and efficient method for conducting structural analysis beyond a mere juggling of words, and with a significant quantitative component.[5]

The Limitations of the Prescriptive-Preferential-Optional Paradigm

Before concluding the analysis of the prescriptive-preferential-optional paradigm of compadrazgo in action, I would like to discuss briefly certain of its limitations with reference to the compadrazgo system as a global institution. I have demonstrated a high degree of correspondence between the ideological and structural orders of the compadrazgo system by showing how effective the system's complex of sanctions and coercive mechanisms is, to the extent that even optional compadrazgo types are subject to certain indirect pressures leading to compliance. On the other hand, in Chapter Nine of Ritual Kinship I, I indicated that the compadrazgo system of Belén has undergone some changes, in that its structural-actual discharge is beginning to deviate significantly in certain identifiable areas, a seeming discrepancy that I wish to explain. The crux of the matter is that the system has at the same time remained highly traditional (there is a high degree of correlation between the ideological and structural orders), and is also beginning to change (the degree of nonadherence to the ideological order is becoming structurally noticeable). This situation, however, pertains to different aspects of the compadrazgo system, and in fact, what I have said implies no discrepancy.

The ideological order of the compadrazgo system has remained basically the same as it was perhaps ninety years ago, when all of rural Tlaxcala was essentially Indian. In addition, the traditional quality of the system has been most noticeable in the actual establishment of compadrazgo relationships. The fundamental sacredness of ritual sponsorship is still very much in the minds of the people, and the introduction of new significant occasions in the life, social, and economic cycles (for example, graduación, BCC, CABP, and so on) has witnessed the establishment of new compadrazgo types. Furthermore, the strong adherence to the directives and injunctions of the ideological order is confined primarily to the preliminary steps and core of ceremonies associated with every compadrazgo type. What has remained constant are the immediate, symbolic, magico-religious aspects of the rites and ceremonies of compadrazgo in action—in effect, the very act of contracting a compadrazgo relationship. On the other hand, what is beginning to change, and has been changing slowly since 1940 or so, are the associated activities and behavior that surround the structural discharge of preliminary steps and the core of ceremonies—above all, the recurrent rites and ceremonies, and the nature of the permanent and temporary bonds and obligations among the various dyads of given compadrazgo relationships. Of course, a point will come at which the cumulation of these small changes will upset the general structure of the ideological order, and the compadrazgo system will cease to be traditional (in the sacred sense of the term) and will adapt itself to a new ideological order, which I have predicted will have a primarily economic nature. Because of the Beleños' cumulative involvement with the outside world, their increasing economic integration into the Mexican nation, and the acquisition of urban ways and attitudes—in short, their increasing secularization— the compadrazgo system is changing from the periphery to the core. When the new secular ideology makes itself felt to the extent that, say, the casamiento, PCE, or PCA compadrazgo types are no longer strictly prescriptive, the traditional ideology will have ceased to be efficacious, and the compadrazgo system will have become adapted to a new structural situation. I can summarize what I have said with reference to diagram 1, and roughly scale the degree of traditionality and departure from it that the compadrazgo system of Belén has undergone.

First, the most traditional aspect of the compadrazgo system remains the event and relationship nodes that extend from the preliminary steps to the pedimento, to the economic, social, and religious arrangements, and finally to the culmination of the core of ceremonies when the compadrazgo relationship offically comes into being. There have been no signficant changes in this domain, and the steps in this symbolic, ritual, and ceremonial chain of events are taken strictly according to tradition. Second, the personnel interaction nodes associated with this domain have also remained traditional, but the quality and quantity of associated relationships and patterns of behavior are beginning to change slightly. For example, promptness and appropriateness in complying with compadrazgo relationships, certain aspects of the etiquette associated with the preliminary steps and the pedimento ceremonies, the intensity of interaction among secondary and even primary actors, and so on, are being slightly altered, and in a few instances noticeably altered. But by the rough standards of the present, this realm of compadrazgo structure still remains quite traditional. Third, the event and relationship nodes below the central complex of ceremonies have changed somewhat. While the recurrent rites and ceremonies are discharged regularly in all compadrazgo types that involve them, this is less the case for the permanent bonds and obligations among the various dyads in a compadrazgo relationship. There are increasing signs of instability in the structure of permanent bonds and obligations that give form to compadrazgo after the central and recurrent rites and ceremonies have been discharged. People are beginning to forget about the prescribed patterns of visiting and formal interaction, and both the quality and quantity of compadrazgo interaction are less than they were in the 1950s. It is in this third more visible domain of the compadrazgo system in Belén that one can see the first clear signs of what is in store for the institution. Fourth, and as a corollary of what has happened to the event and relationship nodes below the core of ceremonies, the personnel and interaction nodes accompanying them are also showing increasing signs of stress. Several traditional patterns of behavior and associated activities are either being diluted or are not being carried out with the original intensity; secondary and tertiary compadrazgo actors are participating less in the traditional manner; in a few compadrazgo types, once the central ceremonies have taken place there is little left for secondary and tertiary actors to participate in; and so on.

The trend implicit in this gradation of various aspects of the compadrazgo system indicates that in the not too distant future the institution of compadrazgo will be confined primarily to the immediate discharge of the core of ceremonies; that is, the ritual (magico-religious) sponsorship itself will constitute the central meaning of the compadrazgo system. (At the moment I cannot compute this point, but the rate of change since the 1940s and the increasing rate of secularization in Belén suggest that it will happen within the next twenty-five years.) Undoubtedly, under the influence of the new secular ideology the compadrazgo system will acquire different functions and be discharged structurally in quite a different way from what I have described here. What this new ideological-structural articulation will be, I cannot say at the moment. I can predict with some confidence, however, that the sacred nature of the institution will be confined exclusively to its immediate magico-religious aspects (the discharge of the sponsorship itself), while permanent or temporary bonds and obligations will no longer be governed by the traditional principles of respeto and confianza (they will acquire new meanings), but rather by principles that will emphasize economic considerations and the extension of social and economic ties (vertically and horizontally), within and outside the community. In summary, the compadrazgo system has remained traditional despite the changes that are beginning to take place in at least two aspects of it, and the overall ideological-structural articulation is still strong enough (that is, traditional enough) to enforce compliance even in those aspects that are showing noticeable stress. The effective transitional stage of the compadrazgo system in Belén and much of rural Tlaxcala will begin when the complex of sanctions and coercive mechanisms is no longer effective in enforcing immediate compliance in those compadrazgo types falling in the category of prescriptive (can never be temporarily refused). Until that moment comes, the system can be regarded as a traditional institution.

The Structural Implications of Symmetrical and Asymmetrical Compadrazgo Relationships

The most common usage of the terms symmetrical and asymmetrical in anthropological literature is associated in one way or another with the presence or absence of reciprocity. The terms themselves, and reciprocity as a concomitant variable, are too inexact to enable me to use them here without at least a brief discussion of their content and range of application, that is, with regard to the personnel or situations to which they are supposed to relate. In this chapter, then, I elucidate the nature of symmetry and asymmetry in the compadrazgo system, and show how these qualities affect the discharge of individual compadrazgo types.

Reciprocity and the Symmetrical-Asymmetrical Context of Personnel

One of the most significant dimensions of the ideological order of the compadrazgo system is the principle of reciprocity—the injunction that all compadrazgo relationships be carried out on a symmetrical basis—which applies to every aspect (event and relationship as well as personnel interaction) of any compadrazgo type. But the very nature and multiphasic aspect of the compadrazgo system, well expressed in its multiple types, conspire against the realization of ideological directives in actual behavior. In addition, several extracompadrazgo variables, such as exogamous selection, labor migration, and new economic constraints, also operate to hamper the ideological implementation of symmetry. Here, then, one finds a rather significant formal discrepancy between the ideological and structural orders in the compadrazgo system. It should be added, however, that the asymmetry that results from this discrepancy plays a rather minor role in the overall configuration of the compadrazgo system in Belén, affecting primarily those compadrazgo types that involve multiple dyads, especially the public-communal ones. The basically egalitarian and horizontal structure of compadrazgo in action is probably the most important aspect of the institution in Belén, which facilitates reciprocity and hence symmetry in certain inherently asymmetrical aspects of the system. Again, it should be noted that the growth of asymmetry in some aspects of the compadrazgo system can be used as an index for measuring change, for it is evident that as Belén moves toward what I have called a secular ideology, the asymmetrical dimensions of compadrazgo will increase accordingly. This is closely tied to the vertical expansion of the compadrazgo system in which economic motivation will play an important role in selecting compadres; and to its horizontal expansion which will bring the people of Belén into contact with communities that are either incipiently or already stratified, to say nothing of the incipient stratification that the village itself is beginning to experience. In short, while the compadrazgo system of Belén today involves networks of social, economic, and religious relationships that are primarily symmetrical, one of the significant effects of an increasingly secular ideology will be to augment greatly the asymmetrical dimension of the system.

Table 17 shows that there are nine asymmetrical and twenty-two symmetrical compadrazgo types in Belén. In addition, marriage compadrazgo involves some asymmetry, while six of the nine asymmetrical types involve a certain degree of symmetry. Furthermore, comparing tables 17 and 18 shows that all six public-communal compadrazgo types are asymmetrical, while only three private-individual compadrazgo types (PCE, CCCH, and CCCA) are asymmetrical. Comparing table 17 to table 1 shows that all nine asymmetrical compadrazgo types, plus marriage compadrazgo, involve multiple compadrazgo relationships, that is, more than the three basic dyads of normal compadrazgo types. The asymmetrical criteria for the classification, then, are given by the ensuing dyads of compadrazgo types, and also to some extent by the nature of the mediating entity and the private-individual–public-communal dichotomy. Thus, the first domain of the compadrazgo system in which asymmetry may come into existence is the actual alignment of compadrazgo dyads. Let me explain this further. In all the compadrazgo types that I have called normal—that is, those with the three basic dyads (compadres-compadres, padrinos-ahijados, and parents-kinsmen-owners with mediating entities), or at least two dyads—there is structural symmetry in the configuration of personnel. Asymmetry arises in those compadrazgo types that have more than the three basic dyads; while the padrinos-ahijados dyad may remain constant, there is a proliferation of compadres–compadres dyads. In such cases, the padrinos become compadres not only of parents, kinsmen, and owners of mediating entities, but also, by extension of a series of other couples. Under these circumstances, asymmetry becomes patent and may or may not have significant structural consequences.

The best way to explain this situation is by a few examples. In addition to all six public-communal compadrazgo types, marriage, PCE, CCCH, CCCA, and to some extent evangelios and parada de cruz in-

TABLE 17. Symmetrical and Asymmetrical Relationships by
Compadrazgo Type

Type	Symmetrical	Asymmetrical
Bautizo	x	
Casamiento	x[1]	
Confirmación	x	
PCE		x[2]
Primera comunión	x	
CCCH		x[2]
CCCA		x
ANDC	x	
ANDI		x[2]
AOI		x
BSI	x	
CSV		x[2]
Escapulario	x	
Graduación	x	
PCA		x[2]
Quince años	x	
Sacada a misa	x	
Compadrazgo de evangelios	x	
Compadrazgo de limpia	x	
BOI		x
Bendición de casa	x	
BCC	x	
BM		x[2]
Parada de cruz	x	
Primera piedra	x	
Compadrazgo de amistad	x	
CABP	x	
Compadrazgo de aretes	x	
CEON	x	
FC	x	
JJ	x	

[1] Some are asymmetrical.
[2] Some are symmetrical.

volve asymmetry by reason of their resulting multiple compadrazgo dyads. Let us take the PCE, marriage, and PCA compadrazgo types as examples. Asymmetry results in PCE when the deceased's parents are dead, and the pedimento is made by brothers, uncles, or other closely related kinsmen. PCE padrinos then become collective compadres of several other couples (for seldom if ever does a single couple undertake the pedimento), thereby giving rise to a multiple-dyad compadrazgo relationship. (If the parents of the deceased are alive, the ensuing compadrazgo relationship is normal and symmetrical.) In the case of marriage, the parents of the bride and groom establish a multiple-dyad relationship with the padrinos. If we consider this a double compadrazgo relationship, there is normal symmetry. But this is complicated by the fact that all subsidiary compadrazgo types (arras, lazo, ramo, etc.) inevitably lead to multiple dyads; hence marriage compadrazgo occupies a rather ambiguous position. Finally, in PCA compadrazgo, as in all other public-communal compadrazgo types, the padrinos of the mediating image or object become the compadres of the entire community. This results in a truly multiple-dyad situation, with the highest degree of personnel asymmetry.

But the personnel asymmetry exhibited in these examples actually means less for the structural discharge of the compadrazgo system than superficially meets the eye. In marriage compadrazgo the subsidiary types are primarily symbolic, and after the central ceremonies have taken place they sink into relative unimportance, although the relationship remains latent and may be activated in a variety of contexts and for the establishment of subsequent compadrazgo types. The double triad of marriage compadrazgo (velación, arras, and anillos), though, can result in a skewed relationship in which one triad predominates over the other; the padrinos and the parents of the bride or groom can constitute the locus of the compadrazgo relationship, while the other triad sinks into unimportance. This is probably the only significant consequence of personnel asymmetry that can lead to conflict in this compadrazgo type. I am not certain how often this split between the triads of marriage compadrazgo occurs, but I surmise that it is not frequent. When it does occur, then after the marriage the parents of either the bride or the groom become tied by compadrazgo in name only. This consequence of asymmetry is conditioned by the selection of compadres, however, arising only when the padrinos are not selected by common accord of both sets of parents. The situation may be more complicated in the case of PCE compadrazgo, but it is essentially the same as that of marriage compadrazgo. When the parents of the deceased are dead, the usual practice is that at least two close kinsmen have the responsibility of seeking padrinos. These kinsmen are either of the same generation as the deceased (brothers or first cousins) or of the generation above (uncles), and they are always close socially. Thus there is usually consensus about the padrinos, which lessens the potential negative consequences of the asymmetrical situation. In both PCE and marriage compadrazgo, however, and in general in all multiple-dyad types that are not public-communal, the nature of the compadrazgo relationship depends not so much on the inherent asymmetry as on the conditions under which the compadrazgo is established and the process of selection. Asymmetry of personnel per se is of only limited significance in explaining operational variations in the formal structure of compadrazgo.

Asymmetry assumes its maximum proportions in all public-communal compadrazgo types, here exemplified by PCA. Theoretically and in practice, the padrinos of a public compadrazgo type become the compadres of every couple in the community. Except AOI and BOI, the padrinos of a public-communal compardrazgo type are effectively the compadres of every couple in Belén for the duration of the ceremonies and for varying lengths of time thereafter. This latent relationship is obviously activated at will by the couples in the community, and in varying ways. Taking ANDI as another example, the padrinos-community compadrazgo relationship is activated during the more than a month that ceremonies last. Throughout this time the padrinos are addressed by the appropriate ritual kinship terms—by the young as padrinos, by adults as compadres. In addition, many couples in the community activate some of the behavior patterns and rites associated with the type, such as visiting the padrinos, or giving them small presents. When the central ceremonies are over, the relationship is deactivated, but the padrinos are remembered as having performed an important service to the community. In the case of public-communal compadrazgo types, then, personnel asymmetry has a definite positive effect, namely, the generation of community integration and solidarity for important ritual ceremonial occasions. In fact, it is the personnel asymmetry of public-communal compadrazgo types that makes them such effective mechanisms of community cohesion.

There is, however, another side of the coin with regard to public-communal compadrazgo types, namely, the more restricted relationships that come into being between the padrinos (and the young madrina in the case of ANDI and CSV) and those who, in the name of the people of Belén, asked them to sponsor the occasion. Here again we have a case of multiple-dyad relationships. Those who ask for public-communal compadrazgo padrinos are invariably either fiscales or mayordomos (see pages 102 and 134 of Ritual Kinship I), and as few as three or as many as six or seven dyadic relationships may result. This multiple-dyad compadrazgo network has a permanent feature, which

TABLE 18. Private-Individual and Public-Communal Compadrazgo Types

Type	Private-Individual	Public-Communal
Bautizo	x	
Casamiento	x	
Confirmación	x	
PCE	x	
Primera comunión	x	
CCCH	x	
CCCA	x	
ANDC	x	
ANDI		x
AOI		x
BSI	x	
CSV		x
Escapulario	x	
Graduación	x	
PCA		x
Quince años	x	
Sacada a misa	x	
Compadrazgo de evangelios	x	
Compadrazgo de limpia	x	
BOI		x
Bendición de casa	x	
BCC	x	
BM		x
Parada de cruz	x	
Primera piedra	x	
Compadrazgo de amistad	x	
CABP	x	
Compadrazgo de aretes	x	
CEON	x	
FC	x	
JJ	x	

survives completion of the ceremonies and not infrequently becomes a permanent compadrazgo bond, tying several of the padrinos-fiscales–mayordomos dyads. What I have said about the possible multiple-dyad compadrazgo relationships in PCE and marriage compadrazgo applies here, too, and resolution of asymmetry will be determined by the circumstances of the pedimento, particularly the personalities involved in it, and the actual process of selection. (Public-communal compadrazgo types are in many ways as much a part of the religious system of Belén as they are of the compadrazgo system. Establishment of public-communal compadrazgo relationships by members of the ayuntamiento religioso is ultimately tied to the structure and function of the rotation of cargos and other administrative aspects of the local religious hierarchy.)

In summary, then, the personnel asymmetry that obtains in all public-communal compadrazgo types, as well as that in various private-individual types, is more apparent than real when we look at the situation from a dynamic, processual viewpoint. There is no question that the personnel asymmetry exists, and that the alignment of triads is skewed in one way or another, in that the relationship of the padrinos to all the multiple couples of compadres is seldom if ever of the same quality. (Here the mediating entity can be disregarded, for, with the exception of marriage compadrazgo, it is an image, an object, or a deceased person, and the padrinos-ahijados bond is the weakest of the compadrazgo types involving children or adults.) But the reason is not the asymmetry per se, but other antecedents I have noted. The asymmetry of personnel in ten compadrazgo types can be regarded as formal; the padrinos, on the one hand, and several compadre couples, on the other, form a naturally uneven multiple set.

Asymmetry and Compadrazgo Selection

Several anthropologists have noted the inherent asymmetry of several compadrazgo situations (see Foster 1953; Gillin 1945; Mintz and Wolf 1950). What they refer to primarily is the asymmetry involved in compadrazgo selection, namely, that there need not be reciprocity between those who ask and those who are being asked to enter into a compadrazgo relationship. In this respect Belén is like countless other communities in Mesoamerica, and probably the whole of Latin America. There is no question that the compadrazgo system of Belén is asymmetrical when it comes to the selection and establishment of compadrazgo relationships. There are no injunctions or directives that make it necessary for couple A, who has been asked by couple B to enter into a certain compadrazgo relationship, to ask the latter into the same or a similar compadrazgo relationship within a specified time. The importance of this perhaps universal, formal, asymmetrical property of the compadrazgo system (I know of no compadrazgo system in which formal symmetry of selection is the rule) must again be assessed in the light of specific circumstances. First of all, there is not yet any significant vertical patterning of compadrazgo in Belén. As a basically egalitarian institution, compadrazgo is almost entirely horizontal, and therefore, every aspect of the compadrazgo system is carried out on an undifferentiated basis. Under these circumstances, the inherent asymmetry of selection is significantly diminished. While there are no rules that say that couple A must reciprocate with couple B, the latter knows that it is a potential source of compadres for the former, and that A will very probably ask B to enter into some kind of compadrazgo relationship. In vertical compadrazgo (Mintz and Wolf 1950:358), on the other hand, superordination is present: socioeconomically, couple A is above couple B, and the latter does not expect to be asked by the former under any circumstances. (In such cases there is obviously some kind of class stratification, or even a castelike situation like several known to me in the Sierra de Puebla.) The relationship is there, but it is asymmetrical both in form and in ideology. This situation is not yet present in Belén, but I see it coming as the community increases it economic and social contacts with the outside world, and begins to depend increasingly on economic and social networks that are basically structured along the lines of incipient or fully formed social classes. Today Belén is still ideologically and structurally egalitarian, and no matter how poor a person may be, he can expect reciprocity in compadrazgo relationships, even with the most affluent members of the community.

How this formal asymmetry of selection is translated into action has to a large extent been described in the discussion of the structural implications of asking and being asked to enter into a compadrazgo relationship, and here I merely expand that discussion. For the average couple in Belén, the frequencies of asking and being asked to enter compadrazgo relationships are more or less equal throughout a lifetime. This is shown clearly in the fifty complete compadrazgo careers I was able to gather. If the specific conditions under which compadrazgo relationships were established by a given couple are taken into consideration, as well as the fact that the number of children, occasions, images, and other mediating entities in a full compadrazgo career are roughly equal for most couples, it can be shown that a couple has asked as often as it has been asked (plus or minus 5 percent). I spoke of a few individuals whose compadrazgo careers included many more occasions when they were asked, but they are either members of the economic elite, or rather prominent by virtue of their participation and achievement in the ayuntamiento religioso and in the general structure of the religious system, and are thought to be especially suitable for certain compadrazgo types. These individuals are exceptions, and the explanation for the asymmetry here must be found outside of the compadrazgo system (see Chapter Eight of *Ritual Kinship* I).

There may be individual asymmetry in compadrazgo selection, but at the level of the compadrazgo system as a whole, and from the viewpoint of the asking–being asked distinction, there is structural if not formal symmetry. Moreover, the informal reciprocity of individual compadrazgo selection, which generates informal symmetry, must also be taken into consideration. When couple A asks couple B to enter into a compadrazgo relationship, the latter may or may not reciprocate immediately for the same compadrazgo type, but in more than 85 percent of the cases couple B eventually reciprocated. This is true also of exogamous compadrazgo relationships, for the compadrazgo system of Belén is essentially shared by most rural Tlaxcalan communities. Furthermore, in perhaps 40 percent of all compadrazgo cases there is direct reciprocity; that is, couple B in turn asks couple A to enter into the same compadrazgo relationship for which it was asked. If to this is added the networks of compadrazgo relationships that result from the concatenation of several cycles of compadrazgo types, it can be seen that the formal asymmetry of selection is further reduced, at both the systemic and the individual level.

Reciprocity and the Activities and Behavior of Compadrazgo in Action

Reciprocity is involved in all the activities and behavior patterns of compadrazgo in action. In all event and relationship nodes from the preliminary steps of a compadrazgo relationship to discharge of the principal ceremonies (see diagram 1), the interaction of personnel (both primary and secondary actors) and all social, economic, symbolic, and religious behavior patterns are strictly regulated by custom and reciprocity, and therefore are quite symmetrical. In many compadrazgo types, of course, the disbursement of cash, goods, or services may be considerably greater for the padrinos or for the parents, kinsmen, and owner of the mediating entity. This kind of asymmetry is, however, an inherent aspect of compadrazgo types, and not relevant to the discussion here. But what about the event and relationship nodes that come after the ceremonies have been completed, and especially the regulation of permanent or temporary bonds and obligations? (So far in the structural analysis I have not emphasized the permanent sociological and economic aspects of compadrazgo, for it is better to structure its antecedents first. Moreover, I do not want to give the impression that the most significant domain of the compadrazgo system is the core of rites and ceremonies. Far from it. In my view this traditional attitude of many anthropologists has obscured the position of the compadrazgo system within the culture and society where it has been described.) This is a quite different matter. In the first place, interaction among the various dyads of all compadrazgo types is directly governed by the principle of reciprocity; hence the permanent bonds and obligations in the relationship tend to become symmetrical in practice, for there are rules and directives that specifically structure the system ideologically. It can be said that the structure of behavior of primary and secondary compadrazgo actors in their permanent bonds is regulated by the injunction of reciprocity. Under these conditions, in practice, if not in theory, permanent compadrazgo behavior is quite symmetrical. This statement must be explained, however.

The permanent bonds of duties, obligations, and privileges of every compadrazgo type are clearly spelled out by the ideological order. What is not spelled out is how and under what conditions these bonds are discharged. In baptism compadrazgo, for example, compadres must visit each other on their saint's day, must invite each other to participate as attendants when elected to an important office in the religious ayuntamiento, and so on. But the way in which these requirements and directives of baptismal compadrazgo are individually discharged is not governed by the intrinsic ideology of the compadrazgo system, but by the higher principle of reciprocity which commands compadres to do everything possible to make the quid pro quo an effective mechanism of behavior.[1] Thus, if compadres do not comply with such requirements or are lax in their discharge, the compardrazgo relationship will grow cold and in time come to an end. Invitations to participate in social and religious events, visiting patterns, patterns of labor exchange, political support for the ayuntamiento religioso, the borrowing of cash and goods, and several other explicitly stated functions binding compadres are discharged quite symmetrically in Belén, for even at this level there are implicit sanctions and pressures that tend to enforce compliance. If a couple does not comply with compadrazgo duties and obligations, word gets around, and the couple acquires a reputation for being selfish, stingy, uncooperative, lacking in community spirit, and on the whole for being deviant members of the community. Few people would dare risk being so labeled, for the complex of pressures and coercive mechanisms will make itself felt in the form of overt social ostracism, religious isolation, and even personal admonitions from kinsmen and other compadres, in much the same fashion as that described for the enforcement of prescriptive and preferential compadrazgo types. There are degrees of compliance, of course, and Beleños are aware of those couples (households) who comply in the highest degree, those who comply adequately, those who comply reluctantly, and those who will try to evade prescribed custom whenever they can. In fact, this constitutes a naturally scaled paradigm of compadrazgo compliance in its permanent dimensions. The higher a couple is placed in this scale, the more it will be respected and esteemed in the community. However, permanent compadrazgo compliance must also be coupled with the discharge of functions in the ayuntamiento religioso and mayordomía system; there again the people scale the performance of individuals and families. When these two scales of performance are put together, there emerges a fairly clear account of status differentials in Belén. In the absence of social classes, except in incipient form, Belén is still a traditional society in which status differentials are not ascribed but primarily achieved by the performance of certain activities and ceremonies that the ideological order dictates as a good for the community and the individual.

It will not be amiss to explain further the functional operation of reciprocity resulting in symmetrical behavior in both individual compadrazgo relationships and networks of compadrazgo relationships. The nature of symmetry and reciprocity in individual compadrazgo relationships is expressed in a clear understanding on the part of the primary actors (and by extension the secondary actors) that customary prescribed duties and obligations such as visiting, invitations, and formal rituals and ceremonials, must be activated automatically, and that if compadres fail to do so, they are breaking the rules and can be called to account. But what about the less explicit duties and obligations that can be activated at will, such as borrowing money, labor exchange, exchange of goods and services, or political support for the ayuntamiento religioso? These may or may not be activated by compadres, but when they are, it is implicitly understood that they will be asked in equal measure in return. Thus prescribed, customary obligations are regulated by the ideological injunctions of the compadrazgo system itself, while potential obligations are immediately regulated by reciprocity. The former are a societal aspect ultimately sanctioned by the community as a whole, while the latter are individually regulated. If you lend your compadre 500 pesos because earlier he had lent you money, this is a private matter, but it is a collective, community matter whether or not you invite your compadres to the annual banquet of a mayordomía of which you are the mayordomo. Only the latter elicits sanctions and coercive measures for noncompliance. (One of the things that strikes the ethnographer in Belén is the clear distinction made by the people themselves between the private-individual and the public-communal. Virtually all aspects of the social, religious, political, symbolic, and even economic life of the community are permeated by this distinction. It has been clear throughout the preceding analysis that Beleños regard certain things as totally within the realm of the individual and the household, while others fall within the realm of interest of the community as a whole, and these are enforced by natural or supernatural sanctions.) The asymmetry of behavior, then, is more marked in the former than in the latter, for it is often difficult to assess the compliance of a particular couple, and the community or a segment of the community is not deliberately looking for instances of transgression.

In dealing with reciprocity and symmetrical behavior in networks of compadrazgo relationships comprising either the sum total of relationships of given individuals, or multiple-dyad compadrazgo types including as many as ten effective dyads, a dyadic analysis is, as I have said, inadequate. Both the temporal and the permanent discharge of functions and activities in such configurations must be analyzed in terms of networks. Reciprocity of exchange among the members of the compadrazgo network is present at all times, for otherwise the configuration of compadres would not work well. For example, in multiple-dyad types such as marriage, PCE, or PCA, the several permanent dyadic relationships that form a compadrazgo network are held together by a series of reciprocal exchanges that might better be called collective reciprocity. In such situations, there are many occasions when the dyadic structure of individual compadrazgo relationships becomes inoperative, and what takes its place is an undifferentiated group of people bound together by certain specified patterns of behavior whose most important structural attribute is collective reciprocity. Again, these networks may not necessarily be permanently organized, but they can be activated at any time, for they are latently structured to function in this fashion. Much the same can be said of the total web of compadres that given couples have at any point in time. This again is a social unit that can be activated to function as an undifferentiated group for specific occasions. When this happens, the sum total, or a considerable part, of an individual's compadres are often more effective in discharging a variety of social, religious, or ritual functions than his kinsmen beyond his household.

The Systemic Implications of Reciprocity, Exchange, and Asymmetry

It is appropriate here to say something about the general context of reciprocity, exchange, and asymmetry in the global operation of the compadrazgo system. The entire anthropological literature on compadrazgo, even before Foster (1961) formulated his theory of the dyadic contract, treated the institution of compadrazgo in terms of dyadic patterns of interaction in which the compadrazgo system is made to appear as a series of rather isolated dyads and never as a system. When the institution is so conceived, we cannot properly speak about the compadrazgo system but only about compadrazgo types, the personnel of which are bound rather informally by certain specified bonds which are discharged unidimensionally. Compadrazgo has been described in these terms as a widespread phenomenon in Latin America, but not necessarily as playing a significant role in organizing community life. Granted, it has often been mentioned that compadrazgo's most significant function may be the expansion of kinship or kinshiplike ties into larger networks of people. This conception of compadrazgo, however, does not maintain that compadre networks come into existence, but only that there may come into existence dyadic relationships which are always egocentrically patterned—that is, that there is a one-many relationship between a certain individual and a series of compadres, but that there is no many-many relationship among the group of undifferentiated compadres. Although the former situation constitutes a significant aspect of the institution of compadrazgo, it is by no means the most important universally. Rather, the compadrazgo system, as a widespread institution in several major culture areas and a significant mechanism for organizing community life, is more appropriately conceptualized in terms of undifferentiated networks of personnel. Once the purely dyadic conception of compadrazgo is transcended, we can in fact organize the structure of community social action around this pervasive institution—not in isolation, to be sure, but in concert with other all-embracing institutions like the ayuntamiento religioso and the mayordomía system. In this view of compadrazgo, the institution plays a role that is analogous and somewhat homologous to that of kinship in more traditional, tribal societies. In other words, in settlements such as Belén, and in countless communities in Mesoamerica and many parts of South America, the compadrazgo system can be profitably used to describe and analyze community structure as mirrored in its multiphasic and pervasive ramifications.

In a different way, compadrazgo can be an effective descriptive and analytical focus for communities in transition, in which kinship is no longer an all-embracing and pervasive institution.[2] Under these conditions, it is important to determine how the actual operation of reciprocity, exchange, and asymmetry affects the structure and functions of networks of compadrazgo relationships, whether egocentrically based or derived from multiple-dyad compadrazgo types. A couple's total number of compadres does form into intermittently organized exocentric groups that may function effectively on a variety of occasions. In such cases, symmetry and reciprocity in exchange transcend personal dyadic interaction, and the whole of a couple's compadres may relate to one another as do kinship units in action. This is particularly the case in multiple-dyad compadrazgo types when, after the principal ceremonies are over, there remain various institutionalized occasions in the ceremonial cycle when all primary actors get together and behave as a corporate group. Out of both of these types of sporadic compadrazgo networks there arise what might be called selective compadrazgo ties which may become constant over long periods. In Chapters Thirteen and Fourteen I describe the developmental cycle of the compadrazgo system, from the viewpoint both of individual couples and of specific sequences of compadrazgo types, showing the formation of selective compadrazgo networks that play a signficant role in the organization of community and extracommunal life, as well as in structuring important sectors of economic and social behavior. Selective compadrazgo networks, for example, channel the acquisition of jobs, movement of personnel out of the village, and several other aspects of Belén's economy. Thus, it is of the utmost importance that reciprocity, exchange, and symmetrical patterns of behavior be accurately conceptualized, so that we can have better mechanisms for understanding social, economic, and religious interaction than those provided by the dyadic approach alone.

Chapter 7

The Permanent and Temporary Dimensions of Compadrazgo Relationships

The Cleavage between Permanent and Temporary Compadrazgo Relationships

In many ways this chapter is a corollary of the preceding one, in that the duties and obligations that bind compadres after the central complex of rites and ceremonies has ended are fulfilled in a reciprocal and symmetrical fashion. It must be realized, however, that there are many differences among the compadrazgo types in Belén with respect to what is temporary and what is permanent. What is always constant are the strict prescriptions that specify customary behavior and the web of duties and obligations, from the preliminary steps to the central rites and ceremonies, for every compadrazgo type in the system. In this area the ideological and structural orders of the compadrazgo system overlap almost completely. After completion of the core of rites and ceremonies, the situation becomes more fluid, and there may be considerable deviation for the prescriptions and injunctions of the ideological order. The principal departures are the subject of this chapter.

The ideological prescription for all compadrazgo types in Belén dictates that once a compadrazgo relationship is established it becomes permanent and lifelong. In practice, however, this is not the case, and several types, of varying intensity, come to an end after varying lengths of time. I do not mean that temporary compadrazgo relationships are terminated in the sense that primary and secondary actors cease to address each other as compadres, and there is no more interaction among them. Rather, these relationships grow cold and only the form remains—the strictly ideological aspects of respeto and confianza in their restricted meanings. Certain patterns of behavior specified by respeto and confianza, such as the use of the prescribed ritual kinship terms, some formal visiting patterns, and the required canons of social and religious respect are maintained, but the real social, religious, and economic bonds of ayuda are no longer active. Thus, in temporary compadrazgo types the most important aspects of the relationship are the central ceremonies and the steps leading to them, while in permanent compadrazgo types the subsequent stages are of equal (in the long run, of greater) importance. Temporary compadrazgo relationships have a primarily symbolic and ritual function; permanent relationships have not only a symbolic funtion, but just as important, social, economic, and ritual functions. The cleavage between permanent and temporary compadrazgo relationships in Belén is not, however, entirely dictated by compadrazgo type, for to some exent it depends on the intrinsic nature of the relationship and the conditions under which it was established. The ideological order scales the compadrazgo types in a continuum of ranked positions, and the higher the position, the greater the permanent dimension of a type. The structural implications of this are shown in table 19. Some of the types listed as temporary in this table may become permanent for a variety of reasons, and the personal factors that to some extent alter the permanent–temporary division are discussed in the next two sections of this chapter. The web of compadrazgo relationships of a given couple at any point in time includes both ideologically determined permanent relationships and temporary relationships that have become permanent for reasons extrinsic to the system itself. It is therefore important in analyzing the developmental cycle of compadrazgo, both egocentrically and multidyadically, to assess the composition of compadrazgo networks in terms of these two kinds of relationships.

Table 19 divides compadrazgo types into permanent types, temporary types, and temporary types leading to or resulting from other types. There are eight permanent types, four strictly temporary ones, and nineteen that lead to or result from other compadrazgo types. The nineteen types include four of the public-communal types, which are special cases. All of these are multiple-dyad compadrazgo types, in which some of the dyadic relationships are permanent (those between the padrinos or madrina and the individuals who officially contract the relationship), while others are temporary (the dyadic relationships between the padrinos or madrina and the community as a whole). Moreover, the compadrazgo types resulting from other types outnumber those leading to other types——thirteen of the former and six of the latter.

I have defined permanent compadrazgo types as those in which ideological prescriptions are strictly discharged. Their primary and secondary actors keep active the right to ask for loans, favors, labor exchange, political support for a variety of purposes, social cooperation on numerous occasions in the life and ceremonial cycles, and in general any type of interaction that requires the expenditure of economic, social, or religious resources beyond the formalities of respeto and confianza (which involve only psychological or symbolic expenditures). The attribute of permanence, of course, comes into existence after completion of the central complex of rites and ceremonies, for prior to this point all compadrazgo types in Belén are the same in ideological-structural articulation. It should be understood, moreover, that I am not saying that per-

TABLE 19. Permanent-Temporary Composition
of Compadrazgo Types

Type	Per-manent	Tem-porary	Resulting From	Leading To
Bautizo	x			
Casamiento	x			
Confirmación	x			
PCE	x			
Primera comunión			x	
CCCH		x		
CCCA		x		
ANDC	x			
ANDI			x[1]	
AOI		x		
BSI	x			
CSV			x[1]	
Escapulario				x
Graduación			x	
PCA			x[1]	
Quince años				x
Sacada a misa			x	
Compadrazgo de evangelios			x	
Compadrazgo de limpia			x	
BOI		x		
Bendición de casa			x	
BCC	x			
BM			x[1]	
Parada de Cruz	x			
Primera piedra			x	
Compadrazgo de amistad				x
CABP			x	
Compadrazgo de aretes				x
CEON				x
FC			x	
JJ				x

[1] Some dyadic relationships are permanent and some are temporary.

manent compadrazgo types must of necessity keep alive the latent patterns of interaction described above. Rather, the personnel of these types feel constrained to comply, thereby producing a high correlation between ideological dictates and structural discharge. In this realm of the compadrazgo system there is no compulsion in the form of sanctions and coercive mechanisms to enforce compliance with ideological prescriptions, and it is probable that some people choose not to activate the latent bonds inherent in this category. Be this as it may, the fact that eight compadrazgo types are unambiguously classified as permanent in table 19 denotes that, statistically speaking, couples in Belén do keep alive the right to call upon each other for social, economic, and religious resources when they engage in these compadrazgo relationships. It is difficult to determine how often they in fact exercise this right, but it is clear enough that the higher the frequency of the requests, the stronger the relationship will grow. Furthermore, the central dyads resulting between the padrinos or madrina of the PCA, ANDI, CSV, and BM compadrazgo types and those who formally ask them, primarily fiscales and mayordomos, must also be included in the category of permanent compadrazgo relationships. These are what I have called the central dyads of the public-communal compadrazgo types. They are not extended to BOI and AOI simply because these two types are primarily practical and utilitarian; they have little symbolic and ritual value, and therefore have only temporary dimensions which de facto come to an end after the principal ceremonies are completed.

Temporary compadrazgo types are the opposite of permanent types in that the permanence prescribed by the ideological order is not structurally realized; after the ceremonies have ended, what remains of the compadrazgo relationship are only the formal attributes of respeto and confianza without their structural implications. Statistically speaking, Beleños generally do not request economic, social, or religious expenditures in their compadrazgo relationships in the four types they classify as temporary. Compadrazgo de amistad, compadrazgo de aretes, FC, and JJ must also be included in this category. Here again, it should be emphasized that since there is no compulsion to enforce any ideological injunctions, particular couples may develop a permanent relationship with compadres in a type classified statistically as temporary. Before I can explain why permanent relationships are sometimes established among personnel of temporary compadrazgo types, and vice versa,[1] I must first clarify the meaning of leading to and resulting from other compadrazgo types. These are relative classifications, of course, but they are useful in determining the statistically variable nature of permanent and temporary.

Leading-to and Resulting-from Compadrazgo Relationships

Nineteen compadrazgo types in table 19 are classified as having relationships that either result from previously contracted compadrazgo ties, or lead to subsequent compadrazgo ties. At the bottom of this twofold classification is the fact that Beleños recognize the affinity of certain compadrazgo relationships associated in various ways with the life and ceremonial cycles, and that certain of the resulting clusters serve as a kind of natural paradigm for the selection of compadres. These natural clusters may affect compadrazgo types regardless of their permanent or temporary classification—for example, the preference for baptism padrinos as PCE compadres when the deceased is a child, or for baptism compadres as marriage padrinos. The same is true of several other compadrazgo types; for example, graduation padrinos are almost invariably related to the parents of the graduate by previous compadrazgo ties, the most common ones being primera comunión and confirmación. Thus, virtually all compadrazgo types in Belén, whether viewed as the main subdivisions of the compadrazgo system as an institution or from the egocentric viewpoint of compadrazgo in action, can lead to or result from other types. (As a corollary, compadrazgo relationships in Belén must be gauged in action in terms of specific structural and ideological features complementing the cumulative effect of sequential clusters.) This statement must be qualified, however. The eight compadrazgo types classified as permanent and the four classified as temporary have a higher statistical incidence of original selection than the nineteen types classified as leading to or resulting from other compadrazgo relationships. This does not mean that the former are subject to formal prescriptions regarding the establishment of original compadrazgo relationships (that is, compadrazgo relationships that did not involve a previous compadrazgo tie with the same couple). Baptism, confirmación, ANDC, AOI, BSI, and BOI are probably the only types that do not result from previous types, but they can and do lead to other compadrazgo types. I can define compadrazgo types that lead to the formation of subsequent compadrazgo relationships as those that are clustered together in a position of anteriority; conversely, types that result from previous relationships are also clustered but in a position of posteriority. Furthermore, resulting-from or leading-to types may become either permanent or temporary compadrazgo relationships in their own right. At the moment I am concerned with the analysis of the nineteen types of table 19, but how the system works will become clear in analyzing the developmental cycle of compadrazgo.

Let us take first as an example a leading-to compadrazgo type. Escapulario is a good example, in that it is almost invariably an original compadrazgo relationship: seldom if ever do those who ask for the relationship select couples already related to them by compadrazgo ties. While escapulario involves a permanent status, this permanence does not result from the establishment of the compadrazgo itself, but rather from the fact that escapulario invariably leads to the establishment of other compadrazgo types. The types associated with escapulario are primarily three: sacada a misa, compadrazgo de evangelios, and especially compadrazgo de limpia. Let us see how this works in practice. Manuel Xolocotzin and his wife wished to give their daughter, an infant of six months, a scapulary medal. As padrinos they chose Pedro Álvarez and his wife, a couple whom they had known intimately for many years and regarded as close friends, thereby establishing the compadrazgo relationship. After completion of the central complex of rites and ceremonies, the compadrazgo relationship continued for more than two years as a temporary one. Neither Manuel nor Pedro invited the other to participate as *componente* (attendant) and mayordomo *secundario* (assistant to the principal mayordomo) in their respective cargos of *fiscal segundo* (second in command) and mayordomo of the Virgen de Ocotlán, which they fulfilled in the interim, nor did they ask each other for specific favors involving outlays of money, goods, or other resources. They did, however, comply with the formal etiquette of compadrazgo involving respeto and confianza in their restricted meanings. When Pedro Álvarez's ahijada reached the age of three years and two months, Manuel Xolocotzin asked him and his wife to become compadres de evangelios by presenting the child in church. After this second compadrazgo, the relationship between Manuel and Pedro became much closer, and they began to ask each other favors involving outlays of money and political resources. When Manuel's daughter was ten, she fell ill and a limpia was effected. Manual asked Pedro and his wife to become padrinos de limpia, thereby establishing with them a third compadrazgo relationship. After this event, the compadrazgo ties binding Manuel's and Pedro's families grew very strong, and the relationship became permanent for life.

In some ways this actual example from Belén is atypical. What usually happens is that by the second time you ask a couple to engage in compadrazgo relationships of this cluster, you have already been asked in return. Thus, the typical situation would have had Pedro Álvarez asking Manuel Xolocotzin to enter into a compadrazgo de evangelios or limpia for one of his children—unless, of course, he had no children of the proper age to take to church, or none of his children became so ill that a limpia was necessary. In any event, given the strong emphasis on reciprocity in compadrazgo in action, a series of combinations could have resulted, but the end product would have been very much like that of the example. In addition, the relationship proceeded from a temporary status to one of increasing closeness and ended in a permanent status. Furthermore, the sequence of the cluster of compadrazgo types in this case moved from one occasion in the ritual cycle to another in a natural way and according to prescribed custom. This order could have been altered, of course, if Manuel's daughter had become ill and needed a limpia before she reached the age of three and had to be presented in church. Also, a couple may not wish to give its children a scapulary medal until they are four or five. If to these variables is added the number of children, the present compadrazgo cluster can have a variety of permutations. Finally, how does sacada a misa fit into the cluster? The scapulary medal is usually given to children shortly after birth; hence escapulario is most often the original compadrazgo established in the cluster. But sometimes the medal is not given until the child is at least a year old, and in such cases sacada a misa becomes the original compadrazgo of the cluster. For this reason sacada a misa may also be classified as a leading-to compadrazgo type. The natural sequence of the cluster goes, of course, from escapulario to sacada a misa to compadrazgo de evangelios, while limpia, being a contingent ritual occasion, can occur at any time in this sequence.

Resulting-from compadrazgo types, on the other hand, are seldom if ever the original compadrazgo relationship binding sets of compadres. It goes without saying that such types from parts of clusters that include an original leading-to compadrazgo type as in the preceding example, in which either escapulario or sacada a misa are leading-to compadrazgo types, while evangelios and limpia are resulting-from types. The most important resulting-from compadrazgo types are primera comunión, graduación, evangelios, limpia, primera piedra, CABP, and FC. Almost invariably these types involve at least one and as many as four previous compadrazgo ties binding the set of compadres. The number of previous compadrazgo ties depends, of course, on the nature of the cluster and on uncontrollable contingent variables such as the eventuality of the ritual occasions (for example, limpias, graduations, acquisitions of important material objects), the position of the ritual occasion in the life of social cycles (as in PCE, CABP, and JJ), and previous compadrazgo ties which are contingent upon individual couples by themselves. However, the nature of compadrazgo clusters in Belén is of great significance because it may not only limit the total number of compadrazgo couples, but also serve as a mechanism for intensifying previous compadrazgo ties. There is probably no compadrazgo type in Belén, except the four main public-communal types, that stands alone and is not part of any cluster. The total of some 200 compadrazgo relationships (approximately 100 asking and 99 being asked) that the average couple in Belén had contracted by the end of its compadrazgo career is established with sixty to sixty-five couples, for an average of approximately 3 compadrazgo relationships per couple. If we discount the repetitive compadrazgo relationships such as baptism, confirmation, PCE, primera comunión, and a few others, in which parents may give their children twice or more to the same couple as padrinos, this ratio of 3 compadrazgo relationships per couple is determined primarily by the clustering of the compadrazgo system in Belén.[2] Thus, the limiting effects of clusters of compadrazgo are amply counterbalanced in quality by the intensification of compadrazgo ties that often result in the strongest and most permanent relationships in Belén society.

The Meaning of the Permanent-Temporary Continuum

I can now analyze the substantive meaning of table 19 and correlate it with other significant structural attributes. In the first place, we have seen that the classification of table 19 in terms of permanent, temporary, leading-to, and resulting-from compadrazgo types is not fixed but rather contextual, and that the classification is primarily a statistical device. When couples establish a compadrazgo relationship in one of the eight types classified as permanent or the four classified as temporary, the relationship does not a priori become permanent or temporary. Rather, there is a strong statistical tendency for the eight and four compadrazgo types to become, respectively, permanent and temporary relationships. The permanent-temporary dimension is even more unstable in the case of leading-to and resulting-from compadrazgo types, in which the status of permanent and temporary will depend on the positions of the types within the clusters of which they are part. Moreover, even the eight and four types categorically classified as permanent and temporary may form parts of compadrazgo clusters, and this will be a significant aspect of their full resolution vis-à-vis the total number of compadrazgo relationships of given couples. Finally, the very terms permanent and temporary are variable in themselves, in that their structural content may or may not become operative at given times. Perhaps active and nonactive would have been more felicitous terms to indicate the variable character of what I have denoted by permanent and temporary.

At any given time every couple in Belén has two sets of compadrazgo relationships: a permanent one and a temporary one—a set with which the couple interacts in terms of the broad spectrum of what the ideological order dictates, and engages in behavior involving economic, social, religious, and even political expenditures; and a set with which it interacts formally in the restricted meaning of respeto and confianza. Given these conditions, several contingent variables always operate to make the temporary-transitory-permanent status of compadrazgo after completion of the central complex of rites and ceremonies rather indeterminate. The transition of a compadrazgo relationship from temporary to permanent status, or vice versa, depends to a considerable extent on personal, contingent factors that I have not yet been able to conceptualize in terms of rules or prescriptions that people either adhere to or break in certain specified ways. I can, however, say something about what these contingent variables or personal factors are. They fall primarily under the rubrics of natural contingencies, such as the number of children a couple might have or the illnesses that befall them, and controllable or accidental contingencies, such as buying new material objects, establishing a business, building a new house, being asked for a public-communal sponsorship, and so on. Of course, the more prescriptive the compadrazgo type, the less likely it is to be influenced by controllable contingencies. Moreover, the permanent-temporary status of an egocentric compadrazgo network will depend also on a variety of accidents that cannot possibly be taken into account by the formal configuration of the ideological-structural articulation, and it is in this context, and under these conditions, that multiple-dyad networks function best and in which we get the best insight into the compadrazgo system as almost a true kinship system.

Comparing table 19 with table 14, we can see a considerable positive correlation between permanent compadrazgo types and the strength of compadrazgo bonds. In fact, these two tables say the same thing in different ways. The correlation is not perfect because of the contingent factors, which cannot at present be subsumed under general rules, and which result in some permanent compadrazgo relationships growing cold. Conversely, there is also a considerable, though weaker, correlation between temporary compadrazgo types and low intensity of compadrazgo bonds. Here again, the correlation cannot be perfect because temporary compadrazgo relationships may develop into permanent ones. Moreover, comparing tables 19 and 16 reveals a significant correlation between resulting-from or leading-to types, and types in which there is a weak or nonexistent bond in the padrinos-ahijados dyad. To some extent this is determined by the fact that several of these types do not have a living person as mediating entity, but in those that do, the transitoriness of the type determines the partial or total absence of a permanent padrinos-ahijados bond. In summary, compared to the highly mechanical situation of every aspect of the compadrazgo system up to and including the central rites and ceremonies, what follows is rather indeterminate.

CHAPTER 8

The Structural and Functional Implications of Interchangeable Compadrazgo Types

The Interchangeability of Prescriptive and Preferential Compadrazgo Types

Several compadrazgo types in Belén are classifed as interchangeable, but this does not necessarily mean that one can be replaced outright by another, thereby releasing a given couple from any prescriptive responsibility the type may involve. Let us explain this in some detail. Table 20 shows that there are eight interchangeable compadrazgo types, namely, escapulario, sacada a misa, compadrazgo de evangelios, compadrazgo de limpia, BCC, compadrazgo de amistad, CEON, and JJ. Only two of these eight types, sacada a misa and compadrazgo de limpia, are classified as prescriptive or highly preferential; all the others are classified in table 12 as preferential or optional. What I must explain first is why a prescriptive type such as limpia has certain interchangeable dimensions.

Table 12 shows that compadrazgo de limpia occupies the lowest (eleventh) rank of all the prescriptive and highly preferential compadrazgo types in Belén. This is in itself significant, and it was an important criterion for drawing the line between the highly preferential and the preferential categories in the total scaling of the compadrazgo system. In the ideological order of Belén compadrazgo de limpia can, under certain conditions, be fulfilled by compadrazgo de escapulario, and this is why I have classified it as interchangeable. But what does this mean substantively? The people distinguish clearly between these two types of compadrazgo, but at the same time the types are sufficiently interconnected to warrant description as a single chain of ritual and sponsoring events (see *Ritual Kinship* I, pp. 129-130 and 148-155). Escapulario is not a type in which compliance can be forced, but the ideological injunction connected with it is strong enough so that the great majority of the people practice it. Limpia, on the other hand, is a highly preferential compadrazgo type and therefore ultimately enforced. Inasmuch as it almost invariably occurs after a child or adult has been given the scapulary medal and the recipient's parents have therefore contracted a compadrazgo de escapulario, Beleños feel that they can use the same padrinos for limpia without going through the preliminary events and central rites and ceremonies (except what is most essential to the situa-

TABLE 20. Interchangeability of Compadrazgo Types

Type	Interchangeable	Not Interchangeable
Bautizo		x
Casamiento		x
Confirmación		x
PCE		x
Primera comunión		x
CCCH		x
CCCA		x
ANDC		x
ANDI		x
AOI		x
BSI		x
CSV		x
Escapulario	x (limpia)	
Graduación		x
PCA		x
Quince años		x
Sacada a misa	x (evangelios)	
Compadrazgo de evangelios	x (sacada a misa)	
Compadrazgo de limpia	x (escapulario)	
BOI		x
Bendición de casa		x
BCC	x (CEON)	
BM		x
Parada de cruz		x
Primera piedra		x
Compadrazgo de amistad	x (JJ)	
CABP		x
Compadrazgo de aretes		x
CEON	x (BCC)	
FC		x
JJ	x (amistad)	

tion at hand) customary for totally new compadrazgo relationships. This is why I consider the compadrazgos de limpia and escapulario to be interchangeable. With regard to contracting the compadrazgo itself, compadrazgo de limpia is essentially transformed into the fulfillment of recurrent rites and ceremonies of the compadrazgo de escapulario. If for some special reason the person who must undergo a limpia has not undergone the sponsorship of escapulario, then of course the compadrazgo de limpia must be originally contracted. These types are also interchangeable in the other direction; if the compadrazgo de limpia takes place first, the compadrazgo de escapulario becomes a recurrent rites and ceremonies node of the compadrazgo de limpia. It must be remembered that the injunction to comply affects only compadrazgo de limpia, and not compadrazgo de escapulario, and it does not matter whether the former is contracted originally or is a recurrent rites and ceremonies node of the latter. In fact, informants assert explicitly that when limpia is a recurrent node of escapulario, the compadrazgo acquires added dimensions of intensification which are not present if limpia is accompanied by the establishment of an original compadrazgo. (We can see here that the intensification resulting from recurrent establishment of compadrazgo relationships with the same couple is a value in itself in the compadrazgo system of Belén.) Thus, there is no inconsistency between the interchangeable nature of compadrazgo de limpia and its highly preferential status in the ideological-structural ranking.

Six of the other seven compadrazgo types in this category are in a sense truly interchangeable. For example, amistad is interchangeable with JJ, and a series of possible combinations results; BCC is interchangeable with CEON, and in fact the former is a subtype of the latter designed to signify the economic and social importance of acquiring such an important material item as a car or truck. However, I say that these are "in a sense" truly interchangeable because, while the ideology prescribes that all thirty-one compadrazgo types must be discharged when the occasion arises, in practice the interchangeability of types becomes structurally adequate without any sanctions coming into operation. This is possible because all these compadrazgo types except sacada a misa are either preferential or optional; that is, compliance cannot be enforced. The ideology of compadrazgo, though, is still strong enough in this domain of the system to enforce compliance by custom without any sanctions coming into play. Thus, although these types are interchangeable, most people in Belén prefer to contract a different compadrazgo relationship for the occasion denoted by each type. People usually take advantage of interchangeability only under difficult conditions (primarily economic difficulties), for the ideology of the compadrazgo system and the concept of supernatural order and propitiation are strong enough even at this level of the system to lead to compliance. Analysis of the compadrazgo careers in the sample indicates that by the end of a couple's career, only about 25 percent of its compadrazgo relationships for these eight types have been interchangeable. Obviously, establishment of independent compadrazgo relationships is still regarded as intrinsically good, which is why people seldom avail themselves of the alternative offered by interchangeability.

In addition to the eight types classified as interchangeable in table 20, there are three other types that have an interchangeable dimension similar to that of compadrazgo de limpia. These are the prescriptive or highly preferential bendición de casa, parada de cruz, and primera piedra. As I explained for compadrazgo de limpia, the interchangeability of these types does not involve any inconsistency vis-à-vis their high ranking in the compadrazgo scale. I did not classify them as interchangeable in table 20 because the incidence of interchangeability is even less than in compadrazgo de limpia. Parada de cruz, primera piedra, and bendición de casa form a cluster of compadrazgo types in the sense explained earlier; that is, the same set of padrinos may be used for several sponsoring occasions in the cluster. The padrinos of one of the several kinds of paradas de cruz are often used in turn for primera piedra, and just as frequently for the third occasion of the cluster, bendición de casa in one of its several manifestations (see *Ritual Kinship* I, pp. 161-165 and 172-181). Customary behavior permits dispensing with certain of the rites and ceremonies as the same set of padrinos sponsor succeeding occasions, and thus the cluster has certain interchangeable dimensions.

It is obvious that, at least in theory, interchangeability tends to reduce the total number of original compadrazgo relationships for any given couple, and thus the total number of egocentrically related personnel. Leading-to and resulting-from compadrazgo types have the same effect. Counterbalancing this reducing effect are the still strong ideological prescriptions for the structural discharge of all compadrazgo types as original, separate compadrazgo relationships. With regard to the changes that the compadrazgo system in Belén, and rural Tlaxcala in general, is beginning to experience, I predict that the reducing effect will increase greatly during the next few years (I can show that this is already happening) and will ultimately result in qualitative changes, that is, changes in ideology. This situation will manifest itself most clearly in a progression from the increasing use of interchangeability, to total use of the practice, to obliteration of the less important symbolic and ritual types, and finally to the retention of traditional types but with a new ideological underpinning and within a primarily economic context. I mention this here because in the changing picture of Belén culture and society, and especially in the case of the compadrazgo system, the people of the area have consistently looked for those junctures in which the ideological-structural articulation permits relaxation of the rules and prescriptions, for purposes of adapting the new secularizing conditions to the exigencies of the traditional system. Many of our informants put this very clearly when they say, "Cada día más, hasta los viejos del pueblo, buscan la oportunidad de usar los compadrazgos que se pueden combinar para no cumplir con sus responsabilidades acostumbradas. Así, primero no cumplen con tal compadrazgo porque ni sus parientes ni vecinos les dicen nada si solamente se contentan con buscar compadres para otra ocasión similar, y por último terminan por no cumplir con ninguno de los dos" (Increasingly, even the old people of the village search for the opportunity to use interchangeable compadrazgos in order not to comply with their customary responsibilities. Thus, first they do not comply with this or that compadrazgo because neither their relatives nor their neighbors complain if they are content with searching for compadres for another similar occasion, and ultimately they end up by complying with neither compadrazgo). The flexibility of structural discharge provided by interchangeable compadrazgo types (and several other similar junctures of the compadrazgo system) is an important interstice in the conceptualizaton of change, through which can be seen the key areas in which the social system is yielding to internal pressures or influences from the outside.

Interchangeability and the Reduction of Compadrazgo Personnel

In this section I discuss briefly what the interchangeability of compadrazgo types means in terms of personnel reduction and the alteration of the prescribed order of rite and ceremonies, as well as its time dimensions and ideological consequences. I have said that although the replacement of one compadrazgo type by another reduces the number of compadrazgo personnel, its measurable consequences have so far not been of major significance. But since, as I have also said, there is every indication that the use of the practice will increase greatly during the coming years, it will not be amiss to indicate how these circumstances will affect new alignments of compadres. Fundamentally, couples in Belén replace one compadrazgo type with another when they feel that there will be no unpleasant repercussions for people closely (or fairly closely) related to them by ties of kinship, friendship, and other compadrazgos. When they use the same set of compadres for two compadrazgo relationships, or undertake one compadrazgo to the exclusion of another, they feel comfortable and within the bounds of social tradition. In the process, however, the specific ideological prescription associated with the discharge of all compadrazgo types as original relationships begins to disappear, and people regard as the norm the discharge of either of the interchangeable types; they are not breaking any traditional behavior patterns by so doing, and therefore there are no sanctions. This is incipiently the case with the younger or more secularized and outward-looking segment of the population. For example, the compadrazgo careers of five couples whose ages range from twenty-seven to thirty-five (and who have engaged in from seven to fifteen compadrazgo relationships) indicate that the interchangeable nature of several compadrazgo types, which include not only the eight preferential and less important optional types but also several prescriptive types mentioned above, is no longer regarded as flexibility in the traditional system but rather as the proper thing in itself. We are witnessing the formation of a new prescription, albeit a mild one, which dictates that it is no longer necessary to discharge a compadrazgo type and that there is actually a genuine option which involves no sanctions of any kind.

This is a neat example of how a change in ideology (regardless of the specification of external factors, involving constraints and adaptations to a new socioeconomic situation) has resulted in a particular change in behavior. If I could pinpoint the several similarly circumscribed, specific ideological transformations that the compadrazgo system in Belén is undergoing, I could fairly accurately ascertain the direction of change. My emphasis on the rather minor aspect of interchangeable compadrazgo types is based on my concern with establishing the mechanisms of change that can be profitably conceptualized within the synchronic matrix, and then complemented with the appropriate diachronic dimensions to give an adequate appraisal of dynamics of, in this case, the compadrazgo system in transition.

The interchangeability of compadrazgo types has a marked intensification effect and virtually the same function as the formation of compadrazgo clusters and the discharge of recurrent rites and ceremonies, namely, a reduction of personnel which results in stronger and more intense ties among primary actors. This alternative in the system has developed as people have come to feel that the intrinsic ritual and symbolic importance of the sponsoring occasion, event, or mediating entity has declined. This fact in itself, of course, is underlain by the secularization and modernization that the community is experiencing, and must be taken into consideration in assessing the importance of interchangeable types as a threshold for measuring cumulative change. I make this point because I do not want to imply that the ideological-structural articulation operates in a vacuum, for the process of action and reaction is always conditioned by extrinsic and external variables—the efficacy of several kinds of secularizing dimensions. Finally, if interchangeability increases, the alignment of compadres will have a significant effect in the formation of both egocentrically based and multiple-dyad networks.

Modernization and Interchangeable Compadrazgo Types

I can safely predict that within the very near future the incidence of interchangeable compadrazgo types will more than double, thereby bringing the total number of interchangeable relationships contracted by an average couple in Belén to more than 50 percent of approximately twelve types. Further, types that are now classified as highly preferential and even prescriptive will become interchangeable. For example, my sample includes four cases of couples contracting an ANDC compadrazgo relationship and neglecting two occasions when they should have contracted BSI relationships, by taking advantage during the former to comply with the latter. This is a telling example which indicates that the structure of interchangeable compadrazgo is being used to manipulate the ideological-structural articulation so as to sidestep the sanctions and coercive mechanisms. At present, about ten of the prescriptive and perhaps two of the highly preferential compadrazgo types in Belén are still discharged strictly according to prescribed custom, untouched by a single instance of the new interchangeability. I can also safely predict that as a corollary, the most traditional, ideological core of compadrazgo types will prove to be the main four public-communal types (ANDI, CSV, PCA and BM), for it is evident that the effects of secularization on the ideological-structural articulation will proceed from the individual to the collectivity. Even individuals who are most susceptible to secularizing influences (among whom I count those who are starting to make extensive use of interchangeability), several of whom I interviewed in depth, are not yet willing even to think about modifying the traditional structure of the public-communal compadrazgo types. Similarly, while many structural changes are now affecting the religious hierarchy of the community, the traditional religious system is still fairly strong because individual deviations resulting in structural modifications at the level of the mayordomía or ayuntamiento religioso systems have not yet made themselves felt. Whether in the realm of the compadrazgo system, the mayordomía system, or the ayuntamiento religioso, individual deviations, either traditionally sanctioned by structural flexibility or made at the risk of censure, have not gained enough cumulative momentum to result in what may be called adaptive social changes. Implicit in this discussion is my assumption that it is possible to measure, at least to some extent, how individual deviations can transform a system qualitatively. Let me amplify this point.

One of the most noticeable effects of interchangeable compadrazgo is the fact that, beyond the reduction of personnel egocentrically viewed, it simplifies and may also reduce the number of rites and ceremonies associated with its types. In fact, when interchangeability takes place, it is common to omit the preliminary steps, and the principal ceremonies themselves are sometimes greatly simplified. When the central ceremonies of the ANDC compadrazgo mentioned above were carried out, the asking compadres took the opportunity to bless two of their images without going through the rites and ceremonies associated with BSI.

Once the ANDC ceremonies had been properly carried out, the padrinos simply went through a very abbreviated version of the principal BSI ceremonies. The cumulative effect of this reduction is most significant, because it not only eliminates the search for original padrinos, but saves money by simplifying the rites and ceremonies. In the long run this will be more damaging to the compadrazgo system than the reduction of personnel, which is to a large extent counterbalanced by the stronger bonds among the primary actors generated by interchangeable relationships. Beleños in fact, are even beginning to think in terms of saving time. The more secularized members of the community—not necessarily the younger, more recently married generation—are beginning to think that the discharge of so many compadrazgo types represents not only an expenditure of money, but equally important an expenditure of time, which is becoming an increasingly significant commodity. Many informants complain that one of the main reasons for not complying fully with their compadrazgo obligations is lack of time, and that they would do many things gladly if time were not of the essence. It is a mistake to think of Beleños, and rural Tlaxcalans in general, as leading placid, timeless lives in leisurely peasant communities. Their lives are as agitated as those of urbanites, and when it is realized that sometimes they have to commute long distances to work, the idyllic picture of the peasant totally disappears. Psychologically also, the life of what I have called the rural proletariat of Tlaxcala (Nutini and Isaac 1974) is tremendously strenuous for the individual, and the pressures and polarization that migrant laborers and their families must endure can be compared easily with those of the most active and disorganized urban life. Interchangeable compadrazgo, then, represents also a means to save time, and as the community finds itself more and more pressed for time, the use of interchangeability will grow.

The Structural Articulation and Ritual-Symbolic Nature of Public-Communal Compadrazgo Types

In previous chapters I have implied that there are certain significant structural differences between private-individual and public-communal compadrazgo types in Belén, but I have not systematically discussed the special structure that characterizes the latter. In this chapter I deal with the distinction between the two types, the structural implications this distinction involves, and above all, the relationship between the social, communal dimensions of public-communal compadrazgo and wider networks of the social structure, namely, the mayordomía system and the ayuntamiento religioso. In the process, I place public-communal compadrazgo in the widest possible framework in order to show how, at this level, the compadrazgo system plays an integrative role which to a large extent parallels that of kinship, and complements the personnel of the ayuntamiento religioso and the mayordomía system.

The Structural Differences between Private-Individual and Public-Communal Compadrazgo Types

Table 18 indicates that there are six public-communal compadrazgo types in Belén, namely ANDI, AOI, CSV, PCA, BOI, and BM. Furthermore, table 12 shows that PCA and ANDI are prescriptive types (can never be refused), that CSV and BM are also prescriptive (can be temporarily refused), and that BOI and AOI are preferential. Thus, the first four rank among the most important compadrazgo types in Belén, while the last two are in the middle range of the scale. All public-communal compadrazgo types have essentially the same structural composition as the normal private-individual types; that is, there are at least one set of sponsors, a mediating entity, and a multiple set of compadres. What are, then, the basic differences? To begin with, the former group has, of course, a communal, public dimension. In both theory and practice, public-communal compadrazgo affect Belén as a whole, and the community can be said to become, albeit temporarily, a social unit tied by the bonds of ritual kinship. Thus, after the pedimento has been made, during the entire period of the principal ceremonies, and in the recurrent discharge of rites and ceremonies (involved in at least three of the most important public-communal types), Beleños constitute symbolically—and to some extent in actual practice—a global ritual kinship unit with specific behavior patterns, its own terminological usage, and well-delineated duties and obligations. In several public-communal types, especially PCA and ANDI, all the adults address the padrinos (and the young madrina in ANDI) as compadres, and all the children address them as padrinos and madrina.[1] Furthermore, the people at large behave in specific ways toward the sponsors throughout the central rites and ceremonies, which sometimes are quite long. This includes giving presents, special attitudes of respect and even reverence, and a conscious effort to honor and identify with the sponsors. In turn, the sponsors reciprocate by giving freely of their time and by collectively giving something to the people: invitations, whether token or effective, to participate in the proceedings, and for the children candy, piñatas, and other small presents. These attitudes and behavior patterns binding the sponsors and the people are in many ways the norm in any compadrazgo relationship regardless of the number of personnel; here, though, they are much stronger than in the average private-individual compadrazgo type.

Of greater sociological significance is what happens to the behavior patterns and the attitudes of the people in general toward one another. It is in this domain that public-communal compadrazgo transcends mere ritual kinship, and comes to be structured and to function like a true kinship institution. After a public-communal compadrazgo type comes into existence, and throughout its entire cycle of rites and ceremonies down to its recurrent aspects, Beleños act toward one another in a fashion that can be characterized as kinship behavior. These are limited periods, of course, which last from a few days to more than a month in the case of ANDI (from December 24 to February 2). In total, for about three months of each year, during the course of the four main public-communal compadrazgo types (from December 15 to February 2 for ANDI and BM, and from approximately mid-April to the end of May for PCA and CSV), the people of Belén are bound by symbolic and actual patterns of behavior into an all-embracing kinship unit.[2] Throughout this time, they not only behave in a manner appropriate to real kinship, but also intensify their normal patterns of community interaction, inviting each other to their homes more often, accentuating patterns of cooperation and labor exchange, and avoiding direct confrontations that could lead to quarrels, in order to achieve the maximum esprit de corps. This attitude was well expressed by one of my informants when he said that "durante las fiestas principales del año [the December-February and April-May cycles] el pueblo se une como nunca, la gente deja sus desaveniencias de lado, y nos comportamos como si fueramos todos de una misma familia" (during the main fiestas of the year, the village becomes highly integrated, people put their disagreements aside, and we behave as if we were part of a single family). In summary, then, for three months of the year public-communal compadrazgo has the function of structurally transforming the community into a truly kin-based community, by symbolically and effectively intensifying latent patterns of behavior. The effects of public-communal compadrazgo are longer lasting, and, together with the mayordomía system and the ayuntamiento religioso, are of great importance as an integrative force counterbalancing the powerful effects of secularization and modernization.[3]

The private-individual compadrazgo types, on the other hand, although endowed with some true kinship dimensions, especially in their multiple dyadic aspects can only encompass a limited number of people in their compadrazgo networks. For example, the compadrazgo network that can result from a multiple-dyad situation such as PCE, or the total exocentric network of a given couple, will seldom involve more than forty-five couples, It must be pointed out, however, that what private-individual compadrazgo lacks in amplitude of personnel, is to a great exent counterbalanced by its continuity of existence and effectiveness of operation. In essence, the differences in kinshiplike attributes between private-individual and public-communal compadrazgo are only differences of degree, but in the broadest context of community life, public-communal compadrazgo acquires a much more significant dimension as an integrative mechanism. It generates social solidarity and integration at the community level, while private-individual compadrazgo generates them at a lower, household-paraje level.

The second difference between private-individual and public-communal compadrazgo types is that the latter includes two distinct sets of compadrazgo dyads, while the former includes only one. In any private-individual type, the compadrazgo dyads constitute a single network in its normal threefold dyadic pattern; for several compadrazgo relationships, such as marriage and PCE, they constitute a network in its multiple dyadic pattern. The multiple dyadic network can be said to be simply a numerical enlargement of the normal threefold pattern, and such an arrangement can have permanent or temporary dimensions depending on specific cases and in accordance with the principles discussed in Chapter Seven. In public-communal types, on the other hand, the two sets of dyads involved have a different structure, with respect to both the permanent-temporary dichotomy of specific dyads, and the general set of dyads at the communal level. The general set of dyads denoted by the padrinos (madrina)–people of Belén as a whole is strictly temporary, and operates during the periods of intensification described above, but it can never develop into a permanent relationship. If it could, then obviously Belén would be structured in terms of ritual kinship in essentially the same way as if the village constituted a clan-community or some other form of compromise kin group. But the fact is that the temporal operation of the sponsors–people of Belén dyadic set acquires kinship-like features intermittently, thereby making the relationship structurally different from what obtains in normal private-individual types. The second set of dyadic relationships that obtains in public-communal types, that is, those between the sponsors and the individuals in charge of selection (fiscales and mayordomos), can—and very often does—develop into permanent relationships binding sometimes quite large numbers of couples.

Let me give an example. The three fiscales and the mayordomos of the Virgen de Mayo are in charge of selecting the sponsors for the CSV, who are a couple and their young daughter fifteen to eighteen years old. When the compadrazgo comes into existence following the pedimento, and is intensified after the central ceremonies have been carried out, the padrinos-madrina become the compadres and madrina of the entire community until the last day of May when the cycle of festivities comes to an end. After that the padrinos-madrina–people of Belén dyadic set ceases to operate and remains only latent. This primarily symbolic relationship accounts for the first set of dyads of CSV. The second set of CSV dyads consists of the couples of the six fiscales and mayordomos and the padrinos-madrina, for a total of seven dyads (disregarding the young madrina, whose postceremonial role becomes latent) organized into an operating network. This seven-dyad network of compadres survives the end of the cycle and develops into a temporary relationship in the same fashion as any normal private-individual type. Moreover, in time, and depending on a variety of conditions, the CSV seven-dyad network of compadres may develop into a permanent relationship, either as a network per se, or by the further establishment of compadrazgo ties binding the CSV padrinos and a fiscal or mayordomo or among the fiscales and mayordomos themselves. The second set of CSV dyads, then, becomes very much like any normal private-individual compadrazgo relationship. In fact, CSV, as well as the three other important public-communal types, is classified as resulting from other compadrazgo types, but almost invariably, it subsequently leads to other compadrazgo relationships, binding the personnel of the seven dyads in a variety of combinations. Thus, the significance of public-communal compadrazgo in Belén stems from its integrative functions at the communal level, and from its leading to other compadrazgo relationships in the developmental cycle of the compadrazgo system.

Public-Communal Compadrazgo and Global Community Structure

For the remainder of this chapter, let us leave aside private-individual compadrazgo types and concentrate on public-communal ones. The four prescriptive types in this category are different from the two preferential types, AOI and BOI. The symbolic and integrative importance of the former derives from their prescriptive and traditional character, while the latter (one of which is a new compadrazgo type in Belén, that is, established since the 1920s; see table 21), being only preferential cannot be ultimately enforced; they are much less traditional and have to do with the ayuntamiento religioso proper, thereby being essentially as much a part of the religious system of Belén as a part of the compadrazgo system per se. Moreover, PCA, ANDI, CSV, and BM are truly universal in Belén; the entire community feels symbolically and actually drawn together by the bonds with the sponsors. AOI and BOI do not elicit total communal involvement; rather, they bind together those individuals who have given money and other resources to improve the local church and maintain objects of the local cult. The number of people asked by the fiscales to become compadres varies considerably, of course, but AOI and BOI seldom involve more than 20 percent of all couples in Belén. The resulting dyads are quite specific, but they are weak from the beginning and always remain temporary, that is, governed by the formal attribution of respeto and confianza. Not even during the height of the ceremonies do the people at large feel or behave toward AOI and BOI padrinos and compadres in the same warm, intense, and reverent way they do toward PCA, ANDI, CSV, and BM padrinos and compadres. In fact, the people themselves regard AOI and BOI as ad hoc means of generating contributions for the maintenance of the local church and cult. (Remember that it would be most inappropriate for a man in Belén to refuse either AOI or BOI compadrazgo because it involved a certain expenditure of money or other resources.) Neither AOI or BOI leads to other types because of the ad hoc nature of the selection process, and because of the kind of cooperation involved; indeed, many couples are not overly happy with the fiscales for having *selected* them as compadres for the sole purpose of eliciting a contribution. In short, then, there is a very clear distinction between AOI and BOI and the four main public-communal compadrazgo types in Belén.

Let us now compare table 18 to the other tables, in order to view the public-communal distinction in a wider perspective. Table 6 shows that Beleños regard all six public-communal types as entirely symbolic or symbolic-religious in primary meaning. This is a clear and definite attitude, which Beleños express in their behavior toward public-com-

TABLE 21. Traditional and New Compadrazgo Types

Type	Traditional	New
Bautizo	x	
Casamiento	x	
Confirmación	x	
PCE	x	
Primera comunión		x
CCCH	x	
CCCA	x	
ANDC	x	
ANDI	x	
AOI		x
BSI	x	
CSV	x	
Escapulario	x	
Graduación		x
PCA	x	
Quince años		x
Sacada a misa	x	
Compadrazgo de evangelios	x	
Compadrazgo de limpia	x	
BOI	x	
Bendición de casa	x	
BCC		x
BM	x	
Parada de cruz	x	
Primera piedra	x	
Compadrazgo de amistad	x	
CABP		x
Compadrazgo de aretes	x	
CEON	x	
FC	x	
JJ	x	

munal types. Table 22 shows that with respect to the regulation of compadrazgo selection, four of the six public-communal types are agamous,
while AOI and BOI are endogamous. It is easy to explain why AOI
and BOI are endogamous, inasmuch as they are used to generate funds
for the upkeep of the cult and the local church building. This is a strictly
community concern which can hardly be extended to include couples

TABLE 22. Community Regulation of Compadrazgo Types

Type	Endogamous	Agamous
Bautizo		x[1]
Casamiento		x
Confirmación		x
PCE	x	
Primera comunión		x
CCCH		x
CCCA		x
ANDC	x	
ANDI		x
AOI	x	
BSI	x	
CSV		x
Escapulario	x	
Graduación		x
PCA		x[1]
Quince años		x
Sacada a misa		x[1]
Compadrazgo de evangelios		x[1]
Compadrazgo de limpia	x	
BOI	x	
Bendición de casa	x	
BCC	x	
BM		x
Parada de cruz	x	
Primera piedra	x	
Compadrazgo de amistad		x
CABP		x
Compadrazgo de aretes	x	
CEON		x
FC	x	
JJ		x

[1] Shows a tendency toward endogamy.

from neighboring communities. On the other hand, the agamous character of the four main public-communal types merits discussion. The
rules concerning selection of ANDI, CSV, PCA, and BM sponsors indicate clearly that the padrinos and madrina for these occasions can be
selected from within the community or from neighboring villages. Ide-

ologically, the people prefer a local couple, but if the fiscales and mayordomos in charge of the pedimento either cannot find the appropriate
couple within the community (mainly because of the financial requirements), or cannot find one who meets with the approval of the majority
of the people of Belén (mainly because of factionalism and rifts within
the community), then it is appropriate to select the sponsors from
neighboring villages. My data show that all exogamous ANDI, CSV,
PCA and BM compadrazgo relationships in Belén have been contracted
with the neighboring municipios of San Bernardino Contla, Santa Cruz
Tlaxcala, and Amaxac de Guerrero, which border community land. As
I explained in the case of PCA (see Nutini and White 1977:374), these
compadrazgo types have been used by Beleños as a means to generate
closer relations with neighboring communities with which they have
had land and other disputes, and also as a way to smooth out impending
disputes. This has been an effective way to improve intercommunity
relations, inasmuch as it is a great honor for a couple from a neighboring village to be asked to sponsor any of these occasions. To some
extent the compadrazgo tie becomes binding upon the sponsoring couple's community as a whole. In fact, the community of the sponsoring
couple is expressly invited to attend the rites and ceremonies associated
with the occasion. According to most informants, this use of public-
communal compadrazgo has had excellent results for Belén, and to it
they attribute their success in weathering land and water disputes with
neighboring communities, especially Contla and Santa Cruz Tlaxcala.

ANDI, CSV, PCA, and BM involve recurrent rites and ceremonies,
which are discharged throughout the year, while AOI and BOI involve
only the central complex of rites and ceremonies (see table 23). Once
the improvements in the local church building or the ornaments of the
cult are blessed there are no more activities associated with these two
types. On the whole, public-communal compadrazgo types involve a
rather high economic obligation (see table 15). The only type with a
low economic obligation is AOI, and this can vary considerably according to what the chosen padrinos are willing to contribute. PCA and BM
involve large expenditures; ANDI involves very large ones. Furthermore, since two of these compadrazgos are contracted for the sponsoring of three consecutive years of ceremonies, padrinos always pay a high
price for the honor of being sponsors. The prestige involved in being
asked for a public-communal compadrazgo, however, always counter-
balances the economic obligations, and few people in Belén and neighboring communities who can afford the expense would not actively
encourage such nomination. (Although specific rites and ceremonies may
be different in, say, Belén and Contla, the common ideological and
structural base of compadrazgo in rural Tlaxcala means that public-

TABLE 23. Compadrazgo Types with Single and Recurrent Ceremonies

Type	Single	Recurrent
Bautizo	x	
Casamiento	x	
Confirmación	x	
PCE		x
Primera comunión	x	
CCCH	x	
CCCA	x	
ANDC		x
ANDI		x
AOI	x	
BSI	x	
CSV		x
Escapulario	x	
Graduación	x	
PCA		x
Quince años	x	
Sacada a misa	x	
Compadrazgo de evangelios	x	
Compadrazgo de limpia		x
BOI	x	
Bendición de casa	x	
BCC	x	
BM		x
Parada de cruz		x
Primera piedra	x	
Compadrazgo de amistad	x	
CABP	x	
Compadrazgo de aretes	x	
CEON	x	
FC	x	
JJ	x	

communal sponsorship has the same symbolic meaning in both communities.) Finally, the four main public-communal compadrazgo types have a compound symbolic objective that may include propitiation, thanksgiving, protection, and intensification (see table 24). The most important symbolic objectives of ANDI, CSV, PCA and BM are propitiation and thanksgiving, but this does not mean that they do not have subsidiary symbolic objectives as well. For example, PCA involves all

TABLE 24. Symbolic Objective of Compadrazgo Types

Type	Protection	Intensification	Propitiation	Thanksgiving
Bautizo	x			
Casamiento	x			
Confirmación		x		
PCE	x[1]		x	
Primera comunión		x		
CCCH		x		
CCCA		x		
ANDC			x[1]	x
ANDI			x[1]	x
AOI			x	
BSI			x[1]	x
CSV			x[1]	x
Escapulario	x			
Graduación				x
PCA	x	x	x[1]	x
Quince años	x			x[1]
Sacada a misa	x[1]	x		
Compadrazgo de evangelios	x[1]		x	
Compadrazgo de limpia	x[1]	x		
BOI			x[1]	x
Bendición de casa	x[1]		x	
BCC	x			
BM			x[1]	x
Parada de cruz	x[1]		x	
Primera piedra	x[1]		x	
Compadrazgo de amistad	x			
CABP	x			x[1]
Compadrazgo de aretes	x			
CEON	x			
FC	x			
JJ	x			

[1] Represents the primary symbolic objective.

four symbolic objectives, namely, protection, propitiation, thanksgiving, and intensification, and it is no coincidence that Beleños unconsciously regard this compadrazgo type as the most significant—which is why I ranked it first in table 12.

The Relationship of Public-Communal Compadrazgo to the Mayordomía System and the Ayuntamiento Religioso

I want to discuss, finally, the relationship of public-communal compadrazgo to the mayordomía system and the ayuntamiento religioso. I have repeatedly mentioned the fact that the compadrazgo system of Belén is part of the general ideological domain that includes the mayordomiá system and the ayuntamiento religioso (the term República Eclesiástica can also be used for these two institutions). I have also implied (and briefly discussed in several connections) that the mayordomía system and the ayuntamiento religioso are structurally connected in various ways to the compadrazgo system. This is especially the case with the six public-communal compadrazgo types. At the level of structural discharge of public-communal compadrazgo, the institution is almost indistinguishable from the mayordomía system and the ayuntamiento religioso, and to a considerable extent it is a matter of choice whether to discuss the ANDI, AOI, CSV, PCA, BOI, and BM compadrazgo types as part of the República Eclesiástica or as part of the compadrazgo system of Belén. The structural interconnections are such that either is an appropriate way to describe and analyze the data at hand. I have chosen the latter because this is, after all, a study of compadrazgo, and also because I think that ultimately the compadrazgo relationship has a higher conceptual priority—that is, it is a more fundamental expression of the general ideological-structural articulation underlying this threefold institution than any comparable relationship obtaining in the República Eclesiástica. In any event, integration among these three institutions lies at the core of Belén culture and society, the core of organizational principles around which virtually everything else is clustered insitutionally and in asociation with which virtually everything else acquires meaning in the life of the people. The public-communal compadrazgo types can be seen both as the mechanisms that structurally connect the three parts of the institutional complex, and as the generators of important functional ties in its actual discharge. Through the discharge of public-communal compadrazgo types the fiscales and the mayordomos of the four most important mayordomias perform a variety of symbolic, ritual, ceremonial, and economic functions affecting the community as a whole, for the four main public-communal types are the only occasions in the social and ceremonial cycles of Belén in which the community becomes an organic unit.

In the selection and pedimento of the sponsors of public-communal compadrazgo types, the fiscales and mayordomos in charge are fulfilling a communal function that is binding upon the whole. In the discharge of the central and recurrent ceremonies, they are activating the will of community action. In the permanent bonds (mayordomos-fiscales–sponsors) that remain after the last recurrent ceremony has been carried out, the fiscales and mayordomos are embodying the latent compadrazgo bonds that come into being. Thus, without public-communal compadrazgo, the integrative structure and cohesive function of the República Eclesiástica could not have been as powerful in maintaining the traditional status quo. It is the network of ideological constraints and sanctions operating upon this threefold institutional complex that results in an effective structural discharge. It would be wrong, however, to regard the compadrazgo system as merely one of the functions of the República Eclesiástica. The former represents a structural system with its own internal consistency, although it shares with the latter its ideological order. Rather, I have regarded public-communal compadrazgo as a part of the ideological order that is equal with the ayuntamiento religioso and the mayordomía system. In this view of things, public-communal compadrazgo can function as a system in itself, as I have regarded it in this section; or it can be conceptualized as part of the mayordomía system and the ayuntamiento religioso, in the sense of being one of the most important manifestations of them. The network of dyadic compadrazgo relationships that obtain in public-communal types, both with the sponsors and among the fiscales and mayordomos, has significant structural implications for the functioning of the mayordomía system and the ayuntamiento religioso. To a large extent, the alliances that result from such compadrazgo ties determine the degree of mayordomía sponsorship and the fulfillment of the offices of the ayuntamiento religioso. (These are discussed in connection with the religious functions of compadrazgo; see Chapter Sixteen.) In summary, then, public-communal compadrazgo in Belén is one of the most significant forces for community integration, both in itself and as part of the República Eclesiástica. For this reason, I predict that the four main public-communal types will prove the most resistant to the secularizing trend of the times.

✳ CHAPTER 10 ✳

The Conscious and Unconscious Nature of Compadrazgo and the Absolute and Relative Importance of Compadrazgo Types

The Need for a Theory of the Social Unconscious in Anthropological Studies

I come now to the discussion of a significant conceptual study question, one I have briefly touched upon, but for which I have no definitive answer. The conscious and unconscious nature of compadrazgo in Belén has underlain much of the discussion at both the conceptual and the substantive levels. It has been my assumption that there is a categorical distinction between what the people should do and what they actually do, and, furthermore, that the former is conditioned by the conscious character of rules and constraints. Thus, three separate conceptual and substantive domains are involved in the description and explanation of sociocultural phenomena, namely, what people should do, what they think they should do, and what they actually do. I have translated this threefold analytical framework into an integrated approach composed of three interconnected levels of analysis that I have called the ideological, the structural-ideal, and the structural-actual orders. I think I have shown how this analytical framework can be applied to a complex system such as compadrazgo in Belén, in which several variables have been used to generate causal links uniting the three levels of analysis. This endeavor has, however, been hampered by the lack of an adequte theory of the social unconscious (a shorthand expression for a theory of the socially conscious and unconscious). Determining the conscious or unconscious nature of the sociocultural phenomena with which anthropologists work is a necessary condition, not only for the implementation of my analytical approach, but for the implementation of any approach that purports to go beyond functional causality. At present, I can only explain why this is so with regard to my own analytical framework, but I think that much of the explanation applies to other approaches.

In the first place, it is almost tautological to say that the conscious or unconscious nature of the data upon which a theoretical construct is based will influence its outcome, that is, will influence the implementation of whatever verification procedures are employed. Even at the purely descriptive level, the conscious or unconscious nature of phenomena will influence the mode and organization of description to the extent that the observer will naturally tend to emphasize the former over the latter. Second, the nature of the theoretical constructs themselves is determined ultimately by the epistemological status of the data upon which they are constructed, and in this respect the conscious-unconscious axis is one of the most important perceptive determinants. So far, I have given equal conceptual status to the conscious and unconscious data presented here, and I have confined myself to the common-sense notions of establishing adequate standards of data collection. In short, I have lumped together data of a conscious and unconscious nature, to form an undifferentiated body of material upon which to construct models and paradigms, on the basis of which we can merely describe. In a sophisticated and mature approach, this would be totally unacceptable.

The epistemological implications here are evident: the physical and the social sciences are no different in logical structure. The same logical principles apply at the level of theory construction, but the gap between them widens tremendously at the second step of the scientific procedure, namely verification. Moreover, one of the main reasons for the inability of social scientists to develop more adequate verification procedures is the persistent confusion between what is conscious and what is unconscious at the most primitive level of conceptualization. What distinguishes the physical from the social sciences is primarily that the former have a undimensional data base, while the latter must be epiphenomenally conceived, not so much because of the multiplicity of variables, as because of the conscious-unconscious character of the data they work with. Thus, the whole problem of verification in the social sciences, and especially in anthropology, revolves around the conscious and unconscious nature of sociocultural phenomena, and an adequate theory about these matters must be developed before we can begin to think about improving verification techniques. For example, the analytical framework presented in the appendix can be only partially implemented until it is determined which elements that entered into its formulation are conscious and which unconscious. I can make no definitive statements about how to construct a meaningful theory of the social unconscious, but in the course of this study I have developed a few ideas. I would therefore like to discuss briefly what I think is a reasonable and realistic attitude to take, illustrating the discussion with examples pertaining to the operation of the compadrazgo system in Belén. The problem has two main components, namely the conscious and unconscious nature of the substantive phenomena with which we work, and the conceptual implications for theory construction that result from employing substrata with different epistemological bases. First, however, let me review what anthropologists have said regarding the conscious and unconscious nature of their materials.

Although it has seldom been explicitly discussed, most anthropologists since the 1920s or so have implicitly assumed a distinction between what is consciously maintained or elicited from their subjects, and what is unconsciously held or elicited by circumlocution. Among other things, this has led to the formulation of practical rules on gathering data and to cautioning investigators in the field not to take at face value what informants tell them, nor to be satisfied with the unidimensionality of both direct elicitation from informants and inferences from observable behavior. It is probably this realization that has led many anthropologists to distinguish contextually between ideology and structure, or ideology and behavior. One of the best examples of this attitude and implicit orientation in anthropology is Lévi-Strauss's distinction between what he calls conscious and unconscious models in the conduct of anthropological inquiry (Lévi-Strauss 1953:526-527). Despite his adequate formulation of the problem, Lévi-Strauss does not, however, present us with either a realistic theory of the social unconscious, or the elements that could enter into its formulation. Moreover, despite Lévi-Strauss's extensive conceptual use of the unconscious, his distinction between conscious and unconscious models boils down to little more than a warning to be careful not to confine ourselves to direct elicitation and to use other indirect techniques to collect data and observe behavior. In other words, the notion of conscious and unconscious models is simply a formal way of expressing what anthropologists have been practicing for many decades with varying degrees of success. Neither Lévi-Strauss nor any other anthropologist who has dealt directly or indirectly with the conscious-unconscious dichotomy has ever formulated a methodology, much less a theory to account for the substantive and conceptual implications involved in this epistemological sine qua non of sociocultural phenomena. The problem has been ignored rather than solved in any meaningful manner—first, by confining its domain of significance to purely practical considerations; and second, by implicitly assuming that it does not play a signficant role in the construction of conceptual tools. This attitude limits the substantive domain of anthropology, and by extension a large segment of the social sciences, to the handling of sociocultural phenomena in terms of a unidimensional perceptive domain; in other words, the data are thought to have no epistemological depth that can be used on different levels of analysis. I am not aware of a single anthropological study in which the raw data of analysis are first classifed in terms of their conscious or unconscious sources of elicitation, nor weighted in terms of a conscious-unconscious scale.

Hitherto, the conscious-unconscious nature of sociocultural phenomena has given rise to little more than the pragmatic rule that behind conscious phenomena there may lie another reality which is more fundamental for the explanation of a given corpus of data. But anthropologists have never questioned the nature of the conscious-unconscious dichotomy itself as perhaps implying drastically different levels of perception and consequently of interpretation. The reason for this prevalent attitude in anthropology is the empiricist bias that makes us regard observable behavior as an ultimate datum of experience. This, on the one hand, hampers the formulation of principles that will reveal the epistemological unevenness of behavior; and, on the other, hinders development of the methods required for measuring the differential significance of the conscious-unconscious continuum. I put it in this way because essentially it is not a matter of a dichotomy, but rather of a continuum along which all primary elicited data are placed, and social consciousness and unconsciousness become limiting parameters. In summary, to achieve substantive and conceptual sophistication we need a theory of the social unconscious that meets the following requirements: at the substantive level, it should specify the kinds of elicited data that can be parametrically regarded as conscious or unconscious, the methods needed to measure degrees of unconsciousness, and above all, what is ideologically and structurally unconscious. At the conceptual level, the theory should specify the differential weight that any construct will give to conscious and unconscious phenomena, and, more important, the role that these data will come to play in the verification of hypotheses.

The Conscious-Unconscious Distinction at the Substantive Level

It must be assumed that no data that can be elicited are either entirely conscious or entirely unconscious, but that these are limiting parameters, given certain measuring standards. Whatever informants tell us tends toward the conscious limit; everything that cannot be obtained by direct elicitation, and any results arrived at primarily by circumlocution, tend toward the unconscious limit. Furthermore, whatever is elicited directly is in itself subject to degrees of consciousness—hence the emphasis on developing measuring techniques and scaling procedures to determine these degrees. The problem is compounded in the case of unconsciously elicited primary data, given the fact that the kinds of circumlocutions used (indirect elicitation, correlation of informants' answers, changing frames of reference, and so on) must be specified, and in these circumstances adequate measuring techniques are even more important. Notice that I have not mentioned the other source of data most commonly available to the investigator, namely the observation and recording of behavior. Here lies the crux of the matter, for it is my contention that observable behavior does not constitute primary socio-cultural data, unless it is interpreted in the light of what is socially conscious and unconscious to members of any group or society as a whole. The fundamental error of empiricists is to assume that behavior by itself is a primary datum, and that direct observation reveals the entire substantive domain. Behavior acquires conceptual meaning only after two things are clearly specified: the ideological (what people should do) and the structural (what people actually do under certain conditions) nature of the actions; and their conscious or unconscious character. It should be noted, furthermore, that the correlation of these two pairs involves a significant dimension in the structuring of the substantive domain. In other words, behavioral facts by themselves are meaningless, and perhaps not even adequate for strictly descriptive purposes; what *really* generates systems is the ideological-structural and conscious-unconscious nature that underlies them, for it is the interplay between observable behavior and these two pairs of epistemological contraries that reveals causal relationships. This has been the dominant theme in the present structural analysis, and the main reason for its inconclusiveness has been the inadequacy of our notions about the social conscious and unconscious.

So far, however, I have looked at the problem from the viewpoint of the subject end of the subject-object continuum, for I have not specified how the structuring or formulation of the investigator's questions and frames of reference may bias the conscious-unconscious character of elicitation. This is primarily a practical problem which can be solved by allowing for the same measuring and scaling techniques that apply to the subjects of the substantive matrix, largely because the investigator in any given situation asks questions with an already specified model or paradigm in mind, and this is almost invariably conscious. (Discussion of whether or not this is necessarily the case would involve psychological arguments that cannot be aired here.) Furthermore, the importance of the object's conscious or unconscious dimensions is really part of the conceptual domain. In any case, it should be clear that what anthropologists are after at the substantive level is the classification of data from the subject viewpoint as a measurable continuum in terms of conscious-unconscious parameters. It is not enough simply to elicit and classify data without this added dimension, as has always been the practice in anthropology. We must first of all construct a general measuring scale with which to determine the conscious or unconscious dimensions of all directly or indirectly elicited data, and on the basis of which we can interpret observable behavior. Although in this study I have been aware of the difficulties involved in this approach, I have not been able to implement the conscious-unconscious scaling beyond a rather coarse and implicit classification. This is the main reason, for example, why there is nothing in those tables of this volume that present structural data that denote the degree of consciousness-unconsciousness associated with the various compadrazgo types in Belén. Given an appropriate theory of the social unconscious, it should have been possible to construct a special table in which all the structural attributes for every compadrazgo type in Belén (tables 1-11, 13-24, and 26-33) would be scaled along this dimension.

In brief, then, the basic substantive problem confronting anthropologists is the development of mechanisms by which we can record directly or indirectly elicited information along the conscious-unconscious scale. Again, this is largely a practical problem, which can be solved without undue difficulty and with a considerable degree of interscientific reliability. Once a corpus of data has been measured and scaled along the conscious-unconscious axis, the other requirements specified above will be more naturally fitted into any analytical framework allowing for the differential depth of primary data. Fundamentally, the consciousness and unconsciousness that people exhibit regarding what they should do or what they actually do represent the most important operational dimension in articulating the ideological and structural orders, and without a thorough knowledge and measurement of this axis we can never completely determine how rules are departed from or adhered to in the conduct of social life. Thus, the scaling of conscious and unconscious primary data must in turn be measured along the ideological-structural axis; that is, it is necessary to determine the degree of consciousness and unconsciousness that people have of what they should do, what they think they should do, and what they actually do.

The Conscious-Unconscious Distinction at the Conceptual Level

The situation becomes more complicated at the conceptual level, because here the lack of an adequate theory of the social unconscious is no longer merely a practical problem, but crucially hinders any analytical approach that purports to transcend functional causality. The first problem that faces us here is to specify how conscious and unconscious phenomena will affect the construction of models and paradigms, and the explanatory value that this differential axis will have, given the degree of relationship we want to demonstrate. Assuming that conscious and unconscious primary data represent different substantive configurations, how can they be used to show causal relationship within the boundaries of specified systems? The answer is complex, and I have only vague notions regarding it, but two points come to mind. First, the differential consciousness-unconsciousness of ideologically and structurally elicited data embodies or exhibits the mechanisms (or at least some of them) that determine why people are aware of certain kinds of behavior and are unaware of other kinds, in which they may nevertheless engage. This in itself can be used as a threshold in constructing models or paradigms purporting to explain behavior in action. In other words, a theory of the social conscious-unconscious would use the interdigitation of the conscious-unconscious and ideological-structural axes as the principal means of explanation, for it is assumed that causal mechanisms can be elicited from the correlation and invariance of the consciousness and unconsciousness of what people should do, what they think they should do, and what they in fact do. Second, the explanatory value of the conscious-unconscious axis lies essentially in the fact that ontologically behavior must be regarded as an expression of different epistemological substrata, that is, that any piece of observable behavior is explained only if we can determine its motivation. If we can determine why a group of individuals or, conceivably, a whole society is consciously or unconsciously motivated, we can in principle explain a good deal about behavior itself. (We must be careful, however, to determine the extent to which any given configuration of behavior is consciously or unconsciously motivated along the individual-social axis by scaling the number of individuals sharing the same degree of consciousness or unconsciousness. This is necessary, for unless we know the shared degree of consciousness-unconsciousness along individual numerical lines, whatever theory we are able to formulate cannot be properly activated. Thus, to the two already specified axes we must add the individual-societal axis.)

I can summarize my ideas on this matter by saying that a theory of the social unconscious should specify conceptually why people are behaviorally motivated by either conscious or unconscious mechanisms— why social groups have conscious or unconscious knowledge (ideological and structural) that is translated into specific configurations of behavior. If this question can be answered, it can clarify many associated conceptual points. I have already mentioned that the conscious and unconscious nature of primary data will play a significant role in the verification of conceptual constructs. I have deliberately distinguished between explanation and verification, to indicate that while conceptual constructs (at least in anthropology) can explain circumscribed substantive domains with a certain degree of accuracy, anthropologists cannot yet *verify* general hypotheses or theories, which is tantamount to saying that we have not yet been able to formulate general theoretical constructs. This again may result from our disregard of the conscious-unconscious dimensions of the substantive and conceptual levels. My next task is to show the relevance of this neglected dimension of sociocultural phenomena to the compadrazgo system of Belén.

The Compadrazgo System and the Conscious-Unconscious Axis

It is obvious that the substantive data of this monograph are not based on any systematic or rigorous scaling and measuring of the conscious-unconscious axis underlying the compadrazgo system of Belén. Most of the data upon which the analysis is based were gathered before I became fully aware of the conceptual importance of the conscious-unconscious axis. Some data were, however, gathered subsequently with this conception in mind, and therefore I can say that to some extent I am speaking with practical knowledge of how the concept works at the substantive level. Nevertheless, all I can do here is to point out some of the implications of my lack of adequate implementation.

First, none of the data presented here can be said to have been exclusively elicited either consciously or unconsciously, nor can I say that a signficant part has been scaled in even a relatively crude manner. For example, the three main bodies of data (namely, the conscious paradigm of the people of Belén regarding compadrazgo as a system, presented in Chapter Two of *Ritual Kinship* I; the systematic description of compadrazgo types presented in Chapters Three, Four, and Five of *Ritual Kinship* I; and the structural payloads of all compadrazgo types presented in tables 1-11, 13-24, and 26-33 in this volume) embodying the structural-ideal and structural-actual domains of the compadrazgo system, and the underlying ideological order presented in the preceding analysis, are a mixture of consciously and unconsciously elicited data that I could not possibly scale or measure at present. If I had had the specified requirements that a theory of the unconscious (at the substantive level) demands, I would have had no trouble in generating a much higher degree of causal relationship between the ideological and structural domains. As it is, I have only been able to show how this can be done in future studies and how the ideological and structural-ideal orders have been adhered to or departed from in actual behavior.

Second, whatever causal relationships I have been able to show between the three levels of analysis have been based not so much on the meager yield of the conscious-unconscious axis, as on the juxtaposition with the ideological-structural axis. For example, the prescriptive-preferential-optional scaling of compadrazgo types is accurate enough, but I have not determined *why* there is no apparent correlation between it and the basic classification of the people in terms of compadrazgo sacramental (or, alternatively, *compadrazgo de grado* and *compadrazgo de fé*), compadrazgo no-sacramental primario, and compadrazgo no sacramental secundario. It is simple enough to say that this represents discrepancies between what the people regard ideologically as important and what they practice structurally. This I have analyzed, but what I have failed to explain are the reasons for the discrepancies. Such an explanation, I submit, must be based on the conceptualization of what the people of Belén hold consciously or unconsciously regarding the institution of compadrazgo and its extensions. Only by the use of such measured and scaled information can this quandary be resolved. Under these circumstances, a second general classification of compadrazgo types rather widely held by the people of Belén (notice that I cannot say whether this second classification is conscious or unconscious, or the percentage of the people who hold it), namely, compadrazgo sacramental, *compadrazgo no-sacramental primariamente religioso* (primarily religious nonsacramental compadrazgo) *compadrazgo no-sacramental secundariamente religioso* (secondarily religious nonsacramental compadrazgo), and *compadrazgo secular* (secular compadrazgo) would also have been adequate for the organization of the descriptive articulation of all thirty-one compadrazgo types. My inability to measure and scale the people's knowledge of the compadrazgo system along the conscious-unconscious axis has prevented me from correlating the ideological and structural attributes of compadrazgo types. This correlation would have enabled me to formulate absolute ranking systems, and thereby to understand the principles that explain the primary rules that involve efficacy.

My third point is a corollary of the second, namely, that whatever I have said about the ranking and scaling of compadrazgo types (the people's own classifications and my classification presented in table 12) and the position of any given type within a given class has been primarily relative, and ultimately subject to the kind of efficacy (which the study sorely lacks) that can only be provided by proper conceptualization of the conscious-unconscious axis. Even the expressions "more important than" and "less important than" which I have often used in positioning a given type in the description are of only relative importance. I have seldom been able to determine whether the behavior that I am describing has been motivated by conscious or unconscious knowledge, thereby precluding the establishment of the correct relationship between the ideological and structural orders, which is what ultimately determines the absolute scaling of the compadrazgo system and the position of each type within each class of the system. It can be seen, then, that the proper substantive and conceptual implementation of the conscious-unconscious axis is of great importance.

CHAPTER 11

Ritual Kinship Terminology

In the remaining chapters I confine myself to substantive and analytical matters related to what I have already established about the structure of the compadrazgo system in Belén and rural Tlaxcala. In this and the following chapter I analyze in as broad a context as possible the ritual kinship terminology of Belén, and the behavior patterns associated both with the institution as a whole and with specific types; above all, I expand what I have said about the differences and similarities between ritual kinship and real kinship within the context of Belén society. I should note that the constant shifting between the compadrazgo system and specific compadrazgo types characteristic of this study is particularly noticeable here, and exemplifies the difficulties of analyzing such a complex multidimensional system as compadrazgo.

The Terminological System

The analysis of ritual kinship terminology is undertaken with reference to table 25, where all current categorical term usages are listed, together with tables 2 and 3, which indicate, respectively, the extensions of ritual kinship terminology and well-defined patterns of behavior to primary, secondary, and tertiary compadrazgo actors, and the extensions of incest prohibitions. However, before I analyze the sociological implications of ritual kinship terminology and place it within the general structure of the compadrazgo system, I would like to discuss its strictly terminological and formal dimensions, as well as some historical implications.

Table 25 lists both Spanish and Nahuatl terms of reference. The people of Belén no longer use the Nahuatl ritual kinship terminology, but according to four of my oldest informants (all of them over eighty-five), it was the only terminology used at the turn of the century. This also applied to real kinship terminology, which was then entirely Nahuatl. This native ritual kinship terminology effectively disappeared between 1910 and 1960 or so, for informants assured me that in 1960 there were still a few people who used it. By now, except in the recollections of perhaps two dozen individuals, it is no longer part of the compadrazgo system of Belén. Basically the same terminological system, however, is still in use in several Indian, or predominantly Indian, villages and municipios on the western slopes of La Malintzi volcano—in, for example,

TABLE 25. Ritual Kinship Terminology of Santa María Belén

Category	Spanish Term of Reference	Nahuatl Term of Reference	Term of Address
Co-Fa	Compadre	Cumpaletzi	Compadrito
Co-Mo	Comadre	Cumaletzi	Comadrita
God-Fa	Padrino	Pilatatzi	Padrino, padrinito
God-Mo	Madrina	Pilanantzi	Madrina, madrinita
God-So	Ahijado	Pilacone	Ahijado, name
God-Da	Ahijada	Pilachpoca	Ahijada, name
So-God-So So-God-Da Da-God-So Da-God-Da	Hermano or hermana espiritual	Pilaicnime	Name
God-Fa Br God-Mo Br	Tío	Pilactio	Tío, name
God-Fa Si God-Mo Si	Tía	Pilactia	Tía, name
God-Fa Fa God-Mo Fa	Padrino	Pilacocoltzi	Abuelito
God-Fa Mo God-Mo Mo	Madrina	Pilazitzi	Abuelita
Co-Fa-Co-Fa Br Co-Fa Br-Co-Fa	Compadre	Cumpaletzi	Compadrito
Co-Mo-Co-Mo Br Co-Mo Br-Co-Mo	Compadre or comadre	Cumpaletzi or cumaletzi	Compadrito or comadrita
Co-Fa-Co-Fa Si Co-Fa Si-Co-Fa	Comadre or compadre	Cumaletzi or cumpaletzi	Comadrita or compadrito
Co-Mo-Co-Mo Si Co-Mo Si-Co-Mo	Comadre	Cumaletzi	Comadrita
Co-Fa-Co-Fa Fa Co-Fa Fa-Co-Fa	Compadre	Cumpaletzi	Compadrito
Co-Mo-Co-Mo Fa Co-Mo Fa-Co-Mo	Compadre or comadre	Cumpaletzi or cumaletzi	Compadrito or comadrita
Co-Fa-Co-Fa Mo Co-Fa Mo-Co-Fa	Comadre or compadre	Cumaletzi or cumpaletzi	Comadrita or compadrito

TABLE 25 (*cont.*)

Category	Spanish Term of Reference	Nahuatl Term of Reference	Term of Address
Co-Mo-Co-Mo Mo Co-Mo Mo-Co-Mo	Comadre	Cumaletzi	Comadrita
Co-Fa-Co-Fa Fa Fa Co-Fa Fa Fa-Co-Fa	Compadre	Cumpaletzi	Compadrito
Co-Mo-Co-Mo Fa Fa Co-Mo Fa Fa-Co-Mo	Compadre or comadre	Cumpaletzi or cumaletzi	Compadrito or comadrita
Co-Fa-Co-Fa Mo Mo Co-Fa Mo Mo-Co-Fa	Comadre or compadre	Cumaletzi or cumpaletzi	Comadrita or compadrito
Co-Mo-Co-Mo Mo Mo Co-Mo Mo Mo-Co-Mo	Comadre	Cumaletzi	Comadrita

Tetlanochca, Cuauhtenco, Xaltipac, Tepatlachco, Teolocholco, San Isidro, San Pablo de Monte, Cuahuixmatla, Acxotla del Monte, and Mazatecochco. Among other things, the survival until recently of this ritual kinship terminology in Belén attests to the immediate Indian past of the community; hence something more should be said about it. The two terms most widely used in the Nahuatl system, *cumpaletzi* (cofather) and *cumaletzi* (comother), are of course nothing more than Nahuatlized versions of the terms compadre and comadre. The other nine terms of reference, on the other hand, are Nahuatl and Spanish compounds. All nine are derivative ritual kinship terms; seven are composed of real Nahuatl kinship terms, and two of a real Spanish kinship term, in both instances preceded by the Nahuatl prefix *pila*, which can be loosely translated from Tlaxcalan Nahuatl as adopted or spiritual kinsman. Thus, padrino (godfather) is *pilatatzi*, or spiritual father; madrina (godmother) is *pilanantzi*, or spiritual mother; ahijado (godson) is *pilacone*, or spiritual son; ahijada (goddaughter) is *pilachpoca*, or spiritual daughter; and so on. The term *pilaicnime* means literally spiritual sibling and stood for the children of compadres, who could also refer to each other as *pilaicni*, spiritual brother, or *pilaihuelti*, spiritual sister. The terms *pilactio* and *pilactia* stood for godparents' brothers and sisters, that is, spiritual uncles and aunts. The terms *pilacocoltzi* and *pilazitzi* stood for godparents' mother and father, that is, spiritual grandparents. Finally, the terms cumpaletzi and cumaletzi were applied to a range of ritual kinship categories basically the same as those covered by the terms compadre and comadre. Thus, beyond the change from Nahuatl terms to Spanish terms, the ritual kinship terminology of Belén has not changed much since the turn of the century. The term for godfather's father and godmother's father is now padrino instead of grandfather, and godfather's mother and god-mother's mother is now madrina instead of grandmother, although bas-ically the Nahuatl term in this category has been preserved in the term of address for these two instances, that is, *abuelito* and *abuelita*, in Span-ish. It is interesting that in several of the communities on the western slopes of La Malintzi, where the Nahuatl ritual kinship terminology is still in use, there is a rather marked distinction between terms of address and terms of reference, across the whole terminological spectrum. For example, to the term of reference pilacone there corresponds the term of address *nocnitzi*; and to pilachpoca there corresponds *nochnictzi*. Also, not infrequently the term for co-parents-in-law (*consuegros* in Spanish), *huehuepohuitl*, applies generically to compadres. These and several other Nahuatl ritual kinship usages in contemporary rural Tlaxcala indicate that ritual kinship terminology has always been intimately associated with and based upon real kinship terminology. This applies also to Be-lén, where the change has been primarily linguistic—that is, a change from Nahuatl to Spanish terminology but with the retention of basically the old kinship associations.

Table 25 shows that there are some fairly significant differences be-tween ritual kinship terms of reference and terms of address. First, the most widespread difference is among compadres, who always use the diminutive as a term of address. In fact, this is a universal aspect of ritual kinship terminological usage in Belén, for I do not recall a single instance of compadres addressing each other except by the terms com-padrito or comadrita. Indeed, to address one's compadres by the appro-priate term of reference is a significant breach of etiquette, and explicitly denotes displeasure and antagonism. Cases have been known in which a compadrazgo relationship came to an end because one of the com-padres thought that the other was angry at him and called him "com-padre" instead of "compadrito." So unusual is this breach of etiquette that in this case it was assumed by the person in question that it was his compadre's intention to terminate the relationship, and nothing more was ever said. Second, on some occasions even ahijados call their pa-drinos by the appropriate diminutive of "padrinito" and "madrinita," but this is not a common occurrence. Third, padrinos may occasionally call their ahijados by their given names, but this again does not happen often. Fourth, padrinos' brothers and sisters are sometimes addressed by ahijados by their given names rather than as *tios* or *tias*, and this terminological usage appears to be gaining wide acceptance in the com-munity. The most significant difference is that ahijados refer to their padrinos' parents as "padrino" and "madrina" but address them as "abuelito" and "abuelita," which is an application of the rule of non-generational crossing, as I discuss shortly. Fifth, ahijados and their padrinos' children refer to each other as spiritual brothers and sisters, but address each other by their given names. Finally, of widespread usage in Belén and rural Tlaxcala are the terms of address and reference *compadrito grande* (elder male ritual kinsman) and *comadrita grande* (elder female ritual kinsman) for the parents and grandparents of the compadres-compadres dyad.

Table 25 also shows that there are six basic ritual kinship terms: compadre, comadre, padrino, madrina, ahijado, and ahijada. The sociological implications of this have been discussed in the preceding chapters. Within the terminological system these six are elementary terms, but, strictly speaking, they are derivative terms composed of a real kinship term plus a prefix or suffix. In addition, there are other terms that are strictly elementary terms, for they are real kinship terms which have a range of application denoting the original real kinsmen. These are *hermano* (brother), *hermana* (sister), *tío* (father's or mother's brother), *tía* (father's or mother's sister), *abuelo* (father's or mother's father), and *abuela* (father's or mother's mother). There are no intrinsically significant sociological implications or correlations attached to the linguistic structure of ritual kinship terms in Belén, except that they clearly show how the real kinship system influences the structure of the ritual kinship system. The latter borrows terms from the former and applies them in real kinshiplike fashion; more important, the configuration of the latter is based on principles fundamentally similar to those of the former.

With regard to the scope and range of application of ritual kinship terms in Belén, they are primarily classificatory. Of the fourteen derivative and elementary terms of the system, only two are really denotative terms, namely ahijado and ahijada. These are never applied to any category except male or female mediating entities, and symbolically to mediating entities that are images, objects, or occasions. The other twelve terms are classificatory in that they apply to more than one ritual kinship category. Hernano and hermana apply reciprocally to ahijados and godparents' children, and are the most denotative. In the same category are the terms tío and tía and abuelito and abuelita (combining both terms of address and reference), while padrino and madrina are slightly less denotative, as they apply to the category of godparents as well as their siblings. The terms compadre and comadre, on the other hand, are highly classificatory, as they apply not only to the compadres-compadres dyad, but to thirteen other dyads of the system. In other words, compadre and comadre are by far the most widely used and sociologically significant kinship terms, as they indicate in a classificatory fashion fourteen of the twenty-two possible single or dyadic categories of the system.

The ritual kinship terminology of Belén, and this is more or less uniformly the case not only in Tlaxcala but in most of Mesoamerica, always takes scrupulous account of the sexual component, for there is no ritual kinship category that does not distinguish the sex of the person in both terms of address and terms of reference. On the other hand, the terminology makes no distinction between consanguineally and affinally related ritual kinsmen throughout the entire categorical spectrum. For example, all the classificatory extensions of the terms compadre and comadre apply to the spouses, at all generational levels and lineally and collaterally, of the categories denoted in table 25 (though for simplicity's sake I did not include them in it). The last formally significant property of the ritual kinship terminology of Belén is that there is no intergenerational crossing within primary ritual kinship; use of the terms ahijado and ahijada, on the one hand, and compadre, comadre, padrino, and madrina, on the other, does not obtain among persons of different generations. I discussed this in connection with the structure of anomalous compadrazgo (see "Compadrazgo Types Including Personnel Who Function As Ahijados and Compadres at the Same Time" in Chapter Two), and I can add here merely that this is not only a terminological property of the system but also a fundamental principle of the institution in action. Intergenerational terminological usage accompanied by sociological generational status can only take place temporarily, as in ANDI compadrazgo. The young madrina is addressed as "madrina" by the compadres of the relationship and by the people at large as she functions as a madrina during the rites and ceremonies associated with the occasion, but when these come to an end she reverts to her status of ahijada, as her generation requires, and is henceforth addressed as "ahijada." Similarly, in sacada a misa compadrazgo the ahijada reverts to her status of comadre, by virtue of being of the same generation as the madrina. These principles apply to primary actors (read ritual kinsmen) throughout the total spectrum of the ritual kinship terminology. The intergenerational principle does not apply to secondary and tertiary actors, however, especially in the classificatory range of the terms compadre and comadre, which may include individuals separated by one and occasionally two generations, as when primary actors (read compadres-compadres) extend ritual kinship terminological usage to their respective grandparents. This is perhaps one of the few really significant differences in the terminological systems of real and ritual kinship in Belén. Finally, the ritual kinship terminology of Belén does not take into account the relative age or sex of ritual kinsmen, with the following exception: the terms compadre and comadre are sometimes extended by padrinos to their ahijados' elder siblings, especially if there is a considerable age difference between the siblings (say, fifteen to twenty years) and the padrinos themselves are not very old. This terminological usage corresponds structurally to the terminological differentiation between "older brother" and "younger brother" or "older sister" and "younger sister" in a real kinship system. The ritual kinship terminology of Belén does not, however, have other formal properties equivalent to the standards generally employed in analyzing real kinship terminological systems, namely, the criteria of collaterality, bifurcation, polarity, and descent.

I have said that table 25 shows the widest possible range of application of the ritual kinship terminology of Belén, but in one sense this is not exact; on some occasions the terms compadre and comadre can be extended to the grandparents of the compadres dyad of primary actors. I did not include this extension in table 25 because these occasions are not numerous, and they can be subsumed under the general rubric of tertiary ritual kinsmen. Furthermore, things get blurred at the outermost limits of the terminological usage, and use of the correct ritual kinship terminology has little more than symbolic value. With this proviso, I can now turn to the range of application of the terminological system to the compadrazgo types of Belén. So far, I have regarded the terminological system strictly as a system involving formal and linguistic properties, potentially applicable to any of the compadrazgo types in Belén. What I want to do now is determine how the system actually applies to the thirty-one types, showing not only the range of application of the set of ritual kinship terms, but also the anomalies and regulations that go with it. More detailed data would be desirable, but I can nevertheless make some meaningful generalizations. To begin with, in table 2 the extension of well-defined patterns of kinship behavior and appropriate kinship terminological usage to the thirty-one compadrazgo types in Belén is shown in terms of primary, secondary, and tertiary relatives or actors. Before I go on, let me explain more fully what I mean by those three categories within the more restricted context of ritual kinship terminology.

Primary, Secondary, and Tertiary Ritual Kinsmen

In the first place, the threefold division of ritual kinsmen in terms of primary, secondary, and tertiary is based primarily on categories of real kinship on both sides of the compadres-compadres dyad; they are not entirely coterminous, however, and this is why I have wavered in calling these categories compadrazgo actors or compadrazgo relatives. The term actor seems to me preferable, since there is no strict correlation between real kinship and ritual kinship. On the other hand, it also seems appropriate to use the term relative in the analysis of ritual kinship behavior, for in this context the term may acquire connotations of real kinship behavior.

For my purposes here, primary actors refer exclusively to the two main dyads of any compadrazgo type, namely, the compadres-compadres dyad—the ritual sponsors themselves, and the owners, parents, or real kinsmen of the mediating entity, on the one hand; and the padrinos-ahijados dyad, on the other. The third dyad of the central core of any compadrazgo type, that is, the ahijados-parents (owners, real kinsmen) dyad, does not play a significant role in this discussion. When it does apply (that is, when the compadrazgo type involves living ahijados), for all intents and purposes it can be subsumed under the parental side of the compadres-compadres dyad, among other things because ahijados in this context are real kinsmen (that is, they are children, parents, or collateral relatives). In summary, then, primary compadrazgo actors or ritual kinsmen or relatives belong exclusively to the above three categories, which under normal circumstances consist of two padrinos, one ahijado, and two parents or closely related kinsmen. Of course, the situation is greatly complicated in the case of multiple-dyad compadrazgo types such as marriage, PCA, or ANDI. In such cases the primary actors may be multiplied as much as tenfold, and analysis cannot be undertaken simply in terms of extensions of kinship terminology. Rather, this dimension shrinks considerably in importance and other considerations enter into the picture, as I note in Chapter Twelve.

Secondary actors may be defined and analyzed in two different ways or from slightly different perspectives. From the viewpoint of ritual kinship behavior it is better to refer to compadrazgo personnel as relatives rather than actors, because the patterns of interaction are more closely parallel, and because the two systems are also more closely coterminous. From the viewpoint of ritual kinship terminology, however, it is better to regard personnel as actors. Thus, in this context secondary actors may be defined as the personnel immediately adjacent to primary actors, both from the viewpoint of real kinship and from that of the skewing elements that in Belén characterize real and ritual kinship alike. (In the ethnographic outline of Belén I pointed out that the kinship system of the community has a rather strong patrilineal bias [see *Ritual Kinship* I, page 45]. While it must be regarded as essentially a cognatic system, it has several ambilateral elements which strongly emphasize the patrilineal line, and especially the recognition of closer association of ego with patrilineal relatives. Moreover, this is reinforced by the fact that the parajes, which in Belén are significant settlement units, are basically conglomerates of patrilineally related households. Under these cir-

cumstances, it is no wonder that the extension of ritual kinship terminology in Belén follows closely this cleavage of real kinship.) Secondary
actors, then, would theoretically include ahijados' siblings, padrinos'
siblings and parents, and parents' or owners' siblings and parents. Given
the patrilineal bias of kinship in Belén, however, the effective extension
of ritual kinship terminology is confined to padrinos' siblings and parents, and fathers or male owners' siblings and parents. Moreover, ahijados' siblings, older or younger, are not important in the terminological system, either from the intergenerational or intragenerational
viewpoints, and for all practical purposes they can be left out. Secondary actors thus involve the following ritual kinship categories: compadres' (padrinos') brothers, sisters, fathers, and mothers; and compadres' (fathers', owners') brothers, sisters, fathers, and mothers, that
is, eight possibly effective categories of real kinsmen on both sides of
the compadre-compadre dyad.

Tertiary actors involve two kinds of personnel: individual categories
immediately adjacent to secondary actors in terms of real kinship; and
real kinship categories left out as secondary actors because of the skewing produced by the patrilineal bias of the real kinship system. Thus,
tertiary actors include the following kinship categories: compadres'
(padrinos') grandfathers and grandmothers; comadres' (madrinas')
brothers, sisters, mothers, and fathers; compadres' (fathers', owners')
grandfathers and grandmothers; comadres' (mothers', owners') brothers, sisters, mothers, and fathers. Furthermore, under the rubric of tertiary actors can be included extensions of kinship terminological usage
to more distant relatives. These occasions are rare and not important in
the total assessment of the extensions of ritual kinship terminology.

It is appropriate at this point to discuss the nature of this threefold
classification with respect to the extension of effective patterns of ritual
kinship behavior, and to determine how they differ from the extension
of ritual kinship terminology. (In this discussion actors are called relatives, for the reasons given above.) Differences between the threefold
classification in terms of actors and relatives, as applied respectively to
the regulation of ritual kinship terminology and ritual kinship behavior,
center primarily on the patrilineal bias of the real kinship system of
Belén. Thus, primary relatives are primary actors plus a few secondary
actors; secondary relatives are secondary actors plus a few tertiary actors; and tertiary relatives are tertiary actors plus the widest possible
extension, both ideally and actually, of ritual kinship terminology and
behavior. In other words, ritual kinship relatives, as embodying fairly
well delineated behavior patterns, are always more extensive than the
kinship terminological range embodied in the same threefold category.
This means that at the outer fringe of any compadrazgo type there are

always individuals who may not be addressed by the appropriate kinship terminology, but to whom fairly well defined patterns of behavior are extended. Still, the patterns of ritual kinship behavior associated with the threefold classification of relatives tend to balance the patrilineal bias of Belén real kinship system by according compadrazgo recognition to matrilateral relatives on a variety of occasions. Thus, when a compadrazgo type requires the participation of the maximum extension of the network of ritual kinsmen, the occasion will include perhaps not as many patrilineal relatives as the normal discharge of the kinship system would, but it will include a considerable number of matrilateral relatives. Such occasions are not infrequent in Belén, and a marriage celebration, for example, may involve the participation and cooperation of the entire spectrum of possible relatives, down to the outermost fringes of tertiary relatives.

In any event, primary relatives include all primary actors plus the compadres' parents, and on occasion, some of the compadres' brothers; secondary relatives include all secondary actors plus the compadres' grandparents, and on occasion, some of the comadres' parents and siblings; and tertiary relatives include all tertiary actors plus the comadres' grandparents, and on occasion, more distant relatives, mostly collaterals. Thus the category of tertiary relatives is virtually coterminous with that of tertiary actors, for, as I have already noted, at the outermost fringes of the system, the differences do not involve any really signficant structural properties. In summary, while the distinction between actors and relatives is meaningful at the primary and secondary levels, it is not really so at the tertiary level. Moreover, other factors must be taken into consideration in analyzing the ritual kinship system (both terminologically and behaviorally), which cannot possibly emerge at this level, but which become explicit when individual compadrazgo types are analyzed. This is another of the differences between the kinship system and the compadrazgo system, and often it is more appropriate to compare the former with a specific compadrazgo type. With this background, I am now in a position to analyze tables 2 and 3.

A word of explanation is, however, necessary. Table 2 really covers two structural attributes under a single entry, for despite the clear notion of the distinction between primary, secondary, and tertiary actors and relatives, I do not quite control the detailed data necessary to activate the distinction throughout the thirty-one compadrazgo types. Thus table 2 really denotes the maximum extension of compadrazgo behavior of relatives. What this extension of ritual kinship terminology to primary, secondary, and tertiary actors means, primarily, is that in five compadrazgo types (bautizo, casamiento, PCE, bendición de casa, and parada de cruz) the appropriate kinship terminological usage described in table 25 applies to primary, secondary, and tertiary actors, that is, the maximum degree of extension; in sixteen compadrazgo types (confirmación, primera comunión, CCCH, CCCA, ANDC, ANDI, BSI, CSV, escapulario, PCA, sacada a misa, compadrazgo de evangelios, compadrazgo de limpia, BM, primera piedra, CABP) the kinship terminological usage applies to primary and secondary actors; and in ten compadrazgo types (AOI, graduación, quince años, BOI, BCC, compadrazgo de amistad, aretes, CEON, FC, JJ) the usage applies only to primary actors, that is, the minimum extension. Thus, in a quince años compadrazgo relationship, only the padrinos, the ahijado, and the parents of the ahijado will be bound to address each other by the appropriate compadrazgo terms. For a variety of reasons, however, such as previous compadrazgo ties, degree of closeness among primary actors and their families, and factors of friendship and neighborhood, it is quite common in these ten types to transcend the strict range of primary actors and call some secondary actors by the appropriate compadrazgo term At the opposite extreme, the five types with maximum extension seldom actually, extend the full terminological spectrum of table 25. There are always categories of ritual kinsmen at the fringes of the system who, for a variety of reasons, are not accorded terminological recognition, regardless of the importance of the compadrazgo type. In the sixteen compadrazgo types in the middle position, on the other hand, the appropriate kinship term is in fact extended to secondary actors. This group of types, which includes slightly over 50 percent of the total, represents the average actual extension of ritual kinship terms.

The people of Belén are always conscious of the terminological extensions associated with each compadrazgo type and when in doubt will extend the use of ritual kinship terms beyond the prescribed extensions. At the same time, there is a conscious tendency to limit the range of application at the outermost edge of the system, for purposes of maintaining a manageable and recognizable individual compadrazgo network, or, in the words of one informant "para que no se chotee el asunto y resultemos todos compadres" (so that the matter does not become a joke and we all become compadres). In any event, the question of the extension of ritual kinship terms revolves primarily around the extension of the terms compadre and comadre, for all other terms in table 25 fall more or less within well-specified and discrete situations about which there can be no mistake. What it means in action to be called by a given compadrazgo term can best be analyzed in connection with ritual kinship behavior. I can finish the discussion here by pointing out that the breakdown of ritual kinship terminology extensions in terms of primary, secondary, and tertiary actors correlates quite well with the scaling of compadrazgo types presented in table 12. For example, four

of the five compadrazgo types (bautizo, casamiento, PCE, and bendición de casa) in which terminological usage is extended to tertiary relatives, rank at the very top of table 12.

Ritual Kinship and the Degree of Incest Prohibition

The other signficant attribute associated with the primary, secondary,
and tertiary division of ritual terminological extensions is the degree of
incest prohibition. Certain incest prohibitions, including both marriage
and mating, obtain in nearly half the compadrazgo types in Belén (see
table 3), beyond the padrinos-ahijados dyad, which always has an incest
prohibition. Before I can analyze this situation, however, I must discuss
in some detail the ideology that underlies the incest prohibition, not
only concerning ritual kinship, but also real kinship, on which it is in
fact based.

I noted in connection with the regulation of marriage in Belén (see
Ritual Kinship I, pp. 46-47) that people are not allowed to marry within
the third degree of consanguinity, or as the people put it, "con primos
terceros" (with third cousins). Moreover, Beleños in general are always
very concerned with not breaking the prescribed extensions of the incest
taboo, and people who have broken the taboo are regarded as little
better than animals. They are treated so roughly, in fact, that they must
leave the community. This, of course, happens very rarely, and in the
memory of my oldest informants it had happened only three times in
the comunity since roughly 1890, the last time being in 1948. In two
cases the couples involved left of their own accord, but in the last incident, the couple (second cousins) went to Tlaxcala to get married and
returned to Belén to live. Immediately upon learning of the marriage, a
large number of villagers, led by the fiscales, forcibly removed the couple from the community with the full consent of the two families. There
is such a dread of breaking the incest taboo that people with the same
name will rarely marry, or at least will be strongly urged not to by their
kinsmen, even when no possible blood relationship can be traced. This
fear of the incest taboo has passed on to the compadrazgo system without decreasing in intensity. Since compadrazgo is a less visible system
than real kinship, the people are especially careful to comply with the
prescription of incest extensions. The immediate ideological underpinnings of this complex of beliefs rest on the fact that the bonds of compadrazgo in Belén bind people together as if they were real kinsmen,
and that basically the same prescriptions and prohibitions apply (or, to
be more precise, apply for specific compadrazgo types). Thus, according to the compadrazgo ideology, the padrinos not only become the
symbolic "parents" of the ahijados, but in a very real sense, ahijados

and padrinos become real kinsmen. At the same time, the relationship among compadres becomes regulated by the real kinship status of siblings; that of secondary actors by the real kinship status of siblings or parents; and that among tertiary actors by the real kinship status of parents or grandparents. All these real kinship degrees of consanguinity involve strong incest prohibitions in Belén, and are thereby extended to compadrazgo relationships according to the symbolic and structural importance of compadrazgo types in a descending degree of extension. Before analyzing how the extension of the incest prohibition works across the spectrum of compadrazgo types in Belén, I must amplify the substantive meaning of the complex.

The marriage prohibition involved in the incest taboo is seldom broken in Belén, even when extended to tertiary actors. Informants could not recall a single case of marriage between ahijados and padrinos of any compadrazgo type in Belén, though individuals related within the secondary and tertiary degree of compadrazgo relationship have been known to marry. In such cases, there is very strong social and religious disapproval, and almost invariably the couples in question have had to leave the community. One notorious case took place in 1952, when a baptismal padrino, upon becoming a widower, married his ahijado's father's sister. This was a serious offense, and the man in question—one of the richest men in the community—made it public after eloping with the woman to be married in Tlaxcala, foolishly hoping that the people of Belén would overlook the incident. This was not the case, however, and the couple was forced to leave the community within a week. Not only that, but the families of the couple in question suffered social and religious repercussions for having been unable to prevent such a flagrant contravention of custom. It is difficult to say how often the compadrazgo incest taboo is broken; it does happen occasionally, but this is usually associated with compadrazgo types that rank rather low in the ideological and structrual scale. In such cases it appears that the immediate public outcry is not violent enough to drive the culprits out of the community at once, but the cumulative social, religious, and economic pressures and sanctions have the same effect sooner or later. Of the twelve cases of ritual kinship incest recorded since the 1880s, only two involved near primary actors (one of whom was the baptismal padrino described above); the others involved either secondary or tertiary actors, and in all ten cases the couples eventually left Belén, The incest taboo is as strong in the compadre-compadre dyad of primary actors as it is in the padrinos-ahijados dyad, and I have no case on record of such a transgression.

Incest in this context refers to both marriage and mating, and the taboo is less strictly observed for sporadic sexual unions. Our informants universally agreed that as long as primary actors are not involved, people generally prefer to ignore such incidents, There are, of course, no permanent or even fairly long-lasting incestuous compadrazgo relationships, only incidental sexual unions, which stop immediately if they become known to the people at large, or even to the immediate families. Here again, no sexual transgression involving padrinos and ahijados or compadres (padrinos) and compadres (parents, owners) has ever been reported. Such a transgression would be regarded as incest committed between siblings or parents and siblings, and therefore most abhorrent to the people of Belén. What does sometimes occur are sexual relationships involving ritual kinsmen in the secondary and tertiary degree of relationship, usually of the same generation, such as compadres' (padrinos) siblings with compadres' (parents, owners) siblings, or tertiary actors on either side of the primary compadres-compadres dyad and ahijados or ahijados' siblings. When these transgressions become known to the people at large there are no public outcries or expressions of disgust, but sub rosa the couple involved, and its respective families as well, may suffer some serious social and religious consequences which can have a permanent effect upon their lives. If the transgression becomes known only to the families involved, these do their utmost to keep it a secret so that they will not suffer in turn. Finally, it appears that more incestuous sexual unions occur than informants were willing to admit, but as long as they remain a secret they do no harm, except psychologically, to the couples involved. Intensive interviewing, especially of old women, showed clearly that incestuous sexual unions of ritual kinsmen cause the culprits a high degree of psychological disturbance: feelings of guilt, inadequate personal control, personal and religious shame, and so on. It is also clear that incestuous sexual unions involving compadrazgo actors are extemporaneous, although they can lead to a fairly sustained sexual relationship, which cannot possibly last for more than a few weeks before being discovered. Most incestuous unions, however, are usually uncontrolled acts occurring under the influence of liquor or in special circumstances, which do not go beyond one or two encounters.

I can now interpret table 3, which indicates that the incest taboo is extended to tertiary actors in two compadrazgo types; to secondary actors in four types; and to primary actors in eleven types; fourteen types involve no marriage or sexual prohibitions, except the universal prohibition against mating or marriage between padrinos and ahijados. Thus, there are varying definitions of what constitutes incest among the thirty-one compadrazgo types in Belén. Here again, there is a high correlation between the degree of incest extension and the general ranking of compadrazgo types presented in table 12. For example, baptism and PCE, extending incest prohibitions to tertiary compadrazgo, rank at the very top of table 12; CEON, FC, and JJ, ranking near the bottom, have no extension beyond what might be termed nuclear incest.

When I say that there are fourteen types in Belén with no incest prohibitions, I mean there are no prohibitions beyond the ahijados-padrinos dyad. In practice, however, the prohibition also applies to primary actors, for although there is no actual injunction against marriage or mating among the members of the compadres-compadres dyad (marriage in the case of widowhood or widowerhood, of course), the people de facto extend the incest prohibition to this dyad, thereby involving the two main dyads of compadrazgo. This, of course, results from the generalized fear of incest, for informants unanimously agreed that primary compadres falling in this category (in table 3 the "none" column) have never customarily married upon the death of their spouses, and their relationship as compadres endured for life. This applies equally to mating. In the eleven cases in table 3 in the "primary" column, those bound by the incest prohibition are primary actors plus compadres-compadres' parents. In the four cases in the "secondary" column, the incest prohibition extends to secondary actors plus the immediate lineal ascendants of the latter. In the two cases in the "tertiary" column, the incest prohibition applies to the whole range of possible extensions of ritual kin bound by ritual kinship terminology and behavior.

This preoccupation with kinship and compadrazgo incest prohibitions seriously constrains marriage selection, for Belén is a small community in which most people are related by some kind of compadrazgo relationship. This explains a good deal about the high incidence of extra-communal compadrazgo in Belén, at least during the past 100 years or so. Beleños try to increase the number of potential marriage partners within the community by establishing compadrazgo relationships with neighboring villages, especially those near Belén. Preoccupation with the incest prohibition has had interesting demographic repercussions in Belén over the past century, and probably in all of the heartland of rural Tlaxcala around the slopes of La Malintzi. It has been an important part of the compadrazgo and kinship system of Belén, but recently (since roughly the mid-sixties) several prohibitions are beginning to weaken. The young people of Belén, and of several outlying communities with which Beleños have traditionally contracted compadrazgo relationships, are now on a modernizing trend. One of the things they find most distasteful is the restriction on marriage partners, with the result that incest prohibitions associated with some of the less stringent types are being disregarded. Belén and the other communites still remain traditional in this respect, however, for all important incest prohibitions are very much in force.[1]

The Extension of Ritual Kinship Terminology and Incest Prohibitions

I move now to some general considerations regarding the extension of kinship terminology and incest prohibtions. The rules and injunctions underlying these aspects of the compadrazgo system are among the most explicit in Belén culture and society. They are internalized by children in early childhood, and can be seen in operation on many occasions throughout the yearly cycle. Consequently, this is one aspect of Belén in which discrepancies between the ideological and the structural orders are operationally held to a minimum. There are, however, exogenous considerations that can, in a variety of contexts and on various occasions, modify this close articulation, and their operation sometimes results in significant departures and omissions. In public-communal compadrazgo types the extension of incest prohibitions and ritual kinship terminology and behavior presents some inherent difficulties. In private-individual compadrazgo types, or at least in the majority of them, the extensions of terminology and incest are clearcut. They result from the outward expansion of the basic compadres-compadres dyad, and there are seldom any problems regarding whom one can marry or mate with, or whom one calls by the appropriate ritual kinship term. There are two reasons why this is not the case with public-communal compadrazgo types. In the first place, all public-communal types involve basic, multiple compadres-compadres dyads, whereas most private-individual types involve single dyads. In the second place, the total number of compadrazgo personnel in public-communal types can be so large that the situation lends itself to natural confusion, whereas private-individual types by definition involve considerably fewer people. What I wish to emphasize is that in public-communal types, the extensions of incest prohibitions and ritual kinship terminology are governed not only by rules and injunctions, but also by other consideratoins. Marriage compadrazgo, because of its multiple-dyad character and the large number of participating personnel, clearly belongs with public-communal compadrazgo.

Some examples may help to clarify this point. In marriage compadrazgo there are at least three basic compadres-compadres dyads, without counting subsidiary compadrazgo types, which implies a large number of primary, secondary, and tertiary actors. The rules of ritual kinship terminology and behavior and incest prohibitions are extended to tertiary and secondary actors, respectively (see tables 2 and 3), in practice the prohibitions and extensions are less stringent. Although the stated rules may apply to the two main dyads, the padrinos–groom's parents and the padrinos–bride's parents, they apply in a milder form to the other main dyad, groom's parents–bride's parents, and to the subsidiary compadrazgo relationships. The complexity and number of personnel involved conspire against full application of the extensions and prohibitions, and the system provides a certain leeway to keep the situation manageable. The two basic mechanisms involved are previous compadrazgo relationships among the senior personnel, which almost invariably exist in marriage compadrazgo, and the potential afforded by subsidiary personnel (padrinos de velación, arras, anillos, and the seven madrinas) for future compadrazgo relationships for the bride and the groom. In such a complicated situation, the most important operating principles are the desire to keep the functioning network manageably small, and to provide possible sources of future compadres.

The situation is even more complicated in public-communal compadrazgo types such as ANDI or PCA, and what I have said about marriage compadrazgo also applies to the multiple dyads that obtain between the padrinos and the fiscales and mayordomos (those who make the pedimento), and among the fiscales and mayordomos themselves. Here again, certain dyads are the locus of greatest intensity, but outside of these, there is a tendency to relax the rules governing the extension of incest prohibitions and ritual kinship terminology and behavior. In CSV compadrazgo, which requires a young madrina, the situation can get even more complicated. In accordance with communal wishes, those in charge of the pedimento try to choose a couple with a young daughter, but sometimes this is not possible and the chosen couple "tiene que pedir prestada una niña para que haga las funciones de madrina" (must borrow a girl to function as madrina). This means that another basic dyad is added to the already large core of dyads, for ritual kinship terminology and behavior and incest prohibitions must be extended to the parents of the "borrowed" girl.

Significant differences in terminological and behavioral extensions result from the dichotomy between the discharge of the central rites and ceremonies and events leading to them, and the permanent and recurrent rights, duties, and obligations of any compadrazgo type. (Incest prohibitions, of course, are set at the start of any compadrazgo type and are egocentrically fixed for life.) In all compadrazgo types in Belén, the rules and constraints of ritual kinship terminology and behavior are scrupulously complied with during the discharge of the central complex of rites and ceremonies and the events leading to it, and there is very little deviation from the ideological order. This is the kind of behavior described in considerable detail in Part One of *Ritual Kinship* I, and with respect to kinship terminology, I can categorically state that the participating personnel of every compadrazgo type go out of their way to address each other in the prescribed manner. This is the essential etiquette of compadrazgo in Belén, which is part play acting and part a deliberate design to impress upon the primary, secondary, and tertiary actors the importance of the rituals and their significance to the subsequent permanent aspects.[2] What follows the core of rites and ceremonies—both events recurring over a few months or a few years, and the permanent alignment of compadrazgo actors—represents the lasting bonds of compadrazgo which acquire the configuration of a system. In this social ambiance, the extension of ritual kinship terminology and behavior tends to shrink from its maximum expression as embodied in the principal ceremonies. The sum total of social, religious, economic, ritual, and ceremonial occasions on which compadrazgo actors subsequently participate on a permanent basis is by far the most important aspect of any compadrazgo type, but to some extent this is because the number of personnel is reduced.

Thus, in the average compadrazgo type in Belén, the permanent bonds, duties, and obligations are effectively extended, terminologically and behaviorally, to a group of compadrazgo actors which varies in size from 25 percent to 50 percent of its ideological maximum. For example, if a compadrazgo type extends kinship terminology and behavior to tertiary actors, in its permanent dimensions this will effectively apply only to secondary actors, and perhaps on special occasions to a few tertiary relatives. As one moves from the most important compadrazgo types with maximum extensions to the least important types with fewer extensions, differences between the discharge of the core of rites and ceremonies and the permanent dimensions of compadrazgo types diminish significantly, and extensions of ritual kinship terminology and behavior to primary actors are fairly equally effective in both the initial and the permanent dimensions of the relationship. I have also noted that some compadrazgo relationships grow cold, but this chill does not affect all compadrazgo dyads. Rather, one must think in terms of specific relationships within the large complex of dyads on the three levels of compadrazgo actors. Moreover, it must always be kept in mind that the average couple in Belén is related ritually to a large segment of the community, either directly as primary actors or indirectly as secondary or tertiary actors, and that although some of these relationships may grow cold, others are renewed by contracting new compadrazgo ties with the same people. It is therefore difficult to speak about compadrazgo extensions and prohibitions in isolation, without reference to the individual and systemic developmental cycle. If one takes into account the developmental cycle of compadrazgo in both of its forms, then it can safely be assumed that few primary, secondary, or even tertiary compadrazgo relationships in Belén really grow cold, except during the very last years of an individual's life. Anomalies such as converting padrinos into compadres (for example in marriage, sacada a misa, and

FC compadrazgo) also contribute to equalizing patterns of terminological and behavioral extensions, and help to keep alive at least the most significant individual relationships of given compadrazgo types.

Finally, I want to point out that the extension of ritual kinship terminology and behavior and incest prohibitions has a different aspect in extracommunal compadrazgo. Here the prescribed extensions and prohibitions are inherently limited by the factor of distance, and the resulting pattern of less frequent visiting and interaction. The differences are minimal in compadrazgo relationships with adjacent communities such as section 1 of San Bernardino Contla or the pueblo of San Matías Tepetomatitlán, but they are signficant in compadrazgo relationships with more distant communities. This concerns primarily the extension of ritual kinship behavior and incest prohibitions, for the application of terminological extensions remains more or less the same. In general, the decrease in the extension of incest prohibitions and especially in ritual kinship behavior is directly proportional to distance, but this again is conditioned by individual considerations and previous compadrazgo relationships. On the whole, however, the structure of participation, visiting, and fulfillment of social, religious, and economic obligations that results from distance is such that extracommunal compadrazgo relationships are seldom extended beyond a few selected secondary actors, either during the principal ceremonies or in the permanent dimensions of the relationship.

In horizontal compadrazgo relationships with personnel from rural Tlaxcala, the structure of extensions and prohibitions is basically the same but conditioned by the factor of distance. I point this out because vertical compadrazgo—contracting extracomunal compadrazgo relationships with personnel of a higher socioeconomic status—has already made its appearance in Belén and will no doubt increase (see "Asymmetry and Compadrazgo Selection," Chapter Six). In vertical compadrazgo, the situation with regard to extensions and prohibitions is not only asymmetrical but also structurally different. Such vertical relationships, usually with people of neighboring cities, fall outside the underlying principles of confianza, respeto, and reliance, and are contracted almost exclusively for economic reasons. In these circumstances, there emerges a picture of compadrazgo that cannot be accommodated within the ideological-structural articulation used in this study. For example, Beleños do not address such vertical compadres as "compadrito" but merely as "compadre," which would be a breach of etiquette in horizontal compadrazgo, both intra- and extracommunal. Moreover, the extension of kinship terminology and behavior is obviously limited to the two central dyads of compadrazgo, and one cannot really speak of extensions, for seldom if ever does the superordinate couple allow its kinsmen to participate in the web of visiting and ritual interaction. In fact, such vertical compadrazgo relationships, at least within the community, are limited to inviting the padrinos to the sponsoring occasion, to which they may or may not choose to bring their kinsmen or friends. In extracommunal vertical compadrazgo, the principal ceremonies generally take place in Belén and thus are attended by the usual actors prescribed by the compadrazgo type. But after that, the compadrazgo relationship will be the exclusive concern of the couple from Belén who sought it (and the ahijado) and the vertical padrinos from outside the community. Hence, after the ceremonies are over, the compadrazgo relationship falls outside the prescriptions of the compadrazgo type in question; the asking compadres interact with the vertical compadres almost entirely outside Belén, although once in a while the latter may be asked to the village for specific celebrations. This asymmetry places vertical compadrazgo relationships definitely outside the Belén system, and such relationships are one of the factors that will change the compadrazgo system of Belén from a sacred to a primarily secular institution in which the main component is economic or social gain.

Ritual Kinship Terminology and the Structure of Compadrazgo

At this point it can be asked to what extent the ritual kinship terminology of Belén reflects the structure of the compadrazgo system. This has been a traditional question in studies of real kinship, and it is pertinent here. Since the beginning of the modern phase of kinship studies, perhaps inaugurated by Kroeber (1909), anthropologists have consistently asked what kinship terminology represents and how it mirrors the kinship system. Many answers have been given, the most common being that kinship terminology reflects the psychology, the language, or the kinship structure of a given society. There is some validity in all three approaches, but social anthropologists must necessarily emphasize the analysis of kinship terminologies from a primarily sociological viewpoint. Thus, without agreeing entirely with Radcliffe-Brown, I think that the most fruitful approach to the analysis of kinship terminologies is to focus on showing how they reflect some structural principle or functional correlation in the corresponding kinship system. The ritual kinship terminology of Belén is essentially analogous and homologous to the community's real kinship terminology, and I can therefore analyze the former essentially as if it were an example of the latter. I confine myself here to sociological aspects, for there is little to be gained, at least within the context of this study, by analyzing ritual kinship terminology in psychological or linguistic terms.

First, the compadrazgo terminology of Belén emphasizes lineal extensions, which is quite in accordance with the general structure of the compadrazgo system. Only at the second ascending generation are there terms for collateral relatives (that is, godparents' siblings and parents' siblings). Furthermore, the lineal extensions emphasize exclusively the ascending generations, for there are no terminological extensions beyond the ahijados' generation. Unlike real kinship terminology, there are no terms that denote descent from the ahijados' generation. Ascendant lineality, then, is the reflection of two central features of the compadrazgo system in Belén: the relative importance of the mediating entity, and the greater importance of compadres' lineal ascendants (parents and grandparents) compared to collateral relatives. Furthermore, the terminological range involving ahijados is confined to six categories of ritual kinsmen (godfather, godmother, godfather's and godmother's siblings, godfather's and godmother's parents), while that involving compadres is twice as extensive (see table 25), which is again an expression of the emphasis on the compadres-compadres dyad at the expense of the ahijados dyad.

Second, while in formal terms the ritual kinship terminology of Belén is extended symmetrically to both sides of the compadres-compadres dyad, in practice it is skewed toward the padrinos' side. The range over which the prescribed terminological usage is applied always includes more kinsmen on the padrino's side than on the parents' or owners' side. Here again, a structural attribute of the compadrazgo system is exhibited in its ritual kinship terminology: those who ask to enter into a compadrazgo relationship (that is, parents, owners, or close kinsmen) bear the greater burden in making the relationship successful, which is tantamount to saying that they take greater care to extend prescribed compadrazgo behavior. The prescriptions indicated in tables 2 and 3 are more stringent on the side of parents or owners than on the side of padrinos. Nevertheless, in the total web of compadrazgo of a given individual, this is balanced by the fact that the average couple in Belén asks and is asked approximately the same number of times throughout its compadrazgo career.

Third, the symmetry of the ritual kinship terminology involving the compadres-compadres dyad (that is, the reciprocal use of the same terms, compadrito and comadrita) clearly exhibits the fundamentally symmetrical structure of the compadrazgo system in Belén. This is also exemplified by the withdrawal of such kinship terminological usage in vertical compadrazgo relationships, when Beleños do not use the diminutive.

Fourth, quite often ritual kinship terminology take precedence over real kinship terminology, and this reflects the fact that within the overall context of Belén culture and society, compadrazgo relationships may become—permanently or temporarily—more signficant than real kinship relationships. A good example is the use of compadre and comadre for the parents of the bride and groom. These terms supersede the real kinship terms *consuegro* and *consuegra* (co-father-in-law and co-mother-in-law) as terms of both address and reference, for in Belén consuegros always address each other and refer to each other as "compadres." The same applies also to other real kinship terms such as *concuño* and *concuña* (co-brother-in-law and co-sister-in-law), if there is a binding compadrazgo relationship. On certain occasions, even consanguines may address each other as "compadre" and "comadre," and in a few exceptional cases as "padrino" and "madrina," rather than by the appropriate real kinship term denoting their consanguineal relationship.

Beleños avoid establishing compadrazgo relationship with kinsmen (see "A Formal Comparison of Kinship and Compadrazgo in Belén," Chapter Twelve); one does not ask a kinsman for sponsorship, but very often consanguines are drawn into compadrazgo relationships by being part of compadres-compadres dyads, and on such occasions ritual kinship terms are used. For example, the fiscal and mayordomo in charge of making the pedimento of the PCA padrinos might well be first cousins or even brothers. Once the PCA compadrazgo is established, they become compadres de jure and de facto, and are drawn into a compadrazgo network that does not come to an end after the ceremonies of PCA compadrazgo are completed, but endures permanently. In such a situation, the cousins or brothers will thenceforth address each other as "compadres," although they may not do so when they refer to each other. Many times I have heard cousins, brothers, and even intergenerational consanguines (uncles-nephews, grandparents-parents, etc.) address each other by the appropriate compadrazgo terminology. This would have been enough to demonstrate that, structually and functionally, compadrazgo relationships—as reflected in ritual kinship terminology—do supersede real kinship relationships, but the people themselves verbalize this attitude by saying, "Muchas veces nuestros compadres se transforman en verdaderos parientes y hay que tratarlos como tal" (Very often our compadres become true kinsmen and they must be treated as such). In summary, then, the ritual kinship terminology of Belén more or less consistently exhibits certain significant operational attributes of the compadrazgo system.

CHAPTER 12

Ritual Kinship Behavior

The Principles and Mechanisms Regulating Ritual Kinship Behavior

I can now address myself exclusively to the patterns of ritual kinship behavior that govern the compadrazgo system in Belén, and here I face a rather difficult task. First, while there is great uniformity throughout the whole spectrum of the compadrazgo system with respect to the discharge of the central complex of rites and ceremonies, there is also signficant variation in the permanent patterns of behavior associated with individual types. Second, and in a sense as a corollary, there is considerable departure from prescribed patterns of behavior within the changing matrix of Belén. The people themselves, in several cases, are no longer sure what the ideological order prescribes, and this is a sure sign that the compadrazgo system is at the threshold of some major changes. This makes the analysis more difficult to the extent that I have not entirely provided a framework for dealing with situations in transition from a traditional stage to what I have called a primarily secular stage, toward which the compadrazgo system is surely headed. A third, purely substantive reason may be added to the effect that compadrazgo combines in itself an inordinate amount of information that I do not entirely command. This is especially the case for the domain of kinship behavior, in which each compadrazgo type can sometimes be regarded as a system by itself. Given these considerations, I would like to concentrate primarily on the mechanisms and attitudes that govern kinship behavior, and not so much on the activities they lead to.

Several considerations are in order before I begin the analysis. First, as I have reiterated several times, the compadrazgo system in Belén is governed basically by the principles of confianza, respeto, and reliance, and this is most noticeable in connection with ritual kinship behavior—the real, daily, observable stuff of which the system is made. Fundamentally, the analysis of ritual kinship behavior consists of the interdigitation and combination of these principles in action. I have thus already said a great deal about ritual kinship behavior, especially in Chapter Two, which deals with anomalous compadrazgo structures, Moreover, in Part One of *Ritual Kinship* I, I described compadrazgo activities and specific modes of action primarily with regard to the core of rites and ceremonies for each type, so the reader already has a broad, general idea of the ways in which compadrazgo actors behave toward one another.

Second, a fairly clear distinction must be made between the specific things that ritual kinsmen do for one another and the required rites and ceremonies that are the attributes of particular compadrazgo types, on the one hand, and the principles and mechanisms of ritual kinship behavior, on the other. Although the former are an expression of the latter, and it may often be difficult to differentiate between them, it is essential to keep them separate. The distinction is similar to the one functionalists make, although in a different context, between function and activity. The difference is that here I am not talking about the functions of ritual kinship behavior, but about the principles and mechanisms that underlie functional discharge.

Third, in the analysis of ritual kinship behavior it is of paramount importance to keep in mind three clear divisions in the structure of the compadrazgo system itself, and in the structure of individual types. The first of these is the distinction between the two main segments of all compadrazgo types: the central complex of rites and ceremonies and events leading to it; and the recurrent and permanent attributes that follow. The analysis of ritual kinship behavior must be conducted with this quasi-dichotomy in mind, for the principles and mechanisms underlying the former are specifically prescribed, while the latter involves individual choices with several variables for which the structural order cannot provide specific prescriptions. I have already described what the various compadrazgo actors do during the central ceremonies, but I have not described the permanent dimensions of the compadrazgo system as a whole. I now want to explain how the same behavioral principles apply to the two main domains of compadrazgo in Belén, and more important, to explain how they differ in application, and why. The second division is that between private-individual and public-communal compadrazgo types, which rests essentially on the fact that these two categories involve primarily single and multiple compadrazgo dyads, respectively, which—all other things being equal—may considerably alter permanent patterns of ritual kinship behavior. Under the category of public-communal compadrazgo types we must also include all anomalous types, such as those in which the padrino and madrina are not a married couple, which lead to the increase of compadrazgo dyads and extensions. These anomalous cases—that is, compadrazgo types that in number of personnel, deletion of prescribed structural attributes, and functional specifications depart from the traditional articulation of the ideological and structural orders—bring about differential changes in ritual kinship behavior, which in specific types may result in the extension, contraction, or absence of specific functions and activities.

Finally, the third division covers the analysis of the enduring aspects of the relationships in terms of the classification of compadrazgo actors into primary, secondary, and tertiary. In substantive terms, I can undertake the analysis of ritual kinship behavior only in terms of this threefold classification. I would have liked to rank the compadrazgo behavior associated with each type in terms of its prescriptive-preferential-optional attribution (see table 12), but this cannot be done at present, for controlling the data fully would have required twice as much time and personnel.[1]

The description and analysis of ritual kinship behavior that follow are thus structured along the vertical dichotomy of the central complex of rites and ceremonies versus permanent compadrazgo attributes; along the horizontal dichotomy of private-individual (single dyad, with the exception of marriage) versus public-communal (multiple dyad) compadrazgo types; and on the basis of the threefold classification of compadrazgo actors. The points of reference are primarily tables 2, 3, 14, and 16. Table 14 indicates the strength of the permanent bonds and obligations of all compadrazgo types in Belén (compadres-compadres dyad and extensions), while table 16 indicates the strength of the permanent dimensions of the padrino-ahijado dyad. These two tables use the terms "strong," "medium," "weak," or "none" to indicate the quality of the relationship. Before I discuss ritual kinship behavior, I must explain what these evaluations stand for behaviorally in some sort of quantitative terms.

The Strength of Permanent Bonds and Obligations

Table 14 shows that there are ten compadrazgo types in Belén with strong permanent bonds and obligations, fifteen types with medium, and six types with weak. This rough quantification of permanent compadrazgo behavior covers behavior above and beyond the specific rights, duties, and obligations associated with each compadrazgo type. In each type there are certain prescriptions (different in every type) associated with its permanent attributes, although for practical purposes they fall into groups which can conveniently be analyzed together. Table 14, however, indicates the strength of these permanent bonds primarily with reference to the nature of the compadrazgo actors themselves (primary, secondary, tertiary). Thus, while baptismal compadres may show the highest form of respeto and confianza, and comply scrupulously with whatever is prescribed, compadres for escapulario or CEON (ideologically less important types) may have a closer and more intimate permanent relationship, as may the extensions of these dyads. In other words, table 14 exhibits the properties that are exogenously modified beyond the intrinsic ideological position of compadrazgo types. This is why it is so important to make the analysis on the basis of primary, secondary, and tertiary actors, on the one hand; and in terms of a horizontal continuum of compadrazgo types, on the other. To analyze in terms of individual compadrazgo types means that closed systems are being considered, which makes it impossible to explore the extensive behavioral network that comes into being when the whole compadrazgo system is taken as the unit of study. The *modus operandi* here, then, is to focus on compadrazgo as a global system, rather than on individual subsystems with their own prescriptions and requirements.

When I say that a compadrazgo type (which is this context means all the compadrazgo actors bound together by recognizable behavior patterns; see table 2) involves strong permanent bonds and obligations, this means that the principles and mechanisms governing ritual kinship behavior are effective in implementing the activities prescribed by the ideological order, so that there is little discrepancy between the ideological and the structural orders. In delineating the principles and mechanisms of ritual kinship behavior in operation, I am able to show to what degree patterns of visiting, economic cooperation, religious participation, and so on, enter in the compadrazgo behavior of primary, secondary, and tertiary actors. When I say that a compadrazgo type has medium permanent bonds and obligations, this means that the principles and mechanisms governing ritual kinship behavior are only moderately effective in implementing the activities prescribed by the ideological order. In such cases, considerations exogenous to the operation of the system itself play a rather prominent role in shaping ritual kinship behavior in all its extensions. These exogenous considerations are variables or individual actions that are not contemplated in the structure of the compadrazgo type per se, but that are a general feature of the institution—for example, the compadrazgo cycle, previous compadrazgo relationships, and the like. When I say that a compadrazgo type has weak permanent bonds and obligations, this means that the principles and mechanisms governing ritual kinship behavior are ineffective with regard to the prescribed activities. While there is a statistically significant correlation between this threefold classification of the permanent strength of compadrazgo types and the ideological ranking presented in table 12, the correlation is gross, because, of course, the strong-medium-weak distinction is itself gross. This is not important at the moment, but I want to emphasize that many of these points become clear only when seen within the context of the developmental cycle of compadrazgo.

A word about the method of analysis is in order. Traditionally, real kinship behavior has been analyzed in terms of dyadic patterns within the nuclear and extended families, but beyond such elementary, domestic units, it has generally been studied (in both unilineally and bilaterally organized societies) in terms of nondyadic patterns (nonegocentrically), to include large numbers of kinsmen. My analysis of ritual kinship behavior follows much the same lines. While it is appropriate to analyze compadrazgo behavior in terms of dyadic patterns for the three central dyads of the compadrazgo system, beyond this group of individuals one cannot use this method. Compadrazgo networks of secondary and tertiary relatives must be analyzed essentially as if they were webs of kinship, in which individuals occupy nonegocentrical loci vis-à-vis the group as a whole. Kinship behavior in real kinship systems (see, e.g., Murdock 1949:37) reflects the basic structural arrangements of the domestic group and its extensions. So too, and probably to a higher degree, does the ritual kinship system of Belén, in which the whole web of primary, secondary, and tertiary actors reflects the basic organization of the central dyads. Hence, the position of any ritual kinship category, and the related compadrazgo behavior, are to a large extent the result of the original structure of the compadres-compadres dyad. What varies is essentially the degree of ritual kinship proximity and the compadrazgo type in question. Since every compadrazgo relationship in Belén, in all its extensions, has real kinsmen for at least 50 percent of its personnel, compadrazgo behavior among consanguines often supersedes real kinship behavior.

In my analysis of ritual kinship behavior I use the term relative which has a less restricted range of application than actor. Primary relatives include two dyads in addition to the central dyads of the institution, namely, those between padrinos' children and ahijados' siblings, and those between padrinos' children and parents or owners. These two dyads, however, do not play a very signficant role at the primary level of compadrazgo behavior, and for purposes of simplification, they can be analyzed separately. There are left, then, three primary dyads (compadres-compadres, padrinos-ahijados, and ahijados-parents or kinsmen) which must be analyzed basically in the dyadic pattern. Moreover, the ahijados-parents or kinsmen dyad is already tied by bonds of real kinship, and for practical purposes can also be left out.

Ritual Kinship Behavior of Primary Relatives: The Padrinos-Ahijados Dyad

As long as the pardrinos-ahijados relationship remains alive and active, and the period varies with the compadrazgo type (but often ends with the ahijados making their padrinos compadres), the relationship must be characterized as one of superordination-subordination. The ahijados must at all times show, privately and publicly, the prescribed respeto (in the literal sense) and deference due to the padrinos. Whenever they interact, especially at social and religious celebrations, the ahijados must wait upon the padrinos, seeing that they get the best seats and the best food, and strive to raise their ceremonial status. Most religious, social, ritual, or ceremonial gatherings or celebrations in Belén are marked by a clear regard for permanent or temporary status differentials among participants. For example, the way in which people are seated at a wedding or burial banquet will indicate both their permanent and temporary status vis-à-vis the occasion, and their relationship to the personnel involved. There is always leeway for honoring people by raising their status temporarily for the occasion, and this is important for ahijados between the ages of ten and roughly twenty-two. Those below that age are too young to be effective participants, while those above are already married or soon will be, and their status as ahijados (vis-à-vis certain specific padrinos) will change to that of compadres in their own right. In the few instances in which people remain ahijados until their padrinos die (there is, of course, a considerable age difference), the relationship usually grows cold, for these are among the least important compadrazgo types such as graduación, quince años, or FC. In marriage compadrazgo, on the other hand, seldom do more than three years elapse after marriage before ahijados make their padrinos compadres. This change in status from ahijado to compadre is an important structural element of compadrazgo behavior, and it is only in this sense that the padrinos-ahijados dyad acquires added importance within the total institution. The deference and respeto of ahijados toward padrinos are also strengthened by the willingness of the former to run errands and perform other small services. They are available on many social and religious occasions for which they may be needed in the house of the padrinos, or elsewhere in the community, to carry messages, chop wood, prepare food, decorate altars, attend at weddings, and take care of a host of other such jobs.

The relationship between padrinos and ahijados is warm and affectionate, and even today, not only young children but adolescents and young adults kiss the hand of their padrinos and always address them very courteously. Padrinos treat their ahijados as if they were their own children, and this often causes some friction in the padrino's family. They make presents to their ahijados and often pamper them "como lo hacen los abuelitos chochos" (like old, cranky grandparents, who play the permissive, benevolent role of "good uncles" in Belén society). As ahijados approach the age of going to work or marrying, their padrinos advise them about proper courses of action. In Belén, a girl who gets into trouble with a boy often seeks advice or even physical shelter in the household of one of her important padrinos, usually of baptism or confirmation. Padrinos intercede for ahijadas with their parents and family, and often serve as mediators in arranging the atonement ceremonies connected with elopements. Padrinos and ahijados may form very close friendships as may madrinas and ahijadas, and mild joking relationships are sometimes established between padrinos and ahijados of the same sex. On the whole the greatest communication and interaction take place between padrinos and ahijados of the same sex, and unless the situation requires action from both padrinos, the ahijado gravitates toward the godparent of the same sex.

The relationship of padrinos-ahijados is happy, evenly balanced, and marked by restraint; they ask little of each other, and both asking and giving are done with pleasure and without ostentation. Neither padrinos nor ahijados can, without grossly transcending the bounds of propriety, ask each other for money, labor exchange, or any other kind of participation or cooperation that demands a large expenditure of money, service, or other resources. (Such behavior is considered appropriate to compadres.) Padrinos and ahijados must be governed by patterns or principles of conduct reflected in respeto, deference, and even admiration on the part of ahijados; and protection, advice, and concern on the part of the padrinos. Participation and cooperation are moderate and always connected to festive occasions. Finally, the only patterns of behavior between padrinos and ahijados that survive the principal ceremonies are confined to the relatively short period of twelve years or so, when the ahijados are between the ages of ten and twenty-two.

The Contexts Involved in Compadrazgo Behavior

Before discussing the compadres-compadres dyad, I would like to describe the kinds of occasions, opportunities, and contexts involved in compadrazgo behavior. There are basically nine sets of activities, listed here in order of decreasing behavioral inclusiveness (that is, from wider to narrower extension to compadrazgo relatives, without regard to compadrazgo type): (1) salutations and patterns of etiquette; (2) patterns of visiting and immediate ceremonial exchanges; (3) ceremonial and ritual exchanges; (4) reciprocal and nonreciprocal social and religious invitations; (5) future compadrazgo intensification leading to new compadrazgo relationships; (6) political participation in ritual and ceremonial occasions; (7) required participation in ritual and ceremonial occasions; (8) direct social, religious, and economic cooperation; (9) ayuda and labor exchange. These nine sets of activities are ranked with regard to intrinsic structural significance, on the one hand; and with regard to the intensity and strength of the compadrazgo relationship, on the other. As one moves from the first to the ninth, compliance makes any compadrazgo relationship in Belén increasingly stronger and more intense; and it is only when one interdigitates this compliance in terms of compadrazgo relatives with that by compadrazgo type that one gets a general picture of compadrazgo behavior in Belén.

Salutations and patterns of etiquette refer to the overt patterns of address, the formal and informal etiquette governing the daily or sporadic interaction of compadrazgo relatives, and in general the behavior patterns of all those bound by a given compadrazgo relationship involving merely the exchange of greetings and signs of respect that express the relationship overtly. While a few compadrazgo types have special patterns of etiquette, there is a high common denominator. None of this involves the expenditure of economic, social, or religious resources, and it is the cheapest commodity in compadrazgo behavior. But as we go down the line from 1 to 9 the cost in resources increases and becomes the main factor shaping compadrazgo behavior.

Patterns of visiting and immediate ceremonial exchanges include whatever is required of a given compadrazgo type, and what the compadrazgo system as a whole prescribes. My concern here is only with the latter. The institution of compadrazgo prescribes that compadres visit each other on certain occasions, thereby leading to ceremonial exchanges. The most common occasions are the compadres' saint's days; ahijados' saint's days; the baptisms, burials, and weddings of compadres' primary real kinsmen; compadres' bendiciones de casa and paradas de cruz; the election and appointment of compadres to religious offices and the ensuing celebrations; and exchange of *ofrendas* (offerings) for the *Todos Santos* (All Saints' Day and All Souls' Day) celebration. During these occasions, the visiting compadres come to offer congratulations or support, extend greetings or condolences, offer their services and their family's—whatever is appropriate to the occasion. This almost invariably involves the presentation of a small gift or flowers leading to ceremonial exchanges. The presentation is more or less a formality, and the occasion does not require a sizable expenditure of any kind of resources.

Ceremonial and ritual exchanges are really a corollary of 2, for to a large extent these exchanges take place during the course of visits, when the visiting compadres may be asked to participate actively in some ritual or ceremonial capacity in the proceedings that are under way. Of course, those who are asked must accept the invitation, which is usually binding on everyone who came with the couple—that is, primary kinsmen, but frequently more distant kin as well. There are many ritual and ceremonial roles that compadres can play at weddings, burials, burial banquets, baptisms, and a host of other such celebrations, which vary in importance according to the compadres' status vis-à-vis the compadres hosting the occasion. All ritual and ceremonial roles are performed by compadres or kinsmen, and since one person is often both, it is difficult to tell whether kinsmen or compadres are more important for a given occasion, even a wedding or burial, in which kinship should obviously overshadow compadrazgo. The most important roles compadres play are those of speechmakers, ritual mediators, masters of certain parts of the ceremonies, ritual attendants (pallbearers for *entregas* of images, attendants in processions, altar decorators, and so on), and prayer leaders (*rezadores*). The least important roles involve helping organize ceremonial banquets, attending at banquets, serving as kitchen coordinators, and taking care of more menial jobs such as preparing food, serving at tables, and the like. This category may involve some expenditures, but they are seldom large, and tend to be confined to the immediate occasion. Sometimes, however, especially at weddings and other celebrations involving drinking and festivities, compadres may be called upon or put under indirect pressure to buy liquor or food, or to pay for more music, and this can lead to major expenditures. In general, however, this category of activities, together with the first two, represents a minimum expenditure of economic, social, and religious resources.

Reciprocal and nonreciprocal invitations to social and religious events and celebrations include invitations resulting from compadres' activities that are not specified by prescribed compadrazgo behavior—except, of course, by the general prescription based upon the principles of respeto and confianza. The first three categories are part of prescribed compadrazgo behavior in general; the other six are not, and they must be conceptualized as falling within the range of options open to compadres and compadrazgo relatives in general. In my previous terminology (see, e.g., "Prescriptive, Preferential, and Optional Compadrazgo Types" in Chapter Five), then, the first three are prescriptive, while the other six are preferential or optional. Included in this category are direct invitations to compadres to participate in specific capacities in religious or social celebrations in which the asking compadres play a leading role. Acceptance is not required, but is almost invariably forthcoming. While it is not predicated on the assurance that the asking compadre will accept a similar invitation, in practice there is considerable reciprocity. The social or religious occasions are essentially the same as those described for the third category, although here there is a greater emphasis on religious celebrations or the formation of groups of officers in the local hierarchy—for example, becoming an attendant or mayordomo of a given mayordomía, assuming a secondary position in the República Eclesiástica, such as fiscal segundo or *tercero* (third in command), or taking on similar positions in several other contexts. Acceptance in this case requires an outlay of resources in kind, cash, or services, and the compadres who are asked can refuse without facing disapproval or sanctions of any kind. What makes the system balanced are the mechanisms of reciprocity inherent in Belén culture.

Future compadrazgo intensification leading to new compadrazgo relationships includes what amounts to the events leading to a new pedimento. If compadres wish to ask as padrinos, usually for a very important occasion, a couple to whom they are already linked by one or more compadrazgo, they deliberately cultivate the couple in question by lavishing upon them invitations and even presents, so that they will be predisposed to accept the new compadrazgo relationship. Of course, Beleños know that prospective compadres, whether previously related or not, must accept whenever asked, given the sacred nature of the institution, but they feel that the sacred must not be abused. Thus, they readily admit that the invitations, attentions, and presents showered upon a couple already related to them are a compensatory mechanism. I include these activities as part of compadrazgo behavior because they are not sporadic, but rather recur again and again in the compadrazgo careers of the average couple in Belén. The invitations do not cost the prospective compadres anything; on the contrary, they profit from the presents they receive, but these activities have to be placed at the middle level of the ranking because they will eventually lead to considerable economic, social, and religious expenditures when the couple becomes for a second or a third time the compadres of the asking couple.

Every individual in Belén who seeks political office, be it in the civil administration or in the República Eclesiástica, either in the group of the fiscales or in the various mayordomias, must generally rely on compadres for support. In fact, to a large extent recruitment for the civil and religious organization of the community is firmly anchored in the compadrazgo system. One asks compadres to support one's candidacy for office, and the more compadres one can muster, the better the chances for nomination or election. It is not altogether simple to get political support from compadres, however, for often there are conflicting interests, and not all of a couple's compadres can or will support a given candidate. Political support involves outlays which can sometimes be high; individuals must often choose between compadres, for more than one candidate may be related to them by compadrazgo ties. Beleños tend to maximize their own economic, social, and religious interests, which may not always coincide with those of their compadres. There is always a price to pay in making choices, be it in withdrawal of future support from the affected compadres, ill feelings, or even economic consequences, if the compadres in question have dealings in common. Nevertheless, the webs of compadrazgo—networks of compadres united by the ties of common interest, neighborhood, and intensified compadrazgo relationships above and beyond the inherent attributes of a single relationship—tend to limit the choices regarding political support for office. For example, there are well-known compadrazgo networks in Belén which tend to limit conflict in the sense that if a couple has compadres who belong to a network other than its own, it simply does not ask for their support. Conflict about choices arises when the networks are not well defined, as often happens in a system as fluid as compadrazgo. This is potentially a critical area of action and behavior. To support one compadre candidate against another is an overt, public choice which often leads to the termination of the relationship between the couples involved, or at least to its growing cold. In any event, one of the most important realities in the social life of Belén is membership in an adequate compadrazgo network, and couples are concerned with this from the very start of their compadrazgo careers.

Required participation in ritual and ceremonial occasions denotes basically what has been described in the third and fourth categories, but with the proviso that participation is not by invitation but rather by reason of certain constraints that oblige compadres to participate on specific occasions, contributing importantly to the event or office being sponsored. The participation, which might better be termed contribution, is often worked out in advance between the asked and asking compadres. The occasions, events, or offices are the same as those described in the third and fourth categories, but with an even greater emphasis on the religious and symbolic, and less on the social. The context is quite different because of the constraints, implicit or explicit, that oblige compadres to accept. These constraints involve reciprocation for previous similar involvements, the intrinsic importance of the compadrazgo type, the position within the compadrazgo network of the couple being asked, and a series of other intangibles which virtually transform this intrinsically preferential kind of participation into a required or prescribed one. The most important of these occasions or offices is becoming a contributing componente to a mayordomía or to the *Fiscalía* (the group of the fiscales), sponsoring a breakfast or other ceremonial event connected with a fiesta cycle of which a given couple is the principal or exclusive sponsor, or simply contributing in kind or cash to any of the major celebrations connected with the religious cycle. This situation occurs rarely in a strictly social domain, with the possible exception of burial and the rites and ceremonies surrounding it. In many ways, these activities become the strongest ties binding compadres together, and once they have been carried out two or three times, the relationship is the strongest in Belén society, stronger even than most kinship relationships. Probably no more than 40 percent of all couples in Belén have such relationships, while the rest must be content with the more sporadic, less binding compadrazgo relationships described in the following items.

Direct social, religious, and economic cooperation denotes no more than the literal meaning of the phrase. In virtually all the categories so far discussed, action and participation are never requested; rather, they are implied by the context. It is true that when, for example, a couple asks for compadres' political support for a certain office in the República Eclesiástica, this is requested directly, but the requisite economic or social expenditures are merely implied. Everyone understands unmistakably, however, and this is part of the formal structure of compadrazgo behavior. This category covers what may be termed outright favors that compadres may ask of each other; these always involve a primarily economic expenditure, which is clearly stated when the favor is asked. These favors may involve both the social and the religious spheres, which—given the importance of the related celebrations and ceremonials—are always in need of contributions that cannot be taken care of by any of the activities described in the other categories. The main consideration here is that asking for participation means that a couple has been unable to generate enough resources by the more structurally prescribed modes. Implicit in this statement is the fact that, ideally as well as in practice, Beleños hope that they will not have to request anything from compadres (at least not directly, although indirectly they let their compadres know if they need help above and beyond expected participation). In other words, the patterns of behavior described in this category indicate that a couple has only a weak network of compadres. Events and occasions included in this category must have more than personal importance, and must concern not only the couple's immediate family but larger numbers of kinsmen or ritual kinsmen in strictly social functions, or a certain segment of the community in religious functions. One may ask compadres for help in raising money or other resources for fulfilling mayordomía obligations, or even for wedding celebrations, but not for the more personal primera comunión or a graduación banquet. This would violate the etiquette of compadrazgo behavior, for being unable to generate one's own resources elicits social disapproval.

Ayuda and labor exchange refer to any occasion on which, as in the preceding category, people may ask their compadres for direct aid or participation. The significant difference here is that such participation may be asked for personal reasons involving only the immediate family of the couple in question. Ayuda means nonreciprocal help in kind, cash, or services, generated on a face-to-face basis, for any occasion or ceremony. Furthermore, ayuda is given primarily in money and occasionally in kind, but very seldom in services. There are probably few couples in Belén who are unable to generate enough services via the structurally prescibed mechanism of compadrazgo behavior, in the sense of being in sufficiently good standing in a compadrazgo network to expect at least the minimal cooperation required. Things seldom get as bad as this, of course, and ayuda even in the form of cash or kind is not often sought. Although ideally the concept of ayuda is nonreciprocal, in practice compadres feel obliged to reciprocate in kind. No person, couple, or group of kinsmen in Belén likes to be permanently indebted to others. The sooner a debt is paid, the better; hence, it can properly be said that even ayuda falls under the principle of reciprocity. On the other hand, labor exchange—*vuelta mano*, as it is commonly known in rural Tlaxcala—is strictly reciprocal in theory as well as in practice, and has to do exclusively with economic matters, that is, primarily with agricultual activities, but with a few other economic pursuits as well. Compadres are the main source of labor exchange, and many couples in Belén have more or less formalized labor exchanges with particular compadres. Especially those who have more than two hectares of land commonly have two or three compadres who help them in the various tasks of the agricultural cycle. This is particularly necessary in Belén, where the great majority of the gainfully employed are labor migrants who cannot spend more than a few days each year in agricultural work. Labor exchange among compadres enables the average couple in Belén to do the agricultural work in its milpas in less than half the time that would otherwise be needed.

I can now make a more quantified interpretation on table 14. This is still not a truly quantitative analysis of compadrazgo behavior, but it is a step in the right direction. The notations of strong, medium, and weak attached to the types with respect to their permanent strength can be gauged by correlating these with the nine kinds of activities that survive the core of ceremonies. This pertains exclusively to the central dyad of the compadrazgo system (the compadres-compadres dyad) and its extensions, for I have already noted that the padrinos-ahijados dyad is relatively inactive and of rather short duration in the permanent dimensions of the institution. Thus a compadrazgo relationship is strong when all nine sets of activities are complied with, whether they are prescriptive or preferential. (In this context, items 8 and 9 are the least important in that they are alternatives to preferred modes of behavior, especially 4-7.) A compadrazgo relationship is of medium strength when six out of the nine sets of activities, three of which (4-6) are fairly insignificant structurally, are complied with. And finally, a compadrazgo relationship is weak when only the first three sets are complied with. Let me analyze this further. Table 14 assigns these indicators by compadrazgo type, which means, statistically speaking, that this is the strength of the type within the total compadrazgo system. This strength is not necessarily fixed, however. For example, an intrinsically weak BCC compadrazgo relationship may be in practice a medium relationship; or an intrinsically medium primera piedra relationship may be in practice a strong one. Conversely, basically strong compadrazgo relationships may be in practice medium or even weak relationships. These variations, which occur often in Belén, must be explained by exogenous considerations. Moreover, my data allow only the classification of compadrazgo relationships into strong, medium, and weak on the basis of types alone, that is, on a rough statistical basis. Finally, the ranking also indicates what is structurally endogenous and exogenous to the compadrazgo system. The first three categories represent elements endogenous to the compadrazgo system as a whole, for these behavioral attributes are part of the structure of all compadrazgo types in Belén. The other six represent the exogenously determined elements of the compadrazgo system; compliance is not specified by the system but by a combination of individual types and external considerations (previous compadrazgo ties, conditions under which the relationship came into existence, and so on). Here, then, we have the internal versus the external view of a social institution—the systemic versus the individual view, which must complement each other if the structural approach is to succeed.

Ritual Kinship Behavior of Primary Relatives: The Compadres-Compadres Dyad

I can now turn to the fundamental dyad of the system, the compadres-compadres dyad, in which behavior is essentially egalitarian and, at least ideally, wholly reciprocal. I say ideally, because there are numerous occasions on which reciprocity cannot be gauged precisely in view of the many intangibles that affect behavior in a particular compadrazgo relationship. But the ideal is always in mind, and compadres try their best to fulfill it. During the central ceremonies there are certain inherent behavioral imbalances that generally put the asking compadres in a slightly subordinate position, but a year or two later this imbalance begins to disappear. Almost inevitably, however, compadrazgo behavior is modified exogenously by a series of constraints that operate to make any given compadres–compadres relationship imbalanced to a certain extent. Thus, the ideological commitment to egalitarianism in compadres' behavior is modified into a situation of subordination-superordination by exogenous constraints, the most significant of which are differences in the compadres' ages, positions in compadrazgo networks, socioeconomic status, religious-symbolic status, and general position in communal life. For example, if a couple in its mid-thirties asks another couple in its mid-fifties, with a long record of religious and ceremonial services to the community, almost inevitably the former will be subordinated to the latter, at least in the outward show of behavior. I do not want to overemphasize this point, for there is never more than a small degree of subordination-superordination, and it is more noticeable in form than in content. Seldom is it translated into significant quantitative or qualitative differences in any of the nine sets of activities outlined in the preceding section.

Although this is ideally a permanent relationship which ends only with death, in fact compadres have significantly more responsibility for keeping the relationship alive than do comadres, and when the former die the relationship and its extensions come to an end, de facto if not de jure. The comadres may continue the relationship, but then it is confined to the first three sets of activities, which are the prescribed elements of all compadrazgo relationships. Upon the death of compadres, compadrazgo relationships classified as strong or medium in table 14 may become weak. Compadres-compadres relationships can of course grow cold or come to an end before death, but this seldom happens, at least in intracommunal compadrazgo, for the community is small and highly inbred. In extracommunal compadrazgo, on the other hand, some relationships do grow cold, and distance and the frequency of visiting are essential factors determining whether the relationship can be kept alive. Within the community, when a relationship is growing cold or is at the breaking point because of serious breaches of etiquette, political disagreement, or even social friction, the compadres of a given network try to bring together the couples in question and revive the relationship, for it is considered bad to terminate relationships other than by death. Couples always try by all means to keep precarious relationships alive, for termination may elicit social disapproval and have unpleasant repercussions. Compadre couples in Belén make strenuous efforts to generate rapport and be in good standing with their compadres—efforts they will not make for real kinsmen.

The compadres-compadres relationship embodies the highest expression of the basic principles of respeto, confianza, and reliance, in both their literal and ideological meanings. In face-to-face interaction, the behavior of compadres is characterized by almost ceremonial respect, even among young compadres. They always address each other by the diminutive, interspersing it frequently in their conversations, and no joking is allowed among them, except perhaps in the privacy of the household. In public, the etiquette associated with respect is definitely ceremonial, and it is amusing to see very young compadres meet, take off their hats, barely touch hands, and bow slightly, much in the manner of old compadres. This aspect of respect is even more accentuated within the context of rites and ceremonies, when compadres must always behave with the utmost gravity and strictly according to the etiquette prescribed for the occasion. There is a definite ranking of compadres associated with the many ritual, ceremonial, social, and religious events, as I have already discussed. After the ceremonialism of a given occasion, compadres usually socialize together, drink together, and in general stay close to each other. In public as well as in private, compadres must be ready to act immediately to make overt their compadrazgo relationship vis-à-vis noncompadres present at any gathering. The highest form of respect is naturally exhibited on religious occasions, regardless of whether or not the compadres are directly participating. Their mere presence at masses, processions, altar decorating, rites and ceremonies connected with specific compadrazgo types, paradas de cruz, burials, and so on, implies what may be called "sacred circumspection." In summary, then, the compadres-compadres behavior patterns rest upon the principle of respeto and are marked by a punctilious effort to proclaim publicly the sacred nature of compadrazgo. Compadres-compadres respeto is thus formal to the point of stiffness; it covers the whole spectrum of compadrazgo behavior (private and public), and is endowed with a certain otherworldliness that sometimes borders on the comic.

On the other hand, compadres-compadres behavior based on the principle of confianza more than compensates for the stiffness and formality of compadrazgo respeto. Certain inherent behavioral contradictions are, in fact, not always entirely resolved, except in the privacy of the home, or when compadres are drunk or in the process of getting drunk. Confianza in compadrazgo behavior can be more or less literally translated as trust, confidence in discussing each other's problems, closeness of sentiment, and above all knowing that one's compadres are always ready to help, advise, support, or console. These are stated ideals which are structurally in contraposition to the ideals involved in respeto. To a large extent, the total ensemble of compadres' behavior is the result of the moderating influence that these rather divergent patterns exert upon each other. Since, however, these two principles operate in rather different contexts, it is no contradiction to say that compadres' behavior can be stiff and formal in its more outward, public aspects, while confianza makes itself felt in the inward, private aspects of the relationship. Adults in Belén always feel a certain ambivalence about these opposing aspects of compadrazgo behavior, and are always a little doubtful as to whether to confide fully in their compadres, ask for special favors, engage in cooperation beyond the prescribed boundaries, and so on. In the end, confianza wins out, and respeto among compadres is generally confined to the more formal aspects of the relationship. Under these circumstances, a compadres-compadres relationship can be regarded not only as a sacred obligation but also as the highest form of friendship. This is especially the case among comadres, who visit each other frequently and without waiting for special events or occasions. They constantly do small favors for each other, exchange small presents, and engage in almost constant gossip about the affairs of the community. Hardly a week goes by that comadres do not see each other, including those who live within walking distance of Belén. The comadres-comadres relationship is unquestionably the closest bond in the entire compadrazgo system, and in not a few cases it is the driving force of the global compadrazgo relationship.

By contrast, the relationship among compadres (males only, that is) does not exhibit to nearly as high a degree the closeness and intimacy of confianza, remaining closer to the formality of respeto. Compadres, however, do sometimes visit each other for strictly personal reasons, and sometimes develop close relationships approximating those of comadres. They are often drinking companions, either in their respective households or in the two or three *changarros* (small stores) in Belén that sell *pulque* (fermented agave juice), beer, and sometimes hard liquor.[2] These gatherings are very illuminating for, among other things, they exhibit some of the behavioral ambiguity inherent in the formal-intimate dichotomy of the compadres-compadres relationship. They usually start calmly and ceremoniously as befits the respeto that compadres must have for each other, but as the degree of inebriation progresses, the intimate, close, almost tender aspects of behavior increase. This is not simply the effect of the liquor, which may affect individuals quite differently, but a patterned, collective expression of culturally shared attitudes. This was expressed by a participant in one of these drinking parties when he said to me, "Que pendejos somos, compadrito, que solo cuando estamos borrachos podemos expresar la gran amistad y cariño que nos tenemos" (How foolish we are, compadrito, that only when we are drunk can we express the great friendship and love that we have for each other).

Confianza among compadres is more easily expressed in face-to-face interaction by the equal sharing of things without bias or favoritism. Although the overt behavior patterns among compadres may be much less close and intimate than are those among comadres, they may well have firmer and more permanent foundations. Behavior patterns between individual compadres and comadres are very limited, for their formal, permanent, and face-to-face interaction always takes place in the presence of the other's spouse. Compadres may interact under any circumstances, and so may comadres, but not compadres and comadres separately; in fact, there are no occasions in Belén beyond casual salutations when this can take place. Compadres and comadres may drink together, dance together, and occasionally joke together, but only when their spouses are present. It is considered very bad manners for a visiting compadre or comadre to stay in the house more than a few minutes if the spouse is not there. Underlying this lack of opportunity for private interaction between compadres and comadres is the fear of potential ritual kinship incest, which leads people to try to reduce the opportunities for temptation. Essentially, the relationship between compadres and comadres is a reflection of individual compadre-compadre and comadre-comadre relationships, and it can be equally formal or equally warm.

Finally, how is the principle of reliance translated into patterned behavior? As a basic principle of the compadrazgo system, reliance is what I have called the activating principle of the triad: the mechanism that underlies and gives form to the basic behavior conditioned by respeto and confianza. Both must first exist, of course, before the principle of reliance can come into operation. In the context of the present discussion, behavior springing directly from reliance requires that compadres know when and how to ask for cooperation, help, or participation of any kind beyond what is structurally prescribed. What is perhaps more significant, they must find out in advance that the compadres who are to be asked, directly or indirectly, will be able to lend assistance without social or economic strain, let alone deprivation. The behavioral aspects of compadres-compadres reliance, then, are structured along much the same lines as the initiation of a compadrazgo relationship; in other words, it is a sacred obligation which cannot be refused. Thus, compadres bound by a given degree of respeto and confianza know that assistance for innumerable social, religious, and ceremonial events and occasions cannot be refused, but at the same time they must know when to ask. They must find out indirectly whether a prospective compadre is able to help, for the etiquette of exchanges and ayuda is predicated on the sacredness of the institution. Compadres in Belén always keep themselves informed about the potential for help within their networks, and comadres play a major role in this. Once a compadre couple has been singled out by another couple as potential donors or partners, the asking comadre talks informally to the prospective comadre about the feasibility of the proposed involvement. If the response is negative, everything stops there and nothing more is said. This seldom happens, however, for by the time comadres get to the talking stage, they are usually already well informed about the situation. In a wider context, within well-established compadrazgo networks, compadres and comadres are always aware of the potential for cooperation or assistance, and most compadre couples in Belén know fairly well whom they can count upon.

Information is exchanged constantly among the members of compadrazgo networks, and again comadres play a prominent role. This exchange works efficiently enough to allow the average couple in Belén to adhere fairly strictly to the compadrazgo system's rules regarding help, participation, and cooperation without undue strain.

Even though I have emphasized the contingency and occasional variability of permanent compadrazgo behavior, from a different viewpoint it must also be regarded as quite institutionalized. This is not a contradiction, but rather focuses the situation conceptually in terms of both its external and internal structure. Once the contingency of respeto and confianza is well established with respect to certain parameters, then it is no contradiction to say that reliance can be translated into well-institutionalized behavior patterns. Finally, it should be clear that these behavior patterns obtain among couples as units, whether a given situation involves primarily compadres or comadres. This is one of the fundamental principles of the compadrazgo system in Belén; once a compadre or comadre becomes involved behaviorally, spouses automatically are drawn in either directly or indirectly.

Ritual Kinship Behavior of Primary Relatives: Subsidiary Dyads

Something should be said about the subsidiary dyads of primary relatives, namely, those obtaining between padrinos' children and ahijados' siblings, and padrinos' children and parents or owners. The best way to delineate the behavior patterns in these two dyads is to regard them as direct extensions of the compadres-compadres dyad, who play roles subsidiary to those of their real kinsmen—that is, their parents. Usually a fairly large number of persons are included in this category, but they are children or young unmarried people, that is, younger than twenty-two or twenty-three. Under certain circumstances, however, especially when there are sizable age differences among compadres, some young married couples may fall in this category. First, with respect to the expression of reliance these two dyads play a passive role. Their members do not initiate actions in their own right, but only indirectly through the involvement of their respective parents. This situation is expectable, given the constitution of the padrinos-ahijados dyad, which the personnel of these subsidiary dyads strongly resemble. They participate in the activities undertaken by their respective parents, and quite often have clearly defined duties to perform. Children and young people in this category can be regarded as adjuncts who actively participate and contribute services, but who cannot provide help or ayuda directly, unless this can be channeled through their parents. This is true of the last six sets of activities, but not of the first three (see "The Contexts Involved in Compadrazgo Behavior and Action," this chapter), for it pertains exclusively to the exogenously modified behavior beyond what is universally prescribed. The pattern of salutation, visiting, and in general minimum cooperation of compadres-compadres' children follow roughly the lines of the primary dyad of compadrazgo, but within these circumscribed contexts they can and do establish some independent behavior patterns of their own. The same holds for padrinos' children and ahijados' parents, in that roughly the same ideal behavior patterns obtain for the first three sets, but with the significant differences that they are weaker. Essentially, then, these two subsidiary dyads are adjuncts to the primary dyad of compadrazgo with respect to the discharge of the last six sets of activities, but independent patterns when it comes to the first three, I must therefore say something more about the latter.

The behavior of padrinos' children and ahijados' siblings is characterized by an open camaraderie which of course includes the ahijados themselves. It is on the whole a close and intimate relationship, especially when the children or young men and women involved live in close proximity. The relationship is strengthened ideologically by the fact that they are regarded as spiritual siblings, but are exempt from the antagonism between younger and older siblings that often characterizes kinship behavior in Belén (see *Ritual Kinship* I, page 38). Ritual siblings who live in fairly close proximity—that is, mostly within the boundaries of the community—often play together or undertake such group activities as pasturing goats and sheep, carrying water, sewing, or preparing some special food. Unlike real brothers and sisters, whose relations are often tense, especially when the brothers are older, spiritual brothers and sisters often develop close ties through the boys acting as go-betweens for the girls and their sweethearts—something that would be unthinkable for real brothers to do. In extracommunal compadrazgo, one of the most pleasurable activities of children and young men and women is to visit their spiritual siblings in nearby communities, which they can do with their parents' consent as long as the community is not more than about an hour's walk away. Parents themselves encourage the interaction of spiritual siblings as a mechanism for keeping compadrazgo relationships active with a minimum effort on their own part. In this respect, spiritual siblings play a rather significant role in the successful operation of compadrazgo relationships. In many ways the interaction of spiritual siblings is closer and friendlier than that among real siblings and first and second cousins, who sometimes live very close to one another. To sum up, some of the young people of Belén's closest ties of friendship come about through their position as compadrazgo relatives. At the same time this serves as a period of indoctrination into the compadrazgo system. It is inevitable that the subsidiary participation of spiritual siblings in compadrazgo, and the close relationships that they develop from a rather early age, will lead to mature compadrazgo relationships. From this viewpoint, the compadrazgo system is more of a closed system than its egocentrical nature might lead one to believe, for one's parents' compadres and spiritual siblings will in turn become one's own compadres, in a fashion that to some extent approximates the generational continuity of kinship.

The behavior patterns among padrinos' children and ahijados' parents, I noted before, closely parallel those of the padrinos-ahijados dyad, but in a more relaxed form. The children of this dyad participate in the ritual, ceremonial, religious, and social occasions of ahijados' parents but via the intervention of their parents, and not necessarily directly as in the case of ahijados vis-à-vis padrinos. Nevertheless, these children and young men and women have certain leeway to act somewhat independently toward their spiritual siblings' parents. Not uncommonly this leads to the establishment of a second compadrazgo relationship between a young person's parents and the parents of his or her spiritual siblings. This is brought about directly by the child; for example, he may cultivate the good will of his spiritual siblings' parents, and then ask his own to ask them to enter into a compadrazgo relationship for the occasion he has in mind. And not uncommonly, children and young men or women have couples in mind whom they would like to acquire as padrinos when the occasion for confirmación, primera comunión, escapulario, graduación, quince años, compadrazgo de aretes, and FC arises. Relations between padrinos' children and ahijados' parents are warm but formal on both sides, underlain on the whole by the same behavioral mechanisms of salutation, visiting, and minimal cooperation as those of the padrinos-ahijados dyad. Rather than regarding it as an intrinsically important behavioral dyad of primary compadrazgo relatives, it is better to regard the padrinos' children–ahijados' siblings dyad as an important stage in the egocentric development of the compadrazgo cycle.

Ritual Kinship Behavior of Secondary Relatives

Secondary relatives include several additional dyads, the most important of which are, of course, related to the compadres-compadres dyad and involve real kinsmen of the opposite compadres, that is, either padrinos' kinsmen or parents' or owners' kinsmen. The most important categories of kinsmen among secondary relatives are: compadres-compadres' parents, siblings and siblings' in-laws, and, of less importance, the children of these kinsmen. None of the multiple dyads among secondary relatives by itself generates any behavioral patterns that can be translated into a dyadic pattern of participation and cooperation among these relatives, unless it is by the mediation of primary relatives, especially the compadres-compadres dyad. Thus, it is impossible to analyze their compadrazgo behavior in a strictly dyadic pattern, unless it is done via their direct relationship to the three main effective primary dyads. Nor do behavior patterns obtain among secondary relatives per se, for the only time this occurs is along the parallel lines of the compadres-compadres dyad, that is, along real kinship lines. It is therefore heuristically necessary to analyze the behavior of secondary relatives in terms of the whole ensemble of relatives and as egocentrically tied to at least the two main primary dyads. The resultant web of relatives can best be conceived as a series of compadrazgo positions which are given expression when the primary dyads of compadrazgo become operative. In such positions, the patterned behavior of secondary relatives may of course cover the whole spectrum of the nine sets of activities, but always in capacities subsidiary to those of primary compadres or ahijados. The number of secondary relatives who will participate on any given occasion in which these activities take place will of course depend on the compadrazgo type and its structural and ideological position within the compadrazgo system as given primarily in tables 2, 3, 9, 14, and 15. The participation and cooperation of secondary relatives can sometimes be important, depending on a series of constraints that I cannot describe in detail here, but which can be subsumed under the rubric of exogenous considerations involving the number of personnel required for a given religious, social or ceremonial occasion, the degree of distinction that the main organizers (compadres) want to give it, and the nature of the occasion itself. For example, weddings, banquets, and ceremonies connected with bendición de casa, parada de cruz, primera piedra, and mayordomía and Repúblic Eclesiástica functions are always large affairs which require the participation of many compadres and kinsmen, and the organizers always want to make the occasion memorable. On the other hand, baptism, confirmación, burial banquets and ceremonies, and a few other occasions occupy an intermediate position; and the rites and ceremonies of tertiary compadrazgo types (see table 8) occupy a low position in which there is little participation except by a few primary compadrazgo relatives of the most egocentrically important compadres.

In view of such a significantly large number of exogenous constraints, it is more appropriate to emphasize the ideological dimensions of secondary compadrazgo behavior. Here again it must be realized that, much as in the case of the less important primary compadrazgo dyads, the nine sets of activities are a necessary aspect of secondary compadrazgo behavior. They are expressed in very much the same way, though perhaps less stringently except when it comes to visiting patterns; but salutations, attending certain events, and in general showing the required degree of respeto and confianza are always complied with. In particular, the parents and siblings of compadres are especially careful to abide by the behavior patterns that are the result of respeto and confianza. This is not only an important part of the ideological order, but a pragmatic attitude to take, in that it is important for every couple in Belén to be on good terms with the largest possible number of even its secondary compadrazgo relatives within the husband's and wife's respective networks. In fact, one of the most common causes of friction among primary and secondary relatives is the failure of the latter to participate in a given occasion when it is required or when the organizing compadres request it. The most significant ideological constraint regarding participation by secondary relatives is underlain by the fact that whenever the presence of primary relatives (usually compadres) is required or requested, secondary relatives are automatically bound to participate. A second significant constraint is that secondary relatives are not bound to give ayuda in either kind or cash; the sacred nature of compadrazgo does not extend to secondary relatives when it comes to direct help, and knowing that secondary relatives can refuse, primary compadres never ask them for direct help in Belén.

In practice, however, the situation may be modified by the web of compadrazgo which often makes some secondary relatives of a given compadrazgo relationship into primary relatives (that is, compadres or ahijados) of personnel in the same relationship. In fact, it is possible that as many as five or six couples of a given compadrazgo relationship may be primary relatives of one another (see Chapters Thirteen and Fourteen). In general secondary relatives are always willing to participate and cooperate (in services) on the many occasions on which they are required or requested to participate. For all practical purposes, this applies only to compadres' (males) parents and siblings, for comadres' parents and siblings seldom participate in any effective fashion. For example, during the first day of celebrations for the average Belén wedding, at least eight to ten different types of primary compadres and secondary relatives of the various participating dyads (the parents of the bride, the parents of the groom, and the several padrinos of the wedding) will be present at the groom's house, but the real cooperation in the form of goods and services will come almost exclusively from the patrilineal side of these dyads. One cannot speak of secondary relatives as discharging specific activities for such multiple occasions, but whatever they do will be determined by their generational affiliation. Compadres–compadres' parents and siblings will participate in capacities commensurate with their generation, serving as intermediaries, speechmakers, prayer leaders, ritual and ceremonial assistants, secondary co-ordinators, and so on, while their children will serve at table, help prepare food, and do a variety of other menial jobs either secular or ceremonial. Secondary relatives of the compadres-compadres generation or the one above (compadres' parents) engage in activities as an extension of padrinos and parents and owners; the younger generation engages in activities as an extension of ahijados and ahijados' spiritual siblings. Thus, except in the matter of direct help, there is no sharp distinction between primary and secondary relatives with regard to participation and cooperation. It is better to regard the situation as a gradient of effective participation determined by nearness to the central compadres-compadres dyad. Irrespective of their egocentric bond to primary compadres, secondary relatives behave toward one another in specific ways, the sum total of which can be characterized as being closer to confianza than respeto; there is less of the formality that characterizes the main compadrazgo dyad, and more of an open and direct relationship which is often translated into a joking relationship. The fact that direct ayuda and labor exchange do not bind them prescriptively leads to a more relaxed interaction, which often constitutes the foundation for future primary compadrazgo relationships. In fact, the most satisfying compadrazgo relationships in Belén are those in which the contracting compadres were previously secondary compadrazgo relatives.

Ritual Kinship Behavior of Tertiary Relatives

Tertiary relatives include an even larger number of dyads, which cannot possibly be enumerated meaningfully for lack of fuller data—if indeed this would be a profitable enterprise. These dyads include compadres-compadres' grandparents, uncles, and sometimes their children and other collateral relatives. Furthermore, in the category of tertiary relatives must be included other more distant relatives of the two primary dyads of compadrazgo who for one reason or another are drawn into some participation in the web of compadrazgo relationship. Tertiary compadrazgo ties represent the maxium extension of compadrazgo behavior and ritual kinship terminology, and while the prescriptions of the latter are well complied with, those of the former are not, for again exogenous considerations conspire against any form of structurally based behavior patterns. Moreover, tertiary relatives do not represent a separate category of compadrazgo extension, but, as in the intermeshing of primary and secondary relatives, they represent a gradation from secondary to tertiary. There is one important difference, however: unlike secondary relatives, tertiary relatives comply structurally with the discharge of only the first two sets of activities but not the third (see "The

Contexts Involved in Compadrazgo Behavior and Action," this chapter). Secondary relatives represent the maximum extension of the three basic, prescriptive behavioral attributes of compadrazgo, while tertiary relatives comply with terminological prescriptions (that is, the use of the appropriate compadrazgo term which is usually compadre or comadre) and attend primary and secondary occasions more or less as guests. Tertiary relatives cannot be asked (nor do they usually volunteer) to cooperate in services rendered at the dozens of events they may attend; their participation consists simply of their presence, which on not a few occasions may give special luster to the proceedings, and for this primary relatives are always grateful. The ideology of compadrazgo here is clear but expressed primarily in respeto by the terminological prescription. In general, the greatest participation always comes from compadres-compadres' patrilineal relatives in the direct line of descent, and this is particularly the case for young compadres who may have not only their parents but their grandparents alive, not infrequently living in the same household. In such cases, obviously, the grandparents of compadres automatically participate very much as if they were immediate secondary relatives. Age and residence always play an important role in the actual discharge of the web of compadrazgo, and can sometimes modify significantly the prescriptive attribution of any compadrazgo relationship. To conclude, then, tertiary compadrazgo relatives can be regarded as a wide variety of personnel who, by their presence, may contribute significantly to the success of religous, social, or ceremonial events, but who at the same time may become temporary participants in a secondary or even primary capacity. This is especially the case in religious and ceremonial events at which large numbers of people are almost a necessity for the success of the occasion, and at which the behavioral dimensions of tertiary relatives can best be seen.

The Personnel Involved in Behavioral Activities Beyond the Dyadic Patterns

A word about the number of personnel involved in behavioral patterns of primary, secondary, and tertiary relatives beyond whatever individual, dyadic behavior these categories entail is in order. Primary relatives vary from a minimum of 5 to an effective maximum of 12 people of both sexes. The average compadrazgo relationship in Belén, however, involves at any given event from 8 to 9 primary compadres and ahijados. I am not taking into consideration, of course, some of the public-communal compadrazgo types (such as ANDI and PCA) and marriage compadrazgo; these may temporarily involve a large number of primary relatives, but in their permanent structure this number tends to decrease to the average size. Secondary relatives can vary from 15 to 30, with an average of a little over 20. These figures, of course, are for what I have called the primary compadrazgo types in Belén, that is, the dozen or so types that recognize and extend kinship terminology to tertiary and secondary relatives. The figures for the eighteen or so remaining types are considerably smaller. The total number of possible primary, secondary, and tertiary participants in the important compadrazgo types averages from 35 to 40 individuals, half of whom will of course be real kinsmen of the primary compadres. These men are individuals that compadres can count on for a variety of purposes and degrees of participation and cooperation. Moreover, assuming (and this is more than an educated guess) that the average couple in Belén has at least 7 primary and 9 secondary compadrazgo relationships active at any given time, it has more than 350 potential compadrazgo relatives. This represents the sum total of compadrazgo personnel for the average couple in Belén, which means that—at any given time and taking into account extracommunal compadrazgo—the couple is related by compadrazgo ties to slightly less than one-fourth of the total population of the community.

Seldom if ever will all the compadrazgo relatives of a given couple participate in a single religious or social event, but the couple knows that if the occasion arises it can count on the majority of some 200 compadrazgo relatives, either by activating prescriptive activities or by asking. This is an egocentric analysis, which must necessarily involve many repetitions of compadrazgo relationships—and this is what ultimately gives rise to compadrazgo networks, which are essentially bundles of couples, perhaps on the order of ten to sixteen, who have been brought together several times by compadrazgo ties. Of the average 350 people to whom a couple may be related, approximately one-third are children below the age of ten who do not participate in any meaningful fashion, and another third are children and young men and women between the ages of twelve and twenty-two who participate in subsidiary positions. Thus, I can realistically say that the average couple in Belén at any given time has access to the participation, cooperation, and ayuda of about 120 adults, or sixty or so couples. Of these personnel, about half are required and half are requested to participate, cooperate, or provide ayuda, further limiting the number of effective couples tied egocentrically to a given couple for varying occasions and events. Moreover, and equally important, personnel tied by required activities may often not be needed, and in such cases the etiquette of compadrazgo behavior prescribes that they be so told. The average compadre couple in Belén knows the extent of both its immediate network of compadres and the total web of couples, and employs certain strategies to activate required or requested behavior, as the occasion demands. The average couple's immediate network and total compadrazgo web, being to some extent egocentrically determined, fluctuate through time. Some compadrazgo relationships come to an end or are discontinued while new ones come into existence. On the whole, the total number or couples remains fairly constant after middle age, but clearly decreases toward the end of the average compadrazgo career, that is, when the couples are around seventy or seventy-five years old.

I have tried to give as complete a picture as possible of ritual kinship terminology and ritual kinship behavior, as a basis for understanding compadrazgo in action. While I lack a significant amount of quantitative data on behavioral patterns, I could operationalize those activities to a limited extent by determining how they are discharged in a ranked order of prescription by primary, secondary, and tertiary relatives. Perhaps more significant, I could not entirely interdigitate this ranked behavioral discharge with respect to the thirty-one compadrazgo types in Belén, except to the extent that I control the extension of behavior patterns in terms of the primary-secondary-tertiary classification. The net result is that the discharge of prescribed, preferred, and optional behavioral patterns is often modified beyond structural control by what I have called the efficacious domains of exogenous considerations. These should be understood as makeshift contexts until additional data enable me to determine the controlling variables and incorporate them into the structural framework. There are so many similarities between the compadrazgo and the kinship systems that I feel justified in undertaking the analysis with a traditional model of the latter in mind, which at the same time serves to pinpoint and exemplify the differences and similarities between the two. I hope to have demonstrated that compadrazgo behavior extends or can be extended to a much larger number of ritual kinsmen than we are led to believe by the ethnographic literature. More than any other part of the structural analysis, this and the preceding chapters show how the institution of compadrazgo in Belén, and by extension in Tlaxcala, stands for a much larger structural and functional complex in organizing community life, quite often extending beyond the confines of the community. I must also point out that the data upon which this and the preceding chapters are based were the most difficult to gather, not only because they are among the most subtle, but because the analysis demands minute attention to detail.[3]

A Formal Comparison of Kinship and Compadrazgo in Belén

I am now in a position to compare formally the compadrazgo and the real kinship system of Belén, in order to determine what gives rise to differences, similarities, and overlappings, and in general to determine how the compadrazgo system is modeled on the real kinship system. I have already presented a considerable amount of data on these topics, both in this chapter and in Chapters Two and Eleven. But before I can bring out the most important points of comparison, namely the structural, contextual, and functional elements of the two systems, I must first discuss the basic principle (perhaps constraint is a better term) underlying much of the discussion.

There is a dictum in Belén that goes as follows: "No pidas a tus parientes que se hagan tus compadres, pues tarde o temprano, bajo pretexto de ser parientes, no cumplen con sus obligaciones de compadres" (Do not ask your kinsmen to become your compadres, for sooner or later, under the pretext of being kinsmen, they do not comply with their obligations as compadres). This dictum is universally followed in Belén, and of the thousands of compadrazgo relationships recorded for a period of nearly seventy years, only ten were contracted among kinsmen (who were rather distantly related at that: four relationships between second cousins and six among collaterals in the third degree of consanguinity). Futhermore, and significantly, these ten compadrazgo relationships were all contracted after 1962 by members of what I have called the economic elite of Belén.[4] In other words, to contract compadrazgo relationships with kinsmen is to violate an unspoken proscription, one that had never been broken until 1962. This is a deeply rooted constraint which has its basis in the belief that compadrazgo is a sacred institution sanctioned both by the supernatural and by the functions it discharges, which affects people directly in varied contexts. The belief leads people to verbalize explicitly that not only is compadrazgo supernaturally sanctioned, but that it involves a large measure of individual control. The strength of what I have called the sacred nature of compadrazgo in Belén is predicated not so much on its sacredness per se as on the element of volition it contains. People feel that the individual and collective choices involved in compadrazgo must never be taken lightly, for, to put it colloquially, you can never have too much of such a good thing, and compadres try to comply with its "sacred" prescriptions to the best of their abilities. In other words, the sacredness of the compadrazgo system is fundamentally a rationalization of its volitional elements.

In contrast the people of Belén believe that kinship is something over which you have no control; you are saddled with kinsmen whether you like it or not, and there is nothing sacred about kinship relationships. Given this state of affairs, kinship in Belén is not an integrative, cohesive force, although there is a fairly well structured social unit beyond the domestic group which I have called loosely the nonresidential extended family. Compadrazgo is, however, without doubt more effective as an integrative, cohesive force within the total social life of the community. Time and again informants expressed their preference for generating participation, cooperation, and ayuda among compadres rather than kinsmen, and they specifically referred to the sacred nature of the former relationship (and all that it implies) and the uncertainty and antagonisms that can exist among the latter. The dictum that "blood is thicker than water" is not significant in such a situation. It is true that the people of Belén are polite and friendly, and try to be on good terms with their kinsmen, but at the same time they seldom trust them or regard them as a reliable source of help. Among kinsmen, strong ties of participation, cooperation, and help obtain only within the domestic group, be it the nuclear or extended family household. These domestic units are always highly integrated socially, religiously, and economically, but outside this domain, compadrazgo is more important in generating and coordinating the participation, cooperation, and ayuda of larger numbers of personnel. Some significant patterns of participation and cooperation exist at the level of the nonresidential extended family, but these activities often take place largely within the context of compadrazgo—that is, on occasions that involve compadres and their extensions, who may in turn be compadres of a couple's nonresidential kinsmen. In any event, if the distinction between the domestic or residential group and nonresidential kinsmen is made, it can properly be said that whenever the latter are effective, it is usually because they overlap with compadres, which is one of the fundamental aspects of the social life of Belén. The ideological injunction against seeking compadres among one's kinsmen (which theoretically means nonresidential kinsmen, for one cannot possibly ask one's own primary kinsmen within the domestic group) is clear; because of the sacred nature of the relationship, the generation of confianza and reliance is always higher among compadres than among kinsmen.

In comparing the compadrazgo and kinship systems of Belén let us take the structural attributes first. To begin with, it is evident that the compadrazgo system has been socially modeled on the kinship system. This is clearly demonstrated in the analysis of ritual kinship terminology and ritual kinship behavior, and also in the extension of incest prohibitions. In these three instances, and especially in compadrazgo terminology and incest prohibitions, starting from a core of terms and prohibitions, the extensions follow outward along the same lines as real kinship extensions. Structurally, there are no signficant differences per se in these three circumscribed domains of compadrazgo and kinship. In fact, one could say that with regard to its formal constitution, compadrazgo is a parasitic structure which uses the established articulation of kinship for achieving certain ends. Moreover, the very nature of compadrazgo (or fictive kinship, as it is sometimes called) makes this development logical, for one can hardly think of another model that compadrazgo could have used to achieve the same structural ends. Once a couple in Belén acquires another couple as compadres (I am disregarding ahijados), the couples and their extensions become reciprocally incorporated into a network that is organizationally that of kinship, but structurally that of compadrazgo. The asking couple becomes ritual kin of the couple asked and its extensions out to what I have called tertiary relatives involving twenty-four possible categories of real kinsmen—and vice versa. This means that in any compadrazgo relationship in Belén (remembering that compadrazgo is symmetrical in both structure and function), primary compadres are related in a certain prescribed extension to each other's real kinsmen, so that there are two sets of egocentrically ritual kinsmen who are inversely each other's real kinsmen.

The net result is that about 50 percent of the global personnel of any compadrazgo relationship is composed of kinsmen, inversely speaking. Also, when either or both sides of a given relationship are in turn related to each other by primary compadrazgo ties, there obtains a much greater overlapping of compadres and kinsmen. In fact, it is often the case that most of the extensions of both sides of an original compadrazgo relationship later become primary compadres (on a couple basis). In such a case, couple A's parents (compadres' parents), grandparents (compadres' grandparents), siblings (brothers), and not infrequently grown sons, will become primary compadres of the same categories of kinsmen on couple B's side, in, of course, a variety of combinations. When this happens, as I discuss in the following chapter, there comes into existence the most efficient corporate network of compadrazgo that is possible in Belén. It must also be remembered that on especially important occasions, such as the República Eclesiástica's and mayordomias' annual celebrations, when compadrazgo ties come most significantly into operation, kinship ties also come into play. There is always a high degree of overlapping of a wide variety of behavior patterns, and under such conditions it is always difficult to differentiate the functions of compadrazgo from those of kinship.

In summary, compadrazgo and kinship, although structurally different systems, merge at several points and involve overlapping in personnel as well as in behavioral discharge. Compadrazgo is based almost entirely on the model of kinship structure, and terminology, compadrazgo behavior, and compadrazgo incest extensions operate essentially like those of kinship. Furthermore, since compadrazgo is a pervasive system related to virtually every aspect of community social life, and since about 50 percent of the average compadrazgo personnel are inverse egocentric kinsmen, the structural discharge of activities overlaps compadres and kinsmen to such a degree that, beyond the confines of the domestic group, it is advisable to conceptualize these institutions together. Compadrazgo, then, is an extension of and overlaps with kinship, but has a functional discharge that corresponds to what is traditionally associated with kinship in societies with effective kinship units beyond the domestic or family group.

There are some differences between compadrazgo and kinship, but they are not very significant. First, the sets of activities analyzed in the section entitled "The Contexts Involved in Compadrazgo Behavior" (this chapter) are the same for both compadres and kinsmen, leaving aside the salutations and visiting patterns peculiar to compadrazgo. However, the prescriptive, preferential, and optional rules and guidelines associated with these patterns of behavior are signficantly more institutionalized for compadrazgo relationships than for kinship relationships. This is in a sense a natural consequence of the inherent preference for seeking out compadres to generate confianza and reliance. Compadres in any degree of relationship know at all times what is expected of them, and what they can expect in return; they know when they are required to do certain things, to participate to a certain degree, or to provide a certain measure of cooperation or ayuda; they also know when it is up to them to offer to participate or cooperate, even though not doing so will not constitute a breach of compadrazgo etiquette. The rules of kinship behavior, on the other hand, are not clearly laid out, and while certain things are expected of kinsmen, the degree of prescription, preference, or option is seldom explicitly stated. (I am speaking, of course, about nonresidential kinsmen.) Kinship terminology is broader and more complete than compadrazgo terminology, which naturally reflects the somewhat more constrained and certainly skewed nature of the compadrazgo system. Kinship terminology is also more reciprocal than compadrazgo terminology, which is essentially asymmetrical when it comes to individuals of different generations. In the case of incest, the immediate prohibitions are essentially the same in both kinship and compadrazgo, but somewhat more relaxed for compadrazgo, especially when the prohibition is extended to tertiary relatives. Unquestionably, the similarities of the kinship and compadrazgo systems are greater than the differences, for essentially compadrazgo deviates little from the kinship model. In fact, even the differences are conditioned by the model. For example, the compadrazgo pedimento is basically the same as the marriage pedimento: it has the same outward form, it is underlain by the same structural components, and its aims are functionally the same; it differs only in personnel and ideological matrix. In their most fundamental aspects, then, the differences between kinship and compadrazgo are shaped by the structural fact that their personnel are dichotomized into inversely related groups, which makes every group of compadrazgo relatives related egocentrically to the nonkinsmen of the total ensemble. These contextual differences are not significant in the actual functioning of the system, and compadrazgo follows the kinship model in action in a fashion which seldom if ever works for the non-kinsmen of the total ensemble.

With respect to the functional aspects of compadrazgo, the situation is even more strikingly complementary, for kinship and compadrazgo in action merge into an undifferentiated personnel complex. Some of the functions of compadrazgo are traditionally discharged in tribal or folk societies by kinship units which stand between the domestic group and the tribe or community as a whole. The explanation of this usurpation of kinship functions by compadrazgo in Belén, and in much of rural Tlaxcala, involves historical considerations of long standing. Of immediate synchronic importance is that in this usurpation, which I have called the extension and complementation of kinship and compadrazgo beyond the domestic group, compadrazgo has employed all the traditional mechanisms of kinship and has retained many of its functions, thereby providing an effective syncretic solution. It is always difficult in Belén to determine the respective functional spheres of kinship and compadrazgo beyond the confines of the domestic group. Even the highly integrated social, religious, and economic nature of the nuclear or extended family in its dealings with the outside world can on occasions in the life, social, and communal cycles be modified by primary compadrazgo ties. Even at this level, in other words, there is a considerable overlap between primary kinsmen and primary compadrazgo actors. Throughout the entire spectrum of the various degrees of kinship and compadrazgo relationship (primary, secondary, and tertiary) there is always an overlapping of functions, which is the natural result of the structural overlapping. Virtually every function of compadrazgo is discharged within the context of potential kinship participation, cooperation, and ayuda, even on those occasions that may seem to fall outside of the realm of kinship—for example, the public-communal compadrazgo types, or graduación, bendición de casa, primera piedra, and so on.

Conversely, compadrazgo and kinship by definition must be functionally interrelated in the discharge of activities. Given the sum total of these interdigitations, conjunctions, and overlappings, it is advisable to conceptualize kinship and compadrazgo as a single institution. The mere fact that the structural form of kinship results from the ideological effectiveness of compadrazgo is justification enough for placing compadrazgo and kinship within a single conceptual framework. The concepts of "compadres" and "kinsmen" are never discrete social entities in the minds of the people of Belén, and although they may talk about compadres and *parientes* (relatives) as individually involving different social positions, this nearly disappears when compadrazgo is observed in action. Moreover, there is not a single occasion in Belén that prescriptively involves the participation of kinsmen only. The reverse is also true, but this is structured by the fact that half one's compadrazgo relatives are necessarily kinsmen. I do not want to belabor the point, but it is necessary to bear in mind that it is compadrazgo that unites the action of kinsmen—either by the discharge of kinship obligations within well-established events in the compadrazgo cycle, or by the fact that events in which kinsmen per se play the leading role are always attended by a large number of compadres who must necessarily modify such roles, especially inasmuch as such kinsmen may be related to attending compadres in their own right—and not vice versa.

A final point of comparison again concerns the structure of these two systems. I have already discussed the compadrazgo and kinship systems from the viewpoints of their systemic and egocentric components, and here I would like to briefly expand that statement. Kinship and compadrazgo have different overall structural compositions with respect to the basic organization of personnel, of course, but in a series of associated attributes, the one is based on the model of the other. Although the kinship system of Belén has a rather pronounced patrilineal bias, it is bilateral in social unit composition; whatever units operate potentially beyond the context of the domestic group are essentially bilateral (that is, primarily the nonresidential extended family) and therefore have a significant degree of egocentric kinship membership. This is also true of individual compadrazgo relationships, the only signficant difference being that here there are two egocentric loci represented by the compadre couples of the basic dyad. As one shifts to the individual couple's total ensemble of compadrazgo relationships, either throughout its compadrazgo career or at a given point in time, then the egocentricity of compadrazgo is significantly reduced and certain systemic elements come into operation. One can say that both the extradomestic aspects of kinship and individual compadrazgo relationships in Belén have a basic interactional structure which is carried on by means of dyadic patterns, with some systemic components. However, compadrazgo transcends this at both the level of the individual, as noted above, and at the level of the community when we conceive of compadrazgo as a system in its own right. In other words, at these two levels the compadrazgo system's nonegocentric, nondyadic components (its systemic aspects, as it were) are preeminent, and they become the most important aspect of analysis. Individual networks, although egocentrically organized from the individual viewpoint, are really exocentric systems in which the component couples no longer interact dyadically but as a global ensemble with fairly well delineated positions within the network. Thus, an individual's network constitutes for compadrazgo something that the nonresidential extended family does not constitute for kinship. The differences between the structure of compadrazgo networks and the nonresidential extended family are striking.

The nonresidential extended family exists primarily as a loosely organized group of related households still predominantly aligned dyadically; the compadrazgo network is composed of several couple households united by repeated bonds of compadrazgo of the most diverse types and functions as a well-organized system. Perhaps another difference between compadrazgo networks and the nonresidential extended family is that the latter has considerable residential unity (within the paraje), while the former does not; its component couple households may be dispersed throughout the entire community and sometimes in nearby settlements.

This comparison of kinship and compadrazgo shows that the nonresidential extended family has limited operational importance, and many of its functions have been usurped by the compadrazgo network. I do not want to overemphasize the point, but in statistical terms, more than 75 percent of all nine sets of activities described in "The Contexts Involved in Compadrazgo Behavior" (this chapter) are attributes of compadrazgo networks, regardless of whether the couple households of the network are related by additional kinship ties; and less than 25 percent are exclusively discharged by households of the nonresidential extended family. I can carry this analogy even further and say that what I have called the total web of compadrazgo of a given couple (all its egocentrically related compadres and their extensions at any given point in time) is, conceptually speaking, what constitutes a kindred in the average bilateral system. This total web of compadrazgo is not really operative in Belén, but neither is the bilateral kindred, and therefore the comparison is given merely for the sake of illustration. Let me add, however, that just as there is an awareness in Belén of large numbers of kinsmen (usually bearing a common name) as "parientes" (such a vague unit is technically some sort of kindred), there is also an awareness of all those individual couples and their extensions who are related by compadrazgo ties to a given couple—but in neither case is this recognition functionally important. Nevertheless, the total web of compadrazgo of a given individual is more important than his recognition of a vague kindred unit; at least he knows that among this undifferentiated mass of compadres he has considerable latitude in activating participation and cooperation, whereas this is not the case among the undifferentiated mass of an inoperative kindred.

I have tried in this chapter to analyze the interdigitation, conjunction, and overlapping of compadrazgo and kinship, and I hope to have demonstrated that while the former is modeled on the latter, they merge at many points, and as they expand outward to encompass the community as whole, compadrazgo becomes increasingly more important than kinship. Moreover, the structural differences and similarities between compadrazgo and kinship are not always translated into commensurate functional discharges, and while the structure of kinship may give an outward appearance of being more integrated and organized than that of compadrazgo, compadrazgo surpasses kinship in overall functional importance. If one approaches compadrazgo as an institution complementary to kinship and basically modeled on it, the institution acquires much greater significance both at the level of the individual and at that of the formation of egocentric units, as well as at the level of the community as a whole. I feel certain that the Belén model of compadrazgo is quite common not only in Tlaxcala but in much of Mesoamerica, and that its structure and functions play a comparable role in the social life of other communities.

✳ CHAPTER 13 ✳

The Egocentric Developmental Cycle of Compadrazgo

I come now to one of the most important parts of the analysis, namely, the developmental cycle of the compadrazgo system. By this I mean to denote essentially its dynamic aspects in operation synchronically, and its diachronic development egocentrically from the viewpoint of an individual couple and exocentrically from the viewpoint of compadrazgo as perhaps the most significant institution in the organization of community life. Like the domestic group, compadrazgo cannot be studied exclusively as a synchronic, static system without running the risk of overlooking a most important dynamic dimension. Just as the domestic group must be studied in terms of its genesis and mechanisms of formation, so the static components (the structural arrangements of types, both egocentrically and exocentrically) and the dynamic components of the compadrazgo system complement each other through a clearly defined development cycle. By studying this cycle I can show how compadrazgo types influence each other, thereby modifying the egocentric structure of the global system (or, if you wish, endowing it with systemic components). At the same time, I must be able to specify the variables that impinge upon the exocentric combination of factors structuring individual compadrazgo careers. This task cannot be accomplished by a strictly synchronic approach, but must perforce involve a sizable diachronic component. Here, I do not use diachronic to refer to historical development over a fairly long period, or to the use of documentary evidence. Rather, it refers to the study of compadrazgo careers within the ethnographic situation, in which one can see the changing compadrazgo perspective from the viewpoint of the individual couple as well as from that of the community over one or two generations— but not necessarily more than two. From the standpoint of both the compadrazgo system in general, and individual, egocentric compadrazgo types in particular, it is a sine qua non for proper conceptualization of this institution to establish the cycles that perpetuate the basic structure of compadrazgo. Once this conceptual standpoint is adopted, the compadrazgo system of Belén looms much larger than a consideration of its synchronic aspects alone might lead the researcher to assert, and one can see more clearly its unifying and pervasive role in the culture and society of Belén. From the very beginning of my fieldwork in Belén I emphasized the dynamic, developmental aspects of the compadrazgo system, and eventually collected more than fifty compadrazgo careers, recording a total of over 10,000 compadrazgo relationships distributed over a seventy-year period. These form the data for the present analysis.

Much of the information relevant to the developmental cycle of the compadrazgo system has already been presented in the chapters on structural analysis, for several of its aspects could not have been analyzed properly without specifying some dynamic components. This applies especially to the interchangeable forms of compadrazgo (see Chapter Eight) and the analysis of the permanent and temporary dimensions of compadrazgo relationships (see Chapter Seven). This and the following chapter try to tie together all the dynamic aspects of compadrazgo discussed earlier, and, more important, to show the mechanisms that affect the diachronic continuity of the institution. In particular, I want to elucidate the following: the configuration of clusters of compadrazgo types and their influence on the developmental cycle of compadrazgo with respect to recruitment, personnel, structural discharge, and the structure of the network and the web of ritual kinship; and the structure of the individual, egocentric developmental cycle of compadrazgo, with special attention to the formation of identifiable and operational compadrazgo units. The structure of the communal, exocentric developmental cycle of compadrazgo as one of the most important institutions causing community action to coalesce; and the structure of the network and the web of ritual kinship and the mechanisms of unit formation within which compadrazgo is functionally discharged as an organic aspect of Belén culture and society are discussed in Chapter Fourteen.

The Configuration of Compadrazgo Clusters

One of the most important aspects of the compadrazgo system in Belén is the fact that there are several groups of compadrazgo types that form into clusters (not necessarily mutually exclusive), both structurally and functionally. The existence of these clusters has a significant implication for the developmental cycle of the compadrazgo system. In fact, the structural attributes specified in at least half the rows in tables 1-11, 13-24, and 26-33 indicate a natural series of compadrazgo clusters. These clusters are related to the developmental cycle of compadrazgo in primarily two ways. On the one hand, the character of the compadrazgo types (their symbolic, religious, and social or other configurations) that form clusters determines to a large extent their position within the compadrazgo career of the average couple in Belén, and structurally they

TABLE 26. Beleños' Conscious Classification of Compadrazgo Types

Type	Sacramental	Primary Non-Sacramental	Secondary Non-Sacramental
Bautizo	x		
Casamiento	x		
Confirmación	x		
PCE	x		
Primera comunión	x		
CCCH	x		
CCCA	x		
ANDC		x	
ANDI		x	
AOI		x	
BSI		x	
CSV		x	
Escapulario		x	
Graduación		x	
PCA		x	
Quince años		x	
Sacada a misa		x	
Compadrazgo de evangelios		x	
Compadrazgo de limpia		x	
BOI		x	
Bendición de casa			x
BCC			x
BM			x
Parada de cruz			x
Primera piedra			x
Compadrazgo de amistad			x
CABP			x
Compadrazgo de aretes			x
CEON			x
FC			x
JJ			x

prescribe certain well specified types of behavior with a high common cultural denominator. On the other hand, and much more significant, the implementation of the types of compadrazgo clusters leads to repetition and intensification, and to the establishment of new compadrazgo relationships, thereby affecting the formation of compadrazgo networks. A look at tables 6, 8, 11, 18-24, and 26-31 reveals a clear or fairly clear configuration of clusters. Of these, the structurally more significant clusters are those in tables 18, 19, 21, 24, 26, and 27, and each is mentioned briefly before proceeding to the overall analysis.

The three basic clusters of compadrazgo types in Belén—sacramental, primary nonsacramental, and secondary nonsacramental—are shown in table 26. Perhaps a more refined account of this row could have been made in terms of sacramental compadrazgo (types 1-7), primarily religious nonsacramental compadrazgo (types 8-13, 18, 19, and 23), secondarily religious nonsacramental compadrazgo (types 15-17, 20-22, 24, 25, and 27), and secular compadrazgo (14, 26, and 28-31), but this classification does not carry more meaning than the one I actually used. This clustering affects the developmental cycle and the compadrazgo network mainly through the polarization of potential compadres in terms of the religious variable; that is, couples in Belén think of different kinds of personnel to fulfill the role of compadres, either initially or recurrently. In terms of traditional and new compadrazgo types (table 21), the clustering has primarily a prescriptive-preferential effect on the developmental cycle, to the extent that new compadrazgo types are relegated to the background in the presence of economic, and possibly other, constraints. The private-individual and public-communal clusters shown in table 18 deserve a separate discussion, for they are of categorical importance to the developmental cycle of compadrazgo. The three clusters based on the nature of the mediating entity (person, image, or object or occasion; table 27) are significant here because again they tend to bring together specific kinds of prospective compadres, thus intensifying compadrazgo egocentrically by repeated compadrazgo relationships. The clusters in table 19 are also of structural significance and are discussed together with those of table 18. Finally, table 24 clusters all compadrazgo types in Belén on the basis of their function for protection, propitiation, intensification, or thanksgiving. These symbolic attributes of compadrazgo types influence the selection of compadres, but it must be remembered that seldom are any of these tables structurally meaningful by themselves. Rather, each must be evaluated in conjunction with other tables. With this background, I càn analyze in detail the five most significant clusters in Belén, which directly and effectively impinge upon the developmental cycle of the compadrazgo system and the formation of networks.

TABLE 27. Mediating Entities by Compadrazgo Type

Type	Mediating Entity
Bautizo	Person
Casamiento	Persons
Confirmación	Person
PCE	Deceased man, woman, or child
Primera comunión	Person
CCCH	Persons
CCCA	Persons
ANDC	Image
ANDI	Image
AOI	Material object
BSI	Image or saint
CSV	Image
Escapulario	Person
Graduación	Person
PCA	Cross (event, object)
Quince años	Person
Sacada a misa	Person
Compadrazgo de evangelios	Person
Compadrazgo de limpia	Person
BOI	Material object
Bendición de casa	Material object
BCC	Material object
BM	Images
Parada de cruz	Material, animal, or vegetable objects
Primera piedra	Material object
Compadrazgo de amistad	Friendship
CABP	Event (silver wedding anniversary)
Compadrazgo de aretes	Person (event)
CEON	Material objects
FC	Vegetable object
JJ	Drinking friendship

The Compadrazgo de Fé Cluster

The first cluster of compadrazgo types involves sacramental compadrazgo vis-à-vis all other private-individual compadrazgo types in the system. Bautizo, casamiento, confirmación, PCE, and primera comunión form a rather noticeable cluster by virtue of the ideological significance attached to compadrazgo sponsorships associated with the sac-

TABLE 28. Presence of Pagan Rituals or Beliefs by Compadrazgo Type

Type	Present	Absent
Bautizo		x
Casamiento		x
Confirmación		x
PCE	x	
Primera comunión		x
CCCH		x
CCCA		x
ANDC	x	
ANDI	x	
AOI		x
BSI		x
CSV	x	
Escapulario	x	
Graduación		x
PCA	x	
Quince años		x
Sacada a misa	x	
Compadrazgo de evangelios	x	
Compadrazgo de limpia	x	
BOI		x
Bendición de casa		x
BCC		x
BM		x
Parada de cruz	x	
Primera piedra	x	
Compadrazgo de amistad		x
CABP		x
Compadrazgo de aretes	x	
CEON		x
FC	x	
JJ		x

raments of the Church, which the people of Belén, and Tlaxcalans in general, refer to as compadrazgos de fé. (CCCH and CCCA, which are essentially variants of marriage compadrazgo, can be disregarded here.) Let me emphasize again that this five-type cluster is not per se the most structurally significant or functionally important block in the total compadrazgo system, for two of its types (confirmación and primera comunión) rank lower than at least seven other compadrazgo types in

Belén. On the other hand, bautizo, casamiento, and PCE do rank very high, and overall this cluster is indeed at the top of the scale. It is the visibility of this cluster that has led to its overemphasis in the published literature on compadrazgo, and the consequent disregard of several other types that may be of greater (or at least equal) overall symbolic, social, or religious significance.

These types form a significant cluster because, on the one hand, they are ideologically the historical model of what compadrazgo should be, and the sacred nature of compadrazgo originally evolved out of their structural implementation; and, on the other hand, the sponsoring occasions of these five types represent the most significant events in the socioreligious life cycle of the individual, thereby giving the cluster a unitary meaning which is not necessarily found in other clusters of compadrazgo types. No doubt this is one reason most compadrazgo studies have been restricted to this cluster. Of more interest to the present analysis, however, is the influence of the compadrazgo de fé cluster on the developmental cycle of the compadrazgo system. Here again the influences are twofold.

First, the general characteristics, expectations, and socioreligious positions, and in general the visible attributes of prospective compadres and the ensuing permanent bonds and obligations are the same for all but one of the compadrazgo types in this cluster (primera comunión, which only appeared in Belén around 1920). Thus, the compadrazgo de fé cluster has clear implications for the individual compadrazgo career, the most specific of which are these: in the career of the average couple there will be a significant repetition of compadres de fé. Invariably, the same set of compadres will be used for two or even three of these types, and not infrequently also for two or three different mediating entities; this is especially the case for baptism, marriage, and PCE. The compadres belonging to the compadrazgo de fé cluster are one of the two main focal points in the formation of compadrazgo networks. The fact of belonging to one of the two focal compadrazgo configurations greatly affects the discharge of the compadrazgo de fé cluster, for it determines the course of the average couple's compadrazgo career. Both as a mediating entity (ahijado and ahijada at marriage) and as full-fledged compadres (baptism and PCE, given the high incidence of mortality before the age of five) the couple begins its career, and acquires its first compadres egocentrically, within this environment. Finally, the tone and general character of the compadrazgo career of the average couple in Belén are influenced by these compadrazgo relationships, the first in which the couple engages as primary actors on its own. The majority of the seven types of compadrazgo de fé (including now CCCH and CCCA) serve as ostensible models in the implementation of compa-

TABLE 29. Primary Reasons for Establishing Compadrazgo
Relationships

Type	Primary Reasons
Bautizo	Already established compadrazgo relationship
Casamiento	Already established compadrazgo relationship
Confirmación	Friends or neighbors
PCE	Friendship or baptismal compadrazgo
Primera comunión	Already established compadrazgo relationship; friendship
CCCH	As a result of casamiento compadrazgo
CCCA	As a result of casamiento compadrazgo
ANDC	Friendship; neighborhood
ANDI	Communal harmony
AOI	Neighbors, or village as a whole
BSI	Already BSI compadres or friends
CSV	Communal harmony
Escapulario	Neighbors or friends
Graduación	Various; the only type in which compadres may be kinsmen
PCA	Communal harmony
Quince años	Friendship; already established compadrazgo relationship
Sacada a misa	Already baptismal compadres, or close friends
Compadrazgo de evangelios	Already baptismal compadres, or close friends
Compadrazgo de limpia	Already escapulario compadres, or neighbors
BOI	Communal harmony
Bendición de casa	Already primera piedra compadres, or friends or neighbors
BCC	Other vehicle owners
BM	Communal harmony
Parada de cruz	Friendship; previous bendición de casa or parada de cruz compadres
Primera piedra	Neighbors or friends
Compadrazgo de amistad	Friends (generally from other communities in Tlaxcala)
CABP	Already compadres of a variety of types

TABLE 29 (*cont.*)

Type	Primary Reasons
Compadrazgo de aretes	Friendship and neighborhood
CEON	Already compadres of a variety of types
FC	Friends
JJ	Friends (often from other communities in Tlaxcala)

drazgo ideology, but perhaps more important, in the discharge of specific activities in future compadrazgo relationships, inasmuch as the various compadrazgo types provide some leeway with regard to making the pedimento, the quantity and quality of the central ceremonies, and the social, economic, and religious constraints in the structuring of permanent rights and obligations. Thus, the compadrazgo de fé types are not only intrinsically important, but as the first compadrazgo relationships in which the average couple engages independently, they form a significant dimension in structuring the developmental cycle both egocentrically and exocentrically.

Second, the influence of the compadrazgo de fé cluster on the developmental cycle of the system is much more important in the area of the repetition and intensification of compadrazgo relationships. One of the main characteristics of all five significant clusters of the system is that compadres almost invariably ask for a second and third compadrazgo relationship and sometimes more, which obviously leads to the establishment of strong, close bonds among the couples in question. This is particularly true of the compadrazgo de fé cluster. Since no prescription is associated with the repetition of compadres, this aspect of compadrazgo structure must be regarded as an optional or preferential dimension that is determined by specific exogenous considerations having to do with the proper conjunction of the determinants of compadrazgo selection. However, the frequency of repetition leading to intensification may lead the casual observer to assign prescription when it does not really exist.

I can make the following generalizations about the compadrazgo de fé cluster. The average couple in Belén has at least four repeated sets of compadres de fé for the same ahijados or ahijadas, during the main part of its career (that is, from about ten years after marriage until the last of its children is married, or from approximately ages thirty to sixty). The number may double when there are repeated compadres for different ahijados; it is not unusual, for example, to use the same set of com-

TABLE 30. Folk-Orthodox or Folk-Pagan Classification of
Compadrazgo Types

Types	Folk-Orthodox	Folk-Orthodox–Pagan	Folk-Pagan
Bautizo	x		
Casamiento	x		
Confirmación	x		
PCE		x	
Primera comunión	x		
CCCH	x		
CCCA	x		
ANDC		x	
ANDI		x	
AOI	x		
BSI	x		
CSV	x		
Escapulario		x	
Graduación	x		
PCA			x
Quince años	x		
Sacada a misa	x		
Compadrazgo de evangelios		x	
Compadrazgo de limpia		x	
BOI	x		
Bendición de casa	x		
BCC	x		
BM	x		
Parada de cruz			x
Primera piedra		x	
Compadrazgo de amistad	x		
CABP	x		
Compadrazgo de aretes			x
CEON	x		
FC			x
JJ	x		

TABLE 31. Primacy of Life, Religious, or Symbolic Cycle by
Compadrazgo Type

Type	Life Cycle	Religious Cycle	Symbolic Cycle
Bautizo	x		
Casamiento	x		
Confirmación	x		
PCE	x		
Primera comunión	x		
CCCH	x		
CCCA	x		
ANDC			x
ANDI			x
AOI		x	
BSI		x	
CSV		x	
Escapulario			x
Graduación	x		
PCA			x
Quince años	x		
Sacada a misa		x	
Compadrazgo de evangelios		x	
Compadrazgo de limpia			x
BOI		x	
Bendición de casa			x
BCC			x
BM			x
Parada de cruz			x
Primera piedra			x
Compadrazgo de amistad	x		
CABP	x		
Compadrazgo de aretes			x
CEON			x
FC			x
JJ	x		

padres to baptize two or three consecutive children. Other practices are
even more visible and well organized, as for example, when the main
set of casamiento padrinos baptizes its ahijados' first child, and they
thereby become compadres. I estimate that this is the case with 80 percent of all married couples in Belén, and it has been a constant for the

seventy years for which I have adequate information. This is an interesting case, in that the situation, which I have called an anomalous feature of the compadrazgo system, has significance for the individual, egocentric developmental cycle of compadrazgo. On the whole, the main effect of this anomalous situation is to reduce the total number of independent compadrazgo sets, but at the same time it intensifies the quality of the compadrazgo relationship, and indirectly helps create more integrated compadrazgo networks on an exocentric basis. A similar situation obtains when the baptismal padrinos become the PCE padrinos, which occurs frequently among children and young adults, since by the time older adults die, their baptismal padrinos are usually already dead. In view of the high rate of infant mortality in Tlaxcala (even today, perhaps 35 percent of all children die before the age of five), this practice acquires significant proportions. The practice of baptismal padrinos becoming PCE padrinos is essentially the same as the practice of marriage padrinos becoming the baptismal padrinos of their ahijados' first child, and both influence the developmental cycle of compadrazgo in the same structural fashion. Finally, there is also some preference for using previous baptismal, marriage, and PCE compadres for confirmación and primera comunión, but this practice does not occur nearly as frequently as those associated with the three main types of the cluster. How the compadrazgo de fé cluster operates in action can best be demonstrated through specific examples, which I provide in subsequent sections.

The Parada de Cruz Compadrazgo Cluster

The second cluster of compadrazgo types in Belén includes several types that have in common primarily some variation of the symbolic act of setting up a cross: PCA, bendición de casa, parada de cruz, and primera piedra (PCE is an anomalous case that is sometimes in this, sometimes in the compadrazgo de fé cluster). These compadrazgo types represent a symbolic act of protection and propitiation, and in some cases intensification, so that the entire cluster is characterized by the same overt function. In fact, not only in form but also in substance the functions and activities connected with these four or five compadrazgo types are essentially homologous and analogous; this makes the present group, which I refer to as the parada de cruz cluster, rather similar to the compadrazgo de fé cluster.

Two things must be noted at the outset. First, the parada de cruz compadrazgo cluster is the other focal point in the formation of compadrazgo networks. (A third focal point, which in many ways is as important as the compadrazgo de fé and parada de cruz clusters, exists, namely, the public-communal types. But since from the individual viewpoint they are of limited distribution, and at least theoretically affect the community as a whole, it is better to treat them separately.) The parada de cruz cluster also ranks high in the prescriptive-preferential-optional scale (see table 12), and overall its component types rank only slightly below those of the compadrazgo de fé cluster.

Second, the absolute incidence of types in the parada de cruz cluster is affected by the fact that it involves several subtypes, especially associated with the parada de cruz itself, in which there are at least nine occasions for establishing a new compadrazgo relationship. In terms of the incidence of absolute relationships, the parada de cruz cluster does not rank as high as the compadrazgo de fé cluster, but what it lacks in numbers it makes up in intrinsic importance and in the individual strength of compadrazgo relationships. The unitary protection or propitiation and intensification function of the types of this cluster makes them a very significant group within the global compadrazgo system, and Beleños overtly single them out as models of compadrazgo behavior in action. It is difficult to say whether the compadrazgo de fé or the parada de cruz cluster ranks higher in the compadrazgo system of Belén because the importance of the two clusters is different, or rather resides in different loci of the institution. The types of the compadrazgo de fé cluster are intrinsically more important ideologically, and fundamentally it is their ideological model that underlies the sacred nature of compadrazgo in Belén. Structurally, however, the types of the parada de cruz cluster are perhaps more important in actual discharge, and this is indicated by the high premium that Beleños place on compadres belonging to this cluster. In any event, these two clusters form the ideological-structural core of the compadrazgo system, and all other compadrazgo types (and clusters), private-individual or public-communal, must be assessed with respect to them.

Much of what I have said about the influence of the compadrazgo de fé cluster on the development cycle of the compadrazgo system applies here also, and I therefore confine myself to the differences between the clusters. In the first place, the repetitiveness of compadrazgo relationships, involving the same or different mediating entities, is considerably less, for there are only so many houses, baking ovens, *temazcales* (steam baths), tiendas, wells, sementeras, and other sponsoring occasions that require the establishment of a compadrazgo relationship. Thus, repetitiveness here is confined to using one set of compadres for two or at most three sponsoring occasions. Of course, the nature of the mediating entity makes a great difference in the structure of primary and secondary personnel of compadrazgo relationships, for in the compadrazgo de fé cluster the mediating entity is always a person, whereas in the parada de cruz cluster the mediating entities are always objects or occasions. In the latter, then, the padrinos-ahijados dyad does not obtain beyond the immediate symbolic occasion, thereby reducing the total number of compadrazgo personnel.

Of much greater significance is the fact that all the parada de cruz types occur after the main part of the compadrazgo de fé cluster has been fully organized—that is, usually fifteen to twenty years after the average couple in Belén begins its active compadrazgo career. Before this, the couple belongs to types in the cluster only as secondary or tertiary relatives, for in one way or another the two are tied economically or socially to parents and even to grandparents, and therefore lack independent occasions for establishing relationships belonging to the parada de cruz cluster. For example, seldom does a man construct his own house before the fifteenth year of marriage, or have his own plot of land through which he may independently contract one of the types or subtypes of the parada de cruz cluster. The fact that parada de cruz types occur in the middle or late compadrazgo career of the average couple in Belén is perhaps the most significant difference between it and the compadrazgo de fé cluster.

The position of the parada de cruz types within the life cycle of the average couple means that the pair already has a fairly wide network of compadrazgo ties, and that to some extent the selection of parada de cruz types will be modified or influenced by these existing ties. The main consequence is that there will be some repetition between the compadrazgo de fé cluster and the parada de cruz cluster, for almost invariably certain compadres belonging to the former will be used for the latter. Most commonly either confirmación or primera comunión compadres will be used for paradas de cruz in any of its forms, but seldom if ever will baptism, marriage, or PCE compadres be used. This is overtly expressed by Beleños when they say that it is not a good thing to mix certain compadres de fé and compadres de parada de cruz. The rationale here points straight to the differences in compadrazgo personnel in the two clusters. The age differences between compadres can sometimes be great in compadrazgos de fé, especially when wedding padrinos become their ahijados' compadres for the baptism of a first child. In parada de cruz types, this is never the case; the compadres belong to the same age group and may have been interacting in positions of social and religious equality for a long period. Indeed, personnel of the parada de cruz types get their strength from the fact that they have either been related by previous compadrazgo ties of long standing, or have been close friends or neighbors for equally long periods.

I can summarize the differences between these two clusters by saying that while the compadrazgo de fé cluster is the initial, overall model of compadrazgo configuration and behavior which guides the early stages of the average couple's career, the parada de cruz cluster represents the paradigm of compadrazgo form and behavior in their later developments. Moreover, the compadrazgo de fé cluster rarely involves antecedent compadrazgo relationships; selection and recruitment are based entirely on the criteria discussed in Chapter Five of *Ritual Kinship* I. In large part, the parada de cruz cluster is underlain by previous compadrazgo relationships involving at least nine or ten types, which tends to present the average couple with stronger candidates. As a result, the strongest compadrazgo ties from middle to old age almost invariably belong to types of the parada de cruz cluster. People generally begin to acquire compadrazgo relationships in the parada de cruz cluster around the age of forty, and this continues until the age of sixty or so. After this, probably the only parada de cruz sponsorships undertaken are those connected with the agricultural cycle, and perhaps occasionally those connected with additions to the house. Thus the compadrazgo de fé and parada de cruz clusters represent not only structural-ideological opposites in the compadrazgo system, but also time opposites in the compadrazgo careers of Belén couples. Although this paradigm is ideologically accurate, it is of course modified in practice by constraints that fall outside the specification of the compadrazgo structure.

The Secondary Compadrazgo Cluster

All the major compadrazgo types and subtypes of the compadrazgo de fé and parada de cruz clusters are primary types (see table 8); that is, in overall importance they rank at the top of the compadrazgo system. The third cluster of compadrazgo types—ANDC, BSI, escapulario, graduación, quince años, sacada a misa, compadrazgo de evangelios, compadrazgo de limpia, and CEON—on the other hand, are primarily of secondary importance (graduation in sometimes secondary and sometimes tertiary, and quince años is a tertiary type). The main reason for considering these compadrazgo types as a meaningful cluster is not, as in the previous clusters, because they derive a unitary meaning from their function or symbolic content, but rather because they are secondary in importance with some types (such as CEON, BSI, and compadrazgo de limpia) that are less tied to the developmental cycle than is characteristic of the other two clusters. In other words, most of the compadrazgo relationships in this cluster, which for lack of a better term, I refer to as the secondary cluster, may be contracted at any time during the average compadrazgo career.

A second, perhaps more important characteristic of the secondary cluster is that its types are most often contracted initially with a new set of compadres. A compadrazgo relationship in the secondary cluster may lead to another relationship of more intrinsic significance, although, as in the case of the other clusters, there can be repetition leading to intensification within the cluster itself. All nine types of the secondary cluster are, however, important enough in their own right to constitute meaningful compadrazgo relationships, and they need not lead to more intensified compadrazgo relationships to play an important role in a compadrazgo network. Most couples have at least five individual compadrazgo relationships in the secondary cluster, but the contracting of these relationships depends on whether or not the sponsoring occasion presents itself. A given couple may never have to make a limpia because the occasion does not present itself, but I am not concerned at the moment with statistical incidence—only with whatever prescriptions or preferences are involved should the occasion arise. In other words, what I have said about all three clusters specifies not only what people should do or must do for any given sponsoring occasion, but also the constraints that impede or facilitate the contracting of a given relationship.

The Tertiary Compadrazgo Cluster

The fourth meaningful cluster of the compadrazgo system involves the intrinsically least important types in Belén: compadrazgo de amistad, CABP, compadrazgo de arctes, ΓC, and JJ. All five types are tertiary, and I therefore refer to them as the tertiary cluster. The main characteristic uniting them is the fact that while they may be regarded formally as meaningful types in themselves, in practice it is better to regard them as steps leading to more important compadrazgo relationships. There is probably not a single compadrazgo relationship in the tertiary cluster that remains independent at the end of the average couple's compadrazgo career. I could perhaps refer to these five types as one of the situational contexts that impinge upon the process of compadrazgo selection and recruitment, but I decided against it because the people themselves clearly identified these as separate types. Again, three of the five types of the tertiary cluster are not associated with any particular period.

The bonds and obligations of these compadrazgo types are per se temporary, but inasmuch as they invariably lead to other compadrazgo relationships, the temporary dimension is translated into a permanent one within the context of another type. From this viewpoint, it can be said that there are really almost no temporary compadrazgo bonds and obligations in Belén, for only four types fail to lead to other compadrazgo relationships and are classified as temporary (see table 19), and these are among the least important types. When compadrazgo relationships grow cold or come to an end, this is not attributable to the intrinsic nature of the relationship but rather to various exogenous considerations. All things being normal—that is, exogenous considerations aside—permanent compadrazgo relationships do not grow cold, and temporary compadrazgo relationships eventually lead to relationships of a permanent nature. The only type in the tertiary cluster that can be said to involve permanent bonds and obligations is CABP. This is understandable given the fact that it comes late in the compadrazgo career, and is also the only type in which the padrinos may have been previously related to the couple.

Whether or not a compadrazgo type leads to the establishment of other compadrazgo relationships is an important structural characteristic of the compadrazgo cycle. Three types not belonging to the tertiary cluster also lead to other relationships (see table 19). There is a difference here, however, that must be established before proceeding with the analysis. In Chapter Seven I discussed the definition and characteristics of the nineteen types in Belén that result from or lead to other compadrazgo relationships. Three of the five types in the tertiary cluster (all but CAPB and FC) are leading-to types, whereas the fourteen other types in this general category are resulting-from types. Several of the resulting-from types fall in the secondary cluster; they not only occupy an intermediate position along the prescriptive-optional continuum of the compadrazgo system, but also in terms of importance their structural position is such that sooner or later they are intensified. The leading-to–resulting-from dichotomy is, however, only relative, for it depends to a considerable extent on the particular form that a given couple's career takes. This involves several alternatives, and only on the basis of these alternatives can leading-to and resulting-from types acquire a more meaningful interpretation. From the viewpoint of the compadrazgo system as a whole, virtually all compadrazgo types in Belén may be regarded at one point or other in the average career as leading-to or resulting-from types. Table 19 simply indicates where each type usually falls in terms of the fourfold classification of permanent, temporary, leading to, and resulting from. When I say that PCE, for example, involves permanent bonds and obligations, I simply mean that were a particular couple not to establish any further compadrazgo relationships, the bonds and obligations binding them to the PCE padrinos would continue indefinitely without any further intensification. When I say that AOI has temporary bonds and obligations, I mean that after a prescribed period these come to an end unless they are properly intensified and the two sets of compadres again become ritually related. Finally, the property of leading to or resulting from indicates primarily the context and direction of intensification—that is, the process that results in the structure of permanent bonds and obligations.

The Public-Communal Compadrazgo Cluster

The fifth or public-communal compadrazgo cluster includes all six public-communal types. While these types are structurally similar to private-individual types and have analogous functions, their public, communal dimensions set them apart as a meaningful cluster. It is important to keep in mind that public-communal compadrazgo types involve two distinct aspects: the structure and organization of primary personnel, that is, the padrinos and young madrina, and those who make the pedimento (fiscales and mayordomos); and the communal dimensions of the sponsorship, that is, the extensions of the compadrazgo relationship to the community as a whole for short periods. Public-communal types are essentially the same as private-individual types in the former aspect; their communal dimensions are, however, functionally different from anything in private-individual compadrazgo. Thus, disregarding the public, community-wide dimensions of public-communal compadrazgo, one can classify its six types into the preceding private-individual clusters according to their intrinsic importance and the nature of their bonds and obligations. In this light, CSV and BM belong to the compadrazgo de fé cluster; PCA and ANDI to the parada de cruz cluster; and AOI and BOI to the secondary cluster. From a different viewpoint, one can say that while public-communal compadrazgo in its wider, public dimensions effectively influences the exocentric aspects of the developmental cycle, in its private-individual dimensions it affects the egocentric aspects. Public-communal compadrazgo differs essentially from private-individual in having a set of added functional dimensions that result in community-wide action and behavior, but in analyzing the egocentric developmental cycle of compadrazgo, both must be treated in the same way. Public-communal types in the restricted sense possess the general characteristics of the clusters to which I have assigned them above, and therefore possess corresponding permanent, temporary, leading-to, or resulting-from properties.

Perhaps a sixth cluster of types can be isolated as bearing directly on the developmental cycle of the compadrazgo system. These are the interchangeable types: escapulario, sacada a misa, compadrazgo de evangelios, compadrazgo de limpia, BCC, compadrazgo de amistad, CEON, and JJ. The structural and functional implications of interchangeable compadrazgo have been discussed in Chapter Eight (see table 20). Here, I only note again that interchangeable compadrazgo types, which belong exclusively to the secondary and tertiary clusters, have a rather significant influence in the egocentric developmental cycle of compadrazgo in that they tend to diminish the total number of original compadrazgo relationships for the average couple in Belén.

From Birth to Adolescence

The compadrazgo career of the individual in Belén begins shortly after birth, when the infant becomes the mediating entity in the sponsorship of baptism and the ostensible cause of this compadrazgo relationship. The child obviously remains inactive in the relationship until the age of three or so, when he begins to follow the prescribed and preferred behavior patterns associated with baptismal compadrazgo. At about the age of five the child is confirmed, thereby acquiring a second set of padrinos and corresponding behavior patterns which he immediately activates. Even now, the compadrazgo careers of perhaps 35 percent of all children in Belén will come to an end before they reach five, when death makes them PCE ahijados. For the 65 percent or so who survive, the following fifteen to seventeen years will witness an increasing involvement in the compadrazgo system, almost invariably as ahijados or ahijadas. The next occasion that requires a compadrazgo sponsorship is first communion, between ages eight and twelve. Thus, by the time a child becomes an adolescent, he has at least three sets of padrinos. I say at least because before the age of ten or twelve, the child can become a mediating entity in a series of other possible sponsorships. If the child is a girl, her mother will usually pierce her ears when the child is between the ages of one and two, and the girl thus acquires a set of padrinos de aretes. Almost invariably, small children find twin fruits or vegetables which also require a sponsorship, in which, after the central ceremonies, their status changes from compadres to ahijados. Again, almost invariably the average child in Belén will undergo a limpia before reaching the age of twelve, thereby acquiring another set of padrinos. If there has never been any need for a limpia, the child most likely was independently given a scapulary, thereby acquiring another set of padrinos.

In summary, then, by the age of twelve or so, the average child in Belén has anywhere from five to as many as eight sets of padrinos, including bautizo, confirmación, primera comunión, escapulario, compadrazgo de evangelios, compadrazgo de limpia, compadrazgo de aretes, and FC. At the end of this period of his life cycle, the child likes to keep active his ties with these sets of padrinos, for they are essentially the only significant ritual kinship relationships in which he engages individually. He is part of several other compadrazgo relationships of a secondary or even primary nature by virtue of being a member of his parents' household, but he is either too young to participate in them, or not interested in participating. Thus, from the age of approximately three to about twelve, the child in Belén is socially introduced to the various aspects of compadrazgo behavior either directly by relating to his several sets of padrinos, or indirectly by observing what goes on in compadrazgo interaction centered around the household. In terms of socializing, this is a significant period in the child's life in Belén.

From Adolescence to Marriage

The second important period in the life cycle begins roughly at the age of twelve, and lasts for approximately ten years or until marriage, which takes place around the age of twenty for women and twenty-two for men. During this period youngsters become increasingly involved in the compadrazgo system both directly and indirectly, in a variety of contexts. Directly they become mediating entities in at least three more compadrazgo types, namely, graduación. quince años, and compadrazgo de amistad. The first graduation occasion, from primary school, comes for the average child at about twelve or thirteen, and most children's parents celebrate the occasion by establishing a compadrazgo relationship. For an increasing number of children, a second occasion arises upon graduation from secondary school, three or four years later; and a third occasion for a still comparatively small number of children, by now young men or women, upon graduation from high school, normal school, or secretarial, business, or nursing school. By the time the average youngster is ready to get married, he has finished whatever education he has been able to afford, and many have engaged in as many as three padrinazgos (ritual sponsorship) de graduación.

The quince años sponsorship is not yet universal in Belén, but more and more girls now have this celebration, thereby acquiring one more set of padrinos. At the end of this second period comes the first opportunity for boys to engage in compadrazgo relationships individually and as primary actors in the category of compadres—the compadrazgo de amistad, which at this stage is exclusively a male prerogative. This is an important event in the developmental cycle of compadrazgo, because for the first time the individual enters the compadrazgo system of his own volition. This most commonly happens at work. By the time a boy is twenty, if he is no longer in school (and generally he is not) he is probably engaged in either daily or weekly migratory work, where he comes into contact with other migrant youngsters from Belén or neighboring communities and in this context acquires his first compadrazgo de amistad.

Throughout what can be termed the adolescent years, youngsters may become ahijados in several compadrazgo types, most commonly escapulario (if one was not given when he was a child), limpia, and FC. I estimate that before the age of marriage, the average youngster has at least one limpia. FC also has its highest incidence during the adolescent years, for children spend more time then in intimate contact with nature in their play and in hiding from their elders, and very often find twin fruits and vegetables. Limpias are also quite common during this period, and they always require ritual sponsorship. Finally, a limited number of girls between the ages of twelve and seventeen become young madrinas for the central ceremonies of ANDI, CSV, BM, and in a much higher number of cases, ANDC. These occasions for young females are somewhat analogous to compadrazgo de amistad for males, but not necessarily homologous, for after the principal ceremonies are over, the young madrinas revert to their roles as ahijadas. (Children, especially young boys, play a role in the parada de cruz compadrazgos, particularly PCA, bendición de casa, and parada de cruz. Not infrequently, one of the children of the padrinos de parada de cruz is asked to set up the cross, and throughout the proceedings he is addressed as "compadrito." After the ceremonies are over, however, the boy does not become a primary ahijado as is the case for ANDI, CSV, or BM madrinas, and for this reason I did not include this aspect of child participation in Chapter Two. In terms of socialization, however, the participation of children in paradas de cruz is significant.)

Indirectly, youngsters may play a role as secondary or even primary actors within the household, as their parents engage in a wide variety of compadrazgo types. I established at the beginning of this section that a youngster begins to play fairly distinct behavioral roles after the age of twelve, and in such capacities the average child in Belén leads a rather active ritual kinship life. Throughout these years the youngsters of Belén continue their indoctrination into the behavioral and ideological aspects of compadrazgo, and by the time of marriage they are thoroughly socialized into every aspect of the institution. To sum up, by the time of marriage, the average young man and woman in Belén has had considerable experience as an ahijado or ahijada, and some limited experience as a compadre. By now he or she have accumulated four to eight more padrinazgos, which together with those of the previous stage make a total that can vary from a minimum of eight to a maximum of fifteen or so padrinazgo relationships—all of which are usually kept.

From Ahijados to Compadres: The Marriage Interlude

We come now to a most important juncture in the developmental cycle, namely marriage. Marriage represents the last important occasion in the life cycle in which young men and women will play the role of ahijados, in a theoretically permanent fashion. (I say theoretical because, as the reader may recall, marriage ahijados are generally transformed into compadres of the marriage padrinos by the baptism of their first child.)

At the same time, and much more important, marriage formally marks the couple's entrance into the active compadrazgo system in its own right, regardless of household membership. This comes almost automatically after the birth of the couple's first child, when the two must either select padrinos or, more commonly, ask their main marriage padrinos to baptize the child and thereby become compadres. The entrance of the husband and wife into the compadrazgo system is a very important event in their lives, which is marked by the most elaborate celebration of their career with regard to the sacramental sponsorship of children—with the exception, of course, of the marriage of their first son. The baptism of the first child is characterized by a larger attendance and a more lavish ceremonial banquet and associated rituals than usual, and by the couple's efforts to generate as much cooperation and participation as possible among its parents' compadrazgo networks—all those primary (mostly padrinos), secondary (mostly their parents and older siblings' compadres), and even tertiary relatives who had become their ritual kin while they were members of their households of orientation. But given the rather strong patrilineal bias of Belén society, in this as in most other compadrazgo celebrations (with the exception of marriage), the ritual kinsmen of the husband and his family always, and sometimes by far, outnumber those of the wife and her family.

Symbolically, the occasion of a couple's first baptism is marked by overt counsel of its parents and other kinsmen, its active padrinos, and in general the most important compadres attending the celebration, to the effect that henceforth the two are more or less free agents in choosing compadres, and that they have entered a new stage in their social and religious development. These admonitions are given in the traditional round of speeches that characterizes the ceremonial banquet of baptismal compadrazgo (see Ritual Kinship I, pages 65-66), which structurally must be regarded as a kind of mild rite of passage. The young parents are advised to take seriously the contracting of compadrazgo relationships, to be aware of the religious and symbolic necessity for complying with the various kinds of compadrazgo types, and above all, to be worthy of respeto and confianza and always willing to generate reliance. In fact, a first baptism is one of the most telling events in the compadrazgo cycle, for throughout the proceedings the nature of compadrazgo is clearly spelled out, as well as what is expected of the couple and what it can in turn expect of its increasing compadrazgo relationships. By our informants' own statements, this is always a most impressive occasion for the young couple, and many of them vividly remember it as an example of what compadrazgo is all about.

Between the birth of the couple's first child and the marriage of its last son or daughter, that is, when husband and wife are roughly between the ages of twenty-four and sixty, the main developmental stage of compadrazgo in Belén takes place. Moreover, these thirty-five years or so are obviously the most active in the couple's compadrazgo career. For heuristic purposes this long period can be divided into two substages. The first substage (henceforth referred to as the first stage of the developmental cycle) extends from the baptism of the first child until approximately the baptism of the last child; and the second substage (henceforth the second stage) from the baptism of the last child to the marriage of the last son or daughter. Both stages are characterized by the contracting of rather specific compadrazgo types, and by certain social, religious, and economic considerations, which need to be analyzed separately.

The First Stage: From Young Adulthood to Early Middle Age

The first stage extends approximately from ages twenty-four to forty, and corresponds almost exactly to the birth cycle of the women of Belén. The average woman in Belén gives birth to seven children, of whom four or five survive past the age of five. This means that they will reach adulthood, for there is virtually no child mortality after the age of five. The usual birth pattern is a child every two years, and not infrequently every eighteen months. This means that women seldom give birth after they are about thirty-eight years old. Give or take a year, the average woman in Belén reproduces for a period of fifteen years. During this decade and a half, the main compadrazgo relationships engaged in by the average couple belong to the sacramental cluster, that is, baptism, confirmation, and first communion; and to the sporadic types of escapulario, limpia, and FC, that is, all those types connected with the life cycle of infants and children from the ages of one to twelve. However, since the last-born will not be confirmed until some five years after his birth and will make his first communion at least eight years later, the first stage in the developmental cycle is, strictly speaking, prolonged another eight years after the birth of the ultimogenit. Nevertheless, most of these compadrazgo types are contracted during the first fifteen years of marriage. After the age of thirty-eight or forty, the average couple will usually have to contract no more than six confirmación, primera comunión, compadrazgo de limpia, and compadrazgo de aretes relationships, while the figure for the previous fifteen years can easily be five times as large. By the end of the first stage in the developmental cycle, the average couple has thus contracted from twenty-five to thirty-five compadrazgo relationships (assuming seven children and counting those who die before the age of five, but who must be baptized, perhaps given a limpia or aretes, and most certainly be buried with the benefit of PCE padrinos).

At the same time, the couple has contracted a rather wide variety of other compadrazgo relationships during these fifteen years, including BSI, sacada a misa, compadrazgo de evangelios, compadrazgo de amistad, CEON, JJ, and possibly at the end AOI and BOI—and in addition, sporadic and unexpected compadrazgos de limpia and FC. The compadrazgos de sacada de misa and evangelios come at fixed times, and generally are not really separate from baptismal compadrazgo; forty days after birth, and again three years after, the mother and child are presented in church, usually with the sponsorship of the child's baptismal padrinos. Throughout this stage the husband may contract several compadrazgo de amistad that result in permanent compadrazgo relationships. Usually no more than two or three are contracted during the first five to seven years when the young couple must make sure of having a good supply of prospective compadres for the more important types. The husband will also contract one or two JJ compadrazgo relationships, also during the early part of the first stage. And during the first stage, the couple always establishes several BSI and CEON compadrazgo relationships, regardless of whether it is living in an independent household or is part of an extended family household.

Shortly after the birth of the first child the young parents set up their own altar, either in the room assigned to them within an extended family arrangement, or in their own main room if they have been lucky enough to start their married life neolocally. This demands that the principal saint of their devotion be sponsored by BSI padrinos, and thereby they acquire a second set of compadres. For about the next fifteen years the number of saints and images on the nuclear family altar will increase considerably (the average middle-aged couple in Belén has an altar with eight to twelve), but probably no more than three will be acquired with a BSI compadrazgo sponsorship. Finally, during the last half of the first stage the couple will buy some significant items of property especially connected with the household, such as stoves, radios, furniture, and more recently television sets. This will require the contracting of CEON compadrazgo relationships, but seldom more than two or three. Occasionally, at the end of the first stage, the husband becomes mayordomo of the least important mayordomias or acompañante (attendant) in the República Eclesiástica in which capacity he will have to enter into an AOI or BOI compadrazgo relationship. This is not common, however, for men younger than forty are seldom nominated or selected for these positions; furthermore, these are not regular or fixed compadrazgo types, but come into being sporadically every three or four years. In summary, taking into consideration the fixed compadrazgo types, the sporadic types, and the repetitions—connected to both the life cycle of children up to the age of twelve, and the life cycle of the parents—at the end of the first stage the average couple in Belén may have accumulated from forty to fifty compadrazgo relationships.

The first developmental stage of compadrazgo in Belén has the following economic, social, and religious characteristics. Economically, these are unquestionably the hardest years for the nuclear family. Although it is becoming increasingly common for couples to start their married life neolocally, patrineolocality still prevails, but the period before separation from the husband's household of orientation is becoming increasingly shorter—perhaps no more than three or at the most four years. The establishment of an independent nuclear family household does not, however, necessarily mean complete economic independence. In one way or another, sons often continue to count on the economic help of the paternal household, which is usually given in kind or cash. Not infrequently, even after separation the land of the paternal household continues to be cultivated in common, with the usufruct divided more or less evenly among it and sons' independent households. The average household agricultural production, however, is not all that important; of more economic importance to separating sons are the cash and goods that they usually need for the frequent ceremonial occasions connected with the compadrazgo cycle and other social and religious activities.

The nuclear family almost never builds its own house until the beginning of the next stage of the developmental cycle—usually when the husband and wife are past the age of forty. Thoughout the first stage, it lives either in an extended family arrangement (very often with sons scaling their period of patrilocal residence according to age) or in a nearby house, generally an old structure, sometimes with only a single room, until it is economically stable and can build a new house. By the end of the first developmental stage, the husband has generally achieved an economic status that probably will not change much until the nuclear family comes to an end. By the end of the first stage the nuclear family has begun to reach a balance between the agricultural economy and labor migration, or become active in some of the alternative modes of subsistence and modest capitalization open to Beleños. Throughout the entire first stage the independent or dependent nuclear family must watch its step economically and look toward the future, when the new house can be built and it can relax a little.

From the social viewpoint, the first stage is a period of intense activity; children are born and must go through the necessary compadrazgo sponsorships, which always require a considerable expenditure of money, to say nothing of the disbursements the average couple must make when it is asked to enter into compadrazgo relationships. Moreover, husband

and wife must participate as secondary and even tertiary actors in the compadrazgo relationships of their parents, siblings, perhaps even grandparents, and nearest kinsmen, which in turn may require the expenditure of time and money. Since the required social involvement of compadrazgo and other aspects of the life cycle are not always compatible with solvency, the family's strategy throughout the first developmental stage is one of cautious spending and careful social involvement. First priority is given to compadrazgo obligations and the contracting of new types, and other social involvements are secondary. It should be pointed out, however, that the economic hardship that gives rise to restricted social involvement during the first developmental stage is often relieved by parental (and to some extent kinship) help, and undoubtedly by the increasing web of compadres that the couple begins to enjoy perhaps halfway through this stage.

Finally, from the religious viewpoint, there is an implicit arrangement in Belén culture and society that religious participation be held to a minimum throughout the first sixteen or so years of marriage, thereby explicitly recognizing the nuclear family's economic struggle. On the whole, direct religious participation is confined to secondary positions in the República Eclesiástica, and the least important mayordomias which do not require much of an expenditure. Only under special circumstances, and largely among the economic elite, will a man be selected for an important mayordomía or become a fiscal tercero before the age of forty. On the other hand, it is quite common for men to participate as acompañantes in a variety of cargos (wives also participate in complementary positions) in which the requirement is largely in terms of services, with only small contributions in kind or cash. In summary, throughout the entire first stage of the developmental cycle the main concern of the average couple is to make ends meet in the discharge of multiple social and religious obligations with the limited means at its disposal. This marks the lives of all the members of the nuclear family, and not infrequently leads to a certain amount of conflict and deprivation, despite outside help.

The Second Stage: From Early to Late Middle Age

The second stage of the developmental cycle of compadrazgo begins roughly with the baptism of the couple's last child, and ends with the marriage of the last son or daughter, while the husband and wife are more or less between the ages of forty and sixty. This is the longest and in many ways the most rewarding stage of the compadrazgo cycle in Belén. The total number of contracted compadrazgo relationships may be as high in the first stage, but in the second the quality and the inherent respeto and confianza of the relationships are probably the highest. Moreover, this is closely related to the more comfortable economic position the family enjoys throughout this stage. The second stage also includes a few compadrazgo relationships contracted on behalf of the children—confirmation, first communion, and perhaps compadrazgo de limpia and aretes—which occur during the first eight years or so, thus, overlapping with the first to some extent.

The following compadrazgo types are all associated with the second stage: casamiento, PCE, CCCH, CCCA, ANDC, AOI, BSI, graduación, quince años, BOI, bendición de casa, BCC, parada de cruz, primera piedra, CABP, and CEON; in addition, there are sporadic, unforeseeable compadrazgo types such as limpia, FC, and even PCE. This is a very large number of compadrazgo types, but they are usually contracted only once, sometimes twice, and seldom more than that. The exception is marriage compadrazgo, which—unlike the sacramental compadrazgo and other types associated with children as mediating entities—can be repeated several times over.

The first eight years or so of the second stage witness the confirmation, first communion, and limpia given to all those children who did not have these sponsorships before the baptism of the ultimogenit. These compadrazgo relationships, however, do not usually number more than six. The first eight years also witness the marriage of the first-born son or daughter, leading to an important compadrazgo relationship. In several ways, the first marriage compadrazgo is as important symbolically as the first baptism compadrazgo, and undoubtedly it marks the second highlight in the developmental cycle of the institution. In Belén ideology, marriage—especially of the first son—is an important occasion because it means that a new social unit has been added to the household, regardless of whether the new nuclear family will reside patrilocally or neolocally, and the occasion must be celebrated with a special compadrazgo. The event is attended by most of the compadres whom the couple has already acquired, and no expense to ensure the brilliance of the occasion is too great. The marriage of subsequent children will never be quite the same. Here again one can see Belén's patrilineal bias, for if the first born is a girl the marriage celebration will not be extraordinary, and the special occasion will be reserved for the marriage of the oldest son.

Throughout the remainder of the second stage the couple will marry off an average of three to four sons and daughters, each accompanied by the establishment of a new compadrazgo relationship. When the last offspring forms his own nuclear family the second stage comes to an end. Throughout the twenty years or so of the second stage, however, the couple engages in many compadrazgo relationships whose mediating entities are primarily images, objects, and occasions. During the second stage the average couple will undoubtedly also have to contract a few compadrazgos de limpia and even FC, but never more than three or four, and usually the same compadres are used after an original relationship has been established. Vastly more important are the compadrazgo relationships established by death in the nuclear family or among parents, grandparents, or closely related kinsmen, in which the couple must find PCE padrinos and thereby become PCE compadres. It is again difficult to estimate how often this happens during the second stage, but probably no more than three times, for the choosing of PCE padrinos is distributed among several sons or closely related kinsmen. Other possible unexpected compadrazgos such as amistad and JJ are not engaged in normally, for there is no longer any real need for them, since the average couple already has a large and active network among which to effect intensification. Moreover, there is usually no occasion for types such as escapulario, compadrazgo de evangelios, and compadrazgo de limpia. Compadres of such types, who were contracted during the first stage, have usually been asked to enter into more immediately important relationships, thereby intensifying the original relationship and keeping intact the primary personnel.

Shortly after the start of the second stage, the couple may contract the first quince años compadrazgo, though it is not yet important in Belén as a whole. Graduación, on the other hand, is an important occasion for contracting new relationships for the next ten to fifteen years, and may involve acquiring as many as seven or eight relationships—which again may mean that two or three sets of compadres are used repeatedly. Compadrazgo de graduación is rapidly becoming universal in Belén, but it is clear that not every graduation for every child will be celebrated with a compadrazgo relationship. Rather, each child will have one ritually sponsored graduación, and perhaps two if education goes beyond secondary school. CEON compadrazgo relationships will be established several times throughout the second stage, but most of the occasions arise during the first half of the period, which is probably when the average couple is in the most acquisitory stage—that is, when husband and wife are from forty to fifty and do not necessarily have the most economic resources, but do have the greatest need to furnish the household and buy certain items of machinery. Throughout the second stage, the couple will probably contract two or three more BSI compadrazgo relationships by adding saints or images to the family altar.

I come now to those compadrazgo types that are almost exclusively associated with the second developmental stage. The most significant material change marking the passage from the first to the second developmental stage is the construction of a new house. This is perhaps true for all couples in Belén except the *xocoyotes*, or ultimogenits, who inherit their father's house. With the construction of a new house, or the extensive reconstruction and improvement of an old one, the couple becomes quite stable economically. This is also an important point in the developmental cycle of compadrazgo. If the husband and wife build a new house, most likely both a bendición de casa and a primera piedra compadrazgo relationship is established; if an old house is renovated, only the former is contracted. In either case, the compadrazgo relationship is an important one and is celebrated elaborately, and the couple tries to generate as much participation and cooperation as possible among compadres and kinsmen. The bendición de casa celebration is always more elaborate than primera piedra, and the couple will spare nothing to show its compadres, kinsmen, and neighbors that it has indeed arrived economically. Shortly after the primera piedra or bendición de casa compadrazgo, the couple contracts the first ANDC relationship. Throughout the first stage, even if the nuclear family was residing neolocally, ANDC always took place in the paternal extended family household. Not until a couple moves into its own permanent home does it feel entitled to have its own ANDC celebration, thereby acquiring ANDC compadres of its own and not merely by extension. This is a highly institutionalized situation that every couple complies with. ANDC compadrazgo must be contracted every three years, but after the second, or perhaps the third three-year period, the average couple loses interest and no longer either intensifies the original compadrazgo relationship or contracts new ones. It is possible, though, that after a period of six to nine years, the couple will again contract an ANDC relationship.

After the couple has settled into its permanent home, a series of new compadrazgo occasions arises, some required and some preferential. The most important are those connected with the variants of parada de cruz compadrazgo. The parada de cruz compadrazgos are intimately related to the physical growth of the household as well as to its improving economic position. Shortly after the bendición de casa compadrazgo—say, a year or so later—a baking oven or temazcal will be added to the house, and this requires a ritual sponsorship. This is a compadrazgo of moderate importance, generally involving the intensification of either the bendición de casa or primera piedra compadres. Within the next two years or so, a lavadero or a private well may become a necessity, and this again will lead to another parada de cruz compadrazgo. These two are the most important parada de cruz compadrazgos, and are invariably complied with. Other instances of prescriptive paradas de cruz are the inauguration of a molino de nixtamal, tienda, pozo, and in general of a place of business such as a taller de costura or a *cantina* (small liquor store). The incidence of these compadrazgo relationships is indeed limited, for there are no more than three dozen such places in the entire community. They are nevertheless definitely prescriptive, for no one in Belén would dare inaugurate such places without benefit of a compadrazgo sponsorship. In these situations, and in general in all parada de cruz compadrazgo variants, the magico-symbolic, protective, and intensification functions of compadrazgo are most clearly exhibited. In this category of parada de cruz compadrazgo I have included several instances of bendición de casa, such as the blessing of a new site (sitio), new public bath (baño), bakery (panadería), barbershop (peluquería), and a few other public places in which the blessing requires setting up of a cross. Except for new house sites, which probably one-third of the married couples in every generation inaugurate, all these types are rare. It is heuristically more appropriate to refer to them as subtypes of parada de cruz compadrazgo and leave bendición de casa compadrazgo to cover only its nuclear meaning, namely, the blessing of the completed new or renovated house.

When children marry, the couple contracts CCCH and CCCA compadrazgo relationships, thereby entering the multidyadic context of marriage compadrazgo. This occurs as many times as the couple marries off sons and daughters, that is, on the average three or four times. (These compadrazgo relationships involve an important exocentric dimension, which is discussed in Chapter Fourteen.) Although, as noted, more affluent couples can become mayordomos and members of the República Eclesiástica during the last part of the first stage, it is during the second stage that the average couple acquires its AOI and BOI compadres. Primarily because of its greater affluence, the couple can now participate more fully in the mayordomía system and the República Eclesiástica, for all positions are at least theoretically open to the husband, except for *fiscal primero* (head of the República Eclesiástica) which is generally reserved for men over sixty. The average man in Belén will contract at least one and possibly two AOI and BOI compadrazgo relationships during the second stage, the majority of them during the second part of it—that is, after the age of fifty or so.[1]

CABP and BCC are among those new compadrazgo types that have not become universal in Belén, the former primarily because of social constraints, the latter because of economic ones. CABP, however, is rapidly becoming widespread, and in a few years more it may become universal. The first CABP compadrazgo relationships were of course established among the economic elite of Belén. I would venture to say that by 1990 or so, every married couple in Belén will contract a CABP compadrazgo relationship. BCC is also associated with the economic elite of Belén, the only people who have been in the economic position to acquire trucks or cars. Although BCC is of limited incidence in the pan-Belén sense, for there are only thirteen motor vehicles in the community, it is intrinsically of universal incidence, for all thirteen vehicles became the mediating entities of BCC compadrazgos. Given the high symbolic, protective attributes of a compadrazgo relationship associated with such a valuable and costly piece of property, I can predict with some confidence that all motor vehicles acquired in the future by Beleños belonging to the economic elite or the economic middle stratum will become mediating entities of CABP compadrazgo relationships. The same is true, of course, of all significant items of property. In this assertion, however, I am assuming that the ideology of compadrazgo in Belén will not have been entirely upset by the rising, primarily economic, secular ideology.

In summary, throughout the twenty or so years of the second stage, the average couple in Belén may have acquired between thirty-five and forty-five more compadrazgo relationships covering the entire range of types associated with that stage. Thus, by the time the couple reaches the age of about sixty (the age difference between husband and wife is seldom more than three years) it has acquired from seventy-five to ninety-five relationships, covering almost the total spectrum of the compadrazgo system.

Let me briefly analyze the economic, social, and religious characteristics of the second developmental stage. The second stage is unquestionably the period of greatest affluence. It corresponds to what might be termed the couple's period of greatest superordinate independence; that is, the couple in turn becomes the economic mainstay of its growing children, or, if it wishes, it can become the center of an extended family network, which may or may not be embedded in an extended family household. This is especially the case during the last part of the second stage, when most or all of the children are married. The beginning of the second stage, on the other hand, can often be characterized as a continuation of the time of struggle. There are heavy expenditures connected with the new house and with compadrazgo obligations, which the couple will find hard to meet, for at this point it is becoming a focal point of social, religious, and economic interaction both in its own right and on behalf of its growing children.

The couple's economic well-being, however, is definitely better some six or seven years after the start of the second stage. For one thing, when the husband reaches the age of about forty-six, the economy of his family is well balanced. The family may be cultivating land that will perhaps account for 35 percent of its income, while the other 65 percent will come from some form of labor migration, or some specialized occupation within the community. In addition, there are almost always one or two employed unmarried sons whose incomes the father is able to control to some extent by virtue of the fact that they are still members of the nuclear or extended family household. The affluence of the couple and the household depends, then, on all these factors, not the least important being economic control over employed unmarried sons and sometimes daughters. The household at this stage includes a rather large number of people who are centered about and organized by the head of the household. There is mutual cooperation between parents and separating married sons, and to a much lesser degree daughters: parents are supposed to help their newly married sons become economically independent, while sons are supposed to contribute to the general economic organization of the household or households separating from the original paternal family. One can regard the parental couple as an effective mechanism of redistribution within the complex. In such an arrangement, the separating married sons must struggle on their own to get their compadrazgo careers underway (which is tantamount to saying that they must get involved in the innumerable social and religious obligations associated with the birth and growth of children and other sponsoring occasions), but at the same time they receive help from their parents—who still control part of their income, especially that connected with agricultural production. From the viewpoint of the parental couple, by now past fifty, the second stage represents a period when it can be less worried about money and start to reap the benefits of having helped its children to establish independent households and to start the cycle all over again. Thus, the developmental cycle of compadrazgo clearly coincides with the developmental cycle of the extended family, and here I am using the term extended family both in its classical, residential sense, and in the derived sense as a conglomerate of households located in close proximity.

Socially and religiously, the second stage of the compadrazgo cycle is the most active period of the average couple's life cycle. Throughout its twenty or so years, there are innumerable social and religious events and occasions to be discharged, as witnessed by the very large number of compadrazgo relationships contracted during that time. Since most important and ritually meaningful religious and social events in Belén require the establishment of compadrazgo relationships, the most accurate index of the social and religious involvement of the average couple during this stage is the number of compadrazgo relationships it contracts. The thirty-five to forty-five compadrazgo relationships engaged in during the second stage covers almost the entire spectrum of private-individual compadrazgo types and one or two public-communal ones. Probably the highest peak of social and religious activity is reached near the end of the second stage, that is, when husband and wife are between the ages of fifty-five and sixty. During these years, and occasionally right after fifty, the average couple contracts its most meaningful compadrazgo relationships, either originally or by the reinforcement of relationships of long standing. This is structurally sound, for it is probably from this time on that—psychologically, and for the individual—the institution of compadrazgo is most important. As the compadrazgo career of the average couple begins to decline and fewer relationships are contracted, relationships already formed and often highly intensified become of great importance in the face of advancing age, whereas in the first stage and throughout most of the second stage, the significance of compadrazgo is largely socioeconomic and religious-ceremonial. But here again, as I discuss below, there is a certain overlapping between the second and third stages of the compadrazgo cycle. At the end of the second stage, the average couple ceases to have a strong interest in the economic coordination of the households of sons who are still tied to the parental household in one way or another, and in general begins to relinquish economic control to its married sons. This is especially noticeable in connection with the cultivation of land, for whatever plots the couple had originally inherited or acquired later are parceled out among married sons, who may or may not cultivate them in common. The husband may continue to work as a labor migrant for a few years longer, and this is usually more than enough to support himself and his wife, for by now all the children are either married or ready to marry. Not infrequently, couples with ambition begin to think about the highest positions in the mayordomía system and the República Eclesiástica, and make a serious effort to accumulate the capital for them, generally when husband and wife are past the age of sixty.

The Third Stage: From Late Middle Age to Old Age

The third stage of the developmental cycle of compadrazgo begins roughly with the marriage of the last-born child, when husband and wife are about sixty, and lasts for about fifteen years, when de facto the compadrazgo cycle comes to an end. The third stage witnesses a clear decrease in numbers of contracted compadrazgo relationships, which simply means that advancing age has released the couple from the need to contract compadrazgo relationships connected with the children's life cycles, on the one hand, and with the social and economic development of the nuclear family, on the other. The types most exclusively associated with the third stage are all public-communal types, namely ANDI, CSV, PCA, and BM. In addition, of course, there are those sporadic and unexpected types over which the couple has little or no control, which can arise at any age, among them PCE, limpia, BCC, parada de cruz, and FC. These occasions are not numerous, and the couple is no longer eager to establish more compadrazgo relationships. It will probably contract one or two other BSI or CEON compadrazgo relationships, but no more than that.

Certain subtypes of parada de cruz, namely, campo, sementera, and almiar, are rather closely associated with the first years of the third stage. All of these are connected with the agricultural cycle, and functionally they should occur just after the couple begins to cultivate its own land, independent of the family lands from which the husband obtained the plot. Thus, these paradas de cruz should come any time after the average couple reaches the age of about forty-six and becomes a separate economic unit, but for reasons not entirely clear to me, the contracting of compadrazgos de campo, sementera, and almiar is postponed for at least fifteen years. Analysis of a dozen couples nearing seventy shows that without exception these compadrazgo relationships were contracted when the couples were between the ages of sixty-one and sixty-seven. My explanation is that when Beleños reach that age, they lose interest in the economy of labor migration and become increasingly concerned with village-centered matters, so it is understandable that they want to establish the agricultural paradas de cruz compadrazgos. In fact, all three of these compadrazgo relationships are invariably contracted in three consecutive years, and the same cycle is often repeated two or three years later, thereby leading to as many as six new or intensified compadrazgo relationships. These parada de cruz compadrazgo relationships are perhaps the only private-individual compadrazgos contracted during the third stage. Their intrinsic importance may not be great, but they acquire importance from the time of life at which they occur.

Although the four most important public-communal compadrazgo types are almost exclusively associated with the third stage, the second and third stages may overlap by five years or so. This is especially the case among the economic elite, who are often represented among the fiscales primeros and the mayordomos in charge of making the pedimento for these types. The ordinary man is invariably over sixty when he is elected to these positions; a member of the economic elite may be younger because his economic advantages enhance his status in the eyes of the people and can win him the election. I am not saying that members of the economic elite monopolize the highest offices in the mayordomía system and the República Eclesiástica of Belén, but given equal social and religious conditions, they do win out over the ordinary man. Other considerations enter into the nomination and election of fiscales primeros and the most important mayordomos in Belén, and there is a fairly equitable balance in which members of the economic elite do not get disproportionately selected. In any event, these public-communal compadrazgo relationships are usually contracted during the first half of the third period, that is, before a man reaches sixty-seven or sixty-eight. Beleños feel that after that men are not able to carry out properly the duties and obligations connected with these important cargos. I have been describing and analyzing the developmental stages of compadrazgo in terms of asking to enter into compadrazgo relationships, and not in terms of being asked. In the case of these public-communal types, I am really discussing the holders of religious cargos, one of whose functions is to select the ANDI, PCA, CSV, and BM padrinos, thereby leading to the establishment of the appropriate compadrazgo relationship. Being asked to enter into these important public-communal types is another story.

The opportunities for being elected to those cargos connected with the contracting of public-communal types are rather limited, for there are only four or five offices per year. Multiplied by the number of years in the third stage, this gives no more than sixty positions for the community as a whole. This means, among other things, that the average Beleño will be able to occupy at least once and perhaps twice, but never more than three times, the positions of fiscal primero and the four main mayordomos connected with the ANDI, PCA, CSV, and BM sponsorships, though this figure may be slightly higher for the economic elite. Thus, during the first part of the third stage the average man in Belén will be able to establish one or two ANDI, PCA, CSV, and BM compadrazgo relationships as a primary actor in his own right. (I am talking about primary compadres, of course, for he may be a componente of the group of the fiscales for the four main mayordomias, thereby acquiring secondary public-communal compadres of these types.) These public-communal compadrazgo relationships are intrinsically and situationally important and always remain lifelong compadrazgo ties.

In summary, then, by the end of the third stage of the compadrazgo cycle, the average couple in Belén has added from 10 to 15 new or reinforced compadrazgo relationships, bringing the total number of compadrazgo relationships to between 90 and 115. Thus, at the age of seventy-five or so, this average couple has engaged in nearly 100 original, repeated, and intensified compadrazgo relationships covering the entire spectrum of the compadrazgo system in Belén.

What are the main economic, religious, and social characteristics of the third stage? First, the couple is no longer in its prime economically; in fact, beginning slightly before the start of the third stage it exhibits a rather marked lack of interest in economic matters per se. By the age of sixty-five or so, the husband has usually quit his labor migrant job and thenceforth his family's subsistence, and the discharge of social and religious obligations, depend upon agriculture and whatever he has been able to save during his long years as a migratory worker. (The average labor migrant manages to accumulate some capital, usually in the form of small plots of land, perhaps in the establishment of a small tienda or changarro, the acquisition of a few cattle and sometimes herds of goats or sheep, and more recently, the purchase of motor vehicles—this last, of course, still of limited distribution.) In addition, he expects some economic help from his married sons, if it becomes necessary. This is rather rarely the case, for the couple's economic needs are small, primarily because it no longer engages in any private-individual compadrazgo relationships that involve heavy expenditures, and has already fulfilled its obligations to its children and other close kinsmen. Nevertheless, married sons feel a certain moral obligation toward their parents, and economic assistance is always provided when needed. Aging parents know this, and to a considerable degree this knowledge gives them a sense of psychological security. Parents definitely do not want to burden their sons unnecessarily, for the sons have economic problems of their own at this stage of getting independently established. Indeed, a surprisingly large number of old couples in the community manage by themselves without any economic help from outside their own household.

In religious terms, however, the first part of the third stage coincides with the involvement of the aging couple in the highest offices in the mayordomía system and the República Eclesiástica. To become a fiscal primero or mayordomo *principal* (main mayordomo) of the four main mayordomias in Belén demands a large amount of money, as well as goods which must be disbursed primarily by the cargo holder himself. This is probably the main preoccupation of aging couples. If they have been provident, they have probably set aside something for these occasions. In a sense, this preoccupation begins during the second half of the second stage, that is, after couples reach the age of fifty or so, and is always very much in the minds of the people of Belén at this time in their lives. It often causes them a good deal of discomfort if they have not been provident enough, or are unable to muster resources among their compadres and kinsmen. This applies also to less important cargos which demand a considerable expenditure. On the whole, however, the aging couple manages fairly well, and anxiety is usually kept within reasonable bounds. If couples cannot manage by themselves—that is, if they cannot demonstrate that they have the necessary resources or can generate enough resources to sponsor any of the five major cargos— they will not be nominated. This is in many ways a dishonor, and no self-respecting son would allow it to happen to his parents. Thus, it is not unusual for married sons to give economic help, in both kind and cash, to make possible their parents' sponsorship of any of the five highest offices in the religious organization of the community. A certain prestige accrues to the family of the cargo holder and his immediate kinsmen, and this helps greatly in gathering resources not only among the elected official's married sons but also among closely related kinsmen. Thus, either essentially by themselves or with the economic help of married sons and immediate kinsmen, the aging couples manage to carry out some of the highest cargos in Belén without economic bankruptcy. Economically and religiously, then, they manage to fulfill their obligations, and although these may be expensive, couples are helped by the decrease in their personal economic needs.

From the strictly social viewpoint, aging couples have far fewer functions. By the time they are sixty-five or even before, they have essentially fulfilled their obligations to their children, kinsmen, and to some extent compadres, although they usually remain active during the third stage. The aging couple continues to participate in the many social occasions of compadres and kinsmen, but much more passively and without having to involve its own social or economic resources. With regard to residential arrangements, there are three alternatives starting about the middle of the third stage. First, the elderly couple may still live in its ancestral house, either by itself or with an older unmarried sister or single or widowed collateral relatives. Second, it may live in an extended family household with the xocoyote and his family. Third, husband and wife (or the survivor of the pair) may attach themselves to the household of a married son, and give up the ancestral house; or they may invite a married son and his family to join them, in which case the son will either rent or sell his own house. The most common situation is that of an extended family household with the xocoyote, who inherits the house when both parents are dead. But aging couples, especially after they reach seventy, usually relinquish social and economic control over the household of which they are part to the son who is living with them, and settle down to enjoy their honored position for the rest of their lives. Even when elderly couples are living independently with only an unmarried daughter or close collateral kinsmen, they may also relinquish much of their social and economic control. It is uncommon for elderly couples to live alone, and practically unheard of for widows or widowers. Beleños believe that once a person reaches a certain age, usually seventy to seventy-five, he should relax and let others worry about subsistence and social and religious cooperation. People who reach this age and still want to be in control of their households and economic affairs are generally branded as "viejos cargantes y metiches" (disagreeable and meddlesome old people), and Beleños often withdraw from them the respect, honor, and high status that the old men and women in Belén possess naturally.

In summary, then, the third stage of the developmental cycle of compadrazgo is characterized by an increasing withdrawal from active social, economic, and religious participation (at least from the viewpoint of asking to enter into compadrazgo relationships), and the principal role is increasingly one of passive participation. At the end of its compadrazgo career the average couple in Belén is in a rather secure socioeconomic position, at least by local standards, and can watch the world go by and play the role of wise men and women—if they do not become meddlesome and overactive. This is a surprisingly accurate model of old age in Belén, for only one of the twenty-nine couples or single individuals over seventy-three was universally described by Beleños as meddlesome and exhibiting antisocial characteristics.

The Final Stage in the Egocentric Developmental Cycle

The average compadrazgo career in Belén comes to an end when couples are about seventy-five, give or take a year or two, for there are really no more occasions for establishing new compadrazgo relationships or intensifying old ones. In fact, my sample shows unmistakably that after that age the individual very seldom asked or was asked to enter into a ritual sponsorship. One of the sporadic, unexpected occasions for ritual sponsorship (mainly limpia and FC) may present itself, but Beleños feel that at this advanced age they have complied fully with the sacred obligations of compadrazgos and no further compadrazgos are necessary; hence the system loses its prescriptive efficacy. I do not mean to suggest, however, that people cease to participate or cooperate in the celebrations, rights, and obligations of the web of ritual kinship; this may continue for a decade or more, given the longevity of many Beleños. Thus, the last decade or so of the average individual's life in Belén in quite comparable structurally to the first twenty years. The only significant difference is that in the last years the individual does not in any sense become a mediating entity, except, of course, to become a PCE ahijado at death. Old men and women in Belén are among the most assiduous participants in the social and religious events associated with the compadrazgo system. While they may cooperate to some extent, their advanced age permits them mainly to participate passively as a welcome addition to the success of any celebration. In fact, old men and women become to a large extent the decorative, visible aspects of compadrazgo celebrations, or for that matter of any celebration.

Our informants universally regarded old men and women in Belén as "los más fiesteros de pueblo" (the most fiesta conscious in the village), meaning that they never missed a celebration. This included virtually all public-communal celebrations and nearly half the private celebrations of all kinds, for in old age the average individual in Belén is related by primary, secondary, and tertiary compadrazgo ties to perhaps half of the community and feels entitled to participate whether specifically invited or not. The people of Belén always welcome old men and women, and would consider it the grossest breach of etiquette not to do so. In essence, then, the last years of life in Belén are characterized by considerable social and religious participation, although in a passive capacity. The aged reap the benefit of their innumerable compadrazgo relationships, active or cold, and in general of the inherent respect for old age and for services rendered to the community in the mayordomía system and the República Eclesiástica. What occasionally mars this rather idyllic picture of old age in Belén are the factional disputes over water and land rights that arise among the various segments of the community.

The Developmental Cycle from the Standpoint of Being Asked to Enter into Compadrazgo Relationships

In this chapter I have presented a fairly complete syntagmatic account of the developmental cycle of the compadrazgo system in Belén. At the same time, I have tried to analyze the social, religious, and economic changes that accompany the various stages of the cycle, in order to determine how the discharge of compadrazgo types interdigitates with the socioeconomic and religious system of the community. In this context, I was able to show that there is a rather close correlation between certain aspects of the developmental cycle of compadrazgo and the developmental cycle of the household. I also tried to show the fixity of compadrazgo types, their repetitiveness, the difference between sporadic and fixed types, and the elements of intensification. My aim was primarily to present those more tangible structural features that constitute the common denominator of the system, at the expense of the more unexpected elements that necessarily exist in such a pervasive system as compadrazgo. The developmental cycle of compadrazgo presented in the foregoing pages is incomplete, however, for it was analyzed exclusively from the egocentric standpoint of couples and from the standpoint of asking to enter into compadrazgo relationships. Two things are needed to complete the analysis: the exocentric analysis of compadrazgo leading to the formation of networks and webs on the basis of multiple-dyad compadrazgo relationships and secondary and tertiary relatives; and the syntagmatic account of the developmental cycle of compadrazgo from the standpoint of being asked to enter into compadrazgo relationships. The former is discussed in detail in the next chapter. The latter, on the other hand, I can dispose of quickly, for as far as the permanent, long-range development of compadrazgo is concerned, there are few significant asymmetries between asking and being asked.

The implications of the asking–being asked distinction have been described in Chapter Three. Therefore, I can discuss the syntagmatic developmental cycle of compadrazgo from the viewpoint of being asked to enter into compadrazgo relationships simply by pointing out the rather minor differences vis-à-vis asking, which have to do mainly with the age of personnel, the fixed or sporadic nature of compadrazgo types, and the public-communal versus private-individual nature of the types in the developmental sequence.

The average couple starts its career by asking to enter into compadrazgo relationships, and not until it has contracted seven or eight such relationships is it likely to be asked in return. (I am not counting, of course, the compadrazgo de amistad type, which compadres enter into by mutual consent, neither asking nor being asked.) Obviously, the being-asked career of the average couple begins some four or five years after its asking career, that is, when husband and wife are near the age of thirty. Thenceforth, their being-asked career progresses steadily but at a slower pace than the asking career. For example, by the end of the first stage the average couple will have accumulated 20 to 35 being-asked compadrazgo relationships, and 40 to 50 asking relationships. In the second stage, however, the situation changes, in that the being-asked relationships soon begin to outnumber the asking ones. By the end of the second stage, the being-asked relationships outnumber the asking relationships; the average couple will have contracted from 55 to 60 of the former, and from 35 to 45 of the latter. But inasmuch as asking outnumbered being asked during the first stage, the numbers are now more or less equalized at a total averaging from 75 to 95. During the third stage, the number of asking and being-asked relationships decrease about equally, varying between 10 and 15, which gives an average of approximately 100 asking and being-asked compadrazgo relationships at the end of the average compadrazgo career.

The quantitative differences in contracting asking and being-asked compadrazgo relationships, then, occur exclusively in the first and second stages of the developmental cycle. For the average couple, the first stage represents a time of struggle, and the people know that the couple should not be unnecessarily burdened with being-asked compadrazgo relationships when it must discharge its required asking sponsorships. By tacit understanding, people in the first and second stages try to avoid asking couples between the ages of twenty-four and forty, thereby producing the imbalance on the side of asking during the first stage. The second stage, when couples are between the ages of forty and sixty, coincides with the period of greatest affluence, and again by tacit understanding, the people of Belén feel justified in burdening couples in this age bracket with requests to enter into compadrazgo relationships. The result, then, is that couples in the second stage are being asked considerably more often than they ask. By the start of the third stage, the number of asking and being-asked relationships have been equalized, and they remain that way throughout the third stage. The greatest economic and social burden of the compadrazgo system falls during the twenty years of the second stage, when the average couple in Belén engages in a very large number of both asking and being-asked relationships. Thus, for economic reasons, and given the fixity of certain compadrazgo types associated mainly with the individual life cycle, the middle period of the developmental cycle accounts for more than half the total number of contracted compadrazgo relationships. No wonder, then, that people have begun to lose interest in contracting new compadrazgo relationships by the start of the third stage.

Ideally, the average couple in Belén wants to contract compadrazgo relationships with couples in the same age group. Beleños prefer this because of the commonality of interests and because the three basic principles of compadrazgo can be discharged in the most symmetrical fashion. One of the risks that every couple in Belén considers upon acquiring a new set of compadres is that the permanent bonds linking it to the other couple will soon become symmetrical. Indeed, the very nature of respeto, confianza, and reliance is predicated upon the symmetry of permanent bonds and obligations, and compadrazgo relationships that do not develop the required degree of symmetry will grow cold or even come to an end without ever having been intensified. Paradoxically, however, the first important relationship (the baptism of the first-born child) is contracted with compadres belonging to the older generation. This is a structural exigency of the system which overrides ideological considerations in the restricted sense of the term; but whenever possible, the Beleños, all other things being equal, will choose compadres among their own age group.

The ideal of contracting compadres in one's own age group is achieved exclusively during the third stage. Couples past the age of sixty are generally in a fairly good position to discharge both asking and being-asked relationships without undue economic strain and fewer required or preferential compadrazgo sponsorships are associated with the third stage than with the first two. In addition, the public-communal compadrazgo types exclusive to the third stage (ANDI, CSV, PCA, and BM) require that padrinos also be of the same age group, that is, at the very least fifty-five, but commonly over sixty. Thus, invariably the ten to fifteen compadrazgo relationships, public-communal as well as private-individual, contracted by the average couple during the third stage are with compadres of the same age group. During the first stage, the majority of a couple's asking compadrazgo relationships are contracted with older couples, generally a generation removed, while most of its being-asked relationships are with couples in the same age group. The reverse is true of the second stage. Structurally, the system is finely tuned, for the initial element of superordination on the part of padrinos (that is, being-asked compadres) facilitates the initial interaction of couples belonging to different age groups. It is an important rule of the compadrazgo system in Belén that one does not ask, nor is one asked by, couples separated by more than a generation and a half, that is, by couples more than thirty or thirty-five years younger or older. Very rarely are compadrazgo relationships established between couples in the first and third developmental stages, unless they are just approaching the second or third stages.

A few additional remarks concerning anomalous cases are in order. First, the ideals of age, symmetry, and equal number of asking and being-asked compadrazgo relationships do not entirely apply to members of the economic elite. The average career of elite couples involves more being-asked than asking compadrazgo relationships, and this can be interpreted, among other things, as an indication of incipient class stratification. And since these couples are in a substantially better economic position than the bulk of the community, much of what I have said about age differentials and the proportion of asking and being-asked relationships at the first and second stages does not fully apply. For example, the position of fiscal primero or mayordomo of the patron saint is sometimes made available to members of the economic elite shortly after they reach the age of fifty, both for socioreligious reasons, and because they have the economic resources to do a good job. Beyond these potentially significant structural anomalies, however, the compadrazgo system of Belén still has a unitary meaning, and its sacred nature applies with roughly the same degree of prescription to the economic elite.

Second, the sporadic or fixed position of compadrazgo types in the developmental cycle has some significant consequences for the age differentials, and for the asking and being asked to enter into compadrazgo relationships during the first and second stages. On the one hand, during the first stage, virtually all the asking and being-asked relationships established within the same age group involve the intrinsically least important compadrazgo types, which require modest expenditures—most often the sporadic, unexpected types such as PCE, limpia, CEON, FC, and even amistad and JJ. On the other hand, the totally fixed compadrazgos—for example, all public-communal types associated with the third stage—by their position in the developmental cycle can only be discharged in the prescribed manner, and no alternative way to comply exists. The relatively fixed compadrazgo types, such as those connected with the life cycle of children and adults, and to a large extent all those belonging to the parada de cruz cluster, are subject to contractual modifications arising from exogenous considerations, and in general provide significantly greater leeway with regard to age differentials and position in the developmental stages. In conclusion, then, the structure of the developmental cycle of the compadrazgo system in Belén, with respect to both its asking and being-asked dimensions, is conditioned not only by age differentials, the symmetrical nature of the distinction, and developmental position, but also by the sporadic, fixed, or semifixed position of types within the system, as well as by certain exogenous considerations such as incipient socioeconomic stratification, and certain socioeconomic exigencies within the community.

Generalizations and Anomalous Features

To conclude the egocentric analysis of the developmental cycle of compadrazgo in Belén, a few generalizations are in order. At the same time, some of the anomalous features, which can affect the developmental cycle, must be taken into consideration.

1. The overall developmental cycles of asking and being asked are essentially homologous and analogous, within the total context of the developmental cycle of the system. What makes the system imbalanced in terms of individual stages are exogenous considerations such as variations in affluence and the social constraints inherent in the sponsorship of events connected with the life cycle of children and adults. Other significant influences are the sporadic, fixed, or semifixed postions of types, which will tend to concentrate the discharge of certain relationships at specific times in the average compadrazgo career. In the end, though, the asked and being-asked systems balance each other in most respects, so that both show a high degree of structural and functional symmetry. In both of its main aspects, the individual developmental cycle of compadrazgo in Belén has an active life span of roughly fifty years, namely, from the time couples are about twenty-two until they are about seventy-five. During this long period, the average couple contracts a very large number of asking and being-asked compadrazgo ties covering the entire spectrum of the system. The period from birth to marriage, and the period after the couple passes the age of seventy-five, can be regarded as stages of apprenticeship and passive participation, respectively. In the former, individuals participate primarily as mediating entities and learn the rules and procedures of the compadrazgo sys-

tem; in the latter, they reap the benefits of an achieved position as a consequence of their innumerable ritual kinship ties, and essentially play the role of honored participants. Inasmuch as the compadrazgo system in its multiple expressions is omnipresent and in one way or another underlies most of the significant stages and landmarks of the life, social, and religious cycles of Belén culture and society, the individual is always directly or indirectly involved in some compadrazgo interaction as he moves from birth to death. Indeed, the individual in Belén begins and ends his human existence by becoming a mediating entity of the baptism and burial (PCE) compadrazgo types.

2. In the description and analysis of the egocentric developmental cycle of compadrazgo, I took as the basic unit of analysis the married couple, for the overwhelming majority (about 95 percent) of compadrazgo ties in Belén are contracted by married couples. (The other 5 percent involve the various anomalies discussed in Chapter Two.) With regard to the developmental cycle, the most important anomalies affecting the alignment of ritual kinsmen occur when the padrinos are not married to each other, or when the sponsoring occasions require either a padrino or a madrina. Only about 3 percent of the total number of compadrazgo relationships contracted by the average person in Belén involve nonmarried couples as sponsors. Furthermore, the only effect of such an anomaly is that the compadrazgo network of primary and secondary actors is almost doubled in size. The structural positions remain the same, and from the viewpoint of the compadrazgo network the anomaly may even have some positive effects. With respect to the occasions requiring either a male or a female sponsor, although de jure a given compadrazgo type may require one or the other, de facto behavioral and terminological recognition is extended to the spouse. Probably the only exception occurs in marriage compadrazgo, for the subsidiary madrinas are generally unmarried and their sponsoring attributes are on the whole temporary. Thus, it is reasonable to analyze the developmental cycle of compadrazgo exclusively in terms of married couples.

3. Analysis of fifty compadrazgo careers in Belén over a seventy-year period clearly indicates that, regardless of the prescriptive-preferential-optional structure of compadrazgo types, the average couple in Belén complies with the overwhelming majority of types throughout the fifty years of its active career. In fact, thirty-two couples in the sample (64 percent) had complied with all compadrazgo types at various stages of their careers. Thus it could be said that all compadrazgo types in Belén are prescriptive in the sense that, barring certain insurmountable constraints (economic position, availability of the occasion, lack of opportunity), they are discharged at least once during the average compa-

drazgo career. (For example, it is possible, although very unlikely, that in the course of a lifetime of active compadrazgo involvement a couple will not contract a limpia.) Most likely to be omitted are the new types and the public-communal ones especially ANDI, PCA, and CSV. The former have not yet been completely internalized, or the occasion for them made available to the majority of the people (as with BCC), and the more conservative elements of the community will tend not to engage in them when the occasion arises. The public-communal types, with the possible exception of AOI and BOI, are intrinsically limited occasions; no more than 75 percent of the couples in Belén are given an opportunity to contract these relationships, and this almost exclusively from the being-asked viewpoint, that is, becoming CSV, PCA, and BM padrinos.

4. The analysis shows that the average couple in Belén, throughout its career, contracts a mean of 102 asking and 99 being-asked compadrazgo relationships. Many of these relationships are not contracted with different sets of compadres, but involve the repetition of compadrazgo sets—the intensification of original compadrazgo relationships. The rare occasions in which an original relationship fails to be intensified usually involve a relationship established near the end of a couple's active career or the premature death of one set of compadres. Given the Beleños' deeply ingrained sense of reciprocity, and the fact that tested compadrazgo relationships decrease the risks involved in establishing anew the proper degree of confianza and reliance, together with the natural prescriptions of the system for intensification, there is a strong tendency to use the same set of compadres for various compadrazgo types. In the first place, reciprocity leads to the exchange of asking and being-asked compadrazgo sets—if you ask me to enter into such and such a relationship, I must ask you to enter into such and such a relationship—which may or may not involve reciprocity of type. In the second place, the decrease in risk that results from using the same compadres several times leads to considerable intensification of both asking and being-asked relationships. The resultant repetition ranges from two to five times for asking to enter into compadrazgo relationships, with a mean of 3.5, and from two to four for being asked, with a mean of 3.0. This means that the average couple in Belén contracts its 102 asking compadrazgo relationships with approximately forty different sets of compadres, and its 99 being-asked relationships with approximately thirty-five sets. Taking into consideration the reciprocity between the asking and being-asked sets of compadres, the asking figure is reduced almost by half. Thus, by the end of its compadrazgo career the average couple has become related by compadrazgo ties to an average of approximately sixty couples, with a mean of 3.25 repeated relationships. (While I have been able

to discuss in general terms the kinds of repetition and intensification this involves—especially in connection with using the same set of compadres for given clusters, and with the inherent attributes of the system as embodying primarily the leading-to or resulting-from types—I have been unable to give the exact patterns of repetition and intensification, for I was unable to obtain the necessary data.)

5. Obviously, the number of acquired compadrazgo sets (couples) is directly proportional to the increasing number of relationships associated with the three main developmental stages, from the viewpoint both of asking and of being asked. By the end of the first stage the average couple has accumulated approximately thirty sets, by the end of the second stage twenty-five more for a total of fifty-five, and during the last stage only five more, for a grand total of sixty couples. Here again, it should be noted that the largest number of sets is associated with the first stage which also witnesses the contracting of more original compadrazgo types. The ratio of couples to contracted compadrazgo relationships is, however, about the same in each of the first three stages. Under normal conditions, and barring the death of compadres, at the end of the average couple's career it is theoretically possible that compadrazgo ties with all sixty couples will still be alive. Primarily because of factionalism and the natural results of age, this is not the case in practice, however. If compadres who originally held the same views concerning some community affair suddenly find themselves in opposite camps, the compadrazgo relationship quickly disintegrates. This is not common, but it does happen. On the other hand, the age of the relationship inherently inhibits its potential for remaining active, especially if it has not been intensified properly, and this probably accounts for most of the cases in which a relationship grows cold without necessarily coming to an end. A couple approaching the end of the third stage will probably have certain compadrazgo ties that have grown cold, or possibly even ended. More commonly, the relationship remains alive in name only. (This can happen even during the second stage.) Attrition does not generally begin until the second stage. At the end of the first stage compadrazgo ties almost invariably remain active, and definite duties, obligations, and patterns of participation and cooperation bind the thirty sets of compadres to the average couple. By the end of the second stage, the average couple will have terminated compadrazgo ties with from three to five sets of compadres. By the end of the third stage, the rate of attrition will have doubled, to involve from six to nine sets of compadres. Thus, at the end of its compadrazgo career, the average couple will still have active compadrazgo relationships with from forty-five to fifty compadre sets.

6. One of the most significant aspects of the egocentric development of the compadrazgo cycle is the fixed, semifixed, and sporadic nature of compadrazgo types. In this context the most important are the sporadic compadrazgo types, followed by those that are indicators of individual economic growth—for example, many of the types associated with the parada de cruz cluster beyond individual houses, and several secondary and tertiary types such as BCC, CABP, compadrazgo de amistad, and CEON. On the other hand, given the even patterns of birth, infant mortality, and several other aspects of the life and social cycles, the fixed and semifixed compadrazgo types have a steadying influence, which ultimately results in a very high actual embodiment of the average developmental cycle presented here. The sample analysis shows that despite many outward changes in the compadrazgo system of Belén, the career of the average couple has changed remarkably little since the turn of the century.

7. The developmental cycle of compadrazgo in Belén mirrors the developmental cycle of the household to a high degree, and many of the social and economic characteristics of the first and second stages in particular correspond to the growth and development of the household and its social composition. The compadrazgo cycle also mirrors the religious development and involvement of the average couple, and in fact its analysis has enabled me to reconstruct fairly accurately the ladder system of religious sponsorship in Belén at the turn of the century. This is not surprising, given the pervasive nature of compadrazgo, and I would only have been surprised if the developmental cycle of compadrazgo had not interdigitated so well with that of the household, or with several other social and religious aspects of Belén that also have cyclical dimensions. More than any other part of the structural analysis, this chapter illustrates the inherent advantage of using the compadrazgo system as the descriptive mechanism for analyzing community culture and society, not only in Tlaxcala, but perhaps in most Mesoamerican Indian and not a few Mestizo communites.

Thoughout the foregoing sections I have tried to show that, even if compadrazgo is regarded as an essentially dyadic construct, which assuredly it is not, it has a definite developmental cycle which affects the ritual kinship involvement of the individual and of couples in quite different ways in different age brackets. Unlike the usual treatment of compadrazgo as a merely static institution, this discussion has shown that compadrazgo is also a processual entity which can be used as the central institution in describing and analyzing the individual's life, social, and religious cycles.

CHAPTER 14

The Exocentric Developmental Cycle of Compadrazgo

The Network and Multidyadic Structure

Just as there is a definite egocentric developmental cycle of compadrazgo, so too there is an exocentric developmental cycle. The analysis
would be incomplete without the latter, and perhaps some of the most
interesting dimensions would not be seen in operation. In the preceding
chapter my point of reference was the egocentric couple, and the analysis proceeded entirely in terms of primary ritual kinsmen—that is, the
immediate actors of the institution, namely, the mediating entity or
ahijado, the ritual sponsors or padrinos, and the parents or owners of
the mediating entity—without taking any notice of compadrazgo extensions or multiple dyadic complexes. The egocentric developmental cycle,
then, refers exclusively to primary actors, or, if you wish, to the nuclear
structure of the institution through cyclical time. Both ideologically and
structurally, primary actors are sufficiently separate in terms of behavioral patterns and terminological extensions to warrant consideration in
terms of separate developmental cycles. The exocentric developmental
cycle of compadrazgo refers essentially to the increase in numbers and
the alignment of secondary and tertiary compadrazgo actors, and at the
same time to the creation of complexes of ritual kinsmen which come
into being through the multidyadic nature of a variety of compadrazgo
types, as well as through certain systemic aspects of the institution connected with the community's yearly social and religious cycles. The
development of the exocentric cycle follows rather closely that of the
egocentric cycle, and its stages and the general alignment of ritual kinsmen are also basically the same; for although there is no longer an egocentric locus, the extension of ritual kinship terminology and behavior
remains to some degree egocentrically determined.

Two fundamental aspects must be considered separately: on the one
hand, the developmental alignment of kinsmen as extensions of primary
compadrazgo relationships, that is, the configuration of secondary and
tertiary compadrazgo extensions; and on the other, the developmental
enlargement of specific compadrazgo relationships in terms of multidyadic complexes, in which the multiplicity of dyads gives the situation
a significant exocentric component. These two aspects of the exocentric

cycle of compadrazgo are closely related to the egocentric cycle. Thus, I can give a brief account of the former on the basis of what I have established for the latter, both syntagmatically and by contraposition, primarily pointing out how the two cycles differ. The relationship of the exocentric aspect of the compadrazgo cycle to the communal social and religious cycles presents a different problem, which is discussed in "The Exocentric Cycle and the Communal Social and Religious Cycles" (this chapter). Before comparing the two cycles, I must first elucidate the intrinsic exocentric elements of ritual kinship extensions to secondary and tertiary actors, and of compadrazgo types with a multidyadic structure.

Chapter Thirteen analyzed the compadrazgo cycle exclusively as an interplay between individual couples, disregarding behavioral and terminological extensions to secondary and tertiary actors. When these extensions are taken into consideration, there emerges a significantly more complicated ensemble of ritual kinsmen in which the individual couple decreases in egocentric importance, and several exocentric dimensions emerge that significantly transcend the dyadic patterns of interaction. Dyadic interaction is substantially replaced by the inherent properties associated with a network system or undifferentiated social unit, in which no specific focus of interaction can be isolated (D.R. White 1977). To a considerable extent, of course, the primary compadrazgo dyad remains the locus of dyadic interaction (assuming always the secondary role of ahijados) in connection with specific social, religious, or economic functions. But when one considers the total ensemble of primary, secondary, and tertiary compadrazgo actors on both sides of the primary dyad, the systemic, exocentric elements of the ensemble, which in some cases may include dozens of individuals, begins to emerge clearly. Well-defined, prescriptively determined behavior patterns, as well as more general, less overt patterns of cooperation and participation are no longer determined with reference to either side of the primary dyad alone. It is these patterns of behavior and cooperation and participation, embedded in specific personnel alignments, that I wish to regard as systemic. As the individual advances through his compadrazgo career, these patterns form into networks and webs of ritual kinsmen.

The exocentric, systemic nature of the ensemble of compadrazgo actors is most noticeable in the establishment of primary compadrazgo relationships among ritual kinsmen who are already related in the second and third degree. When the establishment of such relationships is repeated several times, sometimes during a relatively short period, one can find as many as fifty or sixty people, or eight to ten couples, who are primary compadrazgo actors in relation to one another. Although a certain egocentrism can be associated with one or two of the couples who initiate the developmental sequence, the behavioral and interactional patterns of this ensemble are no longer egocentrically determined. Rather they are determined exocentrically, and the personnel acquire the structure of a system of individuals and couples occupying rather well defined positions and behaving essentially as an undifferentiated and fairly well bounded social unit—as a network or web. Thus, intensification of egocentric dyadic relationships through time leads to the formation of exocentric networks.

Analysis of my career sample shows that the average couple approaching the last part of the first stage begins to acquire effective (primary) membership in at least one such network, which can vary from forty to seventy people, and by the end of its career may be a member of three or four. The creation, development, configuration, and function of these networks are discussed in the last three sections of this chapter. Suffice it to say here that their structural components are based primarily on the overlapping of kinship and compadrazgo, the repetitive establishment of primary compadrazgo relationships with secondary and tertiary relatives, and their intensification through time. By the start of the second stage the average couple has intensified a wide variety of compadrazgo relationships with such a large number of original secondary and tertiary relatives that it soon becomes impossible to identify the couple's secondary and tertiary actors. At this stage of development, in fact, it makes little sense to speak in terms of these gradations, for the exocentric dimensions of the system have overshadowed its egocentric dimensions. The system is simplified somewhat, and the tendency toward repeated intensification reduced, by the large number of extracommunal compadrazgo ties contracted by the average Beleño, for otherwise the community might well be segregated into several very large compadrazgo webs.

Such segregation, in fact, tends to occur at the level of the paraje. To demonstrate the magnitude of compadrazgo networks or webs, a rather extreme example is in order. There are two parajes in Belén that are so intensely inbred in terms of compadrazgo that their twenty-nine component households, including nearly 200 people, are all related to one another by primary compadrazgo ties. The two parajes (the paraje with its *terrenos*, or cultivable plots, is the locality referent for clusters of kinsmen whom I have loosely termed the nonresidential extended family) are adjacent to each other, located in the southeastern part of the community near the Zahuapan River, quite nucleated (that is, none of the households is more than a few yards from another), and separated by a shallow ravine. There are seventeen households in paraje Cuilixco and twelve in paraje Xehuitla, and in both parajes almost all the households are related by consanguineal or affinal ties. About three generations ago, or approximately in 1910, when the parajes were considerably smaller, a couple from Xehuitla asked a couple from Cuilixco to become marriage compadres under rather extraordinary circumstances, for the parajes had been fighting for several years over water rights and constituted two of the factional groups in the community. I have not been able to determine what motivated the couple from Xehuitla, but this unusual and spontaneous establishment of a compadrazgo relationship immediately stimulated the establishment of several others. By the end of a generation or so, the two parajes had established a kind of regular exchange of compadres, perhaps not regulated by any overt principle but, as several informants hinted, operating as a means of keeping peace among the households of each paraje. The social, demographic, and religious factors that have conditioned this longstanding exchange of compadres cannot be described in detail here, but by approximately 1960 all households in the two parajes were related to one another by at least two compadrazgo relationships; in fact, all members of the two parajes had become primary actors in relation to one another. I estimate that from 55 to 60 percent of all compadrazgo relationships are contracted endogamously within the two parajes, and since kinsmen are barred as compadres, the situation continues as a compadre exchange between Cuilixco and Xehuitla. This example is not typical of Belén as a whole, at least in its localization and scale, but it illustrates one of the significant functions of compadrazgo, and more important, the formation of a neat, exocentric network through repeated intensification during two generations and a half, and the interdigitation of kinship and compadrazgo. On a smaller scale, however, and not necessarily within the paraje context, there are at least ten such networks in Belén which, although they may overlap to some extent, have come into existence in a fashion not unlike this example. In fact, this illustrates how several components such as kinship, localization, and factionalism can be instrumental in stimulating the formation of networks that developed originally out of compadrazgo extension and intensification.

As I have mentioned, twelve compadrazgo types in Belén involve more than one primary dyad, with the number of dyads ranging from three to ten (see Chapter Two and table 1). Among these types, the most noteworthy are the majority of public-communal types, and casamiento, CCCH, and CCA, in which the multiple dyadic structure is more complex (for more details see "Primary, Secondary, and Tertiary Actors" in Chapter Two). By any kind of analysis, these multiple dyadic compadrazgo complexes have a significant exocentric dimension, for while one can always regard those who ask and those who are asked as the dyadic alignment, the alignment and interaction of component dyads cannot be explained on a binary basis. Thus, all multidyadic compadrazgo types in Belén give rise to ensembles of actors which must be analyzed fundamentally on an exocentric basis, for just as repeated compadrazgo relationships with secondary and tertiary actors result in an exocentric network, so multidyadic ensembles produce the same result. The multidyadic ensemble has even more inherently exocentric properties than the complex that comes into existence by repeated compadrazgo relationships with secondary and tertiary actors, since it involves from the start several well-defined dyads regardless of extensions. Thus, while the network based on repeated relationships is the result of an, albeit short, developmental process, the multidyadic network is from its inception structured exocentrically or at least has significant exocentric tendencies. Its patterns of behavior and participation and cooperation are not focused around a definite point; for after the principal ceremonies of, say, all public-communal types or even casamiento compadrazgo, the padrinos lose their dyadic focus and the various component dyads become an undifferentiated whole—that is, a primarily exocentric unit in which the component dyads often act corporately and without reference to the original dyads.

One of the important elements of network formation is the extension of compadrazgo ties to secondary and tertiary relatives of marriage compadrazgo and the three most important public-communal types, ANDI, CSV, and PCA. These types combine in themselves some of the most important social and religious dimensions of Belén culture and society. Marriage compadrazgo, for example, is the beginning of a couple's career. It soon leads to baptism compadrazgo, and through this basic complex the average couple in Belén is ushered into effective participation in a compadrazgo network. Later in life, when the couple approaches fifty and the husband begins to hold important mayordomía positions and the posts of fiscal segundo and tercero, the couple in its own right becomes instrumental in initiating other networks or intensifying existing ones by adding new couples, through its involvement in ANDI, CSV, PCA, and BM pedimentos or sponsorships. From the viewpoint of multidyadic compadrazgo types, then, the individual in Belén—in one way or another from birth to death—always belongs to a compadrazgo network, for extensions to secondary and tertiary actors operate throughout the entire spectrum of the compadrazgo system. Separately, the two complexes—compadrazgo intensification among secondary and tertiary relatives, and multiple-dyad compadrazgo types— produce or have inherently a significant exocentric component; in conjunction, they result in the maximum expression of the exocentric dimensions of the compadrazgo network. I am not saying that compadrazgo relationships or networks do not come into being dyadically at the start, either as a potentially expandable single primary dyad or as a multiple or single dyadic complex (for example, the padrinos dyad plus the dyad of the fiscales and mayordomos in charge of the pedimento in ANDI compadrazgo). Rather, I am saying that slowly—or sometimes rapidly—dyadic egocentric interaction gives rise to systemic, exocentric interaction.

Behavioral Patterns in Exocentric Compadrazgo Networks

I can now discuss the behavioral properties and patterns of participation and cooperation that operate in exocentric compadrazgo networks as distinct from egocentric, individual-couples relationships. First of all, the two basic complexes of exocentric network formation discussed above can be effective separately or jointly, but in either case their structural properties are essentially the same. Therefore, what I say applies to multiple-dyad compadrazgo types and the extension and intensification of secondary and tertiary relatives. Strictly speaking, no kind of behavior or interaction in compadrazgo is entirely dyadic. Two sides may be involved, such as the padrinos and those who make the pedimento, but there are always varying numbers of personnel on each side who, in one way or another, affect the outcome of any behavior or interaction. On the whole, however, from the pedimento to the termination of the central ceremonies, interaction and behavior are carried out if not dyadically, at least dichotomously, in the sense that throughout there is an opposition between the padrinos and the personnel associated with them, and the parents or owners of the mediating entity and their supporting personnel.

Because of the single or combined effect of the complexes leading to the formation of exocentric networks, the situation changes shortly after the termination of the principal ceremonies. In this new setting, the moiety locus of action and behavior (for want of a better term) is no longer entirely operational, and individual members of the two originally opposing parts may and do act exocentrically, without reference to the original moiety cleavages. Action and behavior are no longer determined by moiety affiliation, and the individual can behave as an independent actor. Furthermore, the network that has come into existence or been reinforced will eventually acquire certain properties and constraints binding upon individual members, thereby generating group interaction that often approaches the behavior of a true corporate group. Indeed, the process of compadrazgo extension and the intensification of existing ties within the network will increase its operation as an undifferentiated but also quasi-corporate entity. Thus, the personnel of, say, an ANDI or marriage compadrazgo relationship instead of being divided by their dyadic origins, can at times act as a group of couples

united by a common purpose. In such a situation, the distinction between padrinos and those who ask them, or between the parents of the
bride and the parents of the groom, or between the various fiscales and
mayordomos, disappears almost completely, to be replaced by an exocentric ensemble. But it is not until such a complex has been intensified
and expanded, and many of its internal relationships repeated several
times, that compadrazgo networks acquire their maximum expression
and a certain permanence that survives the death or withdrawal of one
or several component couples.

In many ways, the compadrazgo network is egocentrically determined for individual couples, much in the manner of the alignment of
the kindred in a bilateral kinship system, but at the same time the primary compadrazgo relationships among its component couples always
overlap sufficiently for it to function quite effectively as an exocentric
system. In other words, not all compadrazgo relationships of a given
couple are contracted with personnel of the network, but only the 50
percent or so needed to make the system effective.

The main difference in the actual behavior patterns of participation
and cooperation consists in the fact that various mechanisms make the
network function in such a way that all those in a given compadrazgo
category act without specific directives emanating from dyadic interaction, but rather as occupants of specific positions that involve specific
ways of doing things. When a network becomes operative, the behavior
of its members and the patterns of participation and cooperation become
regulated by their being part of the network itself, rather than by their
dyadic relation to specific members. (For details on this matter see the
discussion of the regulation of ritual kinship behavior in Chapter Twelve.)
It is important to remember, however, that dyadic, egocentric behavior
and action are always explicit and personalized, while network, exocentric behavior and action are implicit and generalized. There are many
occasions during the social, economic, and religious activities of the
compadrazgo system when a network becomes operative spontaneously
and without direct stimulus, and on such occasions every member of
the network knows exactly what to do and how to behave. This spon-
taneity characterizes the exocentric behavior of a compadrazgo network
but is usually absent from egocentric behavior, beyond what is perscrip-
tive, which always functions on a dyadic basis. The concerted action
that a compadrazgo network is able to generate spontaneously resembles that of a functioning, effective kinship unit, whose mechanisms of
activation are always latent and need not be specified anew each time.
It is in this sense that after the pedimento and continuing until the termination of the central ceremonies, compadrazgo relationships in Belén,
once they have been properly extended and intensified, become largely

self-regulating ensembles of individuals and couples; everyone knows what to do, how to behave, and what to expect without any explicit activation.

The Developmental Integration of Couples into Compadrazgo Networks

I am now in a position to give an account of the exocentric cycle of compadrazgo. In the analysis in the preceding section I did not intend to minimize the egocentric dimensions of the compadrazgo cycle, but only to put its exocentric dimensions into context. Individual couples tend to become developmentally integrated into exocentric networks that are fairly fixed; one cannot therefore analytically dispense with egocentric couples, although I hope to have shown that this egocentrism is not functionally discharged on a dyadic basis. Thus, whatever I can say about the exocentric development of the compadrazgo cycle must be from the viewpoint of couples moving through the stages outlined in the preceding chapter, for the exocentric developmental cycle of compadrazgo consists simply in the assignment of network membership as the couple progresses through its compadrazgo career.

The individual in Belén is born into a compadrazgo network defined by his parents' compadrazgo involvements, and if the parents are young (less than thirty-five or so), into a network defined by grandparents and possibly great-grandparents, together with several degrees of collateral extensions. Until the age of marriage, individuals do not participate actively in compadrazgo networks—only passively, as mediating entities. Until he is about twenty-four, the average individual belongs to a network of orientation, to borrow the familial term, in which he shapes the development of a network indirectly by being the object of many compadrazgo relationships. After marriage, couples begin slowly to shape the structure of compadrazgo networks, first by establishing new compadrazgo relationships, and later by intensifying established ones.

During the first developmental stage, the average couple in Belén is in a rather ambiguous position with respect to network membership, for it belongs largely to its parents' and grandparents' networks, among which the majority of its relationships may be contracted. It is only to the extent that the couple contracts new relationships outside these networks that it can be said to be shaping its own. And here we come to the most important property of compadrazgo networks, namely, that they are never self-contained, discrete social units; rather, they have a structure that can be homologous to the kindred or other bilateral units. Egocentrically determined to a considerable extent from the structural viewpoint, functionally they may have a large exocentric component. Just as the egocentrism of the kindred can be lessened and the unit become like a discrete social unit with some corporate functions, so the egocentrism of compadrazgo networks can be decreased and the networks transformed into something like discrete units of interaction.

At the beginning of the second stage the average couple already has what can be termed a network of its own, which may be based primarily on the one or two networks that included parents, grandparents, siblings, and other collateral relatives. The dynamic mechanism of network formation in this context is of course the involvement of the couple in relationships outside its networks of orientation. This brings husband and wife into contact with other couples in the same situation, and at the end of a generation or so, a full-fledged network has coalesced. Here again the second stage is the most crucial period for network formation, for during these twenty years or so couples are formally associated with two or possibly three networks, rather compartmentalized in terms of the major compadrazgo clusters in Belén. When, again to use a familial term, the couple acquires its own network of procreation, this overlaps considerably with its networks of orientation, for sibling, parental, and grandparental primary, secondary, and tertiary relationships will always overlap the new relationships generated by the couple. In fact, it is this real kinship basis, on both sides of the compadres-compadres dyad, that gives stability and continuity to the network. It is also the locus on which the network builds to counterbalance the inherent concentration of new relationships, which of course are necessary to the development of the network, for otherwise there would be no exocentric developmental cycle and the network would be a fixed social group bifurcating the compadres-compadres dyad.

What I mean by the dynamic dimension of new compadrazgo relationships established outside the network is simply that the people of Belén tend to compartmentalize their various compadrazgos, and this inevitably leads to the formation of other networks. In this process, the formation of exocentric networks proceeds together with the extensions of compadrazgo behavior and the contracting of multiple-dyad compadrazgo types, as I have already discussed. What is not entirely clear (for it needs more detailed data than I now have) is how the couple structures its position in essentially exocentric ensembles with a minimum of conflict, for seldom will the compadrazgo network associated with a given cluster be the same for any two couples. But here, of course, I am in essentially the same quandary as the literature on the structure of bilateral social units and their corporate and discrete nature (Selby 1976). The fact is, however, that while compadrazgo networks cannot be structurally discrete units, they can function exocentrically with considerable discreteness, that is, with few of their component couples having any serious conflict of interests.

Beginning with the third developmental stage, the average couple in Belén may acquire membership in a fourth compadrazgo network. This is not inevitable, for probably less than 50 percent of the couples who reach that stage become part of this fourth network associated with the main compadrazgos discharged during the last fifteen years of an active compadrazgo career. Rather, the predominantly new compadrazgo relationships couples contract in this stage can be accommodated within the three networks to which they belong by the age of sixty or so. Analysis of my career sample shows that the most common pattern is for people to refrain from getting involved outside their familiar networks after the end of the second stage, and that it is perhaps only in special circumstances—for example, being a member of the economic elite—that a fourth network will come into existence by the middle of the third developmental stage.

In brief, the exocentric developmental cycle of compadrazgo in Belén means that from birth to marriage, individuals are drawn into their parents' one or two networks, exclusively as passive agents. From marriage until husband and wife are in their early forties, the average couple acquires membership in its first independent network, which does not coalesce until a few years later. Between the middle forties and early sixties, it acquires two more networks in essentially the same fashion as the first. The only significant difference is that overlaps with real kinship become less important; the couple, regardless of kinship affiliation, becomes increasingly involved in establishing new, nonkinship–determined compadrazgo relationships, and less involved in intensifying old ones. Finally, less than half the couples in Belén become effective parts of a fourth compadrazgo network in their middle sixties to middle seventies.

I can now correlate compadrazgo networks with compadrazgo clusters. It is not difficult to understand the correlation of developing networks with the clusters described in the preceding chapter, for the clusters occupy fairly definite positions in the various developmental stages of the compadrazgo cycle. The first network with which the average couple becomes associated is composed almost exclusively of types belonging to the compadrazgo de fé cluster and the tertiary cluster, which involve the intrinsically most and least important types in Belén. People begin their careers by engaging in the compadrazgo de fé types associated primarily with their growing children; the tertiary cluster consists of the leading-to compadrazgo types that people contract largely as a means of establishing more important relationships. Associated with the second stage are the parada de cruz and secondary clusters, and here again the correlation is clearly based on the position the types in these clusters have within the compadrazgo cycle as a whole. Finally, the network of the third stage is correlated with the four most important types of the public-communal cluster. The cluster-network correlation is not perfect, for not all compadrazgo relationships belonging to the cluster are contracted within the associated network. Nevertheless, I have evidence that about 60 percent of the cluster compadrazgo relationships are contracted with member couples of the network, a correlation high enough to be significant for the developmental cycle. The formation, structure, and function of the compadrazgo network are analyzed in the last three sections of the chapter. Here I only note that there is also a rather close correlation between the size, secondary and tertiary extensions, and alignment of personnel in the network and position in the developmental cycle.

The Exocentric Cycle and the Communal Social and Religious Cycles

The exocentric aspects of the compadrazgo cycle that have to do with the social and religious cycles of the community at large present a different set of problems related primarily to the public-communal compadrazgo types and their periodic discharge by certain specified members of the community, from the standpoint both of asking (fiscales and mayordomos) and of being asked (padrinos and young madrina, and individual contributors for AOI and BOI). The exocentric properties of public-communal types have already been discussed, and here I would like to show only how they differ from the important private-individual types, with special reference to the third stage of the compadrazgo cycle and to the function of their secondary and tertiary personnel as another source of primary compadres. Of more importance at the moment is the periodicity of public-communal compadrazgo types, and the way in which they generate exocentric extensions at the community level, sometimes for relatively short periods but always with a high symbolic value.

Public-communal compadrazgo types involve essentially three different, isolable groups of compadrazgo actors, which in order of effective functional importance are: the primary actors (the set of padrinos and the set of fiscales-mayordomos); the secondary and tertiary actors of the padrinos and fiscales-mayordomos sets; and the people of Belén as a whole. My concern with the last group pertains to the exocentric-communal aspects of the situation, whereas in the other two I am concerned primarily with the intensifying aspects of public-communal types. In general, all compadrazgo types make a distinction between primary actors, on the one hand, and secondary and tertiary actors, on the other, but this is a matter of gradation rather than of categorical differences. Public-communal types, however, make a more categorical distinction in that secondary and tertiary actors are not brought into the prescribed framework of participation and cooperation. For example, the padrinos and fiscales and mayordomos of, say, the ANDI type do not try to generate participation and cooperation among their secondary and tertiary relatives, nor are the latter customarily brought into the activities except as passive participants—attendants at ritual and ceremonial celebrations. This is understandable, inasmuch as all public-communal types are as much a part of the mayordomía system as of the compadrazgo system, and according to Belén ideology, religious functions and activities involve mechanisms of participation and cooperation that are separate from those of compadrazgo; namely, they are posited on extensions to mayordomía componentes. There are always enough people connected with the mayordomias involved in public-communal compadrazgo types to eliminate the need to use ritual kinship extensions for purposes of active participation and cooperation. This is an important point in the articulation of the compadrazgo system with the mayordomía system and the República Eclesiástica, and Beleños strictly compartmentalize behavior and action within the respective spheres of the systems involved. Thus, of all compadrazgo types in Belén, public-communal types are the most constrained structurally with respect to participation and cooperation into the central ceremonies.

By way of compensation, however, public-communal types have significant, permanent intensifying dimensions, in that they represent a good source of new compadres for the secondary or tertiary relatives of the original padrinos-fiscales-mayordomos set. This is especially the case for couples who are beginning their compadrazgo careers or are in the middle of the first stage, but whose parents are at the beginning or in the middle of the third stage and hence involved in one or two of the important public-communal types. This is also true for AOI and BOI, which may come when couples and their parents are younger, but which the young couples can equally well take advantage of. Once a public-communal relationship has been established, the married children of the padrinos, fiscales, and mayordomos regard the complex as especially well suited to the contracting of primary compadrazgo relationships—that is, intensification of a secondary relationship, or even a tertiary relationship in the case of cousins and other collaterals, into a primary relationship. This is a symmetrical process in that the relatives of both the padrinos and the fiscales and mayordomos engage in it. One of the main reasons that this situation is especially well suited to intensification leading to the creation of exocentric networks is that Beleños strongly believe that if one chooses as compadres people already connected by some religious bond or obligation, the ensuing relationship is bound to be strong and effective. As one of my informants put it, "Los compadritos que han sido fiscales o mayordomos con nuestros padres son los

que mejor resultan" (The compadritos who have been fiscales or mayordomos with our parents are those who yield the best results). This
is one of the junctures of Belén social structure that show clearly the
rather close bonds tying the compadrazgo system, the mayordomía system, and the República Eclesiástica into an undifferentiated complex
underlain by the same ideological order. In the still traditional ideology
of Belén culture and society, the best results and the highest degree of
expectation are found in the conjunction of the social and religious. In
these circumstances, public-communal types as a whole form one of the
most effective compadrazgo clusters for the intensification of exocentric
networks, which unite primary compadres in the third stage and secondary and tertiary compadres who are at the beginning or in the middle of the first stage.

With the exception of AOI and BOI, which have no specific dates
and may be discharged irregularly every five to ten years or so, the
public-communal types have a definite cycle: the ANDI and PCA padrinos are selected for three consecutive years, while the CSV and BM
padrinos are selected on a yearly basis. In the former types, of course,
there are annual celebrations. But regardless of whether padrinos are
chosen annually, triennially, or sporadically, public-communal types have
a definite cycle that creates exocentric networks, which are an important
albeit temporary, means of generating communal solidarity and the
consciousness of being Beleños. I have already pointed out that during
the celebrations associated with public-communal types, the extensions
of compadrazgo behavior and terminology radiate from the primary
actors to include the entire community. Moreover, the feeling of being
tied together into a single, gigantic compadrazgo relationship may affect
the community for some time after the ceremonies are over. From the
communal standpoint, then, one must interpret the public-communal
types as symbolic and social rites of intensification which bring the
community together and solidify it into an undivided entity two or
three times a year—primarily through the ANDI, CSV, and PCA
compadrazgos, covering the months of December and January, and from
mid-April to the end of May. Throughout three and one-half months,
then, the people of Belén are less prone to quarrel, interpersonal relations are close and amiable, and in general Beleños try to generate good
will toward and cooperation among kinsmen, ritual kinsmen, neighbors, and friends, and the community becomes a macrocosm of what a
well-conducted compadrazgo relationship should be. In many ways, this
phenomenon is aided by the fact that these months correspond to the
period of greatest affluence in the yearly cycle, and most of the ritual
and ceremonial activities, with the exception of the festivities connected
with All Saints' Day, take place during this time.

There is a remarkable contrast between these months of intense ritual and ceremonial activity, underlain by the strong corporate feeling of the entire community, and the behavior exhibited by the people during most of the year, which must be characterized as anything but harmonious and equitable. As several informants declared, "Durante los meses de Diciembre, Enero, Abril y Mayo la gente se vuelve buena, cariñosa, y menos pelionera, pero pasando estas fechas, Dios nos libre de chismes, peleas y calumnias" (During the months of December, January, April, and May the people become well behaved, kind, and less aggressive, but after these months God protect us from gossip, fights, and slander). These annual periods of exocentric intensification and the generation of corporate action must be explained by the conjunction of three variables; the economic well-being associated with them, the intensity of the ritual and ceremonial celebrations, and the discharge of the four most important public-communal compadrazgo types. But it is the last that acts as a catalyst and gives rise to the immediate structure of communal action and behavior. While all this takes place every year, the situation is heightened once every three years with the nomination and selection of the ANDI and PCA padrinos, who have the same three-year cycle. Given the importance of the occasion, the mayordomos and fiscales who must seek ANDI and PCA padrinos are greatly concerned with making the right choice. The main reason for the frequent choice of extracommunal padrinos for these types is that often no couple can be found in the community who not only has the necessary qualifications, but will also please the majority of the people. For weeks before the selection of the ANDI and PCA padrinos, Beleños engage in the politics of the situation, which, without exaggeration, constitutes the most significant dimension of any behavior that can be labeled political. They discuss, argue, and engage in controversy over possible candidates. Everything reaches the mayordomos and fiscales in charge of the selection, and in the process the village becomes truly integrated politically.

In this chapter I have analyzed what I refer to as the exocentric properties of the developmental cycle of compadrazgo, with the aim of isolating compadrazgo units that I have called networks (and less often webs). Throughout his lifetime the individual in Belén belongs to a series of changing networks within which he differentially chooses his compadres and in the process acquires both rewards and duties and obligations. In other words, I have delineated a ritual kinship unit in operation.

The General Properties of the Compadrazgo Network

Implicit throughout my discussion of the components of the compadrazgo network in preceding sections has been a consideration of their mechanisms of formation, numerical strength, organization of personnel, and developmental operation. In the remainder of this chapter, I want to bring together all these elements, and more formally describe and analyze the structure and functions of the network. At the same time, I would like to make a distinction between network and web, showing how these two units function in the compadrazgo system, how they represent two levels of ritual kinship integration, and how some of their features are homologous and analogous to those of real kinship units. The quantitative information comes from the fifty compadrazgo careers covering nearly three generations. In effect, I am consolidating what I have said in the four preceding sections with circumscribed quantitative data.

I want to emphasize that the compadrazgo network is a more stable and permanent ritual kinship unit than I may have suggested in the preceding section. So far, I have discussed the network essentially from the viewpoint of the average couple as it moves through the developmental cycle of compadrazgo, and now I want to analyze this ritual kinship unit as a fairly permanent structural entity. The compadrazgo network is the result of, or comes into existence as the confluence of, three main variables: the overlapping of kinship and compadrazgo on both sides of the compadres-compadres dyad; the repetitive establishment of primary compadrazgo relationships with secondary and tertiary relatives; and the intensification of primary relationships through time. Although the average couple acquires membership in an increasing number of networks throughout its compadrazgo career, the network itself is a more permanent social unit which may have taken a generation or two to acquire its form at any given point in time. Thus, it is not really a question of the couple creating new networks as it moves through its compadrazgo career, but rather of asserting its membership in existing ones by contracting relationships with established members of them. In its most important dimensions, the network is a true exocentric social unit which is affected by the cumulative impact of the egocentric compadrazgo relationships of its component couples, especially at the end of their careers. From this viewpoint, the compadrazgo network in Belén is a fairly permanent, fixed unit with some exclusive functional attributes, and a more thorough investigation will reveal its exact structure with respect to pancommunity incidence, and the number of units operating at a given point in time. Unfortunately, my fifty-career sample is not diversified enough to undertake this task here, but I can at least give the general structure of the network in fairly formal terms.

The first question that must be discussed is the formation and development of the network. Essentially, the network is a social unit that comes into existence through the repeated establishment of compadrazgo relationships affecting two groups of kinsmen. It starts with a single compadrazgo relationship, which for various reasons leads to the immediate establishment of other relationships affecting the real kinsmen on both sides of the compadres-compadres dyad. (Obviously, few truly original compadrazgo relationships result in the formation of networks, for otherwise there would simply be a multiple situation of strictly egocentric extensions. What leads to the formation of a network are exogenous social, religious, and economic considerations of the kind discussed in the example of the Cuilixco and Xehuitla parajes.) If, through a period which may vary from twenty to thirty years, the couples on both sides of the now expanded network of real kinsmen feel that it is socially, economically, or religiously advantageous to continue what amounts to an exchange of compadres, the situation crystallizes into what could be called a self-regulating unit, with a considerable degree of permanence. A well-established network is given permanence by the fact that those who are recognized as members of it feel that they must contract a high percentage of compadrazgo relationships within it.

I have found that on the average about 50 percent of a network's relationships are endogamous, that is, contracted among recognized members. It can be seen, then, how real kinship plays an important role in the structuring and growth of the network, but I am not entirely clear about the boundaries of kinship extensions that delimit its formation. It appears, however, that on both sides of the compadres-compadres dyad the maximum extensions lineally are up to the great-grandparental generation, and collaterally to siblings, father's brothers, father's brothers' children, grandparents' brothers, and grandparents' brothers' children. Thus, a network can span up to four generations, starting with ego as a recently married adult. This is the case, for example, with my oldest informants, varying in age from eighty-five to ninety-five, who were participating in networks as far back as the turn of the century. It appears, however, that after four generations the network loses its effectiveness, and new ones come into existence. The Cuilixco and Xehuitla parajes provide a good example, and although the average network in Belén is smaller, it shows clearly its permanence through more than two generations.

In the five compadrazgo networks I was able to isolate, most members (active couples, that is) remembered the couples, the time, and the conditions under which the original compadrazgo relationships of the network took place. There is a striking parallel to descent from a common ancestor in a real kinship system. It is not altogether surprising to find this in the compadrazgo network, for these networks are rather pragmatic entities which come into being for specific reasons and need an ostensible point of reference to define, not only the kinship extensions of compadrazgo ties, but more important the original purpose for which the network was established. One can see, then, how the variables of overlapping between kinship and compadrazgo, the repetitive establishment of primary compadrazgo relationships with secondary and tertiary relatives of an original relationship, and the intensification of many relationships through time, interdigitate in the formation and development of a compadrazgo network.

Networks do not really come to an end; rather, with the passing of the founding generation, their generational emphasis becomes progressively more skewed, which may significantly alter their composition after two or more generations. From this viewpoint, the network can best be conceptualized as extending effectively over two generations, which is the length of the average compadrazgo career; after this, it may be restructured on the basis of a series of more recently intensified compadrazgo relationships. At the end of the average compadrazgo career, the initial compadrazgo network has lost perhaps 30 percent of its membership. This primarily because about 40 percent of the relationships traditionally associated with the network may be exogamous, and secondarily because of the death of network couples.

Also important is the correlation of the network with specific compadrazgo clusters (discussed in "The Developmental Integration of Couples into Compadrazgo Networks," this chapter). I am not entirely certain about the origin and structural significance of these correlations, but it is clear that the compadrazgo network is fundamentally a restricted exchange system between two groups of real kinsmen which is extended over several generations, but limited lineally and collaterally to make it a manageable unit. Given its limitations of personnel and area of interest, a single network cannot possibly accommodate the exchange of all thirty-one types of compadrazgo for two kinship-based groups. Moreover, the thirty-one types differ to such an extent that no network can possibly be formed whose members could provide to the group participating in the exchange appropriate compadres for all the types. This is shown clearly when the average secondary, private-individual type is compared to the four important public-communal types; the former can be discharged by virtually every couple in Belén, but appropriate personnel for the latter may be difficult to find. The multiple network membership of the average couple represents recognition of this impossibility, thus leading to the fragmentation of compadrazgo exchange into a series of networks associated with the four basic clusters of compadrazgo types involving similarity of functional attributes and the requirements for padrinos and compadres.

This static feature of the network meshes well with the developmental cycle of the institution from the egocentric viewpoint of the couple, for there is a fairly high correlation between the various compadrazgo types that form into clusters, and position in the average compadrazgo career. For the average couple, activation of membership in the first compadrazgo network (that is, membership in the network associated with the compadrazgo de fé cluster) involves a fairly rapid integration into the groom's parents' network for the same cluster. From the standpoint of intrinsic importance and permanence, the compadrazgo de fé network (extending the name of the associated cluster to the network in question) is the most stable and fixed throughout the couple's entire career. Not only is it the largest of the four types of networks, it is also exocentrically intensified from the very beginning of the average couple's career. As the couple moves through its career and becomes an effective member of two or three more networks, the process of integration is the same. Again, latent membership is activated as the couple passes from secondary or tertiary compadrazgo status to the acquisition of primary relationships within the network. By the end of its compadrazgo career the couple will have reached the maximum extension of networks both with respect to the number of networks of which it is an effective member, and with respect to the size of each individual network. It can be seen that the network itself undergoes a definite development each generation, which is a direct reflection of the careers of its component couples.

The last point of discussion is the numerical strength of the compadrazgo network and its pancommunity incidence. The network does not have a fixed membership, of course, but fluctuates with each generation as significant numbers of couples move from stage to stage in their careers. It does, however, have a fairly fixed membership core over a period of two to two and one-half generations in the form of couples who activate membership in the network (by becoming primary compadres in their own right) throughout a period not exceeding five years—which in terms of kinship composition involves siblings (mostly brothers), cousins, and perhaps intergenerational kinsmen without great age differences. It must be remembered that the strong patrilineal bias in the social structure of Belén is a significant factor in shaping the compadrazgo network, and gives it considerable integration and self-containment. The fixed membership core of the network is about 40 percent of its average strength; that is, about 40 percent of its personnel go through their compadrazgo careers together. Over time the network varies in size from an average of forty to an average of seventy people, it can include from ten to sixteen couples and from seven to twelve households. There are exceptions, of course; the most notable one with which I became acquainted is the Cuilixco-Xehuitla network, which has more than twice the personnel of the average network. This is primarily because this network is completely localized in two adjacent parajes, which is not the case with most Belén networks.

Generally, members live in two or more parajes quite far apart as distances go in Belén, that is, separated by a kilometer or so. In any event, the average member couple of a compadrazgo network will at any given point in its career have at least ten couples among whom to choose compadres for the cluster associated with it. Further, given the kinship base of compadrazgo networks and the fairly strong localization of the nonresidential extended family in the paraje, Beleños are quite conscious of network affiliation with respect to members' paraje residence.

I estimate that there are from ten to twelve networks in Belén, if forty people is taken as the overall average membership. Of course, when I speak of the numerical strength of the network I am computing only one side of its total membership, that from which the couple on the opposite side must choose its compadres. At least theoretically, the average couple has the right to choose compadres in double the total number of networks minus one, or between nineteen ($[10 \times 2] - 1$) and twenty-three ($[12 \times 2] - 1$) networks. When both sides of the network are counted, the average membership is ninety people. This is to a large extent formal, for the couple's right to activate network membership is determined fundamentally by the husband's kinship affiliation, although there is some leeway in activating membership in other networks. (Sporadic compadrazgo relationships contracted outside the network will not result in activation, for this requires a long process of intensification. I estimate that at least ten new and repeated compadrazgo relationships are needed for the couple to establish membership in a network outside its original kinship-based networks. This does sometimes happen, but it is not common.)

The compadrazgo network is not a neatly circumscribed social group, but changes over generations; nevertheless, the people perceive it as playing a significant role in the organization of the compadrazgo system. It does not have a name, and the closest approximation is "el grupo de nuestros compadritos" (our compadritos' group), but it has a well-defined place in structuring the selection of compadres and the discharge of compadrazgo rights and obligations. Analysis of the fifty compadrazgo careers shows a clustering of compadrazgo relationships in network associations, and upon direct interviewing, component couples were found to regard the network as a fairly well organized social unit with a rather high degree of functional exclusivity.

Ideologically, the network is not necessarily significant, but structurally it has become a necessity for the compadrazgo system, for the highly prescriptive or preferential nature of most types requires the average couple to have a constant and assured supply of prospective compadres. The compadrazgo network is exclusively an intracommunal entity, of course, for distance and the improbability of intensifying compadrazgo relations over a generation conspire against expanding it to extracommunal compadrazgo. Of the fifty some percent of compadrazgo relationships that the average couple contracts outside its networks, at least ninety percent are extracommunal. Thus, of the mean of approximately 100 asking compadrazgo relationships per couple, roughly fifty-eight are contracted within the three or four networks to which the couple belongs by the end of its career, about thirty-seven are contracted with compadres outside the community, and five or so are contracted with compadres in the community who do not belong to any of the couple's networks. The fact that there is little deviation from these averages throughout Belén gives further evidence of the compadrazgo network's significance.

The Structural Definition of the Compadrazgo Network and Web

I can now define the compadrazgo network more formally: the network in Belén is a conglomerate of individuals and couples forming a fairly permanent social unit over a period of up to four generations, which is for the most part structured exocentrically. It has a clear inception, and a developmental cycle that coincides with the two and one-half generations of the average compadrazgo career. Its formation, development, and personnel are determined primarily by kinship, the repetition of a cluster of compadrazgo relationships among primary, secondary, and tertiary actors, and the intensification of primary relationships over at least a generation. The boundaries of the network and its considerable neatness and self-regulation are given largely by the strong patrilineal bias of Belén society, which tends to concentrate the kinship base of the network along unilineal lines. Structurally, the network is fundamentally a system of restricted exchange between two groups of kinsmen biased unilineally, which may include up to four generations lineally (ego being a young adult) and two collaterally. The rules of exchange are not specified, except that reciprocity is of the utmost importance and tends to equalize the number of asking and being-asked compadres on both sides of the network. It has an average membership of ninety people, including twenty couples and about fourteen households, but with significant variations in total membership and couple and household composition at various stages in its four-generation cycle.

Functionally, the network operates with considerable corporate action, and there is always a rather high degree of cooperation and participation among the component couples for the discharge of all the types in its correlated compadrazgo cluster. The functional unity of the network is underlain primarily by the fact that some sixty percent of the compadrazgo relationships of the associated cluster are contracted endogamously, and also by the continuity in the repetition and intensification of compadrazgo relationships. In summary, the compadrazgo network has a structure and functions similar to those of a real kinship unit of a quasi-unilineal variety; the only important differences are that the network has less continuity, and is inherently skewed by the egocentric development of the careers of individual couples. In the overall picture of the compadrazgo system of Belén, the network stands between individual compadrazgo relationships and the community as a whole—a manageable, necessary unit fulfilling certain well-defined structural needs for personnel.

The compadrazgo web, on the other hand, is a rather amorphous conglomerate of individuals and couples, more egocentrically determined than the network, containing more people and having no permanent functional exclusivity. In fact, the web cannot be considered a social unit by itself, without reference to individual couples. Fundamentally, the compadrazgo web is the sum total of a couple's primary, secondary, and tertiary compadres, padrinos, and ahijados. This group varies as the couple moves through the developmental stages, and it includes repeated, intensified, and original but unintensified relationships. In other words, the compadrazgo web is that conglomerate of individuals to whom the couple extends kinship terminological usage, that is, all ritual kinship terms listed in table 25. As such, of course, it is primarily a changing, egocentrically determined body of ritual kinsmen, encompassing a very large number of compadres, padrinos, and ahijados in all three degrees of compadrazgo relationship. The only reason for isolating this conglomerate of individuals as a conceptual entity is that it is composed of people from all of the three or four networks that the average couple has at the end of its career, and less significantly of all those compadrazgo relationships that were never intensified into the formation of another network. It is thus an isolable unit which serves as the reference point in the activation of networks, and their configuration with respect to individual couples. Furthermore, although the compadrazgo web does not have important functional attributes, it is a fairly well-defined entity in the consciousness of Beleños, for people keep track of all their compadrazgo relationships and know at any point the number and network affiliation of all of their primary, secondary, and tertiary compadrazgo relatives. This was well expressed by several informants when they said, "Aquí la gente siempre lleva la cuenta de los compadritos, ahijados y sus parientes, pues es importante saber esto para no hacerse bolas cuando se pide ayuda o se invita a participar" (Here people always keep a count of compadritos, ahijados, and their kinsmen, because it is important to know in order not to make mistakes when one asks for help and participation). The web is important as a reference group because of its significance in the determination of network composition.

When one compares the compadrazgo webs of four or more couples one can see that there is considerable overlapping, which is determined along kinship lines. In other words, a given couple's repeated, intensified compadrazgo relationships in one situation, which are underlain by its kinship affiliation, will overlap considerably with those of another situation. This can be better understood if one conceives of the average couple's essentially egocentric web as being composed of several hundred people, who occupy exocentric loci but interact closely, thereby resulting in an overlapping. The numerical strength of the average couple's web is determined by the size of the three or four networks to which it belongs, plus assorted nonnetwork relationships; in Belén the egocentric compadrazgo web varies from approximately 350 to 450 people. By the end of its career, the average couple is related by compadrazgo ties to at least 25 percent and as much as 40 percent of the total population of the community. The overlapping of egocentrically determined webs is a natural result of the repetition and intensification of compadrazgo ties, in the face of a shortage of potential padrinos and compadres.

As a corollary, within the web there may also be some overlapping with regard to the networks of particular couples, and the relationships involved represent the strongest bonds of compadrazgo in Belén society, for this is an indication of great intensification. From a broader structural perspective, it is quite certain that the web is a group of ritual kinsmen which comes to be structured loosely and with much overlapping, because of a shortage of personnel. In a community with at least twice the population of Belén (say, 2,000 or so), the web would tend to become a more exclusive, more structured social grouping, with a general structure not unlike that of the network—assuming, of course, that the same general compadrazgo principles were operating. In fact, I have been able to verify this in part by comparing the compadrazgo system of Belén with that of San Luis Teolocholco, a community of some 4,500 people sixteen kilometers southeast of Belén. There the web is a more circumscribed conglomerate of ritual kinsmen and has little overlapping, so that the community has about eleven or twelve compadrazgo webs which tend to be endogamous and have fairly exclusive functional attributes. This example helps to justify my isolation of the web as a meaningful compadrazgo grouping, regardless of its functional unimportance.

I can now define the web more formally: the compadrazgo web in Belén is an egocentrically determined social grouping explicitly recognized as a native category embodying all the possible ritual kinship extensions of a given couple at any given point in its compadrazgo career.

As an egocentrically determined grouping, it has a configuration and personnel strength that are coterminously homologous and analogous to the developments during the roughly fifty years of the couple's career. While the web is unimportant functionally in that it does not have or perform (either egocentrically or exocentrically) any corporate or collective functions and activities, as a native category it is an important determinant and reference point for the development of the compadrazgo network. From a strictly structural viewpoint, the compadrazgo web represents the maximum extension of the interdigitation of kinship, repetition, and intensification. The significant status of the web as a native category arises from the Beleños' ideological consciousness of compadrazgo as a sacred institution, for even if a compadrazgo relationship has grown cold, it is ideologically important to keep an account not only of original relationships, but also of secondary and tertiary relationships, which have been extended or intensified. From a more operational viewpoint, the web illustrates the pervasiveness of compadrazgo, in that mapping its extensions will show that at the end of its compadrazgo career, the average couple may be related by ritual kinship ties to as much as 40 percent of the community. It was within the context of mapping the webs of approximately a dozen couples in Belén who were near the end of their compadrazgo careers that I was able to isolate component compadrazgo networks. Fundamentally, then, the compadrazgo web, as a native category, represents the juncture on which I must base the analysis in order to operationalize the compadrazgo network as a well-defined, quasi-corporate social grouping.

A Comparison of the Network and Web with Real Kinship Groupings

Finally, I would like to compare the network and the web with the operation and structure of real kinship groupings, and determine how they function in their respective systems. There are significant homologous and analogous resemblances between the network and web and identifiable kinship units. Let us take the network first. There is no question that functionally, the network is basically an enlarged, multivaried, nonresidential extended family; that is, for certain specified activities and modes of interaction, it operates in an undifferentiated and almost corporate fashion. There are definite patterns of behavior associated with the network, similar to those in the nonresidential extended family. Moreover, the same terminological extensions are used in both the network and the nonresidential extended family; a definite compadrazgo terminology and kinship terminology apply, on the basis of the same principles, to personnel of the two units. Given the patrilineal bias of Belén society, the network is functionally equivalent to the nonresi-

dential extended family on the paternal side—and to emphasize localization in the paraje, I would like to call this the patrilocal nonresidential
extended family. The situation is more complicated structurally, for the
individual in Belén may belong to as many as four networks at the end
of his career, while obviously he has a fixed membership in a single
patrilocal nonresidential extended family. Furthermore, a single network involves two patrilocal nonresidential extended families—the extended kinsmen on both sides of the compadres-compadres dyad. Homologously, then, there are significant differences between the compadrazgo network and the patrilocal nonresidential extended family in
terms of size and the alignment of personnel. A single network includes
two patrilocal nonresidential extended families, and the total number of
networks ultimately acquired by the average couple will include many
more. At least egocentrically, however, the patrilocal nonresidential extended family is the structural basis for the multinetwork involvement
of the average couple in Belén.

Throughout this chapter I have often pointed out the homologies,
analogies, and overlaps between kinship and compadrazgo, and here I
can only add that compadrazgo relationships by themselves, in all their
extensions, have a double kinship component; that is, all extensions of
compadrazgo, except for multiple-dyad types, are strictly along kinship
lines. Thus, analysis of individual compadrazgo relationships and
groupings (i.e., the network) involves a double kinship relationship and
unit (i.e., the patrilocal nonresidential extended family).

Basically the same is true of the web, of course, taking into consideration the fact that it is not a functional, operational grouping, except
perhaps for the reification conferred upon it as a native category. Nevertheless, the compadrazgo web has a structure that is to some extent
homologous to that of what we might call (for want of a better term)
the inoperative kindred, for Beleños recognize all those individuals in
the community who are related to them by consanguineal and affinal
ties. This group may include hundreds of people, but it is largely inoperative except for the regulation of consanguineal marriages. Therefore,
what I have said about the compadrazgo web applies also to the inoperative kindred, which includes all possible real extensions recognized
by the people. In fact, the same ideological principle of keeping track
of all compadrazgo relationships applies equally to the realm of kinship
and the effort to keep clearly in mind the identity of all kin and the
nature of the relationship. In summary, then, it is evident in Belén—
and by extension in most of Tlaxcala—that compadrazgo and kinship
not only overlap but also have significant homologies which are underlain, fundamentally, by the same ideological order, which is reflected in
the structural order in operation.

In several sections I described some of the formal and operational properties of the compadrazgo network and web in an effort to demonstrate that isolating these compadrazgo groupings—or at least the former—can show a social unit in action in the structuring of compadrazgo relationships in Belén. I hope to have shown that the network constitutes a unit of analysis that conforms to most of the requirements generally attributed to a kinship unit, and at the same time that its exocentric, permanent components result in its quasi-corporate functioning as a social unit. The web, on the other hand, is a loose, functionless grouping which it is most useful to isolate as a basis for the structure of the network, and as a conceptual juncture in analyzing it.

I said at the beginning of Chapter Thirteen that it and this chapter were two of the most significant ones in the entire study, for in the analysis of what I refer to as the developmental cycle of the compadrazgo system, my aim has been to show the dynamic aspects of the institution—to show how it can be regarded not only as an egocentrically changing system, but also as an exocentric system with considerable permanence. The literature on compadrazgo has been weakest in this respect, for it has presented compadrazgo as a static institution with no continuity except egocentrically, and in terms of a strictly dyadic pattern rather than as a system. In one context or another, probably most of the properties, components, functions, and attributes of the compadrazgo system that I have discussed throughout this study have been mentioned specifically in one place or another, but no ethnographic source has treated the systemic, exocentric dimensions of compadrazgo. It is fundamentally for this reason that I have attached so much importance to the developmental cycle of the compadrazgo system.

PART II

The Functional Analysis
of the Compadrazgo System

CHAPTER 15

The Political, Economic, and Demographic Functions of Compadrazgo

The preceding chapter completed the structural analysis of the compadrazgo system in Belén. Throughout, apart from description, my aim has been to present compadrazgo as a system in interaction, composed of several definable parts impinging upon each other on a series of planes or levels of structural efficacy. I have tried to demonstrate the reality of the compadrazgo system in terms of the interplay of its ideological and structural orders, on the basis of certain identifiable principles operating upon individuals and associated behavior and actions. My main concern has been with the operational principles that govern the system, primarily as a structure composed of actors occupying certain positions and playing certain roles, and only secondarily as a functional entity. I have made a structural analysis that departs considerably from functional analysis of the classic British variety, but that nevertheless involves several aspects of the latter. Insofar as I have been concerned with function, or functional assignment, it has been indirectly and by way of illustrating certain aspects of the structural analysis. Functional analysis and assignment are indeed important in the conduct of anthropology, but the structure of a system or institution must first be properly established.

In the three remaining chapters I address myself to the functional analysis of the following compadrazgo domains (listed in order of increasing importance): the political, the economic, the demographic, the religious, the social, and the symbolic (including the ritual and the ceremonial). This analysis requires much less space than the structural analysis, for functional assignment, as a complement of structural analysis, can be regarded as essentially a shorthand expression of the structural activities of a system in action, and function is thereby an inference from structural elements that are well specified in the analysis. My approach is, however, somewhat different from that of the traditional functionalist, and I would therefore like to begin by briefly discussing its main tenets, showing how it differs from traditional functional interpretation.

Structural Analysis and Functional Assignment

The fundamental distinction between the traditional functionalist position of Radcliffe-Brown and most of the other more distinguished British anthropologists (many of whom are still active today), and the structuralist position of Lévi-Strauss, is that the former involves a primarily empirical conception of social structure, while the latter involves a primarily supraempirical conception (Nutini 1965b, 1968a). (These are relative statements, however, in that neither functionalism nor structuralism takes a clear-cut empirical or supraempirical position. Rather, the two approaches are scientifically oriented in these ways: the main assumptions and theoretical procedures of functionalism tend to the empiricist limit, those of structuralism to the supraempirical limit.) Despite allegations to the contrary, for Radcliffe-Brown and perhaps all of his students, the structure of the social system is nothing more than the total ensemble of social relations enacted by the personnel of the system occupying specific positions and playing discernible roles. For Lévi-Strauss, the structure of a social system is something quite different, namely, the principles that govern the system translated into relational positions and statements of invariance obtaining among its actors, or rather, their actions and behavior.

The empirical position of Radcliffe-Brown and his followers involves the interaction of structure (the web of personnel in action) and the functional assignment of teleological properties to specific parts, which result in the conceptual formation of the system. Thus, structural-functional analysis, as the name indicates, demands close conceptual interaction between definable parts standing in well-defined functional relationships to one another; otherwise there is no system (Nutini 1970:556-558). In this scheme of things, structural-functional analysis not only requires the elucidation of a system of component parts, but also assumes a priori that each part will contribute something to the maintenance of the system, which very often is not clearly discerned. In this theoretical view of sociocultural phenomena, more often than not functional analysis becomes the primary conceptual focus rather than being subordinated to structural interpretation. The reason is obvious. It is generally easier to ascertain some putative functional variable—isolate it, if you wish—than to delineate accurately the part of the structure to which the variable is supposed to apply. Nagel (1961:510-520) rightly criticizes functionalists, both sociologists and anthropologists, when he says that functional explanations are teleological in that they involve the notion of a system S, and the notion of a state or condition G (the function) which is maintained in a system—but while the system S and the condition G can be clearly specified in, say, biology, this is seldom the case in the social sciences, where such a determination may be extremely difficult. Implicit in this criticism is the notion that structural-functional analysis involves the formulation of closed systems, which cannot generate linear causality but only show functional relationships.

Explicit in the structural approach are the idea of levels of analysis, and the viewpoint that some levels must be operationally assumed in conceptualizing social empirical phenomena. One of the basic tenets of structuralism is that structure involves a more primitive set of elements or terms, and that function is always an inference from structure. This is sound scientific procedure, much in accord with the *modus operandi* of contemporary physical science. This does not mean, as has often been charged, that structuralist anthropologists are not concerned with function, a point I discussed earlier (Nutini 1970:557-558):

Even such an astute anthropologist as Leach (1965b:780) implies this when he says that "Structural interpretations should be complementary to functional analysis and not vice versa," a position which is completely unintelligible to me. Lévi-Strauss is indeed concerned with function, but only insofar as it is a result of the positional and relational arrangements of elements of a contextual social situation; this means that unless we want to run the risk of conjecturing, function can only be assigned after the structure has been thoroughly established. If functional analysis means, as Leach seems to imply, that function is a more primitive concept than structure, then it follows that what we observe and conceptualize are functional attributes, which is patently false. It should be apparent that even at the empirical level, what we observe are social facts exhibiting certain specific arrangements and positions, which according to Radcliffe-Brown constitute the structure of the situation. We never observe functions; they are always elicited from the structural configuration. This obviously applies more strictly to a supra-empirical conception of structure, inasmuch as the relational and positional properties of a construct (model) are verified against a body of social phenomena with an empirical or paradigmatic structure of its own.

Be this as it may, the kind of structuralism implicit in the present analysis definitely relegates function to a subsidiary position that complements structural analysis, but does not become a necessary conceptual activity in its own right or a necessary complement of the analytical framework itself.

But what is the immediate relevance of the empirical position of functionalism as it differs from the mainly supraempirical position of structuralism? Before I answer this question, a few remarks are in order. In the first place, the analysis of the compadrazgo system in Belén is neither Radcliffe-Brownian nor Lévi-Straussian, but involves certain elements of both the functionalist and structuralist positions. I follow Radcliffe-Brown to the extent that I have structured the compadrazgo system basically along the lines suggested above, that is, as a general ensemble of actions and behaviors discharged by actors occupying definite positions and playing various discernible roles. To a large extent, I am still operating at the paradigmatic level of structure, at least with regard to the operation of the compadrazgo system in Belén today. On the other hand, I follow Lévi-Strauss in assigning primacy to structure over function, which is tantamount to saying that whenever functional interpretations are made, they are not a sine qua non for the efficacy and accuracy of the analysis. In other words, to some extent I transcend the paradigmatic level of structure by giving it some modelic dimensions (for the distinction between paradigmatic and modelic structures, see Nutini 1967:10-17).

Second, the general organization of the material follows traditional functional analysis, but to the degree that I have been able to deal with the deep organizational features of the compadrazgo system, I have come closer to the classic structuralist position of searching for structural principles in operation. This has clearly been the case insofar as I have been able to implement my threefold analytical framework (ideological-structural, ideal-structural, and actual).

Third, I have to some extent transcended the unidimensional level of analysis inherent in functionalism, and to a considerable extent achieved a multidimensional analysis which is one of the main characteristics of structuralism. One can now see the immediate relevance of the functionalist-structuralist opposition for the analysis of the compadrazgo system. It has to do primarily with the inability to transcend the paradigmatic conception of structure involved in functional analysis, which has led me to retain several of its organizational features in order to achieve a measure of success in the structural analysis. I have tried to combine what is best in the functionalist position with some of the aspects of structuralism that lend themselves to being integrated into a still somewhat paradigmatic position, namely, the elimination of function as a necessary, superordinate part of the analysis, and the conception of multilevels of analysis which to a large extent play the homologous role of functional assignment. I have discussed in detail what structural analysis involves and have pointed out how it is an improvement on unidimensional functional analysis, but I have not touched on function. Therefore, a brief analysis of the modified notion of function used in this study follows.

My fundamental reason for combining the functional and structural analytical frameworks is my inability to implement the latter fully. Under these conditions, functional assignment has a more important place in a strictly structural study. I am not quibbling about words, but am dealing with a real substantive and theoretical issue. What is achieved by functional assignment in the classic functionalist position is also achieved in structural analysis—not by the attribution of a priori, teleological properties of circular validation, but by the residual interpretation of established regulating principles which govern the positions and relations of invariance obtaining in a social system. Thus, as a denotative term, function is equally important in both the functionalist and the structuralist approaches; the only difference is that in the former it is a circular, largely teleological operation, while in the latter it is an inference from structural components in action. From this viewpoint, then, the concept of function in structural analysis consists basically of empirical configurations of activities engaged in by particular articulations of actors, whose behavior is regulated by rules, imperatives, and constraints which can be discovered and conceptualized, but which are basically outside the realm of what has traditionally been called the social stucture. With respect to my threefold analytical framework, the principles governing behavior and action constitute what I have termed the ideological order, which corresponds in large part to what I have elsewhere called the modelic structure (Nutini 1967). The structural-ideal and structural-actual domains, on the other hand, correspond to paradigmatic structure, which is still basically the same epistemological referent that Radcliffe-Brown regarded as the "social structure."

At the modelic level, the concept of function is totally irrelevant, for this domain has to do exclusively with the principles governing a social system. At the paradigmatic level, however, the concept of function is important, for it enables us to analyze action and behavior as a result of the efficacy of the modelic over the paradigmatic level—or, as I have put it here, of the ideological order over the structural order. Thus, I am using the concept of function in its traditional empirical, paradigmatic sense, but without its teleological, tautological implications. In this new conceptual environment, the notion of function does not play an explanatory role as it does in functionalist theory; this role is played by the causal relationship between the ideological and structural orders. This is what I mean when I say that functional assignment must always be subordinated to structural analysis, and that function is nothing more than an expression of the positional and relational arrangements of actors in a given context which the structure exhibits in its paradigmatic form, that is, at the observational level. This asserts the epistemological primacy of structure over function, and also that function becomes a residual category which may still play a certain explanatory role, but only insofar as it describes behavior as the result of a causal relationship between the ideological and structural orders.

Essentially, this modified structural framework produces causal explanations (at least in principle), whereas the traditional functionalist approach produces only functional explanations, which, albeit useful, are fundamentally not explanations. My main point is that the functional dimensions of this modified structural approach are primarily descriptive and are inferences from what structure reveals in the ordered arrangement of actors behaving according to, or departing from, the rules, injunctions, and commands governing a system or subsystem. There is no longer any concern with function defined in terms of properties necessary to a part of the system, or even the system as a whole, if a certain putative condition or state, which is often impossible to determine accurately, is to be maintained. In fact, I think that by divesting structural-functional analysis of the concept of function as a necessary epistemological entity, this traditional approach acquires a new and more useful conceptual dimension, especially if it is coupled with the concept of modelic structure as I have tried to do here.[1] The combined approach is much more amenable not only to the operationalization of synchrony, but also to the study of change and diachrony.

Finally, I would like to discuss briefly how the derivative, subsidiary conception of function applies to the substantive results of this study, and what this and the following chapters represent. Throughout the structural analysis, and even in the descriptive chapters of Part One of *Ritual Kinship* I, my analysis of the compadrazgo system in its multiple aspects has had two explicit aims: the elucidation of action and behavior connected with well-defined actors or groups of actors; and the establishment of behavioral principles and principles of grouping that govern the system as a whole or its subsystems, namely, compadrazgo types, clusters, and networks. I have not been concerned overtly with function or functional assignment; whenever I have used the term, it has been incidental and to a large extent synonymous with working or operating. Nevertheless, the concept of function has been implicit in many of the descriptions of personnel in action and of the behavior connected with many compadrazgo types, clusters, and networks, denoting the patterned behavior of actors or groups of actors that results from their occupying certain well defined positions and playing varied roles. It has never been used as a statement of what the actors' behavior ostensibly means for maintaining the compadrazgo system, or any of its parts, in a certain state within Belén culture and society. I have used the notion of function to denote the empirical configuration that results from the efficacy of the ideological over the structural order. Hence, in the structural analysis I have referred to the activities rather than to the functions of the compadrazgo system (or subsystems).

The concept of function, however, means more than just the statement of activities of a structural complex. What I have in mind is a more abstract, interlocked account of activities that will give not only an insight into the structure that produces them, but a certain unitary meaning to the system or subsystem. Without endowing the concept of function with teleological, necessary, circular properties, I want it to yield an overall picture of the compadrazgo system, and its parts, in terms of the behavior of its personnel. In this sense, function can be a conceptual entity that has unifying meaning rather than explanatory dimensions. From this viewpoint, the concept of function can be useful for the empirical appreciation of sociocultural phenomena. Thus, when I discuss the functions or functional properties of such and such an aspect of the compadrazgo system, I am denoting primarily an integrated abstraction of the activities that characterize it, and the integrative or disruptive roles they play in the surface structuring of the system, type, cluster, or network, with respect to Belén as a whole or a significant segment of it.

The Political Functions of Compadrazgo

Of all the functional domains to the discussed, that of politics and political behavior is the least significant. Political organization in Belén is probably the least important of all the traditional ethnographic categories, and what I include in this category does not really constitute a separate system that could be analyzed in relative isolation. Like hundreds of communities in the Tlaxcala-Pueblan valley, and in many parts of the Central Mexican Highlands, Belén has a "paper tiger political organization" (Nutini 1968b:60). In practice, the municipal authorities presiding over the community (agente municipal and juez local) have little or no importance within it, and there is no discernible political behavior connected with their positions and activities. Moreover, the political parties (Partido Revolucionario Institucional and Partido de Acción Nacional) and labor unions (Confederación Regional de Obreros Mexicanos and Confederación de Obreros Mexicanos), which are active in the urban areas of the state and in several rural communities, are not yet active in Belén. Thus, there is no political behavior in Belén that can be conceptualized as an independent domain. Whatever passes for political behavior is a subsidiary aspect of a wider and more significant area of community culture and society. As a corollary, the mechanisms of social control that generally come under the rubric of political organization are in Belén based exclusively on kinship, religious participation, and the discharge of the compadrazgo system. Thus, whenever I have spoken of political functions or attributes, I have denoted the political behavior that accompanies the structure of the República Eclesiástica, the mayordomía system, factionalism based on kinship affiliation, and the nomination and selection of public-communal padrinos. In these circumstances, it is not surprising that the compadrazgo system per se has rather unimportant political functions, and that what compadrazgo achieves in this field could better be the function of another institution. I am not saying that political behavior does not exist in Belén, for this would be ridiculous, but only that it must be viewed as part and parcel of the structure of kinship, compadrazgo, and religion.

The main political function of compadrazgo is in generating support for the nomination and selection of the several important cargos connected with the República Eclesiástica and the mayordomía system. On such occasions, a postulant not only calls upon individual compadres for support, but the compadrazgo network immediately becomes operative and unites behind him. If there are two candidates from the same network, an arrangement is usually made, and the full body of the network supports the favored candidate. From the political viewpoint, the compadrazgo network can take effective corporate action, and contrary to what one might expect, on such occasions it is most effective. It is not so surprising, on the other hand, when one considers that the political support of the network as a corporation is not nearly as significant as the same kind of corporate support involving the disbursement of cash, goods, or services for other occasions.

There are well-specified procedures by which the candidate for a religious office lets his network compadres know that he is seeking their support. Usually he invites them to his home for a small *refresco* (repast), and there the matter is settled and a plan of action coordinated. The refresco takes place at least a month before the time of selection, so that the compadres can generate support for the candidate among the people at large. In this circumscribed domain, the politics of religious sponsorship and office selection are extremely active, and make up for the lack of true political behavior. Kinship is here closely tied to compadrazgo, inasmuch as the network is intimately tied to two maximal patrilocal nonresidential extended families. Since a candidate for religious office has usually reached the age of fifty, there will be two or three networks to unite behind him. Now and then there may be splits, especially when two network members vie for the same position, but on the whole the network functions well in providing united political support for religious cargos, in that a choice is clearly made. Moreover, religious politics go on all the time in Belén, and prospective candidates begin to activate political support among their compadres for months before the time of selection. These are the informal aspects of political maneuvering, and they go on constantly. Thus, the context of religious politics is not only formal but also has informal aspects which permeate most of the social and religious gatherings of the yearly cycle.

The discharge of religious cargos is the most significant focus of the life of the community, and its political implications pervade most of the communal activities in which large segments of the population, and sometimes the community as a whole, participate in one way or another. After marriage, Beleños in general take great interest in the many religious cargos connected with the República Eclesiástica and the mayordomía system, and this interest is translated into the political mechanisms that lead to the nomination and selection of officers. Whether an individual asks for or is drafted into the candidacy of a given cargo, the political dimensions of his nomination involve a good deal of maneuvering. This must take into account how acceptable he is to the community as a whole, or at least to a majority of it, for even today Beleños feel that the most important cargos in the community are a matter of corporate importance. This does not apply to all the mayordomias nor to all positions in the República Eclesiástica, but it does apply to the three main fiscales, the mayordomía of the patron saint, the mayordomias connected with ANDI and PCA compadrazgo, and perhaps two or three of the other mayordomias—for a total of approximately eight or nine yearly cargo positions.

It is in this context that compadrazgo has a significant function in rallying support and providing the lines of communication that lead to the discharge of religious cargos. Here, the compadrazgo network plays its most extensive role in that it can effectively generate enough political support to influence a sizable segment of the community. This is especially the case when a given candidate, for various social and religious reasons, is not really an attractive candidate for relgious office. This presupposes, of course, that the average adult in Belén is genuinely interested in the fulfillment of religious cargos, which is still substantially true of the majority of the population. On the other hand, public, community-wide support may often favor a particular candidate, and in such cases the political functions of the network are essentially inoperative. The ideology underlying both the religious organization and the compadrazgo system prescribes that the discharge of religious cargos, as well as of public-communal and to a lesser extent private-individual compadrazgo types, is a sacred obligation of the individual toward the community and the supernatural. The discharge of religious cargos does not confer social and religious prestige (which, nevertheless, the individual latently acquires); rather, the cargos are regarded simply as an obligation. When, however, Belén's ideology is transformed into a secular, primarily economic ideology, the political functions of the compadrazgo system will be much increased.

I have stated several times that there is considerable factionalism in Belén, arising largely from conflicts over water rights, the traditional division of the community into the upper (hill) and lower (river) parts, and, not least, the undertaking of such public works as the building of roads and other communal facilities. In this context of factionalism, compadrazgo plays a rather significant role. To begin with, the factions in Belén are not discrete, permanent groups, except for those springing out of the traditional mild antagonism and rivalry between the upper and lower parts of the village. Rather, factional groups are sporadic conglomerates of parajes—that is, they are territorially based—that arise out of the disputes, and that may last for a generation or two. The Cuilixco-Xehuitla case provides a good example of this function, namely, that a traditional factional split between two parajes is solved by the institutionalization of compadrazgo exchanges leading to the formation of a strong network. More commonly, the exchange of compadres between contending factions (which most often started naturally and despite the split) may smooth out a tense situation for a while, but not lead to the formation of a network between the two contending parajes. Rather, compadres on both sides of the factions will serve as mediators, and can often avert direct confrontations. This is primarily because compadrazgo networks crisscross and overlap paraje affiliation, and usually there are network compadres on both sides of a factional division. In its maximum extension this is the case with the upper-lower division, and the community has been kept from splitting apart by the many reciprocal ties of compadrazgo between these two geographical divisions, in which civic-minded compadres on both sides strive to bring about rapport. All is not harmonious in Belén; from time to time, factionalism and strong dissension threaten the internal cohesion of the community, and in this context compadrazgo ties are still an effective mechanism of political rapport.

The third and final context in which compadrazgo has a political function is in the nomination and selection of public-communal padrinos, especially those for the ANDI and PCA compadrazgo types. These deserve special consideration, for they arouse much greater political involvement than the yearly politics connected with the nomination and selection of religious cargos. It is not surprising that the selection of ANDI and PCA padrinos attracts so much political involvement for they are unquestionably of the highest symbolic and emotional importance to the community as a whole. These two sponsorships are probably the most desired in the religious and compadrazgo complexes of Belén, for regardless of the underlying ideology, they do indeed confer social and religious prestige upon the couples who hold them. The etiquette of the situation, however, does not permit an overt candidacy; rather, the candidates must be proposed by a sizable group of people within the community. There are usually three or four candidates for every such election, backed by well-recognized segments of the community in which the factions especially the upper-lower division, play important roles.

At least two or three weeks before the selection, the various groups begin to campaign for their candidates, and this is unquestionably the period of greatest political activity in Belén; compadres must take sides, networks come into operation, and paraje affiliations are brought to bear. These political maneuverings are conducted informally, but they soon come to the attention of the fiscales and mayordomos in charge of the selection. These cargo officials are in a delicate position, for their only concern must be to reach a consensus that will please the most and offend the fewest Beleños. They must remain completely neutral, and on the whole the people trust their neutrality and judgment. They listen to all arguments on all sides, evaluate the various candidates, and make their decisions on these bases. When, as often happens, they find there is no suitable candidate in Belén, the community generally accepts their judgment and tacitly empowers them to search for padrinos outside—a search for which they have sole responsibility. (This is also an important demographic function of compadrazgo.) The political action involved is very intense and has all the characteristics of political behavior in its nuclear meaning: cajoling, applying pressure, compromising, activating reciprocal ayuda, dickering, and so on. Finally, what I have said about the politics connected with the República Eclesiástica and mayordomía system also applies here, except that compadrazgo cleavage of political support transcends the network and operates on a more individual basis.

In brief, while politics per se are not important in Belén, the political behavior associated with certain public-communal compadrazgo types, religious cargo selection, and factional disputes involves a rather significant compadrazgo function. This, however, is a residual and once-removed functional assignment which does not constitute an immediate reflection of the structure of compadrazgo personnel in action, but rather shows its necessary involvement in activities and behavior that are primarily religious or territorial. The political functions of compadrazgo can best be characterized as facilitating the operation of certain circumscribed domains of religion, and the resolution of territorial, factional conflict; in other words, compadrazgo can be seen as an effective but not the only mechanism for resolving conflict and generating political support.

The Economic Functions of Compadrazgo

The economic functions of compadrazgo are intrinsically more important than its political functions. Here again, I am not concerned with primary functions but with derived functions pertaining to more inclusive domains, namely, religion and kinship and the life cycle. The economic functions of compadrazgo are better viewed as subsidiary aspects of these socioreligious domains. In contrast to the political domain, however, the economic domain itself is in turn brought to bear on the discharge of the "economic" dimensions of kinship, ritual kinship, and the religious organization. The primary economic functions of compadrazgo are to a large extent latent, whereas its derived functions do significantly shape the social and religious behavior of the community through the mediation of the compadrazgo system. An example will make this clear. In terms of maximizing purely economic aims, that is, aims not conditioned by the sacred ideology of the socioreligious core of Belén culture and society—for example, the acquisition of household utensils, house improvement, dress styles, the capitalization of resources—the compadrazgo system does not yet have a detectable functional dimension. Except for members of the economic elite, who (especially in their extracommunal relationships) are tending to use compadrazgo for economic gain, the traditional socioreligious ideology is still strong enough to prevent such secularization. Thus, within the community the economic functions of compadrazgo are confined to the maximization of aims that, although intrinsically economic, are part and parcel of kinship, ritual kinship, and the religious organization. What may appear superficially as a purely economic piece of behavior, such as labor exchange or ayuda, upon closer examination can be seen to be conditioned by the symmetry and reciprocity underlying the socioreligious domain, either through the operation of kinship, or, more important, compadrazgo. It is important to distinguish between primary and secondary functions, with respect both to the intrinsic importance of a behavioral domain and to its independent operation within the societal framework, for otherwise functional assignment may become hopelessly entangled and lose all conceptual value in any attempt to establish the relations of dependence and invariance between the ideological and structural orders.

Essentially, the economic functions of compadrazgo take place within an operational matrix characterized by a scarcity of resources in kind, cash, and even services, and by the generation of participation and cooperation from a significant number of people. The life, social, and religious cycles in Belén often require the expenditure of cash and goods and the provision of services for a variety of celebrations that cannot be the exclusive function of kinship groups or alignments, either for lack of personnel or for lack of corporate action. In this context, the economic functions of compadrazgo have an important role in helping to solve the problem of scarcity of cash, goods, or personnel. Furthermore, given the overlapping of kinship and compadrazgo in Belén, it is always difficult to separate the functions of these two systems. Thus, when I talk about the economic functions of compadrazgo I am also referring to the economic functions of kinship, for while it is sometimes possible to determine exactly what these systems include or exclude, it is conceptually better to make a functional analysis of them as an undifferentiated whole.

The combined kinship-compadrazgo economic functions make themselves felt throughout the whole spectrum of the socioreligious organization of Belén. I am not talking about the economic activities involved in the central ceremonies, for this is an inherent aspect of each compadrazgo type, but about the permanent economic rights and obligations underlying all primary and most secondary compadrazgo types. The economic function of compadrazgo, then, is one of the several ties that keep a compadrazgo relationship in operation for long periods. From the intrinsic viewpoint of compadrazgo, economic considerations acquire a more significant dimension than one may at first be led to believe. The secondary economic functions of compadrazgo are indeed important, for a considerable extent they serve to incorporate the primary functions of the institution into the general framework of a permanent situation—or, structurally speaking, to give individual compadrazgo relationships and networks of compadres a systemic, corporate dimension. Interestingly enough, in Belén latent functions correlate with what I have called primary functions, while manifest functions are always secondary or derived, for Beleños always say that compadres form the political, economic, and even demographic and material web that makes possible most of the ceremonial occasions in the life cycle. I have described in detail the activities underlying the economic functions of compadrazgo (see Part One of *Ritual Kinship* I), and in the remainder of this section I would like to show how these economic functions relate to other areas of the compadrazgo system.

There are many occasions in the life, social, and religious cycles of Belén when the extended family or nonresidential extended family, or just the personnel of a given compadrazgo relationship, can cope with the economic obligations involved. But there are probably just as many occasions that require the economic activation of several pairs of compadres and possibly entire compadrazgo networks. Such occasions are commonly associated with the mayordomía system and the República Eclesiástica; less commonly they are strictly social celebrations, especially marriage and death. The latent economic mechanisms in the various compadrazgo types are always well specified and highly institutionalized. At all times, compadres brought into the web of participation and cooperation, both as individual couples and as network couples, know what to do and how to behave.

There are three mechanisms that regulate economic cooperation and participation. First, it is the duty of compadres, given the degree of prescription (or preference) that binds them to the couple or group of couples sponsoring the occasion, to find out whether economic help is needed beyond what is formally stipulated by custom. This is often a difficult point and compadres are always conscious of it, especially if they are interested in keeping a compadrazgo relationship active or intensifying it. Second, economic help is given either on an individual basis or on the basis of membership in a compadrazgo network. In the former case, the form it takes is regulated by the types of compadrazgo relationships between donors and recipients; in the latter case, it is an inherent, institutionalized aspect of compadrazgo behavior predicated on the degree of intensification, the nature of the occasion, and the extent of the network in operation. In either case, however, economic help is not sought directly by the recipient. When couples activate economic help of their own volition, it becomes an individual action which falls outside the prescriptive or preferential constraints of the compadrazgo system, and it may or may not represent an instance of economic functional discharge. Third, all occasions that require activation of economic functions must fall under the category of the nonutilitarian or traditionally sanctioned, for any other economic implications that may be attributed to the functional discharge of compadrazgo are regulated by the symmetry and reciprocity that characterize the ideological order. In other words, when I refer to the economic functions of compadrazgo, I am referring primarily to its prescriptive and preferential dimensions with regard to exocentric compadrazgo behavior and network operation. Individually, egocentrically based economic behavior is best regarded as an expression of other, more fundamental functional domains. Let me briefly summarize the form and content of the various kinds of economic help and ayuda.

Economic help and ayuda have been defined loosely as being either prescriptively regulated or individually and optionally offered, and of course this dichotomy applies to all functional domains of the compadrazgo system. When economic help is prescriptively regulated, the average couple knows exactly when, what, and how to give; and by extension this applies to the constituent couples of compadrazgo networks, especially when they act as a corporate group. In this sense, then, the economic functions of compadrazgo are better analyzed as a subsidiary aspect of its social and religious functions, for in this context one can see more clearly how secondary economic functions support the primary religious and social functions. To a large extent, in fact, it is the specific economic dimensions of compadrazgo that give form to the social and religious functions. On the other hand, a rather substantial amount of economic ayuda among compadres occurs on an individual optional basis, mostly but not necessarily dyadically. On such occasions, the form and content of economic ayuda acquire a more "economic" function, and ayuda is closer to the primary meaning of the term, for it has elements that fall outside the sacred domain of the compadrazgo system. The economic functions of compadrazgo then transcend its traditional boundaries, and eventually this will weaken the compadrazgo system and its position in Belén culture and society. This trend has been apparent in Belén and most of rural Tlaxcala since roughly the mid-1960s, and there is no reason to think it will stop.

Individual optional compadrazgo help of various forms may be forthcoming on a variety of occasions. Obviously, the most typical occasions are those related to the more optional compadrazgo types, and not infrequently such help is part of essentially secular activities beyond the sacred injunctions of the compadrazgo system. Under this rubric must be included the borrowing of money among compadres and labor exchange for agricultural work, house construction, mercantile operations, and so on. When the limit of these operations is approached, obviously the essentially secondary functions of compadrazgo are transformed into primary functions. Everything else, then, that can be construed as an economic function is secondary in character and must be viewed from the standpoint of the religious and social functions of the compadrazgo system of which it is an integral part. The strictly secondary economic functions of compadrazgo cover a wide range of activities, carried out in specific circumstances and always prescriptively regulated, which cover the whole spectrum of the compadrazgo system in its permanent dimensions, and without which it would lose much of its unitary meaning. From this viewpoint, the secondary economic functions of compadrazgo acquire greater importance in the overall assessment of the institution. This can be seen clearly in the analysis of the economic component of duties and obligations that outlast the principal ceremonies in compadrazgo types with a permanent dimension, when compadres are required to disburse cash or goods and provide services on a variety of occasions (see tables 32 and 33). I have already dealt with these in detail, and I can conclude by saying that the secondary economic functions of compadrazgo are permanently translated into a series of activities that shape and give unitary meaning to the social and religious dimensions of the institution.

Finally, I would like to discuss briefly the incipient transformation of compadrazgo's secondary economic functions into primary ones. In the first place, this is already affecting a small but disproportionately influential segment of Belén's population. I am referring, of course, to the economic elite, which is already beyond the incipient stage in this proc-

TABLE 32. Strength of Postceremonial Economic Obligations by
Compadrazgo Type

Type	Strong	Medium	Weak	None
Bautizo	x			
Casamiento	x			
Confirmación		x		
PCE	x			
Primera comunión			x	
CCCH			x	
CCCA			x	
ANDC		x		
ANDI				x
AOI				x
BSI		x		
CSV				x
Escapulario			x	
Graduación			x	
PCA				x
Quince años			x	
Sacada a misa			x	
Compadrazgo de evangelios		x		
Compadrazgo de limpia		x		
BOI				x
Bendición de casa	x			
BCC			x	
BM				x
Parada de cruz	x			
Primera piedra	x			
Compadrazgo de amistad				x
CABP				x
Compadrazgo de aretes				x
CEON			x	
FC			x	
JJ				x

ess. It is in viewing the compadrazgo system as discharged by the economic elite that one can see most clearly the increasing emphasis on using the compadrazgo system outside its traditional, sacred domain— or, in the context of this section, the transformation of economic functions from secondary to primary. Within the total context of Belén culture and society, the economic elite is on the whole still practicing compadrazgo within its traditional domain. At the same time, however, and to a greater extent than the majority of the community, its members are engaging in compadrazgo activities that are consciously designed to enhance the primary economic functions of the institution, in that they are using some relationships to maximize essentially economic aims.

TABLE 33. Establishment of Compadrazgo Relationships and Participants' Socioeconomic Status

Type	Same Status	Different Status	No Bearing
Bautizo	x		
Casamiento			x
Confirmación	x		
PCE	x		
Primera comunión	x		
CCCH			x
CCCA			x
ANDC	x		
ANDI		x	
AOI		x	
BSI	x		
CSV		x	
Escapulario	x		
Graduación			x
PCA		x	
Quince años			x
Sacada a misa	x		
Compadrazgo de evangelios	x		
Compadrazgo de limpia	x		
BOI		x	
Bendición de casa	x		
BCC	x		
BM	x		
Parada de cruz	x		
Primera piedra	x		
Compadrazgo de amistad	x		
CABP	x		
Compadrazgo de aretes	x		
CEON		x	
FC	x		
JJ	x		

While all of these vertical, increasingly secular compadrazgo relationships are still contracted exogenously, they will have an effect on the community as a whole, for they constitute a model for the individual, optional economic functions of compadrazgo at the expense of its sacred, prescriptive component. The ideological and structural orders will diverge increasingly, until the compadrazgo system becomes essentially a secular institution in which primary economic functions occupy perhaps the most important position in overall functional assignment, and in which the maximization of economic activities will become the primary aim.

The clearest indication of this ideological and structural change in the compadrazgo system of Belén, and by extension in countless communities in Tlaxcala, is the growing number of primarily individual, optional activities binding the economic behavior of specific sets of compadres. This kind of behavior has always been contemplated within the traditional context of Belén's compadrazgo system, but it has now become obvious to the people themselves that the sacred-secular balance of the system is shifting rather dangerously toward the latter. This is explicitly voiced by the most conservative elements of the community, one of whose members said, "Dá mucha pena ver como no pocas gentes del pueblo ya no tienen el respeto debido a la santidad del compadrazgo y lo están usando para ventaja personal" (It is a sad thing to see that not a few people of Belén no longer have the required respect for the sanctity of compadrazgo, and are using it for their personal gain). When one adds the example of the economic elite to the strong secularizing trends now present in Belén, it is safe to predict that in a few years the compadrazgo system will have been transformed into an essentially secular institution.

The second point in this connection has to do with using the transformation of the economic functions of compadrazgo from secondary to primary as an index of sociocultural change. I have already dealt with the theoretical implications of this position (see "Sanctions, Traditionalism, Secularization, and Change," Chapter Five), and here I can only add that this transformation is perhaps the clearest and the most self-contained example of the advantages in focusing the study of sociocultural change in terms of the articulation of the ideological and structural orders. In my opinion, the transformation represents a measurable entity with concomitant properties obtaining between discernible variables, namely, the new exigencies of the Tlaxcala-Pueblan valley delineated in Chapter Nine of *Ritual Kinship* I, and the traditional setting of the compadrazgo system. From the dynamic viewpoint, then, the economic functions of compadrazgo have great importance, and if properly manipulated can yield significant conceptual dimensions for the study of change. It is only when looked at from the static viewpoint that they seem so unimportant.

The Demographic Functions of Compadrazgo

I come now to what I consider the first primary functions of compadrazgo, that is, functions that are not subsidiary to more inclusive and pervasive functions, as was the case for politics and economics. The demographic functions of compadrazgo are primary not only because they involve an efficacious functional domain in their own right, but also because they have been part of the compadrazgo system of Belén for at least 150 years. As such, they must be analyzed without reference to other functional configurations, and be regarded as involving immediate functional assignments. Again, I have already described and analyzed the demographic context of the compadrazgo system, and here I merely describe demographic functions and show how they reflect, to some extent shape and modify, and above all integrate the exogenous and endogenous elements of the compadrazgo system.

Under the rubric of demographic functions I want to include essentially all the extracommunal, exogenous inferential elements and dimensions of the compadrazgo system of Belén. I am not including endogenous, strictly communal dimensions such as paraje population distribution, territorial divisions, and the like, although, strictly speaking, they do have demographic aspects. These endogenous elements are better analyzed as part of the functional aspects of the religious and social domains. From the quantitative, structural viewpoint, compadrazgo has a good many demographic functions, for more than one-third of all compadrazgo relationships in Belén are contracted exogamously; they are not as important from the qualitative, ideological viewpoint, but the structure of both endogamous and exogamous compadrazgo has fundamentally the same ideological basis. Even in the strictly traditional setting the demographic functions of compadrazgo have always been significant, and in the contemporary, changing situation they will become more important.

The people of Belén have contracted extracommunal compadrazgo relationships for nearly two centuries and perhaps longer, and since the 1880s or so these have increased greatly (see Part Three of *Ritual Kinship* I). Starting with nearby communities, the compadrazgo system of Belén has extended its range, and Beleños now maintain regular exchanges of compadres in more than sixty communities in the state of Tlaxcala. The extracommunal, demographic dimensions of compadrazgo have been significant in the historical development of the institution, and structurally speaking, they have both disruptive and integrative aspects that continue to affect its functioning. These functions must be given careful attention, for it is probable that, as the institution continues to develop, they, together with the economic functions, will become its most important, perhaps exclusive, primary functions.

At the highest level, the demographic functions of compadrazgo promote regional integration and the exchange of personnel, and have subsidiary, secondary economic functions. The villages that constitute the heart of the Tlaxcalan area have maintained a considerable amount of contact since the last decades of the colonial period. In this respect, Belén is typical of dozens of communities located between the Tlaxcala-Puebla highway and the middle slopes of La Malintzi volcano. Contact with the outside has always been based on both territorial proximity and economic exchange, for even after the Repúblicas de Indios were established in the middle and late sixteenth century, few Tlaxcalan communities were ever completely self-sufficient and isolated.

So far as I have been able to determine, compadrazgo ties with nearby communities began to be significant and well structured by the last two or three decades of colonial rule, and had primarily an economic foundation. As early as 1790 many Beleños had regular compadre exchanges with the people of the nearby communities of San Pablo Apetatitlán and San Matias Tepetomatitlán.[2] These exchanges have continued without interruption, always expanding, until the present. While the initial contact with specific communities was usually for economic reasons—for example, the exchange of manufactured products (basketry, wooden articles, textiles, and so on) or other economic transactions—it soon led to the exchange of compadres. In time, the initial economic impetus began to be less important, and compadrazgo exchanges acquired an independent status, which is what I have construed as one of the primary functions of compadrazgo, namely, a demographic function. As a result of this structural change, exrtracommunal compadrazgo became a regular and permanent feature of the compadrazgo system of Belén and, by extension, of countless communities throughout the Tlaxcalan area.

By the beginning of the twentieth century, the Tlaxcalan area within a radius of 25 kilometers of the state capital contained at least twenty municipios and 80 to 100 communities, the majority of which were tied to at least 8 or 10 other communities by a variety of social, religious, and economic bonds, in which compadrazgo played a prominent role. Given this historical development, the functions of compadrazgo in Belén have a dual character in synchronic terms: at the regional level, extracommunal compadrazgo promotes integration and helps to break down any traditional isolation mechanisms that may have arisen from various historical factors, originating primarily during colonial times but persisting into republican times; at the communal level, extracommunal compadrazgo has certain disruptive elements arising out of inherent conditions of distance and community size, and the differences that are bound to exist in the local variants of the ideology underlying the pan-Tlaxcalan compadrazgo system. In turn, however, extracommunal compadrazgo has come to represent the solution to certain internal disruptions and dissensions, and its overall integrative functions by far overshadow its disruptive dimensions. This, then, is the general diachronic context of the demographic functions of compadrazgo, and I can now analyze their synchronic discharge.

Extracommunal compadrazgo serves four main, more or less independent, functions. I say more or less independent, because historical developments during the past two centuries have tended to make compadrazgo coalesce into a well-integrated institution in which extracommunal compadrazgo is intimately related to other functional domains, and despite the discrimination between primary and secondary functions, it is not always possible to disentangle them or—what is more difficult—to circumscribe them by assigning them to the proper structural category. In any case, the main primary demographic functions of compadrazgo are these: the settlement of disputes with adjacent communities, or parts of them, over land and water rights; the resolution of compadrazgo selection when no communal consensus can be reached with regard to public-communal compadrazgo types; the structuring of working relationships within the context of labor migration, leading in turn to secondary functions; and finally, the structuring of regional integration and contacts with the outside world on the basis of exchange and outright secondary economic functions. I might add an incipient fifth function, namely, the secondary function of stimulating class stratification.

The use of extracommunal compadrazgo for settling disputes and averting conflict with neighboring communities over land and water rights, and sometimes for less explicit reasons, has a rather long history in Belén, and given the pan-Tlaxcalan ideology of the compadrazgo system, in many municipios throughout the state (see Chapter Nine of *Ritual Kinship* I).[3] Public-communal types are the principal catalyst, but in time, many private-individual relationships are also established, especially among the primary and secondary personnel of the initial public-communal relationships. Thus, over a period of two or three generations, a regular subsidiary compadrazgo network may come into existence. The circumstances under which extracommunal compadrazgo relationships with a demographic function come into existence have already been analyzed, as has the fact that Beleños use this method of compadrazgo establishment with the conscious aim of settling disputes and avoiding conflict, a sentiment that is obviously shared by those with whom they are having disputes. Compadrazgo may also be used in this way within the community, as in the case of contending parajes or factions (see "The Political Functions of Compadrazgo," this chapter). One must distinguish between the initial establishment of extracommunal compadrazgo for the purpose of settling disputes, and the ensuing subsidiary network, for once the demographic function has been achieved, the ensuing compadrazgo relationships—public-communal or private-individual—become an integral part of the normal course of endogamous compadrazgo. On the whole, the functions of compadrazgo in settling disputes and averting conflict have been important in the relationships of Belén with neighboring communities, especially since the turn of the century, and have been instrumental in making possible its peaceful territorial coexistence. At the same time, compadrazgo relationships of this kind have become the model for similar situations within the community, and this demographic function has by now become part of the overall structural-functional picture of compadrazgo in Belén. This function of the compadrazgo system may not be the most important, but it has become the most conscious use of ritual kinship to lessen social, religious, and territorial tension in Belén.

The second demographic function of compadrazgo is in many ways a corollary of the first, for now conflict originates inside the community and is resolved by elements from outside, that is, by selecting compadres from other, adjacent, communities. Here again, the compadrazgo types used initially are always public-communal, but they differ in that they seldom lead to the formation of subsidiary networks, although there may be some compadrazgo exchanges involving the primary and perhaps secondary actors of the original public-communal relationship. As I have already pointed out, (see "The Political Functions of Compadrazgo," this chapter), the contexts of extracommunal selection of public-communal types are factionalism, inability of those in charge of selection to generate communal consensus, and internal religious politics. In all of these, extracommunal selection accomplishes the same ends, namely, avoidance of socioreligious conflict and of confrontations between members of the República Eclesiástica and the mayordomía system and pressure groups from the community at large, which could seriously disturb the yearly cycle of religious celebrations. In some cases, the intracommunal and extracommunal functions are combined into a single complex—for example, the compadrazgo ties of Beleños with the residents of section 1 of San Bernardino Contla, in which the original gravity of the situation led to a rather tight subsidiary network. On the whole, however, these two demographic functions of compadrazgo are separate, and come into operation under different circumstances. This function of compadrazgo may be extended to private-individual types, but this is not nearly as generalized as it is for public-communal types. A couple in Belén may use extracommunal compadrazgo to contract a relationship that, for various reasons, it cannot contract within the community. In such a case, the function of extra-communal compadrazgo is identical to that of selecting the PCA padrinos from nearby communities; the given compadrazgo types cannot be discharged intracommunally without considerable conflict and social or religious dissension. Thus, this demographic function of compadrazgo can be important operationally for the discharge of both public-communal and private-individual types.

The third demographic function of compadrazgo occurs in the context of labor migration, and it is the most important of all the functions in this category both quantitatively and qualitatively. More than 65 percent of the gainfully employed men in Belén come into contact with labor migrants from at least half of the municipios of the entire state of Tlaxcala. Given the pan-Tlaxcalan ideology of the compadrazgo system, within both the work environment and the village itself, many compadrazgo relationships come into existence whose principal manifest function is to create working conditions and a social ambiance resembling the social and everyday life of Belén. Since 1937 or so, as labor migration reached its peak, more than 60 percent of all extracommunal compadrazgo relationships in Belén have been contracted in the context of labor migration. In fact, it appears that even the functions of settling disputes and averting conflict will eventually move beyond compadrazgo exchange with neighboring communities, and take place exclusively within the environment of labor migration. This is one more avenue of secularization that I visualize for the near future, in which even public-communal compadrazgo types will be used vertically and on a communal basis. This view of extracommunal compadrazgo has almost arrived, for couples in Belén are increasing their extracommunal compadrazgo as they become increasingly aware of changes in the ideological order of the institution and of its trend toward secularization. Thus, it is almost inevitable that extracommunal compadrazgo connected with labor migration will acquire important secondary economic and stratification functions, or at least that it will involve activities that will help to accelerate secularization, not only of the compadrazgo system, but of Belén culture and society as a whole. On the opposite side, however, the traditional element in Belén (and the average Tlaxcalan community) is still conservative enough to confine extracommunal compadrazgo to its traditional functions of settling disputes and creating the proper social ambiance away from the community. Secularization will no doubt prevail, but not without a long struggle in which the traditional ideological order will significantly influence the emerging secular ideological order, and there will be considerable overlapping of both structure and functions.

The last demographic function of extracommunal compadrazgo is really a compound of the other three, at least to the extent that Beleños realize that their community has many ties with the outside and that it is best to integrate the community and the region on the basis of some mutual, manageable institution like compadrazgo. This was explicitly stated by one of my informants, and could be replicated in many rural communities throughout Tlaxcala: "El tener compadres en el trabajo, en pueblos vecinos, y el solucionar conflictos importantes por medio del compadrazgo, no solo ayuda personalmente sino que también a mejorar las relaciones entre pueblos" (To have compadres where one works, in neighboring villages, and to solve important conflicts through compadrazgo, not only helps personally but also improves relationships among communities). The implication here is clear: Belén, to exist as a viable community, must *afianzar* (secure) its extracommunal ties, and this can best be done through the ties of compadrazgo. In this context, the overall demographic function of compadrazgo is to integrate community and region into a network or networks of relationships which may include economic, religious, and social ties, but in which the specific attributes of compadrazgo constitute the primary function. To a large extent, this has been the case with Belén, and other Tlaxcalan communities, since colonial times, when compadrazgo acted as a catalyst in shaping economic transactions and the exchange of manufactured products. In the modern setting, however, these subsidiary functions have diminished and will be increasingly replaced by social and religious subsidiary functions, although economic considerations may again become important with the rise of class stratification. In summary, then, the extracommunal demographic functions of compadrazgo may increase in importance in direct proportion to the rise of secularization, and to a significant extent they will shape the development of the process itself.

I have addressed myself here to the least important, secondary functions of compadrazgo, and to one important, primary function which has an anomalous, nontraditional component. The political function is the least significant and most isolated of the three, but the other two are quite closely interrelated. In the changing perspective of Belén, however, the political function is bound to become more important, and will probably become closely related to the other two. It is also probable that when the compadrazgo system acquires a secular ideology, the complex of functions described in this chapter will become the most important primary functions of the system.

CHAPTER 16

The Religious and Social Functions of Compadrazgo

I come now to the primary functional core of the compadrazgo system. In this chapter and the following I deal mainly with the primary religious, social, and magico-religious functions of compadrazgo, and in a subsidiary way with the secondary functions involved in them. In fact, these primary functions are almost invariably accompanied by some of the secondary functions described in the preceding chapter. Moreover, we are entering what have always been regarded as the traditional functional domains of compadrazgo, although they have not been analyzed in their multiplicity of forms. Inasmuch as the compadrazgo system always encompasses several aspects of community culture and society, it seems logical to assume a multifunctional rather than a unifunctional conception of it. This unidimensional focus on compadrazgo may result from a failure to make the distinction between primary and secondary functions. This distinction is essential in dealing with a system as pervasive as compadrazgo, in which functional assignment depends ultimately on the types of compadrazgo being discharged. From this viewpoint, the compadrazgo system is really a metasystem which is articulated to several other systems at specifically designated lower levels of integration. I am not saying that the compadrazgo system is substantively *above*, say, the religious or kinship systems, but only that its pervasiveness tends to impose upon the observer this metasystemic conception. This constitutes both the strength and the weakness of compadrazgo as an integral conceptual system: its strength is that through it one can most clearly see sociocultural dynamics in operation, and compadrazgo becomes a unitary concept by means of which the structure and functioning of a global system can be viewed; its weakness is that one can fall into the reification that such pervasiveness may easily impose upon the observer, which may make it difficult to isolate the efficacious structural and functional domains. Nevertheless, the advantages outweigh the weaknesses, and I have therefore adopted what I refer to as the unitary meaning of compadrazgo. In this and the following chapter I deal with, and try to solve, some of the problems involved in this conception of the institution.

The Religious Functions of Compadrazgo

In Part Three of *Ritual Kinship* I, I show how, in its historical development, the compadrazgo system has moved from an essentially religious institution to an institution with a steadily increasing social component, so that in the synchronic present (beginning about 1820) the latter has become more important than the former. I expressed this developmental change in terms of the increasing importance of the compadres-compadres dyad at the expense of the padrinos-ahijado dyad, which originally embodied the religious essence of the institution. The religious component of compadrazgo is still very important and ranks second only to its social component; in fact it is sometimes difficult to separate the two into meaningful spheres of action. When the full cycle of change is completed, it is evident that the religious functions of compadrazgo will also change from primary to secondary. I think, furthermore, that the religious functions and overall religious importance of compadrazgo have always been overestimated in the literature because too much attention has been paid to its surface components and to the analysis of sacramental compadrazgo. Thus, one of the main purposes of this chapter is to put in perspective the importance and the interrelations of the religious and social functions of compadrazgo.

Under the rubric of religious functions, I am including three main aspects: the role that compadrazgo plays in the administrative (República Eclesiástica and mayordomía system) and theological (ideological, symbolic) conduct of Belén's relations with the supernatural; the ceremonial role of compadrazgo and the activities carried out by its actors; and the ritual role of compadrazgo usually designed to achieve either utilitarian or supernatural ends. The compadrazgo system has religious functions that encompass the whole spectrum of religious behavior, and this is especially the case for all the events leading up to the central ceremonies. It is perhaps in this part of the syntagmatic unfolding of compadrazgo that its religious functions are most important and are most clearly seen in operation. Religious functions are considerably less important in the permanent dimensions of the system, where they are overshadowed by its social functions. One must not overstress this point, however, for religious functions may still have a significant effect on the permanent dimensions, especially with regard to the administrative aspects of religion, in that specific compadrazgo relationships and networks are often the mainstay of religious celebrations. Moreover, the ceremonial and ritual functions of compadrazgo are the most generalized and operate at all stages of the syntagmatic development of the system.

Before I analyze the specific religious functions of compadrazgo, I must describe the interrelationship between the ideological order and the religious segment of the structural order, for only after this juncture is understood can one properly make functional assignments. One of the implicit themes of this study is that religion has been a large component in the historical development of the ideological order of Belén, and by extension the whole of Tlaxcala and much of Mesoamerica. The ideological order of Belén is centered around a series of religious themes which pervade the entire spectrum of community culture and society. It is for this reason that I maintain that the traditional ideology of Belén is essentially sacred, and that contravening its imperatives and injunctions almost invariably elicits supernatural sanctions. In this situation, it is not always possible to separate structurally what is religious and what is not, but I have tried to keep them separate by categorizing elements in terms of the sacred and traditional, on the one hand, and the secular and economic, on the other. This analytical device has yielded good results, especially in the more dynamic aspects of the analysis. In dealing with the functional domain, however, it is more difficult to talk separately of the functions of religion and the functions of compadrazgo. They are generally included in the same efficacious context, and one can easily be led to assign functional involvement to religious and compadrazgo elements indiscriminately. When it is not always possible to say whether or not a complex of behavior, or even a clearly discernible structural arrangement, is part of the compadrazgo system, then it is difficult to analyze it functionally. For example, are the ritual and ceremonial aspects of baptismal compadrazgo more an integral part of the religious system or of the compadrazgo system? And more important, can one assign to this compadrazgo type a specific religious function, or merely one that is part of the overall function of religion?

Here again, the distinction between primary and secondary functions is useful, for it permits the interlocking of functions at various levels of structural integration. The problem can be solved by saying that at the highest level of integration, taking into consideration all of Belén culture and society, the religious functions of compadrazgo are secondary functions of the religious system. Within the context of this study, on the other hand—at the level of the compadrazgo system in relative isolation—one can properly regard the functional complex of religion as primary. Thus, we face once again the basic conceptual viewpoint adopted in this study, namely, that a social or religious institution or unit must be analyzed in both its internal and external dimensions, showing both how it is integrated within itself and how it is embedded in wider contexts. For the moment, then, the religious functions of compadrazgo can be regarded as primary, but without forgetting that they are part of the wider context of religion, both structurally and functionally. For this reason, I have taken pains to illustrate the interaction between compadrazgo and the religious and social systems with which it is most closely associated. In the case of religion, the fact that compadrazgo has the same ideological order has compounded the difficulties, but I hope to have shown that regardless of the hierarchical position of the system, the efficacy derived from a common ideological order produces the same conceptual results. I can now enumerate and briefly discuss the religious functions of compadrazgo without worrying about whether they are primary or secondary, and show their articulation and their subordinate or superordinate positions vis-à-vis other functional domains.

The secondary economic functions of religious compadrazgo derive from the fact that the religious life of Belén includes many occasions that demand large expenditures of cash, goods, and services, and the discharge of compadrazgo rights and obligations plays an important role in generating such resources. In fact, the generation of these resources would no doubt suffer greatly without the compadrazgo system for neither the kinship system nor the religious system per se would be able to provide and coordinate the necessary personnel and economic and social networks. The compadrazgo system is both a religious catalyst and a mechanism for extending economic participation and cooperation in the conduct of religious affairs. These aspects of religious compadrazgo are not only embodied in public-communal types, but are part of the compadrazgo system as a whole. On the one hand, the permanent dimensions of the various compadrazgo types provide for the generation of cash, goods, and services. As I have already pointed out (see "The Economic Functions of Compadrazgo," Chapter Fifteen), this is regulated either by custom or by the specific exigencies of the occasion, but the result is basically the same: compadres always participate and cooperate economically when there is a need for them in religious sponsorships. On the other hand, selections for the cargos of the República Eclesiástica and the mayordomía system are determined largely by ties of compadrazgo. This last is a very important religious function of compadrazgo, which merits further, independent discussion. I am not including under the rubric of the economic functions of religious compadrazgo the economic obligations involved in the religious discharge of the principal ceremonies and events leading to them—for these economic activities are part of other functions—but only those aspects without which the religious system could not operate properly. In summary, then, the economic-religious functions of compadrazgo are a sine qua non for the administrative generation of cash, goods, and services in the conduct of the religious life of Belén.

Religious compadrazgo also has secondary political and demographic functions, most particularly the relationship of various compadrazgo types to the República Eclesiástica and the mayordomía system. In this context, compadrazgo is the most significant mechanism by which alliances are made, compromise is reached, and conflict is averted. Without the compadrazgo system, Belén would be torn by conflicting interests and interest groups which would split the community into irreconcilable factions, and in fact one would hardly be able to speak of Belén as a community in the usual meaning of the term. Let us deal first with the secondary political functions.

The administrative, nonsymbolic aspects of the religious system of Belén are predicated basically on the notion of alliance and compromise. Religious administrative ends are achieved by pressure groups formed on the basis of common interests. At this juncture compadrazgo ties are significant, for they cut across kinship, locality (paraje), and other free-association interactions to become the most important principle grouping people together. Thus, in the nomination and selection for the many cargos of the República Eclesiástica and the mayordomía system, compadrazgo ties are the prime determinant: one is selected for important cargos largely because of the support of compadres; and in turn one selects one's own compadres to occupy the secondary posts associated with a mayordomía or the offices of the fiscales. By extension, this mechanism works in a similar fashion when public-communal padrinos are selected endogamously. This is both a latent and a manifest politico-religious function of compadrazgo, for the occasion itself may determine whether or not it becomes operative. Thus, the fiscales are in some years nominated and selected with the consensus of the community, while in other years there may be serious factional disputes and several candidates. More often than not, the latter is the case, and at such times compadrazgo ties come into play immediately. Thus, compadrazgo alliance, primarily as embodied in networks, is essential to the smooth functioning of the administrative aspects of religion. On the other hand, the notion of social and political compromise is deeply rooted in Belén culture and society, and in every situation imaginable Beleños go to great lengths to reach compromises and avoid direct confrontations. Here also, compadrazgo ties play a significant role. Neither individual compadrazgo ties nor networks are determined exclusively on an ego-centric basis, and there are always overlaps that affect sizable segments of the population. The factional groups in opposition at any given time always contain compadres in common, sometimes many of them. When the occasion arises, these compadres act as mediators in trying to bring about a compromise. In many ways, the compromise functions of compadrazgo are more important than its alliance functions, for avoidance of confrontation is essential to the smooth operation of religion in Belén. The compadrazgo network and web play the role of catalyst in making this possible. Beleños are aware of the alliance and compromise functions of compadrazgo, and assiduously cultivate them. This is well expressed in the words of one informant: "Si no fuera por el compadrazgo, aquí en Belén nunca se llevarian a cabo las mayordomias, porque la gente no se pondría de acuerdo ni habría suficiente cooperación" (Were it not for compadrazgo, the mayordomias could not take place here in Belén, for the people could not get together and there would not be enough cooperation).

How is compadrazgo related to the República Eclesiástica and the mayordomía system as global administrative and ritual institutions? First, to a large extent the networks and webs of compadrazgo determine the composition of these bodies. While sponsorship of most mayordomias (that is, the eighteen or so of medium and low importance) is more or less an individual matter, and depends largely on a modicum of community support in which no compadrazgo networks or webs come into play, sponsorship of the ten most important mayordomias and all the cargos associated with the República Eclesiástica is invariably a community-wide matter in which networks and factions determine the outcome. Compadrazgo again plays an important role, in that factions and networks are essentially structured along ritual kinship lines. While there is no obvious rotation of the cargos and ostensibly no competition for them among factions and networks, these compadrazgo-based pressure groups have great interest in specific positions within the administrative and ritual complexes. In the process of vying for religious positions and the general politics of religion, compadrazgo ties and the proper network membership are essential. When the network and its concomitant faction come into play in this context, they operate very much like a political microsystem.

Second, compadrazgo is an essential aspect of the ritual and ceremonial dimensions of the República Eclesiástica and the mayordomía system, for it is difficult to say whether the six public-communal compadrazgo types, especially ANDI and PCA, are more an integral part of the compadrazgo system or of the religious system. In this regard, one can rightly say that compadrazgo provides the form for an important ritual and ceremonial celebration whose content is essentially religious and symbolic. It is in such situations that one can see most clearly the relationship between compadrazgo and religion, and the functional ties that bind them. Here, and not in the rather superficial embodiment of preeminently religious contexts exhibited by certain private-individual types (for example, baptism and confirmation) lies the real importance of compadrazgo's embodiment of religious functions. To generalize, the discharge of all public-communal types in Belén represents a religious function of compadrazgo that facilitates the ritual and ceremonial enactment of an inherent aspect of the religious system. The compadrazgo system provides the mechanism for selecting the sponsors and governs the ritual form of the celebration, and what is perhaps most important, it generates community-wide support and participation, which the mechanisms of the religious system per se could not do at this level of integration.

The secondary demographic functions of religious compadrazgo are simply a microcosm of the primary demographic functions analyzed in the preceding chapter. What I have said about the primary functions applies to the secondary ones as well, but a few additional remarks are in order. The social structure of Belén requires a fairly high degree of integration for the religious system to function properly. Counterbalancing the *arriba-abajo* (upper and lower divisions of Belén) and paraje factionalism, which has existed in Belén since at least 1900, compadrazgo manages to generate integration between halves and between parajes. With their strong tendency toward social and political compromise and the avoidance of direct confrontation, Beleños overtly seek such compadrazgo relationships. While this is generally on an individual, manifest basis, the results are perceived by the people as communal, latent goals. Beleños are always aware of the need to avoid conflict and unite for a common goal, especially in the religious domain. I have characterized Belén as an open community, but in its reaction to outside pressures and in the face of a common religious goal (the sponsorship of PCA, the celebration of the fiesta of the patron saint, and so on), it becomes, albeit temporarily, a close-knit corporate community. These are the major forces that shape the communal life of Belén, and the community is always wavering precariously between factionalism based primarily on economics and on paraje rivalry, and the integrating force of religion expressed in individual compadrazgo ties and networks. Thus, the most important secondary demographic function of religious compadrazgo is to counteract the disruptive effect of factionalism and interparaje disputes. At this level of integration compadrazgo performs one of its most important functions, without which Belén could probably not have survived the onslaught of secularization during most of this century.

A corollary of the secondary political and demographic functions of religious compadrazgo is that the institution is also instrumental in structuring whatever networks are required for the operation of the República Eclesiástica and the mayordomía system in the yearly religious cycle, beyond the occasions and activities in which compadrazgo plays an immediately formative role. These include the vast networks of cooperation and participation for the Holy Week celebrations, All Saints' Day, the Christmas-New Year celebrations, and a few other fiestas throughout the year. During these festivities, the compadrazgo networks of fiscales, mayordomos, and their attendants come into operation in a customary fashion. There are no temporary or permanent arrangements of personnel in Belén related to the discharge of religious activities that are not underlain by the web of compadrazgo.

Religion and the Ritual and Ceremonial Functions of Compadrazgo

A conceptual problem again arises in assigning the ritual and ceremonial functions of compadrazgo to the proper analytical context. The most obvious place is under the rubric of religion, but ritual and ceremonialism are highly symbolic kinds of behavior and closely related to what I regard as the magico-symbolic aspects of compadrazgo, which is the most ideological function of the institution. I therefore discuss ritual and ceremonialism as part of the magico-symbolic domain (see Chapter Seventeen), except for a few aspects that pertain directly to religion.

In the first place, the entire spectrum of compadrazgo types is pervaded by ritual and ceremonialism, and it is important that rituals be performed in the prescribed manner, for otherwise the occasion has not been sponsored effectively. Moreover, while the ceremonialism of all compadrazgo types is most closely associated with the central ceremonies and events leading to them, that associated with the permanent dimensions of the various types is never as significant prescriptively, and does not necessarily involve efficacious elements; rather, it should be regarded as highly preferential etiquette. Second, one must distinguish between religious and secular ritual and ceremonialism. Obviously, the former characterizes all those compadrazgo types whose primary meaning is religious, while the latter characterizes types whose primary meaning is social or simply symbolic (see table 6). However, most compadrazgo types in Belén have a compound meaning, as table 6 shows, and it is therefore difficult to say whether the ceremonialism accompanying, say, baptism, PCE, or bendicíon de casa, is entirely religious or secular. Some light is shed on the situation when we correlate table 6 with table 31, in which compadrazgo types are broken down according to membership in the religious, social, or symbolic cycles. On the whole, however, it is more appropriate to regard ritual and ceremonialism as constituents of magico-symbolic functions, and to show what these functions mean in the discharge of compadrazgo regardless of their primary social, religious, or symbolic meaning and associated cycle. As functional attributes, ritual and ceremonialism are part of a higher conceptual level of analysis which covers the entire range of compadrazgo irrespective of constituent domains. This is fundamentally what I mean by saying that the magico-symbolic functions of compadrazgo are the most ideological.

Third, the complexity, degree of prescription, and elaboration of ritual and ceremonialism of compadrazgo types are in direct proportion to the position of individual types on the prescriptive-preferential-optional scale presented in table 12. Thus, the ceremonialism of, say, PCE, PCA, and baptism compadrazgo is much more complex, elaborate, and prescriptive than that of primera comunión, escapulario, and graduación. However, the intrinsic symbolic attributes of individual compadrazgo types can alter this picture considerably. Fourth, ritual and ceremonialism as desirable ends in themselves are significant functions of compadrazgo, in that the institution serves as an appropriate vehicle for them. Compadrazgo is unquestionably the most appropriate structural domain, outside of religion per se, in which to satisfy the Beleños' deeply felt need for ritual and ceremonialism. I wish to conceptualize this need as the magico-religious function of compadrazgo, though it may also pervade other structural domains of Belén society. Furthermore, it is this ideological need that to a large extent, gives a certain unitary meaning to the conglomeration of disparate compadrazgo types that make up the institution.

Finally, I would like to summarize the religious functions of compadrazgo regardless of their primary or secondary character. The compadrazgo system, with its strong religious component, is a viable institution for the discharge of several administrative, symbolic, and ritual-ceremonial aspects of the religious system of Belén. Compadrazgo functions as a catalyst in the administrative coordination or the República Eclesiástica and the mayordomía system, by providing the most important mechanism of cooperation, group formation, and the generation of alliance and avoidance of direct confrontation. Symbolically, it embodies many of the most crucial aspects of religion, such as sponsorship of the most important events in the religious cycle, the rallying of religious participation, and the achievement of well-specified symbolic goals. But above all, specific compadrazgo types (especially baptism, PCE, primera comunión; ANDC, ANDI, BSI, CSV, PCA, and BM) serve to enhance and shape some of the most important occasions in the religious cycle of the community, and their rites and ceremonies represent a symbolic high point in the overall cycle. Ritually and ceremonially, compadrazgo has important functional dimensions, but they are unimportant in themselves when seen as part of a much broader and ideologically pervasive complex.

The Social Functions of Compadrazgo

Throughout the structural analysis, I have emphasized the social dimensions of compadrazgo and have often compared the compadrazgo system to a real kinship system. This all-pervasive social dimension of the compadrazgo system has enabled me to use it as the conceptual screen through which to view Belén culture and society. The importance of the social functions of compadrazgo can be seen in the fact that so many compadrazgo types have a social (and symbolic) meaning and belong to the life cycle (see tables 6 and 31). In addition, the structure of compadrazgo is more deeply embedded in kinship and family structure than in any other major domain of Belén culture and society. Further, in the interplay of the ideological and structural orders, the social functions of the compadrazgo system are the most visible and unquestionably have the greatest degree of efficacy. As I have discussed in several contexts, the compadrazgo system is a pervasive social institution which also has religious, demographic, political, economic, and magico-symbolic functions. But these are always carried out behind the social screen of the institution, and are expressed in the behavior of specific temporary or permanent groups of individuals. The main reason, then, for regarding compadrazgo in functional terms as an essentially social institution is that its key conceptual element is the behavior of personnel. Inasmuch as the social functions of compadrazgo parallel its religious functions to a large extent, and much of the structural analysis has been residually concerned with them, I can review the topic briefly.

In Belén, it is hard to distinguish between the functions of kinship and compadrazgo; the main differences are permanence, the ascribed-achieved distinction, and the dichotomy of kinship personnel in the compadrazgo system. It is therefore incorrect to speak strictly in terms of compadrazgo as an extension of kinship, or to maintain that its main function is the extension of kinship ties in the absence of effective kinship mechanisms of cooperation and participation beyond the extended family. True, the effective domain of kinship does not reach beyond the nonresidential extended family, but neither does compadrazgo extend it beyond this kinship unit, in the fashion of larger units such as a lineage or a kindred. Although I have compared the structure of the compadrazgo network to the structure of a lineage and have made some homologous extensions, the functions of compadrazgo expand analogously those of kinship beyond its effective sphere of action. While they are substantially different in structure (at least in the overall arrangement of personnel and the permanance of groupings), in function kinship and compadrazgo not only overlap to a large extent but also represent a fairly uninterrupted continuum. This results primarily from what I have termed the dichotomous arrangement of the kinship-compadrazgo personnel, which means that in every individual compadrazgo relationship as well as in networks, about half of the personnel are related by kinship. There are no significant differences with regard to prescription or preference in kinship and ritual kinship behavior; in Belén, the injunctions and constraints associated with compadrazgo are never less and are often more binding than those associated with kinship. Loyalties, duties, and obligations beyond the extended family are strongest among an individual's closest compadrazgo relationships; and in the functioning of the sometimes unstructured nonresidential extended family, the compadrazgo network can be a more effective, albeit less permanent, corporate or semicorporate group. I can say, then, that the functions of compadrazgo are those of the nonresidential extended family, but that the alignments of personnel are different. This analogy in behavior and action is what I refer to when I say that compadrazgo structures social relations beyond the confines of the extended family, which must be construed as its main social function in the broadest sense.

The Relationship between Kinship and Compadrazgo in Belén, Contla, and Atlihuetzian

A comparison of the kinship and compadrazgo systems of Belén with those of the nearby communities of San Bernardino Contla and Santa María Atlihuetzian can help to determine the relative strength of kinship and compadrazgo and to show how compadrazgo achieves the structure it has in Belén, at least with respect to its social functions. Underlying the compadrazgo system in all three communities in the same ideology, which I have construed as the pan-Tlaxcalan ideological order (see Chapter Nine of *Ritual Kinship* I). The same basic imperatives and constraints govern local systems, the people exhibit the same general attitudes toward the twenty-one compadrazgo types they have in common, and the same potential for expansion exists. But the compadrazgo systems of these three communities are structurally different, and they occupy different positions within their respective cultures and societies. Perhaps of more significance is the fact that these three communities have quite different social (kinship) structures, which I would like to outline briefly. The kinship, community, and economic organization of Atlihuetzian, Belén, and Contla is summarized in table 34.

San Bernardino Contla is a unilineal society in which kinship is overwhelmingly the most important organizational and operational principle in community culture and society (Nutini 1968b). Contla is organized into ten semilocalized, patrilineal, exogamous clans (four of them divided into halves), and each clan is subdivided into localized, patrilineal, exogamous lineages. The lineage is in turn composed of three to fifty-two households. More than 75 percent of the households shelter patrilocal extended families, while the remaining are primarily nuclear family households. In the municipio of Contla the clan (locally known as barrio) is a large group of patrilineally related males with married sons and their children, unmarried sons and daughters, and in-marrying

TABLE 34. Kinship and Community Organization

	Atlihuetzian	Belén	Contla
Descent	Bilateral	Bilateral with strong patrilineal bias	Patrilineal
Residence	Predominantly neolocal	Patrineolocal and bilocal	Patrineolocal
Corporate groups	None	Nonresidential extended families	Lineages and clans
Extended family	20%, noninte-grated	40%, integrated	75%, highly integrated
Nuclear family	Fairly strong social and cere-monial functions	Strong social and ceremonial functions	Embedded in the extended family
Household composition	Single construction predominates, gasto aparte predominates	Single construction and compound, gasto aparte predominates	Compound predominates, gasto junto predominates
Kinship behavior	Noninstitution-alized	Institutionalized	Highly institutionalized
Ultimogeniture	No	Yes	Yes
Barrio organization	None	Weak	Strong
Community integration	Weak, secular	Strong, transitional	Strong, traditional-transitional
Traditional religious organization	Weak	Strong	Strong
Economy	25% agriculture, 75% labor migra-tion	35% agriculture, 65% labor migra-tion	25% agriculture, 30% labor mi-gration, 45% loom industry

women, and its membership ranges from about 250 to more than 1,000. This group corresponds approximately to what Murdock defines as a compromise kin group. The oldest male of the barrio is regarded as the *tiaxca* or head, and he has several important functions: he administers the barrio communal lands, and is in charge of allotting them to barrio members who sponsor any of its big mayordomias; he is the final authority in sanctioning the elected officials of the principal rotating mayordomias and the group of fiscales when it is the barrio's turn to sponsor these religious fiestas; and he acts as arbitrator when barrio members or family groups are involved in litigation over rape, theft, family matters, or ceremonial misunderstandings between lineages.

The barrio also has very important religious and ceremonial functions, and less important social and economic ones. It sponsors the *cofradía* (the group of the four most important mayordomias in the municipio), the ayuntamiento religioso (the República Eclesiástica in Belén), and the mayordomias connected with Holy Week. The barrios take turns (at ten-year intervals) sponsoring the fiestas of the cofradía and ayuntamiento religioso, and in fact all of the most important mayordomias in the community. They also have specific ceremonial functions such as providing pallium bearers, lantern bearers, musicians, and so on. Social and economic cooperation is most often sought among barrio members on the basis of barrio cohesion and a sense of being related. The most important socioeconomic functions provided by the barrio are: the *tlamanal* (alms given to the family of a deceased barrio member); contributions in kind or cash made by barrio members to the mayordomos of the cofradía or to the ayuntamiento religioso when it is the barrio's turn to sponsor these festivities; and contributions in cash for buying incense, candles, flowers, and other ceremonial equipment, or for the improvement of the barrio chapel.

Although there is no Nahuatl or Spanish term to designate the lineage, it is a well-organized body of kinsmen with a high degree of economic, social, ritual, and religious integration. With few exceptions, the lineages are the residential units within the barrios. In formal terms, the lineages in Contla are localized, patrilineal, exogamous kinship units with social, economic, ritual, and religious functions of a corporate nature. Lineage membership is determined by birth, as names are passed from father to son; upon marriage, a women takes her husband's name and is known by it thenceforth. Thus, the lineage in Contla is a kinship group composed of a core of patrilineally related males, their married male descendants and their children, unmarried sons and daughters, and in-marrying women. The lineage is strictly exogamous, and under no circumstances may its members marry within it. It is a close-knit body of kinsmen which varies in number from a few people to as many as 300, since each *apellido* (cognomen) is regarded as a lineage, whether it has 3 or 300 representatives. Members of the same lineage consider themselves to be closely related, and there is a strong feeling of belonging. Lineage members are generally able to trace their common relationship patrilineally through a series of well-known genealogical links. The people of Contla are aware of the possibility of tracing these links to the nth generation, but they seldom remember agnatic ties beyond the great-great-great-grandparental generation.

The lineage functions as an extremely well integrated corporate group in economic, religious, ritual, and social matters. In the absence of a formal head, economic and religious affairs involving the participation of lineage members are coordinated by a group of the most influential members, who take it upon themselves to act as spokesmen for the lineage in dealing with the outside world. The lineage also has important religious, economic, and social functions. Lineage members always lend their material, moral, and political support when one of their number is nominated or elected to a religious office within the barrio, or to a more restricted or private office within the paraje or section. Religious cooperation takes the form of participation in events such as processions, ceremonial banquets, or special masses, and is also expressed in services rendered and contributions in kind or cash for such occasions. From the economic viewpoint, the lineage is a close-knit group whose members turn to one another for help in case of financial distress. Vuelta mano and ayuda are always sought within the lineage. Finally, from the social viewpoint, members of the lineage, and often the lineage as a whole, participate and contribute to some degree in kind or cash in case of marriage, sickness, death, burial, and other occasions in the life cycle. The social, economic, ritual, and religious functions of the lineage are well-defined and highly institutionalized, and lineage members know what to expect and how to behave on any occasion. In this way, the lineage represents the widest possible range of kin within which fully effective social and economic cooperation can be sought, since the barrio or clan has largely ceased to be an effective social unit and has remained principally an effective religious unit.

The structure and functions of the nuclear and extended families—the composition of the nuclear family itself, the overall position of the nuclear and extended families within community culture and society, residence rules, marriage, and so on—are similar in Contla and Belén, except for implications deriving from the fact that Contla has a unilineal structure and Belén a bilateral one. Contla has considerably more extended family households than Belén: 75 percent and 40 percent, respectively. The extended family household in Contla is perhaps more closely integrated, with a higher incidence of *gasto junto* (one expense budget) than *gasto aparte* (separate expense budgets), and in general with a larger individual and nuclear family composition than in Belén. But for fundamental differences between Contla and Belén one must look beyond the domain of family structure.

In summary, the social (kinship) structure of San Bernardino Contla is remarkably uniform and homogeneous, and its integrational levels (clan, lineage, family) are regulated at all times and in every sector by the same principles of patrilineality, reciprocity, hierarchy, cooperation, and their associated mechanisms. Thus, Contla is an organic society in which the various social units in the total structure are simply an expression (or the result) of the various elaborations and combinations of these principles. Kinship, then, is the most important overall principle of organization and unit formation within Contla culture and society. From the viewpoint of the individual, the social structure of Contla may be visualized as a series of ascending concentric circles representing the different levels of integration. The individual views his rights, duties, values, and obligations largely as concomitants of these levels of integration—as an expression of membership in the corresponding social units. In every unit (nuclear family, extended family, lineage, clan, and municipio) of the social structure, the individual fulfills different duties and obligations, has specific rights, and is gratified in a different manner. Each social unit to which he belongs has different functions, which may overlap, since they are governed by the same principles, but which never contradict each other. This high degree of structural homogeneity arises almost entirely out of the fact that there are no irreconcilable contradictions among the society's institutions. This is especially clear when it is realized that there are no permanent socially recognized units other than those based on the principle of patrilineality, for, unlike perhaps the majority of unilineal societies, the cross-cutting of bilateral and unilineal kinship is reduced to a minimum in Contla.

In contrast, the communities of Belén and Santa María Atlihuetzian are bilaterally organized, although the former has a strong patrilineal bias. In these two communities, the role of kinship within the overall culture and society is not nearly as strong, pervasive, and determinant as in Contla, and it is at this point that the compadrazgo systems of the three communities become very illuminating. There are, however, significant differences between the bilateral kinship structures of Belén and Atlihuetizian, which must be explored in order to make the ritual kinship comparison. As an overall principle or organization, and as a means for structuring community culture and society, kinship is less important in Atlihuetzian than in Belén, fundamentally because Atlihuetzian is far less integrated. One does not find in Atlihuetzian the corporateness and consciousness of kind one finds in Belén. Atlihuetzian is a more secular, modernized community than Belén, and the traditional ideological order underlying pan-Tlaxcalan culture and society has undergone more alteration, though not to the same extent in all sociocultural domains. I am not saying that the relatively low efficacy of kinship as an organizing principle in Atlihuetzian has caused the lack of integration. Rather, the former is an expression of the latter: the traditional integrative role of kinship—at the community level—has been significantly decreased, but the causal relationship must be explained in terms of exogenous variables. I would like to outline the way in which this has manifested itself structurally. Atlihuetzian in the 1930s was structured along basically the same lines as Belén; kinship played a similar role in both communities and resulted in the same structural forms. Since then the structural importance of kinship has decreased quite rapidly in Atlihuetzian and remained more or less constant in Belén.[1]

At the level of the nuclear family, there are no significant differences. The size of the nuclear family and the household is about the same in both communities, and so is their physical distribution. The only noticeable difference is that in Atlihuetzian there are far fewer temazcales and *cuezcomates* (storage bins) attached to the household. Furthermore, the same household forms, with respect to social composition, are to be found in both communities. Again there are no significant differences in kinship behavior and internal nuclear family arrangements, except that in Belén the nuclear family household is a more corporate unit in which the division of labor, redistribution of income, and arrangement of daily tasks are geared not only to the exigencies of daily living, but also to the discharge of ritual and ceremonial obligations outside the family per se.

With regard to the extended family, however, there are major differences between Atlihuetzian and Belén. First, the percentage of extended families in Atlihuetzian is roughly half that of Belén, for only about 20 percent of its households harbor extended families. Second, while in Belén the patrilocal extended family predominates by far, in Atlihuetzian the bilocal extended family is most common. There are, however, no significant differences, in the size of the extended family, or in its arrangements in terms of component nuclear families and individuals, except that most extended family households in Atlihuetzian have gasto aparte, while in Belén many have gasto junto. As a corollary, the extended family household in Belén is more highly integrated and has more corporate elements. One gets the impression that the extended family is tolerated in Atlihuetzian, given certain economic and social exigencies, but that it is not a comfortable and relatively permanent arrangement as it is Belén. This is indicated in part by the fact that the practice of ultimogeniture has disappeared from Atlihuetzian, though it is still fully present in Belén.

With regard to residence, there are again no significant differences, except that in Atlihuetzian the patrineolocal rule is of lower incidence, and patrilocal residence seldom lasts for more than two years before couples establish independent, neolocal nuclear family households. Indeed, neolocality is becoming more and more the ideal. This, coupled with the disappearance of ultimogeniture, accounts for the smaller number of extended family households in Atlihuetzian at any given point. Again, there are few differences with respect to descent, marriage, and divorce, and it is in those aspects of kinship beyond the domain of the extended family that the differences between Atlihuetzian and Belén become most apparent.

In Belén, the nonresidential extended family is still a social unit of some importance, and the correlation between the paraje and the nonresidential extended family is the most significant integrative aspect of kinship at the community level. Nothing of the sort can be said about Atlihuetzian, where the structure of nuclear and extended family households is embedded directly in the community as a whole. It is this factor, more than anything else, that makes kinship less important in Atlihuetzian than in Belén. In fact, one can say that the domain of kinship in Atlihuetzian does not extend beyond the extended family household, and even at this level it does not approach the integrative, coordinative, and formative importance it has in Belén. In summary, then, as one moves from the level of the nuclear family to the extended family and on to wider aspects of kinship as exemplified by the nonresidential extended family, the kinship system of Atlihuetzian steadily decreases in structural importance as compared with Belén. At the level of the nuclear family the two communities are essentially the same; at the level of the extended family the differences are significant in both incidence and form; and at the level of the nonresidential extended family (kindred, if you wish), Atlihuetzian has nothing comparable to Belén.

Of course, the functional extent and importance of the nuclear family, extended family, and nonresidential extended family are in large part a corollary of the structural arrangements described above, but a few additional remarks are in order. The functions of the nuclear family are essentially the same in both communities, except that in Belén its religious and ceremonial importance in the life cycle are greater. For example, it is possible in Atlihuetzian for an employed, unmarried son to refuse to participate in the sponsorship of ceremonial activities engaged in by his father. This would be unthinkable in Belén, and any such refusal would be regarded as insubordination and arrantly antisocial behavior. The differences are structurally (prescriptively) significant but not yet fundamental at this level of integration, for this kind of situation is not yet general in Atlihuetzian, and custom is still powerful enough to help enforce compliance.

The situation changes a great deal, however, at the extended family level. While in Belén the extended family is a highly functional social, religious, and economic unit, in Atlihuetzian it is little more than the structural arrangement forced upon young married sons or daughters for a relatively short time by economic exigencies. In Belén, the extended family is the focus of concerted action in sponsoring all the important occasions from birth to death. Within the extended family individuals and constituent nuclear families have specific tasks to perform, and the extended family functions as an integrated unit for the provision of services, goods, and cash. The functional structure of the extended family can be seen even more clearly when it operates as a religious and ceremonial unit. In Belén, as we have seen, the extended family is the most effective permanent locus of religious sponsorship, whereas in Atlihuetzian, the extended family may or may not function as an integrated unit, in some limited capacity, in the life cycle and religious sponsorship. Thus, while the extended family in Atlihuetzian is still a significant structural unit, it has ceased to be an effective, prescriptive functional unit—though now and then it may function preferentially. This again is an expression of the less stringent social and religious requirements in Atlihuetzian, which do not require the generation of the numerous personnel provided by the extended family and nonresidential extended family in Belén.

Finally, the nonresidential extended family does not exist in Atlihuetzian, whereas in Belén it is still a functional unit which partakes of several of the functions of the extended family household; it does not have the integration and corporateness of the latter, but it does function at the paraje level, for a variety of social and especially religious occasions. In summary, then, not just structurally but functionally, as one moves from the lowest to the highest levels of kinship integration, it is evident that kinship becomes increasingly more important in Belén than in Atlihuetzian, and that its role as an organizational principle of community culture and society is also more important.

If the importance and pervasiveness of kinship in these three communities are ranked, Contla is obviously at the top; kinship pervades every aspect of its community culture and society, and in effect there are no principles or mechanisms of integration and unit formation except patrilineality. In principle, there is no need in such a situation for nonkinship mechanisms to cope with the structural and functional exigencies of societal living, primarily as they are expressed in the life and religious cycles. The situation of Contla, in my opinion, represents the maximum expression of kinship for a nontribal society.

In a middle position is Belén, where the kinship system is not as pervasive as in Contla but is strong enough to make itself felt in most aspects of community culture and society. Kinship in this situation may provide the basis for structuring other principles and mechanisms of integration and unit formation, but it never operates in this way by itself and cannot alone cope with the exigencies of societal living, especially in the life and religious cycles. Thus, in Belén it is the compadrazgo system that complements, expands, and amalgamates the basic kinship elements into an organic whole, thereby achieving what kinship achieves by itself in Contla.

Finally, at the bottom of this scale is Atlihuetzian, whose kinship situation differs more from that of Belén than Belén's does from Contla's, even though Atlihuetzian and Belén are bilaterally organized societies and Contla is unilineally organized. Kinship is least important in Atlihuetzian because there is no need for it, either by itself or as a complement to other organizing principles, to cope with societal exigencies, and its effective sphere of action is confined to the nuclear and extended families. The life cycle does not require the formation of either temporary or permanent units with a certain degree of integration or corporateness. The personnel and cooperation and participation in the yearly religious cycle of Atlihuetzian are not provided to any large extent by either kinship or compadrazgo, but by nontraditional mechanisms that are an expression of the strong secularization that has taken place in Atlihuetzian since 1930 or so. As compared with Belén and Contla, which remain traditional to a large extent, Atlihuetzian is well on its way to complete secularization.[2]

Not surprisingly, given the adaptability and flexibility of compadrazgo, these three communities which have different kinship organizations and overall secular development, have the same ritual kinship system. I expressed this by saying that the same ideological order underlies compadrazgo in all three, but that the compadrazgo system is discharged differently and that this is expressed in fundamentally different functions. Ideologically, there are no significant differences between the communities, and this is the principal reason why they have exchanged compadres on a horizontal basis for many generations. The basic attitudes toward the compadrazgo system—especially the principles of confianza and respeto—are essentially the same in the three communities; there are no noticeable differences in ritual kinship terminology or behavior; and in general, most of the immediately perceived aspects of the three compadrazgo systems are uniform. The differences appear, however, as one begins to enter the structural domain along the syntagmatic chain. I said also that as part of their common ideological order, the three systems have the same potential for expansion. In this area there is certainly a gradation of compadrazgo complexity with respect to types, which share basically the same core of rites and ceremonies and associated beliefs. The most complex system is that of Belén with thirty-one types, followed by Contla with twenty-four, and Atlihuetzian with twenty-one, as shown in table 35.

A closer look at table 35 shows that the three communities have in

TABLE 35. Compadrazgo Types by Community

	Atlihuetzian	Belén	Contla	Pan-Tlaxcalan
Bautizo	x	x	x	x
Casamiento	x	x	x	x
Confirmación	x	x	x	x
PCE	x	x	x	x
Primera comunión	x	x	x	x
CCCH		x		
CCCA		x		
ANDC		x	x	
ANDI		x		
AOI		x		
BSI	x	x	x	x
CSV		x		
Escapulario	x	x	x	x
Graduación	x	x	x	
PCA		x		
Quince años	x	x	x	
Sacada a misa	x	x	x	
Compadrazgo de evangelios		x	x	
Compadrazgo de limpia	x	x	x	x
BOI	x	x	x	
Bendición de casa	x	x	x	x
BCC	x	x	x	
BM		x		
Parada de cruz	x	x	x	x
Primera piedra	x	x	x	x
Compadrazgo de amistad	x	x	x	
CABP	x	x	x	
Compadrazgo de aretes	x	x	x	
CEON	x	x	x	
FC	x	x	x	x
JJ		x	x	

common all the compadrazgo types present in Atlihuetzian. Contla lacks CCCH, CCCA, and all public-communal types except BOI, while Atlihuetzian lacks all the above plus ANDC, compadrazgo de evangelios, and JJ. The most significant aspect of this comparison is that in both Contla and Atlihuetzian the only public-communal type is the least important one. "Pan-Tlaxcalan" in table 35 refers to the types present in all rural communities. Communities where the compadrazgo system is least elaborate have the twelve pan-Tlaxcalan types plus at least another four. Communities approaching the traditional limit in the traditional-secular continuum have the fewest types. The number of types increases until communities pass the midpoint of the transitional stage and then begins to decline. Thus, Indian-traditional communities have between sixteen and twenty compadrazgo types; Indian-transitional communities between twenty and twenty-five types; transitional-Mestizo communities between twenty-five and thirty-four; and Mestizo-secularized communities between eighteen and twenty-two (see Nutini and White 1977).

Differences are, of course, bound to arise in the structural discharge of this vast array of types, despite common ideology. The most noticeable and significant differences concern the permanent dimensions of compadrazgo. There are also some differences in the discharge of the principal ceremonies and preliminary events. The most notable of these concerns the ways in which the pedimento is made, specific ceremonies connected with the immediate sponsorship, and the economic obligations involved in the padrino-ahijado and compadres-compadres dyads. For example, in Atlihuetzian the parents of the confirmation ahijado do not have to give a banquet for the padrinos, whereas in Belén this is a requirement; or, in Contla the padrinos de velación must give a large banquet for the ahijados three days before the first wedding day, whereas in Belén this is not a requirement; and so on.[3] The unitary ideology of compadrazgo in Tlaxcala, however, acquires structural uniformity in that (at least in these three communities) there are no significant differences in the configuration of primary, secondary, and tertiary relatives, the configuration of anomalous relationships, the symmetrical-asymmetrical components of the system, the interchangeable dimensions of various compadrazgo types, the basically horizontal, egalitarian nature of the system, and so on. In summary, then, the ideological and structural differences between the compadrazgo systems of Belén, Contla, and Atlihuetzian, are of the kind that will inevitably arise in such communities because of differing kinship structures, size, degree of secularization, economic base, and the like. Thus, Belén, Contla, and Atlihuetzian are structural and ideological variants of what I have called the pan-Tlaxcalan nature of the compadrazgo system.

The Differential Functions of Compadrazgo in
Belén, Contla, and Atlihuetzian

In the functional domain, however, the differences between Contla, Belén, and Atlihuetzian become fundamental. Their compadrazgo systems are essentially the same with respect to ideology, form, and structural discharge; they differ greatly with regard to function and to the way in which the system is embedded in local community culture and society. What this means substantively is that in Belén, on the one hand, the compadrazgo system has temporary (the first part of the syntagmatic chain) and permanent (the second part of the chain) dimensions involving significant and clearly configurated magico-symbolic, social, religious, demographic, political, and economic functions. In Contla and Atlihuetzian, on the other hand, the compadrazgo system has mainly temporary dimensions involving primarily magico-symbolic functions, with some residual social, demographic, and religious functions.[4] Implicit in this analysis is the fact that the primary magico-symbolic functions of compadrazgo are associated largely with the central complex of ceremonies and the events leading to it, and the primary social, religious, and even demographic functions largely with the permanent dimensions of compadrazgo. Thus, when I speak of the ideological unitary meaning of compadrazgo in these three communities (and by extension in all of Tlaxcala), I mean that from the start of a compadrazgo relationship to the completion of the central ceremonies, there are no significant structural or functional differences, and that this domain of compadrazgo is characterized by a magico-symbolic function. The functional difference (and implicitly the structural difference) comes when one moves beyond the first part of the syntagmatic chain and enters the permanent domain of compadrazgo. Here, the compadrazgo system of Belén acquires new primary social, religious, and demographic functions of indefinite duration, while the compadrazgo systems of Contla and Atlihuetzian do not—with the possible exception of the demographic function.

Again, what this means substantively is that in Belén there is an unbroken syntagmatic chain in which the temporary and permanent dimensions of the compadrazgo system are blended into a single entity with the primary social funcitons. Contla and Atlihuetzian are fundamentally different. Up to the point at which the last event of the central ceremomies, including recurrent rites and ceremonies, has been completed, most of what I have said about Belén applies also to Contla and Atlihuetzian. At that point, however, compadrazgo in these two communities has achieved its functional (magico-symbolic) goals, and thenceforth has no social or religious functions—that is, no permanent, primary dimensions. In Contla and Atlihuetzian, after the primary magico-religious functions of the first part of the syntagmatic chain have been fulfilled, any permanent dimensions that can be attributed to the compadrazgo system are entirely secondary, or rather, have secondary social and religious functions. This, however, needs to be explained if we are to understand the differential implications for the global social structure of these communities vis-à-vis that of Belén.

First, what does the absence of permanent primary social and religious functions mean for the individual couple, or in general for egocentrically determined compadrazgo? To be sure, the principles of respeto and confianza, the ideological cornerstones of the compadrazgo system, continue to operate, at least in their superficial meaning. Compadres in Contla and Atlihuetzian continue to address each other by the appropriate kinship terminology, which is essentially that of Belén; they treat each other with careful respect; they may invite each other to their social and religious sponsorships, though not as cooperating members; they may even ask each other favors occasionally. But there are no prescriptive mechanisms governing these kinds of behavior and action, nor are there highly institutionalized principles governing the web of compadrazgo relationships egocentrically as in Belén. Perhaps the only body of behavior and action that can be characterized as institutionalized and prescribed is that related to the recurrence of some compadrazgo types, and the mechanisms of selection that result from recurrent use of compadres, which are similar to what I have described for Belén. These restricted domains can also be regarded as belonging to the first part of the syntagmatic chain, for after all the individual must have a dependable supply of prospective compadres to comply with the prescriptions of various compadrazgo types regarding the selection and pedimento.

It is clear that any permanent dimensions that can be attributed to the compadrazgo systems do not involve the principle of reliance, for this principle is most effective in binding egocentrically determined relationships into some sort of a social, religious, and economic complex based upon customary and prescriptive rules. It is essentially this lack of prescription after completion of the principal ceremonies that has led me to conceptualize compadrazgo in Contla and Atlihuetzian as an institution with no permanent dimensions. I have operationally defined permanent as the prescriptive efficacy between the ideological and structural orders, and in these two communities the efficacy comes to an end after the last event of the central ceremonies. Activities among egocentrically determined compadrazgo dyads are individually contingent and therefore socially impermanent. If certain optional actions are not carried out, there are no social or religious consequences for the continuation or termination of the compadrazgo relationship; in fact, in Contla and Atlihuetzian a compadrazgo relationship can in principle be terminated without deleterious social or religious consequences, something that is impossible in Belén. It can be seen again that the unitary meaning of pan-Tlaxcalan compadrazgo and its ideological efficacy extend only to the first part of the syntagmatic chain; what follows is determined by exogenous considerations in which the prime determinants are the social structure in which the compadrazgo system is embedded and the degree of secularization.

Second, for my present purposes it is the absence, both structurally and functionally, of permanent primary religious functions from the systemic viewpoint that *really* makes the compadrazgo system of Contla and Atlihuetzian differ fundamentally from that of Belén. I have shown that in Belén the principles of temporary or permanent group formation, and the mechanisms that generate cooperation and corporate participation, are based primarily on the compadrazgo system, and in this context I delineated exocentric, systemic units that I called the compadrazgo network and, of less importance, the compadrazgo web. I demonstrated that these compadrazgo-based units operate like true kinship units, with all this implies functionally. Thus, in its permanent dimensions the compadrazgo system of Belén is a combination of egocentric and exocentric relationships, in which the latter often play a prominent role in the organization and discharge of the most varied social and religious activities, thereby analogously expanding and amalgamating the kinship system. Nothing of the sort exists in Contla or Atlihuetzian, where none of the preferential permanent dimensions that may be attributed to the compadrazgo system has any systemic dimensions. There is nothing resembling the compadrazgo network and web. Whenever a group of egocentrically determined compadres gets together for a certain activity, this is always the result of spontaneous behavior designed specifically for the occasion and has no continuity or prescription. Occasionally, the individual in Contla or Atlihuetzian may turn to a specific compadre or compadres for social, religious, and even economic cooperation and participation; but the notion of prescriptive mechanisms affording him these benefits from a stable, permanent (or semipermanent), and clearly discernible group of compadres does not exist. Neither does the concept of collective, multiple-dyad compadrazgo exist in these two communities, and this is exemplified by the absence of the significant public-communal compadrazgo types for which this concept is essential. In summary, then, the single most important difference in the compadrazgo systems of these three communities is the presence or absence of permanent, systemic components.

I can finally ask why the permanent and systemic structure of compadrazgo in Contla and Atlihuetzian does not extend beyond the central ceremonies, while in Belén it does, thereby making the compadrazgo system a global unitary institution. Given certain sociocultural constraints and a certain degree of secularization, the requirements for the formation of social units and the principles and mechanisms of corporateness, participation, and cooperation required in the social and religious domains, are fulfilled by the compadrazgo system—and the most important global function of compadrazgo becomes the expansion and amalgamation of kinship. Thus, the constraints and prescriptions in the global social structure of Belén make it necessary that, in the absence of a truly effective kinship system beyond the extended family or nonresidential extended family, the compadrazgo system come to function as such. I am not asserting that the compadrazgo system is the only institution that can fulfill this function, but merely that given certain constraints and social and religious conditions, the compadrazgo system entails this necessity. In a situation with structural requirements and conditions homologous to those of Belén, a functional solution could still be possible but it would not be the compadrazgo system or a variation of it. In fact, this is the case in Contla. Furthermore, the compadrazgo system in Belén works well as an extension and amalgamation of kinship, because kinship fulfills certain requirements of complexity and expansion beyond the extended family, without which it would have been difficult to base compadrazgo properly. The kinship system itself is sufficiently broad to serve as the basis for the principles and mechanisms of social-unit formation, cooperation, and participation, for with a narrower kinship system, the compadrazgo system could not function as efficiently as it does. This is the case in Atlihuetzian. In summary, then, although they are different homologously, the compadrazgo system and the kinship system of Belén are functionally analogous because of the structural overlapping that binds them into a continuous extension and an undifferentiated configuration of personnel.

The case of Atlihuetzian is the simplest. This community is the most secularized of the three; hence there is no need for the compadrazgo system to function in forming social units or to be the basic principle of participation and cooperation in social and religious affairs. The structure and functions of compadrazgo are thereby limited to its magico-symbolic dimensions. I do not say that no social or religious events in Atlihuetzian require the operation of principles and mechanisms similar to those in Belén—only that these are temporary, preferential, not wholly institutionalized, and the reflection of the rapidly forming new secular ideology. Certain mayordomias or communal activities in Atlihuetzian, for example, require the participation and cooperation of fairly large numbers of people, but these are now the function of secular groups and reflect the new ideology, which must not only be influenced by the receding traditional ideology, but, in the incipient stages, to a large extent be determined by it. Indeed, the limited range of the kinship system of Atlihuetzian would not permit expansion and amalgamation along the lines of compadrazgo, were there a functional necessity for it. The limitations of the kinship system, however, are themselves simply a reflection of secularization. In any event, the point is clear: the compadrazgo system of Belén and Atlihuetzian differ in their systemic dimensions because in the latter there is no need for compadrazgo's permanent attributes, while in the former these attributes are a sine qua non of the traditional ideology.

Contla, on the other hand, is diametrically opposed to Atlihuetzian. Contla and Belén have approximately the same traditional ideology (dynamically speaking, the same degree of secularization) and therefore the same sociocultural constraints and prescriptions, but their compadrazgo systems differ in that the permanent, systemic functions and attributes of compadrazgo in Belén are discharged entirely by the patrilineal kinship system of Contla. Anything I can say about the permanent dimensions of the compadrazgo system of Belén has its homologous counterpart in the patrilineal system of Contla. Thus, the compadrazgo system of Contla, like that of Atlihuetzian but for diametrically opposed reasons, has structural and functional efficacy only until the last event of the central ceremonies has been completed. Naturally enough, kinship as an ascribed system is inherently more efficient than compadrazgo as an achieved system; hence, the permanence, prescription, and degree of configuration of the principles and mechanisms of unit formation, corporateness, and cooperation and participation are more efficient in Contla than in Belén. The strictly kinship system of Contla is more efficient than the combined kinship-compadrazgo system of Belén in coping with the essentially similar global, traditional social structures of the two communities. Here, of course, the all-important variable is the unilineal kinship structure of Contla, for nowhere in Tlaxcala is there a community at the same level of traditional integration as Contla or Belén in which bilateral kinship alone is able to accomplish what the unilineal system of Contla can accomplish. Rather, in the Tlaxcalan communities with which I am familiar, the situation is much the same as in Belén: a fairly effective bilateral system (often with a significant patrilineal bias) which the systemic aspects of compadrazgo have expanded and amalgamated into an organic and fairly permanent whole. I do not know whether unilineal systems in general are inherently more efficient than bilateral systems in this respect, but the example of Contla shows this to be the case for the Tlaxcalan area.

To conclude, in Contla and Belén the degree of secularization is different from that in Atlihuetzian, where there is no functional need for a compadrazgo system beyond its unitary ideological meaning, and where departure from traditionality is shown in the restriction of kinship to family structure. Contla and Belén, on the other hand, have approximately the same traditional ideology and degree of secularization, but differ in that the patrilineal kinship system is the primary principle in the organization of culture and society in Contla, whereas in Belén the combination of a patrilineally biased, bilateral kinship system and the systemic dimensions of compadrazgo is the primary principle.

The Interdigitation of Kinship, Compadrazgo, and Secularization

I have shown how kinship, compadrazgo, secularization, and traditionality interdigitate in three Tlaxcalan communities, to produce three quite different global community structures. This extended discussion warrants several generalizations which apply to the Tlaxcalan area in particular, to several regions of Mesoamerica in general, and perhaps even to other parts of Latin America.

1. The most universal aspect of compadrazgo is what I have called its ideological, unitary meaning, with a primarily magico-symbolic function involving a prescriptive system for the first part of the syntagmatic chain—that is, until the principal ceremonies have been completed. Thus, when I talk about the universality of compadrazgo, or compare individual occurrences of it, I am referring to its magico-symbolic dimensions, with regard both to structure and to function. The primary magico-symbolic functions of compadrazgo constitute its universal features, though it may also have secondary social, religious, and economic functions. What varies from one compadrazgo system to another are its premanent dimensions, and the primary and secondary functions that accompany such structure. Ideology gives unitary meaning to a social institution, thereby exemplifying my contention that one can compare ideological entities more satisfactorily than structural entities. Compadrazgo has been misunderstood as a comparative social instituion; no clear distinction has been made between its ideological aspects as a unitary entity and its local structural discharge, and this has led to confusion about its structural and functional placement in local culture and society.

2. By itself, compadrazgo as a social institution is very uniform, and this uniformity is what I have referred to as its ideological unitary meaning. But it is not an interesting institution in itself, nor does it have broad explanatory dimensions, for having determined that compadrazgo has certain universal structural and functional properties (primarily a series of well-defined types, certain associated ceremonial activities, certain attitudes and behavior patterns, configurations of personnel, and the

magico-symbolic function), one is really not saying much about the institution in its local setting. It is only when it is placed in the context of the local social structure, and one discovers the operative principles and mechanisms, that compadrazgo becomes an interesting comparative institution with a broad explanatory dimension. As a corollary, it is conceptually important to determine both the temporary (primarily ideological) and the permanent (primarily functional) structure of compadrazgo in its particular setting. Thus, only when one has discovered and conceptualized the variables (or exogenous considerations) that determine the degree of permanence of the compadrazgo system in its local setting can one say that the institution has played its explanatory role.

3. While the difference between Belén and the communities of Atlihuetzian and Contla is clear (the permanent dimensions of compadrazgo in Belén are broad and wholly institutionalized, those of Atlihuetzian and Contla are narrow or nonexistent), such a sharp distinction is not typical of the Tlaxcalan area, let alone of Mesoamerica as a whole. Rather, there is a gradation in the degree of permanence of the compadrazgo system, which of course is contingent upon variables exogenous to the system itself. For comparative purposes, it is important to isolate them in order to assess the role, extent, articulation, and saliency of the institution in local culture and society. Differences in the structure of selection, the configuration of primary, secondary, and tertiary actors, the rights and obligations connected with various compadrazgo types, the configuration of the central ceremonies, and so on, will obviously be contingent upon the permanent dimensions of the system, but these differences will never be great enough to overwhelm the unitary meaning of compadrazgo in the first part of the syntagmatic chain.

4. In the Tlaxcalan area, the two most important, readily isolable, exogenous variables that determine the degree of permanence of the compadrazgo system are kinship and secularization, and the two are rather intimately interrelated. When the local kinship system is fully efficacious, the compadrazgo system becomes virtually inoperative beyond the central ceremonies, it has no permanent dimensions. This is the case only with the unilineal system of Contla; for Tlaxcala in general, there is a gradation of bilateral, often patrilineally biased systems which in varying degrees determine the permanent dimensions of the compadrazgo system: the stronger and more extensive the kinship system, the more permanently embedded the compadrazgo system and vice versa. The degree of secularization is more important than kinship as an exogenous variable, for it determines the need for the permanent dimensions of compadrazgo, and all this means structurally and functionally: the more secularized the community, the less need for the permanent dimensions of the compadrazgo system, and vice versa. More-

over, the importance of secularization is enhanced by the fact that to a large extent the kinship system is an expression of lack of traditionality, and the failure of kinship to play a structuring role. In any event, it is unlikely that these are the only exogenous variables, and a comparative study of compadrazgo in Mesoamerica and Latin America as a whole would no doubt reveal other equally significant ones. There may be other exogenous variables even in Tlaxcala itself, but they will probably be secondary and contingent upon the complexity of secularization and its multiple phases.

5. Finally, and as a corollary of 4, for a local compadrazgo system to function effectively as a permanent entity, it must be based upon an appropriately complex and extensive kinship system. The foregoing example did not fully exemplify this point, but I implied that the compadrazgo system of, say, Belén can function as it does, and be embedded as it is, in community culture and society, only on the basis of an effective kinship sytem that reaches beyond the extended family. When the degree of need for the permanent dimensions of compadrazgo has been established by the variable of secularization, its efficacy and extent are determined by its kinship base. Thus, while kinship and the permanent dimensions of compadrazgo may differ significantly in struture, they tend to coincide and complement each other functionally. In this context, differences regarding who may be chosen as compadres (kinsmen versus nonkinsmen), the prescriptions and constraints associated with various compadrazgo types, the verticality and horizontality of the system, and so on, depend to a large extent on the need for the permanent dimensions of compadrazgo, conditioned by the effectiveness and extensiveness of the kinship system. In some situations, there is no need for the permanent dimensions; in others the degree of need covers a wide structural and functional range and is fulfilled by the compadrazgo-kinship complementation; in still others, kinship by itself fulfills whatever systemic and corporate needs there may be. This is shown clearly in the comparative analysis of Belén, Contla, and Atlihuetzian.

This discussion shows how the social functions of compadrazgo in Belén are embedded in the local culture and society and describes the functional principles and mechanisms that determine the social efficacy of the institution. Above all, it explains the structural and functional differences between the permanent and temporary dimensions of the system. There remain a few remarks concerning some of the dimensions implicit in the discussions, especially those relating to the decrease in social tension, the creation of rapport, and the avoidance of direct confrontation. These functions of compadrazgo are secondary, in the sense that they are also part of its general religious functions. This presents no difficulties, however, for the social and religious domains in

Belén (and by extension, all of rural Tlaxcala) are closely interrelated, and whatever has been said about the religious functions of compadrazgo applies here also. I have noted that Beleños take great pains to avoid direct confrontation, and often use compadrazgo to help solve this problem. There are too many situations of this kind to be listed here, but the operative mechanism is the old saying, "If you can't lick them, join them." The decrease in social tension and the creation of rapport are really a corollary of direct confrontation, in the sense that when conflict threatens or is already settled, Beleños act quickly to counteract it by generating socially beneficial patterns of behavior. Here again, compadrazgo is used. The settling of disputes is also part of this general complex, and informants invariably stated that compadrazgo is the method usually employed. Two aspects must be mentioned briefly. First, the settling of disputes, the lessening of tension, the creation of rapport, and above all the avoidance of direct confrontation, take place at both the individual and the communal (networks, parajes, halves) levels. The principle is the same in both cases, and the operating mechanisms achieve the same result, namely, the generation of private or communal integration which is still one of the most important social goals in Belén. Second, inasmuch as Belén is still quite well integrated socially at all levels (except for the two halves into which the community is divided), the function of compadrazgo in generating social integration is more potential than actual, and has a higher communal than individual incidence.

In conclusion, let me summarize the social functions of compadrazgo: the extension, expansion, and amalgamation of the kinship system; the configuration of the principles of unit formation and the structuring of the mechanisms of corporateness, cooperation, and participation; the structuring of socioreligious relationships at the communal level; mediation between the extended family and the community as a whole; the structuring of the ritual-ceremonial matrix of the life cycle; the generation of social integration at the regional level; and the avoidance of direct confrontation, lessening of social tension, creation of individual and communal rapport, and the resolution of conflict. Obviously, the social functions of compadrazgo are the most pervasive of all its functions; they are present in all domains of Belén culture and society, and it is this pervasiveness that gives the institution its conceptualizing value. Finally, primary social functions (those having to do with social-unit formation and the extension of corporateness and participation and cooperation) are almost exclusively the property of the permanent domain of compadrazgo; while secondary social functions (lessening of social tension, and so on) are almost exclusively the property of its temporary dimensions.

✳ CHAPTER 17 ✳

The Magico-Symbolic Functions
of Compadrazgo

The last primary function of compadrazgo concerns the magico-symbolic domain. The magico-symbolic functions are the most ideological, universal functions of compadrazgo, which is tantamount to saying they are its most temporary ones. Of the functions discussed so far, the social and religious functions of compadrazgo are the most permanent, the demographic functions are intermediate, and the political and economic functions are most temporary. But the magico-symbolic functions of compadrazgo are even more associated with specific events of the central complex of ceremonies and recurrent events than the political and economic functions, although the desired results are permanent in nature. Thus, I am concerned now with establishing the universal, but temporary, functional components of compadrazgo, which—more than any other aspects of the institution—give it unitary meaning. In fact, what follows does not apply just to Belén and Tlaxcala, but perhaps to most compadrazgo systems in Latin America in which one finds the particular types being discussed. I repeat that temporary refers to specificity of ritual and ceremonial components, and not to intended results. I do not want to confuse functions and activities, for this confusion is at the root of the trouble in assessing the temporary and permanent importance of the former. The magico-symbolic functions of compadrazgo have been disregarded in the literature, or have been confused with activities of more inclusive functional complexes, especially religion. Thus, it is essential to begin with a working definition of what constitutes the religious attributes, objects, and general elements involved in the compadrazgo system, and then on to discuss the realm of the symbolic and the magic.

The Religious and Magico-Symbolic Domains

When I have talked about the religious aspects or elements or attributes of the compadrazgo system in Belén, I have been referring to the formal, administratively orthodox way of doing things, on the one hand, and to the system of belief and practices that underlies it, on the other. I am referring here to the folk religious system of Belén, and not to the national brand of Mexican Catholicism, from which it differs considerably. When I talk about the religious aspects of compadrazgo I am denoting the folk-sanctioned way of administering the sacraments involving ritual kinship sponsorship, and the celebration of a large number of fiestas in the Catholic calendar that require ritual kinship sponsorship and involve strictly Catholic ceremonies such as masses, processions, rosaries, benedictions, and so on—which may or may not require the presence of a priest or other folk-sanctioned religious practitioners. The functional attribution of this complex has been analyzed in the foregoing chapter, and I want to make a clear distinction between the functional religious components of compadrazgo, on the one hand, and its magico-symbolic functions, on the other. This does not mean that religious functions do not involve, say, symbolic attributes, for obviously they do, but only that the structure and ideology of religious symbolism are somewhat different from what is denoted as the magico-symbolic domain. In the latter context, symbolic attributes and components acquire a different, more encompassing nature than in the former, and this can also be said of what I define as magical attributes and components. Thus, there is a double distinction between Catholic and non-Catholic symbolism (a more general kind of symbolism which may be called magical, which is the result of more than 450 years of religious and social syncretism, and in which pre-Hispanic and Spanish Catholic elements are inextricably mixed), on the one hand, and between Catholic ideology and magico-religious ideology, on the other.

Although I have not explicitly discussed Catholic ideology and symbolism, much of the description and analysis has been concerned with it, and I need not give further details. I would only add that the formal, administrative, and more obvious aspects of Catholic ritual and ceremonial associated with compadrazgo are regulated by the Catholic ideological and symbolic complex. But while this complex regulates the surface structure of religious ritual kinship phenomena in Belén, and is uppermost in the minds of the people, underlying these elements is a magico-symbolic ideological complex that plays an important role in structuring certain kinds of religious and social behavior and action. It is the function of this second complex, and its relationship to the Catholic ideological and symbolic complex, that I want to elucidate. I will make this proviso, however: while one can distinguish the spheres of action of the Catholic and the magico-symbolic ideologies, it is almost impossible to disentangle the symbolic components of the Catholic and non-Catholic domains. This is attributable primarily to the rather asymmetric process of syncretism, which required imposition of the Catholic ideological order but which was laden with latent (and sometimes manifest) non-Catholic structural elements.

The Symbolic System of Santa María Belén

The symbolic system of Belén is a syncretic complex which began at the time of the Conquest and continued to evolve until perhaps the end of the nineteenth century. (For insights into this process of syncretism the reader is directed to Part Three of *Ritual Kinship* I.) It contains pre-Hispanic religious and witchcraft elements, Spanish Catholic elements from the sixteenth, seventeenth and eighteenth centuries, European witchcraft elements, and even some essentially secular elements introduced by the start of the machine age in Tlaxcala about a century ago. Although I cannot at the moment interdigitate all these elements and give a comprehensive picture of the formation and development of the symbolic system of Belén, I do understand how it operates today, and I know its most important structural and functional attributes.

By socioreligious symbol I mean a physical (sign) or social (patterned action) representation that stands for a general or particular concept embodying a single or complex ideological domain. The presence or activation of the symbol involves the functional reinforcement of the denoted ideological complex, which is always translated into specified behavior and action. Thus, the most fundamental property of a socioreligious symbol is the reinforcement of the stated ideological order, acted out in its corresponding structural domain. From this viewpoint, a socioreligious symbol is a mechanism that involves both the ideological and the structural orders: the more effective the symbol, the stronger the causal relationship, and vice versa. By symbolic system, I mean simply the sum total of individual socioreligious symbols composing a reasonably well circumscribed ideological-structural domain—for example, the religious-ritual kinship domain being considered here. In a symbolic system, however, individual socioreligious symbols are not independently efficacious; rather, they have a collective action, and impinge upon each other to form an integrated whole. From the socioreligious viewpoint, however, independent symbols are rarely isolable, and one must instead deal with symbolic systems involving collective representations.

Socioreligious symbols have three additional important properties. First, although they are physically or socially represented and immediately perceived by the polity, the people are not aware of them as evoking the reinforcement of ideological beliefs translated into behavior and action. Thus, when couples who are asked to enter into a baptism compadrazgo relationship accept the candle and chiquihuite, they are aware that the pedimento ceremony is an important event in the syntagmatic chain. They are not aware of it, however, as a symbol that not only maps the future compadrazgo relationship but at the same time formally binds both contracting parties to follow a series of well-established patterns of behavior and action. Socioreligious symbols vary in degree of conscious (or unconscious) evocation; the more physical the symbol, the more conscious the evocation, and conversely, the more social the symbol, the more unconscious the evocation.

Second, the efficacy of a symbol or complex of symbols is always commensurate with its physical or social representation—with the form and position it occupies within the general ideological-structural domain under consideration. The adequacy of a physical or social representation for a given symbol is determined primarily by historical, psychological, and even specific political and economic considerations. The genesis of symbols is an extremely important diachronic consideration, but it is not relevant at the moment. Here I am considering only the way in which the efficacy of a symbol leads to the overlapping of the ideological and structural domains. Let us take, for example, the case of the scapulary as a physical symbol of protection against supernatural evil spirits. The origin, syncretic composition, and specific psychological mechanisms that make this sociophysical symbol an efficacious reinforcer of behavior and action do not matter to Tlaxcalans nor are they conceptually interesting in the present context. What is interesting and conceptually significant is that the sociophysical evocation of the scapulary is an effective reinforcer of certain kinds of behavior and action, among which establishment of the appropriate compadrazgo relationship is one of the most important.

Third, although symbols or symbolic complexes have different individual interpretations, invariably they have a core of unitary meaning, which constitutes their effectiveness at the pansocietal level and makes their functional discharge uniform at all levels of societal integration. To a large extent, it is this unitary symbolic meaning of compadrazgo, coupled with its fundamentally ideological basis, that makes pan-Tlaxcalan compadrazgo a uniform institution. Thus, local constraints may vary from community to community, but what remains constant are the ideological order and one of its most significant mechanisms, the symbolic system. This basically pan-Tlaxcalan system is discharged in accordance with local constraints such as kinship and secularization, and once one has analyzed the basic complex, one need only ascertain and measure these constraints to determine the structure and function of the compadrazgo system in any Tlaxcalan community.

This is what I conceive to be the comparative method: the controlled comparison (more or less in Eggan's sense) of a unitary ideological complex, in which the measurable operational variables are given by what I have called local constraints. My definition of what constitutes a socioreligious symbol and symbolic system is limited, and there are other possible intepretations. But the definition has the advantage over most others with which I am acquainted that it cannot only be operational-ized socially, but also that it does not have the quasi-philosophical, so-cially unmanageable attributes that characterize most anthropological thought along these lines.

It remains now to determine and analyze the actual operation of the symbolic system of Belén. To do so, however, I must first describe the socioreligious ideological system for which the symbolic system serves as the reinforcing mechanism, and whose evocation is translated into actual behavior and action. I cannot at present describe and analyze the global socioreligious ideological system of Belén, but I can give a gen-eral account of the factors that directly affect the discharge of compa-drazgo as involving basically symbolic elements of protection, propitia-tion, intensification, and thanksgiving. This is a primarily cosmological religious system which involves the most fundamental beliefs concern-ing the nature of the world and the supernatural as they affect the life of the individual and society.

The Unitary Ideology of the Catholic and Non-Catholic Belief Systems in Rural Tlaxcala

The ideological predominance of Catholicism in the folk, syncretic re-ligion of rural Tlaxcala may easily lead the ethnographer to think that the region has a basically Catholic religious-ideological system with a few additions attributable primarily to the still rather strong presence of witchcraft, sorcery, and other non-Catholic beliefs and practices. This assessment erroneously presupposes that the Catholic and non-Catholic belief systems are separate. But while this is true structurally—that is, the folk practice of Catholicism shows few points of articulation with non-Catholic practices in ritual and ceremonialism—it is not true ideo-logically. Rather, Catholicism and all non-Catholic practices involving the supernatural share a belief system. In this common system one finds the same attitudes, the same general cosmogonic conceptions, the same conception of supernatural forces, and the same operational mecha-nisms—regardless of structural manifestations. Thus, when Beleños pray to a certain image, sponsor a certain mayordomía, or engage in the various rituals of their folk Catholicism, they are essentially engaging in the same supernaturally directed activities as when they engage in non-Catholic practices such as witchcraft, the propitiation of non-Cath-olic supernaturals, intensification rituals, and so on. From the ideolog-ical viewpoint, then, there is no clear distinction between magic and religion, even though these complexes of beliefs and practices are struc-turally differentiated by the people themselves. I am not entirely certain as to how this unitary ideological system can be expressed structurally in different ways with a minimum of confusion, nor is it really pertinent at this point.[1]

Beleños believe that the world in which they live is controlled and regulated by supernatural powers that they can reach, and with whom they can establish rapport to improve social existence. Furthermore, Beleños could be said to suffer from the fallacy of misplaced concreteness, for seldom do they think about the supernatural in terms of general principles or forces; almost always they think in terms of concrete, often personified, anthropomorphic deities, entities, or things. Although structurally there are several kinds of supernatural domains and levels of religious integration, the whole roster of supernatural deities, entities, and things, be they Catholic (the various manifestations of Christ and the Virgin Mary, the saints, the devil, the angels, Catholic things and rituals endowed with sacred power—rosaries, prayers, the mass, benedictions, processions, and so on) or non-Catholic (supernaturals such as witches and sorcerers, *nahuales* or tricksters, weathermen, tutelary mountain owners, places endowed with supernatural powers, talismans, soul loss, and a rather long list of objects and practices), constitutes a global supernatural complex with a unitary ideological meaning. In this scheme of things, the people definitely distinguish between Catholic and non-Catholic, and consciously try to keep them separate, but the same fundamental ideological elements and psychological processes become operative when Beleños worship, propitiate, intensify, or approach both Catholic and non-Catholic supernaturals. The supernatural belief system of Belén is an undifferentiated ideological whole, but its levels of integration (the main cleavage being between Catholic and non-Catholic) are discharged structurally in different ways. Thus, when the average Beleño undertakes a *manda* (a promise to Christ, the Virgin Mary, or a saint in exchange for a favor) or consults a tetlachihuic, he is engaging in basically the same supernatural activity, his psychological framework is the same, and he expects to achieve the same results, although the Catholic and non-Catholic activities involve a series of distinctly different ritual steps.

The supernatural belief system of Belén has one general, predominant characteristic, namely, to make the individual and collective world of social existence safe and secure by the proper propitiation of all supernatural forces, regardless of the means employed. The relationship between humans and the supernatural, then, is characterized by pragmatic and rather selfish motives for which the individual and the group pay dearly in the sense that the efforts involved demand a great deal of time and both economic and social resources. Regardless of their social or recreational value, nearly all religious activities and behavior are individually and collectively aimed at propitiation of the supernatural in order to achieve certain goals. From this viewpoint, the religion of Belén, and of Tlaxcala in general, is surprisingly lacking in moral (in the ethical sense) attributes, and in this respect it differs greatly from orthodox Catholicism, which is permeated with ethical values. Virtually the sole concern of religion is rapport with the supernatural, while ethics, morality, and appropriate behavior are almost exclusively a social concern.[2] Thus, what individuals and the collectivity should or should not do, what is proper or improper, what is permissible or not permissible, and in general what constitutes acceptable behavior, is regulated almost exclusively by the social structure. Failure to comply with ethics and morality carries social and economic punishment and sanctions, but not supernatural sanctions. If a person engages in antisocial behavior, he is punished by the group and not by the saints or any other supernatural; if a couple fails to marry properly, the pair is punished economically or socially by kinsmen or a sizable segment of the community; and so on. There are many instances in which seemingly social kinds of behavior elicit supernatural sanctions for failure to comply with expectations. Upon closer examination, however, the ethnographer discovers that they are really religious, supernatural kinds of behavior, and therefore punishable by forces beyond the domain of the social. This is the case, say, with failure to contract an important, prescriptive compadrazgo relationship, for this disrupts the human-supernatural order and affects both the indivdual and the group.

This remarkable lack of a moral and ethical component in the religion of Belén, and its overwhelming emphasis on propitiation and pragmatic self-interest, is strongly reminiscent of the pre-Hispanic, polytheistic religion of the region. Clearly, many fundamental ideological beliefs regarding man, the supernatural, and their interrelationship, have survived until the present. The most effective domain of religious syncretism has, however, been the structural, more manifest domain of Catholic ritual and ceremonialism and associated administrative practices; were this not the case it would be difficult to understand the present situation.

I cannot describe in detail the more cosmogonic aspects of the supernatural belief system of Belén, nor are they important here, but I can delineate the main characteristics of the actors and things involved, and the attitude of the people toward them. Beleños conceive of supernatural forces, deities, personages, and things as essentially benevolent. There are exceptions, of course, the most important ones being the Christian devil (who is interestingly syncretized and has several non-Christian components), certain kinds of witches (*tlahuelpochinime*), tutelary mountain owners such as El Cuatlapanga, and a few others. The exceptions, however, are not very significant statistically, and can generally be ignored in this analysis. Furthermore, Beleños do not distinguish Catholic and non-Catholic supernaturals in terms of goodness or predisposition to help. This is clearly specified in the words of an old informant who said, "Aquí en Belén siempre hemos creído que las fuerzas que gobiernan este valle de sufrimientos están la mayor parte del tiempo dispuestas a ayudar, cualquiera que sea su naturaleza. Hay gentes que rezan, otras que buscan las mayordomias, y otras que consultan y se conectan con los tetlachihuics. Todo es lo mismo si se pone el corazón en la súplica" (Here in Belén we have always believed that the forces that govern this valley of suffering, whatever their nature, are most often predisposed to help. There are people who pray, others search for mayordomía sponsorship, and still others consult and get close to the tetlachihuics. It is all the same if one puts one's heart in the supplication).

Supernatural forces, deities, and personages are conceived by the people as existing close to them, in a realm that is never clearly specified. There is no clear distinction between above, or the sky, as the dwelling place of the good forces or spirits, and below, or the depth of the mountains or the earth, as the dwelling place of the evil forces or spirits—a distinction that has been reported for several parts of Mesoamerica. Rather, supernatural forces are supposed to inhabit diverse places, but always close to humans, and they are thought to be able to influence quickly and directly the acts of men and the outcome of future affairs. Given the pragmatic, self-seeking nature of religion in Belén, one would expect to find a good deal of supernatural specialization. This is so not only among Catholic supernaturals (again an inherent characteristic of Catholicism, whose roster of specialized saints must have blended well with the pre-Hispanic, polytheistic religion of the region), but among non-Catholic supernaturals as well. Thus, one not only prays to such and such a saint for such and such a favor, as indicated by his specialization, but the same division of labor concerning powers and favor-granting attributes exists for non-Catholic supernaturals as well. Specific specialized non-Catholic supernatural personages (La Malintzi, El Cautlapanga, Angelina María, La Serpiente Negra—the black snake—and several others), practitioners, and complexes are approached with a variety of supplications. What is never specified is the relationship that holds together this vast supernatural pantheon, nor is there a hierarchical order in which the multiple deities, personages, practitioners, and things can be placed, and which determines how they influence each other. The one vague operational principle here seems to be a conscious effort to keep the Catholic complex more or less separate from the non-Catholic. But not even this is fundamental to the supernatural belief system, for the descriptions of several compadrazgo types show that Catholic ceremonies are sometimes followed by non-Catholic ones.

In general, the people are conscious of the proximity of the supernaturals and of their power to affect human affairs. It is therefore of the utmost importance to keep them content and show them the appropriate deference and respect. Beleños show a certain ambivalence in their relationship to supernaturals: on one hand, the people fear them because they may remain indifferent to supplications when not properly propitiated; on the other hand, Beleños love them and are firmly convinced that they are essentially benevolent. On the whole, the relationship of Beleños (and of Tlaxcalans in general) to the supernatural is governed more by fear than by love—fear that unless the appropriate ceremonies and general behavior toward the supernaturals are forthcoming, the established order binding humans to their nonhuman overseers will be disrupted. Here, then, are the cornerstone of religion in Belén and the most fundamental operational principle in the supernatural belief system: humans and the supernatural are arranged in an established order in which both have rights and obligations, and as long as both sides comply with their part, the world will run fairly smoothly, given the fact that the world of human affairs is at best a bad job. The conceptual, theological sophistication of Beleños is not sufficient to specify what would happen to the supernaturals—the gods, if you will—if humans disregarded them completely, but it most certainly specifies what happens to men if they do not fulfill their part of the bargain.

What, specifically, is man's part of the bargain? First, a certain attitude of mind toward the supernaturals, which includes respect, deference, some love, and above all a firm commitment to try to please them, forms the ideological underpinning of the human-supernatural relationship. On the whole the people adhere to it quite closely, be it out of fear, pragmatism, self-interest, or a combination of these. Second, is a vast structural array of rites, ceremonies, and behavior which must be performed according to specified custom on the basis of a yearly calendar, seasonal variations, unexpected or regular events, and, above all, with respect to individual supernatural deities, personages, or objects. This ritual-ceremonial complex and associated behavior constitute not only the core of Belén religion, but almost its sole concern. The people feel that once they have carried out the prescribed ceremonies, everything else is superfluous or must be taken for granted, for it is this compliance that makes the supernatural predisposed to help individuals and the group and makes the world of social affairs reasonably safe. In complying with ritual and ceremonial prescriptions, individual and collective responsibilities are not entirely separate: what is left undone by individuals may influence the community as a whole, given the fact that it hampers the smooth functioning of the established order—hence the pressure sometimes brought to bear upon individuals by the community with regard to complying with rites and ceremonies, as in the case of several compadrazgo types (see Chapter Five).

Obviously, not all rites and ceremonies rank the same in the ritualistic religion of Belén. Rather, there is a kind of hierarchy of prescriptions, preferences, and options, not unlike that of compadrazgo types, based upon the importance of the occasion, its individual or public nature, and the character and position of the propitiated supernatural. What is constant, however, is the primacy of ritual and ceremonial behavior over whatever other religious behavior one finds in Belén. To reiterate, once Beleños have complied with their ritual obligations, everything else is much less important religiously, for they feel released from further action. In the hierarchy of rites and ceremonies concerning Catholicism, the folk aspects rank considerably higher than the more orthodox aspects. Thus, it is much more important for the average Beleño to sponsor a given cargo and to participate in a certain procession than, say, to go to mass, confession, and communion. Once he has done the former, he feels no compulsion to do the latter, for in his belief system he has already done what is required of him by the supernatural. This lack of interest in the more orthodox practices of Catholicism infuriates the local priests, and it is generalized throughout rural Tlaxcala, where attendance at mass (unless it is associated with a mayordomía) and other orthodox rituals is very low.

The Interaction of the Symbolic and Supernatural Belief Systems

How does the symbolic system of Belén fit into this supernatural belief system, and what are its functions? I defined a symbolic system in general as the global complex of symbols that constitute the principal reinforcing mechanisms operating between a stated ideological order and its corresponding structural domain. Symbols and symbolic behavior in Belén are sociopsychologically designed to create a kind of self-fulfilling prophecy of what the supernatural belief system of the community dictates; in fact, there are really no effective symbols that are not religious or directly associated with the supernatural belief system of rural Tlaxcala. The description in Part One of *Ritual Kinship* I and several aspects of the structural analysis indicate the physical and social composition of Belén's symbolic system, and I need not recapitulate the total array of elements involved. I can, however, say something about how it operates within the global socioreligious context of the community.

Be it a scapulary, a chiquihuite, a pedimento, a round of speeches, or innumerable other physical or social entities, symbols in Belén are clearly identifiable objects or occasions that have two immediate, distinctive functions beyond their evocative, reinforcing functions: to impress upon the people the importance of ideological beliefs in operation, and the necessity to do things according to tradition and custom; and to insist upon the proper discharge of the events that will follow, and the rights and obligations binding the personnel involved. These two secondary functions of the symbolic system, or symbolic behavior, are the psychological corollary of the main evocative, reinforcing function, whose aim is to foster from the start the overlapping of the ideological and structural orders.[3] Under these conditions, the compadrazgo system, as well as the strictly religious domain of the ayuntamiento religioso, includes many occasions for such symbolic behavior, and the success of these institutions in resisting the onslaughts of secularization is to a large extent attributable to the strength of the symbolic system. This may not be an entirely adequate explanation, but at least it illustrates some of the sociopsychological mechanisms at work. Without such an effective, reinforcing symbolic system, neither the compadrazgo system nor the ayuntamiento religioso would have the degree of prescription it still has. Individual symbols, and the global symbolic system, are extremely important self-validating elements in Belén culture and society. I have presented only their most general properties and their primarily social components, without going into their psychological dimensions, for I have neither the proper data nor the competence to do so. But it is evident that proper analysis of symbolic behavior involves an important psychological dimension which must be explored.

The way in which I have defined symbol and symbolic behavior departs somewhat from the generally accepted conceptions of these matters, and the analysis has definitely emphasized the sociological aspects of the situation. Paradoxically, anthropologists who have dealt with symbolism (see Douglas 1967; Leach 1962; Turner 1967) have, very often implicitly and superficially, emphasized the psychological matrix of operation, to the detriment of their avowed sociological aims. My analysis of symbolism sins explicitly on the opposite side, and perhaps I can be rightly criticized for confusing symbolic behavior with what are simply highly structured aspects of social behavior. For example, I called the pedimento a complex symbol, or a bundle of symbolic behavior, but it could also be analyzed as a highly significant event in the syntagmatic chain of compadrazgo. Analyzing it as a complex symbol emphasizes the advantage of my analysis, namely, the articulation of the symbolic system as a mechanism of evocation and reinforcement in sociological terms—which means analogously the same in psychological terms. Hence, the criticisms that could be made of my analysis could equally well be made of the traditional, more psychological analysis of symbolism.

The Relationship of the Magico-Symbolic Realm to Symbolism and the Supernatural Belief System

I come now to the last component of the analysis of the religious and magico-symbolic, namely, the domain of magic, and its relationship to symbolism and the supernatural belief system of Belén. I have maintained that the Catholic and non-Catholic symbolic components in the supernatural belief system of Belén are an undifferentiated whole, but that one can more or less distinguish the spheres of action of the Catholic and non-Catholic ideologies. The elucidation of this point is crucial to the definition of the magico-symbolic and to understanding its functions in the compadrazgo system. Catholic and non-Catholic ideologies are not significantly different; rather, there are differences in detail and in structural discharge. I cannot, therefore, properly call the whole non-Catholic ideological-structural complex the realm of the magical, which underlines the distinction usually made by anthropologists between magic and religion—especially in areas, like Mesoamerica, that have a long and significant syncretic past. Rather, the high common ideological denominator underlying the structural discharge of both Catholic and non-Catholic elements justifies regarding the sphere of the religious and the magical as an undifferentiated whole. Thus, I need to explain why I have coined the term magico-symbolic to refer to several important temporary functions of compadrazgo.

The reason for employing the terms magic and magico-symbolic stems from the distinction I wish to maintain between the symbolic, propitiatory aspects of the more or less *orthodox* folk religion of Belén—expressed in an overt, consciously accepted complex of rites and ceremonies—and a more basic symbolic and propitiatory complex which is unconsciously and covertly practiced but which more adequately illustrates the most fundamental supernatural belief system described in the preceding paragraphs. When the people of Belén engage in the various aspects of their orthodox folk religion in the prescribed symbolic and propitiatory fashion, they are not bringing into play the fundamental tenets of the supernatural belief system so intensely as they are when they engage in magico-symbolic behavior. From this viewpoint, it can be said that the magico-symbolic is the most basic operational principle which, more than any other kind of resulting socioreligious action, covertly structures the relationship between man and the supernatural, thereby creating the greatest stability in the established order. Thus, I am not substantively separating religious from magical behavior, but only separating the level at which they are efficacious, and showing how magical behavior represents a more fundamental ideological-structural juncture in the relationship between man and the supernatural.

I can now define magic and the magico-symbolic. One could say that going to mass or making a manda to a saint constitutes religious behavior, while consulting a tetlachihuic or undertaking certain rites on behalf of El Cuatlapanga constitutes magical behavior; but this does not help us understand what constitutes supernaturally oriented behavior, or the relationship between man and the supernatural. If one cannot meaningfully separate magic from religion, I can only define the former in terms both of its position within the global supernatural context, and of its level of efficacy. Thus, the domain of magic is that kind of supernaturally oriented behavior that to the highest degree exhibits the operational principles regulating the relationship between man and the supernatural, and whose efficacy is greater than that of strictly religious behavior—or what one can traditionally regard as religious behavior within the context of Belén Catholic folk religion. Magical behavior as practiced by the people of Belén (and all of rural Tlaxcala) constitutes a deep, unconscious, and highly symbolic complex of rites, ceremonies, and associated aspects that, in the global socioreligious belief system of the community, are the most efficacious in creating rapport between man and the supernatural. By the magico-symbolic complex I mean simply the total ensemble of magical behavior together with its associated system of symbols, which is an undifferentiated whole operating across the global spectrum of supernaturally oriented behavior. Therefore, by the magico-symbolic functions or dimensions of compadrazgo I mean something quite different from its strictly religious functions and aspects, which are designed either to reinforce certain highly significant religious practices (baptism, confirmation, first communion) or to intensify other religious practices (blessing of an image, coronation of the Virgin Mary, giving a scapulary), which in themselves may have important primary or subsidiary magico-symbolic aspects.

One can see, then, that the concept of the magico-symbolic may operate across the whole spectrum of supernaturally oriented behavior, and may include structural domains that fall under the categories of both magic and religion. To avoid confusion it might have been better to use different terms to refer to magic in its traditional, structural sense (as differentiated from religion) and to magic in my relational, ideological sense (to some extent coterminous with religion). What I want to emphasize most strongly, however, is that my concept of the magico-symbolic cuts across the whole spectrum of what is called the magico-religious domain, the two parts of which are distinguishable only in terms of direct structural manifestations. Because a common supernatural belief system underlies both magic and religion in Belén or rural Tlaxcala in general, the separation of magic from religion, which is necessary in many situations described in the ethnographic literature, is not required. One of the problems in conveying the meaning of the magico-symbolic concept in operation has been the difficult task of transforming structural plurality on the basis of ideological monism. Anthropologists are accustomed to thinking primarily in terms of structural complexes with their own built-in ideological mechanisms. Throughout this study I have disregarded ideology in favor of structure, but it is difficult to devise a methodology for transforming monistic ideology into a pluralistic structural discharge.

The Magico-Symbolic Functions of Compadrazgo within the Supernatural Belief System

I am at last able to analyze the position of compadrazgo in the supernatural belief system of Belén, and the magico-symbolic functions of compadrazgo in the relationship between man and the supernatural. The nature of compadrazgo mediating entities indicates clearly that sacred as well as secular events and occasions, associated with the object of the relationship, are involved. These are important occasions in which the mediating entity, be it religious or social, requires intervention of the supernatural in one form or another in order to achieve certain results inherent in the compadrazgo relationship itself. One must, however, carefully separate the compadrazgo relationship itself—that is, the establishment of a compadrazgo type—from the religious or social event that embodies it. These are quite different things, and in this chapter I am referring primarily to the former. Let us take, for example, the baptism and marriage compadrazgo types. The former is a prescriptive event in the religious cycle of the individual, without which he cannot become part of the Catholic brethren; the latter is an essentially prescriptive social event in the life cycle of the individual, without which he is denied full participation in community life. From the strictly socioreligious viewpoint, an individual in Belén could go through the rites and ceremonies of these events without contracting a compadrazgo relationship, thereby making the compadrazgo relationship a separate, higher belief complex which may or may not be ideologically coterminous with the strictly religious ceremonies. It is the contracting of the compadrazgo relationship itself that has primary magico-symbolic functions (hence its prescriptive nature), whereas the occasion for the relationship may or may not have such functions (though it is also prescriptive by virtue of belonging to another complex)—and if it does, they will be secondary. For example, the rites and ceremonies of baptism, confirmation, first communion, BSI, bendición de casa, and most of the religious compadrazgo types have significant subsidiary magico-symbolic functions in themselves, but these can usually be accounted for separately from the primary magico-symbolic functions of the associated compadrazgo relationships.

On the other hand, one finds that the rites and ceremonies associated with most secular or generally non-Catholic compadrazgo types—such as parada de cruz, primera piedra, aretes, and FC—are in themselves so heavily laden with magico-symbolic functions that these are hard to separate from those of the associated compadrazgo relationship itself. Nevertheless, it is possible to arrange all compadrazgo types in Belén along a continuum according to the degree to which the type's intrinsic magico-symbolic functions blend with those of its rites and ceremonies. One must, thus, consider the degree and level of efficacy in assessing the magico-symbolic functions of compadrazgo types. As a corollary, the greater the blending of the intrinsic magico-symbolic functions with those of the rites and ceremonies, the more temporary the compadrazgo type; that is, the more nearly is the efficacy of the sponsorship confined to the immediate propitiatory or intensifying occasion. Thus, the escapulario, limpia, parada de cruz, and FC compadrazgo types are unquestionably among those in which magico-symbolic functions and values are greatest, but they are also the most temporary. At the other extreme are such compadrazgo types as graduación, quince años, amistad, and CABP, whose associated events have little magico-symbolic value. Between these two extremes are the majority of the compadrazgo types in Belén, whose associated events have magico-symbolic functions that are distinguishable in varying degrees from the compadrazgo relationship itself. This is, of course, tantamount to saying that in the middle range of the continuum I am dealing with two overlapping complexes—compadrazgo itself, and religious and social bundles of occasions—which participate in the relationship between man and the supernatural, but which represent different levels of interaction.

In the socioreligious supernatural belief system of Belén there are many occasions that require the performance of certain rites to create rapport between man and the supernatural, and, by thus reaffirming the established order, to make the world of social relations secure. It is within this context that the compadrazgo system in its most ideological or magico-symbolic aspect must be placed. Most fundamentally, then, from the purely ideological standpoint compadrazgo may be regarded as a magico-symbolic system in which there exists a series of customary, well specified rites and ceremonies designed to achieve certain desired ends (the magical component) exemplified by highly structured behavior (the symbolic component), which can be characterized in terms of protection, propitiation, intensification, and thanksgiving. These four attributes bind man and the supernatural into a covenant, holding them together and specifying their rights and obligations. Ceremonies of all compadrazgo types in Belén are characterized by one or more of these attributes (see table 24). From this viewpoint, the magico-symbolic functions of compadrazgo may be redefined to state that if the appropriate rites are not carried out, not only will there be no individual protection, propitiation, intensification, or thanksgiving, but there will also be a decrease in the degree of collective rapport between man and the supernatural. It is this strong belief that the performance of compadrazgo ceremonies achieves both individual socioreligious ends and collective well-being, that I refer to as the magico-symbolic functions of compadrazgo. This is why I have preferred to use the term magico-symbolic to apply to the whole magico-religious spectrum, and not solely to the beliefs and practices that fall traditionally under the rubric of magic. It is immediately apparent, however, that, in general, the more non-Catholic the compadrazgo occasion, the more primary magico-symbolic functions it has, and vice versa.

I have not really explained why the thirty-one compadrazgo types in Belén have been singled out as occasions for activating the latent and manifest mechanisms for generating individual well-being and collectively strengthening relationships with the supernatural. It can be surmised that these thirty-one occasions represent significant developments in the social, life, and religious cycles of the community, but the question involves primarily historical considerations, and I suggest some answers in Part Three of *Ritual Kinship* I. One must, however, turn to the magico-symbolic component of the supernatural belief system of Belén to understand fully why Beleños comply so readily and so completely with all those events in their relationship with the supernatural that involve any of the attributes of protection, propitiation, intensification, and thanksgiving, be it in the domain of compadrazgo, the ayuntamiento religioso, or the mayordomía system. Interviews reveal that Beleños worry constantly about whether they have done their individual and collective best to keep the supernatural powers happy and predisposed to be helpful. The asking of favors and the creation of conditions for granting them are involved in all four mechanisms of generating supernatural intervention. Thus, one propitiates the supernatural to encourage the granting of a certain request; one may ask for direct supernatural protection on the basis of what one has done in the past to bring oneself and the collectivity closer to the supernatural; one undertakes ceremonies of intensification to prepare the way for propitiation, protection, and direct requests, and in general to keep in close touch with the supernatural; and finally, one undertakes ceremonies of thanksgiving to keep the supernatural favorably disposed toward one's immediate kinsmen, compadres, friends, and the community as a whole. The key principles of behavior regulating this human-supernatural covenant are the Beleños constant, unconscious fear that the supernatural may cease to look favorably upon them; and their constant, conscious preoccupation with the adequacy of the rites and ceremonies.

The individual component is most often foremost in mind, but the collective component is always there, for to a large extent the former depends upon the latter. There are only six public-communal compadrazgo types which are collective complexes of protective, propitiatory, intensifying, and thanksgiving rites and ceremonies, but much of their group spirit and aims are inherent in the twenty-five private-individual types, especially the prescriptive and highly preferential ones—hence, the communal insistence and sometimes outright pressure for individual compliance. In summary, then, compliance with compadrazgo types as well as with every ritual and ceremony in Belén, is designed to keep the human-supernatural covenant and to keep alive the forces propitious to human existence. This is a subtle, largely unconscious process, but once in a while it is lucidly expressed by an informant: "Los santos, fuerzas, y espíritus que velan por nosotros son por lo general buenos, pero a veces caprichosos. Es por lo tanto necesario mantenerlos contentos, hacer lo que ellos quieren, y aun más, ir más allá de lo que piden. Solo así, se puede más o menos vivir en este valle de lágrimas" (The saints, forces, and spirits who watch over us are generally good, but they are sometimes capricious. It is therefore necessary to keep them happy, do whatever they want, and even more, go beyond what they ask. Only thus is it possible to live more or less in peace in this valley of tears). This statement strikes at the heart of the supernatural belief system of Belén and all of rural Tlaxcala, and contains the essential elements that I have discussed here: the supernatural is essentially good, but people cannot take any chances, and it is better to do more than less; the customary, necessary rites and ceremonies are the means of communication between man and the supernatural; the world is at best a bad job, which is made bearable by the intervention and good offices of the supernatural; and no distinction is made between the elements of religion and magic.

Here we have the stabilizing, conservative force that has kept the traditional socioreligious system going since the 1930s in the face of powerful forces from the outside. The success of this fundamental force in Belén culture and society is, of course, a variable matter. Obviously not all inhabitants of Belén adhere to this belief complex, and there are also degrees of adherence. An educated guess is that nearly all people over the age of fifty adhere to it entirely, about 75 percent of those between thirty and fifty do, and significantly less than 50 percent below the age of thirty do. Adherence is not necessarily a function of age alone; several other factors, such as education, labor-migration history, and contact with the outside world, are involved. But were one able to interdigitate individual and collective adherence to the traditional supernatural belief system of the community on the basis of these variables, one would be able to determine the point of that quantum leap at which there is a transition from traditional ideology to a secular, basically economic ideology.

Two more points need to be discussed, one of which is the temporary dimensions of the magico-symbolic functions of compadrazgo, which have two principal aspects. The first of these consists of the temporary aspects of the syntagmatic chain of events through the last event of the central complex of rites and ceremonies. This is obviously the most important temporary sphere of the magico-symbolic functions of compadrazgo. The rites and ceremonies in this part of the syntagmatic chain are the immediate, ostensible motives for the compadrazgo relationship, that is, the prescriptive behavior that will produce the desired effect individually or collectively. This is the most prescriptive dimension of all compadrazgo types, and every step is carefully followed according to custom. The second aspect consists of the intended results of the compadrazgo relationship; these survive the central rites and ceremonies, for the functions of compadrazgo in creating supernatural rapport are cumulative, and may last for a long time—theoretically, for as long as the compadrazgo relationship is kept alive. This is especially evident in the case of recurrent rites and ceremonies, which must be interpreted as reinforcing mechanisms. Thus, the magico-symbolic functions of compadrazgo are structurally the most temporary and are confined to the principal ceremonies and recurrent events, but they are intended to have permanent results. These more permanent results, however, are not translated into any kind of structural behavior, but remain in that subtle ideological domain of the human-supernatural covenant. One can readily see why the magico-symbolic functions of compadrazgo are the most universal, for they arise directly from its most universal feature— its ideological basis. The magico-symbolic functions of compadrazgo are present to one degree or another in all compadrazgo situations described in the literature; the elements of propitiation, protection, intensification, and thanksgiving are present singly or together, in varying degrees, whenever a compadrazgo relationship is established; and basically the same operational principles described here are in effect.

The second point has to do with the roles of the mediating entity or ahijado and the sponsors or padrinos within the magico-symbolic context. Within the context of all the functions of compadrazgo that I have analyzed so far, the ahijados or mediating entities have played a rather passive role. For example, in the general configuration of personnel and intended results of any of the significant social or demographic functions of the institution, the mediating entity is often little more than the original pretext for initiating a series of functional actions, the results of which involve or affect the mediating entity very little—especially when it is an image, object, or event. But with regard to the magico-symbolic functions of compadrazgo, the intrinsic importance of the mediating entity is significantly increased, and it plays a more central role in the total configuration of functional actions and results. The mediating entity, of course, is structurally most important during the core of rites and ceremonies, which also constitutes the most efficacious part of compadrazgo's magico-symbolic functions.

Indeed, one can characterize the mediating entity as both the necessary and the sufficient condition for real effectiveness of the magico-symbolic functions. The ahijado not only embodies the central ideological motive for the compadrazgo, but is also the structural basis for undertaking it, for the intended results are centered on the ahijado. Thus, in the BSI compadrazgo type, an image is the ostensible reason for the relationship, which is also contracted to propitiate the image and assure the compadres-compadres dyad (and extensions) of propitious conditions for their relationship to it. The same can be said of virtually all compadrazgo types in Belén, whether the mediating entity is a person, image, object, or event. The only perceptible distinction is between persons and all other mediating entities, in that the protective, propitiating, intensifying, and thanksgiving attributes associated with the former are more easily identifiable and more concentrated.

Comparing the functional dimensions of the mediating entity and the compadres-compadres dyad, especially the padrinos, one finds some significant differences that are important for the assessment of magico-symbolic functions. The magico-symbolic functions centered on the mediating entity can be characterized as embodying primarily the individual dimensions of the compadrazgo system—the individually beneficial results people hope to achieve by establishing a ritual kinship relationship. The compadres-compadres dyad embodies primarily the collective dimensions of the compadrazgo system, namely, elements that transcend the mediating entity and acquire a more permanent form, and above all are an integral part of maintaining the proper human-supernatural relationship. From a slightly different viewpoint, one can say that the permanence of the compadres-compadres dyad is what maintains the appropriate degree of rapport with the supernatural; at the same time, compliance with what the compadre-compadre tie involves structurally—rights, duties, rites, and ceremonies binding compadres permanently or leading to reinforcement—is seen as increasing the collective bargaining power of the community with respect to the supernatural. Hence, compliance with the permanent dimensions of compadrazgo still involves a high degree of prescription. In essence, then, the compadrazgo prescriptions associated with the first and second parts of the syntagmatic chain—its temporary and permanent dimensions—are based, respectively, on the individual and collective discharge of all compadrazgo types and their aims to propitiate, protect, intensify, and give thanks on behalf of specific persons, images, or objects; and on the general maintenance of the established supernatural order.

The Most Salient Components of the Magico-Symbolic Functions of Compadrazgo

Let us conclude this discussion with a summary of the most important magico-symbolic attributes of the various compadrazgo types in Belén. Tables 24, 28, 30, and 31 are the most significant with regard to the magico-symbolic functions of compadrazgo. Although the magico-symbolic functions of compadrazgo in Belén and rural Tlaxcala comprise a complex of attributes that transcend the Catholic–non-Catholic cleavage and the usual ontological distinction between religion and magic, it is evident that these functions are always more apparent in compadrazgo types that have overt non-Catholic rites and ceremonies, and are primarily folk in general structure. For one thing, magico-symbolic attributes are often hidden behind the trappings of Catholic rites and ceremonies, which tend to obscure the elements of protection, propitiation, intensification, or thanksgiving that underlie many compadrazgo types. Thus, while there are no significant ideological differences between the pagan and the Catholic, structurally the pagan has more apparent magico-symbolic attributes, and for conceptual purposes, is somewhat easier to pinpoint.

Table 28 divides compadrazgo types according to whether or not their ceremonies include pagan rites, that is, rituals not contemplated even by the pan-Tlaxcalan folk religion. Thirteen compadrazgo types include varying numbers of pagan rites, from a single ritual act as in ANDC, primera piedra, and compadrazgo de aretes, to rather elaborate complexes of rites as in PCA, compadrazgo de limpia, and parada de cruz. On the other hand, eighteen compadrazgo types do not include any pagan rites, and the ceremonies are conducted according to orthodox or folk Catholicism. It must be noted, however, that what I have defined as folk Catholicism often approaches the pagan, as, for example, in a variety of rites connected with the offering of fruit, food, and other items to the dead (in PCE compadrazgo), when the items themselves are charged with pagan meaning which definitely transcends the standard practices of folk Catholicism in rural Tlaxcala. While it is easy to separate the functional elements of folk and orthodox Catholicism, it is difficult to separate folk from pagan elements. Folk Catholicism itself had been strongly influenced by pagan elements, and it is more appropriate conceptually to regard orthodox Catholicism, folk Catholicism, and the realm of the pagan as a continuum rather than as compartmentalized spheres of action. Thus, the breakdown of types in table 28 has structural but not ideological significance.

Table 30 presents compadrazgo types in terms of folk-orthodox, folk-orthodox–pagan, and folk-pagan. There are four folk-pagan compadrazgo types, seven folk-orthodox–pagan types, and twenty folk-orthodox types. These categories need clarification. First, the classification of compadrazgo types as folk-pagan denotes that their rites and ceremonies are primarily non-Catholic in nature, or at least that their ideological component approaches the parametric limit of the pagan. Thus, in all four types (PCA, parada de cruz, compadrazgo de aretes, and FC) the primary functional meaning of compadrazgo is essentially non-Catholic, even though two of them (PCA and parada de cruz) include some significant Catholic elements. Second, the compadrazgo types classified as folk-orthodox–pagan are primarily folk-Catholic in nature, but they include some significant pagan rites and ceremonies which vary from type to type. In these seven types it is most difficult to determine what is folk-Catholic and what is non-Catholic or pagan. The gradation within this category is significant, and escapulario, and compadrazgo de limpia, for example, approach a folk-pagan status. Third, the twenty types classified as folk-orthodox adhere most closely to orthodox Catholicism; they include no pagan ceremonies of any significance, although there may be some latent pagan elements. Comparing tables 28 and 30 one can see that there is a high correlation between folk-orthodox compadrazgo types and types without pagan rites, on the one hand; and between folk-pagan and folk-orthodox–pagan compadrazgo types and types with pagan rites, on the other.

Table 31 breaks down compadrazgo types on the basis of whether they belong to the life (social), religious (ceremonial), or symbolic cycles. The preceding discussion makes clear what the life and religious cycles are, and what they denote structurally and functionally, but the symbolic cycle needs clarification. I have used the term to include a rather large area of ritual kinship religious behavior which cannot properly be included within the life or religious cycles. The best way to describe it is to attach to it the symbolic attributes, for per se it is unquestionably the most symbolic complex of behavior in the compadrazgo system of Belén. A type classified as a part of the symbolic cycle may sometimes appear to have important religious or social components, but its purpose is essentially that of symbolic evocation. This is the case with ANDC and ANDI compadrazgos, for example; superficially they may be classified as part of the religious cycle, but their symbolic meaning warrants placing them in the symbolic cycle.

Finally, the symbolic objectives associated with compadrazgo types in Belén are shown in table 24. Every compadrazgo type includes at least one such objective, and, at least latently, as many as three. Of the four main symbolic objectives of compadrazgo, those of intensification and thanksgiving are least common, while those of protection are most common. The symbolic objective of the compadrazgo types is of course determined by the intrinsic nature of the mediating entity, and by the position of the type within the social and religious domains. The functional objectives of protection, propitiation, intensification, and thanksgiving do not depend directly on the magico-symbolic elements of the human-supernatural covenant, but rather on extrinsic variables that govern activation of mediating entities. Hence, one can only determine the conditions under which these four functional objectives are discharged structurally. With this in mind, I can briefly review the magico-symbolic functions of all compadrazgo types in Belén.

The Magico-Symbolic Attributes of Compadrazgo Types

With baptism, the individual is incorporated into the Christian community, original sin is erased, and he is assured of entering heaven if he dies before puberty. Children who die without baptism go to limbo, a neutral place where there is neither suffering nor enjoyment. Hence, it is necessary to baptize children as soon as possible, and if they become ill they must be baptized immediately. If parents do not baptize a child within six or seven months and the child dies, this is considered "un gran pecado" (a great sin), and even though the child "murió angelito" (died as a little angel), his parents "cargan con la culpa" (bear the blame). The underlying belief follows orthodox Catholic ideology, but the ceremony of baptism involves rites with magico-symbolic ojbectives through which supernatural protection of the child is sought. It also affords protection against "las tentaciones del demonio" (the temptations of the devil) and other evils that the devil could cause the child. To let a child go without baptism for more than the prescribed time is strongly disapproved, and social pressure is always brought to bear against malingering parents.

In addition to participating in all the ceremonies, baptismal padrinos also share with their compadres certain risks related to the luck (*suerte*) of the child. With baptism, Beleños not only comply with a sacrament of the Church, but through the ritual sponsorship the luck of the padrinos is converted into protection for the child. If the child dies before reaching the age of four or five, it is thought that the padrinos "no fueron de suerte" (lacked luck), and they are called *metepalca* (unlucky). Parents will seldom ask such padrinos to become baptismal compadres again, or as one informant put it, "Se le morian los ahijados y por eso lo cambiamos" (His godchildren died and therefore we changed him). The padrinos share with the comadre another kind of risk until *la sacan a misa* (she is taken to church). Until this ceremony is performed the mother finds herself *al borde* (or *a la orilla*) *de la sepultura* (at the edge of death); she must not go out of her house, or at least she must not go to church until she is accompanied by the compadres of sacada a misa. Thus, the magico-symbolic functions of baptismal compadrazgo are not confined to the ahijado but extend to protecting the mother until she is taken to church and passes the critical postpartum period, which in Belén's belief system is the most dangerous in the life of a woman.

Confirmación and primera comunión compadrazgo are best regarded as an intensification of baptism, that is, as the way of sanctioning and reaffirming the participation and membership of the individual in the Catholic church. In Belén they are not important intrinsically or in the life cycle of the individual. Although they are regarded as compadrazgos de grado, they are not important ritually. All children are confirmed and they receive first communion with the benefit of ritual sponsorship, but after the ceremonies there is no emphasis on the religious or ritual importance of the occasions; despite the constant exhortations of the visiting priest, communion is received less than once a year by most of the adult population of Belén. While ritual sponsorship of confirmation and first communion does not appear to have magico-symbolic functions, these two compadrazgos are regarded as requirements in the human-supernatural covenant and have latent magico-symbolic attributes—otherwise, one could not explain their prescriptive nature. One informant explained it by saying, "Los compadrazgos de confirmación y primera comunión, y lo que representan, no serán muy importantes, pero siempre ayudan a mantener contentos a Dios y a los santos" (The confirmation and first communion compadrazgos, and what they stand for, may not be very important, but they always help to keep God and the saints happy).

With the ceremonies of marriage (and by extension, those of CCCH and CCCA), people comply with an important religious obligation and traditional custom of Belén. In addition to the velación padrinos nine other padrinos and madrinas can be involved. Each of these individuals or couples has a symbolic function, but the most important one is that of the velación padrinos, whose presence is a necessary condition for the wedding ceremony. The ceremony sanctions the institution of marriage socially and religiously, and this must always be done according to the prescribed ritual and ceremonialism, through which supernatural blessing and protection are sought for the couple and for the nuclear family being established. If a couple is living in free union or was only married with a civil ceremony and begins to suffer illness or poverty, or experiences a death in the family, this is generally attributed to the fact that the couple has not received the blessing of the supernatural. From this viewpoint, the ceremonies of marriage and its compadrazgo sponsorship may be regarded as a form of propitiation to obtain protection for the couple, with the padrinos as intermediaries. The element of risk is explicit: the velación padrinos (who usually double as arras and anillos padrinos) share with the ahijados the dangers of the años noviciados (see Chapter Three of *Ritual Kinship* I). If the ahijados do not experience suffering, bad luck, and struggle during this period, the padrinos will. If the años noviciados do not occur for either the ahijados or the padrinos (an extremely rare situation), it is said that the former are lucky people, and they become the most sought-after sponsors in the community. The other marriage padrinazgos do not involve any apparent risks; they are simply elaborations of the wedding ceremonies, which have a certain social status value and symbolism but lack truly magico-symbolic functions. "Dan lujo a la ceremonia" (They are a luxury in the ceremony), but they are not essential to the entire complex.

All the rites and ceremonies that surround death and burial and the erection of a cross on the grave are full of magico-symbolic meaning. In general, the burial rites are folk interpretations of elements of orthodox Catholicism, such as the wake, the *misa de cuerpo presente* (mass with the deceased lying in state), the burial ceremony itself, the *novenario* (rosaries on nine consecutive days), the mass on the ninth day after burial, the responsory, and the setting up of the cross. Nevertheless, all these rites have as their primary objective the propitiation of the supernatural "para que el alma del difunto no sufra" (so that the soul of the deceased will not suffer). The PCE padrinos must be present when the cross is set up on the ninth day and must also participate in all the other ceremonies, which are carried out scrupulously to make sure the objectives in such a delicate rite of passage are achieved. The padrinos, as the main symbolic and social personages of the burial rites, also run a risk; if they do not perform to the best of their abilities (and this goes also for the kinsmen of the deceased) in propitiating the supernatural elements that will determine the fate of the deceased, his soul will return to remind them of their obligations, or sometimes to ask them for specific favors to ease his unfortunate position in the afterlife. The return of the soul is not desirable, for it disturbs the human-supernatural order. In fact, preoccupation with the deceased after burial involves all primary PCE actors, who take special care to continue offering masses and prayers, and arranging non-Catholic rites and other supernatural activities.

For example, they remember the deceased often in consulting weathermen or tetlachihuics, and most particularly in preparing and arranging the family altar for All Saints' Day, when he is remembered by the presence of a favorite article of clothing, drink, or food, or by some other item that he especially liked. The PCE padrinos as well as the deceased's immediate kinsmen may maintain their concern for several years. The magico-symbolic concern with death and burial accords with Beleños' belief that the dead have joined the supernatural and can, therefore, have an unfavorable influence on the outcome of human affairs if they are not propitiated. Thus, the magico-symbolic functions of PCE compadrazgo and the large ritual and ceremonial complex surrounding death and burial, are among the most explicit examples of the human-supernatural covenant. The magico-symbolic functions of this compadrazgo not only involve individual propitiation of the deceased mediating entity, but just as important, the generation of rapport between man and the supernatural via the intercession of the dead. Functionally speaking, then, the great concern with the dead, shown not only in Belén but in most of Mesoamerica, can be explained as one of the most significant mechanisms for keeping the balance of the human-supernatural order tipped favorably toward human existence.

The ANDI and CSV celebrations have important magico-symbolic attributes and functions, although the rites and ceremonies connected with them involve essentially Catholic elements and only tangentially a sprinkling of pagan elements. These celebrations purport to propitiate the Christ child and the Virgin of Belén in order to obtain their protection throughout the year. The public-communal character of the ANDI and CSV celebrations greatly enhances their magico-symbolic value, for it is on such occasions that the individual and collective interaction between society and the supernatural is seen most clearly. At the same time, ANDI and CSV constitute forms of thanksgiving for individual and collective favors received during the year, or even for the mere fact that it was possible to celebrate the occasion. This is a good illustration of the Beleños' basic attitude toward the supernatural, which includes some degree of uncertainty about the natural world and the need to keep the supernatural happy. As one elder of Belén said of ritual celebrations: "El mero hecho de que estamos aquí haciendo esta fiesta quiere decir que las cosas van regular y que nuestras súplicas han sido oidas" (The mere fact that we are here celebrating this fiesta means that things are coming along fairly well, and that our supplications have been heard). Inasmuch as ANDI and CSV are celebrated annually, one can also regard them as rites of intensification. ANDI and CSV padrinos share with the fiscales and mayordomos, and with the community in general, not only the responsibility for the rites and ceremonies, but also the risk that the functional objectives of the compadrazgo celebrations may not be achieved, an outcome that affects them directly if they are from Belén, and indirectly if they are from another community. The overt manifestations of failure can be drought, bad crops, dissension within the community, intensification of disputes with nearby communities, and so on. This feeling of failure is projected not only onto the padrinos, but also onto the fiscales and mayordomos in charge of the compadrazgo selection; they are charged with causing the bad luck by not having fulfilled their ritual and ceremonial obligations properly. This outcome reflects upon the future religious and compadrazgo careers of those involved, and they may become unpopular as prospective religious officials or padrinos. On the other hand, if the ritual sponsorship is successful, Beleños—individually and collectively—cannot do enough for the padrinos and those who selected them. This attitude applies to all public-communal compadrazgo types, which, except for AOI and BOI, always have significant magico-symbolic functions. To a considerable extent, the attitude applies as well to private-individual types, in which the luck of the padrinos in past sponsorships may play an important part in their selection.

The ANDC and BM compadrazgo types are essentially derived from ANDI, but although BM is a public-communal type, both have an essentially private-individual character and thus involve fewer magico-symbolic elements than ANDI. The rites and ceremonies of ANDC and BM are fundamentally the same as those of ANDI, but their magico-symbolic functions are more latent. The ANDC celebration is important as a family fiesta; in a sense it must be regarded as a complement to ANDI, for although they have separate sets of compadrazgo actors, many of their specific ceremonies are closely related. The risk involved in ANDC compadrazgo is low or nonexistent because its propitiatory, intensifying, and thanksgiving objectives are modest and do not involve large numbers of people.

AOI and BOI are not only the least important public-communal compadrazgo types, but also have no apparent magico-symbolic functions. They are essentially social occasions, with a strong economic component (from the communal viewpoint, and on the part of those in charge of the administration of the cult, that is, the fiscales); beyond the mildly symbolic act of blessing a material item or activity, they do not involve any supernatural risks, either individually or collectively. These types, of course, are new, were introduced from the outside, and do not have a history of local development.

With the blessing of a saint or image (BSI) Beleños ask protection from or seek to propitiate a particular Catholic supernatural; this is done to ask for a specific favor because the saint is the particular devotion of the owner, and frequently it is an act of thanksgiving for favors already received. Ritual kinship sponsorship of this compadrazgo type does not imply a risk on the part of the padrinos; even though they, too, are propitiating the saint or image indirectly, their ritual responsibility ends with the termination of the principal ceremonies and any recurrent events. Whether or not the saint or image complies with the request is a matter resting with the owners, and it is they who incur the risk. Thus, BSI compadrazgo has few magico-symbolic functions.

The magico-symbolic content of the rites and ceremonies of the sacada a misa compadrazgo complex is obvious and important. Until the ritual is carried out, the mother is in imminent danger, but once it is complied with, the danger disappears. The mother's risk is shared by the sacada a misa compadres (who most often are the baptismal padrinos of her child), but once her danger is past, so is theirs. The sacada a misa, as a derivative of baptism, can rightly be regarded as an intensification of the latter. It should be noted also that the magico-symbolic functions of leading-to or resulting-from compadrazgo types may involve all four objectives in sequence, as in baptism to sacada a misa or baptism to confirmation.

The compadrazgo de evangelios type seeks protection for the child upon being presented in church. The padrinos are participants and mediate between the child and his parents and the supernatural to whom the child is commended, usually the child's namesake saint or another Catholic supernatural of the parents' special devotion. The ritual sponsorship risk is minimal, and the padrinos share it to only a small degree with the parents of the ahijado.

Presentation of the scapulary, and its compadrazgo type, are among the best examples of seeking direct aid from the supernatural, in which the magico-symbolic functions are shown clearly in the general structure of the rites and ceremonies. The wearing of the scapulary assures the bearer that he will enter heaven in case of sudden death; it is also protection against certain evils such as *mal aire* (bad air) and *mal de ojo* (evil eye). In general the bearer has a better chance of surviving adverse supernatural interference of any kind. (This is a case in which an essentially Catholic element—the scapulary itself—achieves supernatural protection regardless of the Catholic-pagan distinction.) Once the padrinos have handed over the scapulary they no longer participate in the risk; the scapulary itself has inherent protective properties over which they have no influence, so whether or not the padrinazgo objectives are achieved is beyond the scope of the sponsorship itself.

All compadrazgo types that involve setting up a cross have important magico-symbolic structural elements and functions which include protective, propitiatory, and intensifying elements. This is especially the case when there are recurrent rites, as in PCA and certain variations of parada de cruz connected with the agricultural cycle. The padrinos of most of these types incur considerable risk, and in PCA, the risk is quite high. PCA and parada de cruz are essentially folk-pagan compadrazgo types. They include a large number of ritual elements that are clearly non-Catholic in origin, such as the ritual participation of weathermen (*tezitlazcs*) or sorcerers (tetlachihuics) after the folk-Catholic ceremonies at the spring of Actiopan have been concluded, or the ritual manipulation of these non-Catholic practitioners after the parada de cruz has been carried out in a cultivated field. Furthermore, the ideological content of the PCA and parada de cruz compadrazgo types involves more pagan than Catholic elements, but at the most efficacious level in the human-supernatural relationship, there is no clear distinction between the two. Structurally, the pagan and the Catholic are carefully kept separate, but the propitiatory, protective, and intensifying objectives are directed toward an undifferentiated supernatural which embodies, say, El Cuatlapanga as well as specific Catholic saints.

The ritual kinship sponsorships of quince años and CABP have essentially social and religious objectives, although to some extent they can be considered to have the objectives of giving thanks and seeking protection for the future of the ahijados. As new compadrazgo types, they do not have the sanction of tradition, nor are they of universal incidence. They have not yet become an inherent part of the ritual and ceremonial apparatus that surrounds the human-supernatural covenant, nor will they ever, for secularization will have destroyed the sacred nature of compadrazgo before this can happen. The same can be said of compadrazgo de graduación, another new type.

Again, compadrazgo de limpia is one of the types in which magico-symbolic elements and functions can be seen most clearly, and in which the religious content is minimal but strongly characterized by magical elements. When a limpia is undertaken, it is expected that in one way or another the cleansing implement (usually a bouquet of three different branches or plants), when placed in front of the altar of the saint being asked to effect the cure, will absorb the illness afflicting the patient. Not infrequently, a weatherman or sorcerer undertakes the limpia and buries the cleansing implement in a particular spot endowed with certain supernatural powers, which has the same effect as asking for a saint's intercession. Through magico-symbolic propitiation, the limpia seeks to end the illness and protect the person being cleansed, this latter usually by presentation of a scapulary. The good luck of the padrinos is important in achieving these compadrazgo objectives, and they share with the ahijado and the parents the risk of the cure. Beleños believe strongly that the padrinos for compadrazgo de limpia must be especially worthy individuals, from the religious and social viewpoints, for their impeccable and traditional ritual performance will favorably influence the result of the limpia.

With the blessing of a car or truck, protection is sought to ensure both the vehicle's proper functioning and the driver's safety. BCC padrinos incur no supernatural risk, but if the car or truck does not function properly, people will say that the padrinos "no tuvieron buena mano" (did not have a good hand). Neither is there any risk attached to CEON compadrazgo. A failure of the implement or appliance to work properly is attributed to the envy or greed of persons other than the padrinos, for the padrinos' envy has been neutralized by the establishment of the compadrazgo relationship. Two points should be noted in this connection. First, whether or not the ideology of a given compadrazgo type involves risk for the padrinos, Beleños tend to blame the failure to achieve functional objectives on certain things inherent in the sponsors, or on something that was left undone. Their faith in the efficacy of ritual kinship sponsorship is such that they must find a specific explanation for a failure. Second, Beleños also believe that ill feelings, envy, greed, antagonism, and in general, all antisocial behavior, are neutralized among compadres when a compadrazgo relationship is established. This belief is posited on the sacred nature of compadrazgo, and the conviction that serious supernatural punishment may be visited upon compadres who violate this precept. Nevertheless, antisocial behavior does occur now and then among compadres, and if it becomes public it may have serious consequences for the culprits. Compadres who have fallen out with each other often prefer feigning respeto and confianza to formally terminating a relationship, for although a formal alternative is allowed by the system, this may exact a rather high social and religious price.

Compadrazgo de amistad and JJ may or may not have significant magico-symbolic elements and functions, depending primarily on the circumstances under which they are contracted. If either type is contracted between two persons (and by extension their spouses) to avoid social or religious friction or to neutralize aggression, the relationship involves mutual protection and the shared risk is conditioned by the relationship itself. (The reader should note that this review of the magico-symbolic functions of all compadrazgo types in Belén is addressed to those specific properties above and beyond the intrinsic value of establishing compadrazgo relationships in the creation of rapport between man and the supernatural. This is a general ideological property of the compadrazgo system irrespective of types, but when I note that a given compadrazgo type has a certain magico-symbolic function, I am referring to structural properties at a lower level, on the basis of which I have classified all compadrazgo types in Belén with regard to varying degrees of magico-symbolic functions or elements.)

Finally, compadrazgo de aretes and FC are essentially folk-pagan types; like PCA and parada de cruz, they have the highest degree of magico-symbolic elements and functions, in both ideology and structure. Giving a child a pair of gold or silver earrings protects her, for metal has the property of guarding the wearer against the evil eye and bad air, and in general against the manipulations of sorcerers and other supernatural practitioners. In aretes the padrinos to a considerable degree share the ritual sponsorship risk with the ahijada.

In FC compadrazgo, the same risk exists and is sometimes extended to the sacramental padrinos or the compadres of the person who finds a twin fruit or vegetable. Twinning is always undesirable and full of evil connotations. The birth of twins, whether human, animal, or vegetable, is regarded as an aberration of nature and is always associated with impending disaster for those involved. It must, therefore, be counteracted immediately with the appropriate ritual kinship sponsorship, which is the only way to neutralize the event and minimize the risk and bad omens. If, for example, the finder of a twin fruit or vegetable eats it without sharing it with another person or does not establish a compadrazgo relationship by means of it, he or she will procreate twins, and so may some of his padrinos or compadres. Twins in Belén and all of rural Tlaxcala are thought to possess *de nación* (by nature) certain supernatural powers, according to which *uno pone y el otro quita* (one inflicts and the other takes away). One of the twins may, of his own volition, adversely affect a living person—for example, cause a constant pain in the part of the body that has come into contact with him, or cause the symptoms associated with the evil eye. Removal of the pain or neutralization of the evil eye can be effected only by the good twin, "el que quita"; however, he need not be the brother of the bad twin, but any good twin—that is, any twin "que quita." To bring about relief, the good twin must rub the affected part of the body with his own saliva. What is not clearly specified is how one identifies good and bad twins, except by trial and error.

The beliefs and practices associated with twinning are clearly of pre-Hispanic origin, for they have no overt associations with either orthodox or folk Catholicism, and they operate today in a manner quite similar to that of pre-Hispanic times. In cases such as these the magico-symbolic functions of compadrazgo are most clearly exhibited; this does not necessarily mean, however, that within the general framework of the human-supernatural covenant, a compadrazgo type with more visible magico-symbolic functions is more richly endowed with these functions.

The Element of Risk in Ritual Kinship Sponsorship

Throughout this description and analysis I have spoken of the risk involved in ritual kinship sponsorship, for the padrinos as well as for the ahijados and parents or owners, but I have not defined what the risk is and what it involves ideologically and structurally. Obviously, all the occasions in Belén (and rural Tlaxcala in general) for which a compadrazgo relationship is established represent some significant event in the life, soical, religious, or even economic cycle which must be sanctified and dignified with the addition of ritual kinship sponsorship. At the same time, such occasions almost invariably represent either well-established rites of passage or propitiation for the mediating entity, or situations of imminent danger which may or may not make a change in the social, religious, or symbolic status of the person, image, or object in question. In either case, there is always an element of uncertainty which can best be described as the actors' knowledge that unless things are done properly and according to prescription, the functional result will not be favorable. Although present for all primary actors, the danger, uncertainty, or apprehension that characterizes all occasions for ritual kinship sponsorship is generally greater for the mediating entity than for the padrinos and the parents or owners. In essence, the risk run by primary actors in Belén's compadrazgo system is fundamentally that inherently associated with transitional stages in the life, social, or religious cycles—naturally dangerous rites of passage involving symbolic, ritual, or ceremonial change of status. The element of risk varies, of course, according to the nature and relative importance of the occasion and according to the intrinsic nature of the mediating entity as involving *more* or *less* danger, change of status, and specific difficulties associated with certain aspects of the supernatural belief system. The risk of kinship sponsorship notwithstanding, the sacred nature of compadrazgo compels a person or married couple in Belén to accept the sponsorship when asked.

Upon accepting a ritual kinship sponsorship, a person or couple in Belén incurs varying degrees of risk. The risk is conditioned by the occasion itself, but there is another aspect of risk that is centered on the padrinos: the inherent property of being lucky, which they may or may not have. The padrinos' luck, or lack of it, is shared with the mediating entity and with the parents or owners, Conversely, the inherent risk of the mediating entity, generally manifested in a specified state of danger (as in the sacada a misa and FC compadrazgo types), may also be shared with the padrinos. Padrino-centered risk has important repercussions for compadrazgo selection and the development of compadrazgo careers. Risk centered on the mediating entity denotes little more than the inherent characteristic with which the compadrazgo occasion itself is endowed, and I therefore deal primarily with the former.

The clearest case of padrino-centered risk is the marriage padrinazgo, in which the velación padrinos consent to share with the ahijados the risk of the noviciado. The element of risk is less evident in many other compadrazgo types, but invariably it is there. For example, the baptismal padrinos share with the parents the real risk that the child may die before reaching the age of five, the period of highest infant mortality in Tlaxcala. As I have said, if the child dies, the padrinos are invariably blamed, and people say that "no fueron de suerte" (they were not lucky) or that "son metepalca," a term that signifies "to break" and applies exclusively to persons whose ahijados die before reaching the age of five. If this happens, other padrinos must be selected. On the other hand, there are persons who have a reputation for being lucky, and they are much sought after for baptism, PCE, and several of the most important compadrazgo types in Belén. The property of being lucky, or "tener buena mano," means that certain persons are thought to have inherent beneficial powers which help the compadrazgos to achieve their objectives; they serve as intermediaries with the supernatural and as protectors of the compadrazgo object.

As I have said, the padrinazgo risk, regardless of how explicit it is, is present to one degree or another in all compadrazgo types. Padrinos accept the risk voluntarily, but there is a certain amount of implicit social pressure which cannot be ignored. More important, however, in moving them to accept the risk and make the acceptance appear voluntary, is the covert pressure of possible supernatural sanctions. Those who ask to enter into a compadrazgo relationship also run a risk, above and beyond that they share with the padrinos and the mediating entity, but this risk is entirely of a social, economic, or personal nature—for example, will the padrinos comply with the prescriptions, will they have the economic resources to fulfill their obligations, will they be able to generate the proper degree of respeto and confianza? Considered in the aggregate these risks clearly point to the highly significant structural and functional component of chance and uncertainty which permeates the selection, discharge, and permanent dimensions of the compadrazgo system in Belén and rural Tlaxcala generally.

Finally, it is interesting that in Belén and much of rural Tlaxcala there is a series of compadrazgo types—especially those connected with the setting up of a cross, and in general those I have classified as folk-pagan—that require the additional performance of a tetlachihuic or tezitlazc. In Belén, for example, upon building the foundations of a house or upon setting up a cross, the owners of the mediating entity also hire a tetlachihuic or tezitlazc to perform certain rites of propitiation, protection, or intensification to non-Catholic supernaturals. In these cases, the tetlachihuic or tezitlazc shares the risk with the owner of the mediating entity in the fashion described for the padrinos, for if the functional objectives are not achieved, they are blamed. This is also true at the communal level. In many communities in rural Tlaxcala, local tezitlazcs are entrusted with keeping an eye on the weather, for which they are paid a yearly sum. It is their job to watch for storms, especially hailstorms, and give the community warning to prepare for them. When a storm approaches, the tezitlazc "debe salir a conjurar el mal tiempo" (must go forth to ward off the bad weather). In 1960, after the ritual performance of the official tezitlazc of Cuauhtenco (a community on the western slopes of La Malintzi, some eleven kilometers from Belén), a tremendous hailstorm completely destroyed the corn crop, and the people were so enraged that the tezitlazc narrowly escaped death. Thus, it is evident that the padrinos of many compadrazgo types may be regarded as functional substitutes for the tetlachihuic or tezitlazc, for they share the objective risk of the compadrazgo or the occasion for which ritual sponsorship or supernatural manipulation was undertaken. As spiritual sponsors, then, padrinos and tetlachihuics and tezitlazcs have the same fundamental relationship to the mediating entity, namely, to help it undergo the dangerous aspects of transformation and to serve as intermediaries between man and the supernatural on its behalf.[4]

Inasmuch as the magico-symbolic functions of compadrazgo and the associated elements of risk are among the most obvious functions of the institution, and certainly the most universal, it is strange that they have never been analyzed in the ethnographic literature. The magico-symbolic functions of compadrazgo, or whatever one may wish to call them, are the most important properties of the institution in terms of giving it unitary meaning and the necessary universality—at least in rural Latin America—for comparative purposes.

In these chapters I have tried to give the thorough account of the functions of compadrazgo that is warranted by its great pervasiveness in Belén culture and society. I have tried to show the multivaried functions and activities that characterize the compadrazgo system, and to point out that these are its most important assets in regarding it as the central institution around which to organize conceptually local culture and society. I have stated that the functional structure of Belén is not only a good common denominator of compadrazgo in rural Tlaxcala, but that this approach can be applied to countless other regions in Mesoamerica and South America as well.

Conclusions

In this monograph I have presented a thorough analysis of the compadrazgo system in Santa María Belén Azitzimititlán and rural Tlaxcala in its widest conceptual implications. Together with the first volume, it constitutes the most exhaustive descriptive and analytical treatment of the institution in the literature. The ethnographic, ethnologic, comparative, and historical dimensions of compadrazgo have been discussed in a large variety of contexts, but all the discussions have been centered on the diachronic-synchronic continuum and the ideal-structural dichotomy. I have labored to present compadrazgo as an integrated domain, systemically and institutionally, emphasizing simultaneously the structural and changing components in operation throughout a wide contextual spectrum. Combining the most advantageous theoretical and methodological features of structuralism and functionalism, I have implemented, albeit incompletely, an analytical framework that I think transcends what has been accomplished by the modern practitioners of these classical positions. Throughout the entire study I have tried to strike a balance between the qualitative and the quantitative, and this *modus operandi* has served to illustrate the several levels of meaning involved in anthropological research.

Although the mode of research exemplified by my work on compadrazgo still has a place in anthropological inquiry, it seems to be coming to an end and is being replaced by more restricted and methodologically controlled studies. In concluding this monograph, I would like to address several questions centered on the raison d'être of my research, the conceptual significance of the compadrazgo study, the rapprochement between ethnographic-ethnologic and quantitative-mathematical approaches in anthropology, and the way in which these two approaches complement each other. In this endeavor, I discuss primarily three topics: (1) the preservation of the ethnographic record and the descriptive and anayltical signficance of Belén and rural Tlaxcala for compadrazgo studies elsewhere in Latin America; (2) the network analysis of compadrazgo and multiple role systems in Belén and rural Tlaxcala, examining how we can transcend descriptive integration and generate more powerful explanations that will specify the structure and content of compadrazgo networks as an expression of social, economic, religious, and political action; (3) prospects for compadrazgo studies, briefly discussing how the general approach developed for compadrazgo in Belén and rural Tlaxcala, complemented with its mathematical treatment now in progress, can be applied to similar situations elsewhere.

The Significance of Belén and Rural Tlaxcala for Compadrazgo Studies in Latin America

It is astonishing that compadrazgo, one of the most universal institutions in Latin America, has never been described and analyzed in all its multidimensional complexity in terms of the institution's place at the local, regional, and national level. The ethnography of compadrazgo is deficient insofar as it is a part of wider community studies, nonexistent at the regional level, and downright confusing when used for generalizing purposes. All these drawbacks have resulted in a superficial and often contradictory knowledge of this pervasive institution. The reverse is equally true: the lack of solid ethnographic descriptions and analyses has resulted in the poor conceptual understanding of compadrazgo as an institution and of the role it plays in the many horizontal and vertical social milieus in which it is found. I have already discussed the inadequacy of compadrazgo studies in Latin America in the first volume (pages 405-428), and I wish only to reiterate here that much remains to be done for the proper understanding and conceptualization of the institution. The two volumes of *Ritual Kinship* thus represent not only the first detailed and in-depth description and analysis of compadrazgo, but also a kind of salvage ethnology: the preservation of the ethnographic record for this institution and its regional, comparative implications. I say this because compadrazgo in rural Tlaxcala is changing rapidly, and many of its traditional, sacred attributes are disappearing. It is my belief that the compadrazgo system of most of the communities in the region will be transformed into secular versions of the institution within the present generation; that is, from a strictly egalitarian basis compadrazgo is evolving into a vertical, secular system. Moreover, this is probably the rule rather than the exception in most comparable regions of Mesoamerica and the Andean area, where compadrazgo has developed its most complex, pervasive, and socially significant forms. A generation ago, probably all the comparable regions in Nuclear America would have been amenable to the kind of treatment I have given compadrazgo in rural Tlaxcala. But it is doubtful that anthropologists today could find a large number of comparable regions in which compadrazgo as an institution remains sacred, horizontal, and an effective mechanism of integration at the regional level. It is therefore of the utmost importance that this study be replicated in at least five other regions of Latin America. The continuation of this salvage operation would constitute a good beginning for a general theory of compadrazgo and how it develops and functions in secular, vertical, and essentially urban and national contexts.

One of the pervasive themes of my ritual kinship studies has been the structured and often highly formal kinds of behavior and actions associated with compadrazgo couples, units, and networks. In several contexts, compadrazgo approaches the inherent structure of kinship. For example, ritual kinship behavior and ritual kinship terminology may not be as complex as kinship behavior and kinship terminology, but they certainly approach such complexity, and they are amenable to the same procedures of description an analysis. It is inexplicable that nearly a century after anthropologists "discovered" the institution of compadrazgo they have not yet devised a technical vocabulary comparable to that developed for kinship since Morgan's time. Technical nomenclature is not an end in itself, but it is necessary for efficient analysis and for comparative purposes. I do not wish to stretch the analogy too far, but it seems evident to me that compadrazgo studies during the past fifty years would have benefited significantly from the development of a nomenclature pinpointing the key domains, bundles of behavior, and groups of personnel of compadrazgo in action.

From this viewpoint, my compadrazgo studies represent a step in the right direction. Throughout the two volumes, but especially in this one, I have tried to delimit a dozen or so domains that have yielded a more structured and systematic analysis than has been traditional in compadrazgo studies. At the same time, I have developed a nomenclature for several concepts that begins to approach the tool kit of kinship studies. These methodological operations have resulted not only in a more comprehensive picture of compadrazgo in its multidimensional components, but have also increased the potential interscientific reliability of comparative studies of the institution. In other words, by systematically employing the nodes and domains delineated in this monograph in terms of a still rather crude nomenclature, one can undertake the comparative study of compadrazgo in Latin America with greater prospect of success. I do not claim to have formulated for the study of compadrazgo the structural equivalents of the extended family, the kindred, or the lineage, but surely my somewhat crudely operationally defined concepts of "secondary compadrazgo relatives," "the compadrazgo web," and "the compadrazgo network" are better tools than the rather amorphous and unsystematic behavioral and structural attributes previously used as the basis for describing and analyzing compadrazgo. What follows is a list of the most salient domains, features, and nomenclature of compadrazgo which can be profitably used for comparative purposes and the description and analysis of the institution in Latin America:

1. The overlapping of compadrazgo and kinship. Cognizance of this

overlap is essential for understanding the functions and structure of compadrazgo. The overlap obtains in all possible combinations involving compadrazgo and kinship: when compadrazgo and kinship are exogenous (there is an effective interdiction against choosing one's compadres among one's kinsmen; this occurs mostly in basically egalitarian, horizontal situations, as in rural Tlaxcala); when compadrazgo and kinship are endogenous (there is a strong preference for choosing one's compadres among one's kinsmen; found mostly in stratified, vertical situations, as in most urban forms of compadrazgo); and when compadrazgo and kinship are agamous (there are no significant prohibitions or preferences underlying one's choice of compadres; this variation is widely distributed in both egalitarian and stratified situations).

2. The general overlapping of compadrazgo and kinship for the definition of compadrazgo personnel in action on the basis of operationalizable exocentric units, networks, and webs. The main idea here is to transcend the dyadic, egocentric bias that has been a permanent feature in the analysis of compadrazgo. While there is no question that in many situations the dyadic, egocentric focus must constitute the main way of looking at compadrazgo, there are just as many situations in which an exocentric focus must be used. The compadrazgo network and web— as exemplified for Belén and rural Tlaxcala—in many traditional and transitional communities may exhibit the permanence, structure, and behavior patterns associated with real kinship units. In such situations it is essential to play down the dyadic components and emphasize the exocentric operation of the compadrazgo in action. Only by taking such a stance will it be possible to determine how compadrazgo complements kinship, how compadrazgo may tend to replace kinship, and how compadrazgo and kinship accommodate each other in a wide spectrum of community types in Latin America.

3. The description and analysis of ritual kinship terminology and ritual kinship behavior. Given the similarities, overlappings, and spheres of action of compadrazgo and kinship, it is important to undertake the above operations in order to position compadrazgo properly and refine its analysis. Two examples may serve as illustrations. The analysis of ritual kinship terminology may not only reveal unsuspected ties binding particular categories of compadres but is essential for understanding the extension of compadrazgo behavior. This operation alone should make clear that every compadrazgo system, no matter how simple and limited, involves structural and behavioral exocentric dimensions that transcend dyadic patterns of interaction. Still more significant is the analysis of ritual kinship behavior as it obtains in the various categories of compadrazgo actors as the result of extensions and intensification of compadrazgo ties throughout the career of individuals, couples, and groups.

My analysis of the problem in terms of primary, secondary, and tertiary actors has yielded good results in understanding the different levels of compadrazgo in action.

4. The developmental cycle of compadrazgo as an institution and as a system. Like the domestic group, compadrazgo cannot be studied exclusively as a synchronic, static system but must also be examined in terms of its genesis, mechanisms of formation, and development through definite time sequences. By the development of compadrazgo I mean its dynamic aspects in operation synchronically, its diachronic development egocentrically from the viewpoint of individuals and couples, and its development exocentrically from the viewpoint of the institution as it unfolds in the life and ceremonial cycle of the community. Thus, the most detailed chapters in this monograph are on the developmental cycle of compadrazgo in which I analyze the most salient components of the institution: the egocentric development of compadrazgo as individuals and couples progress from birth to death; the exocentric formation of networks and webs as the result of repetition, intensification, and the implications of multidyadic relationships; the delineation and structural implications of compadrazgo clusters; and so on. The compadrazgo literature does not contain a single instance in which the institution has been conceptualized in this fashion, and this is probably the main reason anthropologists know so little about its dynamic, pervasive components. From this viewpoint, the developmental cycle of compadrazgo presented in Chapters Thirteen and Fourteen is a good model for replication in many contexts and regions of Latin America.

5. The sacred and secular nature of compadrazgo. This is a significant dichotomy that clearly delimits the two fundamental kinds of ritual kinship in Latin America: compadrazgo relationships characterized by a sacred content that emphasizes reciprocity, exchange, and the absence of any type of intrinsic maximization; and compadrazgo relationships characterized by a secular context that emphasizes the maximization of social, economic, and even political goals. While sacred compadrazgo is most commonly found in traditional, small-scale rural communities and secular compadrazgo is most commonly associated with large-scale, mostly urban environments, there is a wide range of variation along the total societal and cultural spectrum. In any reasonably adequate theory of compadrazgo, it is of the utmost importance to determine the sacred-secular composition and the ideology, sanctions for compliance, and constraints that go with it.

6. Egalitarian-horizontal and stratified-vertical compadrazgo. This is another significant dichotomy which characterizes a wide spectrum of compadrazgo systems, communally and regionally. My review of the literature on compadrazgo indicates that there is a high correlation be-

tween this and the sacred-secular dichotomy: the more egalitarian-horizontal the compadrazgo system, the larger the sacred component; and the more stratified-vertical the compadrazgo system, the larger the secular component. Several telling exceptions, in which, the context of compadrazgo selection, exchange, and reciprocity is essentially egalitarian but involves a modicum of social or economic maximization, are described in the literature. There are no reports of the opposite case, but it is not unlikely that basically stratified compadrazgo systems without social, economic, or any other kind of maximization do exist. Be this as it may, the functions and place of compadrazgo within the context of the community, the region, and possibly the nation cannot be determined properly without reference to this pair of dichotomies.

7. The symmetrical and asymmetrical structure of compadrazgo systems. This feature of the institution interdigitates with 5 and 6 in various ways. Some are obvious but others would have to be explicitly formulated and tested against comparative data. For example, the literature is clear in demonstrating the high correlation of sacred, egalitarian-horizontal, and symmetrical compadrazgo; but there are several other correlations involving these three attributes that must be explored conceptually. Another aspect of the symmetrical-asymmetrical structure of compadrazgo that must also be examined is the symmetry and asymmetry that obtain in a variety of domains of compadrazgo in action: recruitment and selection of compadres; reciprocity of rights and obligations; the temporary-permanent cleavage; and so on. Only when these contexts are analyzed is it possible to determine and assess the much-talked-about malleability and adaptability of compadrazgo.

8. The permanent and temporary dimensions of compadrazgo. One of the difficulties in assessing the functions of compadrazgo arises from the rather unidimensional fashion in which the institution has been described and analyzed. This applies particularly to the lack of analyses in terms of compadrazgo's temporary and permanent attributes and components. Compadrazgo relationships of all types always include temporary and permanent dimensions. These must be clearly specified and positioned with respect to the egocentric and exocentric development of the institution inasmuch as these dimensions affect individuals, couples, and groups of compadres throughout their compadrazgo careers. Looked at from this viewpoint, compadrazgo has a complex of functions that are essentially determined by the permanent and temporary nature of specific relationships and the process of repetition and intensification to which they are subjected. Thus, in Belén and rural Tlaxcala, the temporary functions of compadrazgo are essentially magico-symbolic, while its permanent dimensions are mostly social and religious. One can easily imagine the various possible combinations that obtain in

different communal and regional contexts, but the principle remains the same: the functions of compadrazgo can only be assigned after the temporary-permanent continuum has been established with respect to specific compadrazgo types and in relation to the life and ceremonial cycles of individuals, couples, and groups.

9. Ritual kinship (compadrazgo) and ritual kinship sponsorship (padrinazgo). Assessment of the relative structural importance and functional saliency of the compadres-compadres and padrinos-ahijados dyads is essential for the comparative analysis of compadrazgo. In the Old World the structural importance of the institution is centered on the padrinos-ahijados dyad, while in the New World it is centered on the compadres-compadres dyad, and it is this feature that leads to the formation of networks and webs based on extensions, repetitions, and intensification of original subject dyads. Here again, there are several possible combinations obtaining at all levels of Latin American society in which the compadres-compadres and padrinos-ahijados dyads will structure various temporary and permanent exocentric extensions. These combinations may range from the basically Old World model, in which padrinazgo is temporary and involves no social or economic functions, to the almost exclusive predominance of the compadres-compadres dyad leading to the formation of permanent or fairly permanent network and webs.

10. Prescriptive, preferential, and optional compadrazgo types. The complexity and elaboration of compadrazgo systems in Latin America vary greatly, and this variation is most apparent in the contexts and constraints underlying the processes of recruitment, selection, and establishment of a large gamut of compadrazgo types. In this domain, the compadrazgo system of Belén, where most of the alternatives associated with the institution are found, constitutes a good model for compadrazgo studies. There are probably no compadrazgo systems in Latin America in which all types are prescriptive or truly optional; rather varying combinations along the prescriptive-preferential-optional scale exist. This variation is especially evident with respect to the decision to establish a particular compadrazgo type, but it also has significant implications for recruitment, selection, ritual kinship behavior, network extensions, and so on. The prescriptive-preferential-optional scale is a pivotal element in the analysis of compadrazgo and in gauging its structural and communal pervasiveness.

11. The asking–being-asked distinction and its implications. This is another key juncture in the analysis of compadrazgo, which is hardly hinted at in the literature, and yet it entails several structural implications. The asking–being–asked distinction constitutes an integral part of the analysis and interdigitation of 6, 7, 8, and 9. It determines the initial

structure of the compadrazgo tie, the degree of asymmetry involved, and whether it will develop into a permanent relationship. Within the widest context of the compadrazgo system, the asking–being-asked distinction exemplifies the symmetry or asymmetry of compadrazgo careers and the elements of repetition and intensification in the formation of compadrazgo networks. In a basically contractual institution such as compadrazgo, it is of paramount importance to harness those junctures that structure the system in as "natural" a fashion as possible. This is the utility of the asking–being-asked distinction and of several similar distinctions analyzed here.

12. Private-individual and public-communal compadrazgo types. More than any of the other salient structural features of compadrazgo, this basic distinction of compadrazgo types exemplifies the complexity, pervasiveness, and communal and regional importance of the institution. At least in Nuclear America, there are probably few communities in which public-communal compadrazgo types are not present, and yet this aspect of compadrazgo has barely been noticed in the literature. Moreover, under this rubric I would like to include those padrinazgos or ritual sponsorships that take place at the regional and even the national level, which have significant vertical and horizontal implications, socially and politically. What I have in mind here are such ritual sponsorships as the *apadrinamiento* (sponsoring) of "the high school class of 1980," or the apadrinamiento of "those who attended the seminar on tropical agriculture in Zempoala, Veracruz during the summer of 1981." These are common forms of ritual sponsorship in many parts of Latin America; they are on the fringes of compadrazgo as an institution and may be significant in understanding its operation in its widest possible context.

13. The structure of interchangeable compadrazgo types. This feature of compadrazgo systems is not central to the analysis of the institution but it exemplifies several other features important in elucidating ancillary aspects. In this context, the structure of interchangeable compadrazgo types illustrates the traditional baseline of the system, changing trends, and the adaptation the institution is undergoing at the communal and regional levels. Although the literature is silent on this aspect of the institution, my acquaintance with several compadrazgo systems in the Central Mexican Highlands indicates that it might be a widespread phenomenon in many regions of Latin America. At least from the diachronic viewpoint, it is important to determine how compadrazgo systems have changed in the short-range historical perspective, and in this connection, the analysis of interchangeable types is signficant.

14. Compadrazgo choice and its situational contexts. This is another aspect of compadrazgo that is intimately related to the wider context of

community culture and society. The structure of compadrazgo choice and the situational contexts which it is embedded illustrate how compadrazgo is articulated with several other systems and domains, at both the communal and regional levels. In Volume One I demonstrate how compadrazgo choice articulates with labor migration, friendship, neighborhood, and common interest groups in Belén and ramifies throughout rural Tlaxcala. Although there are no comparative data on this subject, it is warranted to assume, at least for most of Nuclear America, that compadrazgo is always linked to several systems and domains with wide ranging implications, communally and regionally. Within this context of interaction with other domains, the structure of compadrazgo choice constitutes yet another juncture for the conceptualization of the institution as the structural equivalent of kinship in a significant number of contexts.

15. Ritual kinship nomenclature and the compadrazgo system. Given the lack of comparative information for Latin America, it has obviously been impossible to develop a systematic nomenclature dealing with all the structural contexts and domains discussed in my compadrazgo studies. But I have made some progress in developing a tentative nomenclature for several domains discussed above, among which the most significant are the following: (a) "primary," "secondary," and "tertiary" compadrazgo actors or relatives; (b) the compadrazgo "network" and "web"; (c) the compadrazgo "cluster"; (d) "egocentric" and "exocentric" compadrazgo relationships; (e) the "egocentric developmental cycle" and the "exocentric developmental cycle" of compadrazgo; (f) "sacred" and "secular" compadrazgo; (g) "egalitarian-horizontal" and "stratified-vertical" compadrazgo; (h) "symmetrical" and "asymmetrical" compadrazgo types and relationships; (i) "permanent" and "temporary" compadrazgo types, relationships, and attributes; (j) "compadrazgo," "padrinazgo," and "compadrinazgo"; (k) "prescriptive," "preferential," and "optional" compadrazgo types; (l) "asking" and "being asked" compadrazgo relationships; (m) "private-individual" and "public-communal" compadrazgo types. Some of these have been briefly discussed or hinted at in the literature (g, h, j, and l), but the comparative discussion of compadrazgo have never employed the implied nomenclatures. It is my contention that the efficient description and analysis of specific cases and the comparative study of compadrazgo must be conducted on the basis of a standardized and operationally defined nomenclature as exemplified here.

The foregoing contexts and domains do not exhaust the list discussed in Volumes One and Two, but they are the most significant and worthy of replication ethnographically and comparatively. Some of them have been discussed in the literature (3, 6, and 9), others have been implied or hinted at (7, 10, 11, and 12), but the majority (1, 2, 4, 5, 8, 13, 14, and 15) have been considered here for the first time. Compadrazgo in Latin America is still a vigorous and widespread institution in innumerable vertical and horizontal contexts, and any future ethnographic or comparative studies should be based on a set of clearly delimited domains and operationally defined nomenclature. This is the only way to achieve the degree of interscientific reliability that knowledge of this institution in the New World warrants.

My two volumes on compadrazgo are also significant for the conduct of similar studies elsewhere in Latin America because of the mode of analysis I have used, particularly in this volume. One of the principal aims in Part One has been to isolate operational principles that can be used as the basis for expanding the merely descriptive and for generating better explanations in circumscribed domains. At the same time, the principles that I have been able to isolate, and to some degree operationally define, transcend the ethnographic situation, and they may prove to be the most useful in the comparative treatment of compadrazgo. These principles fall basically into two categories: substantive and operational (or analytical). An example or two will suffice to illustrate the advantages of my approach.

The conscious and unconscious character of compadrazgo data and of the people's conception of the system is a good example of a substantive principle. The majority of anthropologists during the past sixty or so years have implied that there is a distinction between what is consciously and directly elicited from informants, and what is unconsciously elicited by circumlocution. This in turn has led to the specification of practical rules for the collection of data, and subsequently, to their elaboration analytically. Thus, the distinction has both substantive and conceptual implications. Substantively, the distinction should specify the conditions under which the data were gathered and the uses to which they can be put analytically. It should also specify the mechanisms by which anthropologists can record directly or indirectly elicited information along an operationally defined conscious-unconscious scale. Conceptually, the distinction has significant implications related to the task of delimiting the ideological and structural domains and demonstrating their interrelations. At the same time, the conscious-unconscious distinction should specify the nature of the models or paradigms that can be constructed on the bases of given bodies of data. The substantive and conceptual implications for the compadrazgo system of the conscious-unconscious distinction have been illustrated extensively in this volume, I can only add that this point is highly significant for both ethnographic and ethnologic purposes: on the one hand, for establishing the ideological and structural parameters for specific cases of compadrazgo; and on the other, for isolating the ideological elements that must be employed in comparative constructs of the institution.

Confianza, respeto, and reliance are the most salient examples of operational principles affecting the dynamics of compadrazgo systems. I have defined these as dynamic, activating principles with a large component of covering properties. Confianza, respeto, and reliance are probably the most universal conceptual properties of compadrazgo insofar as the institution entails permanent bonds and obligations. In the literature, however, although they have been amply described as substantive properties of compadrazgo systems, they have never been construed as operational principles. Rather, confianza, respeto, and reliance have retained little more than their common-sense meanings within specific ethnographic settings. These principles embody a high degree of semantic homogeneity applying to large bodies of sociocultural phenomena, and are therefore most suitable for comparative purposes. From the viewpoint of ethnographic description and analysis, confianza, respeto, and reliance, as covering terms for large bodies of compadrazgo data whose parts can be construed as forming more structured wholes, are important thresholds in helping to generate causal entailment. The behavioral and structural scaling of confianza, respeto, and reliance—that is, their configuration as dynamic, activating principles—constitutes the single most important operation that can be performed on probably the most universal components of compadrazgo in Latin America. By retaining the common-sense meaning of these compadrazgo attributes one loses a significant opportunity for advancing compadrazgo studies to a mature stage of conceptualization. Thus, the analysis of compadrazgo in terms of substantive and operational principles, as I have defined them in this volume, represents a significant descriptive and comparative conceptual improvement.

Finally, I would like to reemphasize one of the main themes of Volume One, namely, the use of compadrazgo as the central institution in the conceptualization of transitional communities in Nuclear America. A vast spectrum of community types is no longer "traditional," and yet these communities are not "secular," "modern" "nationally integrated," or whatever one may wish to call them, either. In such communities, kinship is weak, religion is in various stages of disintegration, ritual and ceremonialism are no longer sacred, but compadrazgo may still retain a measure of sacredness and vigor in the organization of community action. Under these conditions compadrazgo, as a most pervasive institution, one that is highly interconnected with other aspects of society, is the best candidate for anthropologists to use in describing and analyzing the community in its regional context. I believe the demonstration of how this conceptual operation can be achieved is the most solid contribution of Volume One. In conclusion, I hope to have shown the reasons why the two compadrazgo volumes present several viable paradigms for the study of compadrazgo in Latin America.

The Network Analysis of Compadrazgo and Multiple Role Systems in Rural Tlaxcala

I have indicated that in the two volumes I have tried to balance the qualitative and quantitative aspects of anthropological inquiry, as they are commonly defined in structural and functional studies. Here, however, the term quantitative indicates the use of an extensive corpus of quantifiable data covering a large number of topics for structural analysis, not the construction of formal models and algorithms for solving specific structural problems, now common in several anthropological quarters. For example, the egocentric and exocentric developmental cycles of the compadrazgo system in Belén are based on fifty compadrazgo careers and thousands of compadrazgo relationships, while the extra-communal structure of compadrazgo in rural Tlaxcala was analyzed with reference to more than sixty communities. In several places in the text I indicated that operationalization will require the mathematical formalization of circumscribed domains, which by myself I am not qualified to undertake. The operationalization of "secularization" in the compadrazgo system of rural Tlaxcala, for example, requires the measurement of at least a dozen variables that can only be achieved in the formal mathematical sense. This and many other examples maintained my interest in the formalization of many compadrazgo domains for years after I began writing the first volume in 1970.

The two volumes on ritual kinship, which were finished by 1974, opened up new lines of inquiry by demonstrating the multidimensionality, complex structure, and many stranded nature of compadrazgo at the communal and regional levels. It became increasingly apparent to me that network analysis was the most efficient and potentially rewarding approach to the conceptualization of compadrazgo, many problems of which had been impossible for me to solve during the writing of the monographs, both for lack of personal competence in mathematical formalization and for lack of appropriately developed methods and techniques. Significant theoretical and methodological breakthroughs in network analysis had been achieved by 1975, and this made possible the tackling and solution of many intractable problems that I had delimited or hinted at. Thus, in September 1975 I joined forces with Douglas R. White, a mathematical anthropologist keenly interested in network analysis. Since 1976, with the support of a five-year grant (BNS 76-08386) from the National Science Foundation, we have been engaged in research on compadrazgo and kinship networks in rural Tlaxcala. We have completed the first of a series of monographs on compadrazgo networks and multiple-role systems entitled *Social Structure and Ideology: Social Networks in Rural Tlaxcala*. In the remainder of this section I briefly discuss what White and I expect to achieve with this work now in progress, and how my description and analysis of compadrazgo complement network analysis.

Description and comparative analysis of the forms of social organization in Mesoamerica have been complicated by the many-stranded character of social relationships like compadrazgo, bilateral kinship, and economic and political alliances, and by the lack of clear-cut structural units resulting from such open-ended relationships. Foster's (1961) characterization of the "dyadic contract" identifies the process by which many social relationships are formed in peasant communities, but he did not clarify the types of social configurations that may result from such open-ended contracts. Etnographic work on the structure of social networks in societies that emphasize many-stranded relationships, and on the consequences of different types of network structure for role behavior is badly needed. This is particularly the case in Latin America, from the village to the nation.

My studies in the understanding of compadrazgo links and the methods of network analysis (MSSB 1974; D. R. White 1975) suggested to White and me that network analysis can be an extremely fruitful approach to many problems in the study of many-stranded social organization, of which the compadrazgo system is in many ways an ideal example. We are not employing the concept of social network in a loose or metaphorical sense. Barnes (1974), in tracing the development of metaphorical usage of the network concept, notes that for most problems of social organization, a detailed network analysis of social relationships may be redundant in that other analytical concepts, such as social roles or corporate groups, could serve equally well in the exposition of social organizational data. This is not the case for compadrazgo in rural Tlaxcala, as has been made abundantly clear throughout this monograph. It should be emphasized, however, that network analysis is meaningful in its own right only where the behavior of actors in the social setting is related not to roles or characteristics of individuals or groups, but rather to the particular configuration of relationships within a network. Thus, network analysis, if applicable to a problem, should be able to elucidate (and predict) certain types of individual and group behavior, which are not a function of individual attributes or even dyadic relationships per se.

White and I believe my ritual kinship studies make a strong case for the applicability of network analysis to the compadrazgo system of rural

Tlaxcala. While the various types of compadrazgo are either dyadically or communally contracted, and are related to the life, ceremonial, and economic cycles of individuals or the yearly religious cycle of the cummunity, the resultant exocentric patterns of social relationships tend over time to form structures that acquire a dynamic of their own: clusters of individuals with a high density of compadrazgo ties emerge, and for certain purposes they exhibit behavioral regularities at the community level, sometimes in relation to concerted economic, religious, and social action, sometimes in relation to conflict resolution or the avoidance of direct confrontation. In other words, there exist strong exocentric patterns in network formation hitherto unnoticed in the Mesoamerican literature, and coherent sets of behavior predicated on the structure of such networks. Without refined tools for the analysis of clustering, the decomposition of a finite population according to network linkages, and the compounding of role relationships (D. R. White 1974), it is impossible to define and specify the structure of social networks beyond their merely descriptive integration as I have already done. The aim of our current research is to transcend descriptive integration and generate more powerful explanations that will specify the structure and content of compadrazgo networks as an expression of social, economic, religious, and political action.

In order to move to the level at which the effects of network phenomena may be studied, the research has been organized so as to: (1) generate data on the full dyadic matrix of social relationships defined by compadrazgo and necessarily also by kinship (since compadrazgo relations build upon kinship and their network structure cannot be understood without considering kinship as well); (2) apply specific methods of analysis to detect structural properties that hold across the network in a particular community; and (3) isolate critical variables in terms of the antecedents and predicted consequences of different network structures.

To demonstrate network consequences, White and I centered the research on the impact of emergent compadrazgo-kinship structures on other important aspects of sociopolitical organization: the movement of personnel into positions in the civil-religious hierarchy, changes in local political organization and the outbreak of factional disputes, the process of recruitment into labor migration, and the territorial, occupational, and language-maintenance aspects of social organization as affected by the structure of social networks. The focus of the research, then, has been on compadrazgo networks, but only as these are generated in conjunction with kinship networks, and as both together impinge upon other aspects of social organization.

An important subsidiary problem that developed shortly after we began this research is the extent to which individuals, who are knowledgeable about social relationships within any particular community, are aware of the exocentric strucure of compadrazgo links, where these differ from territorial or kinship organization. It may well be that no group of individuals within a community is fully cognizant of the complex exocentric structure of many-stranded compadrazgo relationships, or of the effects of network structure upon individual and group behavior within the local setting. On the other hand, if—as we were able to ascertain—there are individuals who are aware of the overall patterns of clustering and complex linkages built up through compadrazgo networks, this may suggest ways in which complex social organizations could be studied through individuals' perceptions of social organizational linkages (the cognitive study of complex social systems; see White and Nutini n.d.).

For our research White and I have used the following three basic techniques: (1) blockmodeling, developed specifically for the analysis of the structure of multirelational social linkages; (2) graph theory applied to multirelational directed digraphs as a representation of social linkages; and (3) statistical entailment of social linkages.

Blockmodeling, developed by Harrison White and his students and colleagues at Harvard University (Boorman and White 1975; H. C. White 1969; White, Boorman, and Breiger 1976) is based on the inductive analysis of network linkages, and proceeds in two stages: Blockmodeling I identifies sets or blocks of individuals in structurally equivalent positions, and Blockmodeling II analyzes the network structure of different types of links that hold between these positions, including role reciprocity, compound roles, the interlocking of role structure, and the comparison of role structures for different populations. Because of the power of blockmodeling to abstract relevant features, not only from the network structure of compadrazgo, but also from role and behavioral structure, it has been our main technique of network analysis. Recent findings from blockmodeling analyses of large social networks (Breiger 1976), and from considerations of network sampling (Granovetter 1976), also indicate that a subset of the network linkage data from a relatively bounded and densely connected social group, can serve as well for empirical analysis as complete linkage data. This facilitated the collection of network data at the community level.

Second in importance to blockmodeling for the analysis of compadrazgo networks are the techniques for measurement of network structure derived from graph theory (Harary, Cartwright, and Norman 1965). These have been extensively employed by British social anthropologists (Barnes 1974; Mitchell 1969) and in sociometric studies (Doreian 1970). If we represent the matrix of choices for particular compadrazgo types (for example, baptism or scapulary compadres) as a directed graph with arrows connecting askers to those being asked, we can define structural indices that apply to persons, dyads, triads, or global properties of the graph as follows: personal attributes (indegree, outdegree, span, centrality, zone density); dyadic attributes (reinforcement, reachability); triadic attributes (balance, transitivity); global attributes (number of cliques, number of clusters, size of cliques or clusters, density of cliques or clusters, and centralization of cliques or clusters). Many of these indices of the structural position of individuals, or the structural properties of networks, have been very useful for our analyses of compadrazgo.

Statistical entailment analysis (D. R. White 1975) allows a direct measure of the extent to which particular compadrazgo relationships are subsets of other relationships, and the extent to which the existence of one type of compadrazgo entails the absence of another type, across the network of individuals in particular communities. I have identified ethnographically many types of compadrazgo that in specific communities lead to or result from other compadrazgo types. Such entailments are not detected by blockmodeling or graph theory analysis, and yet may be important for the structure of compadrazgo linkages. This is the context in which we have expanded entailment procedures to analyze several aspects of compadrazgo networks.

White and I selected four communities and a small factory in rural Tlaxcala, and for four consecutive years (1976-1980) we gathered complete relational data on compadrazgo for nearly 2,000 married couples. The communities range from traditional to secular, and are representative of the acculturative continuum for rural Tlaxcala. In addition to relational data (that is, the total number of compadrazgo relationships of every married couple in the four communities and the factory up to the time they were interviewed), we collected several kinds of other data, directly or indirectly related to network structure: kinship links for all interviewed compadrazgo couples up to the grandparental or great-grandparental generation; cognitive data on compadrazgo networks for selected samples (about 25 percent of interviewed couples) for each of the four communities and the factory; linkage data on labor migration careers, civil-religious participation careers, and other social and political activities of selected samples for each of the four communities and the factory; control group data sample for each of the four communities involving baptism and marriage compadrazgo relationships as recorded in the local church registers; and so on. This enormous body of network data, containing hundreds of thousands of linkages and attributes, is being handled by specifically designed computer programs developed by White and his associates at the University of California at Irvine.

In conclusion, the advantage of the network approach is that it makes it possible to consider social structure from the aggregate of individual viewpoints and from a global structural viewpoint simultaneously. Compadrazgo networks are constructed from the individual perspective, yet they function as a global network in which community roles are interlocked and articulated within the larger regional context. Network analysis allows structural positions in the global network to be identified on the basis of patterns of connections and understanding of the relationship between individuals and positions. How are social positions defined and articulated? How are individuals "recruited" for positions? How do individuals "seek" or construct positions? How does the structure of positions evolve over time?

Prospects for Compadrazgo Studies: Descriptive Integration and Network Analysis

I hope to have demonstrated that my descriptive integrational studies of compadrazgo in rural Tlaxcala and network analysis complement each other well. Indeed, it would have been difficult to collect reliable relational, linkage, and network data on compadrazgo without the descriptive studies. This lack of a solid ethnographic base has been one of the notable weaknesses of the network studies that sociologists have undertaken since the mid-1960s. It is also very difficult to interpret the analysis of formal relational, linkage, and network data without a firm ethnographic foundation. Thus, the complementation of formal, mathematical with ethnographic, mechanical techniques and modes of analysis is a necessary condition for the study of multidimensional, many-stranded institutions such as compadrazgo. These were the considerations that led White and me to undertake the network study of compadrazgo in an area that was already well investigated, institutionally and ethnographically. In addition, our experience suggests that for a thorough understanding of differential network formation and impact, the future of compadrazgo studies must be regional and multicommunal.

Despite the claims of functionalists and structuralists of several persuasions, their methods and results remain basically descriptive and integrational. To a large extent, this is also true of my two volumes on ritual kinship, although in several domains I was able to transcend the limitations of the descriptive integrational method. By descriptive integration I mean essentially that, regardless of its logical underpinnings, the method does not generate linear causality, or, to put it more modestly, global entities cannot formally be operationalized. It is also true, however, that the functional and structural positions, and what they entail descriptively and conceptually, can never be dispensed with entirely in sociocultural studies, for descriptive integration provides the general framework within which systems can be isolated, explained, and interpreted.

Had White and I not had the benefit of the two volumes of *Ritual Kinship* our study on compadrazgo networks would have suffered in several ways. First, the data base would have been weaker, for we would not have been able to construct the right questionnaires to elicit maximum network amplitude and cognitive representation. We would have missed the complexity of compadrazgo types and the natural clustering involved in the developmental cycle of the system, and thereby not taken into consideration key network junctures. Second, the application of entailment analysis, and possibly graph theory, would have been difficult if not impossible. Without a thorough understanding of interlocking types, the mechanisms of compadrazgo recruitment and selection, and the religious and economic implications of compadrazgo for communal structure, the application of these two basic techniques in network analysis would have been reduced to rather empty formalizations. Third, the intepretation of compadrazgo network structure (or the network structure of any system) is best undertaken in terms of the system's full articulation to the salient comparable system at both the local and regional levels. Thus, position in compadrazgo networks, role structure, and role behavior to a significant degree become a function of the many-stranded participation of individuals and groups in many social, economic, religious, and political systems at both the community and regional levels. I could enumerate other disadvantages, but I have made my point: network analysis *in vacuo* is not nearly as powerful in generating explanations as it is when complemented with a thoroughly described and structurally well-positioned study of the system under consideration.

The work on network structure now in progress in both anthropology and sociology and my own collaboration with White suggest a division of labor for future studies. I see anthropologists performing basically three tasks, all related and forming part of a meaningful whole. At the first, or ethnographic level, they will work much as they have in the past, incorporating advances in the sophistication of data gathering. (Volume One of my ritual kinship studies constitutes a good example of this task.) At the second, or analytical level, anthropologists will be concerned with the analysis of fairly broad problem areas; the results will be rather like those that sophisticated functionalists and structuralists of today hope to achieve with their monographic studies— again with the refinements required by the theoretical framework underlying this threefold division. (This volume on the structure of compadrazgo represents an adequate example of this level of analysis.) Finally, at the third, or theoretical level, anthropologists with different configurations of data from the first two levels will be concerned exclusively with theoretical constructs or models of varying degrees and scope. Without this threefold division, it makes little sense to talk of models as distinct from paradigms, for I fail to see the relevance and immediate connection of models to, say, even the most sophisticated studies of kinship structure now in existence. This third level is well exemplified in White and my work on network structure in rural Tlaxcala, in which on the basis of my ritual kinship studies, we are able to operationalize a circumscribed problem area and generate explanations not quite within the reach of the essentially descriptive and qualifying methods of traditional anthropology.

Needless to say any attempt to reach a theoretical level must be problem oriented and essentially comparative. In other words, the aim of generating models of network structure is not simply the emic explanation of particular instances—for example, the explanation of compadrazgo in rural Tlaxcala—but more important the formulation of etic generalizations that can broadly function as deductive-nomonological constructs—for example, the formulation of a general theory of compadrazgo in Latin America that can account for specific instances of the institution. The alternatives for achieving these goals are numerous, and I cannot possibly discuss them here. I suggest, however, that at this stage in the development of anthropology the alternative most likely to succeed involves the collaboration of anthropologists with skills in the three levels of description and analysis delineated above. This has been the strategy that White and I have been using in our work. It would be ideal if we could train students to be full-fledged professionals in all three levels of conceptualization, but this is not a realistic goal. Rather, this threefold endeavor can best be achieved by the collaboration of structural and mathematical anthropologists with an understanding of and sympathetic feeling for each other's craft.

Finally, the institution of compadrazgo in Latin America will not be properly conceptualized and explained in its many contexts and expressions unless the strategy suggested here is replicated for all major culture areas, vertically and horizontally. This means at least five, and as many as ten, structural and historical studies of the institution followed by corresponding network analyses for, say, Mesoamerica, the Andean area, the Circum-Caribbean area, southern South America, Brazil, and so on. The advantages of this approach are many, and for the first time there is the opportunity to generate truly interscientific reliability and implement properly the comparative approach, that much talked about but elusive and hitherto unrealized method. I hope that my compadrazgo work and its network analyses with Douglas R. White will have presented a paradigm worthy of emulation for an institution that warrants intensive comparative treatment.

Appendix: The Epistemological and Ontological Foundations of the Analytical Framework

Scope of the Problem

In a forthcoming book entitled *Structure and Ideology: The Epistemological and Ontological Basis of Their Interrelationship* (Nutini n.d.), I analyze the theoretical and methodological foundations of this monograph and *Ritual Kinship* I in particular, and of several structural and ideological problems in general. I address myself to the fundamental assumption that has underlain the entire compadrazgo study, inasmuch as it is in this central feature that what has been achieved in these two volumes departs significantly from similar structural-functional studies. The basic premise of this assumption is that there are two fundamental orders in the conceptualization of sociocultural phenomena, the ideological and the structural, and that it is heuristically and operationally soundest to regard them as separate. Only under these conditions can better descriptions and explanations of the synchronic dimensions of sociocultural systems be generated, and, more important, can their synchronic and diachronic dimensions be integrated into a single conceptual framework, thereby avoiding the rigidities that the classical structural-functional approach imposes on the conceptualization of social and cultural change. Throughout this study it has been my cardinal principle of analysis to keep these two conceptual orders separate, but without losing sight of the fact that they impinge upon each other and are in some fashion causally related. This *modus operandi* has advantages over the primarily synchronic matrix that underlies the majority of structural-functional studies. Beyond the immediate ethnographic and ethnological levels, my approach seems to come closer to fulfilling the requirements for successful formulation and eventual operationalization of the comparative method. This method, which is the most characteristic theoretical contribution of British social anthropology, has so far remained largely unrealized, despite many efforts on the part of the most outstanding practitioners (Eggan 1950; Evans-Pritchard 1956; Firth 1963; Fortes 1953; Gluckman 1950; to name a few).

My aim in this appendix is to discuss, in the light of these considerations, the epistemological and ontological foundations of a limited-range theory of the integration of and the efficacy binding together the ideological and structural domains, but as part of a single theoretical and methodological matrix. This appendix, then, has a dual purpose. On the one hand, I present an outline of the perspective and substantive components of a limited-range theory of the synchronic-diachronic, which can be used in a variety of contexts to endow structural-functional studies with the dynamic dimensions of change. On the other hand, I analyze the axiomatic justification of my *modus operandi* with respect to the independence of the ideological and structural orders, and their causal relationship to each other. This second aspect is important because it forces us to examine several of the fundamental assumptions underlying social anthropology, which are either not clear or not necessary for an adequate theory of social structure and social action.

In this appendix I summarize the first three chapters of my forthcoming monograph, concentrating on the following conceptual areas: (1) the historical and analytical bases for the distinction between the ideological and structural domains, including a general discussion of the stand anthropologists have taken with regard to this fundamental aspect of the conceptualization of sociocultural phenomena; (2) the nature of custom, values, and ideology, and the definitions of these terms in order to ascertain their interrelationship and their role as conceptual entities; (3) the ontological status of sociocultural phenomena and the epistemological viewpoints that anthropologists have adopted in studying them, paying special attention to the level of conceptual integration; (4) the conception of sociocultural systems as ideological systems, and the operations that must be undertaken in passing from the ideological-ontological conceptual level to the scientific (structural)-epistemological conceptual level; (5) the logic of and reasons for operationalizing the ideological and structural orders as separate conceptual domains, but also as the bounding and limiting parameters of sociocultural systems, in which the explanation of behavior is a function of the efficacy obtaining between the two orders. These points are discussed in approximately this order, but it must be emphasized that they are not independent conceptual matters, and some of them must be discussed together. In particular, 1, 2, and 3 must be analyzed in a block, whereas the other two can be discussed with a certain degree of independence.

The Conceptual and Historical Perspective

One of the most persistent themes of anthropology since the discipline crystallized as a scientific field about 100 years ago, has been the implicit distinction between the realms of nature and culture—between man, the possessor of symbolic behavior, and the rest of the animal, vegetable, and mineral kingdoms. This concern has found its most elaborate expression in the so-called American school of anthropology, and especially in the work of Lévi-Strauss. The majority of British social anthropologists have never adopted this ontological position, although they have not escaped the influence of some of the implications of the nature-culture distinction. Such implications permeate much of the anthropological work from Morgan to Boas, to Kroeber, and to Lévi-Strauss. It seems to me that the basic ontological assumption underlying this epistemological position is that the possessors of culture cannot be directly and entirely acquainted with the natural world, but must always see it through the screens of symbolic behavior. Furthermore, these screens tend increasingly to distort perception, both collectively and individually, as one moves from the physical to the cultural—from the non-organic, to the organic, and on to the superorganic or symbolic. Two points must be noted in this connection.

First, what I am saying here about the implications of the nature-culture distinction has seldom been spelled out explicitly by anthropologists, with the possible exception of Kroeber and of course Lévi-Strauss, but the conceptual implications of this position are clear in what has been achieved by American anthropology. What this anthropological tradition reflects is a philosophical position that has been prominent for the past 400 years, and that has been reinforced by the scientific advances of the past century or so (Nutini 1971b). This position holds that we are not directly acquainted with the external world and that, as percipients, we contribute something to the conceptualizing matrix. Thus anthropologists, whether they like it or not, are "Kantians without a transcendental subject," as Lévi-Strauss aptly puts it about himself (1964:19). Furthermore, it means that in talking about ourselves or about most aspects of the external world, we cannot depend solely on empirical evidence and induction, and that deduction (intuition and introspection are associated aspects) also plays a prominent role. Thus, to call something a good piece of observation and analysis—a piece of good science, if you wish—means simply that the proper proportions of these two conceptualizing activities have been achieved.

The second point is really a corollary of the first, and can best be understood in anthropological terms. The acquisition of language, or symbolic behavior, in the evolution of man must be interpreted primarily as a requirement for social communal living, which means most significantly that consensus about what the group experiences, as a collection of individuals, be uniform so that serious discrepancies affecting the life of the group cannot arise. Looked at from this epistemological viewpoint, the acquisition of language brings with it the considerable disadvantage that consensus about what the world really is can be achieved only at the societal level. Otherwise, communication among individuals is impossible; hence no culture is possible. In other words, it is only as individuals, and therefore subjectively, that we can experience what the world really is, for as we begin to communicate with other individuals we are immediately drawn into the symbolic screens that give meaning to and interpret the world collectively.[1] There is no question, of course, that societal, collective perception embodies a high common denominator of individual perceptions. Nevertheless, collective perception is something more than this common individual perceptive denominator, and it is precisely this "something more" that constitutes the screen that gives meaning to what anthropologists call cultures and societies. Furthermore, the degree of individual consensus and collective or societal consensus is not the same at all levels in the external world. Rather, it increases as we descend the ontological scale from the superorganic, to the organic to the nonorganic; or, as Kroeber would say, as we move from the study of epiphenomena to phenomena and their intermediate stages. It is evident that the explanatory and predictive success of the various sciences is directly proportional to the position of their subject matter in this scale, that is, as we move from the study of physics, to chemistry, to biology, to zoology, and finally to the so-called social sciences. The complexity of the phenomena at hand, however, need not be the necessary condition for a given degree of scientific success in their conceptualization, but most philosophers of science would agree that it is a very important consideration.

The whole point of this discussion, in summary, is that around the individual and the collective, and how they perceive and conceptualize the external world, revolve the understanding and solution of most of the fundamental problems of our science, and of science in general. The problem at hand can be seen in terms of two intersecting axes: on the one hand, the collective-individual axis involving primarily ontological properties; on the other, the percipient-perceived axis entailing primarily epistemological properties. This problem has never been properly analyzed, for we have been content to postulate broad concepts which have not been carefully axiomatized, even though some of the most prominent American anthropologists of this century have occasionally addressed themselves to the systematic analysis of the ontological and epistemological dimensions underlying the science of anthropology. His concern for these problems, and not necessarily the substantive contributions he has made to the discipline, is what makes the work of Lévi-Strauss important at this point in the development of anthropology as a science. The British social anthropologists, on the other hand, have remained staunchly empirical, more so than their American colleagues, and on the whole they have declined to leave the narrow course pioneered for them by Radcliffe-Brown and Malinowski. This is paradoxical indeed, for as the contemporary heirs in anthropology of the French sociological school, they should have been more receptive to the so-called rationalistic elements in the position of Durkheim and his followers. Let me say in fairness, though, that this also applies to many post–World War II American anthropologists, for whom behavior is an ultimate empirical constituent. When this is combined with a kind of naive materialism, the results are not very promising. The best example of this position is the work of Marvin Harris (1964), in which the ultimate constituents of the sociocultural universe are entities that can be determined and measured, and that can form into efficacious systems by themselves. This position means no more than a return to a kind of nineteenth-century positivism.

The Concept of Values and the Interdigitation of Custom and Ideology

Since the beginning of the discipline, anthropologists have been aware of the concepts of custom, values, and ideology. An attentive reading of the anthropological literature shows that most of the prominent anthropologists who have advanced the discipline conceptually have taken a stand on the role of these concepts in the practice of anthropology, and in one way or another have come to grips with their implications. Furthermore, at least the concepts of custom and values have been assigned a kind of efficacy or causal action, in the sense that they have been thought to regulate sociocultural behavior in one way or another or to set the parameters within which sociocultural behavior takes place—conditioned, of course, by the discoverable constraints regulating the relationship between man (culture) and his environment (nature). Anthropology has not used the concept of ideology in any important or encompassing fashion to refer to basic regulatory processes; rather, it has been implicitly assumed to be part of the realm of values, and the terms have generally been used synonymously. In other words, anthropology has postulated the concepts of custom and values as all-encompassing, constant efficacious entities that not only regulate behavior but also give unitary meaning to sociocultural systems. These two constants, for the majority of anthropologists, are given primitives. Some anthropologists have gone so far as to define anthropology as the science of custom, evidencing a significant lack of conceptual interest. The most sophisticated anthropologists, on the other hand, have tried to elucidate the nature of these two concepts, but usually by defining and explaining their roles as the regulators of behavior. There has been no study of how custom and values originate and are shaped as efficacious domains, let alone any elucidation of the mechanisms that hold and constrain these two domains in the actual conduct of social life.

Nevertheless, despite the anthropologists' lack of interest in the relationship between custom and values and the conduct of sociocultural life, they have given us a fairly clear idea of how they view these concepts vis-à-vis organized culture and structured social life. Let us first take the concept of values. To the best of my knowledge, no anthropologist from Morgan to the present has specifically defined and systematically analyzed this concept as a cultural societal phenomenon. Some anthropologists have talked about the nature of values as being predicated in the interrelationship between man's reaction to and interaction with his natural environment, but they have never discussed and formulated a theory of values—an anthropological ethical system, if you wish—that is comparable to any of the ethical systems known to philosophy.[2] Rather, anthropologists who have concerned themselves with values have done little more than echo a kind of common-sense view, which has a philosophical aspect to be sure, as to the place of ethical norms and rules of conduct in specific cultural domains, or to indicate the organizational aspects of values within total systems. In other words, the anthropological work on values has been eminently descriptive, but directly or indirectly, explicitly or implicitly, the anthropological literature reveals two main positions with regard to values.

First, there are those anthropologists who regard values as mainly outside the physical, material, and social framework of culture and society. For them, values constitute an independent domain, which is best thought of as a body of ethical norms and cultural rules, which underlie social structure and the organization of material culture, but cannot be predicated as conversely reflecting causal efficacy. In this view, the domain of value underlies and in one way or another regulates the sociocultural domain per se. But while values are indeed a part of culture and society, they are primitive constructs which cannot be explained as reflecting a causal efficacy in the opposite direction—that is, that in some sense values in turn reflect the global sociocultural framework. This appears to be the position of most anthropologists who call themselves "cultural anthropologists," that is, the great majority of American anthropologists for whom culture is a global concept that subsumes the physical and material as well as the social. While in many ways most cultural anthropologists have regarded the concept of values as being outside the province of their empirical inquiries, a few, by the very nature of their manner of looking at the concept, have specifically tried to deal with it, and have even made it the cornerstone of their anthropological theory and practice. This is the case with such anthropologists as Kroeber (1952), Benedict (1946), Opler (1945), and a few others who have written during the past fifty years or so. They all share a concern with general sociocultural characteristics—patterns for Kroeber and Benedict, themes for Opler—that underlie the organization and the social process of cultural phenomena. These characteristics are supracultural, in the sense that somehow they are ultimate givens, not necessarily part of the sociocultural stuff of life, which seems to represent a rather extreme case of reification. Nevertheless, many cultural anthropologists share this position implicitly, and in many ways it is a sound position. It is clear that whether these general characteristics are called patterns, themes, or any other such term, they are intended values which are the most primitive constituents of the constructs of culture and society. The trouble with this position is that it seems to be implicitly postulated to get rid of values as an important component in the conceptualization of phenomena. In essesse, then, cultural anthropologists tell us very little about values, except for rightly placing them outside the realm of organized cultural and social life.

Second, there are those anthropologists who deny the ontological, independent existence of values outside the domain of organized social and cultural life, or in a more restricted sense, outside the domain of the social structure in its broadest definition. This position is almost universal among British social anthropologists, and in general among those who call themselves "social anthropologists," for whom there is a rather sharp distinction between culture and society. These anthropologists maintain that values are no more than a kind of residual aspect of the interplay of organized cultural life and the structure that gives form to social systems in the context of particular environments. For them, values conceived as normative, regulatory dimensions of sociocultural life have no place in the theory and practice of anthropology, for in whatever way one may wish to define and handle the concept, it must be ultimately interpreted and understood in terms of actual social and cultural processes and actions in operation. Social anthropologists believe that if one can pinpoint a certain sociocultural value, that value is little more than the formalization by custom of a certain process, interaction, action, or reaction of social and cultural mechanisms in operation. It is, then, in the interrelationship or interaction between man's organized social life (the social structure) and organized cultural environment (culture at large) that certain values are formed, and one need not postulate an independent realm of values. While cultural anthropologists reify the domain of values (and global culture in a sense), social anthropologists reify society as by itself producing normative rules and regulatory mechanisms.

The Concept of Custom and Anthropological Theory

I have said that the concept of custom has been regarded by anthropologists in general as almost synonymous with values, or at least as part of the same conceptual domain. This is not the whole picture, however. Anthropologists have been much more explicit about custom than they have been about values. In analyzing this problem one must take into consideration both the ontological and epistemological aspects of the concept of custom, with reference to its individual and collective components. In the case of values, it is evident that as one of the limiting parameters of organized cultural life and the social structure, this conceptual category is almost exclusively an ontological category. The concept of custom, on the other hand, is more than that. It embodies some significant epistemological properties, in that it plays a role in structuring our perceptions of sociocultural phenomena in a variety of ways. I can put matters in perspective by saying that custom is a direct causal entailment of values—the objective representation of causal efficacy which directly affects the discharge of organized cultural life and the social structure. It is in this efficacious dimension that the concept of custom goes beyond ontology and acquires its epistemological dimensions, to the effect that it may be interpreted either as the objectivization of moral imperatives and jural rules themselves, or as the subjectivization of the actual conduct and operations of organized cultural life and the social structure, according to one's perceptual viewpoint. The conceptual screens through which we view the sociocultural domain will be different, of course, depending upon which position is adopted.

The concept of custom is in many ways at the heart of anthropological theory, and it has played a sizable role in modeling the relationship of conceptual constructs to empirical data. The concept of custom is one of the most universal categories with which anthropologists have concerned themselves, but while it has been more systematically analyzed than values per se, it remains in most contexts a vague construct that either is implicitly assumed as a constant in the description and analysis of sociocultural phenomena, or acquires a more definite and systematic dimension when it is used to differentiate empirical sociocultural facts from conceptual schemes (paradigms, models). In most cases, the concept of custom has been left deliberately vague for the simple reason that it does not need to be refined or operationalized, given the loose and unsystematic constructs that are often the product of the anthropologist's toil. I have in mind here the generalizing work of classical anthropological theory à la Kroeber or the work of most of our nineteenth-century forefathers. When anthropologists are concerned with conceptual categories, however, their work invariably leads to the refinement, and to some extent the operationalization, of the concept of custom. This is the case with contemporary anthropologists concerned with holistic description and analysis, such as the functionalists, or with those concerned with the application of formal methods to anthropological studies, who are trying to some extent to axiomatize some of our fundamental concepts.[3] The situation is more complicated and varied than this mere sketch of these two positions would suggest, but for my purposes here, it is sufficient to indicate the extent to which anthropologists rely implicitly on custom as a concept giving a certain primitive form to, and sometimes even structurally preconditioning the handling of, sociocultural data. However, the concept of custom by its very nature forces anthropologists to assume that all sociocultural systems involve moral imperatives or jural rules, and that these are discoverable no matter how implicit or disguised they may be. As a corollary, it follows that the norms and imperatives of sociocultural systems are bound to be broken, given the fact that inasmuch as sociocultural systems are predicated on the controlled relationship of man to his natural environment they are always contingent. Looked at from this standpoint, the concept of custom plays a central role in all the sciences dealing with human behavior (although it may sometimes be camouflaged and far removed from the explicit formulation I have given it here), not only in setting the parameters of social and cultural life but more important, in dichotomizing behavior in terms of ideal and actual behavior, the *what is* and *what should be*.

I have discussed the concept of custom elsewhere (Nutini 1965b). Focusing the problem of custom on the ethnographer-ethnologist distinction, I came to the conclusion that the concept does not have much heuristic and theoretical value at either the experimental or observational level, and that anthropologists who work with structural problems would be well advised to ignore it in its present form (see Leach 1961b). The concept of custom, as it stands, may be useful in delineating the permissible parameters of conceptualization of broad social theorizing characteristic of most anthropological approaches, but any approach that purports to achieve what are called concepts by postulation, or anything approaching the degree of axiomatization entailed by this endeavor, cannot use such an imprecise and basically amorphous concept. Thus, we must use another concept or construct standing for much of what values and custom do. In my opinion, this is the concept of ideology, which denotes and connotes roughly the same referents as custom and values, namely, a body of moral imperatives or jural rules— what should be—in the conduct of social and cultural life. Fundamentally, these referents are the ontological and epistemological separation, for analytical purposes, of the domains of "what is" and "what ought to be" in dealing with sociocultural phenomena.[4]

The Definition of Ideology and Its Epistemological and Ontological Components

The term ideology is by no means a precise one, and it is used in at least three different senses. First, it is virtually synonymous with ethical behavior or ethical norms; or as philosophers are fond of saying, there is a transcendental distinction between what is and what ought to be, which they construe into the distinction between epistemology and ethics. The implicit assumption here seems to be that while what ought to be is always an immediate result of or is directly based on what is, human beings living in society must of necessity formulate perceptual codes in order to communicate successfully and lead an orderly life; in other words, unless there are implicit moral codes governing individual behavior, neither culture nor society is possible. From this viewpoint, all sociocultural systems are ideological systems in the sense that what ought to be gives unitary meaning to the individuals composing the system, thereby permitting communication, and at the same time it assigns values to the system's physical components. As social beings we cannot be primitively acquainted with what the sociocultural universe "really is," and we must necessarily view it through the ideological screen of what ought to be. Only as individuals can we perceive the sociocultural universe as it is. The existence of sociocultural systems must therefore be predicted on the notion that consensus about what the world really is can only be achieved by arbitrarily establishing what it ought to be. This notion of our lack of real acquaintance with the "external world" of social relations, or rather the realization that we view the world through "coded screens," is one of the central ideas of structuralism, and one that pervades its conception of the relationship between nature and culture. As I have already pointed out, in recognizing the characterization of structuralism as "Kantianism without a transcendental subject," Lévi-Strauss clearly asserts that his endeavor is not in any sense idealistic (1964:19).

The second use of the term ideology is largely a corollary of the first. Although this use is underlain by the what is–what ought to be distinction, the concept here must be interpreted primarily as an ethical-moral imperative to action. The concept of ideology in this sense is not directly concerned with the epistemology-ethics distinction, but rather with changing a context, a sociocultural system, or perhaps the entire fabric of human society on the basis of a specific what-ought-to-be construct. Let us note, however, that although this use of the term is the most common, it is at the same time the most imprecise. More often than not, what is denoted by the concept from the epistemological point of view is consciously relegated to the background, given the fact that the accent is on the practical and not on determining how what ought to be is anchored in the relevant contextual what is. But it must be indicated that sometimes this use of the term may indicate conceptually both a clearly laid out ethical-moral code, and its practical implications. This does not mean, of course, that the followers of an ideological creed are aware of the what is–what ought to be distinction in the pursuit of its practical implications. Thus, while the ethical–moral conception of ideology is primarily philosophical and concerned with the exigencies of societal living, the practical-dynamic conception is primarily pragmatic and concerned with strategies of how a context can best be changed, given a certain end in view. That is, theories of culture, insofar as they limit themselves to global societies, are ethical–moral ideological constructs that make it possible to conceptualize the primitive ensemble of individuals in orderly systems. Capitalism, communism, humanism, and other similar ideologies, on the other hand, are practical dynamic ideological constructs at a subcultural level, which purport to transform a part of the societal structure, or to reorganize some aspects of the total societal structure, according to some ethical–moral construct that may not always be clearly postulated.

The third use of the term ideology may be characterized as scientific-epistemological. Here again the conceptual meaning of ideology is underlain by the what is–what ought to be distinction, but I call it scientific-epistemological because the emphasis is entirely upon verification and bridging the gap between nature as individually perceived and nature as socially perceived. This is primarily an epistemological and not an ethical question, and the concept of ideology in this sense may be properly termed scientific ideology. (By contrast, the ethical–moral conception of ideology involves primarily ontological considerations.) One of the persistent themes in Western philosophy throughout more than 2,500 years has been the unreliability of the senses in experiencing the external world, a theme that runs deeply even through so-called empiricist philosophies. Furthermore, non-Western philosophies, and the information that can be culled from the ethnography of nonliterate peoples, also point in the same direction. This unreliability of sensible experience is what I mean by saying that we cannot become directly acquainted with natural phenomena. Furthermore, as one moves from the realm of the nonorganic to the organic and on to the superorganic, the screens through which we view natural phenomena become increasingly complicated and verification more difficult to attain. In this meaning of the term, ideology is opposed to science in the sense that science represents the realm of what is (or of what can be verified, verification being operationally defined so as to indicate the extent to which it bridges the gaps between sensible experience and rational experience), and ideology the realm of what ought to be. From this viewpoint, then, every theory, physical or social, is basically an ideological construct until it is properly verified. It goes without saying that verification is impossible at the level of sensible experience, for an operation at such a level would simply constitute consensus primarily about what ought to be. Verification is a rational operation that can take place only at a postulated supraempirical level. Otherwise, a true science is not possible, and any endeavor using the name will remain largely ideology or perhaps more accurately, an unrealized scientific ideology at the intuitional level of concept formation. It should also be obvious that the science-ideology dichotomy obtains only in the metalanguage (supraempirical level); at the level of sensible experience, science is just another ideology, developed within the confines of a given culture, namely, that amorphous entity we refer to as Western culture.[5]

Let us note that there can be other conceptual usages of the term ideology, but they are always corollaries of either the first (ethical-moral) or third (scientific-epistemological) usages. Furthermore, any well-established and comprehensive ideological system, or even ideological viewpoint, can be a compound ideological construct in that it can involve any two, or sometimes all three, of the analytical usages of the term described above. For example, humanism involves a well thought out ethical-moral conception of what society should be, and at the same time it is a practical-dynamic endeavor, or at least it involves pragmatic considerations as guides to action. Marxism is a practical-dynamic program for political and social reform, and at the same time it is a fairly well thought out scientific-epistemological theory of culture and society. It should be clear that I am not discussing ideology from the actor's viewpoint and the philosophical implications that its different usages imply, but rather from the universal viewpoint that, given the nature of man as a superorganic entity, we cannot at particular levels of conceptualization escape the what is–what ought to be distinction. To transcend ideology, we must raise ourselves to higher analytical levels, in the same manner as, in a logical context, it is impossible to solve semantic paradoxes (e.g., "All Cretans are liars; I am a Cretan") without the notion of a metalanguage; that is, any statement about any object language must be made in its metalanguage. The theory of levels of language is a consequence of Russell's theory of types (Reichenbach 1946:39), and I believe that it applies equally to the epistemological context of finding the appropriate levels of analysis at which the what is–what ought to be distinction does not obtain. The only analytical level at which this takes place is the theoretical level of contemporary science, which involves both an object language (organization of empirical facts) and metalanguage (theory construction and verification). No "scientific ideology" that persists in reaching consensus about what is at the strictly empirical level can attain the status of science. (By "reaching consensus about what is" I mean the verification of a theoretical construct.) Sensible experience is a true datum for individuals, but it is not consensually true at the societal level.

The Passage from Ideology to Science: The Anthropologist's Dilemma

In the preceding section I discussed the main terminological usages of the concept of ideology, and at the same time delineated its most important attributes, by itself and vis-à-vis the concept of science. Before I proceed, however, I would like to discuss this pair of concepts in more detail, and show how they may sometimes be confused or be in seeming opposition in the conduct of inquiry.

Anthropology is ostensibly a scientific discipline, and I must therefore determine how the confusion of science with ideology can arise in the conduct of anthropological inquiry, and how this affects its results. I established that sociocultural systems are ideological systems, and I think that few anthropologists would disagree with this statement. In short, cultures or societies determine what life should be by presenting man with carefully worked out ethical imperatives. Cultural relativists express this proposition by saying that sociocultural systems must be judged and understood in their own terms, and not by universal ethical standards. Thus, while ethical imperatives—or rather, sociocultural imperatives—are firmly based in actual properties of the external world, they cannot be justified with reference to cultural facts alone. They are neither true nor false beyond the confines of the system that produced them, and only in these systems can they be efficacious, that is, in contexts in which terms as ought, should, right, good, duty, beautiful, can have specific meaning.

It can be argued that since sociocultural systems are ideological systems, they cannot really be studied scientifically. This does not follow, for anything can be subjected to scientific inquiry so long as the study complies with certain standards of objectivity, and the ends are clearly stated. One must agree with cultural relativists that it is quite proper to study cultures or societies scientifically so long as we confine ourselves to establishing how they are organized, and to giving general accounts of how they funtion. But anthropologists not only describe and try to explain particular cultures and societies, they also try to determine what cultures and societies throughout the world have in common, and try to arrive at generalizations. In this fashion, the cultural diversity disclosed by ethnography leads us to the concept of cultural relativity, but at the same time, the common cultural denominator apparent in sociocultural systems throughout the world compels us to search for categories with universal characteristics in order to account for the similarities. Implicit, I think, in the outlook of most anthropologists is the idea that cultural universals are only broad, formal categories, whose content and expression vary so much from society to society that it is impossible to arrive at sufficiently objective criteria to permit the formulation of these universals in meaningful general statements. For example, anthropologists talk about kinship and the family as universals of culture, in much the same terms as, say, duty, morality, or beauty, but, they add, these cultural attributes are given such diverse expression as to render meaningless any absolute standard of measurement. This kind of reasoning involves both good and bad logic: good logic insofar as it regards sociocultural systems as ideological systems; bad logic insofar as we hope to arrive at intersocietal, general constructs on the basis of ideological facts. Thus, the dilemma of anthropologists: how do we proceed to formulate scientific, value-free general statements about sociocultural phenomena, using the value-laden facts of ideological configurations?

The dilemma is resolved in two ways. While cultural relativists allege that there are broad universal categories, such as those mentioned above, they are strict pluralists insofar as they can be said to be practicing science: they study particular ideological systems and disregard the formulation of general statements. In this category are included the majority of anthropologists, including functionalists, for despite their insistence that functionalism must lead to the formulation of a comparative method, and ultimately to the formulation of social laws, they have been unable to develop truly scientific techniques of comparison. On the other hand, the minority of anthropologists who seek to transcend cultural relativism put matters into an epistemological framework and insist that anthropology as a science must assume comparative categories. They are mistaken, however, when they try to construct comparative categories out of sociocultural facts that are vitiated by belonging to ideological configurations. Cross-culturalism is perhaps the only important example of this group. Thus, via the science-ideology dichotomy we have arrived at the fundamental problem: how do we construct truly scientific concepts of inquiry?

It can be seen, then, that both solutions to the anthropologist's dilemma are inadequate, for both the pluralist functionalist and the monistic cross-culturalist sell the science of anthropology equally short. The former does so by engaging solely in a descriptive metalanguage of ideological configurations, the latter by trying to formulate explanations exclusively on the basis of ideological sociocultural facts. To regard sociocultural systems as ideological systems, and to engage in the scientific activity of formulating general statements about the nature of sociocultural phenomena, are two quite different things. The scientific assumption that there are intercultural, comparable categories cannot be verified at the level of ideological facts, but such facts are the primitive data of all sociocultural inquiry, and we must always begin by their metascientific study. Furthermore, since it is inevitable that scientific facts, or what is, will always be colored to some degree by ideology (or more properly, will be colored by the sociocultural tradition of the percipient), it is of the utmost importance to devise measuring scales so that we may know the degree of subjectivity involved. From this viewpoint, the concern of anthropologists, especially during the thirties and forties, with trying to justify cultural relativism and to cope with the scientific limitations it imposes on anthropology, was both redundant and misplaced. It is redundant because ideological systems cannot be judged by a priori standards, nor is there any need to do so, unless one is bent on formulating a universal ethical code. Any well-informed ethnographer or cultural historian knows that there must be a considerable common ethical denominator, at least in the basic biological and social needs of individuals living in the context of cooperation and mutual dependence, in order to account ethically for specific acts or ends—as, for example, whether in the name of cultural relativity we should refuse to condemn the genocide of the Jews by Nazi Germany. It is misplaced because the broad, amorphous cultural universals that anthropologists are willing to admit have little scientific value, and more important, because cultural universals cannot be formulated with the facts of metascientific constructions.[6]

I have talked about the science-ideology dichotomy in terms of the ethical and epistemological components and implications of both. I would like now to put aside ideology per se and concentrate on science. The fundamental question here is: what facts, or configurations of facts, yield truly scientific constructs, or what are the proper ontological referents of the scientific method? I have already answered the question both negatively, by arguing that we must discard ideological facts per se or specific sociocultural configurations, and positively, by arguing that scientific facts are really value-free facts, or what is. The next important questions are: where do value-free social facts come from, and how can we determine the epistemological level that makes possible the conceptualization of such categories in order to pass from particular to general systems? I think the answer can be found by distinguishing, as Chomsky does for linguistic phenomena, between the deep and the surface structure of sociocultural phenomena.[7] Value-free facts, what is, or epistemological entities as the material for truly scientific constructs, can emerge only from the deep structural level of phenomena. The distinction is vaguely envisaged by empiricist anthropology as the distinction between ethnography and ethnology; it comes close to the epistemological crux of the matter, and its consequences are more clearly envisaged in the distinction made by ethnoscience between emics and etics. But it appears that Lévi-Strauss is the first major anthropologist to have made the distinction between the deep structure and the surface structure of phenomena by committing himself to a supraempirical theory of social structure, that is, to the bifurcation of the sociocultural universe into the empirical reality of ideological configurations and the analytical constructs built after them. If the distinction is not made, we are doomed to a metascience of culture and society which can amount to little more than the generalization of common sense. The interdependence of the value-laden facts of ideology and the value-free facts of science is apparent, and it is beside the point to argue that those who make the distinction between deep structure and surface structure are antiempirical or rationalistic merely because they want to go beyond the confines of sensible social experience in formulating analytical constructs.

The Bifurcation of Nature: The Justification for Distinguishing between Deep and Surface Structure

I must justify the adequacy of the distinction between deep structure and surface structure within the context of modern science, in order to show why science and ideology constitute different systems of knowledge with their corresponding conceptual domains. It could be argued that the distinction between science and ideology cannot really be justified, for it is evident that what we call science is part of, or was developed within the confines of, Western culture and is ultimately the product of Western ideology. This is true, but it says no more than I have already conceded, namely, that granting the contingency of all empirical phenomena, physical and sociocultural, science begins with ideology and is grounded in it as a source of primitive data. Granting, then, that ultimately (philosophically?) science is ideologically based, since it is the product of culture, is there a point at which certain ideological conceptual activity becomes what in the modern world is called "science"? Let us point out that objectivity, exactness, public verifiability, and the several other requirements associated with science are not enough to determine the fundamental characteristic that sets it apart as dealing in value-free facts. Its fundamental characteristic is that science is supraempirical; that is, although firmly based in empirical phenomena (as the initial point of departure and final point of verifiability) it transcends them by postulating a higher level of analysis underlying sensible experience, a level at which, and only at which, truly universal constructs are possible. Science begins with common sense, that is, with what should be, for even the simplest perceptual operations are culturally determined, but its ultimate aims are realized only on the basis of culture-free facts.

From this viewpoint, science began when Galileo and Newton bifurcated nature into the "immediately sensed" and the "postulated but not sensed," or nature as immediately given in sensible experience and nature as conceived according to the postulates and principles of physics (see Northrop 1945; Nutini 1970). Whatever was characterized as "science" before Galileo and Newton (and much that was so characterized after them, even to the present day) was not science in the strict sense of the term, but rather metascience, for want of a better term, for it worked largely with the materials of sensible experience and did not involve the bifurcation of nature. This may be a restricting conception of science, but I think it is a necessary one, for without it the great triumphs of twentieth-century physical science are not intelligible (see Nutini 1971a; Whitehead 1922:53-71). We now know that it is inconceivable for a physical scientist to work with the facts delivered by sense perception in order to arrive at laws or theories, and it was the genius of Galileo and Newton to have realized this, and to have made it possible to combine deductive (mathematical) and inductive (empirical) elements in a single analytical framework in the conceptualization of the world around us. (This is what Galileo called the "idealization" of the problem.) Since we must inevitably assume the methodological and theoretical unity of science, it follows that the bifurcation of nature must also take place at the sociocultural level. I think that this assumption is logically more parsimonious and pragmatically more productive than assigning a nebulous ideological status to the sociocultural domain of inquiry on the grounds that the nature of man precludes studying him in the same fashion as the rest of nature.[8]

These views on the bifurcation of nature must, however, be qualified in two ways. First, the logical and epistemological consequences of the distinction made by Galileo and later by Newton between sensible experience and scientific experience were not fully manifested until the late nineteenth century, but they resulted in the scientific miracle of the twentieth century. The period between the time of Galileo and the late nineteenth century must be characterized as one of gestation. During these centuries, physical science made many false starts, achieved limited successes, and gained a considerable insight into the nature of physical process, until it reached the takeoff point represented by the great work of Planck, Einstein, Bohr, and a few others. The disciplines dealing with the study of man may not require as long a gestation period, but they will need considerable time to achieve a takeoff point. Second, the bifurcation of nature must not be construed into a rigid analytical *modus operandi*, for even in pre-Galilean science it is possible to detect a tendency toward bifurcation. This must be interpreted, however, to mean simply that in any conceptual activity or generalization, it is inevitable that in one way or another we must go beyond sensible experience. Only when sensible experience is categorically transcended, that is, when a scientific domain is established with its own rules of discourse independent of mere common sense, can we say that the bifurcation of nature has taken place. In anthropology, for example, the distinction between the particularity of ethnography and the generality of ethnology does not point to the bifurcation of the sociocultural universe, nor does the emic-etic distinction of ethnoscience. But Lévi-Strauss's supraempirical conception of social structure, on the other hand, and most certainly Chomsky's distinction between the surface structure and deep structure of linguistic phenomena, do indeed envisage the bifurcation of sociocultural phenomena. This is only the beginning, of course, but for this very reason the work of these scholars is important to the formulation of true sociocultural bifurcation.

A last point must be carefully stressed. Since science always begins with common sense, that is, with ideology, it is important to distinguish between the epistemological properties of science and ideology. Thus, it is an ideological matter whether, say, the conceptualization of social anthropological phenomena may be "best" (and this "best" must be interpreted with a clear end in view) achieved by the employment of exclusively traditional anthropological methods or by the grammatico-structuralist method implicitly assumed in this study. It becomes a scientific matter only when appropriate verification procedures have been, if not devised, at least envisaged in order to test the adequacy or inadequacy of the methods. In the metalanguage, then, the traditional empiricist method and the grammatico-structuralist method, like contending scientific hypotheses, can be proved true or false only by adequate verification. Of course, it all depends on the anthropologist's ends, for those who conceive of it as a kind of specialized history, or aim simply at very broad, ultimately unverifiable statements about the activities of man, are well within their rights. But then, as Lévi-Strauss has demonstrated in discussing the relativity of history (1966:251-263), anthropology falls almost entirely within the realm of ideology.

Let me give a concrete example to clarify how ideology, outside its primarily ontological context, can constitute an impediment to the proper conduct of scientific inquiry. The fundamental notion of Lévi-Strauss's structuralism is the opposition between nature and culture which is mediated by the structure of the human brain. The nature-culture opposition plays a very important role in Lévi-Strauss's conceptual system, not only as an ontological property of sensible sociocultural experience, but also as an epistemological device in the analysis of that experience. What does the nature-culture opposition mean in the light of our two main usages of the concept of ideology (ethical-moral, scientific-epistemological)? On the one hand, as an ethical-moral conceptual tool the nature-culture opposition not only implies a clear distinction between what is (nature) and what ought to be (culture), but at the same time it implies the fundamental notion that at the level of sensible experience, we cannot possibly bridge the gap between these two ontological levels—hence Lévi-Strauss's insistence that cultures are coded screens that enable men to organize the facts of nature, as a projector is needed to make sense out of a filmstrip. This is of course a sound view of the interplay between man and his natural environment, and an ontological view with a long tradition in Western philosophy. On the other hand, the nature-culture opposition as a scientific-epistemological conceptual tool asserts that to achieve *true* consensus regarding sensible experience, that is, universal agreement irrespective of individual social perception, we must postulate a metalevel of analysis. It asserts, in short, that epistemological consensus can only be arrived at by transcending both individual sensible experience (nature) and social sensible experience (culture).

We can see that the ontological (primarily ideological) and the epistemological (primarily scientific) implications of the nature-culture opposition in Lévi-Strauss's system do not really conflict, and that they are in a sense complementary. But what, then, constitutes the dichotomy of structuralism with respect to ontology and epistemology, that is, with respect to sociocultural phenomena and method? Lévi-Strauss knows that science is primarily method, and that this basically epistemological activity cannot possibly succeed at the ontological level of sensible social experience. Why, then, does he seem to persist in searching for epistemological constructs at the level of sociocultural facts, much as his empiricist counterparts do, when he knows that this is impossible? Thus, the paradox of structuralism: Lévi-Strauss is clearly aware of what constitutes good science and yet he seems unable to practice it, or at least to carry its implications to their logical conclusions. All anthropologists should know that no contextual situation ever involves constructs based strictly on what is or on what ought to be, for these are limiting parameters, so I am simply saying that Lévi-Strauss has chosen to practice what his ideology dictates to him rather than what he knows science to be.

The Conceptual Foundation of the Distinction between the Ideological and Structural Orders

I am now in a position to delineate the ideological and structural domains or conceptual orders. In the preceding paragraphs I attempted to give the concept of ideology the broadest possible basis, to determine what the concept means by itself, and to ascertain its relationship to germane or nearly synonymous concepts such as values and custom.

Before delimiting the ideological and structural domains and making them into efficacious parameters of conceptualization, however, it is necessary to qualify the "philosophy" of anthropology as a science that I have implied here. The conceptual distance between what anthropology should be as a scientific discipline and what anthropologists are actually able to do at the present is great, and I do not want to be charged with meaningless speculation because of this conceptual gap.

In the study of the sociocultural universe one must always start with the axiom that there is a transcendental difference, arising out of the very nature of societal living, between what is and what should be, which always permeates the perceptions, actions, and products of individuals living in a collectivity. I conceptualize this basic and most general constraint and attribute of man, the social entity, as the distinction between nature and culture in an ontological context; as the distinction between science and ideology from an epistemological viewpoint; as the distinction between ideal and actual behavior from a theoretical viewpoint in the conduct of anthropological inquiry; and as the assertion that all sociocultural systems have rules but that these rules are broken from a methodological viewpoint. In other words, we move from the basic constituents of the sociocultural universe to the way in which we perceive that universe as individuals and as members of collective groups, to the way in which we conceptualize it as members of that "ideologically defined" group we call scientists. As to the method of study itself, I concluded that to avoid "ideologicalization," the scientific method of approaching sociocultural phenomena must be conceived as a series of ascending metalanguages. Viewing sociocultural phenomena and their conceptualization unidimensionally plunges us immediately into contradictions, and prevents that transcending of the ideological domain that is the ultimate goal of science.

In a still different way, separation of the ideological and structural domains as conceptual, limiting parameters has no other objective than to achieve the eventual formulation of concepts by postulation in anthropology. It is my contention that once anthropology is defined as a scientific discipline, we are committed to the ultimate bifurcation of the sociocultural universe. To be sure, this cannot be achieved immediately. Fortunately, there are indications that a substantial segment of the anthropological community is consistently searching for the appropriate methods and techniques. There have already been some significant results; and although it is still inconclusive, the work of certain ethnoscientists, structuralists, mathematical anthropologists, and formalists in general, is a step in the right direction. It seems to me, however, that these new approaches, in their impatience for immediate results, have emphasized methodology and technique at the expense of theory construction and the delineation of the foundations of a philosophy of anthropology as a science. This could be detrimental in the long run. No matter how laudable we may think the endeavor of, say, the ethnoscientist in trying to achieve interscientific reliability at the level of observation, or the mathematical anthropologist seeking explanatory formalizations, they may not be concentrating on the correct domains, they may confuse levels of analysis, or they may apply tools of analysis that are not the best for a particular level or pay insufficient attention to complementary conceptual tools. Thus, at the moment, anthropologists should concentrate on delineating what theory construction consists of in anthropology, and on comprehending both its epistemological foundations and the ontological materials with which we work.

What I have said here may be interpreted primarily as a rather loose and tentative formulation of some of the parameters that must guide the conduct of anthropological inquiry within a certain narrowly defined context, namely, the ontological-epistemological parameters that limit the interaction of what we have defined as ideology and structure. I have, in fact, said what anthropology *must do* to achieve certain ends, namely, formulate true concepts by postulation, or elaborate theoretical terms. In view of my own conception of science and ideology, this statement remains an ideological construct until it is adequately verified, or perhaps, more modestly, proven either adequate or inadequate. My next task, then, is to determine how much of this what ought to be is translatable into what is in this particular conceptual domain. In other words, I want to verify my theory in some way, and if I can operationalize at least its main tenets, I will have succeeded in part. At this level of conceptualization, then, I am conceiving operationalization as an adequate procedure leading toward verification. Here, I am primarily concerned with operationalization, while the study as a whole may be interpreted as a test of my *modus operandi* in comparison to other approaches to analyzing sociocultural complexes similar to the compadrazgo system. Obviously, I cannot possibly translate the whole of my theoretical scheme into its methodological applications. Rather, I can operationalize only a few of its important components, but if I can succeed with even one or two of these components, I will have accomplished my task here. What I want to do is devise a paradigmatic construct that is still essentially empirical, but that could be expanded into a modelic structure by narrowing down the complex or through complementation by other axiomatic complexes. I want also to extend the application of my theoretical stand from the compadrazgo system to a variety of social-structural situations, and indicate what results may be expected from distinguishing between the ideological and structural domains, especially in the realm of change and the articulation of the diachronic and synchronic in approaching this dynamic aspect of sociocultural systems.

The Conceptual Comparability of the Ideological and Structural Orders

The first problem that must be faced here is the intrinsic and methodological comparability and symmetry or asymmetry of the ideological and structural orders. The structural domain is well established analytically and has been perhaps the main conceptual apparatus shaping sociocultural studies since anthropology emerged from its data-gathering ethnographic stage around the turn of the century, and entered its classificatory stage (Nutini 1968a). It is true that there are several conceptions of what constitutes the structural domain, and these are known by various names: social structure, social organization, the organizational framework of society, the jural rules and statistical norms governing organized behavior, and so on. There are some significant conceptual and methodological differences among anthropologists who employ one or another of these terms (or perhaps others) in the actual practice of anthropology, depending on their particular epistemological and ontological positions. Thus, at one extreme, British social anthropologists conceive of social structure as the total ensemble of social relations in a given system, ordered and efficaciously arranged in terms of components having specific functional attributes. At the other extreme, Lévi-Straussian structuralists maintain that social structure, at least ideally, cannot be found or conceptualized at the level of the observational facts, but rather that it is the embodiment of social relations at a higher conceptual level. Between these two extreme empirical and supraempirical positions are several intermediate positions of varying degrees of importance, but all of them have a high common denominator with regard to the nature of the constituent elements and the degree of abstraction that goes into formulating social-structural entities. Thus, in operationalizing the structural domain I can address myself to the common denominator, for at this stage I cannot account for the distinctions involved in the various positions. Furthermore, I do not deal directly with the operationalization of the structural domain beyond delineating its most important properties. My aim, in fact, is the tentative and broad operationalization of the ideological but not the structural domain, and I have two reasons for this stand.

First, anthropologists already know how to handle many aspects of the structural domain successfully, regardless of what theoretical position we may take, and many specific principles, elements, or concepts could be operationalized with considerable success. For example, we could give an operational definition of such social units as the nuclear family or the lineage, and such concepts as descent or residence, which would come to replace present nominal definitions with significant improvement, especially in comparative or cross-cultural studies. Second, and by contrast, anthropologists know almost nothing about whether the ideological domain is indeed a genuine and not a spurious conceptual domain, about how its components are organized, and about the operating principles that give it form and govern its efficacious relationship to the structural domain. It behooves us, then, to concentrate on it almost entirely to the exclusion of the other, passive member of the efficacious relationship between the two. By passive I mean that the ideological domain is efficacious over the structural, at least within the context of my operationalization. In a diachronic context, however, the relationship of efficacy may become symmetrical, and this is one of the problems that must be investigated. In the following analysis I want to concentrate on the ideological domain so as to make it comparable to the structural, both in the organization of constituent elements and in the elucidation of operational principles, and my primary focus of analysis is the delineation and possible taxonomy of the relationship of efficacy between the two.

The Substantive Configuration of the Ideological Order

Before I can analyze the relational properties and the properties of efficacious invariance of the ideological order vis-à-vis the structural order, I must describe the substantive configuration of the former. The amplitude and organizational configuration of the ideological domain must be clearly defined in terms of substantive constituents. When anthropologists speak of values or custom, they are implicitly asserting the dichotomy between what ought to be and what is. In this sense, I am saying nothing new, for from the time of Morgan and Tylor to the present, we have been implicitly—and sometimes quite explicitly—making this empirical claim about the fundamental nature of sociocultural phenomena. When Malinowski speaks of custom, Benedict of patterns, Opler of values, they are not venturing beyond our fundamental substantive predicament. Their assertion that sociocultural systems are ultimately dichotomized in terms of imperatives and action does not say much about how the two halves of the dichotomy are efficaciously and functionally related. Few anthropologists have done more than state vaguely that, say, values mold the social structure, that patterns shape the nature of culture, or that custom is a compulsory or efficacious spring to behavior, and so on.

The majority of anthropologists, regardless of whether or not they adhere to a deterministic position on human behavior (that is, regarding whether man has free will or not), have explicitly and purposely left the relationship between the ideological and structural domains vague, on the grounds that it is not amenable to scientific investigation. Instead, they have thought to solve the problem of formulating generalizations, and sometimes even lawlike statements, by concentrating exclusively on structure and ignoring ideology, except, of course, in its pragmatical-practical aspects. This course has hampered the development of anthropological theory, and perhaps of a modicum of formalized prediction (if we make prediction and explanation logically symmetrical), which may hinge on the efficacious relationship between the ideological and structural domains. I think this is unacceptable, and even if I cannot now operationalize even a small part of the ideological domain, the present *modus operandi* is valuable. First, it emphasizes that human behavior is not the most primitive referent and data of our conceptualizations, and that it is always a relational property of the what is–what ought to be distinction. And, second, it shows the avenues of research that may lead to the measurement and formalization of the lines of efficacy between the ideological and structural domains.

As a corollary of what I have said above, it follows that the ideological domain as an absolute entity, or as a global ensemble for given sociocultural systems, cannot really be handled in a meaningful analytical manner. Perhaps it must always remain a what–ought-to-be entity giving unitary meaning to a system, and it is in this sense that anthropologists have always recognized cultures and societies as ultimately ideological systems. Thus, by confusing levels of analysis, and by rightly regarding global ideological domains as essentially unanalyzable from a meaningful scientific stand, we have thrown out the baby with the bath water. From a philosophical viewpoint, however, the study of global ideological domains of specific sociocultural systems can be useful. But even here, anthropologists have missed an opportunity to usurp one of the traditional tasks of philosophy and conceptualize general, universal ethical systems, which I think we are better equipped to formulate than philosophers. It is not my intention to talk here about the ideological domain in its philosophical dimensions. I am concerned only with isolating and delineating subideological parts that can be construed as adequate constituents of an integrated approach in terms of the ideology-structure dichotomy.

The general description and explanation of the ideological domain as an efficacious conceptual entity vis-à-vis the behavior and action of the structural domain must involve the right combination of psychological and sociocultural variables and dimensions, and as a general *modus operandi* the superorganic will eventually be conceptualized in terms of a combined psychocultural theory. I count myself among those who think that ultimately the sociocultural domain will be largely reduced to the psychological. At present, though, this cannot be done, for the reduction rules from the sociocultural to the psychological have not even begun to be envisaged operationally. To phrase our explanatory constructs in terms of psychological variables is meaningless at present, although we can, with varying degrees of success, describe sociocultural phenomena in terms of limited psychological mechanisms as effective variables of behavior. Neither social psychology nor psychological anthropology has been very successful in harnessing the individual and the collective into a single explanatory conceptual framework, even for limited domains. Both remain essentially dichotomous, without benefit to the interrelational links of the dichotomy, and such studies amount to little more than fairly simple psychology or bad sociology. Given these circumstances, I am taking the sociocultural as an independent scientific domain, and I am making the empirical claim that the dichotomy of ideology and structure is intelligible in terms of its own mechanisms and operational principles. Let me add, however, that I am aware that this is simply a makeshift *modus operandi*, for lack of adequate methods and theoretical procedures for giving the system psychological dimensions. To explain action and behavior, especially as embodied in decision-making processes—which are at the heart of the dynamics of sociocultural systems—operative psychological mechanisms are a sine qua non. From this viewpoint, Durkheim's distinction between psychology and sociology has hampered the progress of anthropological theory and practice.

It might be useful to describe the organizational configuration of the ideological domain as a functional entity in terms of the empirical and supraempirical conceptions of sociocultural phenomena, in order to ascertain which elements can be incorporated into the present approach. First, ontologically and from the broadest viewpoint, the ideological domain must be regarded as everything that falls under the category of what ought to be from a pansocietal and pancultural standpoint—the sum total of cultural rules and imperatives governing the conduct of man throughout the world—worked out in behavioristic form and seen as the instrinsic responses of man to his natural environment. This represents the external interaction and oscillation between nature and culture, which is the ultimate bounding parameter of the superorganic. The conceptualization and adequate scientific control of this broadest of domains can be compared to the formulation of a universal grammer of language as envisaged by Chomsky in his transformational generative grammar approach to linguistics. This will probably constitute a hard conceptual nut to crack in linguistics, but it will be an even harder one in anthropology. At present we cannot begin to think realistically about achieving such a goal, and I therefore leave it totally outside the discussion.

Second, at the strictest level of sociocultural systems, we may again ontologically conceive the ideological domain as the sum total of the rules, moral constraints, and imperatives to action that govern and give form to a specific sociocultural system. From a scientific viewpoint, then, at the moment it is best to leave out the global conceptualization of specific ideological domains, although such studies could be more valuable were anthropologists to undertake the philosophical task of devising universal ethical systems. I can again compare the conceptualization of global ideological domains to the formulation of the grammar of a particular language. While linguists are able to do this as a matter of course, we are not yet in the position to do the same in anthropology. Our data are intrinsically more complex, the linguist begins his conceptualization with a higher degree of phenomenal structuring, and we have not yet devised the tools and techniques for addressing ourselves to the study of sociocultural phenomena in a grammatical fashion.

Third, at present we have adequate conceptual techniques for analyzing specific ideological domains at a subglobal sociocultural level, and from this viewpoint, we can ontologically delineate them as the functionally related elements of a what-ought-to-be complex that is efficaciously related to another complex structurally and functionally bounded. With reference to the data in this monograph, I do not think that giving a general account of the value system, or general ideological configuration of Santa María Belén, would necessarily be conducive to better explanation and description. However, even the informal operationalization of the ideological domain underlying and affecting the operation of the compadrazgo system (and unquestionably other subsystems) has yielded significant results. My intention here, then, is to operationalize a carefully bounded and circumscribed system of rules in order to explain some aspects of the compadrazgo system in operation. In a different ontological context, this piecemeal approach to the grammatical conceptualization of sociocultural phenomena has been tried by several anthropologists with some degree of success (see Buchler and Nutini 1969; Buchler and Selby 1968; Werner 1970).

The Boundaries of the Ideological Order: The Empirical and Supraempirical Viewpoints

With these provisos in mind, how can I substantively define bounded, efficacious segments of the ideological domain at a level below global sociocultural systems? The answer may be put in this way: once a structural configuration of phenomena has been worked out in terms of functionally related ideal and actual behavior, representing primarily the observable, behavioristically formulated abstraction of a subsystem in operation (say, the kinship system, the religious system, and preferably smaller subsystems such as compadrazgo in Belén or the mayordomía system in the average Mesoamerican community), it is necessary to generate a deeper conceptual structure which represents the basic organizational principles and elements underlying and giving form to the observable, structural configuration, which is regarded as the surface component of the subsystem under consideration. The ideological domain, then, represents the ontological substratum which gives meaning to the operation of the structural domain empirically observed.

Explanations of sociocultural phenomena that are based solely on the structural domain, aside from simple functional causality or correlations, are inadequate, even if at this level one makes the distinction between ideal and actual behavior. This procedure leaves out the efficacious dimensions of the ideological domain, which is the level at which meaningful relations of invariances are most likely to be obtained. For practical and methodological reasons, it is at the ideological level that we can truly compare, and eventually formulate a genuinely comparative method. At the structural level we are almost by definition forced to deal with entities and particularly arranged behavioral facts that are most difficult to deal with in a relational manner, for one cannot ultimately compare sociocultural facts, but only relations and positions of invariance. Structural facts, either as referents of what people actually do or as embodiments of the constraints of what people should do, are in a Pickwickian sense unique, and they must always be viewed with reference to the system of which they are part. Thus, the actual components of, say, any given lineage system cannot be compared, much less the lineage as a whole. The component parts of the lineage system as specific structural entities, behavior patterns, and even actual physical parts, have meaning only with respect to the total organization of this social unit, and the same goes for the system itself vis-à-vis the global society of which it is a part. That we do use the concept of the lineage as a comparative and cross-cultural category simply betrays a neglect of scientific precision.

The ideological domain, on the other hand, offers a greater possibility for eliciting truly comparable and cross-cultural categories, but in the form of relational or positional properties of systems or subsystems, which is the only way to transcend the monistic predicament of the functionalists. In fact, I am asserting that within the context of this study, it is more appropriate scientifically to compare cross-culturally the ideology or ideological domain of the compadrazgo system, than the categories of actual sociocultural facts associated with it. I do not think that even the most refined, nominally defined (that is, embodying the lowest common denominator) structural attribute of compadrazgo can be used to construct a model or paradigm of this institution that will explain compadrazgo as it operates in, say, most of the Latin American ethnographic area. Furthermore, given the diachronic context of any ideological domain, it is obvious—at least in the case of the compadrazgo system—that at this level one has a much higher common denominator to start with than at the level of specific structural domains, inasmuch as the compadrazgo system in this broad ethnographic area has a common historical inception.

In brief, then, I can operationally define the ideological domain of a particular structural domain at the level below global sociocultural systems, as the conceptual task of arranging the patterns of interaction, relations of invariance, and positional properties into an integrated whole. On the one hand, this enables us to explain the system in terms of the two limiting parameters of ideology and structure; and on the other, we should be able to construct comparative categories that would eventually yield adequately verifiable generalizations—adequate, *ceteris paribus*, sociological lawlike statements. I want to make it clear that I am not reifying the ideological domain into a category or entity comparable to a manipulable empirical construct. The ideological domain is simply a conceptual category that has reality only insofar as it is a better tool for explanation. One could say also that the ideological domain is an entity twice removed from empirical reality, while the structural domain is only once removed, but to say that the former is less real than the latter is a non sequitur. There are no degrees of reality when dealing with conceptual entities.

I can now discuss my specific conception of the ideological domain from the viewpoint of both the empirical and supraempirical approaches. First, from the viewpoint of the former the ideological domain comprises the total ensemble of jural rules, moral constraints, imperatives to action, and value directives that underlie and shape the actual structural discharge of a bounded system or subsystem at a level below global sociocultural configurations. All these rules, constraints, imperatives, and directives can be empirically harnessed by observation and experimentation on the sociocultural facts themselves and on the constructions that are devised from them. (By experimentation, I mean the conceptual manipulation of the component parts of a system in order to discover their articulation. It can be interpreted as being almost synonymous with functional attribution, although the same concept can be used in its classical meaning of actual physical experimentation.) In the metalanguage, then, we could say that the structure of the ideological domain is composed of the total ensemble of these components. This conception of the structure or organization of the ideological domain simply would not do, however, for an empirical attribution of the ideological domain is inadequate. What I can use from the empirical position for my conceptual purposes is the realization that the factual and intuitive materials with which to elicit the ideological domain must be sought initially in actual configurations of sociocultural facts, and based firmly on them.

It is inevitable that one must turn to the supraempirical position for an adequate account of the ideological domain. From this viewpoint, I am no longer concerned with the exhaustive categorization of constituents, but rather with establishing the relations of invariance and the positional properties that make the ideological domain a separate, efficacious conceptual entity and its relationship to the structural domain a parametric limit. The supraempirical, substantive conception of a circumscribed ideological domain is best viewed as an efficacious complex of variables arranged as an invariance-relational configuration or hierarchical order, which can effect the operation of its corresponding structural order either directly or indirectly by setting up norms of behavior that cannot be entirely ignored. It should be obvious that there is never a one-to-one correspondence between the ideological and structural domains, for this would mean that the system or subsystem under consideration is in a complete state of equilibrium. One need not concern oneself with the actual configuration of the ideological domain in terms of specific variables and how they are arranged. This may be difficult to establish, for the ideological and structural domains have fundamentally different ontological referents. The former is a function of the diachronic dimension, while the latter is a function of the synchronic dimension, and although the efficacy of one over the other is exerted at concrete moments in time, the ideological is more permanent as an essentially diachronic entity. From a different viewpoint, one need not worry overmuch about the substantive constituents and organization of the ideological domain. The crucial point of my analysis is the relationship between the ideological and structural domains, and the establishment of the lines of efficacy that make the system operational.

The Concept of Efficacy Collectively and Individually

When I speak of social efficacy I am not necessarily using efficacy, as the term is most frequently used in the physical sciences, to refer to necessary connections between two objects or entities tied by the relationship of cause and effect. In a certain sense, though, social efficacy, insofar as it transcends functional efficacy or functional causality, does involve elements that may be construed as embodying to some degree the attributes of necessary and sufficient causation. From this viewpoint, when I say that there is an efficacious relationship between the ideological and structural domains, I mean to imply that in varying degrees the ideological domain involves the necessary and sufficient conditions for the discharge of its corresponding structural domain. The ideological domain can be said to be the necessary cause of the discharge of its corresponding structural domain to the extent that the former involves a command or imperative to do such and such. Correspondingly, the ideological domain can be said to be the sufficient cause of the discharge of the structural domain to the extent that the former provides the conditions under which individuals may choose certain alternatives of behavior. Were I to leave the analysis here, I would be saying little more than what several anthropologists have said regarding the role of custom or habit in shaping individual and collective behavior. But the whole point of separating the ideological and structural domains is not only to delineate clearly the efficacious relationship that holds them together, but to elucidate the external and extrinsic factors that impinge upon this relationship. To maintain simply that custom is efficacious or that the structural order suffices by itself as an explanatory domain, will not allow the determination of the external and extrinsic factors and conditions that bear upon individual and collective behavior, for the structural domain by itself as a global entity is circular, and does not allow linear causality.

The operationalization of efficacy here stands basically for the determination of those factors and conditions in which the causal relationship (both in its necessary and sufficient aspects) is embedded. The aim is ultimately to devise the rules that will tell us when, how, why, and under what conditions individual and collective behavior departs from or adheres to the dictates and imperatives of the ideological order. (Let me note, however, that I have not really devised any rules that will permit me to do this for the compadrazgo system. The construction of even a primitive grammar of compadrazgo is beyond the scope of this study. I think, however, that I have given all the elements necessary for doing so in the future, and in addition have set down the conditions under which and the possible ways in which this task can be performed. As I have noted before, here I am still working at the paradigmatic level of analysis, but the analysis is already conceptually removed from mere empiricism.) It goes without saying that the configuration of the ideological order can be ascertained and made into a postulated conceptual domain, which is a shorthand expression for saying that behavior per se can never be the raw data of our conceptualizations. From a different stand, the framing of the anthropologist's task in these terms offers many possibilities for the study of problems of change, and the eventual construction of limited-range theories. In other words, what I have in mind here is that the degree to which actual operation of the structural domain departs from or adheres to the ideological domain can be made into a measuring scale and fundamental taxonomic system for wide areas of anthropological inquiry.

From the heuristic viewpoint, social efficacy means basically the explanation of the decisions that cause individuals (and groups of individuals can always be endowed with a "collective action" without violating the empirical evidence or reifying a conceptual domain) to choose this or that course of action from among a series of alternatives with which they are presented by the lack of one-to-one correspondence of the ideological and structural domains. Thus, it is not of primary importance to determine the actual composition of these domains, but rather to ascertain the causal links for their degree of departure from a one-to-one correspondence. It is evident that the ideological and structural domains, because they embody respectively the what ought to be and the what is, are always analogously different, and we should not concern ourselves too much with scaling the degree to which the two domains overlap. Rather, our efforts should be directed toward heuristic determination of the lines of articulation that bind them together efficaciously. Let me first address the general conceptual framework that holds these two domains together in an efficacious whole. In the study of all sociocultural systems we are dealing basically with three levels of analysis with their corresponding empirical or analytical spheres of action: the undifferentiated ideological domain, the structural domain embodying ideal behavior, and the structural domain embodying what people actually do under specifiable circumstances.

The ideological domain must be taken as an integrated complex of rules and imperatives that are either consciously or unconsciously regarded by the people as the guide to structural and actual behavior and action. At the restricted level at which I am operating, this is synonymous with saying that, *ceteris paribus*, there are certain well defined ways of behaving and acting, and were one to deviate from them, the result could be measured in terms of undesirable consequences involving specific sanctions varying in social significance depending on the degree of deviation and on the circumstances in which it takes place. Under perfect conditions, there is obviously no deviation, and what people should do is coterminous with what they actually do, at least at this highest ideological level. Let us note here that the constraints that impede the complete actual discharge of the moral or jural directives of a specific ideological complex are always determined by conditions that are not part of the structural complex being discharged. It is these extrinsic and external conditions that we want to ascertain, for in this way we can determine the degree of deviation and the available alternatives that result in structural or actual behavior and action. In fact, it seems to me that what I have delineated here corresponds to the logical method of explaining and to some extent predicting behavior involved in the use of such techniques as game theory. The ideological complex of a specific structural system constitutes the rules of the game, among which the players (the individuals who compose the system) may choose certain combinations or permutations in order to discharge (or maximize) the system in action in accordance with what has been preordained—that is, in accordance with the maximum degree of overlapping between the two domains permitted by operative external and extrinsic variables.[9]

One of the main reasons, I believe, why the application of game theory to many sociocultural problem areas has not been entirely successful is that ideology has been regarded as synonymous with structure, which has led to a serious confusion as to what in fact constitutes the rules of the game. In the application of game theory to anthropological problems, the rules of the game have been erroneously regarded as the second level of analysis, that is, what I have called the structural-ideal aspects of the structural domain (see Barth 1959; Buchler and Nutini 1969; Davenport 1960); and the strategies that people devise in playing the sociocultural game are really *tactics*, that is, the making of choices among alternatives that are twice removed from the ideological domain per se. In my view of how the sociocultural game is played in terms of choices and decision making, strategies can only be chosen among variables that result from interaction between the real or most primitive rules of the game and the standardized discharge of the rules as they are shaped by determinable external and extrinsic variables. I am placing the ideological domain totally outside the structural domain, and, in Lévi-Straussian fashion, I am dividing the latter into mechanical or ideal behavior and statistical or actual behavior.

From this viewpoint, the task of the anthropologist is to explain and describe actual behavior, and occasionally to predict it. We must go from this lowest conceptual level to two higher levels to find the causal relationships to achieve this goal. Furthermore, the causal relationships are different at higher levels; they share the property of not being part of the construct that obtains at each respective level, but are the specific, ascertainable variables and conditions that are the ultimate objects of conceptualizations. If one maintains that these variables and conditions are always part of the constructs that obtain at the two levels of analysis (the third ideological level is seldom granted conceptual existence), one could only generate functional causality and not linear causality. Functional causality may be significant within certain analytical contexts, but primarily in the form of makeshift, preliminary generalizations that will serve a more explanatory purpose. It is often important to determine how the constituents of a system are put together, which is all functional explanation permits us to do.[10]

The Substantive Composition of the Structural Order:
The Ideal-Actual Distinction

I can now move to the substantive and organizational configuration of the structural domain, and to its constituent parts. The ideological domain, which can also be referred to as the ideational order (a fairly common usage), is not directly observable, nor is it deductible from the raw data of social and cultural experience. Rather it is an ontological entity (with its corresponding epistemological referent) which is twice removed from sensible sociocultural phenomena. One can regard the ideological domain as a largely unconscious sociocultural sphere in Lévi-Straussian terms, and in this context the term ideational order fits in very well. The ideological domain is unconscious, not only to the extent that the actors who participate in any given system or subsystems are unaware of its basic tenets and efficacious properties, but also to the extent that the observer—the anthropologist—becomes acquainted with it only after a prolonged period of time and analysis, and after he has assigned functional interpretations to the structural domain. But perhaps more important, what really shapes conceptual awareness of the ideological order is the diachronic, historical dimension of the synchronic system being studied. Only in this context can the anthropologist properly say that he has the ideological domain under control and properly conceptualized.

Again, in Lévi-Straussian terms, both the structural-ideal and the structural-actual aspects of this domain are not only conscious sociocultural experience (or at least primarily conscious), but we are primitively acquainted with the latter, and the former is directly deduced from it. These two contexts or levels of analysis correspond to the otological categories of what people ought to do and what they actually do; hence I have called them the structural-ideal and the structural-actual. At the same time, the epistemological entities associated with these two ontological levels of analysis result in what Lévi-Strauss calls mechanical models (paradigms), involving coercion or efficacy; and statistical paradigms, or accounts of what people actually do. This is one of the basic tenets of structuralism, and a significant part of it is also embodied in functionalism. The structural-actual context is little more than a descriptive statement based on our primary data, which must always be presented in terms of the right combination of quantitative and qualitative dimensions, and the sum total of the constituents of any such combination will constitute a paradigmatic description of a given complex or sociocultural system. Most anthropologists know how to do this very well, and as a conceptual operation this level presents no problems. Realization that the discharge of the structural-actual context is in varying degrees delineated or influenced by another conceptual level brings us to the structural-ideal context. The structural-ideal context of analysis does not have any intrinsic quantitative dimensions, but rather consists of the analytical description of the jural rules and imperative constraints that dictate what ought to be, given the specific configuration of the system or subsystem under consideration. The structural-ideal complex is thus a conceptual entity that is deduced from actual behavior, but at the same time it is often verbalized by participants in a series of descriptive statements. Thus, the structural-ideal context is the sum total of the rules of a system worked out in behavioristic terms and spelling out alternatives with regard to deviation.

It should be said that since the beginning of anthropology most of its sophisticated practitioners have been theoretically aware of the distinction. In practice, however, their descriptions and explanations have been based entirely on either actual or ideal behavior; that is, they have produced studies that are either mechanical, ideal or statistical, actual paradigms. Functionalists, on the whole, lean toward mechanical, ideal paradigms, while many American anthropologists tend to present statistical, actual paradigms. I have shown elsewhere that such polarized descriptions and explanations are inadequate and lopsided, and tell only half the story (Nutini 1965b). To make adequate and scientifically meaningful explanations, we have to account not only for what acually happens but also for the ideal patterns of behavior that underlie it. In fact, the explanation of a body of sociocultural phenomena consists of the extrapolation of ideal and actual behavior structured in terms of mechanical and statistical paradigms. In summary, then, I have explained what my three levels of analysis mean conceptually, and how they are organized substantively. But before I can proceed to the crux of the argument, one aspect of the interrelationship between these three levels must be clarified.

As analytical conceptual levels, neither the structural-ideal nor the structural-actual context presents any problems. Elucidation of these separate contexts falls within structural theory and methods and I need not concern myself with the details, but the reader may wish to consult the standard presentation of the structuralist position (see Leach 1961a, 1965a; Lévi-Strauss 1953, 1955, 1964; Nutini 1965b, 1970). The links or efficacious relationships between the structural-ideal and the structural-actual contexts present no difficulties, but I have not made entirely clear the form of the links or relationships between the ideological domain and the structural-ideal context (I am using the term context here to stand for subdomain). To understand this relationship, and the conceptual use of my third level, the significance of diachrony and synchrony in the functionalist and structuralist positions must be recognized.

The functionalists (especially à la Radcliffe-Brown) and the structuralists (à la Lévi-Strauss) have in common a disregard for diachrony or historical considerations in general as complements to the conceptualization of synchronic contexts. At best they tend to subsume diachronic dimensions within the generalizing matrix of synchrony. Radcliffe-Brown and his followers, despite protestations to the contrary, maintain that history is superfluous to the formulation of comparative generalizations and the explanation of specific sociocultural systems, or at best assign little value to any diachronic dimensions that may be apparent in their synchronically conceived systems. Thus, they inhibit the formulation of an integrated synchronic-diachronic matrix, which is a sine qua non for any scientific conceptualization involving epiphenomena. On the other hand, Lévi-Strauss's statement of the primacy of structure over history, or of synchrony over diachrony, not only inhibits such a formulation but also maintains that true generalizations must be formulated without the benefit of a time dimension, and that relationships of invariance can be meaningfully formulated within a strictly synchronic matrix. I disagree entirely with this antidiachronic, or at least ahistorical, perspective in the conceptualization of sociocultural phenomena. If it could be demonstrated that the contention of both functionalists and structuralists is valid, and that we need not concern ourselves with significant diachronic variables in the formulation of general statements at either the individual sociocultural level or the comparative level, then the dichotomization of sociocultural phenomena in terms of ideal and actual behavior (with their corresponding referential constructs) would suffice as a conceptual framework. But this is not possible either ontologically or epistemologically, for synchrony and diachrony are the limiting parameters of the sociocultural universe, and must be used as complements.

It is in this context that postulation of a third ideological domain is necessary, for it enables us to accommodate the diachronic dimensions and variables which, depending upon the availability of historical data, determine the proportion of these ontological components or the viewpoint from which it is most profitable to look at a given body of sociocultural data. As ontological limiting parameters, synchrony and diachrony determine the conditions, methods, and procedures for handling a given body of epiphenomena, and the postulation of a separate ideological order becomes a necessary condition for the most advantageous organization of analytical considerations. Analysis of the structural domain in its ideal and actual aspects may involve the necessary and sufficient conditions for the conceptualization of epiphenomena in terms of functional causality of specified systems or subsystems frozen in time. If, however, the demonstration of linear causality is our principal goal, the necessary and sufficient conditions are supplied by analysis of the ideological order, as outlined in the preceding pages.

The Concept of Articulation: The Efficacious Links Connecting the Three Analytical Levels

I would like now to analyze the efficacious links between the ideological and the structural-ideal. The first problem is the obvious double dichotomy in the analytical framework: the ideological-structural dichotomy, and the structural-ideal–structural-actual dichotomy. The latter presents no difficulties, and I hope to have shown what it means empirically and theoretically. The former, however, immediately points out the fact that both dichotomies include elements that fall under the ontological category of what ought to be, in that they specify rules, imperatives, and constraints involving varying degrees of coercion. The next question is why these what–ought–to–be complexes must be conceptualized separately when they involve essentially the same ontological constituents. The answer can be given in this way: the structural-ideal domain constitutes the immediate synchronic conditions for the discharge of actual sociocultural behavior, whose expression is in standardized, directly elicited behavior patterns, and whose articulation to other subsystems within the total sociocultural system can again be specified in synchronic terms. The ideological domain, on the other hand, constitutes a metalevel of analysis which embodies primarily diachronic conditions shaping the structural-ideal context directly or the structural-actual context indirectly, and whose articulation with the broadest aspects of the total sociocultural system falls outside what anthropologists have traditionally called the social structure. Thus, the structural-ideal domain is a language level of analysis that is immediately anchored in the observational level; the ideological domain is a metalanguage level of analysis that is essentially a postulated conceptual entity designed to encompass epiphenomena in time as well as in sociocultural space. Were we to combine the elements of the ideological domain with those of the structural-ideal domain, we would be confusing the dynamic and the "static" components of a given sociocultural system or configuration. Let us pursue this further.

The key conceptual points in these two levels of what ought to be are denoted by the opposing terms of synchrony and diachrony, and the language and metalanguage levels of articulation—the immediate and the once-removed levels. The ideological domain is articulated con-

ceptually at the highest societal level and given form within the diachronic context, while the structural-ideal domain is articulated conceptually at a lower level and given form within the synchronic context.
What I mean by articulation is, essentially, the interconnection between
the various substantive empirical levels of a system or subsystem and
other constituent systems or subsystems of a global situation—and
sometimes other global sociocultural systems that have a common cultural denominator. In brief, then, it is necessary to distinguish between
the ideological and structural-ideal domains as embodying different what-
ought-to-be configurations (although with the same ontological constituents), or configurations which have a different origin and are efficacious at different conceptual levels, for otherwise it is not possible to
determine the external and extrinsic variables that activate the explanatory framework.

In using the concept of articulation, I am not making the a priori
assertion of the functionalists that all sociocultural systems, and their
constituent subsystems, are integrated wholes and that in fact we can
determine how functional changes in one constituent will affect the rest
of the system. I can define articulation more or less formally in terms
of ascertaining which external and extrinsic variables and conditions, at
different analytical levels of a given system or subsystem, make it possible to assign a causal relationship. In practical terms, they enable us to
determine why, how, and under what conditions ideological imperatives and configurations of rules are broken or deviated from in the
standardization of structural-ideal forms; and in turn, why, when, and
how structural-ideal standards are broken or deviated from in actual
behavior. Articulation in this sense is almost synonymous with the efficacious links connecting the three levels of analysis, but it is easier to
visualize this conceptual process as an ostensible property of the three
levels themselves, and for purposes of exposition I can approach the
problem in this fashion. For the moment, then, I would like to address
myself to the three levels of analysis, and especially to the ideological
and structural-ideal domains and determine what role they play as substantive conceptual entities.

Starting at the top, the ideological domain can be said to articulate in
two ways with any given system or subsystem. Internally, the ideological domain is a shorthand expression for determining what constraints
(in terms of specific variables and conditions) or jural injunctions are
involved in a particular system. The ideological domain as a concept
must specify, in behavioristic terms, not only the rules, imperatives,
and moral commands that make up its substantive empirical content,
but more important it must specify the connections of the system with
broader aspects of the social structure in which it is embedded. This

specification consists primarily in establishing the social, religious, ritual, ceremonial, symbolic, economic, and even political components of the well-delineated ideological domain, and showing how these extrasystemic ties (which in their own right can be construed as other well-delineated and circumscribed domains) can and do activate deviations from or adherence to the ideological domain in the structural-ideal and structural-actual contexts. This is the most significant articulatory function of the ideological domain in action, and in conceiving the what-ought-to-be complex in this fashion, I need not establish exhaustively what its substantive empirical composition *really* is, as long as I can specify the external and extrinsic variables that are the operationable elements of the conceptual scheme. In this fashion, once the basic form or configuration of the ideological domain of a given system has been determined in the manner described here (it is in this context that the percipient's intuition plays an important role, and it is at this level that theory construction is at its creative best), the next task is to work the operative external and extrinsic variables into an integrated complex; this is the hardest part of the task, and it can be carried out only after functional causality has been assigned to the constituent elements of the complex. In this context functional analysis is useful as a steppingstone to the assignment of linear causality. Functional causality, as defined above, does indeed tell us how any given structural element is integrated into a given system, and if this property can be determined for all the constituent elements of the integrated external and extrinsic complex, we can then establish more readily how it is likely to affect the departure from or adherence to the ideological order in the actual discharge of the structural order. In summary, then, the internal articulation embodied in the ideological domain involves the discovery of relations of invariance, and especially the positional properties of the system under consideration which place it in the global sociocultural system of which it is a part.

Externally, the ideological domain also has some important articulatory functions, and what I have said for internal articulation also applies here; the only difference is that the articulatory mechanisms operate between the system and the external world; that is, in one way or another extrasocietal variables and conditions always affect even the most isolated sociocultural systems. For example, within the context of this study, in which the compadrazgo system is a very significant component of a vast array of primarily folk sociocultural systems, the external articulatory aspects of the ideological domain are of capital importance, not only because folk cultures are part cultures, but more important because the ideological order underlying the innumerable expressions of the compadrazgo system in the Latin American ethnographic area has a unitary meaning, a common inception and origin, and a discernible historical development. Furthermore, in sociocultural systems that are undergoing rapid change, which is often effected by external factors (and this is the case for most folk societies, and even the remaining tribal societies), it is important to determine which external and extrinsic factors activate the ideological-structural causal links. Implicit in my analysis here is the assumption that change, whether brought about by internal or external factors, is best regarded and conceptualized as a departure from a more stable and permanent ideological order. In this view, change must be measured by the degree to which structural discharge departs from or adheres to a certain ideological order, with the external and extrinsic variables regarded as the all-important activating mechanisms for change or stability. The external articulatory dimensions of the ideological domain are conceptually homologous and analogous to its internal dimensions, but the full implications of the external aspects can best be analyzed within the diachronic discussion of the ideological order that follows.

The structural-ideal domain always overlaps with the ideological domain to a considerable extent, for the former seldom departs significantly from the latter. It stands to reason that, both being what-ought-to-be complexes, their causal relationships will permit little deviation. But regardless of whether deviations are small or large (under certain specified conditions), they are very important to the total discharge of the integrated system on all three analytical levels, and from a strictly synchronic viewpoint, this is the key conceptual threshold for a complete analysis. We can regard the structural-ideal domain operationally as the standardized, normative network of behavior patterns that result from the dictates of the ideological domain modified by the immediate constraints that represent the influence of the external and extrinsic variables which articulate the system with its immediate matrix. This matrix represents only the predominant substantive components of the system under consideration, and not the articulation with the global situation in terms of general sociocultural categories of phenomena, which I described for the higher articulatory level. For example, the immediate components of the compadrazgo system are primarily in the social realm, but they can also can be considered religious, at least in a complementary fashion. One can say, then, that the structural-ideal context represents an efficacious, immediate what-ought-to-be complex at a lower conceptual level, and that in the absence of any higher sociocultural articulation, it would come to play the role of a full-fledged ideological complex in its own right. This is never realized of course, for it is a conceptual impossibility to achieve truly explanatory dimensions within an independent, closed system at this level of sociocultural integration.

In any event, as the pivotal analytical level between the ideological domain (or highest normative-behavioral level) and the structural-actual level of behavior, the structural-ideal context is the prime objective of our analytical manipulations, and it has an upward dimension of constraints and regulatory mechanisms, and a downward dimension of efficacious relationships.

By prime objective I wish to signify that the structural-ideal domain, as the most obvious analytical level with some kind of efficacy, often becomes the sole explanatory construct with which we concern ourselves; and while this is necessary and beneficial, we must not assign to it explanatory qualities it does not have, thereby halting the search for the upward and downward causal relationships. This is another way of saying that the structural-ideal context is the analytical pivot that coordinates the impingement of the external and extrinsic variables, thereby activating their explanatory power. From this viewpoint, the structural-ideal context represents the largest body of empirical and conceptual operations that the anthropologist has to contend with. Abiding by my general *modus operandi*, let me simply reiterate that the structural-ideal domain is the conscious, behavioristic body of jural rules, moral injunctions, and imperative constraints that directly regulate the system in operation. Furthermore, this is also the traditional realm of explanation of both the functionalist and the structuralist position, but I must emphasize that it plays different roles and stands at different levels of abstraction in these approaches, which in turn differ from my integrated approach. First, unlike both the functionalist and structuralist positions, in my approach the structural-ideal domain is the product of both synchronic and diachronic dimensions, and this constitutes the advantage of my approach. Second, unlike the functionalist approach, my conception of the structural-ideal domain does contain several elements necessary for supraempirical constructs, and unlike the structuralist model, it includes the necessary diachronic dimensions.

The Conceptual Elements of the Theoretical Framework

In the preceding paragraphs I delineated the substantive composition and analytical properties of the two levels that involve causal efficacy. Finally, I wish to discuss briefly how this theoretical account can be actualized methodologically. On the whole, I am reasonably certain that the main tenets of my theoretical approach are correct and consonant with the canons of modern science. I refer, or course, to the threefold division of levels of analysis; the efficacy of causal relationships as embodied in external and extrinsic variables and conditions; the adequacy of the linkages uniting the different levels; the heuristic and methodological reality of these substantive and conceptual entities; and most important, the discoverability and adequacy of the empirical claims that I make for the explanatory system. (That is, I argue that we can *in fact* clearly delineate an ideological complex of rules and imperatives as distinct from the structural-ideal context; that we can *in fact* pinpoint and isolate external and extrinsic variables and conditions; and most fundamentally, that it is possible, directly or indirectly, to discover that there are always rules governing people's actual behavior.) What the approach lacks at the moment is a set of heuristic guidelines which can only be developed with practice; this study represents an attempt to point out some of the paths we might follow. It is likely that some of my conceptual entities and procedures will have to be modified, but the main structure of the approach should not require substantial alteration. I suspect that the greatest number of modifications will be in the practical and heuristic realms, and will have to do with the difficulty of obtaining specific data or making several of the conceptual distinctions substantively sound. An example will help to clarify what I mean.

I said that the ideological domain has two sets of articulatory mechanisms which involve two complementary sets of external and extrinsic variables and conditions. I termed these external and internal articulation, and said that they articulate the ideological domain with the outside world and with the broader aspects of the global sociocultural system. Conversely, I said that the structural-ideal domain articulates the system under consideration with the other constituents of the global system. There are two difficulties here that will modify the application of the scheme to more sophisticated empirical data gathered with the former in mind as its explanatory construct. First, it is best that each of the two conceptual levels with causal efficacy be assigned only one set of external and extrinsic variables and conditions; hence the two sets of variables of the ideological domain must be collapsed into one. The external and extrinsic variables corresponding to articulation with the external world must be regarded as causal impingement acting alone upon the ideological domain, while the variables articulating the ideological domain with broader aspects of the global sociocultural system are best seen as part of the causal relationship acting upon the structural-ideal domain. Second, it is also better heuristically to view the immediate matrix of the structural-ideal domain in terms of the complex of systems and subsystems (that is, the related segments of the global situation) that make up the general fabric of the social structure of the global system under consideration. What I am proposing, in other words, is to transpose all the internal articulatory dimensions of the ideological domain to the structural-ideal domain for heuristic reasons, in order to obtain a more symmetrical analytical framework. In summary, the links connecting the ideological domain to the structural-ideal and to the structural-actual, are best regarded as embodying respectively, those external and extrinsic variables and conditions that have causal efficacy by way of their articulation vis-à-vis the external world; and those that have causal efficacy through their articulatory properties vis-à-vis the broader aspects of the global sociocultural system under consideration.

I have tried to give a complete picture of all the substantive and conceptual elements that enter into the threefold scheme, and the emphasis has been on two key aspects. These can be subsumed under the limited conceptual terms of activation and efficacy; they are closely interrelated, and their operation can be described as follows. What I am activating are the various links that connect the three levels of analysis in terms of measurable quantities. I want to determine the degree to which a what-actually-happens complex departs from or adheres to its corresponding what-ought-to-be complex, and the measurable degree of departure or adherence is what I call efficacy or causal relationship. Therefore, in the efforts to operationalize a concrete and well-delineated conceptual entity, I have thought it best to do so in terms of efficacy or causal relationship predicated on variables external to the system itself. There are two reasons for this: first, external and extrinsic variables are more visible and easier to pinpoint than those that are part of the system itself, or at least regarded as part of the system itself; and second, a closed system can only be activated from the outside, thereby endowing it with linear causality. I have also determined that the best way to look at the conceptual scheme is from the central position of the structural-ideal domain as involving an upward and a downward dimension. From this standpoint, the operationalization must be conducted in terms of the double connecting link that unites the structural-ideal domain in a position of efficacious subordination to the ideological domain, and of efficacious superordination to the structural-actual domain. Finally, although theoretically the conceptual entities that I have designated as the mechanisms of articulation have slightly different methodological and heuristic properties, they can be regarded as analogous and homologous. I have tried to present the reasons it is of fundamental importance to expand the ideal-actual analytical dichotomy, already well accepted by most anthropologists, into my threefold conceptual scheme, as well as the general *modus operandi* for doing so, and in this endeavor I have thought it best to go from the substantive-empirical composition of the three levels or conceptual nodes, to their theoretical structure in terms of specified conceptual elements, and finally to the activating mechanisms that endow the system with causal efficacy.

In my forthcoming monograph, *Structure and Ideology: The Epistemological and Ontological Bases of Their Interrelationship* (Nutini n.d.), I informally operationalize and substantively implement the analytical approach postulated in this appendix. On the basis of historical data gathered by myself and compadrazgo network data gathered by White and myself (White and Nutini n.d.) I implement the present analytical framework, centering on the following problems: (1) interdigitation of the primarily diachronic nature of the ideological order with the primarily synchronic nature of the structural order, leading to formulation of the operational principles involved; (2) the distinction between ideal and actual behavior at the strictly structural level, and how this affects the articulation of the ideological and structural orders; (3) the interrelationship of ideological and structural constraints as a joint causal explanation of actual social behavior, in a system of deep and surface phenomena regulated by generative rules at the ideological-structural level, and by transformational rules at the ideal-actual level; (4) exemplification of the integrated theory with regard to the synchronic personnel and the diachronic development of the compadrazgo system in rural Tlaxcala; (5) tentative formalization of the limited-range theory of ideological and structural integration, and the advantages of adopting a basically grammatical approach to the conceptualization of sociocultural phenomena.

Notes

Chapter 1. The Sacred Nature of Compadrazgo in Belén and the Characteristics of the Mediating Entity

1. If one considers the three sets of structural constraints that operate in determining the structure of compadrazgo choice, and the fact that each set contains at least five variables, one can readily see the difficulties in trying to apply a mathematical solution to such a situation.

2. Most anthropologists who have made community studies in the Mesoamerican and Andean areas have been ahistorical in that they have paid little or no attention to the diachronic dimensions of their communities, and it seems paradoxical that they have been influenced surreptitiously by the diachronic aspects of compadrazgo. However, the diachronic dimensions of compadrazgo have been presented to them via superficial published sources and through the oral and local traditions of the Catholic religion, and they have seldom investigated original archival materials on the diachronic aspects of the institution. Instead, they have accepted a historical tradition that might have been true in early colonial times and in Europe, but that has developed into something quite different synchronically over 400 years of acculturative and syncretic change.

3. The analytical position taken here is predicated on the assumption that most social institutions have such junctures which are of great conceptual importance, and that they can also be found in the functioning of many institutions. For example, the *entrega* (handing over the bride) in the marriage ceremonies of San Bernardino Contla (Nutini 1968b: 288-291), is a good case in point. The position of the bride and the principles that will regulate her future life, and that of married life in general for both husband and wife, are set down in a series of speeches made by the kinsmen of the bride and groom. With respect to the compadrazgo system itself, the pedimento is one of the junctures that sets the tone of the relationship and outlines the ensuing rights and obligations. Still another example, from the Tlaxcalan area in general, is the position of the *mayordomía* (the religious sponsorship or stewardship) of the patron saint with respect to the total ayuntamiento religioso. Analysis of such junctures, of a primarily social or religious nature, can yield important results.

4. In the conclusions I discuss several comparative problems involved in the analysis of the compadrazgo system. The inadequate knowledge

of compadrazgo in Mesoamerica, and by extension the whole of Indian and rural Latin America, is attributable primarily to this polarization.

5. In general, anthropologists working in Latin America have been remiss in devising conceptual and methodological tools for dealing with the compadrazgo system, an institution that contains kinship elements together with socioreligious and symbolic elements, thereby neglecting an opportunity to make significant contributions to the difficult area in which kinship, religion, and ritual mingle inextricably.

6. The reader may want to check the breakdown of mediating entities. Of the thirty-one mediating entities (or compadrazgo types), fourteen are persons, one of them deceased (PCE); six are saints or images (one of them a cross), and eleven are social, religious, and economic things, objects, events, or occasions. Analysis of this breakdown indicates that it is sometimes difficult to classify a mediating entity as either a social, religious, or economic object, event, or occasion, but its symbolic value indicates the reason for its existence (see table 27).

Chapter 2. The Personnel of the Compadrazgo System

1. When table 3 is correlated with table 2, the entry "none" means in fact "primary," for the title of table 3 should read "extensions of incest prohibition to compadres' primary and secondary relatives." In other words, the compadres themselves are primary actors, their primary relatives are secondary actors, and the primary relatives of secondary actors are tertiary actors. Moreover, in even the least important compadrazgo types that involve living ahijados, under no circumstances may the padrinos marry their ahijados or have sexual relations with them. The breaking of this prohibition in even the least important compadrazgo types can still elicit strong sanctions from the community as a whole, or at least strong disapproval.

2. The use of children as ritual sponsors in the compadrazgo system varies considerably from community to community in Tlaxcala. I am acquainted with several communities in which the use of children as sponsors is much like that in Belén, but in perhaps a larger number of communities they are used in other than strictly religious compadrazgo—in, for example, types of primarily symbolic meaning such as PCA or escapulario in Belén, and even in types such as CEON, primera piedra, and JJ.

3. According to the folk ideology of rural Tlaxcala, a child is not entirely human until he begins to talk, and the closer the child is to the womb, the more vulnerable he is to evildoing and external influences. This is the reason, the people believe, the tlahuelpuchis always suck the blood of infants under one year old.

4. No matter how compact and logically connected a description or analysis may be, it will always contain a certain amount of repetition, and I am aware that mine may include more repetition than is necessary. My justification is that I am trying to look at the compadrazgo system of Belén from several standpoints as well as from several levels of analysis, which results in more repetition than one normally encounters in less multidimensional analyses. I feel that it is excusable to exchange elegance and conciseness of exposition for depth and breadth of analysis, especially in dealing with such poorly understood institutions as compadrazgo.

5. On several occasions I have pointed out that one of the failings of traditional structural-functional analysis has been its overemphatic concern with social statics and its inability to account for change and the dynamics of culture and society, and that this has been largely attributable to the exaggerated role that the concept of equilibrium has played in its conceptualizations. I have contended that the structural-functional method of analysis can be endowed with a diachronic component which may well result in an appropriate way to look at change and at the more processual aspects of culture and society. At several points in this study I have tried to focus the analysis by including both synchronic and diachronic components, and in trying to articulate what is mainly permanent (equilibrium) and what is mainly changing (dynamic) in the structure of the compadrazgo system, I have sought to give an added dimension that is lacking in most structural-functional studies. I think the above instance is a good example of the conceptual mistake that would be made by simply taking the exogamous-exogenous aspects of the compadrazgo system in Belén (and Tlaxcala in general) and making them a part of a postulated state of equilibrium in which one could construe the institution to be at present because they have been one of its important features for such a long period. If this were the case, one would freeze the system and not allow for the dynamic dimensions that are presently working to transform it, and which are mostly exogenous to the system itself. Under these circumstances, I would be missing an opportunity to determine, to some extent, the direction of change, and more important, the dynamic principles in operation that may in the foreseeable future upset the total structure of the compadrazgo system and its articulation with the broader aspects of Belén culture and society. In my particular view of structural-functional analysis, it is important to endow the analysis of a social unit or social institution with an account of how changes in the foundations of the system—its ideology—will result in changes in the structure and functions of the institution or unit. It is even more important that one ascertain the exogenous considerations governing the articulation of the ideological and structural-

functional orders, which are the efficient causes regulating the change-equilibrium balance.

6. In fact, only in the most acculturated communities in rural Tlaxcala (those that have been entirely Mestizoized and, structurally speaking, can no longer be regarded as in any sense Indian or as including significant traditionally Indian institutions or complexes of traits) is the ideology ambivalent about exogamous compadrazgo relationships. In such cases, there may still be more endogamous than exogamous relationships (obviously enough, explained as a functional constraint of distance and locality), but the people may by now prefer to contract exogamous relationships. Here there is a change in ideology that has not become fully formalized in the collective consciousness, but that points to the constraints that bear upon ideological changes, and upon the articulation of the ideological and structural orders.

7. Structural-functional studies, especially of the British variety, have uniformly disregarded the anomalous and have been concerned exclusively with equilibirum. The concept of equilibrium, once more, has been too pervasive in anthropology. Under the guise of helping to establish the basic structural principles and components underlying and giving form to sociocultural systems, most social anthropologists have overemphasized the permanent aspects of conceptualization, to the detriment of the processual aspects that must always accompany it.

Chapter 3. The Structural Implications of Asking and Being Asked to Enter into a Compadrazgo Relationship

1. For simplicity of exposition I refer to the primary actors in a compadrazgo relationship merely as individuals or persons, for it goes without saying that spouses are an important part of the relationship. Only when spouses have different structural and functional attributes do I refer to them independently. In only three or four instances is structural and functional attribution not extended to spouses not directly or immediately involved in the compadrazgo relationship.

Chapter 4. Confianza, Respeto, and Reliance

1. In his essay on deductive-nomonological explanation, Hempel (1965:335-376) discusses the advantages of explaining in terms of general principles. He also maintains that the deductive-nomonological type of explanation can be used in the social sciences, contrary to what William Dray (1957:105-135) has vehemently maintained. I think that Hempel is essentially correct, and have made his deductive-nomonological kind of explanation my model. I also think that in the absence of general

laws or lawlike statements in anthropology, the explanatory model in terms of general principles can work best at the level of specific socio-cultural systems. Under the controlled conditions of well-delineated systems, general operational principles can be formulated with a certain degree of success, and these principles can play the conceptual role of general laws in the deductive-nomonological model of explanation. This has been the idea of searching for what I have called activating, dynamic principles, that is, those substantive junctures that can be made into theoretical terms by a process of successful operationalization. Of course, in the present study much of this remains an ideal. Nevertheless, without the notion of what constitutes activating, dyanamic principles, one can hardly expect mathematically or formally inclined anthropologists to achieve real success with their constructions, for they purport to explain in terms of the complementing of deductive and inductive elements, which is the fundamental property of explanation by the deductive-nomonological model.

2. At the moment I am unable to say what these reasons are, but elucidating what is conscious and what unconscious in social behavior is one of the most important epistemological problems that anthropology will have to face in achieving an adequate stage of conceptualization. Lévi-Strauss and several other anthropologists have addressed themselves to this problem, but none has been able to enlighten us as to the epistemological components of the conscious-unconscious distinction in sociocultural phenomena, let alone give any adequate substantive or theoretical reasons for the unconscious nature of a sizable segment of sociocultural behavior. An adequate theory of the social unconscious in the realm of sociocultural behavior is of paramount importance in solving a variety of problems that have not yielded to the unidimensional analysis usually employed by both sociologists and anthropologists.

3. The covering nature of many terms is widespread in Mesoamerican rural Indian and Mestizo society, and I imagine in many other ethnographic areas of the world. This is the result of the conscious-unconscious dichotomy in the verbal aspects of sociocultural phenomena. It corresponds roughly to what Lévi-Strauss (1953:527) has discussed as conscious and unconscious models and the widespread tendency for societal "self-mystification," or the fact that, by different means, societies may unconsciously denote behavior by conscious covering terms. In Tlaxcala, and much of Mesoamerica, this can be bothersome to the ethnographer in the field, and no doubt it has led to much misinformation and to taking at face value the conscious verbalizations of our subjects. The terms confianza, respeto, and reliance, and many similar ones, always have a much heavier substantive payload than their con-

scious, common-sense meaning as elicited by the ethnographer. It must be admitted, though, that when, for example, informants keep repeating that "los compadritos deben respetarse y tenerse confianza" every time the ethnographer wants to elicit a specific behavior pattern or structural attributes associated with a compadrazgo type, it can be a frustrating experience. This kind of situation is most common in Mesoamerica in the domain of social organization, where every complex is plagued by covering terms (screens, in the Lévi-Straussian terminology) with a substantive payload far transcending common-sense interpretation, which the ethnographer cannot elicit directly but must infer from the interrelationship of a variety of contexts. This is not the case with religious organization, either at the ritual-ceremonial or hierarchical level. I am not certain why this is so. Most institutions and behavior patterns associated with religion in Tlaxcala, and probably in most of Mesoamerica, are quite conscious—that is, not as amenable to being subsumed under defined covering terms. Furthermore, the conscious or unconscious character of a people's knowledge of specific domains has, in my estimation, nothing to do with the intrinsic position of the domain in the total configuration of the sociocultural system. Questions such as this can only be solved in the light of an adequate theory of the social unconscious. The main objectives of such a theory should be, on the one hand, to establish why there are degrees of explicitness about one's sociocultural knowledge, and on the other, how unconscious knowledge is subsumed under covering terms.

4. Of fundamental importance for the correct conceptualization of sociocultural phenomena is the realization that the articulation of the ideological and structural orders changes from system to system, for unless one is aware of this, one cannot generalize beyond individual systems. The rules of the game and the strategies employed for achieving certain ends always vary from system to system—or, more accurately, what binds these two fundamentally different entities may vary greatly in different systems.

5. The success of mathematical anthropologists in certain domains of sociocultural phenomena bears me out. Only in the domains in which culture itself presents more naturally structured configurations—such as kinship, some aspects of economics, cognitive categories, and the like—have they been successful in implementing inductive-deductive constructs. The empirical data of such domains may be naturally regarded as a covering term, or as embodying covering terms, with a significant degree of semantic content. This example also makes clear the need to advance through a series of abstracting steps before one can reach the point at which the data are sufficiently distilled for the formalists to take over.

6. Anthropologists know that the description of a system is never complete, nor is it possible to explain every aspect of it with the same degree of exactness. One can always elicit new properties by looking at the system from a different perspective, which in turn imply new phenomena, perhaps more difficult to explain. From this viewpoint, sociocultural systems are quite different from physical systems, in that the latter are more controllable to the extent that the perspectives from which one can look at them are always limited, while the former can almost always be expanded as soon as one changes standpoints slightly. The problem of completeness and circumscription in the explanation and description of sociocultural phenomena will limit the application of deductive techniques.

Chapter 5. The Preferential and Prescriptive Structure of Compadrazgo

1. One of the most fundamental ideological beliefs of the people of Belén (widely shared in rural Tlaxcala) is that the universe is essentially unstable, and that it is the duty of the individual, and the social group as a whole, to generate harmony and stability by establishing good relations with the supernatural powers. Both Catholic and non-Catholic supernaturals are further conceived as essentially good, benevolent, and predisposed to help man and his universe, but it is believed that they are much concerned with being propitiated correctly, often, and according to custom. Only under these circumstances are the supernaturals willing to exercise their powers to keep harmony in the community and grant individual favors. From this viewpoint, the most important institutions in the community, the mayordomía system, the ayuntamiento religioso, the compadrazgo system, and some non-Catholic ceremonial practices are the mechanisms through which the people of Belén propitiate the supernaturals and keep them happy and predisposed toward Belén. Thus, virtually all symbolic actions, rituals, and ceremonials in Belén have a direct or indirect element of propitiation to bring about rapport between man and society and the supernatural. The religion of Belén and its associated aspects are essentially devoid of what might be called theological beliefs and practices, and little concerned with sin, damnation, and otherworldly matters. For the people of Belén the significance of religion lies in ritual, symbolic action, and ceremonial in the here and now; it is concerned exclusively with propitiation and the need to maintain an orderly social life. Once the average Beleño has discharged his traditional religious duties, ritual occasions, and ceremonial sponsorships, he has little interest in religious matters which have usually come from the outside through the influence of the priest and the process of secularization the community is experiencing. Given this state of affairs,

the discharge of the rituals and ceremonials of the compadrazgo system plays a prominent role in generating rapport with the supernatural, thereby facilitating societal and individual living. As I discuss in Chapter Seventeen, this is what I call the magico-symbolic function of compadrazgo.

2. It is interesting that all the legends with this theme involve exclusively non-Catholic supernaturals. The most common is La Malintzi, who is usually depicted as a moral cosmic overseer upholding the religious and social orders, and at the same time dispensing boons and favoring those who are especially well-behaved. For example: "There was once in Belén a very miserly and uncouth man who refused to search for a padrino for the death of one of his children, and the poor child was buried without the benefit of the parada de cruz de entierro sponsorship. The day after he took his child to the cemetery, he went to the mountain to gather wood. When he got to the mid-slopes of the mountain, he climbed a tree in order to cut a hanging branch. But on the way up to the branch he was imprisoned by a thick twig which kept him on the tree unable to move. He spent the entire night there shivering with cold. Early the next morning, a beautiful lady [La Malintzi] dressed in a white blouse [huipil] and a blue skirt [titixtle], and accompanied by several white dogs, passed by and asked him why he was imprisoned on the tree. The man answered that he did not know, and asked her to help him to get down by breaking the twig. She did not pay any attention, and kept on walking down the slope. Exactly the same thing happened for two consecutive days. On the fourth morning, the man was nearly dying of thirst and hunger, and it finally occurred to him, when the lady asked him why he was kept on the tree, to say that it was perhaps because he had not buried his child with the benefit of the parada de cruz sponsorship. The lady stopped and told him that that was exactly what she wanted him to say. She immediately told one of her dogs to release him from the tree, and another to give him food and water. Before sending him home, the lady admonished him to be a good, kind, and generous man, and above all to comply with his obligations of sponsorship to himself and the community. From that day onward, the man became a model citizen of Belén."

3. It is difficult to refrain from straying occasionally into the changing, diachronic dimensions of the situation. While in principle it is a good idea to keep separate the conceptualization of synchrony and diachrony, this is not always possible or desirable. There are many junctures, such as the present one, at which the synchronic and diachronic components of a situation need to be treated in a single conceptual reference. Problems of change, obviously diachronic, are most often for-

mulated within the synchronic situation, and it is only their conceptual implementation that must be undertaken historically.

4. Throughout the structural analysis it has been explicitly assumed that the compadrazgo system—together with the mayordomía system and the ayuntamiento religioso—forms the core of Belén culture and society, not only because it is their most significant, all-embracing manifestation, but also because all three are based in a common ideological order. The acculturative development of the compadrazgo system, and especially that of the ayuntamiento religioso (the mayordomía system is essentially part of it) presented diachronically in Part Three of *Ritual Kinship* I, establishes the reasons for this assertion. Until about ninety years ago, when rural Tlaxcala was still fully traditional in the colonial sense and not yet influenced to any significant extent by outside secularizing economic influences, these three structural components were effectively brought together by the ideological order. But during the past ninety years, the mayordomía system and the ayuntamiento religioso have been transformed more than the compadrazgo system; that is, their structural discharge has been adhering less and less to the formal rules, directives, and injunctions of the ideological order, while the structural-ideal articulation of the compadrazgo system has remained essentially the same. For this reason I have maintained that the latter has remained more traditional than the former. But as I discuss below, this pertains exclusively to its formal structure, for in its functional aspects and activities, the compadrazgo system has also changed. What has remained constant, then, is the discharge of the ritual-ceremonial core of compadrazgo types, but not the ensuing rights and obligations binding compadres into dyads and into networks of compadres. In the final analysis, this differential change in compadrazgo is a counterbalancing factor in comparing it with the ayuntamiento religioso and the mayordomía system as part of the same ideological complex.

5. Let us note, however, that the result delineated here can also be achieved by a column analysis of the thirty-one compadrazgo tables (tables 1-12, 14-24, 26-33). I have not attempted this task, but several combinations of columns would be significant in scaling compadrazgo types for three or four constructs similar to the model just described.

Chapter 6. The Structural Implications of Symmetrical and Asymmetrical Compadrazgo Relationships

1. I am saying in effect that the ideological order of a particular institution, system, or subsystem is not necessarily a self-contained entity. In the majority of cases, in fact, one cannot speak of the ideological order of a global sociocultural system, for seldom can one successfully

conceptualize such an entity. Reciprocity as an ideological principle is at the core of values of Belén society, and it therefore permeates more circumscribed ideological complexes in the sociocultural system. Moreover, while one could perhaps isolate other principles such as reciprocity that belong to the general ideological order of Belén culture and society, at this stage of the analysis it is conceptually more adequate to determine how they are discharged in specific instances.

2. The compadrazgo system operates very much as it does in Belén throughout the rural sector of the entire Tlaxcala-Pueblan valley, with possibly one exception—nearby San Bernardino Contla. (It is possible that other communities in the valley are still strongly organized on a kinship basis, but I doubt there are more than a handful.) It is immediately apparent that one cannot describe and analyze Contla's social structure and social life in terms of compadrazgo. For details of the differences between compadrazgo in Belén and Contla, see "The Relationship between Kinship and Compadrazgo in Belén, Contla, Atlihuetzian" and "The Differential Functions of Compadrazgo in Belén, Contla, and Atlihuetzian" in Chapter Sixteen.

Chapter 7. The Permanent and Temporary Dimensions of Compadrazgo Relationships

1. Here I wish to note that throughout the foregoing analysis I have frequently used the terms compadrazgo type and compadrazgo relationship as interchangeable. On the other hand, in many contexts I have tried to make clear that compadrazgo relationship refers to a specific instance of a given compadrazgo type. No confusion need arise if the context of the situation is specified.

2. If one calculates that only about half of the total number of compadrazgo relationships established by a couple throughout its career involves living mediating entities—that is, 50 ahijados—the total network of personnel egocentrically computed includes from 170 to 190 primary actors per couple (including the ahijados). In addition, one must take into account secondary actors who may number twice as many, so the total number of primary and secondary actors in the compadrazgo career of the average couple in Belén may range from 300 to as many as 400 individuals. Inasmuch as 40 percent of all compadrazgo types are established extracommunally, the personnel network is reduced to approximately 180 to 240 individuals from the community itself. One must realize, of course, that this is at the end of a couple's career, but taking into consideration the fluctuation of personnel attributable to death, compadrazgo relationships that grow cold, and other contingent factors, the number of personnel does not vary much from middle age, when

compadrazgo involvement reaches its peak, to retirement around the age of seventy-five. On the other hand, even when couples start their careers shortly after marriage, usually with the birth of their first child, they already have a backlog of secondary compadrazgo relationships through the involvement of their parents and other household members in the compadrazgo system. (Because of the strong patrilineal bias of Belén culture and society, and of Tlaxcala in general, after marriage the bride ceases to participate effectively in the compadrazgo network of her family of orientation and is incorporated into that of her husband and household.) These relationships may involve as many as 75 to 100 people. Thus, at no point in the career of any couple will the total number of primary and secondary compadrazgo ties be less than 75. Changes in personnel, alignments of compadres, and the functioning of clusters are discussed in Chapters Thirteen and Fourteen and the structure and functioning of compadrazgo networks as quasi-kinship units in Chapter Twelve.

Chapter 9. The Structural Articulation and Ritual-Symbolic Nature of Public-Communal Compadrazgo Types

1. By adults, the people of Belén mean all the married people, and in a few instances old bachelors and unmarried women. This represents an extension to the ritual kinship terminology of the kinship terminological practice of noncrossing generations. ANDI compadrazgo, which includes as sponsors two adults and a young girl, is an exception to the rule. During the cycle of festivities, the adults of Belén call the ANDI padrinos compadres, while the children call them padrinos; the adults call the young madrina comadrita, while the children call her *madrinita* (little madrina). The structural implications of this and other anomalies in ritual kinship terminological usage are discussed in Chapters Eleven and Twelve. Right now, I only wish to point out the homologous and analogous similarities of certain public-communal types to a true kinship unit in operation.

2. These two periods account for the two most important cycles of festivities in Belén. During this time, the most important ritual and ceremonial celebrations in Belén take place, and the community reaches its annual peak expenditure of symbolic, social, and religious resources. The third important occasion in the yearly cycle of festivities is the week before and the week after All Saints' Day, and here again, the people of Belén exhibit the same kinship patterns of behavior described for the other two.

3. What I am saying here applies also to the great majority of Indian and Mestizo communities in rural Tlaxcala. Given the long history of

labor migration, the continuous contacts with the outside world, and the insidious pressures of secularization and modernization, it is astonishing that these communities have managed to retain such a high degree of closeness and integration. The explanation lies in the great integrative force represented by the compadrazgo system, the mayordomía system, and the ayuntamiento religioso, which have traditionally constituted the main organizational elements of Tlaxcalan culture and society. But this is not an adequate explanation until it is well understood why this threefold institutional core has remained strong and effective in resisting secularization and modernization. Here again, I can give a few tentative answers, one of which is that the disruptive forces of secularization and modernization have not yet presented the people of most of rural Tlaxcala with a true economic alternative that will lead ultimately to the formation of what I have called a secular or economically oriented ideology.

Chapter 11. Ritual Kinship Terminology

1. In the ethnographic discussion I established that around 1880 Belén was a traditional society, which had not changed fundamentally since colonial times (see Part Three of *Ritual Kinship* I). Thus, "traditional" denotes a long period of stability (although I have not quantified what stability signifies) preceding a given point in the development of a sociocultural system—in the present case, the community of Belén. Moreover, I have implicitly assumed that it is best to apply the concept of traditionality to specific components or configurations of components, and not to whole cultures or subcultures. I have spoken about traditional times regarding, say, the ladder system (before 1900), certain demographic aspects (prior to 1920), and compadrazgo pedimento (prior to 1940); now I speak of traditional times regarding incest prohibitions. By this shifting of traditional baselines, I am taking cognizance of the fact that the development of a sociocultural system, as expressed in social and cultural change, is never even. There are always fluctuations which must be dealt with in what might be called a differential approach, in which the differences in traditional thresholds can give us important insights into the nature of change itself.

2. Most anthropologists who have dealt with compadrazgo have studied primarily the core of rites and ceremonies and the events leading to it, but have generally disregarded what follows—which, in the wider context of a given situation, is more important sociologically. Thus, most studies of compadrazgo have disregarded the permanent aspects of compadrazgo types, sometimes for lack of evidence about them, and sometimes because anthropologists have been overly impressed with the im-

mediate significance of the often dramatic core. As a single ritual and ceremonial complex, the core of any given compadrazgo type can never be matched afterward, but the cumulative effect of personnel interaction over a long time is more important sociologically. Furthermore, it has often been erroneously assumed that after the core of ceremonies comes to an end, little more than respeto (in its literal meaning) remains among compadrazgo personnel.

Chapter 12. Ritual Kinship Behavior

1. This is one of the perennial methodological problems in anthropology. Many sound methods have failed because they lacked an adequate data base, and several new methods that have appeared recently (for example, ethnoscience, componential analysis, and most aspects of Lévi-Strauss's structuralism) have failed or have not been analytically successful because they have not been able to generate this data base. This is paradoxical, because now, more than ever in the past, there exist the technical apparatus and resources for producing adequate data bases for virtually any method. What is at work here is the traditional conservatism of anthropologists, which permits little deviation from established but largely obsolete techniques. For example, many social scientists accept as sound the detailed techniques of participant observation, and some have even internalized these techniques themselves. But after they have done this, many sociologists, political scientists, and demographers say, "And then what?" Apparently, anthropologists themselves have not gone beyond these techniques, nor have they refined them to fit increasing methodological sophistication.

2. Drinking parties in Belén are to compadrazgo what the handing over of the bride (entrega) is to marriage, namely, one of those important occasions on which certain central features of the institution are played out. Drinking in Belén, when it takes place outside of formal events in the life cycle or the ritual and ceremonial cycles of the community, is structured along lines of friendship and compadrazgo. Compadres in particular seek each other out as drinking companions—not only individually, but often as sizable groups of compadres belonging to the same network. Much of my data pertaining to the structure of the compadrazgo network was gathered at these drinking occasions, both by counting the assisting compadres and by observing their collective behavior.

3. The data were collected during the months of May, June, July, and August of 1971, when more than half of the two-volume monograph had been written. They were specifically gathered with the threefold

analytical framework (which had not entirely crystallized until the fall of 1970) in mind.

4. This is significant not only because it indicates a departure from the traditional structure of compadrazgo, but more important because of the segment of the population that has engaged in this unorthodox practice. The economic elite of Belén is definitely not a clear social class, but it is rapidly acquiring modes of behavior whose cumulative effect puts Belén almost at the threshold of stratification. Its members are acquiring city ways, such as contracting a few compadrazgo relationships outside of the community for primarily economic reasons, or choosing compadres among kinsmen. Such behavior falls outside the traditional compadrazgo system of Belén with its sacred ideology and is part of the secularizing trend, which will affect the economic elite of Belén more than the rest of the community, and which will usher in stratification within less than a generation.

Chapter 13. The Egocentric Developmental Cycle of Compadrazgo

1. The ladder system described by Carrasco (1961) has disappeared from Belén, but it was a functional aspect of the religious system of the community at the turn of the century. The ladder system has survived in slightly modified form and is practiced today in the nearby villages of Ixcotla, Tepatlachco, and Tetlanohca, all of which are well known to me. By observing these ladder systems, I have been able to reconstruct the situation in Belén at the turn of the century. But even synchronically one can get a good idea of Belén's turn-of-the-century ladder system by analyzing several aspects of the developmental cycle of the compadrazgo system, especially the public-communal types. Several steps and age brackets in the discharge of the offices of the mayordomía system and the República Eclesiástica undoubtedly represent a survival of the strict and well-specified developmental cycle of the ladder system. For example, during the first developmental stage of the compadrazgo system, married men may become secondary officials such as secundarios of mayordomias, or perhaps even mayordomo segundo or tercero, and of course they may become *topiles, tequihaus, sacristanes*, and *porteros* (all offices of the República Eclesiástica). Near the end of the first stage, say after he is thirty-eight, a married man may become mayordomo of the less important mayordomias and perhaps fiscal cuarto. During the first half of the second stage, married men may become any kind of mayordomo, and during the second half any official in the religious system, except fiscal primero. This age gradation of mayordomía and República Eclesiástica cargos fits very well with what I have

observed in the villages in which the ladder system is still functioning in a well-organized fashion.

Chapter 15. The Political, Economic, and Demographic Functions of Compadrazgo

1. I say "tried," for I have never claimed that the structural analysis of the compadrazgo system involves the full notion of modelic structure. I postulated an ideological order and was able to delineate some of its properties and the nature of its rules and injunctions, but I have not been entirely successful in demonstrating how it is causally related to the structural domain. I have shown how the threefold analytical framework can be implemented, at least in its more paradigmatic dimensions, and this has compelled me to combine a primarily structural approach with a functional one.

2. This information comes from partial analysis of the death, birth, and marriage records of the parish of San Pablo Apetatitlán, of which Belén was an *iglesia de visita* (visiting church) starting in 1765. Prior to this date, it was an iglesia de visita of Santa Ana Chiautempan, which has birth, death, and marriage registers for the preceding 200 years. I have not yet fully analyzed these registers, but I suspect that regular exchanges of compadres among communities may have started before 1790.

3. My comparative information on the compadrazgo system in Tlaxcala comes from the intensive study of San Bernardino Contla, San Juan Totlac, and Santa Cruz Tlaxcala and from in-depth surveys of Santa María Atlihuetzian, San Luis Teolocholco, San Francisco Tetlanohca, San Rafael Tepatlachco, San Esteban Tizatlán, San Juan Ixtenco, Acxotla del Monte, San Miguel Tenancingo, San Pablo del Monte, and San Isidro Buen Suceso. I have been observing these and several other communities since 1966, and on the basis of my knowledge of these communities feel justified in generalizing, both substantively and ideologically, about Tlaxcala as a whole.

Chapter 16. The Religious and Social Functions of Compadrazgo

1. This is a good example of differential change that cannot be explained in terms of available anthropological theories of sociocultural change. It is in such cases that the distinction between the ideological and structural orders is potentially of great value. It is evident that several structural forms are still present in the two communities, but their functions and incidence have changed significantly in Atlihuetzian while they have remained more or less constant in Belén. At such a point

change can be conceptualized in terms of the efficacy holding between the ideological and structural orders, or, in the present case, between the traditional pan-Tlaxcalan ideology and the structural forms present today in these two communities.

2. The structural and functional comparisons of Contla, Belén, and Atlihuetzian imply a fairly clear typology of secularization in rural Tlaxcala. I have in mind, of course, not the kinship systems of these communities per se, but rather their overall communal culture and society. In a mature form, this typology would have to be refined (especially by the addition of a fourth, fully traditional type), but the procedure would be the same: the efficacy of kinship and compadrazgo as principles and mechanisms of integration and unit formation would be used as an expression or index of communal secularization.

3. It is curious that one of the most important, specific functions of the padrinos de velación in Contla disappeared around 1920 or so, namely the sexual indoctrination of the bride and the groom the night following the banquet in the house of the padrinos (see Nutini 1968b:286).

4. Fundamentally, this temporary-permanent difference in the compadrazgo systems of Belén, Contla, and Atlihuetzian is a structural difference. Nevertheless, I have chosen to put it in functional terms for economy and clarity of exposition, for the structural sphere of action of magico-symbolic functions is essentially the first part of the syntagmatic chain, while the structural sphere of action of primary social, religious, and demographic functions is the second part of the chain.

Chapter 17. The Magico-Symbolic Functions of Compadrazgo

1. Two points must be noted here. First, while these generalizations about the common socioreligious belief system in rural Tlaxcala are statistically valid for the majority of communities (especially Indian communities and those in the first stage of transition to Mestizo culture and society), one must take into consideration the comparative effect of secularization, both intra- and extracommunally. Not all members of a single community, not even the most traditional, share in this system, but statistically speaking my generalization is valid to the extent that even in fully Mestizo communities it is possible to detect a rather high degree of traditional ideology. Secularization in this context means primarily modification of the manifest structural order, especially its physical components, and only when the latent ideological belief system is transformed into an essentially secular ideology will one be able to say that the secularization process has come to an end. Second, it is evident that the common ideological system underlying Catholic and non-Catholic beliefs and ceremonials regarding the supernatural has been molded

by a process of syncretism that may have been significantly modified after the middle of the seventeenth century (see Part Three of *Ritual Kinship* I). There appears to have been a renaissance of non-Catholic elements and dormant pre-Hispanic elements starting shortly after the middle of the seventeenth century, which, coupled with the introduction of elements of European witchcraft, may have significantly modified the ideological synthesis achieved up to that time.

2. I say "almost," because there are a few instances in which religion may become the arbiter of ethics and morality. However, this is by no means the attitude that pervades orthodox Catholicism and regulates every domain of social behavior. A case in point is the fact that a man in Belén cannot discharge some of the most important religious cargos unless he is properly married. In this case religion does regulate a segment of social behavior, but on the other hand, in Belén and in all of rural Tlaxcala, religion is not a moral deterrent to polygyny or concubinage. The global analysis of religion clearly indicates that it has remarkably little influence on social ethics and morality and supports my contention that religion (defined as propitiation of the supernatural) and the social structure (in the restricted sense) are separate domains with few overlapping areas.

3. On the basis of what I have said about the primacy of the folk over the orthodox aspects of Catholicism, one can easily imagine the greater effectiveness of symbolic behavior regarding folk religion. The mass, for example, is not an effective symbol, whereas the cross, a strictly orthodox symbol, has acquired interesting folk and even pagan dimensions.

4. I am grateful to Jean Forbes Nutini for her suggestive thoughts and analysis of the magico-symbolic functions and general aspects of compadrazgo in Belén, and for her insightful comments on the elements of risk which permeate the compadrazgo system. I have incorporated into this analysis details from her excellent M.A. thesis for the Iberoamericana University entitled "El Sistema de Compadrazgo en Santa María Belén Azitzimititlán." I am also grateful to Angel Palerm for his thoughts and suggestions on the same topics, and for pointing out that they have never been analyzed in the anthropological literature on compadrazgo.

Appendix. The Epistemological and Ontological Foundations of the Analytical Framework

1. It seems to me that if this had been taken into consideration by philosophers of the past, the history of philosophy would have been quite different, and many an epistemological position would never have seen the light of day. Classical epistemology almost until the present

has been extremely individualistic and subjective, and seldom if ever has it accounted for the collective dimensions of perception. Witness the philosophical discourse of most of the major philosophers who have dealt with epistemology: they referred to custom and the social group for enlightenment and insight only when everything else had failed and they found themselves in an impasse that introspective analysis could not solve. This is also true in ethics, where custom is the last refuge of the philosopher.

2. Although Western philosophy has been developed within and is an integral part of Western culture, and therefore subject to the limitations of a particular instance of the nature-culture societal screen, philosophers have postulated ethical systems that purport to be universal. Indeed, some contemporary philosophers have been working for decades on the development of what may be called a "scientific theory of values"; that is, they are ostensibly trying to divest themselves of their own cultural values in order to achieve value-free, scientific dimensions. It seems to me that this task could be performed much more adequately by anthropologists, who should be aware of the great cultural variety throughout the world, and hence of the variety of value systems. Whatever anthropologists have said about values, beyond what I have noted above, is confined to the description of particular value systems, or cultural systems, which are almost synonymous. I know of no other area of anthropology in which one can make a more substantial contribution than in the domain of values or ideology, a contribution that will transcend the boundaries of the discipline. It seems paradoxical that all those "committed" anthropologists, who quite rightly worry about the present state of the world, should spend so much effort campaigning for private value systems and limited ideological viewpoints, when they should be addressing themselves to the more fundamental problems of formulating the new, scientific ideology that sooner or later must become universal, given the unprecedented cultural leveling that is taking place today.

3. Lack of formalization, by the way, seems to be one of the great maladies of anthropology. Most of the important operations and activities, and the delineation of specific constructs, are left purposely vague on the excuse that this is best, given the fact that it is maintained a priori that effective axiomatization is not possible in dealing with sociocultural phenomena.

4. The following discussion is based primarily on Nutini 1971a and 1971b. The reader should consult these articles for a more detailed analysis of the concept of ideology and its relationship to science.

5. I think this basic idea is what Lévi-Strauss has in mind when he maintains that at the perceptual level there are no fundamental differ-

ences between scientific constructs and the constructs of primitive peoples, that is, taxonomies, classifications, and so on.

6. Interest in the ideological aspects of cultural relativism seems to have died out since the 1940s, but its epistemological implications are still very much with us. Little progress has been made during these years in formulating analytical tools that would enable us to pass from particular ideological constructs to general scientific constructs. This is the central problem of anthropology, and I have expressed it here in several ways: sometimes emphasizing methodology, sometimes theory, and at other times the level of analysis or the ontological and epistemological dimensions of the problem at hand.

7. For a detailed analysis of what it means conceptually to adopt a grammatical conception of sociocultural systems, and the implications of the surface structure–deep structure distinction, the reader may want to consult Nutini 1974.

8. Elsewhere I have compared the theory and methods of Lévi-Strauss and Chomsky, and elaborated the distinctions between the deep and the surface structure of social phenomena, between paradigmatic and modelic structure, between particular grammars of culture and a universal grammar of culture, and so on (Nutini 1974). This is an effort to determine how the bifurcation of nature may be achieved in the science of man in order to ensure the successful combination of deductive and inductive elements that would yield results falling within the search for concepts by postulation.

9. If one had a taxonomic system sophisticated enough to measure the degree of overlapping—or conversely, the degree of departure—one could very well formulate a *ceteris paribus* law of correspondence (that is, a lawlike statement that specified the conditions under which a measurable degree of overlapping would occur) of the two domains. This would be a powerful tool in the conceptualization of change and the general dynamics of sociocultural systems, which would involve a significant degree of linear causality.

10. The severe criticisms leveled against functional analysis to the effect that its arguments and explanatory analyses are circular and tautologous (Nutini 1968b:384–392) have their origins in the insistence of functionalists that structural-functional systems are closed systems that do not allow for linear causation. I could say that at the highest theoretical level the main purpose of the threefold analytical framework is to endow functional analysis with external variables in order to allow for linear causation, thereby permitting the conceptualization of change. The solution to the problem of sociocultural change presented by or latent in several functionalist practitioners (see Smith 1962)—that change can be conceptualized in terms of a series of historically determined

structural-functional cross-sections at specified points in a time sequence—is not adequate, for the time between cross-sections must still be accounted for in terms of extrinsic and external variables and conditions. In the historical account of the ayuntamiento religioso and the compadrazgo system of Tlaxcala presented in *Ritual Kinship* I (pages 288-367) I was able to achieve this conceptual goal, at least in outline form, by separating the ideological from the structural order. This takes this study out of the structural-functional matrix per se and puts it on its way toward determining the necessary external and extrinsic variables.

Glossary

Most of the Spanish and Nahuatl terms included in this glossary are used at least twice in the text and explained as they occur, but for the convenience of the reader I have compiled them in one place. The thirty-one compadrazgo types and their variants are listed separately in Chart 1.

Acompañantes   Attendant in the República Eclesiástica

Acostada   The act of bedding (placing) the child Jesus in the holy manger, either in church or at home

Ahijada   Goddaughter

Ahijado   Godson

Ahijados   Godchildren in general

Almiar   Haystack

Altares   Altars

Anillos (padrinos de)   Wedding rings; godparents of

Años noviciados   The first nine years of marriage; characterized as a "dangerous" period for the couple

Apadrinación   Sponsorship; godparent sponsorship

Apadrinamiento   The sponsoring of

Arras (padrinos de)   Earnestmoney; godparents of

Ayuda   Religious, economic, and social assistance. Nonreciprocal labor exchange. Outright donations in kind or cash

Ayuntamiento religioso (República Eclesiástica)   Religious government. Body of officials elected by the people of Belén on January 1 each year

Casamiento   Marriage, and its rites and ceremonies

Chiquihuite   Basket; a ceremonial gift basket of bread, fruit, and liquor presented to prospective padrinos

Cofradía   The group of the most important mayordomias

Comadre   Comother; female ritual kinsman; term of reference for female ritual kinsman

Compadrazgo   Ritual kinship. The ritual sponsorship of a person, image, object, or occasion, together with a whole complex of temporary and permanent social, religious, economic, and symbolic attributes binding its personnel (parents, owners, kinsmen, sponsors, and mediating entities)

Compadrazgo no-sacramental primario   Primary nonsacramental compadrazgo

Compadrazgo no-sacramental secundario   Secondary nonsacramental compadrazgo

Compadrazgo sacramental   Sacramental compadrazgo

Compadrazgo de fé   Baptismal compadrazgo; by extension, the main sacramental compadrazgos (marriage, confirmation, erection of a burial cross, and first communion)

Compadrazgos de grado   Baptismal and confirmation compadrazgo; sometimes by extension, the other main sacramental compadrazgos (marriage, first communion, and erection of a burial cross)

Compadre   Cofather; male ritual kinsman; term of reference for male ritual kinsman

Compadres   Coparents; ritual kinsmen; term of reference for ritual kin in general

Compadrinazgo   Act of cosponsorship

Componentes   All the religious officials of a mayordomía or hermandad assisting the principal mayordomo

Compromiso   Religious or social agreement. Social, religious, and economic obligations contracted by ritual kinsmen. Obligations contracted by a religious official when nominated or elected to a religious office

Confianza   Trust; reliability; rapprochement. One of the three dynamic, activating principles of the compadrazgo system

Consuegra   Co-mother-in-law; term of reference between the mothers of husband and wife

Consuegro   Co-father-in-law; term of reference between the fathers of husband and wife

Consuegros   Co-parents-in-law; term of reference between the parents of husband and wife

Entrega (de una imagen)   The handing over of a mayordomía image to the incoming officials

Escapulario   Scapular. Sometimes a medal with a picture of the Virgen del Carmen on one side and the Sacred Heart of Christ on the other

Fiscal primero   The leading official in the República Eclesiástica

Fiscal segundo (mayor)   Lieutenant fiscal; second in command of the República Eclesiástica

Fiscal tercero (escribano)   Scribe; third in command of the República Eclesiástica

Fiscales   The four principal officials of the República Eclesiástica. The integrated group of the four main officials of the República Eclesiástica and their assistants (five assistants, five messenger boys, two sextons, two doormen, and four altar boys)

Fiscalía   Group of the fiscales

Gasto aparte   The maintenance of separate expense budgets by the component nuclear families within an extended-family household

Gasto junto   The maintenance of a common expense budget by all the component nuclear families within an extended-family household

Hermandad(es)   A special type of mayordomía which includes among its annual religious celebrations a pilgrimage to the place where its image is venerated

Iglesia de visita   Visiting church

Imagen   Wooden or plaster image

Lazo (madrina de)   Ornamental tie, used during the wedding ceremony; godmother of

Madrina   Godmother; female ritual sponsor; term of reference and address for female ritual sponsor

Manda   A promise to Christ, the Virgin, or the saints in return for a certain favor

Mayordomía(s)   The sponsorship of the religious fiesta in honor of a given saint, together with a whole complex of ceremonial, administrative, and economic functions

Mayordomo   The principal official of a mayordomía, steward

Milpa   Cultivated plot of land; crops growing on the plot

Nahual   Individual endowed with the supernatural power to transform himself into a donkey, turkey, coyote, and sometimes small animals. A trickster of sorts

Nixtamal   Ground corn soaked in lime

Padrinazgo   Male ritual sponsorship

Padrino   Godfather. Male ritual sponsor; term of reference and address for male ritual sponsor

Padrinos   Godparents. Ritual sponsors; term of reference and address for ritual sponsors

Paraje (terreno)   The five to ten hectares of land into which the entire community is divided. More specifically, the areas associated with the eighteen name groups and sometimes with nonresidential extended families

Parientes   Relatives. People bearing the same name and having a certain sense of identification

Pedimento   Formal request for ritual kinship sponsorship. Betrothal. Legal or traditional marriage

Principal   Old man. A man who has reached the top of the ladder system. A man who has discharged important civil and religious cargos

Pulque   Fermented agave juice

República Eclesiástica (ayuntamiento religioso)　　Ecclesiastic republic. The group of the fiscales and their assistants

Respeto　　Respect; veneration; honor. One of the three dynamic, activating principles of the compadrazgo system

Rezador　　Prayer leader

Rosario (madrina de)　　Rosary used in the wedding ceremony; godmother of

Secundarios　　Attendants or secondary mayordomos: first, second, and third. The varying number of assistants of the principal mayordomos

Sementera　　First seeds

Taller de costura　　Sewing shop

Temazcal　　Steam bath

Terrenos　　Cultivable plots of land

Tetlachihuic (hechicero)　　Sorcerer

Tezitlazc (conjurador)　　Weatherman; rainmaker. Also known as tiemperos and campaneros

Tienda　　Store

Tlahuelpuchis　　Male and female witches

Velación (padrinos de)　　Nuptial benedictions; godparents of

Vuelta mano　　Reciprocal labor exchange

Xocoyote　　Ultimogenit; last-born son

References Cited

Barnes, John A.
  1974 "Network Analysis: Orienting Notion, Rigorous Technique or Substantive Field of Study?" Mathematical Social Science Board (MSSB), Advanced Research Symposium on Social Networks.

Barth, Frederick
  1959 "Segmentary Opposition and the Theory of Games: A Study of Pathan Organization." *Journal of the Royal Anthropological Institute* 89:5-21.

Benedict, Ruth
  1946 *Patterns of Culture*. New York, Mentor Books.

Boorman, S. A. and H. C. White
  1975 "Social Structure from Multiple Networks: Part II. Role Structures." Cambridge, Mass. Harvard University mimeo, Department of Sociometry.

Breiger, Ronald L.
  1976 "Sampling Large Social Networks for Blockmodeling." *American Sociological Review* 41:117-135.

Buchler, Ira R. and Hugo G. Nutini, eds.
  1969 *Game Theory in the Behavioral Sciences*. Pittsburgh, University of Pittsburgh Press.

Buchler, Ira R. and Henry A. Selby
  1968 *Kinship and Social Organization: An Introduction to Theory and Method*. New York, Macmillan Company.

Carnap, Rudolf
  1939 "Foundations of Logic and Mathematics." *International Encyclopedia of Unified Science*, vol. 1. Chicago.

Carrasco, Pedro
  1961 "The Civil-Religious Hierarchy in Mesoamerican Communities: Pre-Spanish Background and Colonial Development." *American Anthropologist* 63:483-497.

Davenport, William
  1960 "Jamaican Fishing: A Game Theory Analysis." *Yale University Publications in Anthropology* 59:3-11.

Doreian, Patrick C.
  1970 *Mathematics and the Study of Social Relations*. London, Weidenfeld and Nicholson.

Douglas, Mary
  1967 "The Meaning of Myth." In *The Structural Study of Myth and*

Totemism (E. T. Leach, ed.). Association of Social Anthropologists Monograph no. 5. London, Tavistock Publications.

Dray, William
1957   *Laws and Explanation in History*. London, Oxford University Press.

Eggan, Fred
1950   *The Social Anthropology of the Western Pueblos*. Chicago, University of Chicago Press.

Evans-Pritchard, E. E.
1956   *Social Anthropology*. Glencoe, Ill. Free Press.

Firth, Raymond
1963   "Bilateral Descent Groups: An Operational Viewpoint." In *Studies in Kinship and Marriage* (I. Shapera, ed.). Occasional Paper of the Royal Anthropological Institute no. 16. London, Oxford University Press.

Forbes Tanner, C. Jean
1971   "El Sistema de Compadrazgo en Santa María Belén Azitzimititlán." Universidad Iberoamericana, M.A. thesis. Mexico, D.F.

Fortes, Meyer
1953   "The Structure of Unilineal Descent Groups." *American Anthropologist* 55:17-41.

Foster, George M.
1953   "Cofradía and Compadrazgo in Spain and Spanish America." *Southwestern Journal of Anthropology* 9:1-28.
1961   "Dyadic Contract: A Model for the Social Structure of a Mexican Peasant Village." *American Anthropologist* 63:1173-1192.

Gillin, John P.
1945   *Moche: A Peruvian Coastal Community*. Institute of Social Anthropology Publication no. 3. Washington, D.C., Smithsonian Institution.

Gluckman, Max
1950   "Kinship and Marriage among the Lozi of Northern Rhodesia and the Zulu of Natal." In *African Systems of Kinship and Marriage* (A. R. Radcliffe-Brown and D. Forde, eds.). London, Oxford University Press for the International African Institute.

Granovetter, Mark S.
1976   "Network Sampling." *American Journal of Sociology* 81:1287-1303.

Harary, Frank, Dorwin Cartwright, and Robert Z. Norman
1965   *Structural Models: An Introduction to the Theory of Directed Graphs*. New York, John Wiley and Sons.

Harris, Marvin
1964 *The Nature of Cultural Things.* New York, Random House.
Hempel, Carl G.
1965 *Aspects of Scientific Explanation and Other Essays in the Philosophy of Science.* New York, Free Press.
Kroeber, Alfred L.
1909 "Classifactory Systems of Relationship." *Journal of the Royal Anthropological Institute* 39:77–84.
1952 *The Nature of Culture.* Chicago, University of Chicago Press.
Leach, Edmund R.
1961a "Lévi-Strauss in the Garden of Eden: An Examination of Some Recent Developments in the Analysis of Myth." *Transactions of the New York Academy of Sciences,* series 2, 23(4):386–396.
1961b *Pul Eliya: A Village in Ceylon.* Cambridge, Cambridge University Press.
1962 "Genesis as Myth." *Discovery* 23:30–35.
1965a "Claude Lévi-Strauss: Anthropologist and Philosopher." *New Left Review* 34 (November–December): 10–28.
1965b Review of Claude Lévi-Strauss's *Mythologiques: le cru et le cuit. American Anthropologist* 67:776–780.
Lévi-Strauss, Claude
1953 "Social Structure." In *Anthropology Today* (A. L. Kroeber, ed.). Chicago, University of Chicago Press.
1955 "The Structural Study of Myth." *Journal of American Folklore* 78:428–444.
1964 *Mythologiques: Le cru et le cuit.* Paris, Plon.
1966 *The Savage Mind.* Chicago, University of Chicago Press.
Mitz, Sidney W. and Eric R. Wolf
1950 "An Analysis of Ritual Co-Parenthood (Compadrazgo)." *Southwestern Journal of Anthropology* 6:341–368
Mitchell, John C., Ed.
1969 *Social Networks in Urban Situations.* Manchester, Manchester University Press.
MSSB
1974 Conference on Social Networks. Organized by R. Bernard. Cheat Lake, W. Va.
Murdock, George P.
1949 *Social Structure.* New York, Macmillan Company.
Nagel, Ernest
1961 *The Structure of Science.* New York, Harcourt, Brace.
Northrop, F.S.C.
1945 "Whitehead's Philosophy of Science." In *The Philosophy of Alfred*

North Whitehead (P. A. Schilpp, ed.). New York, Tudor Publishing Co.

Nutini, Hugo G.

1965a "Polygyny in a Tlaxcalan Community." *Ethnology* 23:123-147.

1965b "Some Considerations on the Nature of Social Structure and Model Building: A Critique of Claude Lévi-Strauss and Edmund Leach." *American Anthropologist* 67:707-731.

1967 "A Synoptic Comparison of Mesoamerican Marriage and Family Structure." *Southwestern Jounral of Anthropology* 23:383-404.

1968a "On the Concepts of Epistemological Order and Coordinative Definitions." *Bijdragen Tot de Taal-, Land-, en Volkenkunde* 234(1):1-21.

1968b *San Bernardino Contla: Marriage and Family Structure in a Tlaxcalan Municipio.* Pittsburgh, University of Pittsburgh Press.

1970 "Lévi-Strauss' Conception of Science." in *Echanges et communications: Mélanges offerts à Claude Lévi-Strauss* (Jean Pouillon and Pierre Maranda, eds.). The Hague, Mouton and Company.

1971a "The Ideological Bases of Lévi-Strauss' Structuralism." *American Anthropologist* 73:537-544.

1971b "Science and Ideology." *Bijdragen Tot de Taal-, Land-, en Volkenkunde* 127(1):1-14.

1974 "A Comparison of Lévi-Strauss' Structuralism and Chomsky's Transformational Generative Grammar." Pittsburgh, University of Pittsburgh mimeo, Department of Anthropology.

n.d. *Structure and Ideology: The Epistemological and Ontological Bases of Their Interrelationship.*

Nutini, Hugo G. and Betty Bell

1980 *Ritual Kinship: The Structure and Historical Development of the Compadrazgo System in Rural Tlaxcala.* Princeton, Princeton University Press.

Nutini, Hugo G. and Barry L. Isaac

1974 *Los Pueblos de Habla Nahuatl de la Región de Tlaxcala y Puebla.* Instituto Nacional Indigenista, Serie de Antropología Social no. 27. México, D.F.

Nutini, Hugo G. and Douglas R. White.

1977 "Community Variations and Network Structure in the Social Functions of Compadrazgo in Rural Tlaxcala, Mexico." *Ethnology* 16 (4):353-384.

Opler, Morris E.

1945 "Themes as Dynamic Forces in Culture." *American Journal of Sociology* 51:192-206.

Paul, Benjamin D.
  1942 "Ritual Kinship: With Special Reference to Godparenthood in Middle America." Ph.D. dissertation, University of Chicago. University of Chicago Microfilm Series no. 1,686. Chicago.
Ravicz, Robert S.
  1967 "Compadrinazgo." In *Handbook of Middle American Indians* (Robert Wauchope, ed.). Social Anthropology 6:238-252. Austin, University of Texas Press.
Reichenbach, Hans
  1946 "Bertrand Russell's Logic." In *The Philosophy of Bertrand Russell* (P. A. Schilpp, ed.). Library of Living Philosophers. New York, Tudor Publishing Co.
Selby, Henry A.
  1976 "The Study of Social Organization in Traditional Mesoamerica." In *Essays in Mexican Kinship* (Hugo G. Nutini, Pedro Carrasco, and James J. Taggart, eds.). Pittsburgh, University of Pittsburgh Press.
Smith, Michael G.
  1962 "History and Social Anthropology." *Journal of the Royal Anthropological Institute* 92:73-85.
Turner, Victor
  1967 *The Forest of Symbols*. Ithaca and London, Cornell University Press.
Werner, Oswald
  1970 "On the Universality of Some Lexical/Semantic Relations." Paper presented at the 68th annual meeting of the American Anthropological Association. New Orleans.
White, Douglas R.
  1974 "Mathematical Anthropology." In *Handbook of Social and Cultural Anthropology* (J. J. Honigmann, ed.). New York, Rand-McNally.
  1975 "Communicative Avoidance in Social Networks." Mathematical Social Science Board (MSSB), Advanced Research Symposium on Social Networks.
  1977 "Material Entailment Analysis: Theory and Illustrations." In *Classifying Cultural Data* (Herschel C. Hudson, ed.). New York, Jossey Press.
White, Douglas R. and Hugo G. Nutini
  n.d. *Social Structure and Ideology: Social Networks in Rural Tlaxcala*.
White, Harrison C.
  1969 "Notes on Finding Models of Structural Equivalence: Drawing on Theories of Roles, Duality, Sociometry and Balance."

Cambridge, Mass., Harvard University mimeo, Department of Sociometry.

White, Harrison, C., Scott A. Boorman, and Ronald L. Breiger
1976 "Social Structure from Multiple Networks. I." *American Journal of Sociology* 81:730–780.

Whitehead, Alfred N.
1922 *The Concept of Nature.* Cambridge, Cambridge University Press.

Index

acculturation, 4

achechando, 101-102

acostada del Niño Dios en casa (ANDC), 7; adolescents as ahijados, 258; children as sponsors, 56-58; and interchangeability, 158-159; as leadng to relationship, 147; magico-symbolic dimensions, 392; as preferential compadrazgo, 112-114; religious function of, 345; role transformation in, 43; and second stage of developmental cycle, 266

acostada del Niño Dios en la iglesia (ANDI); adolescents as ahijados, 258; asymmetry in, 133-135; behavior patterns, 160-163, 227-228; children as sponsors, 56-58; defined, 7; dyads in, 188-192; as global exocentric relationship, 37-38; and incest prohibition, 197-198; magico-symbolic dimensions, 391-393; multiple dyads in, 33-35, 289-290; and noncompliance, 102; as permanent relationship, 146; political functions, 321-323; as prescriptive compadrazgo, 112-115; religious functions of, 342, 345; ritual symbolism in, 161-163; role transformation in, 43-44; seasonal cycles in, 297-298; and secularization, 158-159; structure of, 164-170; terminology of, 186-187

actors. *See* primary, secondary, and tertiary actors

Adolescence, and developmental cycle of compadrazgo, 257-258

agente municipal, 319

ahijados: as mediating entities, 24; defined, 6

altars in house, 261

Alvarez, Pedro, 148

Amaxac de Guerrero, 167

ANDC. *See* acostada del Niño Dios en casa

ANDI. *See* acostada del Niño Dios en la iglesia

Angelina María, 374

anomalous compadrazgo, 64-67; and asking-being asked distinction, 279-280;

and behavior patterns, 204-205; developmental cycle, 249, 280-284; terminology of, 186-187

años noviciados, 20

anthropological theory, 425-427

AOI. *See* apadrinación de ornamentos de iglesia

apadrinación de ornamentos de iglesia (AOI): asymmetry in, 133-135; defined, 7; and developmental cycle, 267; as leading-to relationship, 147-148; magico-symbolic dimensions, 392-393; and ma-yordomia system, 296-297; structure of, 164-170; as temporary relationship, 146

articulation, 454-458

asking-being asked distinction, 68-70, 406; and developmental cycle, 272-273, 276-282; dynamic and temporal implications of, 70-73; permanent implications of, 73-74; and reciprocity, 282-283; symmetry in, 136-137

asymmetry: and compadrazgo choice, 135-137; context of compadrazgo personnel, 129-135; and incest prohibition, 199-200; structure of compadrazgo, 405; systemic implications of, 140-142; table, 131

ayuda, 104, 143, 209, 214-215, 326-327

ayuntamiento religioso: coercive mechanisms, 104-105; and community organization, 349; and compadrazgo ideology, 4-5; public-communal compadrazgo, 135, 164-171; reciprocity in, 139-140; secularization, 471 n.4

baptism: in development cycle, 259-260; religious function of, 345

baptismal compadrazgo: behavior patterns, 138; and clustering, 244; defined, 7; and incest prohibition, 194-195; as leading-to relationship, 147; magico-symbolic dimensions, 388-389; and noncompliance, 109-111; reciprocity in, 138; strength of associations in, 205-206

Library of Congress Cataloging in Publication Data
(Revised for vol. 2)

Nutini, Hugo G.
   Ritual kinship.

   Includes bibliographies and indexes.
   Contents: [v. 1] The structure and historical development of the compadrazgo system
in rural Tlaxcala.—v. 2. Ideological and structural integration of the compadrazgo system
in rural Tlaxcala.
   1. Nahuas—Kinship.   2. Sponsors—Mexico—Tlaxcala (State)   3. Indians of
Mexico—Tlaxcala (State)—Kinship.   4. Tlaxcala (Mexico: State)—Social life and cus-
toms.

I. Bell, Betty, joint author.   II. Title.
F1221.N3N89   306.8'3   79-3225
ISBN 0-691-09382-2 (v. 1)
ISBN 0-691-09383-0 (pbk. : v. 1)
ISBN 0-691-07649-9 (v. 2 : alk. paper)
ISBN 0-691-10144-2 (lim. pbk. ed. : v. 2)